JOHN FURLONG

with Gary Mason

PATRIOT HEARTS

INSIDE THE OLYMPICS THAT CHANGED A COUNTRY

Douglas & McIntyre

D&M PUBLISHERS INC.

Vancouver / Toronto / Berkeley

Douglas & McIntyre
An imprint of D&M Publishers Inc.
2323 Quebec Street, Suite 201
Vancouver BC Canada V5T 4S7
www.douglas-mcintyre.com

Cataloguing data available from Library and Archives Canada
ISBN 978-1-55365-794-1 (cloth)
ISBN 978-1-55365-795-8 (ebook)

Editing by Trena White
Jacket and text design by Jessica Sullivan
Jacket photographs: Portrait of John Furlong by Shannon Mendes;
background image by Randy Lincks/www.randylincks.com
All interior photos courtesy of the author, Jim Richards and VANOC, except as noted.
Photo of VANOC executive by Vincent L. Chan
All torch relay photos by Jim Richards
Photo of Stephen Harper © The Canadian Press/Jonathan Hayward
Photo of John Furlong with Jack Poole by Kim Stallknecht
Printed and bound in Canada by Friesens
Text printed on acid-free, 100% post-consumer paper
Distributed in the U.S. by Publishers Group West

We gratefully acknowledge the financial support of the Canada Council
for the Arts, the British Columbia Arts Council, the Province of British
Columbia through the Book Publishing Tax Credit and the Government of
Canada through the Canada Book Fund for our publishing activities.

PATRIOT HEARTS

To Catherine
and the Canadian spirit

Contents

The **Golden** Goal

FROM THE MOMENT I woke up on Sunday, the last day of the 2010 Winter Olympics, I had a gut feeling that it would be historic. That 17-day-old knot in my stomach was gone. I'd had zero sleep, but on this day it just did not matter. Call it an old athlete's intuition, but I liked Canada's chances in the men's gold medal hockey game.

Even though the United States had defeated us earlier in the tournament, I felt strangely relaxed and confident about the outcome of the rematch that would be played that afternoon. It was a game I had dreamed about even before we won the bid to host the Games in Prague, back in July 2003.

I walked out onto the balcony of the suite I had been staying in at the Westin Bayshore during the Games. As I had every morning since the Olympics began, I checked on two things: the Olympic cauldron at the waterfront and the weather. Today, as always, I was relieved to see the flame still burning. A clear sky made me feel even better.

Sometimes the entire Olympic experience felt like a dream, one I would wake up from and discover had all been a fantasy. This morning was no different. Had this experience really happened? So many days had felt surreal, knowing I was part of something so massive in scope, so dramatic in its telling, so important to entire nations. The biggest event ever to be organized on Canadian soil.

I could tell by the number of Canadians who were watching the Olympics on television and devouring daily accounts of the Games in the newspapers that interest was off the charts. A day earlier, somewhere in the neighbourhood of 80 per cent of the country had tuned in to watch the coverage. Those were never-before-seen-or-imagined numbers. Ecstatic Olympic broadcasters expected them to be even bigger for the gold medal hockey game.

Faceoff was set for noon.

Before the game started I had to attend a Vancouver Organizing Committee meeting to review the plans for the many challenges the final day posed. The team seemed energized, almost younger, and was certainly feeling more confident. Today would be huge for us. There would be 80,000 people cramming into two arenas for the hockey game and closing ceremonies in the space of four or five hours. Getting everything to start on time was going to take military precision and discipline. After that meeting finished, I had to attend a windup news conference at the Main Press Centre.

I was struck by how different the questions at the final session with reporters were from the ones I had had to handle a couple of weeks earlier, when the common perception, certainly among the British press, was that the Games were in trouble. Now many of those same reporters were writing that we had staged perhaps the best Winter Olympics in history. As press conferences go it was pretty much a love-in.

Shortly before 11 AM, I headed to Canada Hockey Place, where the game was being played. On the way I passed several downtown restaurants and bars, outside of which stood hundreds of customers clad in red and white, waiting to get in. I'm sure records were set across the country for the most beer ever sold on a Sunday.

By the time I arrived at the arena it was jammed with people wearing the now-iconic Team Canada jerseys. Even though it was more than an hour before game time, people were already blowing horns and chanting "We Want Gold! We Want Gold!"

This was the one event where I had hoped to be sitting with members of my executive team; it was the last day of the Olympics, and we'd been through so much together. This was going to be perhaps the most historic hockey game in the nation's history. If we won, I wanted to be celebrating with the people who had become family to me over the last several years.

But I had been asked to sit with the big bosses, Dr. Jacques Rogge, president of the IOC, and René Fasel, president of the International Ice Hockey Federation. It was a request I felt I couldn't turn down.

After taking my seat I reminded René of a conversation we'd had in 2002 at the Salt Lake City Olympics, when Vancouver was still bidding for the Games. It was the day of the men's gold medal game, Canada versus the United States, which we would ultimately win. Imagine the same final in Vancouver, on Canadian soil, I told René at the time. It would be one of the biggest things ever to happen in the country. It would be one of the biggest things ever to happen to international ice hockey. René didn't need to be convinced. I think from that moment on he wanted our bid to succeed.

While confident of the outcome of this Olympic rematch, I had some nervous energy to burn off so I walked to the concourse and decided to go looking for some Blue Jackets, the tireless volunteer army that had played a pivotal role in making the Games such a triumph. I wanted to thank each one of them for their incredible service. I spoke to as many as I could before it was time to drop the puck.

Everyone in the country wanted Canada to win, but there was more at stake than just bragging rights. The Games weren't going to be judged a failure if we lost. I knew what we had accomplished, was aware of the unprecedented nationalistic fervour the Olympics had ignited across the country. But I felt winning would mean the difference between everlasting glory and memories of a wonderful fortnight. A gold medal would be Canada's fourteenth at this Games, establishing a new Olympic record for any nation at the Winter Games, a record that would be difficult to break. Victory on this Sunday afternoon would also give the country what it most wanted: men's hockey gold. A win would go down in our history as a uniquely Canadian moment that would be written about in books and talked about for generations. It was much more than just a hockey game.

By the time the puck was dropped the crowd was on its feet, chanting, making more noise than I'd ever heard in a hockey rink. Imagine a 747 revving its engines inside a hangar—that's how loud it felt. All around me were adults and children screaming their hearts out. I could only shake my head in wonder at how sport could transform a cross-section of Canadians into a roiling unified mass of kinetic energy.

I knew nothing about hockey before arriving in Canada from Ireland. But I had quickly learned what the game means to people here. It was to Canadians what Gaelic football was to those back home. And the more I came to understand the game, the more I realized Canadians had rallied around a sport that defined them and their spirit. Hockey players are among the toughest, most fearless athletes of any sport. Canadians are among the most resilient and courageous people. In so many ways, the sport and the people who love it are a natural match.

Large parts of the gold medal game remain a blur to me. I had a million things on my mind, as I did most days during the Games. There was still a cross-country skiing race to get off up at Whistler. The closing ceremonies would be taking place just a few hours later. Getting 60,000 people into BC Place Stadium was a massive undertaking. I worried about that. I had a speech to give as well and was fretting about how my French was going to go over.

So my focus wasn't entirely there when Canada went up 1–0 in the first period and then 2–0 in the second. I couldn't have told you who scored the goals at the time, but now I can, of course. So thank you, Jonathan Toews and Corey Perry. I will never forget, however, the sound in the rink when the pucks went in, the blast of the horn, the spontaneous delirium of the crowd. Jacques Rogge, normally so reserved and stoic, even cracked a smile. I thought that he quietly wanted Canada to win because he understood what it would mean, ultimately, to the Games and the place that would be reserved for them in the annals if the Olympic experience was capped off by hockey gold.

Before the second period was finished, however, the United States would make the score 2–1 on a goal by Ryan Kesler, whom I had often watched play in this building for the hometown Vancouver Canucks. Now he was the enemy, no doubt an odd feeling for him and the many Canucks fans in the rink that day. After his goal I felt the energy seep out of the crowd a little bit. I could sense the worry and dread but remained cautiously optimistic. René, in contrast, was absolutely delighted. "All we need now is another American goal," he said during the second intermission.

"Another goal!" I screamed at him. "Are you out of your mind?"

"No, no, John," he said, smiling. "It would be unbelievable for the ratings. We need this game to go to a shootout. That would be perfect."

"No it would not," I screamed. "Now you stop that right now, do you understand? We do not want or need overtime. We do not want a shootout. We want this game over, finished, and wrapped up, now."

I spent most of the third period tightly clutching the edge of my seat. I wasn't alone. I could hear my own heart beating—or maybe it was the collective sound of everyone else's. The last minute of regulation time was pure torture. When the Americans' Zach Parise tied the game with 24 seconds left, I closed my eyes and covered my face in my hands. Nearby, Prime Minister Stephen Harper was doing the same. I looked over at Jacques. His face was ashen. I looked at René. He couldn't stop smiling.

"René, I'm just telling you that if the U.S. scores in overtime I'm going to stab you in the heart with my pen. I am, René. I am going to do that." I took my pen out of my jacket and held it high in the air. "Remember," I said.

I'm not sure I was smiling.

I don't remember leaving my seat during the intermission. I was paralyzed with fear, like most people in the building. We all wanted a win so badly. We could all read the tension on each other's faces. No one was smiling. People rubbed their hands nervously. Others chewed on fingers. The religious prayed.

I'm not sure I took a breath again until seven minutes and 40 seconds into overtime. When Sidney Crosby scored I jumped up and raised my hands in the air. The place exploded, releasing a beautiful energy in the process. Everyone was hugging and kissing and jumping up and down. I saw many people crying. People looked so relieved. Some looked exhausted, as if they had played in the game themselves. On some level they had: all of the country was on that bench alongside the players.

I looked at Jacques Rogge, and he too seemed relieved. I looked at René, and he was still smiling. Despite his hopes for a shootout I believe that, like Jacques, in his heart René wanted Canada to win. He loved hockey and he knew how much the game means to our hockey-mad nation.

As the crowd continued to sing and chant and immerse themselves in the moment, I stood watching, saying nothing. I thought of that wonderful scene in *Chariots of Fire*, my all-time favourite film that I've seen 20 times or more, when Eric Liddell, the devout Scottish Christian, lines up as the underdog in the 400-metre sprint at the 1924 Olympics in Paris. He had been the favourite in the 100 metres, but because the race was held on a Sunday it was against his religion to compete—so he didn't. Against all odds he wins the 400 metres. The camera pans to the crowd where his coach, Sandy

McGrath, is standing amid all those cheering and celebrating, his hands in his coat pockets, a satisfied smile breaking across his face. Rather than going nuts, he is calmly soaking it all in.

That's kind of what I did as the crowd continued to sing and wave Canadian flags. I wanted to look and admire and immerse myself in the moment. Suddenly, I felt a tug at my jacket. It was my 12-year-old grandson, Henrik, the son of my daughter Maria.

"How did you get here?" I asked.

"Mom sent me," he said.

"So," I said. "What did you think of that?"

"Awesome," Henrik answered.

I put my arm around his shoulders and we both looked out at the ice, where the players were celebrating and taking turns skating around with a giant Canadian flag supplied by a fan.

"Why don't I go get Mom?" he said. Off he went.

A few minutes later Maria was by my side. Maria is a tall, tough, disciplined cookie who runs marathons. I often thought she had inherited her competitiveness and intensity from me. There was a time in our lives when our relationship wasn't the best. It had taken some time for it to grow back into something that resembled a normal, healthy father-daughter bond. Now we stood looking down at the ice, not saying much. The red carpet was rolled out. Jacques Rogge was getting ready to hand out the gold medals.

He started with goaltender Roberto Luongo, the Vancouver Canucks goalie and local hero whose play is often celebrated during games by chants of "Luo-o-o-o-o-o." When Jacques put the gold medal around Roberto's neck the chant began: "Luo-o-o-o-o-o." Eventually he got to the overtime hero, Sidney Crosby, and the place went crazy. Jacques hesitated a few seconds before putting the medal around Sidney's neck so Canada's newest hockey hero could enjoy the moment. And then it was time to play the national anthem.

The crowd started singing as the Canadian flag was raised. I looked over at Maria and put my arm around her. Tears streamed down her beautiful face as she sang along. It was such a warm, happy moment for us both. After it was over, Maria and I hugged and said goodbye. Behind my seat was a bank of televisions showing scenes of celebration taking place on streets from Halifax to Victoria. CTV had sent its helicopters to the skies to shoot the instant euphoria. Then they cut to what was going on in downtown Vancouver. Thousands of people had poured out onto the streets to join in a massive party.

I couldn't help thinking that the celebrations would be mixed with a little sadness that the Games were coming to a close. For two weeks the entire country had been on a very rare kind of vacation. Now it was over. Now it was time to go back to work. For life to return to normal, but maybe a new normal.

Something profound had taken place. Thanks to the Olympics, thousands of Canadian children would get out of bed the next morning with new heroes and new dreams. They would now want to be on that Olympic stage one day themselves, playing hockey or blasting down a mountain on a snowboard. These Games would be a gift to the country for generations.

The Olympics were going to be judged a success regardless of how the men had done that afternoon. I knew that. Everyone at the Vancouver Organizing Committee knew that. But we wanted more. In order for people to feel as if they'd woken up in a new country the next day, we needed something extraordinary. Sidney Crosby made it happen.

I couldn't help but think about the complex and sometimes difficult road I had travelled to arrive at this moment. A journey that began in Ireland and that was powered by my own thoughts of Olympic gold.

1

"Welcome to Canada—Make Us Better"

MY OLYMPIC DREAM began when I was 14 years old. It was October 14, 1964, to be precise. I was sitting in the living room of our family home in Dublin watching television. I had been glued to coverage of the Tokyo Summer Olympics since they'd begun a few days earlier. On this afternoon, I was watching the men's 10,000-metre race. The favourite was a fellow named Ron Clarke of Australia. At the time, he held the world record. Clarke took an early lead in the final, and by halfway through the race four runners were within striking distance of him, including Native American Billy Mills.

With two laps to go, Clarke still held a convincing lead. There were only two runners close enough to challenge him—Mills and Mohammed Gammoudi of Tunisia. As they took the final turn, Gammoudi soared in front, with Clarke straining to keep up. Mills looked like he was losing steam. Down the final stretch the American tapped into some miraculous well of energy and power and sprinted past a bewildered Gammoudi and Clarke to win.

The announcers were stunned by what they had just witnessed. Most in the stadium were in the same state of disbelief. Mills had run faster than he'd ever run in his life; his time was 50 seconds better than his personal best—an almost unthinkable accomplishment. It was also a new Olympic record.

For whatever reason, the race would have a profound influence on me. Maybe it was Mills's underdog story, one a kid from a working-class Irish family could relate to. Maybe it was the mesmerizing finish. But from that moment on I wanted to go to the Olympics. I remember throwing on an old pair of Keds right after the race was over and taking off down the streets of my neighbourhood, imagining myself in the Olympics. I ran four kilometres to Phoenix Park, the biggest and most famous public space in Dublin. By the time I ran home I was an Olympic champion.

I watched a lot of the 1964 Tokyo Olympics. Many athletes made an impression on me: American sprinter Bob Hayes; Peter Snell, the great middle-distance runner from Australia; Joe Frazier, the boxer from the United States. But none left quite the same mark as Billy Mills.

At 14, life was a giant possibility, and I was probably more of a dreamer than most kids growing up in Ireland. I was born in Clonmel, in the county of Tipperary, on October 12, 1950. The town is situated on the northern bank of the River Suir and rests in a valley surrounded by the Comeragh Mountains. In Irish history, Clonmel was noted for its resistance to Cromwell's armies, which had successfully sacked other communities nearby.

My father, John, who went by Jack, was a prison warden, or, as they were called in Ireland, a governor. Governors typically lived on the jail grounds, which meant I was raised, quite literally, in prison. We bounced around a bit. When I was six we left Clonmel for Dublin, where we stayed for three years before relocating to Portlaoise, in the Irish countryside. When I was 12 we returned to Dublin for good.

Living in a home that was attached to the walls of a prison was different. There's no other way to put it. Depending on which prison my father was working in at the time, our house could be separated from the jail by bars. At one stop, I remember being able to look through my bedroom window into the prison yard and watching the inmates playing soccer. In Clonmel, the jail was for low-risk inmates, and some prisoners would work on the grounds of our house. I would see them all the time but be forbidden to talk to them.

As my father moved up the ranks of the penal system, the prisons we lived in housed more dangerous prisoners. Perhaps the most notorious of all was Mountjoy Jail in Dublin. Not far from our house at Mountjoy was a stone cross that marked the grave of Kevin Barry, a member of the Irish Republican Army who was hanged by the British on November 1, 1920, when they ran the prison. Barry was among a group of IRA members killed at the prison between 1920 and 1921, who collectively became known as the Forgotten Ten.

My father felt that Mountjoy was not the kind of prison that should be housing serious political criminals. It was too old, and its technology wasn't sophisticated enough to thwart the creative minds inside and those inspired to spring them out. Not long after my father retired from Mountjoy, three Provisional Irish Republican Army volunteers escaped from its walls aboard a helicopter that actually landed in the prison's exercise yard. The escape created a worldwide sensation and a major scandal in Ireland. My father had been right.

I was the third of five boys. My brothers were Jim, Eamonn, Brian and Terry. I had a younger sister named Rosemary who would become the closest of my siblings.

Like most families in Ireland, we never had a lot of money, but my dad did have a reliable job so we were better off than many. But nothing was ever wasted in the Furlong household. When I eventually grew to share the same shoe size as my father, I inherited his hand-me-downs. They were always laughably ugly. I was teased mercilessly at school whenever I wore them. Mortified, I eventually scraped together enough money to buy a brand new pair of running shoes. I would carry the runners in a plastic bag, and out of sight halfway to school I would change out of my father's second-hand office shoes and put on my new ones. On the way home, I would change back.

My father was a towering figure. Almost six feet tall, he was handsome, dignified, humble, extremely intelligent and fiercely disciplined. He was an avid reader and a wonderful musician. He would lead singalongs in which we were all expected to participate. Little was grey in my father's world, certainly not when it came to what was right and wrong. Perhaps that's not all that surprising, given his job. Growing up, there was never much ambiguity about what we should and shouldn't do. We never helped ourselves to seconds at the dinner table without asking. We never did anything outside the home that could embarrass the family, like steal or destroy property. Our rooms were expected to be spotless. My father would inspect them on weekends. He was a Latin scholar and expected nothing less than A's from us in Latin at school.

In his day he was a great athlete. When I began to take athletics seriously, eventually making top teams and representing Ireland in various sports, he became both my biggest fan and biggest critic. I remember returning home in the wee hours of the morning from trips I went on with my sports teams. Often, Dad would be waiting up to dissect every minute of the game, homing in on my mistakes over my triumphs. While it may not have been clear to me at the time, my father wanted me never to be too satisfied with a performance. There was always room for improvement.

My mother, Maureen, was a gentle soul. Tall, elegant and reserved, she was a wonderful cook and took pride in making the home as comfortable as possible. She was also extremely religious, as was my father. We lived in a typical Catholic home, with crucifixes and pictures of Christ and saints everywhere. There was church every Sunday, and mass before school was common during the week.

When I think of my parents, I think about how loving their relationship was. There was never any conflict in our household, at least not between them. In fact, I don't remember a single argument between the two. I can say that I enjoyed a loving upbringing. But that doesn't mean my childhood was without its troubles.

I was a quiet introvert, scared and often nervous. Whenever a teacher called my name in the classroom I was horrified I might have to speak. Part of that fear, I think, stemmed from the fact that we were never in one place long enough for me to establish meaningful friendships with other kids. I hadn't been at St. Vincent's School more than a couple of days after we moved back to Dublin when the homeroom teacher barked out my name. *Oh, God, no, I* thought. He walked between two rows of desks before stopping in front of mine. I felt ill.

"I presume you play Gaelic football," the teacher said.

I hadn't yet taken up the sport. Scared to admit it, I replied that I did.

"Good," he shot back. "Because we're playing tomorrow and I expect to see you suited up."

I raced home after school and told my mother what had happened. I had to have Gaelic football boots—now, today. Although we didn't have much money, my mother always found a way to get us what we needed. She always had a few pounds stashed away for emergencies. So we walked into town that afternoon and bought a pair of shiny new football boots.

I had watched Gaelic football on television. The game is played on a field similar to a rugby pitch but much larger. There are 15 players a side, and the object is to kick or strike the round soccer-sized ball into the other team's net or over the crossbar. Players advance the ball up the field by passing or kicking.

But back then I didn't know anything about strategy or even all the rules. The next day, before my first-ever game, the coach came to me and said, "Okay, Furlong, your job is to make sure number 13 doesn't get his hands on the ball. Do you understand?"

I let my instincts take over. I did pretty much what the coach had asked, sticking to the other team's left corner forward like fog on an Irish coast. After the game I was sitting in the dressing room listening to the coach talk about what we did right and wrong. Then he stopped and walked right up to me.

"And you played a great game," he said.

I was hooked.

After getting changed, I walked by an outdoor basketball court where some kids were playing. I stopped and watched and couldn't take my eyes off the play. "God," I thought to myself. "Does that look like fun!" A man named Bill Casey, who was coaching the kids, came over and asked if I'd like to give it a try. "Boy, would I ever," I said. Within minutes I was addicted to another sport.

By my early teens I was obsessed with athletics. The field of play, whatever the game, was the place I always had the most fun. I enjoyed everything about sports: the teamwork, the intensity, the way games were built around a code of honour and fairness. When you grow up as an introvert, you get pushed around and teased quite a bit, and life doesn't seem fair. Sports levelled the playing field. No one bullied me. Sports changed my life.

There was a grass tennis court outside our home in the prison compound. Tennis was considered an English game, so people in Ireland didn't play it. The court, I discovered, was the perfect size for a five-on-five soccer match. For some reason, our school banned the playing of soccer, so this was the only place to play it. It crossed my mind that if we took the net down from the middle of the tennis court and used it to fashion two soccer nets, we would have a pretty decent pitch. And then someone came up with the brilliant idea of marking the court somehow so we could have out-of-bounds lines. One of my friends told me that pouring gasoline on grass burned it. If we could find some gasoline we could literally burn perimeter lines onto our new soccer field.

Our family didn't own a car, but a friend of my dad's did. Whenever Mr. O'Donovan, the prison's deputy governor, came to pay Dad a visit, I would take a hose and siphon gasoline from his tank. My friends played lookout so I wouldn't get caught. We then used the gasoline to line our field. All was fine until one day I overheard Mr. O'Donovan telling my dad about how hard his car was on gas. I turned white. I imagined my father finding out about what I had been up to.

That was the last time I stole gas from Mr. O'Donovan's car.

There were many life lessons that I would take from sports and use long after my playing days were over. In my late teens, I was named captain of a pretty good Gaelic football team. At the time, I didn't fully appreciate the honour, or for that matter understand a captain's role and responsibilities. I mostly thought I'd been given the distinction because the coaches happened to like me. In my captaincy debut, our team played what I thought was a solid game. Even better, we won. The coach, however, saw things differently and went around the dressing room after the game just ripping into people. He saved his bluest words for me.

He pretty much said I was a big fat zero who had contributed nothing to our victory. I felt humiliated and went home afterward discouraged by the dressing-down I'd received. The next day I woke up determined to bounce back from my subpar outing. I trained hard all week and barely slept. I couldn't shake the empty feeling I was left with following my coach's tongue-lashing.

The next game finally rolled around. I scored several times. I was in on key tackles. I left the field exhausted and covered in mud. Although we won fairly easily, I could see that our team was still struggling on several fronts. Against a stronger opponent, we'd be in big trouble. Still, I was happy with the way I'd played and figured I had saved myself from a roasting by the coach.

The dressing room went silent as the coach strode in. Within minutes he started in on different players. Eventually, his gaze settled on me. "Furlong," he said, "is there a chance you will be making a contribution anytime soon?"

I was stunned. A *contribution?* I'd just had the game of my life. What on earth was this man talking about? I'm not sure how much later it was when the light went on, but eventually it did. My coach wasn't talking about how many points I scored or tackles I made. He was talking about leading. As captain, I had to concern myself with more than just my own little world. "Your job is to help this team succeed," my coach said. "Your job is to lead this team in all respects." What he was talking about was finding a way to imbue my teammates with the belief that they could be the best in the country. I had to teach them that when someone falls down it is a teammate's job to pick him up. When someone falters it is a team-mate's job to cover for him and not be blind to the needs of others in pursuit of one's own success.

That is the contribution to the team that my coach wanted from me. It was one of the best lessons on leadership I ever received.

BY MY EARLY TWENTIES, I had represented Ireland in basket-ball and European handball, and I had played Gaelic football for Dublin. I would discover years later that I scored the very first goal for Ireland in a European handball match. My experiences on the Gaelic football field were the most memorable, however, for the sheer magnitude of the events, if nothing else. We would often play in front of 80,000 people, and when we screwed up on the field they'd let us know it.

I'll never forget walking toward the dressing room after a game early in my career and being met by a man and his son. The man said I was his son's favourite player and that his boy would often wear a team sweater with my number on it. He wondered if I'd sign an autograph for his son. That was the first time that I understood the impact an athlete could have on a child. Instantly, I recognized the role model responsibility the athlete bore. But I also remember thinking what an honour it was to be in that position, to have the power to shape someone's thinking and outlook for the good.

When it came to sports, I was fanatical. I trained hard, I played hard. I was never the most talented guy on my team. If I were to compare myself to a player on a hockey team, I was a second-liner.

Not a star but a notch above the third- and fourth-line grinders. I think I was often asked to be captain of my teams because of my heart and desire. Few people were going to outwork me.

At 23, I was asked if I wanted to coach Ireland's women's basketball team. The women weren't very good. In fact, they were beaten pretty badly most times they played. But I saw the offer as a challenge, something I rarely passed up.

I became possessed with the idea of turning this disparate group of women into something resembling a real team. I decided I was going to make them better no matter what. I remember realizing that when I stood in the middle of the gym floor, looking them in the eyes, making demands of them that they initially thought were impossible to meet, every one of the players looked directly back at me. They were paying attention. That may not sound significant, but for someone who was 23 and a little intimidated by the job I'd taken on, it was. It told me I'd made a connection with these women, giving me confidence that I could make them believe in things they hadn't believed in before. It also gave me some assurance that I could hold a room. I became conscious of the importance of words and the influence they could have on people. Thanks to these women, I also came to understand that if you lead the right way, people will follow.

By the time our first game came along, the women were ready to run through walls for me. I coached them for only two games before events changed the direction of my life, but I would always be proud that we won both of them.

LIVING IN IRELAND, we were somewhat immune to the problems going on in Ulster. Most nights when you turned on the television, there would be some story about "the Troubles" that plagued Northern Ireland, but for a teenager it was a story on television, nothing more. The violence was so commonplace that there would be stories about milk prices, bus fares and telephone strikes before those about someone dying in Belfast because of the Catholic–Protestant war. That would change on the afternoon of May 14, 1974—the day that my family's world changed forever.

At 5:30 PM, as most people were heading home from work, three car bombs exploded in Dublin's city centre. I remember feeling the blasts through my feet as I walked along a street far from where the explosions occurred. Within minutes I could hear the sound of ambulances making their way to the locations of the bombings, which happened on three different streets. In all, 26 people would die.

In the immediate hours after the explosions, everyone in Dublin was frantic to hear from family members and loved ones. I was quick to assure my parents that I was okay. But as afternoon turned into night, my mom's sister, Josephine, and her husband, Ned, hadn't heard from their daughter, Siobhan, who would have been leaving her job downtown about the time of the explosions.

Siobhan was among the dead.

Those who were missing family members were urged to go downtown to a temporary mortuary to identify the bodies. For my aunt and uncle, that task was too much. Besides, they lived 130 kilometres away. My father volunteered for the assignment. He later described a scene at the provisional morgue that was night-marish beyond belief. The bombs had ripped people into pieces. Body parts were stuffed in bags. It was a ring on a finger that helped identify Siobhan.

Many of the dead had been young women who were employed in the civil service and were leaving their offices just as the blasts occurred. There were also 300 injured, many of whom would be permanently disfigured. The Ulster Volunteer Force would claim responsibility for the bombings almost 20 years later.

It would be said that there was no family in Ireland that wasn't affected in some way by what happened that day. I feel the country lost something that it never fully recovered. Bad history biting us again.

My cousin's funeral was difficult to sit through. I remember looking around the church at tear-streamed faces. My aunt and uncle were broken and almost unrecognizable in their grief. So was my father.

I wouldn't realize until later the extent to which the whole appalling chapter in the country's history had emotionally ravaged my poor father. In the weeks that followed, he could barely talk about what had happened. He was haunted by the gruesome images he encountered at the morgue. He was never able to shake the feelings he was left with after having to see his niece's body torn asunder. It was as if he was in a perpetual state of shock.

Less than a month later, on June 4, my father was felled by a heart attack.

He lapsed in and out of a coma. I remember sitting at his bedside by myself and praying that I could have one more conversation with him. He stirred and looked at me.

"What are you doing here?" he said in a whisper. "Don't you have things you should be doing?"

It was so typical of my dad. *Don't you have things you should be doing?* Which meant something better than sitting in a hospital waiting to talk to him, preferably something that would help me get ahead in life and make me a success. During an earlier talk my father had said to me, "We sent you to good schools. We taught you the difference between right and wrong. You know that when something isn't yours you shouldn't take it and if you break something you should fix it. But all these values together aren't going to make you a success. What's going to separate you from the others is how hard you are prepared to work."

I will never forget that.

My father died the next day, June 5, 1974. He was buried beside my cousin, Siobhan. And there would be few days in the following years when I wouldn't see something, or hear someone talking, that didn't make me think of him. I missed him terribly. He was just 63 years old when he died. It would take me a long time to stop feeling angry that my father's life had been cut so short, that he'd been robbed of an opportunity to enjoy life after working so hard for so many years.

Not long after my father's death I was enticed by an unexpected offer. A recruiter from a high school in Prince George, British Columbia, had come to Dublin in search of someone to set up an athletic program. I was a young teacher with just two years' experience. The job intrigued me. My cousin's death, followed so closely by my father's, had left me feeling a little empty, and open to new adventures. I was definitely receptive to the idea of leaving Ireland after what had happened a couple of months earlier.

I decided to take the position, thinking I would return to Ireland in a few years.

IT WAS A FALL DAY in 1974 when my wife and I bundled up our son and daughter and boarded a plane to Canada.

I don't recall much about the long haul over the Atlantic other than looking out the window occasionally at the great white expanse below and pondering just how cold it was going to be when we landed. I spent part of the flight second-guessing my decision. At one point, I pretty much convinced myself that I had made a colossal error—and I had dragged three other people along with me on this misadventure.

But it was too late to obsess about that. Our plane touched down in Edmonton, and we approached a customs agent with our passports and a letter of introduction from the school I would be working at. I will never forget the parting words of the man who interviewed us. "Welcome to Canada," he said as he handed me back our documents. "Make us better."

Soon I was in Prince George starting a new life. My job offered plenty of challenges, but I dove into it with everything I had and made some real headway in getting an athletic program up and running. I had only been at the school a couple of years when I received a call about a position with the city as director of parks and recreation. Compared with what I had been doing, this was a big leap. The city owned arenas and tennis courts among its many recreational properties. I would be in charge of them all. And I would have to deal with unions almost daily. I was 26. I got the job.

If there was a highlight from that time it was in 1978 when I received a call from someone in the provincial government. He wanted to talk to me about the Northern BC Winter Games, which had been started a few years earlier. The Games bring together athletes from across the north to be part of a friendly competition. The government rep asked me if I'd lead a committee to restructure the event, with an eye to moving it around to different communities. In the three years since their inception, the Games had been held in Fort St. John twice and were heading for neighbouring Dawson Creek, provided we could get a new structure in place. So I took it on and with a few colleagues overhauled the structure and set the new course. It was a lot of fun.

Prince George later followed Dawson Creek as host city, and I was handed responsibility for staging those Games. I desperately wanted the Games in my adopted city to be a success, but I didn't have a clue how to do it. It was all learn as you go. Two months before the Games were to open, I decided to phone Iona Campagnolo, who was the Member of Parliament of the northern B.C. riding of Skeena. She was also minister of amateur sports. To my surprise, the minister took my call and when I asked her if she'd consider coming out to open the Games later that year she didn't hesitate to say yes. I couldn't believe it.

It got better.

A day or two later, the minister phoned back. "John," she said, "how would you feel if I brought the prime minister along?"

I nearly dropped the phone. The prime minister was Pierre Elliott Trudeau. I might have been relatively new to Canada but I was aware of Trudeau's star power; most everyone in Europe was. He cut quite the glamorous figure. Now he was going to be coming to this event that I was organizing. At the time, Trudeau was dealing with any number of issues. There were loud noises emanating from Quebec about separation. I didn't fully understand the debate, and I couldn't figure out why anyone in any province would want to leave this amazing country.

Over the next couple of months there was lots of communication with Iona and the Prime Minister's Office. Trudeau wanted to make a speech to help launch the Games. He wanted to skate with the athletes one day. He would need to be briefed on what the Northern Games were all about and why they were important. That would be my job.

The big day arrived, and I was directed by the Prime Minister's Office to go to such and such a room at the Inn of the North hotel. I was sitting there by myself when the door swung open and in walked the prime minister. He shook my hand and we made small talk for a couple of minutes before I started filling him in on the brief history of the Games. He was warm and funny and personable. I, however, was an awestruck wreck who couldn't believe to whom he was talking. I remember thinking about my father and wishing he was still around so I could tell him this story.

After about an hour we walked to the hall, and the crowd was already on its feet. I was behind the prime minister feeling like a 3-million-dollar man. We bounded up the stairs of the stage, and before long I was introducing the guest of honour. I remember acknowledging the problems in Quebec and saying that Trudeau never had to worry about anyone in this part of the country wanting to leave Canada. I even got a bit of a cheer for that line.

Soon it was Trudeau's turn to speak. He'd only been speaking for a few minutes when I was left flabbergasted. His speech touched on almost all the points I had raised during our hour-long meeting, during which he barely took a note. As I listened, I remember thinking I'd never met a smarter person.

A month later I got a letter thanking me for helping him out with his speech and the trip. The letter included a picture of the two of us, taken while I presented him with a token of our appreciation. Only much later did I realize the impact his speech had had on me. I'd never heard someone in such command of an audience before. He didn't have a line written for him, yet the crowd was enthralled. I eventually realized his secret: he spoke from the heart. He talked about the country, his country, and the need for all of us to band together if we were going to be a great country.

I matured 10 years from my Trudeau experience alone. Part of it was listening to him talk; part of it was the pressure I was under to get right everything connected with his visit. And certainly part of it was the enormous responsibility I had at the age of 28, organizing such a huge undertaking. I got a headache on the second day of the Games that has never gone away. It got so bad at the time that I was admitted to hospital, where doctors tried to break up what they told me was a massive migraine. Now I carry medication everywhere I go to manage the headache pain. Most days it's tolerable; some days it's terrible. But it is always there, a constant reminder of a heady time in my life when it all started.

SHORTLY AFTER TRUDEAU'S visit I moved to Nanaimo, on Vancouver Island, to take the job of regional director of parks and recreation. The centrepiece of the region's recreational properties was a new multiplex in Nanaimo called Beban Park. It had an ice rink, swimming pool, playground and tennis courts, among other amenities. It was losing money by the sackful and had become a bit of an albatross for the city. It was my job to turn that situation around.

I figured it would take an entrepreneurial spirit to accomplish this goal. I quickly concluded that we needed to be in the marketplace competing for various entertainment acts that were coming to town. And if I could up the ante a bit and somehow convince bigger names to visit our blue-collar town, we could really turn things around. I didn't know a thing about staging concerts but I would find out, and before long we were attracting the likes of singers Johnny Cash and Glen Campbell.

My biggest early coup was landing the Beach Boys, whom I booked to play at a local car racing track. We had to build the band a $25,000 stage, a lot of money at the time. Still, the concert made a six-figure profit, and I was learning a lot about the entertainment business.

I also got the city involved in the fight business, another thing I was clueless about until I started doing a bit of homework. In the late '70s and early '80s, cities around Canada were staging amateur boxing events called So You Think You Are Tough. There was a kid from Nanaimo who had built up a bit of a legend and had turned professional. His name was Gord Racette. A real-life Rocky, Racette was a security guard by day and a serious brawler by night. He had had success at the professional level in fights throughout the Pacific Northwest, and his exploits were often written about in the local paper. I'm not sure where the idea came from, but I pitched a crazy notion to Racette's manager, Tony Dowling: a fight between the reigning Canadian heavyweight champ at the time, Trevor Berbick, and the hometown hero, Racette. We would stage it at Frank Crane Arena, and it would be a smash success. At least in my head it would be.

But I would need to convince Berbick's camp it was a good idea and not something that would sully the boxer's reputation. I thought a hefty paycheque might persuade him. So I jetted off to Halifax to meet Berbick's people, knowing that I was completely out of my league. We met at a local hotel and I laid out my proposition: Berbick would get $100,000 and Racette, $30,000. Berbick's camp said no deal and ranted on and on about needing more. I wasn't prepared to offer a cent more, so I figured I'd flown across the country for no reason. After hours of high drama and banter, I told them I was sorry we couldn't make a deal and left. It was around 4 AM by this point and I had a flight in five hours. I decided to hop in the shower to wake up. I wasn't in it five seconds when there was a loud knock on my door. I grabbed a towel and answered it. Standing there was one of the guys who had been in

Berbick's room, a six-foot-five-inch bruiser himself. He said Berbick's gang wanted to talk again.

I went downstairs and Berbick's lawyer started haggling again over the take. I said, "Look, I told you that it was my best offer and I wasn't kidding." With that I got up to leave. Berbick walked over to the table, grabbed the contract and signed it. "We're on," he said.

I couldn't believe it. Nor could most of the people back in Nanaimo when I phoned with the news. The fight sold out within hours, and folks still talk about it today. Berbick won by a TKO in the eleventh round, and after it was over he knew he'd been in a battle.

BY THE SPRING of 1982, the economy had gone in the tank and mill towns like Nanaimo had been particularly hard hit. The chamber of commerce decided to put on a forum for local business in an attempt to get people inspired about meeting the challenge the recession was posing. The chamber approached me, of all people, to be emcee and a keynote speaker. They asked me to talk about "what it took to be a winner."

I was petrified. I had never given a major speech in my life. The night before I had stomach pains I was so nervous. I jotted down some thoughts on little cue cards, and before I knew it I was walking onstage to face 600 people, many of whom I knew were skeptical about my ability to say anything remotely motivating. After three minutes I noticed something—the place was completely silent. I took this as a good sign. They were listening. I told them that as a group we had to stop thinking we were all doomed because the economy was bad. It meant only that we had to work harder and be more creative. No one was going to drive up and dump a load of money on our lawns. We were going to have to find ways to create that money ourselves.

Forty minutes later, I was done and found myself awed by the reaction of the audience. I received a standing ovation. It was a big moment for me. Looking back, I have no doubt that listening to Trudeau speak had helped me immensely. The lessons derived from his speech were universal. Speak about what you know. Speak from the heart. Speak with passion. Little did I know that my talk in Nanaimo would be the first of thousands I would give over the coming years.

Outside of work, I was pursuing the sport of squash with the kind of focus and enthusiasm I had brought to Gaelic football, basketball and handball back in Ireland. I kind of stumbled upon squash. While working in Prince George, I decided to give the game a try, and it had grown on me to the point of addiction.

By the time I got to Nanaimo with more losses than wins under my belt, I had set a goal of becoming Canada's national squash champion for my age category. I went at my training hard, often playing six or seven hours a day. I would go to the local club and play the top five guys one after another. On May 2, 1986, the day Expo 86 opened in Vancouver, I took the court in the men's final of the national squash championship in Vancouver. As was often the case, I wasn't the most talented or naturally gifted player in the tournament, but I wouldn't allow anyone to work harder. As usual, that well-worn philosophy paid off.

My involvement in the Northern Games, plus connections I made through squash, helped to get my name known in amateur sport circles. Shortly after arriving in Nanaimo, I got a call from the provincial government asking me if I'd consider taking on a role with the B.C. delegation for the Canada Games, which were being held that year in Thunder Bay, Ontario. The position was assistant chef de mission. My job was to help the chef de mission, doing a lot of his grunt work so that he could concentrate on overall strategies. It wouldn't exactly turn out that way.

The chef that year began exhibiting some rather odd behaviour and suffered nervous exhaustion. It became clear to many of us with the B.C. delegation that he was in trouble, and it was agreed that he should return home. This meant I was now the chef de mission, whose job it was to ensure that our B.C. team had what it needed to perform at its best and that the many needs of the athletes were being met. I had never done anything remotely close to this in my life.

I relied on instinct. It ended up being an incredible learning experience on many levels. Ontario and Quebec edged British Columbia out by a hair to win the Games.

In a nutshell, I had been thrown into heading up an athletic delegation with no previous wisdom to draw upon. On the positive side, I did learn a lot about the Canadian amateur sports system: how it was structured, who made key decisions. I would end up being part of the B.C. delegation at the next six Canada Games.

In late 1987, I left Nanaimo to take a job with the Arbutus Club, a private recreational club in the affluent west side of Vancouver. I had been headhunted for the position and was ambivalent initially about sitting for an interview. But curiosity took me to the club, and before meeting with the hiring committee I walked around the premises. I was shocked at their condition. This was a place that once had a reputation as one of the best private clubs in the country. But as I toured the facilities I saw a club in decline, one that was dull, dated and in disrepair. And I told the members of the committee exactly what I thought.

I got the job.

It didn't take long for me to realize that the place was being scammed by some of the staff. The food and beverage section was losing buckets of money, and when I read the financial statements the figures didn't add up. Something was going on. I hired a private investigator to go to our lounge and watch the bartender. Over a period of three hours she caught him stealing 18 times. So I fired him. When I went to the club on weekends I noticed there were always fewer staff than there should have been. I uncovered a scheme whereby a couple of guys from the maintenance crew would come in and punch the clock for five or six others who were at home. So I fired them too. Not a lot of fun.

My biggest challenge was persuading the board that the club needed a new vision and a major multimillion-dollar facelift. It was time to stop putting good money after bad. I campaigned hard for a new direction. After exhaustive discussion and debate over 18 months, we organized a members' meeting where my proposal was to be debated and voted on. It was one of the largest turnouts in club history, and by the end of the night only 11 of the 950 people who cast a ballot voted against the new direction.

We soon went public with our plans and let it be known we were looking for new members. Within days, people started arriving at the club to join. All our renovations were paid for with cash from our membership drive. During my time there, the club won several industry awards and was able to substantially hike its membership fee to maintain the premier services we began offering.

My time at the Arbutus Club taught me about building a vision and getting people to believe in it. It provided me with some real insights on consensus building. The Arbutus Club was full of wealthy, powerful people who were all wildly successful. These were serious people who were used to getting what they wanted. When it came to running a club, they all had different ideas about how that should be done. It was my job to navigate through those murky waters.

While I was working at the Arbutus Club, I also took on a volunteer role with the BC Games and became involved with the Western Canada Games, which helped broaden my Rolodex of contacts in Canada's amateur sport world even more. I helped evaluate presentations of cities bidding to host the Western Canada Games. It was during this process that I came to understand that when a city is trying to land a major athletic competition, the final decision is rarely based on its planning ability. More often the intangibles make the difference: Who are you? Can you be trusted? And the value-added proposition: What will the Games gain if we give them to your city? I remember Abbotsford's bid to host the Western Canada Games, how they absolutely wowed everyone in the room with their presentation. It was full of passion and vision. I had no choice but to vote for its bid even though Prince George, a town I had sentimental reasons to support, was also in the competition.

After a term as chair of Sport BC, the umbrella agency for sport in the province, I got a call from John Mills, who was CEO of the organization during my time there. It was early summer 1996, and a local group was trying to drum up support for a bid to host the Summer Olympics. A local television station wanted to interview someone from Sport BC about the idea. John couldn't do it, so he asked if I'd stand in for him.

"But I don't know anything about this," I said.

John convinced me that I could shadowbox my way through the interview, and I did. I talked about how the Olympics would open up a new world for amateur athletes in Canada. Somehow, I managed to sound as if I knew what I was talking about. I waxed on a bit about the beauty of Vancouver and the stunning backdrop it would provide. I tried to give those watching some idea of the colour and atmosphere the Games would create. It was a bit of a "can you imagine?" moment that might have sounded good but was pure fly-by-the-seat-of-your-pants stuff. Heavy on the blarney.

I hadn't really thought much about Vancouver hosting an Olympics until then. Little did I know what I would be talking myself into.

2

Enter **Jack** Poole

P EOPLE HAD BEEN talking about hosting an Olympics in B.C. as far back as the 1960s. But in the run up to our Games, it became accepted wisdom that Bruce MacMillan, a vice-president at Tourism Vancouver in the mid-1990s, was the person who got the whole ball rolling.

As the story is told, he walked into the office of his boss, CEO Rick Antonson, and suggested trying to land the 2010 Winter Olympics. Task forces were formed and feasibility studies commissioned as the idea gained currency and real enthusiasm and momentum began building up behind it.

Others, however, insist the first person to bring up the idea in the 1990s was Gary Young, who was director of parks and recreation for North Vancouver. After the district successfully hosted a BC Games, Gary called John Mills at Sport BC and asked him what, if anything, was being done to perhaps bring the Olympic Winter Games to British Columbia. (The idea of a Summer Games bid had been dismissed by now.) The two met and then invited Bruce MacMillan to a later lunch to discuss the idea further, and afterward plans were launched that resulted in B.C. vying for domestic rights to challenge for the 2010 Winter Olympics.

Arthur Griffiths, the former owner of the Vancouver Canucks and someone who had good business connections in the city, was asked to chair the Vancouver/Whistler 2010 Bid Society. The first hurdle was securing the domestic rights. Quebec City was seen by many as the clear and early favourite, and Calgary was in the race too.

I became involved and was given the task of securing votes among the Canadian Olympic Association delegates who would determine the winner. Many of those votes belonged to the heads of various amateur sports organizations I had come to know through my volunteer work with the Canada Games and later the BC Summer and Winter Games.

The elephant in the room for all three Canadian cities was the fact that Toronto was in the hunt for the 2008 Summer Olympics. Many people in the amateur sports world thought Toronto had a decent chance and that going after the 2010 Winter Games for Vancouver was a waste of time and money. I didn't see it that way. I thought the allure of bringing the Olympics to China for the first time would be too great for the International Olympic Committee (IOC) to resist. This was a country of over a billion people, nearly half of whom were children. The emotional dimension of the 2008 Beijing bid was just too compelling.

On November 21, 1998, Calgary, Quebec City and Vancouver made their pitches to the Canadian Olympic Committee (COC). Vancouver's ace in the hole was the B.C. premier at the time, Glen Clark. Clark became an enthusiastic supporter of the bid early on. He loved sports and could see the potential benefit to the province, even though many members of his New Democratic Party caucus didn't like the idea. Clark was also an excellent public speaker and often at his best when he was talking without notes. He gave a command performance in front of the COC. He focused on how

Vancouver had a better chance than Calgary and Quebec City of fending off the other cities around the world that would be going after the Games. It had an allure as a dynamic destination. Besides, Calgary had already hosted the Winter Olympics and the chances of the IOC giving them to the Alberta city a second time were slim. And Quebec City had earlier made a bid for the Winter Games and lost badly.

In December, the COC announced that Vancouver was the winner.

Now things really became serious. All of a sudden we had a major project on our hands. Money would need to be raised. A bigger organization would have to be built. A grand vision would have to be mapped out. A bid committee would have to be formed that included different stakeholder groups, including governments, Tourism Vancouver and relevant amateur sports organizations.

Above all else, the bid needed a chief executive officer to lead the project. My name came up as a possible candidate. I was surprised and extremely flattered and thought it would be a marvellous opportunity. I also thought I could do the job. By this point I knew a fair bit about Olympic sport and I thought I had the right mentality for the position. Suddenly, my mindset changed. I went from being a casual believer in the plan to land the Games to being obsessed with the idea.

I knew one of the big issues that would be on the minds of the hiring committee would be the CEO's ability to raise money to fund the operation until July 2003, when the IOC would make its decision. It was estimated we would need almost $30 million to hire staff, travel, commission studies and draw up plans, among other things. I assumed the committee would be looking for someone with strong corporate connections. In other words, someone who had a more distinguished business pedigree than I. Still, I thought I could make a good case for the job.

The night before I was interviewed I went to see a movie about the Nagano Games that was playing at Science World in

Vancouver's False Creek. I remember sitting through it with a handful of patrons and not being moved by the experience at all. It seemed that the Nagano Games lacked soul. After it was over I went out to my car, sat for a few minutes and decided to go back in and watch the film again. I needed to better formulate in my mind what it was about Nagano that wasn't going to be good enough for Vancouver.

After watching a second time, I realized that to win our bid had to centre on people. We had to reject the traditional model that this was about building infrastructure and boosting the local economy. Those were benefits undoubtedly. The physical and financial legacies of the Games would be enormous. But that wasn't a vision. That wasn't going to get people to buy into what we were selling.

My interview was at 11 o'clock. I was nervous. I walked into a boardroom in a building downtown, where there was a clear view of the North Shore Mountains and the homes that dotted the hillsides below them. The committee chair, Arthur Griffiths, asked me right off the top what I thought these Games should be about. I pointed to the window.

"If the Games don't mean anything to the people living in those homes over there," I said, "if those people don't talk about them in their kitchens, if we don't touch and inspire human beings with the idea of hosting the Games, then our chances of winning will be greatly diminished."

I talked about how we had to offer the IOC something no one else could: an Olympics that included the entire country and that would make its presence felt in every corner of its vast expanse. Our advantage over our rivals was our geography, our sheer size. It was a canvas upon which we could design a Games none of our competitors could match.

Finally, I talked about money. While I didn't have the corporate connections that others did, I believed I could sell a vision for these Olympics that would get the business community excited and eager to climb onboard. I believed I could raise money by being passionate and articulate about what these Olympics could deliver to the country—that would be the easy part.

On the way out of the interview, one of the committee members followed me to the elevator and told me I had been the only candidate to provide a real vision of what the Games could do. Not that it did me any good, as it turned out.

The next day I was told I didn't get the job. It went to Don Calder, a former president of BC Telecom. Don was a solid guy with impeccable corporate credentials. I was disappointed, no question. I wanted the job and thought I could do something special with it.

However, the committee saw something in me and asked if I would sit on the executive and chair the strategic planning committee. I agreed. I felt a little awkward at first, as Don knew I had been a finalist for his job. But that feeling soon passed, and I dug in to help as much as I could. After a year, however, there was a feeling that not enough progress was being made. Things were uneasy and we were limping along. I don't think Don and the job were ever a particularly good fit. He decided to step down, and the search for a new CEO began. Again, I was asked to throw my name in.

I was hesitant at first. What's that old adage? Once burned, twice shy? And I thought the hiring committee might be asking me so it could fill the quota of candidates it needed. I nevertheless agreed. This time the interview process was more rigorous, the questions tougher and more probing. I elaborated on the vision I had outlined the first time around. I presented some new ideas for raising money, uniting the country and engaging Aboriginal Canadians. Overall, however, my presentation hadn't changed much in a year.

The next day I got a call from Rusty Goepel, a senior executive with the investment firm Raymond James Financial, Inc., and one of the most connected businesspeople in town. He headed up the hiring committee.

"I've got good news and bad news, John," Rusty said. "The good news is we found a great guy for the job. The bad news is it's not you. We have selected Jack Poole. However, the committee believes it's a job for two and thinks you and Jack would make a great team. So we want you to sit down and talk to Jack about the two of you working together."

The news left me more disheartened than it had the first time around. Losing twice in a row really stung. I didn't know much about Jack except that he was a big-name developer in town. I wasn't much in the mood for sitting down with the winner to talk about how I might work with him. Besides, I didn't think it was fair for the bid committee to be foisting someone on the new guy. But Rusty was insistent, so to be a good sport I agreed.

I had put down the phone no more than 10 seconds when it rang again. "John," the voice said, "Jack Poole. I've heard lots about you."

He was warm and friendly, as if he'd known me a lifetime. We talked for five minutes, and he asked if we could get together to chat further. We agreed to meet at his office in two days.

When I turned on my car radio that Tuesday morning on my way to the meeting I thought I was listening to an old broadcast from the Second World War. It was real-time coverage of the terrorist attacks on the World Trade Center in New York. I would never forget the date of my first meeting with Jack.

We carried on seamlessly from our telephone conversation. Jack was just an impossible guy to dislike. He had some of the halo effect that Trudeau had and a Kennedyesque charisma. He was a good-looking guy, tall, athletic. We talked about everything: the task ahead, sports and people in town whom we both knew. He joked a lot. He asked me what I thought the vision for the bid should be. I gave him a brief version of my pitch and he agreed. At the end of our conversation he looked at me and said, "John, if you don't agree to work with me on this project I'm not going to do it either."

It would occur to me later that in that moment I had been "Jack Pooled," a phrase I used to describe the man's ability to get people to do things for him. How could I say no? We shook hands. I walked outside and stood on the sidewalk for a moment looking up at Jack's office. He wanted me to be his second-in-command, in charge of several key aspects of the bid's operations. That was an enormous responsibility. And as I stood there, I couldn't help thinking about the significance of this moment. I'd spent my whole life dreaming I'd be part of something this big, but never in a million years had I thought it would happen. I was elated—and a bit scared.

I left for Europe a couple of days later on a golf holiday. I spent most of that time away calling Jack from various pay phones, talking about people he wanted to hire and other matters. I had to get my board at the Arbutus Club to agree to a sabbatical, so I asked Jack to write a letter outlining why he needed my services. I thought the board would be honoured to have its CEO seconded for such a cause. The directors agreed.

In mid-October, on my first day in our sparse offices on Dunsmuir Street in downtown Vancouver, Jack walked into my office, eager to explain how our partnership was going to work. "My desk, no paper," he said. "Your desk, all of the paper." He wasn't joking.

One of the first things we had to prepare for was an event being held in Singapore called SportAccord, a five-day gathering of 1,500 of the most important people in the world of international sport. Among them would be the heads of over 100 international sports federations and almost every IOC member who would have a vote on the 2010 bid. We needed to be there to start introducing ourselves to those who would be deciding our fate. Our competition was attending. This would be the beginning of our international campaign for votes. It was big. I knew enough about the IOC and how it worked to know that delegates didn't waste a lot of their time with underlings. That's why Jack needed to be there. He asked me to accompany him, and I agreed because I knew it would make him feel more comfortable if we were two at a convention full of strangers. But two days before we were to leave Jack walked into my office and announced he wasn't going.

"What do you mean?" I said. "You have to go! You have no idea how important it is that you be there, Jack."

Nope, he said. He had come down with a cold and just didn't feel up to it. We argued some more before I finally gave up. He wasn't going, I was, and that was the end of it.

A few days later I was walking into the conference hotel in Singapore with a knot in my stomach. I didn't have a clue how I was going to penetrate this gathering. It was like bringing a rowboat up to the *Queen Mary*. Overwhelming.

There were a few familiar faces. One was Paul Henderson—not the famous hockey player but rather a champion for the Toronto bid for the 2008 Summer Games, a former Olympian and an IOC delegate. Toronto had lost out that summer to Beijing, and Paul wasn't happy about it. He did not warm much to me, at least not there. He thought our bid had hurt Toronto's chances because of the mixed message he believed it sent to IOC delegates: Canada couldn't make up its mind if it wanted the Summer or Winter Games.

What Paul didn't accept was that as soon as China threw its name in the ring for 2008, it was over for everyone else. Even though Toronto put together a world-class bid that was technically superior to everyone else's, it lost in a landslide. I could understand why people on Toronto's bid committee might be bitter, but being upset at us was unfair. Singapore was not the place to argue about it.

Another Canadian there was Bob Storey. Bob was from Ottawa and head of the International Bobsleigh Federation. He was brilliant and fiercely direct. As such, he was a man of major influence in this arena and knew all of the delegates who would be casting votes for the 2010 Games. We had met earlier in Vancouver, but I introduced myself again and it wasn't long before he was letting me know what he thought of our bid: not much. One of his criticisms was that we hadn't reached out to well-placed Canadians living outside British Columbia. This had created resentment in the rest of the country. He thought we were naïve and without focus.

Without people like Bob on our side, the challenge we faced was going to be even more formidable. I pleaded for his help.

After a long conversation, he agreed. It was one of the most pivotal developments in the bid phase, though I didn't know it at the time.

For the five days I was in Singapore I would shake as many hands as I could. If I saw someone identified as an IOC delegate I'd walk up and say hello. It was cold-calling at its worst and a bit like selling dictionaries in Oxford. No one wanted or needed one. Being a hardcore introvert I was lost, but I had no choice. It was my job, at least on this trip.

On the way home I thought about the nightmare that lay before us. Singapore made me realize what a monster this process was, how much work was going to be involved. While I had met many IOC members, I didn't think the trip had gone particularly well. Votes secured—none. I phoned Jack as soon as I touched down in Vancouver and told him what a mistake it had been for him not to go. Never again, I said.

The next day I went over the trip with Jack almost hour by hour, reciting the names of every person I had met. I told him the process was too unforgiving for blunders and miscalculations. There were going to be dozens and dozens of similar occasions that he was going to need to be at to press our case to IOC voters.

Jack looked at me. "John, I'm not going to do this," he said.

I looked at him, astonished. "What in heaven's name do you mean?"

"It's young person's work, John, and you're young and have lots of energy so you're going to do it."

But what about the work that I was supposed to be doing in Vancouver? I was the chief operating officer. There were technical plans to organize and sponsors to recruit. Who was going to do that?

"You are," he said. "When you absolutely need me I will be there."

I was flabbergasted. I couldn't believe he was asking me to take this stuff on. We went back and forth for another 30 minutes before I gave up trying to convince him why it wouldn't work. He was going to look after the significant, sometimes unpredictable politics of the bid, dealing with the provincial and federal governments, and I would focus on international voters and do the best I could with everything else. This would be the genesis of my transformation from chief operating officer to president. My role was now fundamentally different. As far as IOC delegates were concerned, I was the head guy they were dealing with. I would end up handling huge numbers of the media interviews from this point on too—something I didn't relish.

THE SALT LAKE CITY Olympics were a few months away. That would be another key milestone for us. Throughout any calendar year there are events where IOC people gather. In an Olympic year, there are even greater opportunities to buttonhole them. By the time the Games rolled around in February 2002, we had developed our strategy for hunting down votes.

We decided on a humble Canadian approach. We would tell IOC members that we'd never been involved in anything like this before, and solicit help and advice. We felt it was far more seductive to ask someone for their assistance than to give the impression that we were cocky. We also didn't want anyone to confuse us with the U.S., who, we had discovered, had big issues within the IOC.

We needed to build relationships. The stronger the relationship the harder it would be for that delegate to vote for another city, and the stronger the rapport the greater the degree of trust we would have between us. The one thing we insisted on was not asking delegates for their vote directly. I thought that would be cheesy and too aggressive. We preferred to convince them we were trustworthy and then have them volunteer that we had their vote.

As the months went on, the international team we formed at the bid corporation developed profiles of every IOC member. We amassed massive amounts of useful personal information on each one, never knowing when a single piece of information might come in handy. If asking a delegate about a daughter's graduation from high school helped seal a bond between us, it was worth it.

Salt Lake gave our team a chance to put our strategy in action and see a Winter Olympics up close. Organizers gave us good access. It was fascinating and scary at the same time. I spent a great deal of time flitting from one social and sporting event to another, trying to shake hands with as many delegates as I could. I felt far more at ease than I had in Singapore.

By now I had formed a good relationship with Bob Storey, the Bobsleigh Federation president. I often kidded him about his sport. "Anyone can jump in a canoe and slide down a tunnel of ice," I would say. One day in Salt Lake City I got a call from Bob. "So, want to see if you're man enough to try our sport?" he said. "I've got a ride for you, but you have to be here in half an hour. And by the way, you're going to be in the sled with Princess Nora of Liechtenstein." In an instant, my bravado disappeared.

Driving to the Sliding Centre I was terrified. Sure enough, Princess Nora was there. I knew she was an IOC delegate and it was going to be beneficial to share this common experience—if we survived. Besides the pilot, an American, there would be one other person in the sled with us, a fellow from England. A bobsleigh official gave us instructions about where to hold onto the sled and to put our feet. He told us how to keep control of the head so it would not rock back and forth and smash into the back of the helmet of the person in front of us.

We started down at a reasonable pace, and after making the first turn I thought everything would be fine. Then our bobsleigh fell off a cliff, or so it seemed. Suddenly, we were rocketing down the course. I had my legs wrapped around Princess Nora, who was in front of me and screaming as I'd never heard a person scream before. The helmet of the English guy behind me smashed into the back of mine 50 times, just as the instructor had predicted it would. It didn't take long to get to the bottom, where we were all elated to be alive. I told Princess Nora that I thought I heard her screaming for her mother. She laughed. I was confident we had sewn up a vote.

The highlight in Salt Lake was the men's gold medal hockey game. The Canadian team had been under so much pressure during the entire tournament, and now there was the chance to win gold for the first time in 50 years. Canadian golfer Mike Weir was sitting behind me at the arena. I was astonished to see the number of Canadian flags and jerseys in the crowd. We ended up beating the U.S. quite handily, 5–2, which helped produce a wonderful moment late in the game when people from all nations embraced each other and started singing "O Canada."

The bid team's experience in Salt Lake was beneficial but also sobering. IOC President Jacques Rogge neatly summed up the bottom line for all the bidders. "There's only one gold medal," he said, as he urged us to compete fairly and within the rules. At that point, there were still eight countries looking to win. Many hearts would be broken before this process was finished.

By now there were some internal frustrations inside the bid corporation. Even though we hadn't been at it that long, Jack could see problems on the horizon with how things were structured. He was used to clarity of command. Now he had to answer to a board, in this case one that had not fully gelled. He thought the decision making was too slow. Far better for him to be chair so he could communicate more easily with the board and move operational decisions along at a greater speed. It would mean the current chair, the former Olympian Marion Lay, would have to step aside. Jack was insistent and the board accepted his instincts right after we returned from Salt Lake. Marion remained a director. I became president.

Our next big task was to draft a mini–bid book. This was to give the IOC a general idea of what we planned to deliver, what our venues might look like, how we intended to look after the athletes. It wasn't to be accompanied with precise dollar amounts, but there needed to be enough information in it for the IOC to shortlist the real contenders.

This is one time when Jack and I had a pretty major disagreement. He wanted to make the contents of our bid book public, even though we had no obligation to do so. Bid books were normally handed to the IOC in private, but Jack thought that because this was ultimately a public enterprise, using a lot of tax dollars, there was an onus on us to be as open as possible. I understood, but this was also a competition. Why would we reveal our plans to our competitors? How did we know that they wouldn't try and steal our best ideas or at least devise a way to nullify their impact? I believed there were a couple of areas in which we were going to be vastly superior to our opponents, and I didn't want them scrambling to come up with something with an equal "wow" factor. I compared Jack's proposal to a hockey player telling a goalie which corner he was going to shoot at.

But the day the Austrians submitted their bid book they also put it on the Internet. The Koreans did too. The media in Vancouver rightly began demanding we do the same. We had no choice. I quickly realized I'd made a significant mistake and hadn't demonstrated good judgment. It would only dawn on me later that the jewels we had in our bid, like the Athletes' Village, were going to be impossible for our competitors to match or copy. How was anyone going to duplicate False Creek, one of the choicest pieces of real estate in the world? Similarly, how could they copy our plans to bring the entire country together? None of our competitors had the geography to do something as grand and all-encompassing as we were planning.

If I learned a lesson, though, it was to be as transparent as possible. Worse was looking like you had something to hide.

IN AUGUST 2002, the IOC announced the four finalists, and to few people's surprise, we advanced, along with Salzburg, Austria; Berne, Switzerland; and Pyeongchang, South Korea. The next stop would be a five-day Olympic initiation course in Lausanne, Switzerland, at IOC headquarters on how best to navigate the process and a presentation by the ethics committee on what you could and couldn't do in the company of IOC members. We sent about six delegates. I sat with Terry Wright during the sessions. Terry was one of our best team members and a logistical wizard. He was the person instrumental in putting together our technical bid, which covered venues, transportation and accommodation. He'd worked on countless provincial, national and international sporting events before this. We felt lucky to have him. He had the heart of a lion.

In Lausanne, we sat through many different sessions. During one, Terry had a question that was answered by an IOC official. I then asked Terry if he understood the response and expected him to say, "Yes, thanks very much," or whatever. Instead, he whispered a little too loudly, "Yes, what he's really saying is they are going to ding us for a bunch more money." Well, the whole room heard the aside. My jaw dropped. By the end of the day, word had spread about Terry's retort. Committee officials weren't impressed, and more than a couple told me so. They said that the comment had made us look like rude, arrogant know-it-alls.

That night I went to Terry's room and told him what people were saying. He felt sick. It could never happen again, we both agreed. That's the way this thing worked. The smallest setback seemed like a bid-threatening development that could throw us into depression.

We managed to right the ship in Lausanne. Terry worked extra hard to make sure people didn't think he was too self-assured or cocky. At the end of the final session, I got up and thanked the IOC officials on behalf of all of the bid cities for their time and guidance. We took a lot of notes. We realized our competition was extremely tough.

The next few months I would have to maintain a brutal pace. I would be flying around the world a couple of times. *Votes. Votes. Votes.* That's what it was all about.

Our international strategy was pretty straightforward. We would have to count on Europe to get us over the top. We knew we weren't likely to get far in Asia or most of South America or Africa.

We had the U.S. onside—or so we thought. That left Europe, which we felt optimistic about. And our odds of making inroads there improved after Berne dropped out when an Olympic plebiscite in the city failed to produce the required number of votes to go ahead. Little did I know we would be facing a similar referendum of our own in a few short months. With Berne out, Salzburg and Vancouver were chasing many of the same delegates.

The bid process could hardly be described as logical. Sometimes we sought out Hail Mary opportunities on the off-chance something might work out. Delegates were scattered all over the world, so face time with them was often hard to arrange. When we had an opportunity, we pounced on it immediately. One such occasion occurred that August. Canada was hosting the women's U19 World Cup of soccer. Sepp Blatter, the iconic head of the International Federation of Association Football, or FIFA as it is commonly known, was in the country and, we were told, was going to be passing through Vancouver on his way to Edmonton, where the tournament was being held. Working with our friends at the Canadian Soccer Association, we arranged to squirrel him away for an evening to talk Olympics. Sepp was an IOC member and an influential one at that. We wanted to make an indelible impression on him. We decided this would be a night for Jack Poole and his wife, Darlene, to put on the ritz at their sprawling estate in Mission, a rural community 90 minutes east of Vancouver. The plan was to send a helicopter for Sepp and fly him to Jack's place, while showing off a little of the local geography at the same time.

We met Sepp when he touched down on the estate's landing pad. Yes, Jack had his own landing pad. The Pooles poured on the charm. The steak was brilliant and so was the apple pie. We had a great evening talking to one of the most influential sports kings in the world, who waxed eloquently about sport politics, including those that surrounded the IOC.

Sepp was in his element—at the centre of attention with no pressure. I asked him at one point what his vision was for the game of soccer. "I will not be satisfied until every child on the planet owns a soccer ball," he said. And he meant it. Sepp was a formidable man, short and stocky and with an imposing face, who seemed to dominate his surroundings the way someone much bigger might. By the end of the night we were friends. As always, we didn't ask for Sepp's vote but we were all smiles when he told us we could count on him.

One person who became important to our effort in Europe was Pat Hickey. I didn't know much about Pat, only that he was from Dublin and was a heavy-hitter in the IOC. I figured if I couldn't wrap up the vote of a fellow Irishman we were doomed. I phoned up my brother-in-law, Padraig MacDiarmada, in Dublin and asked him what he knew about Hickey. Padraig said he didn't know much other than that Hickey was often in the news and seemed to be a controversial fellow. Padraig said he'd do a little more digging and get back to me. He phoned back a couple of days later. "You're never going to believe it. Guess where Pat Hickey went to high school? St. Vincent's!"

Pat had graduated four years ahead of me, but it was a wonderful tidbit and gave me a great conversation starter when I called to see if we could meet. A month later Bob Storey and I met him at a restaurant in Dublin. Pat is one of those guys who fills a room when he walks in, a real bon vivant. I told him we were new at this Olympics game, and didn't have enough confidence and needed his help. I wanted him to adopt his former schoolmate. Take me under his wing. It worked. Pat would sign on to "help an old friend" as he often put it, doing as much intelligence work for us as he could.

He became an important insider for us. Whenever he heard any negative scuttlebutt about our bid, he passed it along. One time he told me that someone, likely another bidder, was spreading a rumour that we had no intention of fixing the road from Vancouver to Whistler, which needed to be widened in order to give our bid a shot at success. The B.C. government had committed to making it happen. Pat's tipoff was important because it allowed us to go out and address the misinformation that was being spread.

It had become clear that the Russians would be crucial to our bid. They had six or seven votes, and we had already done quite a bit of spadework to get their support, telling their officials that we'd be happy to help them launch a later bid of their own. The person who ultimately influenced where their votes would go was a man named Yuri Luzhkov. Luzhkov had been mayor of Moscow since 1992, having been appointed by Boris Yeltsin. Since then, he had consolidated his power base in the region and had become one of the most influential people in the country. He owned all the McDonald's restaurants in the city and was quite wealthy.

Late in the game we had arranged to meet Luzhkov during a trip to Moscow. His office was near Red Square. There were about a dozen people milling about in the foyer an hour before the meeting was to start, though I wasn't sure who they were or what role any of them played. We weren't there long before a message was delivered that Luzhkov wasn't going to be able to make it and was sending his deputy. I choked. We had come halfway around the world for this. He was the key guy. He was the one who influenced all of the Russian votes. The room quickly cleared after that news arrived.

Bob Storey and I were then told of another change of plans and were soon escorted into a large, ornate room with massive chandeliers and billboard-sized oil paintings. Within minutes the door swung open and who should walk in but a short, powerfully built man with a bald head and a general demeanour that suggested you didn't want to mess with him. It was Luzhkov.

As it turned out, the earlier message had been a ruse. If he said he wasn't coming, all the would-be power chasers, sycophants and hangers-on would disappear, we were told. We quickly got down to business. Moscow was now fully declared and bidding on the 2012 Summer Olympics. Luzhkov said the country wanted our help with the planning of its bid. We talked about the deal we had earlier worked out with Russian officials: we would show them the ropes, explain how a bid was prepared, and give them our campaign strategy in exchange for their votes.

It seemed perfectly reasonable to me. Bob had structured the deal, and we had spent months finessing it. There was certainly nothing illegal or unethical about it. When we shook hands I never doubted for a second Luzhkov would be good for his word. Say what you want about various aspects of Russian life, the people are loyal. We kept our word and staged a formal workshop for the Moscow 2012 team. We got Russia's crucial support in return. Moscow would lose out to London for 2012.

By the time the bid phase was over in July 2003 I had travelled nearly 2 million kilometres chasing down votes. There were days I could really feel it and had to push myself to go out to some restaurant or cocktail party in Madrid or Reykjavik or Mexico City to have a chat with an IOC member. But I figured that as long as I was asking my staff to test the limits of their endurance, to work harder than they'd ever worked before, I had to do the same. Also, I believed that the tiniest, seemingly most inconsequential gesture or conversation could affect us. That extra mile we went to get a single vote could be the difference between utter joy and utter dejection.

There were days, though, when I was seriously beat. I remember one trip to St. Moritz. It was at the end of a long European jaunt, and I had travelled by car through the mountains most of the day and evening to get to the famous Swiss resort town. It was almost midnight when I finally checked into some no-name hotel, got to my room, threw on my pajamas and flopped into bed. In seconds I was out cold. I woke up around 3 o'clock in the morning in an utter fog. I honestly had no clue where I was. I looked around the drab room for hints, but nothing helped me.

I walked downstairs to the lobby, but there was no one working at the front desk. I still had no idea where I was. I went outside and started walking down the street. I was in my pajamas. I had no shoes on. I remember thinking: *What on earth are you doing, man?* But I was genuinely lost until I came across a confectionery shop a couple doors up from the hotel. I looked in the window and there were some cakes with little bobsleds and curling rocks on top of them. Bobsleds. That's right. I was at the World Bobsleigh Championships in St. Moritz! I felt like such an idiot. And I was scared. I scampered back to the hotel on the balls of my cold feet, praying no one would see me.

MOST OF THE FALL of 2002 was spent preparing our bid book. The organization was just over 50 strong by now. Linda Oglov, our marketing chief, had raised over $30 million and signed many sponsors big and small. So our bid book would be top-drawer and we could afford a world-class campaign. The bid book had to include our definitive plans and cost estimates. This was the document against which the IOC and the Canadian public would hold us to account. It was a massive undertaking and we had been working on it for the better part of three years. It would be made public in January 2003 and be the basis of a major presentation to the IOC's evaluation commission in the spring.

But the civic elections of November 2002 threw us a curve. Mayoral candidate Larry Campbell had promised during his campaign that if elected he would hold a referendum on whether to host the Olympics. It was a pure populist move, and I was livid at Larry. Still, I didn't think he'd follow through if he got elected. Well, he won in a landslide, and he quickly made it known he had no intention of backing off his pledge to voters.

Jack went to visit Larry to see if he could move him off this promise. He had no luck. So I decided to take a run at him myself, two Celts going head-to-head. I didn't mince my words. "You know what you've done, don't you?" I said.

"What?" responded Larry.

"You've sent a message to the IOC that their time is worth nothing," I continued. "You've indicated that everything we've said so far about the city being behind this exercise is questionable. You've suggested that we don't fully believe our own story anymore, that we're second-guessing if we should be in this thing. And in the process we've tied up the IOC's time through visits and presentations and now we're saying that we may not have really meant it after all."

Larry was having none of it. He said his position was a matter of trust and integrity; he'd made an election promise and he was going to honour it. I told him he could easily tell the public he'd reconsidered his position on a referendum and had decided it would not be in the best interest of the bid for a vote to go ahead. Or he could say it was too expensive. But he was adamant. The best he could do was promise me that he'd campaign for the Yes side.

I was furious. A similar vote had killed Switzerland's bid, and now there was a chance the same thing could happen to us. Publicly, I took a different position because I felt I had no choice. If I railed against the plebiscite it would look as if I was worried about the outcome. Instead, I chose to take a positive view, suggesting that I was convinced that the vote would be overwhelmingly in our favour. Others weren't so sure.

David Podmore, a local developer who headed up Concert Properties, the firm he had founded with Jack Poole, came to our offices one day shortly after the referendum was announced and offered us some blunt advice: if we didn't have a Vote Yes campaign the 2010 bid corporation was going to be out of business. Even though a majority of Vancouverites might be in favour of hosting the Games, he said, they might not feel it was important enough to waste part of their day going out and casting a ballot. And if those people stayed home, the bid was going to be in trouble.

He was right. Thankfully, David agreed to chair the campaign and bring his trademark energy and focus to the project. With David out front, Jack was sure we would succeed. There were few people in the city with David's skills package. It was why he was so often asked by government to help turn around troubled projects.

In the run-up to the plebiscite, he was relentless. He went on radio talk shows to debate those opposed to the Olympics. He opened up a Yes campaign centre that hundreds of canvassers he recruited used as a base. He raised an estimated $700,000 to finance the campaign. I don't even want to think what might have happened without David's efforts.

I continued to have serious words with Larry right up until voting day. I think he came to realize how ugly it would have been if the No side prevailed. It would have tarnished his term as mayor, without a doubt. The business community would have been furious. So he was probably as relieved as anyone when on February 22, 2003, the Yes side prevailed, 64 per cent to 36 per cent for the Nos. It was not a landslide, that's for sure, but it was a solid victory. And more importantly, the bid corporation wasn't put in the position of deciding what to do if the vote had gone another way. Jack was of the opinion that no matter the outcome we were going ahead. I didn't agree. I felt that if we lost it was pretty much over. I just couldn't see how we could go ahead without a mandate.

WE NOW HAD just a couple of weeks to prepare for the visit of the IOC's evaluation commission. This was going to be a seminal moment. It was the commission's job to take stock and compare the relative merits of each bid city's plans. The visit would mean driving up to Whistler and not only showing commission members the infamous road we vowed to fix but the sites we had chosen for various sporting competitions. The climax of their visit would be a day-long presentation on 18 different aspects of our bid.

The commission's opinion was hugely influential. If it liked what it saw, word spread, not just among members of the IOC executive in Lausanne but among all voting delegates. A thumbs-down would almost certainly be the kiss of death.

To prepare, we had months earlier put together a mock commission made up of several members of our international team, plus a few people who had experience working on other Games. The group included people like George Hirthler, an Olympic bid consultant from the U.S.; Charlie Battle, an executive member of the organizing committee of the 1996 Summer Games in Atlanta; Richard Bunn, a former Swiss television executive and insider with the International Ski Federation; Roger Jackson, a Canadian with loads of Olympic bid experience; Petter Ronningen, the chief operating officer of the Lillehammer Games in 1994; Bob Storey and others.

We wanted our presentation team to be ready for anything, so in that spirit we asked our mock commission to be tough and unrelenting. It was. Almost too much so. Some of the sessions got derailed by the caustic manner of some of the faux commissioners. "Your plan is shit," I recall someone saying about one presentation. "It's garbage and you sound arrogant." The harsh tone was not helping build confidence among members of my executive team. I decided to step in and get our mock commission to dial back some of the caustic remarks. "You need to cool it," I said to Richard Bunn after one particularly gruelling and testy session. "We're not going to perform open-heart surgery in that room. We're two weeks away from the real evaluation commission being here. You're supposed to be helping this team, not making them a bundle of nerves."

The head of the evaluation commission was a guy named Gerhard Heiberg. He was from Norway and a bit of a legend in Olympic circles. He had been brought in to help rescue the Lillehammer Olympics when organizing went off the rails. He did a masterful job and Lillehammer became the gold standard against which all other Winter Games would be compared. Early on, it was suggested I get to know Gerhard because he was such an important figure within the IOC. I set up a meeting with him in Oslo before new rules were brought in prohibiting bid cities from visiting IOC officials in their home towns. We met for breakfast in a hotel and talked for a few hours. I was well prepared and knew lots about his life, from his time in the military to his career as a successful businessman. I knew his opinion carried enormous weight with the IOC. It was the beginning of a strong and lasting friendship. It was after Gerhard and I had established ties that the IOC announced he would be heading up the evaluation commission for our bid. I thought our ship had come in. It was a huge break.

He would turn out to be one of the key individuals upon whom I relied heavily for advice along the way. And because he was head of the IOC's marketing committee, he had top-level corporate connections all over the world and was clearly someone who would be able to help us over the long term were we to succeed in Prague. I liked him very much as he had great values and deep integrity. I also wanted him to have a soft spot for us. And while I didn't expect him to play favourites, I was hoping he would help us avoid a bid-ending mistake.

The 18 IOC evaluation commissioners arrived in Vancouver at the beginning of March. The visit was tightly scripted, with almost every minute of every day accounted for. The second day included the trip to Whistler. The weather was magnificent and the drive up magical. It would be the one occasion where my friend Gerhard didn't do me any favours.

We knew he was going to get questions from the media about the road to Whistler. It was a lingering issue. It was narrow and unsafe. But the province was committed to improving it so it could accommodate more traffic more safely. Still, as Jack Poole had once put it to reporters, it was the Achilles heel of our bid. "Rocks as big as Volkswagens are falling on the road," he'd said.

When Gerhard was asked by a reporter about the road, he said, "It's too far to Whistler." I was standing beside him at the time. My heart sank. Gerhard had just given the media a juicy sound bite that would reverberate around the world in a matter of minutes. We now had a problem on our hands, one we needed to remedy quickly. I found some time alone with Gerhard to discuss what had happened. I knew he was not feeling good about what he'd said and I didn't want to rub it in, but I was honest. "Our team is a bit ruined by what you had to say and they're not sure what to make of it," I said. He nodded understandingly.

"Look," I continued, "it's not for me to say ultimately, but if I were you I think you could rectify the situation by saying that the distance of the road is a given. But efforts to make it safer and more efficient would materially affect the bid and you are confident it will get done." He agreed.

Gerhard would later clarify his comments, which some media took as backtracking from his earlier remark. But the tempest wouldn't last for long. We had arranged for Prime Minister Jean Chrétien to be in Whistler at the same time as the commission. I asked the Prime Minister's Office if it was possible for Chrétien to spend a little time alone with Gerhard, maybe over a beer. I knew that the prime minister would be comfortable in that setting and, more importantly, I knew Gerhard would be thunderstruck by the honour. So we made it happen. The pair spent more than an hour drinking beer and talking. I waited outside the pub praying it was all going well.

What I wanted the prime minister to impress upon Gerhard was just how committed the country was to this bid. When they shook hands at the end, I wanted him to feel that there would be no problems with support from the federal government. That was an important stipulation in the minds of the IOC. It was pretty clear talking to Gerhard on the drive back to Vancouver just how much his time with the prime minister meant to him. He'd never get easy one-on-one time with the prime minister of Norway, a country a fraction the size of ours. From that point on, I thought he had a quiet personal desire to see us succeed. He liked us. As we moved forward, I thought we could count on him to sing the praises of our bid in private conversations with his IOC colleagues around the world. That was huge.

After Whistler, we returned to Vancouver, where we had to make our presentations to the commission, covering plans for everything from transportation and sponsorships to tickets and venues.

We had built a stunning presentation hall at the downtown Pan Pacific Hotel. We put the commissioners in big padded seats on an elevated dais to make them feel special. I thought we really nailed our presentations. After we were done, Gerhard told me there were two or three aspects of our plan that we should not make public again because they were so good. The next time you talk about these things, such as the torch relay, should be in Prague, he said. Why reveal our best weapons to competitors?

The final day was going to be capped off with a dinner planned by Darlene Poole, a consummate hostess, and an entertainment extravaganza at the Queen Elizabeth Theatre. The commissioners would be leaving the following morning, so the idea was to send them off feeling as positive about Vancouver as possible. We packed the theatre with almost 3,000 friends of the bid. While Gerhard and the commissioners were at a reception, I slipped over to the theatre to prepare the crowd for their arrival. I went onstage and told the audience how important it was to make the commissioners and, in particular, the chair, Gerhard Heiberg, feel important.

Prime Minister Chrétien, Premier Gordon Campbell and the commission members arrived and were waiting outside the auditorium doors for their introduction. When the commission members entered, the place went bonkers. It was just the kind of over-the-top reaction I was hoping to get. The astonished look on Gerhard's face said it all. He looked over at me and broke into a wide smile. The commissioners took their seats for the show, which included Aboriginal performances, singing and, of course, speeches.

Acclaimed music producer David Foster came up from Los Angeles to perform. The passion was a mile high that night. At one point during Jean Chrétien's speech, he said, in fun, "What's all this talk about if, if, if we win the Games? There's no *if*, there's only *yes*." The crowd ate it up. (One commissioner from Japan was less than impressed and suggested the next day at the airport that we keep that kind of bravado under control in Prague. A little more humility would reflect better on us, was the message.)

Eventually, it was time for me to speak and to introduce Gerhard, and when I did the crowd stood on its feet and cheered as if Brad Pitt had arrived. He couldn't even begin to talk for several minutes because of the ovation. Over the next 10 minutes he would be interrupted constantly by screaming and clapping and shouts of "We want the Games, We want the Games." At one point, Gerhard raised his hands and said, "Okay, okay, stop, we'll give you the Games." Mission accomplished.

The next day, we took the commission members to the airport. We were in the Maple Leaf Lounge when Prince Willem-Alexander of the Netherlands took me aside to say he had a problem: "I have a bit of a rip in my pants." He then bent over and showed me a tear that went from the top of his pants to his crotch. One of our team members, Andrea Shaw, was nearby and realized what was going on. She told the prince that she was a seamstress and that she could probably find a needle and thread somewhere in the airport if the prince was willing to surrender his pants. So right there in the middle of the lounge, the Prince of Orange stripped down to his boxers. For the next 20 minutes he sat in his chair, white-legged, reading a paper as if nothing had happened. Eventually Andrea returned with the pants sewn up nicely and the crisis was averted.

"You know," I said to the prince as we walked to the gate, "if we don't get the Games this story might get out."

He laughed.

"I hear you," he said. "I hear you."

3

Flight **2010** to Vancouver

W ITH THE EVALUATION commission gone, our
focus turned toward decision day in Prague.
It was less than three months away, and if
I thought about it long enough I began feeling queasy. At stake
was nothing less than the dreams of millions of Canadians. Polls
showed the country supported our efforts. And while there were
people in Vancouver and Whistler who were not Olympic boosters,
I knew that on July 2 the big city and the small town would stand
still when Jacques Rogge strode to the podium to deliver the verdict.

Before then, there was plenty of work to do. I still had a couple
of big trips, including another SportAccord conference, this time
in Madrid. When I walked into the conference this time, however,
there were few people I didn't know. My nervous introduction to
the IOC world in Singapore two years earlier now seemed ages ago.
I knew that in Madrid our two rivals would be making strong final
pushes for votes as well, especially the Koreans, who many felt
were in third place heading down the home stretch.

I didn't share this view. All of our closely guarded intelligence
indicated that we were in front, with South Korea a nose behind.

If what we were hearing was correct, and the promises that IOC members were making held up, we had Salzburg a distant third. But in the often murky world of the IOC, you never knew.

The meetings we had internally to discuss delegate support sometimes got rowdy. They usually involved Bob Storey and I and certain members of our international team, many of whom had been on the mock commission we formed to test our presentation to the evaluation commission. We would go down the list of IOC voters, from top to bottom, discussing where we saw each one of them: solidly for us, solidly against us, on the fence.

Disagreements about where a particular delegate stood often got loud. "You're full of shit," you might hear someone bark. I didn't care too much if feelings were hurt. I just wanted an honest debate; if we couldn't reach consensus around a particular person, we had to go back out and see if we could find additional information or focus on a new strategy that might help us land that extra vote. It was a thankless process. Even when you thought a vote was secure, it took about five minutes for doubt to creep in. Trust was in short supply.

I was worried about the Koreans. I thought they were walking a fine line when it came to honouring the IOC's rules around gifts or incentives you could give voters. Everything had been tightened up in this area after it was revealed that organizers of the Salt Lake City Olympics had offered IOC delegates an estimated $10 million in cash and gifts in exchange for their votes. Now the most you could offer an IOC member was a present of trinket value.

I remember a key gathering in Buenos Aires. A full complement of sport delegates would be there, but I was going down to focus on the eight IOC members in attendance. I went to Argentina with just one person, Carlos Garcia, a Toronto-based colleague and a member of our international team. He had strong South American roots and was fluent in Spanish. The Austrians had a delegation of three. The Koreans had more than 20. My eyes grew even wider when a squad of beautiful young Korean women walked into the presentation hall carrying gift bags full of goodies. I saw one delegate pull a watch from one bag. Someone lifted a compact disc player out of another.

More than one person had asked me if I wasn't concerned that we were losing ground to the Koreans because of their blatant tactics. The flip side of that was the implicit suggestion that perhaps we should start employing the same tactics. I was never going to do it and was never convinced it was a guaranteed strategy anyway. My feeling was that if you were inclined to accept something that effectively amounted to a bribe, then you were just as likely to take it, promise something in return, and renege on that promise 10 seconds after you walked away.

While the IOC had certainly cleaned up its protocols since the debacle in Salt Lake City, there were still some marginal characters around the organization. One who represented the worst of the IOC was a fellow by the name of Ivan Slavkov. Slavkov was an IOC member from Bulgaria who did not have a sterling reputation. He had been investigated by the IOC in connection with bribery allegations levelled by officials from Cape Town who were bidding to stage the 2004 Games that went to Athens. The South African officials had said Slavkov had promised to deliver votes in exchange for money. After an inquiry, the IOC decided not to pursue the matter.

I met Slavkov at a restaurant in Sofia in the winter of 2002 while attending a meeting of the International Sports Press Association there. As a courtesy I brought him a small gift, a corkscrew that had a First Nations design on it. It came in a beautiful box that also had a Native motif embossed on it. The whole thing might have cost $25. I noticed that Slavkov had two bags beside his chair, one more full than the other.

During our conversation he talked about how expensive the bidding process was for cities and how difficult it could be to get IOC members onside. Reading between the lines, I thought that he was suggesting there was still work to do and people to influence if we were going to be successful. Then he talked about his son and how he wanted him to get into Canada. That's when I started to feel a bit uncomfortable and began wrapping up our conversation. I presented him with our token gift. He opened it and examined the corkscrew, seemingly in disbelief. He took the arms of it and moved them up and down slowly a few times, as if he'd never seen one before. I imagined Ivan in a T-shirt that read "I MET JOHN FURLONG AND ALL I GOT WAS A LOUSY CORKSCREW."

He set the wine opener down and reached for one of the two bags beside him, the smaller one. "And this is a little something from me," he said.

I waited to get back to my hotel room before peering inside. In it was a T-shirt with a picture of Slavkov embossed on the front. If I was being generous I'd say it probably retailed for $2.50. I guess this was his way of saying he didn't think too much of the corkscrew.

The meeting with Slavkov gave me the creeps. What an over-sized ego. He was definitely old-school IOC and the type of member the committee was trying to rid itself of. In 2004, the BBC would secretly film Slavkov offering to deliver votes for London's bid for the 2012 Summer Games in exchange for bribes. A year later, Slavkov would be charged with bringing the organization into disrepute and kicked out.

There were all sorts of strange characters out to make a buck from the Olympics. We were constantly approached by people who were essentially influence peddlers promising to deliver votes in exchange for money. Some were subtle, others downright blunt. These weren't IOC members but people who operated on the periphery of the committee and were apparently tight with people on the inside—or so they would tell you. I liked to call these guys secret agents because they always seemed so mysterious. The IOC had warned us about them.

We heard about this one guy who boasted that he had sway in the ski world and beyond. Former Canadian Olympian Steve Pod-borski, who was on our international team, had suggested we meet with him. The guy claimed to have worked at one time for the Israeli secret service and to be well connected. That was enough to make me reluctant to even talk to him, but Steve convinced me that it might be worthwhile so we set up a meeting in Zurich.

Bob Storey and I met him in the courtyard of a hotel. He was a stocky, tough-looking character and not exactly brimming with charisma. We listened to his pitch, regretting every second of the rendezvous. He claimed he had connections throughout the IOC and could put us in a position where we would know with certainty how many votes we had. And, he said, he could also help secure votes we didn't have. And just to make sure we understood how vital he was to our success, he told us we would likely lose without his services.

I felt utterly uncomfortable. All I could think was this was some sort of set-up—that hidden cameras were trained on our conversation. Out of curiosity, I asked him what he was looking for. He wanted $40,000 a month, and for that he would provide us with regular reports as well as other documentation that would give us all the intelligence we would need to win. I didn't say much but could not wait for the meeting to end. Bob and I thanked him for his time.

I felt sick as we walked away. Bob too. The experience left me feeling so grimy I wanted a shower.

That man would not be the last foreigner who offered to help us out. But I felt that relying on a lineup of internationals said you didn't have much confidence in people in your own country—which looked horrible. These guys were everywhere and I wasn't interested. If we lost because we didn't hire them, so be it. I was prepared to live with that. We all were.

LIKE OTHERS ON our team I was giving speeches everywhere by this point, at IOC-sanctioned events and also across Canada as I attempted to drum up national support for our project. Most of my speeches were based on a document I wrote in September 2002 entitled "What Dreams May Come." I had written it in the hopes it would be published in the *Vancouver Sun*—it was rejected. The editors felt it was too long and also that it was too rah-rah. Maybe it was, but it was really the outline of the vision we had from the start for these Olympics, one that admittedly might have seemed audacious back then. In it, I asked people to imagine a six-week period in which the entire planet would stand and watch "in amazement as the spirit of higher-faster-stronger sweeps Canada off its feet."

"Volunteers," I wrote, "will come from small towns, villages, hamlets and big cities. Not just ordinary volunteers either. The blood of generations of pioneers flows in the veins of this generation too... We carry their flame, their inspiration and their legacy of drive and tenacity."

I said that for the people of the world coming to Canada would be like coming home. That's the kind of people we were. The word *Canada*, I noted, was derived from the native word *Kanata*, meaning "meeting place." How appropriate. I imagined what the Games might do for our country. "The Games will come and go... And as they pass into memory we will emerge uplifted for the experience and our country will seem a little better, a little taller than before. Folks may use the words 'the best there has ever been.' And we hope we will have earned that distinction."

When I first started talking publicly in these terms, there were far more skeptics than believers. But the document would become my Olympic manifesto, the credo of our bid, the inspiration for our business plan, the foundation upon which the 2010 Games would stand.

Before the vote in Prague, I decided to send all IOC members a letter thanking them for the time they had shared with me over the previous couple of years. Even if I knew they were not going to be supporting our bid in Prague, I thought it was important to acknowledge the journey we'd all been on and to express, in a heartfelt and personal way, my gratitude for the role they had played. This was going to be a huge job: almost 120 letters I'd need to write by hand. I thought I could do a lot of them while on planes, jetting from one place to another, and I was happy we had good files on each member.

My hand began cramping up after the tenth letter, but I was determined to get them written and sent off a month before Prague. While I wasn't really expecting to get any votes in return for the gesture, you also never knew. It might help sway a fence-sitter. Plus, I thought it would reflect well on the bid and on Canada generally. I thought it might say something about the type of people we were.

One day, I was flying back from Mexico via Los Angeles with 50 or 60 letters neatly stacked on the empty seat beside me. The flight attendant came by with a tray loaded with water and proceeded to stumble and dump it all over my letters and me. Honest to God, I could have opened the door of that plane and thrown her out. She was mortified. She ran and got some paper towels and frantically started drying the letters. Some we were able to salvage, many we weren't. What I didn't know at the time was that she had been trying to drum up the courage on that flight to pitch her case to leave the airline and work on the 2010 Games if we won the bid.

Fast forward several years. We were having an open house at my office so I could spend time face to face with our staff, many of whom were slaving away day and night on the project. About 600 or 700 people came by that day. A woman who looked vaguely familiar came up to say hello. "Do you remember a time when you were on a flight from Los Angeles and the flight attendant spilled water all over some letters you were working on?" I did, I said. "That was me." She told me about losing the courage to ask me about working for us after she'd spilled the water. We managed to have a good laugh. She was a great catch for us too.

Five days after I put those letters in the mail I had a call from an IOC member from the United States. He wanted to tell me how touched he was by the letter. He then said, "Stop worrying about me. I'm onside and will help any way I can." I was beaming. If his was the only win I got, it was worth all the pain and suffering.

As we got closer to Prague, I grew concerned about the quality of our presentation. Establishing the right mood in the conference hall where our final pitch would be delivered was going to be essential. Beyond the speeches, we hoped to knock people out with a breathtaking video that captured the beauty of Canada and the wonderful spirit of our people. From the second our team walked through the door we needed to own that room.

There would be a massive screen upon which we would be casting images of our country. I had decided with Jack's support to use the song "Here I Am" from the movie *Spirit* as our main anthem. It was a beautiful piece, sung by B.C. rock star Bryan Adams, which made its use even more salient. I thought the lyrics would strike a chord with the IOC members too.

> Here I am—this is me
> There's nowhere else on earth I'd rather be
> Here I am,
> Just you and me
> And tonight we make our dreams come true.

But it was going to be essential that the images in the video strike the hearts of everyone in the room. We needed to find a way to take their breath away. On a Saturday less than two weeks before we left for Prague, I went to our cramped offices, now located in the historic Landing building on Water Street in Gastown, to take a look at the video that our creative wizard, Marti Kulich, had put together. There were about 10 of us in the room. Marti darkened the lights and turned the video on. For the next few minutes we all sat in silence as dozens of images crossed the screen.

I began getting worried. Others were too. It was awkward.

What Marti had put together was fine, but it didn't wow me. If you took out the iconic images of the Mounties and the Maple Leafs, it could have been put together by any country. I also didn't think it was nearly inspiring enough. There were no children. There wasn't enough soul or talk about hopes and dreams and aspirations for Canada. So when the lights went up I looked at Marti and told him how I felt.

"This is just not going to work," I said. "We need to light up the screen and we're not doing that. It just isn't nearly human enough, Marti. It doesn't connect with our vision. It lacks the thunder that we need."

One of the ideas we were tossing around at the time was having a ring of fire around the roof of BC Place Stadium, where the opening and closing ceremonies would be held. It would effectively become the Olympic cauldron, the biggest in history. I wanted to show delegates what that would look like in our video. Possible or not, it would make for stunning imagery. There was a lot of arguing and people talking about all the reasons why we couldn't do the video revisions, how much money it would cost and how little time we had. "I don't care how much money it costs," I said. "If it's technologically possible, then we must show it. For starters we need the ring around the stadium to explode into flames."

The discussion developed into quite a row. There was a screaming match at one point before I stopped it all. Marti was deflated. "Marti," I said, "that's it. We've got 10 days. Let's get it done. You are the only one here who can pull this off." A few days later, Marti had a new video ready that was everything I hoped for.

(There were other people in the building that day who could hear the yelling going on inside our conference room. As I was walking down the hall, an assistant came up and asked me what had just happened. "I think maybe we just became a real team," I said.)

The next big issue that had to be resolved was who would be onstage for the presentation, to give us the best shot at winning. This was always going to be a dicey proposition and highly political. I was dreading it. Rules allowed 11 people onstage, but because of time constraints it wasn't going to be possible or practical for all of them to talk, so there were going to be some bruised egos. But some people *had* to be up there: Jack Poole, the chair of the bid; me; the prime minister; the premier; some recognizable athletic stars.

We had commitments from Wayne Gretzky, gold medal speed skater Catriona Le May Doan and Steve Podborski, who was not only the first man ever to win an Olympic skiing medal for Canada but who had also put in a lot of work on our bid. We also wanted Jamaican-born Charmaine Crooks, a former Olympic track star and IOC member, to talk about cultural diversity. We felt we needed to have Vancouver Mayor Larry Campbell onstage and Chief Gibby Jacob of the Squamish First Nation, on whose hereditary lands much of the Games would be played out. Finally, we believed that Michael Chambers, president of the Canadian Olympic Committee, had to be there.

That meant there would be no Paul Henderson, who was an IOC member, and no Dick Pound, also an IOC member and probably one of the most recognizable Olympic names in the country. The decision to leave Dick off the ticket was very touchy. Dick wasn't shy about expressing his opinion about anything, anytime. He was direct and could rub people the wrong way. He'd been around the IOC a long time, handled some controversial issues such as doping, and had made himself a few enemies inside the organization as a result. That was evident when he ran for the IOC presidency in 2001. Jacques Rogge won. Dick finished a disappointing third behind South Korea's Kim Un-Yong, who was implicated in the Salt Lake City bribery scandal and would later be prosecuted and jailed by the South Korean government.

Dick's name seemed to come up in most conversations I had with IOC delegates, and not usually in a flattering way. Over the closing months, one of the members of our international team had a discussion with Juan Antonio Samaranch, the former IOC president, about our bid. Samaranch told our guy that if Dick Pound stood to benefit from the Games being in Canada in even the slightest way our chance of success would be diminished. It was evidence of the sometimes bitter rivalries that exist within the IOC.

Dick didn't offend me in any way and he was unquestionably one of the IOC's brightest minds. The modern IOC owed him a lot too and, while I wanted to remain on good terms with him, I didn't want the awkwardness of his situation to be a detriment to the bid. I remember one time I was in Manchester for the Commonwealth Games, which always drew an IOC crowd. It was late July 2002. I was sitting in the lounge of the hotel with a few people when Dick came over and sat down. My paranoia kicked in. I was a little worried about being around him to be honest, not because he wasn't a decent guy, but because it could create a guilt-by-association problem for me, and we couldn't afford that. A few minutes after he arrived I got up to leave. As I walked away Dick yelled out: "What's wrong, afraid of being seen with a real live IOC member?" It was a bit of a shot but I ignored it. It wouldn't be the last uncomfortable encounter with Dick before the bid announcement.

The final days leading up to Prague were mostly a blur. One job I remember was phoning the Prime Minister's Office to book a time to talk to Jean Chrétien about the speech he would be giving as part of our presentation to the IOC. We had only an hour, including time for questions and answers. A lot to cover and everything had to be tightly scripted. There was no room to veer off course and start to ad lib. We were a little concerned that Chrétien might just do that. He had a penchant for talking off the cuff, or "straight from the heart" as he liked to say. Straight from the heart was fine as long as he did it within the time parameters we gave him. Ideally, we wanted him to deliver the words we were giving him, which I had drafted subject to his approval. The question was how to tell him.

Just days before Prague I got the prime minister on the phone. "I just wanted a few minutes to go over our Prague strategy with you," I began.

"Our strategy?" he replied. "Our strategy is to win, no?"

I laughed. Yes, our plan was to win. But the presentation had to unfold precisely as we drew it up. We needed the prime minister to eloquently convey to the IOC that the bid had the backing of the federal government and that he, personally, had an unshakable commitment to the project and to us.

At one point he said, "You know, John, I'm a pretty good public speaker. If things aren't going well over there, I will improvise." Which is exactly what we didn't want him or anyone else to do. So I told him something that, perhaps, stretched the truth a little. I told him we had to submit the speeches to the IOC ahead of time. Once we did there couldn't be any big surprises. I told him I'd written some remarks for him and would be grateful if he would deliver them verbatim if he was comfortable doing so.

He said, of course, he would do whatever we needed him to do. Getting to Prague was going to be hell for the prime minister, who had to be in Ottawa for Canada Day celebrations. He was going to have to board a plane as soon as his obligations there were over and fly through the night to arrive in Prague one hour before we were scheduled to go onstage. The man was a warrior who wanted to win the bid as badly as any of us.

ON THE GROUND in Prague it was nail-biting time. The Koreans had set up shop well before us. Samsung, the Korean electronics giant, had seemingly bought up every inch of billboard space in the city. It was as if the company, and by extension Pyeongchang, had taken over the place. Not only were their signs everywhere, but so were members of the Korean delegation. It seemed as if there were hundreds of them, spread out all over the city looking for an IOC voter to corner. We were all staying in the same hotel as the IOC members, but the floors they were on were off limits to everyone else. Whenever a few of them went downstairs, officials from Pyeongchang would be on them like fruit flies on a peach.

I grew concerned that members of our group might be tempted to lose their discipline. I didn't want anyone, under any circumstances, changing anything, promising anything, no matter how seemingly innocuous, to an IOC member in exchange for his or her support. We had been meticulously clean throughout the race, and I was determined that we were going to continue being that way to the end.

Most days our team assembled in the dingy, dark confines of the Charles University Faculty of Law, where we had rented space for run-throughs of our presentation. Premier Gordon Campbell was terrific, working with people on their speeches, quietly reassuring everyone they were going to be great once the spotlight hit them. It was a side of Campbell that the public rarely gets to see, and I thought that if people did they would undoubtedly feel differently about him. He had a warm, funny, compassionate dimension that really shone through in Prague.

Wayne Gretzky arrived with his family a few days before the vote. Wayne has a legendary fear of flying, so agreeing to hop on a plane for 16 hours was incredibly kind of him. He showed up at the daily practice sessions and then disappeared. He told me he didn't want the media swarms to become a distraction for the group. I really wanted Wayne there after hearing an interview with him and CTV's Rod Black in which he talked about the thrill of playing in the Olympics for the first and only time in Nagano. He said it surpassed any of the four Stanley Cups that he'd won, which was a pretty amazing statement. Hearing that sentiment coming from such a world-recognized athlete would mean an incredible amount.

We set up a little war room in a space adjacent to my room in the Intercontinental Hotel, and each day a small group of us—Bob Storey, Jack and I, mostly—went over the delegate list, checking, double-checking, our support and talking last-minute tactics. The way we had it figured, Salzburg would be out on the first ballot. We thought we might be close to a first-ballot win but probably wouldn't get there. After Salzburg went out, we figured to pick up almost all of their votes.

I didn't get much sleep most nights. Meetings would go late, and I had a million things running through my mind. It was like that scene in *The Wizard of Oz* after Dorothy has been struck on the head during the tornado. She dreams she's looking out her window and all these people she's encountered pass by. Well, that was the inside of my head. All these people and concerns just kept passing by and I couldn't do much to stop it.

The night before our presentation in Prague, a group of us were at a restaurant when Dick Pound and his wife walked in and joined us. It was awkward as hell. Dick leaned over to tell me he was prepared to go onstage the next day and introduce the group. I felt terrible. I didn't like being put in this position and I had to tell him no, that the list of those who would be onstage was finalized and had been submitted to the IOC. Dick sloughed the rejection off, but I knew it bothered him. It was a slap in the face, even though it was not intended to be. He was the leading IOC official in Canada, a name recognized around the world, and we hadn't asked him to be onstage with us. How else was he to interpret it?

The morning of the vote everyone was nervous, which was understandable. We would be first up among the three bid cities, not the ideal position. I wanted to be last, but Pyeongchang drew that straw. We were to be onstage at 10 AM. The prime minister arrived at 9 AM, all smiles, telling everyone he was raring to go even though he must have been exhausted. The 11 of us who were going to be onstage lined up outside the hall in the Hilton Hotel, in front of the hundred or so lucky Canadians who got to watch the presentation live.

Before we went in I went down the line and thanked everyone individually for their contribution. I wanted them to know that, win or lose, what they each had done had meant a great deal to me, the project and their country. For me this was the best day ever. We were at the finish line in one piece, together, inspired and proud. We had made it, hurt no one, cheated no one, promised only what we could deliver—as truly Canadian as we could be. There would be no shame whatever the result. I was never more content—a bag of nerves yes, but morally completely at ease.

Jack Poole had given every one of the Canadians who would be entering the hall behind the presentation team a "lucky loonie" to stuff in their pockets. The lucky loonie had a fabled heritage, of course. One was put under centre ice in Salt Lake City by the Canadian who was in charge of maintaining the ice surface for the Olympics. After the men's and women's teams won there, the lucky loonie became the stuff of lore.

And then the doors opened to soaring, powerful music from the movie Spirit. On a big screen in the room were glorious images of Canada and its people. Two minutes of pulsating energy to help us take the room over. It was the perfect mood-setter.

Now it was game time.

Jacques Rogge made some introductory remarks and then stopped and looked at me: "Mr. President, the floor is yours."

I stood at the podium microphone and for a few seconds seemed to be frozen as I looked out over the crowd, centurions of the most powerful sport parliament in the world in whose hands our fate rested. The cameras were rolling and the world was tuned in. "I am John Furlong, the president of Vancouver 2010, and as I stand before you today I must admit I'm extremely nervous."

I have no idea why I decided to tell people that I was shaking in my boots. I guess I thought honesty was the best policy. It was funny how many people would later comment positively on that small admission. They felt it showed a vulnerability they could relate to. Who wouldn't be nervous under the circumstances?

It was my job to introduce our team and I started with Jack. He conveyed how ready we were to get started. We could begin construction the next day, he assured them with confidence. He talked about some of the infrastructure improvements that were already underway, including work on the Sea to Sky Highway.

Premier Campbell was next. He was the guarantor. It was his job to tell the IOC that the Games would not get into financial trouble, because they were backed by the provincial government. He was completely convincing. The prime minister followed and talked about the federal government's commitment and the commitment all Canadians were making on this day. He made it personal and also spoke of trust and Canadian values. He was utterly on his game and nailed the emotion we needed.

Because of time constraints, we had had Larry Campbell, Gibby Jacobs and Michael Chambers tape comments, and we showed their videos. Then Charmaine Crooks talked about Canada's multicultural heritage and her own immigrant history. She assured the IOC that athletes from around the world would receive a warm welcome from a country made up of people from around the world.

I was up next.

"Although my accent might lead you to believe that I am an Irishman," I began, "I stand up here today a proud Canadian. The day I arrived in Canada a Customs and Immigration officer looked me in the eye, and as he handed my passport back said to me, quite simply: 'Welcome to Canada—make us better.' He challenged me to contribute to the greater good of Canada and for the last three decades, while I built a career in sport, this national culture of giving became a real force in my life. I came to realize that to give is the Canadian way... and it is expected from every one of us."

I went on to talk about everything Vancouver and Whistler had to offer, from a wonderful airport to world-class hotels and some of the most impressive sports venues a Winter Games had ever seen. I said ours was a worry-free plan based on stability and reliability.

Steve Podborski followed me and talked about how he was the first Canadian man to bring home an Olympic medal in downhill skiing. He said the facilities we planned to build for the athletes would be second to none. And then Steve introduced The Great One.

Wayne Gretzky talked about the magic of stepping onto the ice in Nagano, not knowing the impact it would have on him. "There is no greater honour than the Olympics because there is no greater movement than the Olympic movement." Out in the audience I could see a big smile cross René Fasel's face. He knew how powerful Gretzky's statement was inside that room.

Catriona Le May Doan gave part of her speech in French while talking about catching the Olympic spirit as a child and how that transformed her life. She talked about the thousands of dreams that would be ignited in children in B.C. if we received the privilege of hosting the Games.

And then it was back to me to wrap up our presentation. "As a boy, I dreamed of becoming an Olympian," I started. "It was all I could think about. While I never made it to the Olympics, this bid has given me and my colleagues a chance to be Olympians of a different kind. We share the values of the Olympic ideal as a powerful platform for building a better world through sport. And we very much want to be your partners in building that better world."

I thanked our opponents for making the Vancouver bid a better project, for helping many people visualize a better future for our city and for the country. I promised we would be the best partners the IOC could possibly imagine, partners it wouldn't have to worry about, that could be counted upon. I asked the IOC members to imagine a torch relay arriving in Canada above the Arctic Circle, farther north than it had ever been before, and then travelling from sea to sea to sea, unifying our vast country in the process.

"We are ready to be an Olympic city... We believe that for generations to come, these Games will be a catalyst for immense promise for Vancouver... We believe that through sport there can be a chance for peace. That we might distinguish ourselves in the greater cause of sport and humanity. In the end we hope that you might look back on the Vancouver Olympic and Paralympic Winter Games with great pride and affection. Our Olympic dream has transformed us and captivated our nation. Our dream is embedded in the heart of every Canadian athlete, every Canadian family, every Canadian child. Our dream, like your dream, is a dream forever."

We had to reserve some time for questions from IOC members. We had a pretty good idea whom they would be coming from. All of them allowed us to accentuate positive aspects of our bid and address lingering concerns like the road to Whistler. No damage done.

WHEN I FINALLY sat down in my seat I felt an enormous weight lift. My speech was the culmination of years of hard work by so many people. I honestly believed we had given the campaign everything we had. Coaches ask hockey players to leave everything they have on the ice. I believed that our team had left everything it could in Prague. I couldn't have asked for more.

As our group began walking out of the conference hall, an elderly man with glasses approached me with an outstretched hand. "That was a wonderful speech, Mr. President." It was the famous U.S. statesman Henry Kissinger, an honorary IOC member. "I wish you well." Our team congregated outside the hall. Everyone was happy. Some people were planning to watch the other presentations. I had no interest. Why put myself through that just to worry even more. I needed to get away and clear my head so I went for a long walk along the river. Later in the afternoon, some of our team started assembling in my hotel room. All the presentations had been made by that point, and we were about to learn the results of the first vote by closed-circuit television. And soon enough Jacques Rogge was on the screen. My hotel room fell silent.

"After the first round of voting the City of Salzburg has been eliminated," said Dr. Rogge.

And for a city that had the same Olympic dreams we had, that had poured thousands of hours into its bid and spent tens of millions of euros, it was over just like that. *See ya, goodbye.* I couldn't fathom what that moment must have felt like for the members of the Salzburg team. Devastating for sure.

We knew that we were poised to gain most, if not all, of the votes that Austria received in the first round. But then, when you were dealing with the IOC you could never be absolutely sure about anything. Yes to your face could really mean no; it was like grabbing a handful of Jell-O.

The final announcement was going to be made at 5:30 local time. When we got to the hall, most of the Korean delegation was already there, looking supremely confident. A rumour started circulating that there was a report on the Internet that Pyeongchang had already won, and someone from the media asked me about it. "I don't believe it for a second," I said. "And no one will know until Jacques Rogge opens that envelope."

The last minutes before the announcement were excruciating. My stomach was a mess. I was confident but the wait had a way of messing with a person's head. At this point, all of the IOC members were onstage. A small girl in braids and traditional, brightly coloured Czech dress walked to the stage holding a pillow upon which lay the envelope that would seal our fate. Dr. Rogge walked toward the stage. The tension in the room was unbearable. The president opened the envelope and seemed to take a few seconds to digest the results. More tension. The entire IOC was standing behind him—rows of them.

"The International Olympic Committee has the honour of announcing that the 21st Winter Olympic Games are awarded to... the City of Vancouver," he said.

There was a momentary delay in my response. The way Dr. Rogge had pronounced *Vancouver* sounded like "Pyeoncouver," but that confusion lasted only a second before I realized we had won. The place went crazy. I was standing beside one of the two Mounties in red serge who had escorted our delegation in for our morning presentation. Constable Chantal Jung turned to me and put me in a bear hug that nearly broke my ribs. "We did it," she screamed. The next several minutes were just chaos. I was hugging and shaking the hands of everybody on our team.

"Today we moved a mountain," I said to Jack Poole. Jean Chrétien, the exhausted warrior, looked 10 years younger. I thanked him for flying through the night to give a guarantee to the IOC that I felt had been vital to the bid.

It was a coming-of-age moment for me. I had been second-guessed a thousand times along the way and now, it seemed, I had been vindicated. It was as if my whole belief system had been validated. I suddenly could relate to every athlete who was part of a big win—a Stanley Cup, the FIFA World Cup, an NBA championship. Plus there was an immediate, palpable feeling of relief.

I WAS SURPRISED at how close the final vote was. Three votes. We were behind after round one but grabbed all of Austria's 16 votes to sneak by the Koreans 56–53. Scary close. Only a couple of other decisions in IOC history had been closer than ours—both of those determined by one vote.

There would be a lot of talk about the role geopolitics played in our victory. How European countries wanted the 2012 Summer Games, so were not going to vote for a European city to win the 2010 Games. I never put much stock in that theory. I thought we won because of the quality of our bid, pure and simple. The IOC trusted us and liked us. Sure, there may have been a few people who voted for other reasons, but overall I think that if Salzburg had had a superior plan and strategy, it would have prevailed. Same with Pyeongchang. Honestly, though, after the way the Koreans played the margins I was happy they were going home empty-handed. With the help of Samsung, they had probably spent over $100 million on their bid to our $35 million, but in the end it didn't matter. That outcome made me feel better about the IOC and the way it operated.

As I was walking out of the hall, the Prince of Orange approached me with a big smile. "Are we good now?" he asked, a reference to my threat to leak the story about his ripped pants if we didn't get the Games.

"Yes," I said. "We're good."

We attended a reception hosted by the IOC at the Hilton before we joined a bigger party for all the hundreds of Canadians who had made the trip. Dr. Rogge and his wife, Anne, were in a greeting line. When Jack and I got to the president, he reached out to shake our hands. "So," he said, "are you going to be another one of those cities that make a whole bunch of glowing promises you don't plan on keeping?"

Humour aside, I was a bit taken aback by the remark. "No," I said. "You won't have a problem there, I can assure you. The Canadian public will insist that the promises we made here will be kept."

A little later on, I headed over to our victory celebration, where I was greeted by a lovely ovation when I walked through the door. I felt embarrassed and quickly slunk into a corner to banter with some guys from NBC. Among them was Dick Ebersol, the charismatic chair of NBC Universal Sports and the network's longtime Olympic guru. The network had paid an astounding US$2.2 billion for the rights to the 2010 and 2012 Olympics, and Ebersol told me part of the equation was the assumption Vancouver would win the bid to host the 2010 Winter Olympics. He had bet the farm on us.

Ebersol was wearing the biggest smile. "It's a goddamn good thing you won," he said. "Or I would have been living in exile in a house floating on an iceberg in the North Atlantic for the rest of my days."

I didn't have a hard time sleeping that night. I was completely spent. Most of the team was heading home the day following the vote. I felt that too much of the attention had been on me in Prague. I wanted Jack to get the accolades he deserved. He had empowered this effort with such class. I told him I wanted him to return to Vancouver a hero for everything he'd done. I also needed to thank every IOC member for trusting us, so I stayed behind an extra day. Jack and the premier and others landed in Vancouver and received a star's welcome.

Along with a few other members of the team and the media, I flew home a day later aboard an Air Canada flight. I was on a complete high, still not quite believing what we had just accomplished. The last 48 hours had been emotional for everyone. It was difficult not to think about how life-changing the result was going to be for many of us.

I took my seat on the plane, feeling more relaxed than I had in months, maybe years. Everyone in the delegation got an upgrade. As we began to taxi over to the main runway the captain came on the intercom. "Good morning, ladies and gentlemen," he said. "Welcome aboard Air Canada flight 2010 to Vancouver."

The words gave me the shivers.

4

Employee **No. 1**

GOT A TASTE of the euphoria surrounding our win when our plane landed at Vancouver International Airport. We had been told by our pilot that there was a mob waiting for us, but to see the thousands gathered in the international arrivals area when we got through customs was still a shock. People had signs. Many were outfitted in red and white. My eight-year-old daughter Molly sprinted past everyone to greet her dad, still not sure what all the fuss was about. But she was not about to be left out. There was media everywhere. Dozens of friends showed up as well. I was flabbergasted.

It was one thing to pick up the phone to say thank you, or write a card, but to make the trip to the airport to say it in person meant a great deal to me. It was like nothing I had ever experienced. I was asked by the media about my future and whether I was interested in being CEO of the Vancouver Organizing Committee that would put on the Games. I said I was but that if Prague was my last day working for the 2010 Olympics, I was good with that too. Others were going to decide my future.

A number of events were held over the next few days in recognition of the honour that had been bestowed on Vancouver. It was impossible to walk down the street without being stopped by someone who wanted to say thank you for what our group had achieved.

Shortly after returning home I received a phone call from Brian Burke's office looking for a meeting. Brian was the president and general manager of the Vancouver Canucks at the time and one of the most recognizable personalities in town. When I showed up at the boardroom at GM Place, I was met by Brian and his chief operating officer, Dave Cobb. I sat down to hear what this was all about.

"John, I just wanted to thank you personally for an extraordinary performance in Prague," Brian began. "I wanted to thank you for doing incredible good for the country and just wanted to say it was a genuine delight to see you guys win."

He told me how he and Dave had been in GM Place for the announcement at 5 AM and were a little miffed that the cheer that went up inside the stadium was louder than any he had heard at a hockey game. Before I left he said that if there was anything he could do to help us out, all I had to do was call. It was an offer he lived up to often in the years that followed. Many like Brian were already stepping up to say "Well done" and "Count me in if you need any help."

While it was fun basking in the glow of our victory for a few days, there was also work to be done. There was a huge transition to make between being a bid city and a host city. The Vancouver-Whistler 2010 Bid Corporation would now make way for the Vancouver Organizing Committee, or as it would eventually be known, VANOC. It would mean a new board would have to be chosen and the jockeying to be on it would be fierce. While it was understood that Jack would be chair of that board, at least initially, what wasn't known was who the CEO would be. That was the big job, the ringmaster of everything that would happen over the next seven years.

Over the next couple of months, newspapers and television and radio talk shows were consumed with the project. There were never-ending debates about the amount of money that was going to be needed. There was much speculation about who might be on the board and who would get the CEO's job. The rumours, gossip and conjecture seemed to be endless. As the weeks rolled on, I could sense the euphoria of Prague beginning to evaporate among the office staff, which was composed of a small group of us from the bid phase who were managing the transition. People were wondering if they were going to fit into future plans. There were a few trying to position themselves for certain jobs. It made for an uncomfortable environment, and the Irish worrier in me triggered more sleepless nights than I could count. It was energy-sapping in the worst way. I had no idea how long it would be before a CEO was chosen, but we couldn't afford to put the organization in neutral while we waited for a decision. Meanwhile, I was driving the transition and was involved in all major decisions related to the project. We tried to press on.

Construction to improve the Sea to Sky Highway began almost immediately. Talks were also heating up over the possibility of building a new rapid transit line from the airport into downtown. While it wasn't promised to the IOC during our bid, we had certainly dangled it as a possibility. It was a commuter link that needed to be built at some point; we were hopeful it could get done in time to help deliver Olympic visitors to downtown hotels. Critics, of course, put what came to be called the Canada Line at our feet—especially the cost.

On October 3, 2003, the VANOC board was announced. As expected, it was a group that included heavyweights from government, sport and business. The Canadian Olympic Committee had seven spots at the table. Canada and B.C. had three each; Vancouver and Whistler each provided a pair, with one each from First Nations and the Canadian Paralympic Committee and one at-large member, Jack Poole.

With the board in place, hiring a CEO was expected to be its first priority. The IOC, meantime, had announced that my good friend René Fasel would be heading up its coordination commission. This was another huge break for us. It was the commission's job to monitor the progress we were making—or not making—in delivering on the promises we made in our bid. René had been a huge supporter of our project going back to our first Olympic conversations in Salt Lake City. He wanted us to succeed and would more often than not give us the benefit of the doubt as we moved forward. With René in that job we felt like we were up 1–0 early in the game.

Also, the stakes were very high for René. He was the head of the International Ice Hockey Federation. Having the Olympic hockey tournament on Canadian soil represented a huge opportunity for him. If we failed, he failed. So there was a big incentive for him to become a partner in our success. He had once been a top referee and had an even temperament, making him an ideal chair. The stars were aligning nicely for us.

That fall, René, Gilbert Felli, who was Olympic Games executive director, and other members of the commission visited Vancouver to begin their oversight and see what progress we had made since Prague. They wanted to take a look at where the venues would be built, meet team members and sit down with our various political leaders to establish relationships.

We organized a trip to Whistler and thought it would be fun, efficient and novel to fly rather than take a car. So we hired a float plane out of Vancouver Harbour and headed up right over the top of Grouse Mountain and some jaw-dropping geography before landing in Green Lake in Whistler. René and Gilbert seemed a little puzzled about the route we were flying. I'm quite sure they took this as a sign that we hadn't started work on the highway that we'd promised would begin right away.

It was just as baffling to us that there were doubts, especially this early. I think it was more to do with the IOC's history with other Olympic cities and the many broken promises the committee had to deal with over the years, in different countries. In Whistler, René asked me if it would be possible to take a different route back to Vancouver so we could fly directly over the highway. He was pretty blunt about it: you've told us there is progress being made on improving it so we'd like to see for ourselves.

I was happy to oblige, and when we flew back down René and the others could see bulldozers and construction workers all over the place. There were plenty of nods of approval inside the plane. When they left town, I was confident they felt good about the partner they had in us. I reminded them what I had said in Prague—a promise made here is a promise kept in Canada.

THE NEXT FEW months would be one of the most difficult periods of my professional career. Not a day went by when there wasn't something in the media about the search for a CEO, including lots of speculation about who might be in the running for the job. Media commentators offered their views about the kind of résumé a person needed to oversee what would be the largest project of its kind in Canadian history. There were indeed people who felt I deserved the chance to take on the job based on my performance throughout the bid phase. But there were plenty of others who didn't think I had the skill or the horsepower.

I remember a column written by Daphne Bramham of the *Vancouver Sun* that pondered the type of candidate she felt was being sought for the CEO position and why it would almost certainly not be me. The headline screamed: WHY JOHN FURLONG WON'T WIN GAMES' RACE. The story went on to suggest I was a nice guy, but there was nothing in my résumé that showed I was ready to run a multibillion-dollar project. Daphne even apologized to me later about the scorching headline, telling me it was the work of another.

I won't deny how much that hurt. Deep down I was confident I could not only do the job, I could do it well. And I didn't think anyone possessed the passion for the project that I had, or the vision for what it could do for the country.

At the board level I was aware that some directors weren't comfortable with the relationship I had with Jack Poole. A small group felt there wasn't enough distance between us to allow for the kind of objectivity a chair needed to have with a project as grand as this. Without that distance and objectivity there wouldn't be the necessary level of accountability—or so some believed. I thought the opposite was true. It probably didn't help that shortly after we won the bid, Jack had come out and said I would be his choice to be CEO. To many, that was just another sign that the two of us were too close.

In November, the formal process to recruit the CEO got going in earnest. I was contacted by Kyle Mitchell, with whom I had had several dealings during the bid phase. He was the organization's recruiter of choice from the beginning and knew the inner machinations of the project well. I sat down with Kyle and provided him with everything he needed from me, including a synopsis of the approach I would take as CEO and my overarching vision for the project.

In December, I wrote Kyle a letter that outlined why I wanted the job, and why I thought I was the right candidate for it. "Success will not come down to the ingenuity and drive of one person but to the sterling performance of many," I wrote. "It will take a talented, comprehensive, star-studded team to give the world great Games in 2010."

I also addressed a perception held by some that it took a different type of team to organize an Olympic Games than it did to win the bid. "Such a belief caused enormous grief in Athens until finally the bid leader was recalled after three years of organizational pandemonium and poor performance," I wrote. "Frank King was with Calgary for the duration and was viewed in the most positive light in both roles. Indeed, Calgary went the distance with mostly the same team that they started with.

"I cannot imagine approaching this opportunity without some form of trepidation, perhaps even a little fear... The challenge has been defined in countless ways and, yes, although there are many complex elements to the project, in summary, it primarily comes down to leadership. The leader will be the passionate, loyal custodian of a major trust. This someone will guard and protect and will instill a spirit of relentlessness in the team. This is someone who others will believe in and be prepared to follow. This person will have unassailable human values, known integrity and a never quit attitude."

I also made it clear that I didn't want this job just because people felt I deserved the opportunity due to our success in Prague. I wanted it only if people felt I could do it.

There was much speculation about who was in the running and many of the names of those mentioned hadn't even applied, I would learn later. I thought my interview with the selection committee had gone well. The questions were tough and penetrating. I really felt I was in a dogfight for the job. I had the sense that I was proving myself all over again. One thing was certain: no one was cutting me an inch of slack.

I tried to make clear to the selection committee that if it was looking for the perfect candidate who had all the qualities needed for this job, it was never going to find that person because he or she didn't exist. The best they could hope for was the right leader who would surround himself or herself with the right people and then lead them to the finish line. But it had to be a leader who had the capacity to build a unique team, and who could successfully ask extremely prominent people to abandon great jobs to take a big risk on a project that was going to reflect on our country's reputation around the world.

There were times during the interview when it felt as if the committee was looking to fill the job of CEO of a construction company, someone whose top priority was to get venues built on time. Yes, that was vitally important. But I thought the CEO's most important job was selling the Games to the country. I was going to hire people who could get the venues constructed on time. That would be one of the easier challenges.

Eventually, I heard that the board was deadlocked around two candidates: me and another person who was rumoured to be a senior executive in the hotel industry. I was frustrated because I could see that the delay in choosing someone was paralyzing the organization. I could sense morale slipping. It was now February 2004, eight months since Prague, and the organization still had no CEO and no real budget to speak of, and there were people who needed to be hired.

At one point, Jack walked into my office obviously frustrated himself and said that the winning candidate needed the approval of three quarters of the board and I was a vote or two short. Jack said that an idea had come up that he wanted to talk to me about. What if the board appointed the other person CEO and I took any other position I wanted in the organization? In Jack's words this was an opportunity for me to have plenty of responsibility and influence on the Games with none of the pressure associated with the top job. Although he had the best of intentions I was extremely annoyed. I asked him if the same question had been posed to the other candidate. It hadn't. We both knew he would have rejected it out of hand.

That was almost the final straw for me. I drew up a letter of resignation dated February 10, 2004, which I handed to Jack and copied to Mike Phelps, who was chairing the search committee. In it I wrote: "It is very clear to me that the way must be made clear for the board of directors of Vancouver 2010 to unite behind one candidate for the position of CEO. Although I hoped it would not come to this, it is clear I cannot achieve such support. But someone must. I believe that a unanimous decision on leadership is essential.

"To facilitate this I hereby withdraw my name as a candidate for the position of CEO and tender my resignation as a member of

Vancouver's Olympic team to take effect on a date mutually agreeable to the board of directors and to myself.

"I will explain my decision in more detail in a separate letter to the board. I have been privileged to be part of this historic achievement and wish you all great success."

Jack came to see me almost as soon as the letter arrived on his desk. There would be no resigning, he said. He understood my frustration—he was angry and frustrated himself. He knew the project was bleeding and in desperate need of a decision on the CEO. Jack vowed he would get the matter resolved one way or the other. But I knew where he stood. He wanted us to continue on in this together.

Within days I was told that a vote had been taken and that I was the successful candidate and would be recommended to the board. I was told to expect to be named CEO shortly, likely within days.

I was more relieved than elated. The drawn-out process had zapped any feelings of elation right out of me. I knew that I wasn't a unanimous choice, which bothered me a lot. But I wasn't going to dwell on that. It was time to get on with things. I just had to prove my detractors wrong. Outwork them all, as my dad would have urged me to.

That night, Thursday, February 19, I was at home contemplating the road ahead when the phone rang. It was a reporter from the *Vancouver Sun*. He said the paper was going to be running a story the next day quoting Dick Pound as saying the CEO selection process was rigged in my favour. And for good measure, Dick was quoted as suggesting I wasn't up for the job. I couldn't believe it. I told the reporter I had no comment. I tried to get to sleep while anticipating what the full story was going to look like the next day. I was also mad that someone on the board had obviously leaked the news. I don't remember sleeping much.

I got up before 6 AM the next day and immediately went out to grab the papers off the front step. It didn't take long to find the story—it was on the front page, right across the top—a gulper. "PREMIER 'RIGGED' CONTEST FOR 2010 GAMES CEO, BACKS INFERIOR CANDIDATE: POUND," the headline roared. In the story, Dick was quoted as saying the selection process had been hijacked by Premier Gordon Campbell's office. "My belief is always that when you hire somebody for a very senior position, what you look to is a record of dealing with challenges similar to what will be faced in the job for which you're recruiting. Mr. Furlong is a perfectly capable person and a nice person, but he doesn't have the experience that you need for this job."

I could scarcely believe what I was reading. I felt ill and incredibly angry at the same time. To be rebuked in such a public way was worse than a punch to the gut. I couldn't help feeling that Dick was motivated to say these things because I hadn't found a role for him during the presentation in Prague or because he felt I had avoided seeking his counsel throughout the bid phase. Either way, it was ugly and humiliating, and all I wanted to do was buy up every paper in the city so my family and friends didn't have to read the story.

I knew the board was meeting that morning to ratify the decision. There was a possibility that the whole thing could still have gone sideways, especially in light of Dick's rant. But I got a call just after noon asking me to come down to the office. Once there, I was told by Mike Phelps, in the presence of Jack, that I was the new CEO and a news conference was going to be held almost immediately to make the decision public. There was no discussion about a contract. I didn't even know what the job paid.

The next thing I knew I was walking into a room full of reporters and television cameras being introduced as the CEO and being presented with a sign that said "VANCOUVER 2010—EMPLOYEE NO. 1."

It was difficult to be upbeat and euphoric, or for that matter even a good sport, given the events of the previous 24 hours, but I tried my best. At one point a reporter asked how much I would be getting paid, and I said I honestly didn't know. At this point Mike said to everyone: "We already told them it's $300,000 a year." So I said, "Well, I guess there you have it."

It wasn't a classy way of dealing with the matter, but at this point I just wanted to move on, put the drama of the selection process behind me and start getting to work in earnest, with a new mandate.

I learned later that Dick was one of those on the board who had been holding out for the other candidate, as were France Chrétien Desmarais (the prime minister's daughter) and Patrick Jarvis and possibly one other. I knew the fact I wasn't bilingual bothered France and a few others a lot. My Gaelic did not count, I guess. And I couldn't help feeling that there was some Central Canada bias at work. But I didn't have time to obsess over what was done. As a result of the delay in selecting a CEO we had lost some ground.

Dick phoned the same day, referring to himself as Darth Vader, and left a message explaining what he had done and promising his support now that we had a decision. He said he hoped to one day eat his words. When we finally talked, I told Dick I accepted his story and said we needed to meet to clear the air. Within a week I was in his Montreal office letting him know what I thought of his attack. I told Dick what bothered me the most about it was the fact he really knew nothing about me and yet he had made assumptions about my character and ability. His suggestion that the premier had pushed for me was too much to take when I had always held the position that I would win the job on merit or not at all.

Around this time, I sat down with my family to explain what this assignment meant. It was going to require an enormous sacrifice for everyone: it would eat up massive volumes of time, and I was not going to be around much. It was going to be tough on my close relationships, no question. The highs and lows would surely be severe. Everyone was supportive and very encouraging. My children recognized that this was an assignment of a lifetime, that Dad was about to do something important for the country.

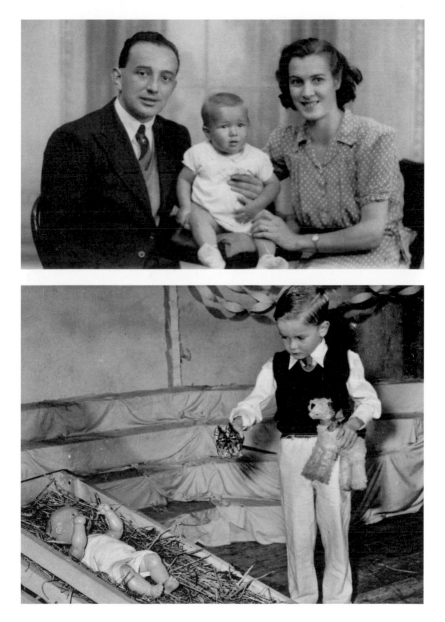

TOP My proud mom, Maureen, and dad, Jack, on one of my quieter days.

ABOVE Following Mom's orders at Christmastime in Clonmel, Ireland.

ABOVE Prime Minister Trudeau and me at the launch of the Northern BC Winter Games in Prince George, 1978.

TOP RIGHT The VANOC executive committee: (back left to right) John McLaughlin, Ken Bagshaw, Terry Wright, Dan Doyle, Cathy Priestner Allinger, David Guscott, me; (front) Ward Chapin, Donna Wilson, Dorothy Byrne, Dave Cobb.

BOTTOM RIGHT Sumi making new friends. The official mascot of the Paralympics was beloved by children around the world.

TOP LEFT Governor General Michaëlle Jean signs VANOC posters.

BOTTOM LEFT On the floor of the United Nations, reading into the record the 2010 Olympic Truce resolution calling on all warring nations to cease fighting during the Games.

ABOVE Actress Maria Nafpliotou ignites our flame from sun rays in Olympia, Greece.

TOP Carrying the Olympic flame from the field of the Panathenian Stadium in Athens, heading for Victoria.

ABOVE The Calgary Islamic School welcomes the torch.

RIGHT Aboriginals across Canada welcome the torch into their communities.

Proud parents from north to south cheered their athletes on.

Jack called the next day and suggested we spend a few days in Palm Desert, California, to talk about where we went from here. He thought I looked exhausted and might benefit from a few days in the sun, away from the daily calls from the media. So we went south in a small plane he chartered. I told Jack over those days that it was important that the people on the transition team who had been doing Olympic-related work since Prague knew where they stood, what roles they may or may not play in the organization in the future. I was determined not to make any personnel decisions quickly that I might regret later on. I was more preoccupied with mapping out how the organization might be structured so that it could cope with anything thrown at it. I had a few visits from key players on the bid who had, in their own way, advised me that if they were not given senior assignments of the kind they felt qualified for they would move on.

One of those people was Terry Wright, who had done a lot of the key planning work for us during the bid phase. On the surface, Terry would have had the first right of refusal to be VANOC's chief operating officer, a job he coveted. But I wasn't prepared to make that appointment so early in the process—besides, there were no operations to be chief operating officer of. I wanted to put together an executive team and then wait and see if the COO emerged from that group. The position didn't have to be filled until much closer to the beginning of the Games in any event.

Terry wasn't happy. At one point he said he was going to leave. I think Terry thought I didn't have confidence in him. It was nothing of the sort. He was eventually going to be given an important area of responsibility: services and Games operations. I told him he needed to understand I was going to build a great organization with great people and he was going to be one of them. But Terry was pretty insistent that he was going to pack it in.

"Before you do I want you to go home and have a conversation with your wife," I told him. "You live in Victoria, you have young kids, this is the biggest project you have tackled in your life and you're thinking of walking away from it? I don't want you a year from now looking back and regretting this decision, especially given you had so much to do with our success. And we need you. So you go home and sit down with your wife and tell her: 'I've been offered this very senior, high-profile, executive vice-president position. I'll be first among equals, side by side with a team of passionate Canadian stars, involved in every key decision in the organization, and I can come home on weekends, and I will get extra financial support to go back and forth.'"

I knew what would happen if he did. Terry's wife, Monique, had a way of getting to Terry—they were best of friends. After the weekend, Terry walked into my office wearing a sheepish grin.

"Count me in," he said.

I was happy to have his signature and his fearless commitment.

Over the next couple of months I spent countless hours with Kyle Mitchell trying to find the right people to fill out the executive team. I told Kyle that ultimately I wanted to have a team of seven to nine executives, each one capable of managing a large, diverse portfolio, each one enthralled with our vision for the Games, each one ready to hit the ground running, each one madly in love with Canada. I envisioned an organization that was, on almost every level, pretty flat. No silos and no walls to interfere with building the kind of teamwork we would need. I wanted my vice-president of marketing to be fully cognizant of what was going on with construction. I wanted my vice-president of construction to be able to ask penetrating questions about marketing issues or HR.

By the time the Games arrived, almost every person on the executive was capable of doing anyone else's job. That is what I had imagined and hoped for from the outset.

While I hoped that every member of the executive we chose at the beginning would stay the course and have a major impact on the organization, in retrospect it was probably a bit naïve to think every person we picked would succeed. After all, we were asking them to sign up for something that had never been attempted before—in scope, anyway—and to figure out how to become loyal teammates in a high-stress organization. I think for Kyle it was one of the most challenging assignments he'd ever had, especially with my insistence that we find people of sterling character who could stare down fear; to me that was the number one asset a candidate had to have. Finding such people is not as easy as it sounds. Normally you'd say to a search firm, "I need a guy to dig holes. He needs to be strong, over 250 pounds and needs to have a shovel." I was looking for skill, sure, but the core strength needed to be something far less tangible.

I felt we should be looking at Canada's best companies for the kind of executive members we needed at VANOC. We talked about looking at non-traditional candidates, people who had drive, determination, integrity and spirit that stood out. Sleepers ready to show off their stuff.

One of the people I had my eye on was Dave Cobb, COO of the Vancouver Canucks. I had first met Dave during the bid phase when he helped out with our presentation to the evaluation commission on GM Place, the prospective site of men's and women's hockey. I was immediately impressed with his unflinching, confident, gung-ho attitude and crackling intelligence. He was to me what I was not. He had stepped in front of the commission with little time to prepare and given a stellar performance about what a superb venue GM Place would be for Olympic hockey.

When Kyle and I started talking about the qualities we needed in a marketing executive, Dave's name was the first that popped to mind. But honestly, I thought our chances of prying Dave away from the Canucks were minimal. The Canucks were the biggest thing in Vancouver, and Dave, who grew up in the shadow of the arena where the Canucks once played, had always dreamed of one day working for the organization. Now he was basically running the operation.

Luckily for us the Canucks were going through a period of upheaval. Brian Burke had been let go since I met him after Prague, and there were questions about the direction in which Seattle-based owner John McCaw and his right-hand-man, Stan McCammon, were taking the team. So the door was open a nudge. Dave had maple syrup running through his veins, so I thought I would sprinkle a little Olympic dust on him. I had hoped the opportunity to be part of a once-in-a-lifetime event such as the Olympics would capture his imagination. He could not resist and agreed to join the team. It was a huge announcement for the organization, one that caught the attention of the local business community and helped put us on the map. A few more like him and we could take on anything, I thought.

Over the coming months we assembled our team. For the most part, we picked wisely. Most of those we selected for the executive ended up staying until the end. Unfortunately, there were a few people who did not make it. Jeff Chan, our first vice-president of human resources, was gone in a year. But that opened up the door for Donna Wilson, whom we nabbed from Vancity credit union—which was regularly named one of the top companies to work for in the country. Cathy Priestner Allinger, the speed skating medallist, became vice-president, sport. Cathy had loads of Olympic experience and sports savvy at the executive level and had been discussed in some circles as a potential CEO candidate. She oozed calmness. I thought the sport world would celebrate her appointment and it did.

Ken Bagshaw was secured as our general counsel, a crowning role in an impressive law career; Ward Chapin was in charge of technology and systems, a role with zero tolerance for failure of any kind. We found Ward in France, and I went to Paris to interview him and sign him up. We recruited Steve Matheson from Dominion Construction to head up venue development. Steve is a wonderful guy with impeccable values and a solid track record. Unfortunately, as painful as it was, I would eventually have to replace him too.

The only other change we had to make was our chief financial officer, Rex McLennan. We hired Rex in 2005, and he would stay with us 18 months. The fit was not the best. I was looking for someone who wanted to be in on the ground floor, who was a great teacher and who would help promote the idea throughout the organization that we had to be careful with every dime we spent. We replaced Rex with John McLaughlin, who had been our comptroller almost from the beginning but initially did not seem ready for such a heavy burden. Now he was.

One of the fonder memories from my early days as CEO was renting the Capitol 6 theatre in Vancouver and assembling all members of our transition team one afternoon to watch the movie *Miracle.* It was the story of the 1980 United States men's Olympic hockey team that won a gold medal against all odds. I thought there was so much for our group to take from the movie, not the least of which was the message it sent about the power of teamwork. The American coach, Herb Brooks, epitomized leadership and I closely studied the motivational tactics he used to select and get his team ready for its epic showdown with the Russians.

I found the movie extremely moving and deeply inspiring. It was a rags-to-riches story about a group of very human, dynamic but in many ways flawed individuals assembled from college teams. They embraced a collective dream to do something many thought was impossible. After the movie, I remember having a conversation with the group about what they had just seen and how this hockey team's story was, in some ways, a metaphor for the compelling challenges we would face.

I told everyone that day that if they wanted to be on such a team they could stay and be part of this journey we were embarking on. But if they felt they couldn't make such a commitment, could not pour their hearts and souls into this project for a sustained period of time, then they should probably not show up the next day. More than anything, I wanted them all to understand what I was asking them to sign up for. I told them that they were going to be asked time and again to do things they were not going to think were possible. But I also said the sum of the parts of our team could, on any given day, overcome so many obstacles and challenges that at first blush would seem too formidable to scale.

I told them that afternoon that if we didn't bring the Olympic spirit to the front door of every home in Canada, if we didn't share this experience with every Canadian family, every Canadian child, then we would have failed. And although on the surface our work might look to others like an Olympic success, it would, in fact, be a tragic Canadian failure and we would always know this. This was not about constructing venues and providing jobs and sparking tourism, but about doing something profoundly human for our country and showing the world what could be achieved when the people of a nation come together to do a great thing.

I was not naïve enough to think everyone bought what I was saying and that everyone necessarily agreed with me. At least not yet. I'm sure there were some in the room that day who thought that over time this grand plan of mine would change, and we would have a sober vision correction, and that practical realities would temper my hyped-up ambitions. But I also knew that there were many who wanted in on the action because the adventure I was proposing was just too compelling to pass up—even though the road to our final destination was likely to be tough and bumpy and fraught with danger.

Happily they all showed up the next day, just as I had expected.

AT THIS POINT there were about 50 of us. I didn't have my entire executive team in place yet. I was going to be relying, to a large extent, on this core group to build much of the greater organization, one that would swell to more than 1,300 full-time employees by the time the Games rolled around in six years' time. If this first group really took ownership of the vision, if they understood and believed it was a great privilege to be part of this operation from the outset, they would remind others around them why we were all here. They would ensure we never lost our way. They'd be the leaders who would protect the vision from others who didn't share it or were working at odds to it.

One of my early concerns was how my executive team would respond when the first crisis struck. As part of trying to understand and anticipate what that reaction might be, we decided to make a real investment in exploring the strengths and weaknesses of the various team members through a number of different workshops. If we were to be a team then we'd better practise hard.

I have attended different leadership workshops over the years. I remember one in London, Ontario, at which I experienced fire walking—that is, walking on 950-degree hot coals in bare feet and not burning. The course helped cure my fear of flying—actually my fear of anything. We did other crazy things there, like cramming as many people as we could inside a scorching hot pup tent. The idea was to see how long we could last in that stifling, claustrophobic environment. The exercise was supposed to measure tolerance, focus and commitment. In another drill, we fed someone else dinner and vice versa. No talking allowed—a real test of patience. For my Olympic team we had everyone do the Myers-Briggs personality test designed to measure how people perceive the world and make decisions, among other things. It was incredibly revealing, showing that we were blessed with an extraordinary amount of diverse talent but that almost everyone was fiercely competitive. Oddly, I was the only member of the team who was confirmed to be an out-and-out introvert. A "Feeler" is how I was described. Leads with the heart first. I was in one corner of the chart with the rest of my team as far away from me as one could get. Most of the others were heavily Type A: driven, ambitious and tenacious, and typically more detail-oriented than me. My team—rational and logical. Me—driven and aspirational.

Understanding the individual players on the executive team allowed for an environment that was more open, understanding and effective. Books on team building and team dysfunction were circulated for reading. When I talked to my team, I drew on my experiences as a coach. Players who are not prepared to declare their vulnerabilities, such as an injury, fear or lack of confidence, will cause great grief in the dressing room—and on the field. By not being upfront and honest they hurt their team. I told my team it was really important that if people weren't sure of themselves they were to raise their hand and declare it. I didn't give a damn how badly they felt about it—on this squad it was a sign of strength not weakness.

I was not about to allow the vision for the project, or our mission and values, to be overpowered by a strong lineup of assertive individuals. That is why it was so important to embed these ideals as deeply into the organization as possible and to constantly reaffirm them. As a group, we decided that the vision, mission and values would always be our moral compass, the thing that we would use to strengthen ourselves when we were tested or feeling lost. And we agreed that no individual would be allowed to join the company if we felt that person couldn't live our culture.

Our vision for the 2010 Winter Games had always been that they would be Canada's Games—even during the bid phase. We recommitted to it when we became an organizing committee. Our mission was to touch the soul of the country, get inside its heart. After the Summer Games in Beijing, many people asked me how we were ever going to top that. My answer was easy: that's not what we were trying to do. We were not looking to provide a spectacle; we were looking for something that was deeply moving, that would leave behind an emotional legacy for the country. If people didn't care deeply about these Games, our legacy wouldn't last a weekend.

Establishing the values that would guide our organization was serious but invigorating. We wanted principles that would allow us to build a consistent code inside the company, and provide us with a yardstick against which we could measure potential partners. If we felt Company A didn't share our values, we would leave money on the table and walk away. Our values would be so ingrained that we would know instantly if something was off with a potential business partner.

Teamwork was our number one value but not something we were particularly good at in the beginning. Coming out of the bid phase, we were a bit arrogant and self-satisfied. We didn't immediately embrace new partners like Bell Canada and the Royal Bank when they came aboard. We had to grow a bit as an organization before we could see that we were at times standing in our own way to the detriment of the overall project. Every partner represented a teammate who could do something to help us succeed. So it was best we treat them like friends. Our mantra became "We all cross the finish line together."

Trust was another of our values. If you were working outside my door, it was important that you knew I had faith and trust in you. We needed every employee to know and feel that it was up to them to make the Games great. Whatever their job we wanted them to feel it was the most important one in the company and that what they produced must be perfect. We tried to get people to look at their work and never be satisfied, never settle.

When we came home from Prague someone asked me to describe the culture of our organization. I said if you put a sign over the front doors it would read: BEYOND HERE EVERY SINGLE THING MATTERS. Excellence and creativity were our other values, for obvious reasons. Everything needed to be first-rate, and we were surely going to need non-traditional solutions to everyday problems. More than once we had to pull a rabbit out of an empty hat.

The last value was sustainability. One member of the board, Jim Godfrey, was adamant on this. He had allies in board member Judy Rogers and several members of the executive. I wasn't so sure. I thought it was one of those politically correct words that didn't have a clear meaning. Did it mean the greening of the Games? Cutting down fewer trees? A smaller this and a smaller that? What does *sustainability* really mean, I asked. From Jim came the answer I will never forget: "It means you do what's right every time, period." That principle couldn't be any more evident than it was a few years later when we were involved in some construction in Whistler. At one point, our staff had to move dozens of frogs and tadpoles by hand to a location 40 metres upstream. They would do this, at great cost, on five different occasions during work on the men's and women's downhill runs.

That's what was meant by doing the right thing. In front of the camera or behind it our behaviour needed always to be impeccable. No exceptions. Our reputation was the one asset we had that was priceless, so we needed to protect it at all costs. Lose it and we would lose ourselves.

DESPITE ALL THE team building that we had done, life was far from smooth for us. The first few years in the life of an Olympic organizing committee are always challenging, but we had an additional problem that was making our job even harder: an underlying tension was building between the executive and the board of directors. We were like oil and water sometimes.

We felt that some of our board members were putting the needs and desires of the stakeholder group he or she represented ahead of those of the organizing committee and the Games. If we were going to succeed we needed everyone to be united and on the same page.

The other issue that had emerged was leaks, much like what had happened before my appointment as CEO was announced. Sensitive information we were providing to the board was getting out and sometimes appearing in the press. It was as unsettling as it was infuriating. We did not feel that the boardroom was a secure environment to discuss matters that had, on occasion, the potential to impact a company's share price if made public.

I also felt there was far too much politics going on. We would make a presentation before the board and often come away feeling that we had not taken advantage of the considerable expertise in the room. On the contrary, we sometimes felt the information we were providing the board was being traded and used to our disadvantage by certain stakeholder groups, such as a city council or a government partner. There were just so many conflicts around that boardroom table. My feeling was that if the board's modus operandi was to allow seven different stakeholder groups to fish for themselves we were going to be in big trouble. We wouldn't be able to put on the Games we wanted to. Their job was to be a good team too and to help us be successful.

By early fall, I'd had enough. I was frustrated beyond words. We needed to change the dynamic in the boardroom and convince the directors they were supposed to be on our side—that was the only way it could work. My team needed to be better too. I had talked to Jack about this on many occasions, and he completely agreed. He knew we had a problem and that something had to be done—but that did not make dealing with it any easier.

In mid-October 2004, we were going to be announcing our first major sponsorship initiative and we'd come down to two bidders. The board was holding a retreat in Whistler before its October meeting and that is where we were making our presentation on the deal. Outnumbered though I would be, I thought that this might be the best time to speak to the board about our concerns. I began by telling the directors that I understood how difficult their job was—on the one hand, they were representing entities that were negotiating with VANOC; on the other, they were supposed to be looking out for the greater interests of the organizing committee. But, that said, we were all supposed to be playing for the same team. Unfortunately, I continued, my executive was worried about the sanctity of the boardroom. We felt that some directors couldn't be trusted to keep the information we were giving them confidential; there had been too many leaks.

I had to give them examples of what was going on, which meant awkward innuendo and finger pointing. Some board members resented being told they weren't trusted and said so. One director later called me borderline impudent. I told them that regardless of whether they felt the charge against them was warranted, the executive was having a hard time and morale was suffering. Although I acknowledged that the scattergun approach had annoyed the innocent members, at least now the healing could start.

(I knew I was taking a personal risk in being this direct. But I figured it was better than trying to solve the issue behind the scenes, working one director off against another. Still, there was a good chance I had offended a lot of people in that room, and depending on how it turned out I may or may not have a job after it was over.)

By the time I finished, the divide between the executive and the board was as wide as the Grand Canyon. A team? I don't think so. Not even close.

Later on, Jack and I met in my hotel room. "My God, you're unbelievable!" he said. Jack did not much like conflict so he couldn't fathom how strident I was with the directors. It was a side of me he'd never seen before. But he still agreed something had to be said.

Members of the executive drove up from Vancouver that night to have dinner with the board. Everybody was polite and friendly, but there was an undercurrent of tension. No one was happy, least of all me. After dinner I had a separate meeting with my team and told them what had transpired earlier in the day. I warned them that the sponsorship presentation to the board the next day was going to be challenging, and we needed to perform at our best.

The meeting would have its noisy moments, but ultimately the board signed off on our proposal. We had received so much pushback on our recommendation that it did not feel much like a win for my team. Before leaving the room, I reminded the directors that this was a strictly confidential matter and that we would be advising the two companies of our decision as soon as we could meet them face to face. I figured that after my earlier conversation with the board, we didn't need to worry about any more leaks.

Wrong again.

Dave Cobb and I drove to Vancouver right after the meeting. We hadn't been in the car 15 minutes when my phone rang. It was a good friend who had been heading up what turned out to be the losing bid. "So," he said, "I understand you've made a decision. You might have had the courtesy to let me know in advance, given our long-standing relationship."

I felt an inch tall. A grenade went off in my head.

I couldn't believe it. Someone on the board had struck again—even after my warning about leaks. I was furious. I had no choice but to deny that a decision had been made, but my friend knew beyond all doubt this wasn't the case. When I got off the phone I called Jack and told him what had happened. We agreed that we would investigate fully and confront the board with this information as soon as we could.

I told the directors when we finally did meet that we had a pretty good idea who leaked the information and that as soon as we had it 100 per cent confirmed we would be reporting back to them. Mostly, I wanted to drive home that we were on top of what was going on and determined to root out those who were not working in our best interests. The strategy worked: this would be the last time such a breach occurred. The boardroom became airtight. Score a point for team building.

Our problems with the board didn't end—not entirely anyway. During the next couple of years, I picked up rumblings about a power move to replace Jack with someone else. There was a feeling among a minority of directors that he and I were too close and that Jack wasn't objective enough about the job I was doing and the decisions the executive was making. There were some on the board who had the mistaken impression that Jack was meant to be chair only for a couple of years before stepping aside. That was never meant to be the case. Or if it was, it was news to me. For his part, Jack insisted on being reappointed as chair every year. He wanted to earn his spot the old-fashioned, democratic way, by a majority vote of the directors, and did not accept a lengthy term on the board like everyone else.

The executive was made aware of the chatter about replacing Jack, and as a group we made a decision to rally around his leadership. I certainly made it clear to the board, through back channels, that if Jack went I would be gone and some members of the executive team would probably leave too, which would lead to an incredibly messy and unstable situation at the organizing committee. To us Jack was a rock, a giant.

Luckily, that disaster never came to pass.

5

Calls for **My** Head

I WASN'T LONG into my tenure as CEO when I realized there was a massive problem lurking on the horizon. Not the distant horizon, either. It was barrelling right toward us.

At the time we were bidding to stage the Games, we had to build a plan as if we were holding them in 2002. That meant that our $470-million construction budget was not going to be enough for us to build the sport venues in five or six years' time. I knew this was going to be an issue from the beginning, but those were the rules by which all the bid cities had to play, and we followed them. The explanation we were given was that this stipulation allowed the IOC to evaluate the relative merits of each bid without having to factor in inflation and other economic elements, which could be radically different from country to country, from year to year.

Bid cities provide dramatically different construction programs because they all have different visions. Some undertake massive infrastructure projects—such as Sochi, Russia, which is building almost everything from scratch—while others don't. We focused on using existing structures and building as little as possible. We were all about sustainability, and for us less was more. Still, we were going to have to do some construction and we knew the cost was going to be greater than what we projected it would be in the bid book because of inflation alone. It had to be. What we didn't know when we were designing our original budget was the multiplier impact a red-hot economy would have on the construction industry. The price of everything was sent soaring.

Looking back, if I have any regrets, it's that we didn't better explain to the public at the beginning that our construction budget was probably going to need to be increased. We should have better clarified how the IOC bid process worked and why our financial plan was going to have to be reworked to account for a rise in the cost of labour, materials and other inflationary elements of the construction industry. Here we were, an Irish minute into the project, faced with having to ask the federal and provincial governments for more money—and having to tell the public that our costs were going up. Talk about having a queasy feeling in the pit of your stomach. I could picture the screaming headlines about cost overruns and the comparisons with other Olympic cities that had ended up mired in debt.

Everyone at VANOC knew this was going to be one of those storms we were going to have to just get through. Perhaps our first big test.

As an organizing committee, we were unique in that we had asked upfront that the construction program be our responsibility. Most Olympic organizing committees delegate that duty to another company altogether. That company then carries responsibility for all costs, and if there are overruns it—not the organizing committee—has to go cap in hand to some level of government for more money. But we felt that model hadn't worked well in the past. Most recently, construction on venues for both the 2004 and 2006 Olympics was still being done mere weeks before the start of the Games. Costs went way over budget, and the headlines were ugly.

In both cases, the overruns would taint the Olympics. We wanted to control our own destiny, especially given that our reputation was our single biggest asset.

Before we announced that we were looking for more money, we had to demonstrate that we had already tried to trim construction costs as much as we could. This meant taking an almost forensic look at every project and seeing if we could cut something out of the original design to save a few bucks while not harming the integrity of the venue itself. It was vital that we demonstrated to taxpayers that we understood and respected the fact that this was their money and we were not going to be frivolous with it in any way.

The evolution of the Richmond Olympic Oval is a good example of our taking a hard second look in light of the funding challenges that were confronting us. In our original plan, the Oval was slated to be built at Simon Fraser University for an estimated cost of about $63 million. But by the spring of 2004, that projection was already out of date and under pressure. We now estimated the Oval could cost as much as 20 per cent more, given that a lot of construction materials, such as concrete and steel, were rising at ridiculous rates almost weekly. Steel prices had more than doubled over the previous year, and concrete costs were three to five times higher. Greater Vancouver was in the midst of a construction boom, so workers were in high demand and their rates were going up as well. We were facing this perfect storm of circumstances that was attacking our bottom line.

It didn't take long for the media to conclude that if the costs to build the Oval were up 20 per cent, the cost of everything else was probably going up by a similar rate. And every time the media went to a provincial or federal politician, the answer was "There's no more money," which we read as we'd better pull out all the stops. The punditry portrayed us as being in trouble and perhaps in over our heads. The situation forced us to be ultra-creative.

We had hoped that the Oval would be a major contributor to sport programs at SFU long after the Games were over. It was expected that the university would also make a significant investment in the project. But it quickly became apparent that almost the entire cost of the project was going to be borne by us. The university was going to come up with $5 million and no more. With costs rising at the rate they were, that wasn't going to be enough unless we were prepared to put up a building that resembled a giant shed.

One day I was driving home to suburban Richmond and got stuck in a rush hour traffic jam. I started daydreaming about the Oval challenge. It occurred to me that the City of Richmond had invested $500,000 to help us secure the bid without any expectation it would get something in return. Sitting in my car, I mapped out on a scrap of paper the potential sports legacy a structure like the Oval might have in a community like Richmond. I figured Richmond, with its entrepreneurial partnership-like spirit, might be interested in taking this project on.

The next day, Terry Wright and I sat down with Richmond's top official, George Duncan, a towering man and at one time a helluva squash player who wore his community pride on his sleeve. I drew up my concept on his whiteboard, gushed on about the potential benefits to the community of such a venue and suggested that if Richmond took the project on it would get a $63-million gift from VANOC and ownership of a one-of-a-kind sports facility. We suggested the Oval would allow the city to rethink its long-term recreational sports facility strategy. George was intrigued and more than a little excited but said he'd need to talk to Mayor Malcolm Brodie and members of city council. Soon we got a message back that the city was interested in entering any competition we commissioned to land the rights to the Oval.

We now had to have an uncomfortable conversation with the folks at SFU. They were not happy when we advised them we were planning to put the Oval up for grabs through a competitive bidding process. We tried to get other municipalities interested, but in the end it came down to SFU versus Richmond. It was no contest. Richmond put an enormous amount of effort into its submission. City staff had flown around the world to look at other ovals. They proposed using a magnificent piece of land along the Fraser River, easily the city's premier site, to build on. The architectural renderings of the structure the city envisioned would clearly make it the most celebrated venue of the Games. After the Olympics, the city planned to convert the Oval to a magnificent recreational complex, probably the best in the country with a focus on high-performance and community-based activities.

The final price tag would turn out to be $178 million. The city paid for it by selling roughly 20 acres of land it had around the site of the Oval for about $140 million. The architects planned to build the structure, in part, with wood from trees in B.C.'s interior that had been killed by the pine beetle, which would eventually help make the project even more popular with the public. It would be an architectural marvel. The crown jewel of the Games. The "wow" structure that every Olympic Games wants to have.

Simon Fraser's proposal wasn't at the same level as Richmond's. That was a simple fact. There just wasn't going to be anywhere near the same communitywide legacy as Richmond was envisioning. We had suggested the university try to enlist the help of the City of Burnaby, where the school was located, to get additional funding, but that didn't go anywhere. Burnaby's mayor, Derek Corrigan, was not a fan of the Games, so the likelihood of his becoming a champion of SFU's quest for the Oval was pegged at about zero. It was a shame, because our polling confirmed that Burnaby was a major hotbed of support for the Olympics. We had little choice but to go with Richmond.

I wanted to tell the university's president, Michael Stevenson, about our decision in person. The timing meant flying home from Athens, where I was attending the Summer Games. I went up to the school with Dave Cobb, who had graduated from SFU and was a favourite son. I was hoping his presence might defuse some of the anger and tension I anticipated. It didn't.

Michael was pretty miffed. The next day we announced our decision publicly. Michael was quoted in the newspaper as saying he was looking forward to getting an explanation from VANOC about why we had decided on Richmond—making no mention of our face-to-face meeting a day earlier. Derek Corrigan, true to form, used the occasion to take some more shots at us. Most of the media coverage was positive, with many people suggesting we'd pulled off a major coup. We had done our duty and protected taxpayers from a huge cost increase. We felt badly for SFU, but our mandate had become extremely challenging and we were playing for keeps.

It wouldn't get any easier moving forward.

Since returning from Prague, we had trimmed about $85 million from our original capital costs budget of $470 million by refining designs, cutting out elements that were difficult to build, and by deciding to house the broadcast media in the new Vancouver Convention Centre downtown. Originally, the plan had been to put the broadcasters in a temporary building in Richmond and the print media in Canada Place on Vancouver's waterfront. NBC's head honcho, Dick Ebersol, hated that idea and told us so every time he came to town to talk about 2010. He was furious that the broadcasters, who had paid billions of dollars for the right to cover the Games, were being "stuck out in Richmond." Once we were convinced that the new Convention Centre, which had been plagued by delays and cost overruns, was going to be built on time for us, we made the move. It was going to save money too, because we were not going to have to build a $20-million temporary structure in Richmond. So Richmond lost the broadcasters but had a lock on the Oval.

We were determined that we were not going to provide the two levels of government or the media a whiff of any new numbers until we were satisfied they were ones we knew we could count on until the end. We simply could not afford to get it wrong. We would have only one chance to make a case for more funding.

Meanwhile, we had also decided to see if we could convince the International Ice Hockey Federation (IIHF) to allow us to stage the Olympic hockey tournament on an NHL-sized ice surface, instead of the larger international one. Most of the men's hockey tournament and some of the women's would be played at GM Place, home of the Vancouver Canucks. Reconfiguring that ice surface to international dimensions was going to cost up to $20 million to get the job done properly, which would entail ripping up cement and taking out seats. If we could convince the IIHF's board to allow us to hold the tournament on the existing ice surface, we would save money, time and headaches.

We also thought it was a more responsible decision that should have been up for debate anyway. It seemed ridiculous to tear apart a perfectly fine structure just to have to put it back together again later. That wasn't living up to one of our values—sustainability.

In 2004, I flew to Riga, Latvia, where the IIHF board was meeting during their world championships, and arrived late the night before the meeting, exhausted. I immediately went to see René Fasel, the IIHF president, in his hotel room. He was waiting there for me with his CEO, Jan-Ake Edvinsson. Everyone was tired. René sat in his chair in his stocking feet, looking as if he'd rather be in bed than briefing me on what to expect the next day. It was the first time I'd spent serious time with Jan, who was a hockey lifer, a stocky guy with a big face and warm smile. But make no mistake; he was tough as battleship steel.

My conversation with the two helped me frame what I would explain to the board the next day. For instance, they told me that the Russians and some other European countries might resist the idea of keeping the NHL ice surface, as they would see it as a move designed to give the North American teams added home-field advantage. My answer to that was simple: most of the world's top players already played on NHL ice. I just needed to be convincing.

It was made clear to me that if the IIHF was to give us a break, there would have to be a quid pro quo. In other words, enough of a benefit to calm any anxiety expressed by the Europeans. From my end, that meant giving an outright guarantee that hockey would have a spectacular stage at the Games, and that IIHF officials would be treated extremely well and given access to top-notch hotels conveniently located close to the hockey venues. That wasn't an inducement. It was the least we could do, I figured, given the multimillion-dollar break we wanted them to cut us. Not to mention the fairly radical departure from tradition that the organization would be making.

The next morning, bright and early, I went before the IIHF board and laid out our proposal and suggested it was not reasonable to ask an organization to take existing venues, tear them apart for a one-time use and then endure further costs to restore them to their original use. I suggested that it was contrary to our value system and probably contrary to the value system of the IOC as well. I went so far as to suggest the IIHF would seem heavy-handed and out of touch with the times if it was to press us to deliver wider ice. I wanted to place a burden on them that was too heavy to carry, and to appeal to their social conscience and better judgment. I pitched hard and took my leave. An hour later, I was on a plane for Vancouver.

I thought the discussion went well, but the directors took my presentation under advisement. It wasn't long, however, before we got word that the IIHF was, in principle, okay with our plan to keep GM Place as it was, subject to some fine-tuning of our proposal. It was a huge win at a time when we were looking to save every dime we could.

By this point in the project, I had already indicated publicly that although we were performing surgery everywhere we could we were going to need more money for construction than we had indicated in our bid. In a speech to the Vancouver Board of Trade in November 2005, I said that with construction costs expected to increase by 50 per cent on comparable major projects and infrastructure, we might need some additional help from government.

Discussions with federal and provincial partners had already started. We had made a detailed submission asking for a lift of $55 million from each. We outlined all the different ways we had trimmed costs, from doing away with our plans to build a temporary broadcast centre in Richmond to reconfiguring cross-country ski trails in the Callaghan Valley southwest of Whistler, and a score of other initiatives. Still, those efforts were mostly overlooked in the ensuing coverage, which focused largely on the call for more funding. The 2002-dollars argument was being ignored.

It bothered us that, even though the construction projects were mostly on schedule and on budget (if you factored in inflation), our message didn't seem to be getting out. Public confidence in the project was taking a beating. It made no difference that we were outperforming almost every other major project in the province. No matter what we did, it seemed, it was a public relations battle we were losing. The level of scrutiny we faced was intense.

We were even getting negative comments from some elected officials who were pretending they were caught by surprise. Both levels of government knew all along that our original construction budget wasn't going to be enough because it was in 2002 dollars and did not factor in inflation and rising costs. They knew. We told them enough times. Although I understood the politics of some of the public remarks, it didn't make them any less galling to swallow. My team felt pretty beaten up and for good reason.

I could have responded to some of those comments, but doing so would have meant throwing our government partners under the bus, and I wasn't prepared to do that. In part, I think politicians in both Victoria and Ottawa were feeding off concerns the public had about costs and whether we were going to complete the project on time—or if we even knew what we were doing. If the public was unhappy with us, ipso facto it was unhappy with the government.

I spent a great deal of time talking to Jack about this problem. He knew the construction business inside out and had great instincts. We agreed that something dramatic needed to be done, a seismic event of such significance that it would help rebuild public confidence. After a great deal of soul-searching we decided to sign a new head coach for the construction team.

Jack and I both admired Dan Doyle, who had recently retired as B.C.'s deputy minister of transportation. Dan was highly regarded and had successfully spearheaded a number of high-profile provincial initiatives. I first met Dan during our discussions with the government over the Sea to Sky Highway. He had come to Prague for our closing presentation and had a real spirit for the Games. He was a guy who instilled confidence in people and organizations. He was solid, no-nonsense, composed, durable, trusted and respected. We knew he would have a calming effect on the organization and help dissipate the growing panic about our construction program. We knew he could hit the ground running.

As a bonus, Dan knew the inner machinations of the B.C. government. His appointment was going to give us instant credibility in Victoria and probably get government officials off our backs over the cost of the venues. Personally, my plate was overflowing. I just wanted to sleep at night knowing the construction program was in the hands of someone who could deal with any issues that might arise, who would not accept failure. An unflappable, stoic commander.

This meant removing a great guy in Steve Matheson, who was incredibly capable and had done a stellar job on the construction side. Dan Doyle said as much soon after he'd had a chance to assess where things were. Unfortunately, Steve wasn't able to instill public confidence in what was going on in the way we knew Dan could. Informing Steve of the change was one of the tougher decisions and conversations that I would ever have with anyone, especially as I had earlier convinced him to abandon a great career to join our team. He deserved to cross the finish line with us, having given his heart and soul to the project. It was heartbreaking to ask for his keys.

Dan's presence on the team had the immediate desired effect, inside the organization at least. He took bear-trap control, declared the construction program sound and then quickly appointed a quarterback for the indoor venues and another for the outdoor ones. He was adamant that all construction would have to be done within our revised $580-million budget and declared victory on that number. The two levels of government eventually approved the $110 million in extra funding. The new budget was the one our organization believed we should be measured against. This was an important distinction, because we planned on saying we had constructed the venues on time and on budget. Others would disagree.

AS GOOD AS we tried to feel about the direction we were heading, there always seemed to be a challenge or mini controversy around the corner.

In September, the provincial auditor general released a report by Pacific Liaicon, a subsidiary of construction powerhouse SNC-Lavalin, which was commissioned to look at our building plans. It questioned whether our $580-million budget was going to be enough to deliver a venue package that the IOC was going to be satisfied with. The auditor general said in another report released at the same time that the true cost of the Games should be pegged at $2.5 billion and not the $600 million the B.C. government was saying was the cost.

Needless to say, the opposition New Democratic Party jumped on the reports, suggesting they pointed to mismanagement, planning errors and cost overruns and harkening back to the massive debt piled up by the City of Montreal for the 1976 Summer Olympics. I thought this was blatant gamesmanship. They did it because they could.

I met with Harry Bains, the NDP's Games critic, one morning at the Waterfront Hotel and outright accused him of making up facts. I used pretty strong words to remind him of the damage he was doing to the Games by spreading fictitious information. Harry would hang out in our lobby after press conferences looking for the cameras, and when he found one he'd sound off on us. It didn't matter what we did; it was never good enough for Harry or his party. He would just swing the bat as hard as he could and it didn't matter who he hit in the process.

A few days after the auditor general's report, there was a front-page headline in the *Vancouver Sun* suggesting that people were calling for my head. This was mostly based on NDP leader Carole James's statement that I should be fired in light of the reports released a few days earlier.

It rattled me a little, I won't lie. I expected more respect from Carole James, who had never asked for a walk-through of our finances. It burned me even more that the auditor general was sounding off and yet had never once asked to meet with me or members of my team to talk about the facts. It all felt pretty cheap and opportunistic. We had no choice but to sit there and absorb the blows.

Although the temperature around the project seemed to be rising, I felt that we were on the right track. I could see miles of progress that others couldn't. I tried my best to drown out the background noise, focus on the job and look after my team, which was vicariously under attack too. What else was I going to do? We had a strong set of values upon which we were trying to build the whole organization. And during troubling times like these, it was those values of honesty and decency and trust and hard work that guided us. My dad used to say, "When your world is falling apart and people are saying bad things about you, and the walls are caving in, to survive you must ask yourself the one and only question that matters: 'What is the truth?' That will sustain you." He was right.

All I could do was continue pushing forward. If someone decided it was time to change the CEO for the Games, I had no control over that. What I could control was my ability to lead, be a good example to my troops and continue to work my butt off from five in the morning until I collapsed in bed at midnight.

IT WAS A little-known fact that during the bid phase we had allocated a certain amount of our construction work to First Nations companies and crews as part of Aboriginals' broad participation and partnership in the Games. There were certainly some doubts within the organization about the capacity of First Nations companies to construct at this level, while staying within the cost parameters and time constraints we had set out. To make certain we kept the situation under tight control, we chose to allocate construction work to First Nations groups upfront, to test the waters, so to speak. That would allow us to see how capable their teams were, and if we saw a problem there was still time to rectify it. As it turned out, we didn't need to worry.

The First Nations construction crews were first-rate. We began by having them do some earth-moving work on the Nordic cross-country ski trails in the Callaghan Valley. They finished below budget and before their deadlines. They were good. And they were excited to be in on the serious action of building the Games. Everyone was so pleased with the quality of the work that we ended up awarding them about $50 million in contracts, a far leap from the $15 million that was first envisioned. Fact is, they gave us an early edge by saving us money and getting us ahead of schedule. The result was outstanding construction, beautiful venues, full First Nations participation, additional jobs and job training. It also gave these companies a new confidence and new capacity to compete for high-level construction work in the future and worked wonders for our relationship with the four host First Nations.

I was told a great story about a Native father and his son who were part of one of the construction teams in the Callaghan Valley. At one point, the father noticed the son taking a break, sitting on a rock admiring the scenery. He got off his machine, walked over and told him to get back to work. They were there in the service of their country, he told his boy, and there was no time to waste. Such was the spirit of the men and women who came to work on the project from First Nations communities in the Sea to Sky corridor from North Vancouver to Whistler.

AT VANOC, WE worked extremely hard to ensure that the culture at all these projects was healthy and that there was a keen focus and desire to complete the facilities on time and on budget. We needed to make all construction workers feel as much a part of our Olympic family as the person working on logo designs or the one putting together our ticketing program. We were all striving for the same thing and needed to be guided by the same principles.

To make sure that the workers felt included, I would visit construction sites often, and if not me then another member of the executive. We instituted a program in which the workers were given Olympic jackets by one minister or another and were awarded beautiful medals by the premier, who thanked them personally for their work. It was a small thing to remind the workers, who had come from across Canada, of the key role they were playing in helping to prepare the region and the country for the extraordinary experience we were about to have.

By the end of 2006, most of the concerns about construction costs had waned. At least the public debate had quieted down. We were ahead of schedule on many venues. Finding enough accommodation in Whistler still presented challenges, but overall we were being given high marks by the IOC for stability. We felt we had weathered the first early storms that every organizing committee faces and had come out even stronger as an organization. We were finding a second wind. I could feel morale improving.

Our first venue was completed in early 2007—that was the freestyle skiing and snowboarding stadium at Cypress Mountain. By the end of the year, all of the venues at Whistler would be finished—including the ski jumping facilities, the Sliding Centre and the cross-country ski course in the Callaghan Valley. The last venue to be completed was the new curling rink in Vancouver, which opened in 2009, a year before the Games began but just when we needed it.

THE BIGGEST CONTROVERSY surrounded the construction of the Athletes' Village in Vancouver. We had entered into an agreement with the city early on to provide $30 million toward construction—any costs beyond that were the city's responsibility. The plan was to build the village on an iconic site on the south shore of False Creek, just across from where Expo 86 was staged—by any measure it was a jewel of a location. Under the plan envisioned by the city, the condominium units would be used by the athletes during the Games and then sold at market prices afterward. The plan called for more than 200 units to be set aside for social housing.

Millennium Development Inc. won the right to build the village complex and they soon produced plans for a state-of-the-art community built to the highest environmental standards in the world. The cost was about $1 billion. Rumours aside, everything seemed to be going fine with construction until fall 2008 and the beginning of the worldwide financial panic. Millennium had arranged financing with a New York–based hedge fund company called the Fortress Investment Group. Fortress, also the parent company of Whistler-Blackcomb ski resort, was really feeling the pinch and was increasingly concerned about overruns that Millennium was incurring at the Athletes' Village. That fall, it stopped making its monthly loans to Millennium, which forced the City of Vancouver to step in and provide a financial lifeline to the developer. It really had no choice since our deal to provide the village was with the city, not Millennium.

But the decision to provide the financing was made on camera and leaked to Gary Mason. Mason's stories in the *Globe and Mail* were published on the eve of a civic election. The governing Non-Partisan Association (NPA) bore the brunt of the scandal that erupted around the secret loan, and the party was all but wiped out at the polls. The election ushered in Mayor Gregor Robertson and his Vision Vancouver party, which took swift political advantage of the situation. Behind the scenes, bureaucrats would lose their jobs, including City Manager Judy Rogers, who sat on our board and had been a champion for the Games from day one. It was a shame to lose Judy because she was smart, savvy and had done a great job for us. Penny Ballem, a formidable administrator, succeeded her.

Eventually, the city would completely take over financing for the project. It wasn't ideal from the city's perspective, but there were few other options. The complex would eventually get finished on time and would become easily the best Athletes' Village in the history of the Olympics. It would be a marquee project for a twenty-first-century global city.

Although we weren't directly involved in the problems the Athletes' Village experienced, we couldn't help but get a little wet when the story splashed over the front pages of the papers for months on end. The new mayor didn't help by trying to play politics with the situation he inherited, making the NPA look as bad as possible in the process. He suggested that taxpayers had been left with a $1-billion nightmare. I thought it was a lot of overhyped rhetoric that wasn't particularly helpful or especially fair. In fact, it would come back to haunt him a bit. By the fall of 2010, the Athletes' Village was back in the news for all the wrong reasons. A suddenly soft real estate market had stalled sales, which whipped up more doom-and-gloom stories about how much money the city was going to lose over the project. The mayor's handling of the issue was coming under constant attack.

The Athletes' Village controversy did seem to ignite a whole new round of negative publicity about the cost of the Games. I won't ever forget the morning I woke up to see the front page of the *Vancouver Sun* and the massive headline: "ADD IT ALL UP, AND YOU'LL FIND THE OLYMPICS IS GOING TO COST US $6 BILLION (SO FAR ANYWAY)." The story was by Daphne

Bramham, the same reporter who had suggested I wasn't qualified to be CEO. It seemed to spark a whole new round of negative stories about the cost of the Games.

The $6 billion in costs accusation was patently unfair, an exaggeration on steroids. It included the cost of Vancouver's new Convention Centre, but we had never included the centre in our bid proposal because it wasn't being constructed for us or by us. It was being built regardless, and we had had no idea if it was going to be on time for the Games. Now that we were confident it would be ready, we were going to pay a considerable rent to use it for the broadcast media.

The same went for the new rapid transit line from the airport into downtown. This was another project that had been on the province's radar for years, long before the Olympics was being discussed. Originally the hope was it would be built by 2012, if I'm not mistaken. After we won the right to host the Games, an effort was made to move up the timeline so that the line would be in place for the Olympics. After all, the world was coming. But we never made the Canada Line part of our presentation in Prague, and I never mentioned it in a single bid speech.

Now, admittedly, we did include the upgrade to the Sea to Sky Highway in our bid presentation. It was a well-known fact that the road was a killer stretch of highway. The provincial government had been promising to fix it, and there was a timeline to get the work done. Did the province agree to accelerate that timeline for us? Yes, absolutely. If critics wanted to ding VANOC for the cost of the acceleration, fine. What would that be? Maybe $20 or $30 million at most. But to say the project was only in the works because of the Olympics was simply not true. And the people writing those stories knew that.

In the end, these were battles we were never going to win. And frankly, after a while we just gave up trying. There was nothing we could do about what people wrote and said. All we could do was focus on staging the best Games possible. Besides, most of the people working for newspapers or radio or television were complete professionals. And even if I didn't always agree with what they wrote or said, I respected the fact that they carried out their duties honourably and, for the most part, fairly.

The rage I sometimes felt about the misinformation constantly being spread by the organized opponents of the Games was much harder to suppress. On that front, I had little time or respect for Chris Shaw, the de facto head of the Olympic resistance movement in B.C. Chris was a professor of ophthalmology at the University of British Columbia and author of an anti-Olympics book called *Five Ring Circus*. Almost from the beginning of the bid, he led the campaign against us, trashing Jack, me and anyone who came within a country mile of the work we were doing.

One time, I was invited on Bill Good's talk show on CKNW to debate Shaw. Bill is a local broadcasting legend, and has the number one talk show in B.C. Well, right on cue Chris did his thing, ranting about how much the Games were costing, how much damage the Games had left behind in every country that had hosted them, the poverty the Olympics caused, how the poor were booted out of their homes and communities to make way for the rich and powerful. He had statistics that apparently showed the damage that Expo 86 had done to the poor in Vancouver. There was nothing good about the Olympics. All they did was cause chaos and pain—and ruined Christmas for children. Or maybe that was the one thing he didn't accuse the Olympics of doing...

I tried the best I could to maintain my cool and give thoughtful answers. The last thing I wanted to do was to sound as if this guy had succeeded in getting under my skin. I was not going to give Chris's tiny legion of supporters any cause for celebration even though I wanted to push their man out of the window. When it was time to leave, however, I looked at him and said: "You call yourself a man of science. You should be ashamed of yourself. You should care much more about getting it right and being dead certain you are. That is the one thing that your students should be able to count on from you. But you don't seem to care about the facts or about getting them straight. You just care about the agenda that you have. It's a disgrace, quite frankly, that you get away with this."

Bill Good looked at me with a wry grin.

"Darn it anyway," he said. "I wish the microphones were still on."

EVERYONE AT VANOC was now facing a huge workload and attendant pressures. A lot of our staff members were young and enthusiastic, but few had ever faced this kind of stress before. In a project that spanned several years, there were going to be emotional peaks and valleys. It was my job to keep spirits up and, in some cases, put jobs in perspective.

Every year, I sent out a Christmas card to staff containing a letter with a message that I felt might be useful to them. The letters usually got a good response, but the one I sent in Christmas of 2006 really hit home. I talked about how my mother and I had enjoyed an extraordinary relationship over the years, even when we lived thousands of miles apart. We would phone each other, write letters and see each other at family celebrations. We had an intense bond. Then one day, we had our first argument ever and it was a bad one.

"For the first time the phone was placed on the receiver with a blunt thud," I wrote to my staff. "And it was all my fault. Four months passed without a word or a letter... too stubborn and all over nothing. Then my brother phoned. Mum was dead. And I was filled with remorse, tears and guilt. For one more hug, one more smile, I would have given anything."

After her funeral, I was alone in her apartment going through old photo albums and other family history. I came across a sealed envelope on top of the mantel with my name on it.

"I picked it up almost trembling," I wrote. "Inside was mum's last letter to me, written as if nothing had happened at all. Words of compassion, kindness and love, as if she knew we might not see ach other again. It was carefully folded around her photos of me growing up, our happy memories from times long past. It was her final but lasting lesson on how to live better... her gift of peace and joy."

My point was to share my mother's lesson with my Olympic family at VANOC. Each year represented a new beginning, a chance to get a fresh start, make wrong things right. I wanted to make sure that those working with me didn't make the same mistake I had.

"So go on," I wrote. "Make your mother proud. Celebrate the gift of family and friends. A kind word, a warm hug, a long overdue call. Spread some joy. *Semez de la joie.*"

6

Diving for **Pennies**

THE DOOR SLAMMED with a loud crack. A picture hanging on the wall of the boardroom crashed to the floor. Those of us left behind at our Gastown headquarters looked at one another self-consciously in the wake of Terry Wright's emotional departure. The silence was deafening.

In the early going, dust-ups over the value of corporate sponsorships were fairly common. VANOC was responsible for two very different budgets. One was the budget to build the venues. The second was to run the Games—money for transportation, staff, accommodation and a myriad of other costs. While the public perception seemed to be that taxpayers' dollars were being used to finance this budget as well, it was not the case. Only about 10 per cent came from government. The majority of the funding came from the private sector, which included our share of the money the IOC received from the sale of television rights to broadcasters. There was also money from ticket sales. But the bulk of the budget would derive from our ability to convince corporations to pony up millions of dollars to become Olympic partners.

During the bid, our target for corporate sponsorships was set at a sobering $450 million—the most we thought we could raise. Many thought that was a wildly unrealistic goal. Even the IOC had its doubts and said so. Terry Wright, my top lieutenant, and Linda Oglov, who headed up our marketing team during the bid phase, both felt that the maximum amount we were likely to get out of the biggest corporations in the country would be between $20 and $30 million. That is what history had shown. Canada was not known for deep pockets like those found in corporate America.

I knew that if these estimates were true we were going to be in big trouble. We would never be able to stage the kind of Games that I and others envisioned. Even with $450 million we would be putting on the Low-Cost Games. Or worse, we would be in a nasty deficit position when it was all over, with the public screaming bloody murder.

Terry and Linda often became exasperated listening to me ramble on about the value a company could derive from an association with the Olympics. I'm sure there was more than a little violin music played when I was not in the room. Terry, in particular, grew tired of me constantly challenging his assertion that Canadian companies had a fairly modest ceiling when it came to sponsorships. It was during one such meeting that Terry, having had enough, slammed the door behind him with enough force that it caused a picture to fall off the wall.

Linda thought I'd been a bit rough on Terry and told me so the next day. What's more, she thought Terry was right when it came to forecasting what we'd be able to raise through sponsorships—give or take a few million. We agreed to disagree. Clearly, our visions were not aligned. Some of us were thinking about two great weeks of sport—others were dreaming about taking the Olympic spirit into every home in Canada, nation building, one Canadian at a time if necessary. I was among the latter.

To me, the first deal that we struck with a corporate partner was going to establish the bar against which all other partnerships would be measured. We had many conversations about which business sector would give us the best chance at success in this regard. We finally agreed it would be telecommunications.

It was clear to us that Telus, based on the West Coast, desperately wanted to be associated with the Games. The company had generously donated nearly $5 million to help us put together our bid. It was evident in some preliminary discussions that I had with Bell Canada that it wanted in too, badly. Bell also didn't want Telus seizing the Olympic spotlight at its expense. At the time, Bell was the telecommunications partner of the Canadian Olympic Committee.

It was important to us that we not only get a deal that was a runaway financial hit, but that we also attract a new teammate that was aligned fully with our values and our vision. We wanted a company that had the capacity and desire to help us take our story to all corners of the country. Telus and Bell both set up teams inside their respective companies to work on their bids.

I have a wonderful memory of walking into Bell's executive offices in Montreal and sitting down with the company's CEO, Michael Sabia, a man with a deep love for the country. I talked about our vision for the Games, the many challenges we faced, the once-in-a-generation opportunity the Olympics presented Canadians. I looked him in the eye and asked him if Bell could become a champion for these Games. I remember Michael's passionate response. He told me how much Bell wanted to be our partner, how much the company, and he himself, believed in the nation-building adventure we had embarked on. He said Bell would be a partner VANOC could count on to help spread the Olympic spirit throughout the country and deliver a flawless telecommunications set-up for the Games. He gave me his word that Bell would live this experience with us moment by moment if we were to accept it as our first partner.

I believed him.

Michael saw the Games as an opportunity to take a company that had been in Canada for almost a century and revitalize it. It was a chance for Bell to rebrand itself in a more youthful, relevant image and connect with younger customers. His biggest concern, and one he expressed many times in different ways, was that the bid process be fair. I think there was a worry in the executive ranks at Bell that we might try and give Telus a bit of a hometown discount and award it the deal no matter what Bell put on the table. I gave Michael my word that the winning bid would be the winning bid even if the distance between the two was a dime. We shook on this promise.

Telus, of course, was just as enthusiastic. The company saw the Olympics as an opportunity to take Canada by storm and come out as the number one telecommunications company. The guy Telus put in charge of its bid was a ferociously competitive fellow named Rob Cruickshank. Rob was a good friend of mine. I had helped train his son, Greg, who would become a nationally ranked squash player. Rob had always been good to me. He was someone I never hesitated to call during difficult times. I wasn't sure Rob's appointment to head up Telus's bid team was coincidental, but it did make the situation awkward at times, especially at the end.

My goal was to build as much competitive tension between the two companies as possible and elevate the level of public interest around the bids in the process. It was high drama. Financial commitments notwithstanding, either company, we were convinced, would deliver the telecommunications solution for which we were looking. I hoped we would not have to decide the outcome through a type of shootout. I preferred that the winner was a mile in front.

By the time the deadline had arrived, I was convinced we were heading into uncharted waters as far as sponsorship deals go. I could sense how desperate both companies were to sign on and spend the next five-plus years taking advantage of an association with the Olympics. When it came time to receive the two bids, I contrived a reason to be out of the office so that Terry Wright would be the person who would open the envelope. Devilishly, I wanted to hear his voice when he looked at the numbers. And I also sensed Terry wanted to be the one with the letter opener in his hand.

The envelope, please!

The day the bid offers arrived, Terry got me on the phone in Harrison Lake, B.C., where I was doing some business. Out of instinct I told him to open the Telus bid first. The package contained an extremely sophisticated proposal that conveyed the passion the company had toward the Olympics. Then Terry came upon the dollar value of the bid. There were a few seconds of dead air.

It was valued at about $135 million—an unheard of amount in the history of Canadian corporate sponsorship deals.

I could tell Terry was stunned. I felt like a child who had just discovered a new bike under the Christmas tree, though I tried not to show it over the phone. I felt Terry was going to be even more dumbfounded in a few minutes.

He then opened the Bell offer, which also contained a beautifully packaged set of materials that outlined their telecommunications strategy for the Games and articulated the promise the company was making to help sell these Olympics to the country. The Bell proposal screamed commitment. And then Terry told me what the value of the Bell bid was: $200 million. It included $90 million in cash, $60 million in telecommunications services and $50 million in tangible promotional support for the Games, including a $15-million cash investment in Own the Podium (OTP). A new high-performance athlete program that brought science to bear on training and preparation, OTP was just coming out of the gate. We needed a partner to invest big if we were to have a genuine shot at raising enough money to achieve our goal of topping the medals table in Vancouver for the Olympics, and placing third at the Paralympics. The federal government had committed $55 million, and we were on the hook to match. The program was seen by VANOC as vital to achieving our vision of bringing the country together. With Bell's proposal, we'd hit the jackpot and had a new ceiling.

Terry chuckled as he read and the significance of the moment was not lost on him. He had in his hand the largest sponsorship deal in the history of the Olympics—Summer or Winter—period. It was an extraordinary moment in the life of the 2010 Games, and the one during which I think Terry realized the power of our vision. We were incredibly excited—this wasn't just a home run; this was a grand slam early in the game. We agreed it was crucial that the contents of the bids remain confidential until we completed a full analysis and audit of every detail.

We had former B.C. chief justice Allan McEachern, whom we had hired as a fairness monitor, evaluate the two bids himself. He too concluded the Bell offer was easily the best proposal. It didn't take long for my executive team to endorse the Bell bid.

Right after our board approved the deal, I phoned Michael Sabia with the good news. He was, as expected, over the moon. It may well have been the first day he completely trusted VANOC, despite the assurances we had given him that the process would be fair and carried out with integrity. Michael had grand plans to make the announcement to all of the company's employees via a simulcast in a week's time.

Before then, we would have to tell Telus officially that it had been unsuccessful. I made a call in person to the company's downtown office, along with Dave Cobb, to see Darren Entwistle, the CEO of Telus. Darren, an impeccable dresser, was a legendary figure among the Canadian business establishment. He had done wonders with Telus since taking over the helm. But he had a reputation for not suffering fools gladly. He did not like to lose. Everything I had heard about him suggested a person whose veins bulged from his neck when a decision didn't go his way. Maybe that wasn't the case, but that was the image I had in my head as we walked into a boardroom to give him the bad news. I was nervous and shaking. Darren was already red-faced. He knew what was coming.

I thanked him for Telus's support throughout the bid phase and for the company's interest in the sponsorship deal. But I told him that the VANOC executive had recommended the Bell bid to the board and it had been approved, and I gave him all the reasons. Looking into Darren's eyes at that moment was like looking into the burning fires of hell itself.

"Is that it?" he said.

Yes, we said.

"Okay," he said. "Thanks for coming and best of luck."

And that was it. Dismissed. Short and painful. My friendship with Rob Cruickshank would never be the same, unfortunately. He would be quoted as saying that we had "elected to go with the cash." That's not the way I saw it at all. It sounded like sour grapes to me.

We made the announcement official on the afternoon of October 18, 2004. Bell employees across the country were ecstatic when Michael Sabia and I appeared on their computer screens to deliver the surprise news. It didn't take long for the news to filter into boardrooms across the country where other sponsorship bids were being prepared for our evaluation. I would later learn that the Bell offer made companies pause and rethink their proposals, jacking them way up in many cases and maybe causing a few to abandon their plans entirely. One thing was certain: It was game on.

The IOC was astounded at the Bell result. We were already halfway to the number we had targeted in the bid—the one the IOC was skeptical we might not hit. Now we needed a few more big victories on the sponsorship front to really create some momentum and take the financial pressure off the organization.

Our next target was the banks.

At the same time that the Bell and Telus battle was unfolding, we were talking to a number of Canadian banks about becoming a premier national sponsor of the Games. Many took a look, but in the end it would become a contest between the Canadian Imperial Bank of Commerce and the RBC Financial Group.

The Royal had been a supporter of the Canadian Olympic Committee for well over 50 years, the world's longest uninterrupted Olympic partner. It was determined to secure the sponsorship.

CIBC was hoping to dethrone the Royal as the so-called Olympic bank. Both put together excellent presentations, though I will admit that the Royal's struck me for its passion but even more so for its alignment with our values and vision. It had that irresistible human touch. RBC president and CEO Gord Nixon impressed upon us that his bank was an institution we could trust. He emphasized this many times. He left us with words we would never forget: "Canadians will judge you by the company you keep," a humble but pointed reference to the fact that RBC was at the time regarded as Canada's most trusted company.

After listening to CIBC and Royal's pitches in Toronto and getting the substance of their offer, Dave Cobb, Andrea Shaw, our vice-president of sponsorship sales and marketing, and I flew back to Vancouver. We worked on the documents throughout the flight and continued our work in an airport lounge. It was our view that the Royal was probably the right partner, but it would need to up the value a bit. We sat for hours talking strategy. A little drama was called for, I thought.

It was decided that I would phone Graham MacLachlan, RBC regional president for B.C., at the crack of dawn the next day. I asked for an immediate meeting so I could outline our concerns. I'm pretty sure Graham was still in his pajamas when I called. I told him we had a few challenges with their proposal, but that we would like to try and work them out. He agreed to turn his morning upside down, and I met him in a room on the thirty-sixth floor of the bank's downtown offices in Vancouver. I told him that based on the proposal we had it would be difficult to cut a deal. But if RBC could rework the numbers a bit we felt there was an agreement to be had—that day.

We bantered back and forth and eventually got Dave Cobb on the phone to talk details. To further add to the drama, I asked Dave to jump in his car and come down to where our meeting was taking place. He was standing next to me in 15 minutes. We pitched hard for a recalibration of their proposal. Graham said he would see what he could do and make some calls. We went to a waiting room. Graham got Gord Nixon and the bank's top marketing executive involved. Soon we were all on a conference call and batting ideas back and forth. Once again, we were banished to the waiting room. Twenty minutes and one more conference call later, the bank agreed to amend its proposal, which improved our cash position by $26 million.

Dave and I left absolutely delighted with the deal we had managed to strike. We high-fived each other in the elevator, two kids who had just landed an extra scoop of ice cream.

The Royal was an enormous force in the country, and Gord Nixon was a universally trusted CEO who we felt confident would help us elevate our standing in the corporate community across the country. When he spoke, people listened. We announced the deal to great fanfare at an RBC annual general meeting in Halifax in late February 2005. The package ended up being worth more than $110 million and gave the bank Canadian marketing rights to the next four Olympic teams.

The deals started to come fast and furious now. The one that followed the RBC announcement had interesting roots, as it were. In the fall of 2002, I was named Canadian Sports Leader of the Year in Toronto. As it turned out, the person who had been chosen to present the award that night was George Heller, an old friend and president and CEO of the Hudson's Bay Company. George was a formidable fellow with a solid sports background. He had been CEO of the very successful Commonwealth Games in Victoria in 1994.

Afterward, we were sharing a few laughs backstage when I just came out and told George there had to be a way for Canada's oldest company and largest retailer to become partners with Canada's Games. George agreed and we shook hands, determined to make it happen. A handshake with him I would take over a contract anytime. That little backstage meeting would cement our friendship and become the first of many over the next couple of years that would eventually lead to HBC's becoming the third big sponsorship deal that we announced in 2005. It was a package worth more than $100 million, which not only gave the company the rights to design, manufacture and provide clothing and luggage for Canada's Olympic teams over the next eight years, but also make The Bay the official Olympic department store and VANOC's merchandise retail partner. Also, it was the first deal of its kind in Olympic history.

Yes, we were doing it our way.

The Bay announcement wasn't without controversy. Many people thought we would stick with the popular Canadian clothier Roots, which had made a name for itself with the "poorboy" hats it designed for the Salt Lake City Olympics. Roots founder Michael Budman was not happy about The Bay deal and with no evidence at all cried foul. In financial terms, the Roots offer was empty for us. Zero cash, plus we were not just looking for a clothing retailer. The Bay's story and our vision for the Games meshed perfectly.

The Bay began designing outfits for Canadian Olympians in 1936 and continued until 1968, when it was supplanted as the official clothing supplier by other companies. George saw this deal as central to The Bay's vision for becoming new again. For The Bay, it was also paramount to its emerging business strategy of reconnecting with Canadians. In an instant, the company's army of employees became 2010 Olympic messengers.

In the first three deals, totalling in excess of $400 million, we had doubled the amount we anticipated getting from selling 10 top sponsorship packages.

AMID ALL THE wheeling and dealing and travelling on the sponsorship front, a group from VANOC attended the 2006 Winter Games in Turin, Italy—a last chance to learn before the world's attention would be on us. Our team took plenty of notes in Turin, noting the many problems that the folks there were experiencing and how they addressed them. From a marketing and fundraising prospective, Turin was our polar opposite.

The Games were never sold to all of Italy; they were completely local. In some parts of the country the level of awareness bordered on lack of interest. You got the sense at times that even the city of Turin itself wasn't all that excited about the Games, certainly during the build-up phase.

There were three big Canadian stories in Turin, two positive, one a little less so. One of the positive stories was the success of our athletes—the men's hockey result aside. We ended up winning 24 medals, a new Winter Games record for Canada. More importantly, it was a sign that the fledgling Own the Podium program was already paying dividends, even though it was just one year old. The other big moment for us was the closing ceremonies, where the Olympic flag would be handed over to Vancouver Mayor Sam Sullivan.

Sam's presence on the stage became the focus of worldwide media attention because he is paraplegic. He was the first Olympic mayor to receive the Olympic flag, and wave it in front of 60,000 cheering spectators and a massive global television audience, while seated in a wheelchair. It was a wonderful moment that I thought reflected well on Canada and spoke to our values as a country and our sense of fairness and inclusiveness. Sam was beaming.

As part of any closing ceremonies, about eight to 10 minutes are given over to the organizing committee of the next Games to introduce themselves to the world. We chose a light approach and decided to poke a bit of fun at ourselves, play up some of our stereotypes and then undermine them a bit by showing the young, dynamic face of the country in the image of singer Avril Lavigne.

The trouble began days before the closing ceremonies arrived. The weather was horrible, which made rehearsing in the open-air stadium absolutely brutal for our performers. And the Italians didn't treat us all that great either. Our eight minutes was just not important to them. They gave us rehearsal times in the middle of the night. Many of our people were in lousy moods as a result and not exactly motivated to practise long and hard. They just wanted to get on with it.

All things considered, the ceremonies came off pretty well. Our montage began with a scene of a guy ice fishing and included images of igloos and Mounties, a deliberate attempt to poke a little fun at the Canada of the past. Even though our performers seemed to pull it off with few hiccups, we expected some abuse from the media. It seems that throughout Olympic history, these presentations by the cities next hosting the Games are always ripped in the home press. No one is spared. Ours would be no exception. It was a little different in our case, as it wasn't just the media attacking us; even Premier Gordon Campbell got into the act and let us have it for a performance he thought was cliché-ridden and didn't speak to the "new Canada." This was one of the few times I was disappointed in Gordon. Not that he didn't have the right to his opinion, but I wished he had spoken to me first before taking a stick to us in public.

I mean, did the premier and others really think we were trying to promote ice fishing in Canada? It was simply a way to start our production by saying "This is the Canada that was," and then move to the Canada we are today—youthful, vibrant, hip, fun. (Although having said that, there are still parts of Canada where ice fishing is important—I have letters from those folks to prove it.) But remember we had only eight minutes. It's very difficult to tell a full story in eight minutes, even though we had some of the brightest cultural minds in the country helping us.

Others criticized us for portraying Canada as an ice-locked deep freezer. Well, we never did that. But we did want to say that we Canadians love winter, we embrace it and we overcome it every year. The Winter Games are supposed to be about winter. Hockey and curling are not for the beach. I found it interesting that the only place we got royally ripped was at home. "Bravo, Canada!" was NBC's sign-off that night.

If I had to do it over again, I would hire three great performers, put them on the stage and have them sing three great Canadian songs and go home.

AFTER TURIN, OUR focus continued to be on raising as much money as we could through sponsorships. We knew we needed a landmark deal in the automobile sector, though that proved a greater challenge than we anticipated.

Almost from the day we got the Games, General Motors had indicated a strong willingness to partner with us. That sounded good, but in order for us to make the right deal we needed to create the impression that there were a number of other automakers who also wanted in—which wasn't exactly the case. The fact is no one we talked to was offering what GM could and would put on the table, which made creating the illusion of a major competition that much tougher. In the end, we signed a fairly lucrative deal with GM Canada that was valued at about $67 million. The company ended up supplying us with 6,000 vehicles, cash and support for Own the Podium.

General Motors had become our sixth national Tier 1 partner. Besides GM, Bell Canada, RBC and The Bay, we also managed to put together strong pacts with RONA and Petro-Canada. The RONA deal was interesting because the company's CEO was trying hard to unseat Home Depot as the top home renovation company in Canada. He saw the Olympics, traditionally an event Home Depot sponsored, as a way to help pull it off. So we created a pretty strong competition between the two companies, and thanks to some last-minute bargaining RONA won out with a bid that amounted to $68 million. I will never forget the company's emotional pitch in Montreal as its French-speaking CEO, Robert Dutton, stood atop a Canadian loonie for good luck. A bonus of the deal was that we were now firmly grounded in Quebec and expanding our influence among francophones.

Ultimately, our sponsorship total would amount to more than $750 million, which completely stunned the pundits and especially the IOC. We signed nearly 70 partners, and in each case the company had pretty much written the largest cheque it ever had for a sponsorship. It showed how important the association with

Vancouver 2010 had become. An added bonus throughout this process was seeing what a company's involvement in the Olympics meant to its employees. I recall flying to Calgary with Dave and Andrea to meet with the executives of Petro-Canada. The employees came down by the hundreds to the lobby, where they staged an in-house demonstration to let us know how badly they wanted to be Olympic partners. A sea of singing red-shirted employees was there to make an impression that would tug our heartstrings and touch our Canadian pride. And it worked. I had tears in my eyes.

Still, I believe we could have raised tens of millions of dollars more from sponsorships if we had had greater authority over the entire process. But the IOC controlled business categories that would have been lucrative for us but were sold internationally by the Olympic committee itself. When the IOC sold a category, say to Coca-Cola or McDonald's, we would get between 15 and 20 per cent of the deal and for that the company would get the same rights as Bell or RBC. We would clearly have done far better operating on our own but had to play by the IOC's rules.

One of our biggest disappointments was not being able to convince the IOC to allow us to have a competitive bid process in the beer category. God knows we tried. The IOC had signed a one-off deal with Budweiser that gave the company Olympic marketing rights up to 2008. That left us little time to negotiate a deal with Molson's or anyone else after it expired. We did ultimately sign an agreement with Molson's for a few million dollars, but it was nowhere near what we could have secured had we done a Tier 1 sponsorship deal with Molson early on. Molson's still ended up being great partners.

In the end, the IOC saw the situation for what it was and realized we had been hurt badly by the deal it signed with Budweiser and that we probably ended up losing tens of millions as a result. It was not one of the IOC's better deals, for sure.

Domestic television broadcast rights to our Games were also the IOC's baby, but we were obviously intensely interested in the outcome. We believed that the more eagerness and passion we stirred up around our project, the more the networks in Canada would want to be involved. This would attract more lucrative bids, which would mean more revenue for us—in theory anyway.

Negotiations had become complicated by the fact that we had signed the massive deal with Bell Canada. Bell was a corporate partner of CTV and desperately wanted the network to win the rights—it would make the telecommunication giant's life simpler on so many levels.

Bell CEO Michael Sabia phoned me up one day to ask if there was anything I could do to help CTV. I told him the best I could do was meet with the network's CEO, Ivan Fecan, and talk to him about what we were trying to achieve and how they might best fashion the company's presentation to the IOC. In fact, I met with representatives from CTV and CBC to talk about our goals and dreams. The reception I received from the two networks couldn't have been more different.

The CBC didn't seem at all interested in what we were trying to achieve. Its president presented CBC as a company that had done this many times, knew the drill, and frankly, thought Canadians *expected* them to cover these Games. The company was happy to talk partnerships but left little doubt about who would be calling the shots. Its executives didn't seem to be moved by the fact that we were looking for a more collaborative approach. We wanted to work with a company that shared our values and was interested in helping us make our vision a reality. We also wanted to introduce every athlete on the Olympic team to every person in the country.

CTV, in contrast, was widely enthusiastic about what we were trying to accomplish and completely open-minded. We quickly concluded that CTV would be the best broadcast partner for us, whatever the financial commitment it was prepared to make. The network would assure the Games received the saturation we had hoped for and saw the business advantage that went along with it. Still, we were extremely worried that the IOC might still favour the CBC, even if the bids were a distance apart in value. The IOC knew the CBC and felt comfortable doing business with the highly regarded, award-winning broadcaster.

As the two companies gathered in Lausanne to pitch the IOC, I received an eleventh-hour call from Michael Sabia, who was sweating buckets and was especially worried about mobile-rights issues if CTV lost. He asked me to help. So I called Ivan Fecan, who was in Lausanne getting ready to give his final pitch. He too was biting his nails. Michael had asked me to give Ivan some frank advice about the company's presentation the next morning. I told him it needed to be like the one we presented the IOC in Prague, as much about heart and soul as business. It needed to be respectful of the IOC and embrace the broad spirit of the Games. It had to be filled with emotion and energy, had to make people believe they desperately wanted the opportunity to make these Games special. Mostly, it needed to stress partnership. It was important that the company impress upon the IOC that it shared our values and ideals.

As it turned out, Ivan and his group completely nailed it. I think it would have made a difference had the gap between CTV's and the CBC's financial offers been close. But it wasn't. The CBC was outplayed by the new kids on the block, ones who radically altered their approach so that no Canadian would miss a minute of the action. It was good for us and good for business.

CTV bid $151 million for Olympic rights from 2008 through to 2012. Of that, $90 million was for the rights to 2010. It was the first time ever that a Winter Games bid had topped a Summer Games bid. The entire package was a record for Canada. It seemed as if almost every day of the Games the network set new records for viewership.

We at VANOC were operating all along under the mistaken belief that a bigger television deal in Canada would mean more money for us. Otherwise, why would we be working so hard to drum up such intense interest in the bids, to create a competitive dynamic in order to drive up the price, if there was nothing in it for us? In fact, when you added CTV's offer to what the IOC got from

NBC and others around the globe it added up to almost $4 billion, a new record. In our original bid, we expected the IOC to contribute roughly US$348 million toward our Games, money that mostly came from television revenues. Our number was based on what the IOC had shared with previous Winter Games. But now, the IOC had decided to put us and London on fixed amounts based on what it gave to Turin 2006 and Beijing 2008, plus inflation. We didn't think this was fair and bluntly told the IOC so.

We weren't able to convince the Olympic committee to give us a greater percentage of television revenues. It didn't want to set a precedent, which would mean London would be asking for the same thing a few years down the road. But the IOC did give us more money overall than it originally said it would and continued to help us when we were in very stormy seas.

ONE THING THE sponsorship phase made clear was just how important our vision of uniting the country was in enticing national companies to join us in our mission. I sat in on dozens and dozens of meetings with CEOs who spoke passionately about wanting to be part of this great Canadian story. If the 2010 Olympics had been marketed as Vancouver's or B.C.'s Games, we wouldn't have received nearly the same level of interest from corporations across the country. In fact, I believe the Games would have been a financial disaster. A lesser vision and many of our friends would likely have sat out the experience.

I think the radical approach we took will be one of the legacies from our Games—how it changed big-event marketing to some extent. We were able to prove to the country that marketing doesn't have to be just about selling the rights to use a logo, but rather selling the rights to have a complete engagement, a complete affiliation. Ultimately, the companies that signed on helped us stage the Olympic Games. Yes, they put our logo on their products, but their men and women were involved in every way with the staging of the Games. They were in the trenches with us and worked hard for our success. Many loaned employees to VANOC for a period of time. They were our everyday ambassadors and were everywhere—just as we had hoped.

Our licensed products, in the meantime, also became runaway favourites. Our executive was stunned by the ever-growing numbers we were getting from sales, whether it was replicas of our mascots, pens, watches, water bottles or the famous Red Mittens.

We unveiled our logo first. We called it Ilanaaq, the Inuit word for friend or buddy. The logo was based on the Inukshuk, the stone landmark figure the Inuit people have relied on for centuries as a signal. It was chosen by a panel of nine judges and picked from more than 1,600 entries. I was thrilled with it. I thought it represented the entire country, but particularly the North, and it was rooted in a profound and caring spirit. It was a stone beacon that visitors looking for the Games could rely on to guide them. A new Canadian icon, and it was ours.

We were going to be making the announcement on a Saturday, live, on national television and in all time zones. I was watching Global BC news on the Friday night before the announcement when they led with an item about our new symbol. Apparently, someone told a reporter there he had seen it and described it for him. This was the foundation for a story filed by Ted Chernecki that mocked the design, which someone had sketched out on a piece of paper. The story just completely trashed what we had come up with, even though no one at the station had actually seen it.

I was furious, as mad as I think I had ever been during my entire association with the Olympics. I phoned up the station right after taking a run at Dennis Skulsky, Global's top executive on the west coast at the time. Dennis shared the view that Global had misbehaved badly and apologized unconditionally. When I got the news director, Ian Haysom, on the phone, I let him have it. I told him I was so angry watching the item I wanted to throw my cellphone against the wall. Not only did the story ridicule the design, but it also got the name of the winning designer wrong and ruined the real winner's moment in the spotlight. My voice grew so loud and animated that my wife took Molly outside the house so she didn't have to listen to my rant. If Ian got a word in I did not hear it. That was one of the few times I really lost my cool with the media.

But while the logo was criticized initially, mostly by those expecting to see the Maple Leaf, those opinions quickly faded into the background as its popularity gained momentum across the country. Pretty soon there were school groups from Parker's Cove, Newfoundland, to Port Coquitlam, B.C., building or designing Inukshuks in the classroom. You could drive down the Sea to Sky Highway or country roads in Quebec and Ontario and come across a stone replica of our logo.

When it came time to unveil our mascots, we hired a local entertainment company, led by Patrick Roberge, to design a show that would be staged in a Surrey school theatre. We brought in a bunch of kids to welcome Sumi, Quatchi and Miga to our Olympic family. Mukmuk, a Vancouver Island marmot, was introduced as a sidekick. The media were placed strategically in the audience of children so they could see their smiles up close. It would be hard to be critical amid the hysteria generated by happy, screaming kids. As hoped, Quatchi and company didn't attract the kind of criticism some Olympic mascots initially invite—to my great relief. (Unlike the poor folks in London, whose one-eyed mascots, Wenlock and Mandeville, were trashed by everyone but children.)

Quatchi was a sasquatch with boots and earmuffs who had the commanding presence of a hockey goalie. Miga was a mythical sea bear. Sumi, part whale, part bird and part bear, was the official mascot of the Paralympics. We originally thought we'd need a few sets of the mascots to make appearances around the country. The demand for them ended up being so great we had to increase the number tenfold.

Like everything that was important at VANOC, the mascots had a champion, a mastermind lurking in the background. His name was Leo Obstbaum.

Before Leo arrived on the scene at VANOC, there had been months of loud banter inside the organization about the "look" that we wanted to create, a look that would be evident in everything from backdrops to torches, a trail-blazing design that would separate us from all the other Olympics before us.

In a perfect world, we would have had our own design team working inside the walls of VANOC to have greater control over what was produced—provided, of course, we had the horsepower and creative proficiency to deliver the kind of results that were needed. Ali Gardiner was heading up our young, fairly inexperienced brand and creative team. Well aware of our vulnerabilities, she was hunting for senior talent to help get us to the next level. That is when she came across Leo.

Leo was from Buenos Aires and had done some creative work on the Summer Games in Barcelona in 1992. He had quite a bit of experience in designing mascots, specifically. Ali was convinced this was the guy we needed to inspire and build our design team, but English wasn't his first language, and he also lacked experience working in Canada. An interview was set up with Dave Cobb and me.

Leo was a charming guy, mid-thirties, thin, with a goatee. At first glance, he could easily have passed for a Spanish painter or a matador. I could tell he was nervous but I could also tell he wanted this job desperately, even though his résumé didn't stop us in our tracks. But over the years, I have found myself in rooms with a lot of guys just like him. When I worked at the Arbutus Club, this 26-year-old Belgian kid, Patrick Marchal, walked in wanting the chef's job we were advertising. His résumé was thin, but his heart was the size of a mountain.

"Give me the job for six months," he said to me. "You don't even have to pay me. And if at any point I'm not working out you can kick me out the door."

Well, he knew I was going to pay him. But I gave him a chance and he worked out brilliantly. He now owns his own winery in France.

There was a bit of that guy in Leo. He was just looking for a chance. We gave it to him, and he turned out to be a stunner who managed to steal the hearts of just about everyone whose path he crossed. He really was a complete genius who saw beauty in the most nondescript things. Everything he touched seemed to win rave reviews. The IOC had to sign off on every design we came up with, whether it was the mascots or the medals. And every time Leo put something in front of them, the box was ticked minutes later.

When it came time to design the medals, Leo and Ali spent months consulting with athletes and others. He researched medals through the ages. He came up with the idea of making each medal unique, something that had never been done before. "Imagine," he said one day. "Imagine an athlete showing his medal to a bunch of kids and telling them there isn't another one like it anywhere in the world."

Leo had a bit of child in him, that innocent spirit of wonder. He revelled in the happiness of others. At staff gatherings when we honoured the performance of a teammate, you would always spot Leo standing on the side wearing a huge grin. In meetings, if he was showing us something and it wasn't working or he wasn't getting the feedback he was looking for, he'd stop and say, "Okay, we're not ready. This is not good enough. I'll come back." And he would, with something better. But when he felt he was dead right he would pull out all the stops to get you to his point of view.

Then one August morning, Ali asked to see me and Dave Cobb. She started to talk but couldn't get the words out before breaking down. Leo had passed away the night before in his sleep. It was his heart. The irony was lost on few of us. The guy had one of the biggest ones around.

At his memorial service in the packed atrium of our company headquarters a few days later, I asked those assembled to cast their eyes around the very place we were standing and see how much Leo had touched. The look of the Games was everywhere. He was buried on a lovely warm Vancouver day, and as we stood around his grave taking turns tipping soil on top of his coffin a rapid transit train with one of Leo's Olympic designs on the side whizzed by. We all smiled.

THANKS TO OUR merchandising and sponsorship deals, by the fall of 2008, the financial health of our organization was fairly strong. Our construction woes were behind us. We were optimistic about the revenue we would get from ticketing. Every week or two we seemed to be announcing another deal, tacking a new name up on our wall. One week it was beds, another hand sanitizers or chewing gum. Companies everywhere wanted in. The project was humming along, mostly controversy free. Media camping out on our lawn to catch us mucking up were getting frustrated.

Then, on September 15, 2008, New York–based investment house Lehman Brothers filed for bankruptcy. Over the next few days, coverage of the collapse was like watching the outbreak of a war. It was wall-to-wall mayhem. People were scared. The headlines in the newspapers were gigantic. The evening news was inevitably filled with images of stock traders burying their faces in their hands. No one was sure where this was all heading, but it didn't look good.

At first it was unclear how Canada might be affected. But it wasn't long before the downfall of Lehman's triggered big problems at other institutions. It became evident that other U.S. investment houses were in trouble, and banks too, mostly because of subprime mortgages. Foreclosure signs began popping up from Pensacola, Florida, to Salinas, California. The daily reports of the widespread damage to the U.S. economy became numbing after a while.

While the carnage certainly caught the attention of those of us at VANOC, there was little evidence that the problems down south were seeping into our backyard. Payments from our corporate partners were being made on time. No one was calling to renegotiate the terms of their agreement with us. No one was even phoning to sound the alarm, put us on notice. The levee was holding. A false confidence set in that the financial panic in the U.S. might miss Canada entirely. But there was a growing unease in our boardroom.

The directors began growing worried about the health of Olympic partners such as General Motors. The American automobile industry was on life support, or so it seemed. The CEOs were being summoned to Washington to meet with President Barack Obama to figure out a survival plan.

It was ugly.

Jack Poole was sweating too and wanted me to get a more ironclad assurance from General Motors that it wouldn't renege on our deal. I honestly didn't know what more GM could do or say that would make our deal with them any safer. I thought it would be almost insulting to ask, that we were best served by standing by the shoulder of a good partner, while others were trashing them. I remember heading east to see Arturo Elias, their president and CEO of Canadian operations, and asking if there was anything we could do to help. I suggested at one point that the company use the Games to show off their next generation of vehicles and that we were ready to do pretty much anything we could to give GM a hand—for free. He appreciated our loyalty and support and assured me everything would be fine, that we needn't worry. And GM was true to its word, despite the fact the company was fighting for its life.

The growing worldwide gloom began to cast a shadow over our programs, and the optimism that had filled the organization for years disappeared. Companies and governments everywhere were now being affected. This, in turn, meant that some of our own directors were fighting fires of their own.

Prompted by instinct and a growing nervousness in the boardroom, we decided to behave as if this tornado was going to hit us soon. It was time to prepare for something quite dire: the failure of one of our major partners. Chasing replacement revenue 18 months before the start of the Games would be like chasing needles in a haystack. What-if scenarios were being sketched out almost daily in our executive meetings. To prepare for what was to come, I tagged on the title of Deputy CEO to Dave Cobb and asked him to lead an aggressive internal review of just about everything, a task he would take on with ferocity, supported by his executive colleagues. This move was a sign to all that it was time to hunker down.

We decided to take the organization and essentially turn it upside down and shake it in the hopes enough dimes and nickels would fall out to make a difference. Everything that wasn't absolutely essential to our survival would be cast off. This may sound simple. In truth, it was a migraine of a process that included hundreds of painful choices. Rather than cut people we froze hiring. Huge savings were realized when we stalled new hires for even a month. We did that as often as we felt we could sustain the punishment that followed: fewer people meant that those already working had longer days, but it was better than a pink slip.

Over the years, we had built our budgets fairly logically. Reasoned estimates of cost and revenues were refined as data hardened. So budgets were always moving to some extent but generally in the direction of more certainty, not less. But not in times like this. Every meeting we had, every discussion, was about money. Those with room in their budgets had to surrender their surplus, every penny of it. Contingency funds were disappearing faster than beer in an Irish pub. We went after new revenue sources—although there were precious few—and trimmed big-ticket programs to the bone. We advised our government partners that we might need their help if we were going to survive this and still put on a spectacular Games.

We appealed to our staff for creative ideas to get around our funding dilemma. We were not going to run a deficit under any circumstances. A culture of survival took hold. We reduced all travel and hunkered down, hoping the economic storm would blow over soon. I decided not to attend a SportAccord conference in Denver, where I was supposed to give a progress report to the IOC. The IOC was not impressed and told me so. I didn't care. I had to lead by example.

Scheduled pay increases for members of the executive were cancelled voluntarily, other contracts curtailed or shortened. We looked at our ticketing program, and if there was any way to jam another seat into a venue we did it. That's how desperate we were to find an extra $20 of revenue. We set aggressive new revenue targets for licensed products and found new suppliers to help us reach them. If you could put an Olympic logo on something and sell it, we did. We even looked at how we could make money when it was time to wrap up everything after the Games were over. We had to get top dollar for every item we had acquired.

Against all odds, but in line with our most daring predictions, there was one major win coming for us—ticket sales. Tickets were put on sale to staggering global and national demand, and it became clear that we were heading for a virtual sellout. Caley Denton, our vice-president of ticketing, whom Dave Cobb had lured away from the Vancouver Canucks organization, had judged the market perfectly. He did two things that were exceptionally smart: he decided to release the tickets in three stages and he created the fan-to-fan marketplace. In the first stage, he only put a limited number of tickets on the market, which were gobbled up quickly, creating a demand frenzy. This led to an even greater appetite for tickets during the second and third releases.

The fan-to-fan program worked brilliantly. Even an attempted ticket fraud scheme conjured up by Latvian hucksters did not diminish the value of this program. Let's say you had a ticket to the men's quarter-final hockey tournament, in which you were hoping to see Canada play Norway. If Canada didn't make the play-offs and instead it was Switzerland playing Norway, suddenly you were unlikely to want that ticket as badly. So Caley created a system where you could throw your ticket back in the mix so someone else, maybe a Swiss fan, could get access to it. We collected a small fee as part of the transaction, which helped us derive more revenue. Everyone won.

The success of the Olympic Red Mittens campaign helped take some pressure off us as well and allowed us to meet our obligations to the Own the Podium program. What was originally intended to be a simple fundraiser for our athletes became a phenomenon. The mitts became the number one stocking stuffer in the country. The factory where they were being produced couldn't keep up with the demand, even though it was going 24/7 for months on end. The mitts even made an appearance on *Oprah*, where the queen of American daytime television gave a pair to each member of her studio audience. We ended up selling more than 3.6 million pairs. Even I couldn't get my hands on them for friends. We needed every cent from them.

Then, as the Games edged ever closer and the market conditions began to gradually improve, we realized that with a bit more belt tightening we just might survive this financial windstorm in one piece. Both levels of government helped us recoup some of the losses we incurred as a result of what was being called the Great Recession. We also went to the IOC and asked them for one final gesture of support—never an easy thing to do.

While the IOC was sympathetic, it was also a little wary. It had been burned before. The organizers of the Games in Salt Lake City pleaded poverty and got a last-minute infusion of cash from the IOC. Months later, the organizing committee declared a $100-million profit, to the complete fury of the IOC. But our relationship with the IOC was strong. They saw the pain we were in and the measures we had taken to deal with this crisis on our own. The IOC is criticized often for not being caring enough, but that was not the case here. In the end, the Olympic committee protected us to the tune of over $50 million beyond what it had originally committed to. Through this time, the IOC had suffered too. Its own revenues and investments were down and the organization had some belt tightening of its own to do.

This was an exhausting period involving endless strategizing. Dave Cobb and I wrote dozens of letters and proposals to the IOC, making all sorts of pleas for help. I used to joke to Dave that if we didn't get help we might have to record "Danny Boy" in 50 languages and use it as the official music for the opening ceremonies. But in the end we survived one of the worst economic maelstroms anyone could remember.

We proved that we were more than a worthy adversary for bad times. Yes, we were helped by the amazing team of accountants we had at VANOC, who were pretty good scroungers. But I think it was street smarts over spreadsheets that won the day, as we got all of our thousand-plus staff goring away at budgets the way you would in your own home during tough times. I was in awe of the performances of individual members of our team, especially the leadership shown by a battle-weary executive.

While this period was easily the darkest, it ended up making us stronger, really giving us our wings. With the weeks clicking down rapidly toward February 12, 2010, we were more fearless and more together—our training was done. But battling through the first few months of the recession took a toll, no question. I also had to get some benign lesions removed from my face that left me looking like I had gone 15 rounds with Muhammad Ali. The entire team, including me, was falling-down tired. Everyone needed a break.

I had scheduled a week off in late December of 2008, mostly to sleep. It was the first week I'd had off in a very long time, and I was really looking forward to it. My calendar was completely clear of appointments. They would be my first Olympics-free days in years. The next morning, I couldn't get out of bed. I was sicker than I could ever remember being. My system seemed to completely crash. Maybe the adrenalin drop brought it on, I don't know. I would end up spending my week in bed with severe flu symptoms, but weird as it sounds I was happy to be there. I managed to get some work done that I wasn't planning to do otherwise. So at least I didn't have that waiting for me when I returned to the office.

But there were some awkward stories circulating about my health at the time. I had taped a Christmas message to VANOC staff that was posted on our website. Well, I don't know what happened this time around, whether it was bad lighting or what, but I looked atrocious. I made Casper the Ghost look like George Hamilton. It was as if they had found me living in a cave for 20 years and threw me in front of the camera. If people wondered how much longer I had to live—and one or two asked—I couldn't blame them. Even I was afraid to look at me.

I assured reporters that I was fine, though I had definitely lost some weight and needed to start working out again. I had to take better care of myself and I would. The board also had concerns that I looked weary and expressed to Jack that he might intervene. Jack told them, "I have tried to get his attention. If you think I can convince this guy to slow down you are seriously mistaken. This is who he is."

He was right. I was not about to slow the pace—how could I? The Games were coming like a freight train. I didn't know how to slow down anyway and there wasn't the time. When I went back to work that January I felt just fine. We had a year to go. About 400 sleeps before the flame arrived—the very thought filled me with the energy to push through anything.

7

The **Power** of the Flame

WHILE MANY VIEWED my job as glamorous, the highs were often followed by bouts of soul-searching anguish.

It could be a lonely experience. There was hardly a moment along the way when I was not worrying about something. Some days were pure hell and I'd feel the weight of an entire country on my shoulders. Other days we'd get a big win and I'd feel invincible. It was rollercoaster stuff. I tried to grow a tougher skin but I took most everything personally for years. To sustain my spirit, I stopped reading newspapers, only perusing those articles and columns I was told I had to look at. To avoid plunging into darkness, I often read *It's How You Play the Game*, a behind-the-scenes account of the Calgary Olympics written by its CEO, Frank King. While much about the Olympics had changed since 1988, there was still a lot I could learn from Frank's insights and observations. Like me, he was a real believer in the power of sport.

One of the more memorable sections in the book concerned the torch relay. Calgary launched one of the most ambitious relays in Olympic history to that point—18,000 kilometres over 88 days.

After its arrival in Newfoundland, the torch made an appearance in all 10 provinces and two territories. (Nunavut didn't become a territory until 1999.) Calgary's relay stood in stark contrast to the only other one ever held in Canada—Montreal's in 1976. Back then, the torch travelled from Ottawa to Montreal, a distance of 200 kilometres, believed to be the shortest torch relay in modern Olympic history.

I remember Frank talking in his book about the excitement associated with deciding who would run with the torch. But the best parts focused on the energy that the relay gave the Games themselves. Frank talked about going out on the route, running alongside some of the torchbearers and seeing their passion. He said those sojourns were a nice respite from the negative jaw-wagging that was going on back in Calgary, where the air was often filled with despair over various aspects of Games preparations. On the road, the mood was magical and it lifted him. He returned to Calgary completely charged up.

To me, the relay was the secret to delivering Canada's Games, and while 18,000 kilometres was certainly impressive, I thought we could go farther—much farther. I wanted to reach every Canadian I could. Coca-Cola, RBC and Canada had signed on as full partners, so we had the support we needed to make a seemingly impossible mission possible. But it wasn't until we started mapping the route out in detail that I began realizing what a monster challenge I had set for my team.

The primary group assigned to deal with the relay included Dave Cobb; Andrea Shaw; Jim Richards, who was named torch relay director; and Vidar Eilertsen, head of operations and a genuine road warrior. Vidar was an impressive Norwegian import, a general, who knew more about relays than just about any other person on the planet, having worked on several. He was the guy with the whip and chair who made sure the buses left on time—in his own charming way. There would be many other hands that would help shape the journey, but this was the core group forced to listen to my constant harping and insistence that we perform magic and extend the relay to its far-out, far-off limits.

Over the months the relay took shape, there were plenty of tense meetings. The sparks would often fly over my saying that the plans as they were didn't push the boundaries far enough, didn't get the flame close enough to enough Canadians. In the early going, much of the push-back I received from Andrea, Jim and Vidar involved simple logistics. There was concern the relay would never end if we tried to get the torch into all the communities I wanted it to appear in. It was not lost on me that Canada was not Luxembourg—but this wasn't an adventure for the faint-hearted either. And then there was the inevitable bad weather and other unforeseen problems we had to allow for.

In my heart, I was pretty sure that once on the road it would be a frosty Friday in the Sahara before Vidar would let the relay get as much as 10 seconds off schedule. I thought we should just go flat out and if we had to modify on the fly we'd do it. But let's not model the whole program around having to rest the tour every six days because we might be a little tired or encountering a week's worth of bad weather and planes not able to fly or land when we needed them to. I was having *none* of it. I felt the team could pull it off and told them so a hundred times.

We were going to plan on everything going right. There would be lots of time to sleep after the Games.

I admit I didn't make it easy on this group. I pushed them to the brink. In the years that followed getting the bid, I was speaking several times a week across the country, drumming up support for the project. It seemed everywhere I went people wanted to know if there was any chance the torch was going to be making an appearance in their town. I wasn't above getting some cheap and immediate applause, so I said, "Of course it's coming here," wherever "here" happened to be that day. I'd get a standing ovation and lots of pats on the back afterward, and the next day my guarantee would appear in the local press. The members of my torch-relay-planning team would shake their heads and curse me and wonder where I'd be asking them to go next.

Our vision for the relay forced us to be creative. We would have to be in more than one place at the same time, which meant having teams that would splinter off from the main relay to get into other smaller nearby communities. This was trickier than it sounds. There are strict rules governing the activities of the torch and one states that it can never be burning in two places at the same time. You could take a lantern that contained the Olympic flame to a remote community; you just couldn't light a torch there until it had been extinguished in another. But we managed around this dilemma, and there would be several days during the relay in which the Olympic flame seemed to appear in two different places at the same time. It was carefully orchestrated but ultimately vital to our mission to get the torch or flame within an hour's drive of almost 95 per cent of the Canadian population.

The route would undergo many redesigns before we finally settled on one that would be 45,000 kilometres—the longest in Olympic history—and last every second of 106 days. But the truth is, having the longest route was never what got the team excited— rather it was the idea of bringing the torch close to so many people.

AFTER LOOKING AT what seemed like a thousand scenarios, we decided to kick off the relay in Victoria. There were a couple of reasons we went this way: first, starting off in the B.C. capital offered us a better chance of getting more runners involved in the relay. That was a primary objective: get the torch in the hands of as many Canadians as possible. More than 12,000 people would have a chance to walk, run and even paddle with it, which was an astounding number when compared with the 6,000 or so who ran with it in Calgary—a Herculean feat itself at the time.

But there was another reason we liked Victoria as a jumping-off point: the relay would start in the province where the Games were being held. This, we felt, might help address the unease in some quarters about our sharing the Games so enthusiastically with the rest of the country. It also harkened back to the origins of the relay itself, when runners were dispatched from Olympia to inform people in outlying areas about the sporting festival the Greek city was hosting in honour of Zeus. So in a sense, we were now doing the same thing: setting runners off from Victoria to invite the rest of the country to the 2010 Games.

Another part of our planning involved travel to Greece, where we would need to be present for the official lighting of the flame in Olympia and again a week later in Athens, where the flame would be handed over to us for transport back to Canada. So much of the Olympics are laden with protocol but none more so than the handover of the flame in Athens, a ceremony that has evolved over centuries. A large group of us would need to—and want to be—in Greece for both ceremonies, which posed transportation issues. How would we get there and back and stay true to the exceedingly tight deadlines we would be operating under to get the torch everywhere we promised in the time we had? Flying commercial to Athens was going to be extremely difficult and costly, so I offered to find us alternative transportation.

Early on in the Games planning, I had a meeting with representatives of the Canadian Armed Forces, including chief of the defence staff Gen. Walter Natynczyk. It was a great chat, and from the outset he made clear just how important it was for the military to have a presence in Vancouver in 2010. I think he understood what an opportunity it presented the military to be part of something so big that meant so much to the country. He could imagine his men and women in uniform taking part in the many flag-raising ceremonies, protocol and other events. They would have a front-row seat to the festivities. What an opening to promote the brand. He wanted in, and we were happy to have them.

Within days the forces assigned a senior officer to us, Capt. Matt Barlee. He sat outside my door, immersed himself in the VANOC culture, and had access to military personnel across the country.

He would be our liaison to the army from here on in. I wanted the military involved because if we needed special jobs taken care of, I figured we could count on them because the word *fail* is not in their DNA. Over the next couple of years after that initial meeting, I would be a little disappointed when the armed forces said it couldn't provide this or that service to the Games. They were extended pretty thin given their commitments around the country and abroad, so were unable to commit to anything big in the run-up to the Games. So I thought that maybe we could get a plane from them to take to Athens.

There were a number of reasons I liked the idea. First, it would help us get around some of the logistical challenges that flying a big team to Greece via a commercial airline was going to pose. I also thought that getting the military involved would elevate the importance of the relay in people's minds. I liked the image of the military escorting this ancient flame from Greece to Canada. It would turn a trip into a mission. Just thinking of that plane lifting off to secure the flame gave me goose bumps. I knew the men and women in uniform would take this duty seriously and that the travel time would be organized to the minute if the military was flying the plane.

It didn't exactly unfold that way...

The Greece segment of the relay was another one of those high-profile situations where big-name politicians expected to play a role. I thought it best if we spread them out and gave each a lead role at one of the events. They agreed. In the end, we decided that Premier Gordon Campbell would be on hand in Olympia for the lighting ceremony and that Vancouver Mayor Gregor Robertson would be in Athens for the handover a week later. The prime minister, in the meantime, would be on the tarmac in Victoria for the arrival. Initially, everyone seemed good with this arrangement, but one day I got a call from the mayor, who was freaking out about not being part of the ceremony in Olympia. He told me that Greek friends had informed him that part of the ceremony in Olympia involved the passing of something or other from a representative from Olympia to the mayor of the host city. All news to me. Gregor said it was now vital he be there. He insisted on it. I was taken aback, as this change would mean more surgery to the protocol plan. "Gregor," I said, "I think I would know if that was supposed to happen." He persisted and I gave in. (The information Gregor received never was validated in Olympia.)

By this point, our staff handling this portion of the trip had already informed Victoria that Premier Campbell was going to be on first in Olympia, our delegation leader. I had told him that myself. Now we had to phone back and say, ah, well, he's now going to have to share the stage with the Vancouver mayor. It made us look like amateurs who didn't know what we were doing, but it was par for the course when dealing with political delegates.

There would be more arguments about who should carry the flame off the plane in Victoria. Should it be federal Minister of Sport Gary Lunn, a real team player who deserved a role? Should it be Gregor? Maybe an Aboriginal chief? Many people wanted me to do it. I honestly didn't care; I just wanted peace. Ultimately, Gregor carried it off, but there had been far too much politicking behind the scenes for us to feel good about the outcome.

Political aides were always arguing about who would speak first and who would speak second at various events. It was exhausting dealing with this stuff and my least favourite aspect of the Games, in many ways. We had to have a full-time person—make that a team—looking after protocol, just to manage those in public office who craved the limelight.

On that front, I should say that throughout the entire Olympics, including the lead-up to the Games, Gordon Campbell never insisted on centre stage. While he would face cheap shots and criticism for his boisterous, some would say over-the-top, displays of Olympic fervour during the Games, Gordon never once asked to be accorded any special favours as the lead politician in the host province. He had put more on the line, politically at least, than any other elected official connected to the Games and yet asked nothing in return, except that we deliver a wonderful experience for the country. He went way up in my estimation.

IN THE MONTHS leading up to our trip to Greece, I endured one of the toughest periods of my professional career—probably my life. Jack Poole, the guy who had mentored me and had become my number one confidante throughout the organization of the Games, was dying of cancer.

Jack had been diagnosed with pancreatic cancer a couple of years earlier. I remember him telling me when he got the news. I would forever be struck by how poised he was in describing how he discovered he had the disease. He had been at a dinner with Darlene and gone to the bathroom not feeling particularly well. When he looked in the mirror he noticed he looked jaundiced. Several trips to the doctor, lots of tests and the eventual diagnosis followed.

Pancreatic cancer is one of the deadliest forms of the disease. A person's chances of surviving it are less than 5 per cent. But for Jack, 5 per cent was like 50 per cent: enough to work with. If it took sheer guts and determination to be among the lucky survivors, then Jack was there. But it wouldn't be easy. Treatment would involve complex surgeries and a stay in a Seattle hospital that used a particularly harsh treatment protocol to enhance the chances of survival. It involved radiation every day for 40 days and chemo three times a week on top of that. Jack would have climbed Kilimanjaro three times a day to get better, such was his raw inner spirit.

The day Jack described to me what the treatment would entail, he could have been describing changing the oil in his car. The guy was tough as nails. I will always remember seeing him in Seattle after a particularly punishing day of treatment, on his knees, throwing up. Even after that, Jack could manage a smile and make some wiseacre remark about how much fun he was having. As sick as he was, he wanted to hear all about what was going on back at the office. Funny how those visits to make him feel better ended up making *me* feel better.

Eventually, Jack would be released from hospital and resume his duties with the board. But there was always the chance the disease would return, and sure enough it did in the summer of 2009. Jack was stoic as usual when he told me, but this time I sensed something different in his voice. There would be no second round of treatment such as he had undergone in Seattle. Enough already.

For those close to him, it was a question of how much longer he had. Darlene was by his side 24 hours a day, praying for a miracle. He lamented time and again to her how much he regretted not being able to pitch in more when I needed him most. I took the changing news hard, knowing I would soon be losing my best friend. Quietly I prayed he would hang on until the Games, imagining the two of us together in the front row.

As the weeks passed, Jack spent more and more time at home, in bed or on the couch. The phone was his lifeline. He wasn't going to be returning to work as chair of VANOC, though I used to say underestimating him was a mistake. Count him out and he'd walk through the door. I would visit him to update him on where things stood with various aspects of the project. He was always ready with advice, but it was terrible to see such a vibrant, strong man so weak. There were a few moments in every day, especially when I was on an airplane or sitting in an airport terminal, when I thought about Jack and our friendship and the crazy journey we had embarked on together eight years earlier. I would call him often and without reason just to laugh and chat.

We certainly had our disagreements over the years. More than once I hissed at Jack for saying things to the press that I knew would not translate well in the hyper-sensitive world of the IOC. He would enjoy the ribbing and do it again. Almost every time we disagreed on an issue, he would tell me he thought I was wrong but he'd let me make the call, saying: "Look, it's your show. You do what you think is right." Coming from a corporate titan like Jack, that meant a lot. Win, lose or draw, he always had my back. When the going got rough he'd make me think twice before pulling the lever on a major decision. I was determined never to make him look foolish for sticking by me the entire way. Often when I thought of Jack I was reminded of a line my father sometimes trotted out: "If I was twice the man I am, I'd still only be half the man he is."

Jack had a wicked sense of humour and little tolerance for people feeling sorry for themselves. I remember once when he was convalescing from a round of cancer treatments and I visited him at home to talk about a tough issue. He had a card for me sitting in an envelope beside a glass of fresh orange juice. Inside it said something like "It is always darkest just before it goes black." In other words, bad as you think it is, it will surely get worse. That was Jack.

A few days before we were leaving for Greece for the lighting of the torch in Olympia, I went to the hospital. He didn't look good when I entered his room but he still managed a smile. He had lost so much weight and had a few more tubes attached than the last time I visited. I filled him in on what was going to be happening at the ceremony and some of the logistics involved. I told him that I would be back in a few days and planned to show him pictures and video from the ceremony. I told him that day that no matter what happened, we would deliver a great Games, make him proud and keep every promise we made. I gave him a hug, knowing I might not see him again.

On my way to Olympia I stopped in New York to attend the UN's adoption of the Olympic Truce, which calls on all nations in conflict to embrace peace and to cease fighting for the period of the Games. In ancient times, this was done to allow athletes to get to the Games safely. Today, while some see this initiative with cynicism, it is a reminder of the power and example of sport to foster harmony and peace.

Canada, along with the IOC and VANOC, had prepared the draft resolution, and I was the proudest Canadian alive when our ambassador to the UN deferred the floor to me to read the resolution into the record, from the same podium that numerous world leaders had spoken from—and then to see it approved unanimously. That night I spoke with Ban Ki-moon, the secretary general of the UN, who insisted that our work was more important than ever. Good enough for me.

A COUPLE OF DAYS later, a group of us landed in Athens and made our way to ancient Olympia and the Temple of Hera for the official flame lighting, a four-hour ride late at night. It was an incredible setting, seemingly unchanged in centuries, a hallowed ground with a beautiful grassy seating area from which to watch the proceedings.

The ceremony was simple and yet rich—a re-enactment of a centuries-old tradition full of moving protocol and symbolism. It was the job of actress Maria Nafpliotou, playing the part of a high priestess and dressed in a long, flowing gown, to ignite the flame from sun rays captured in a parabolic bowl. It was somewhat overcast, and there were concerns there wouldn't be enough sun to light the flame. But some timely prayers to Apollo, the Greek god of the sun, and sure enough the clouds parted, the sun arrived and the flame was lit. We were standing in a roofless temple watching a miracle—the gods had somehow blessed us and sent us on our way to do a great good. I was pinching myself with excitement.

Soon Vassilis Dimitriadis, officially the first torchbearer of the 2010 Games, lit his torch from the original flame and set off to begin what would be an eight-day relay through the mountains of Greece. Seeing him run out of the ancient stadium into a field and over the surrounding hills before going out of sight gave me shivers.

The exchange brought my torch relay director, Jim Richards, to tears. I had to work hard not to shed a few myself, the moment was so powerful. I pulled out my BlackBerry and found a quiet corner of the grove to phone Jack and tell him what had just happened. It was 2 AM back in Vancouver, so I had to leave a message but it was a long one. I gave Jack an almost minute-by-minute account of the ceremony. I really wanted to bring him there and put a smile on his face if I could. I told him again I would see him in a couple of days.

Gordon Campbell and I rode in a van together back to Athens. A rumour surfaced en route that Jack had passed away. I received a query from someone in the media. I choked but told the caller it could not be true or I would have heard about it immediately. A bit shook up, I called Deborah Prior, Jack's long-time and much adoring executive assistant, who was walking into the hospital at the time. She put Jack on. I could barely make him out. It was good to hear his voice nonetheless. He said little but that he looked forward to seeing me upon my return. We were all elated just knowing he was still with us.

The premier and I flew home the next morning through Amsterdam, where we had a stopover of six hours. We decided to grab a hotel room to do some work while we waited for our flight. Gordon went down to the business centre at the hotel, and I was getting ready to exercise when my phone rang. It was Deborah Prior. Jack was gone.

I sat on the bed for a few minutes trying to digest what I'd just heard. Even though I had known this day was coming, I was still heartbroken and trembling. I couldn't help thinking that Jack had hung on long enough to know that the torch had been lit and was on its way to Vancouver. It was okay for him to go now so he did. For Jack, the 2010 Games had started. His mission accomplished. His service fully rendered.

I had to make arrangements to get a VANOC press statement sent out, as the news wouldn't remain a secret for long. I got Renee Smith-Valade, our vice-president of communications, on the phone along with a couple of others, and an hour later we issued our statement. The premier wrote his own. It would be a heavy, tearful day.

Gordon and I spent the plane ride to Vancouver sometimes talking about Jack, sometimes locked in silence. His experiences with the man were different from mine, but they went back decades. When we landed 10 hours later, there was a mob of media at the airport. The premier and I sat down to address them. I told the reporters, as did the premier, that the province had lost a giant and so had our Olympic team. I think those members of the media who dealt with me a lot could tell how rattled and shaken I was.

Jack's funeral was held on Tuesday, October 27, 2009, and it was as close to a state funeral that a layperson gets in this country. Hundreds squeezed into Vancouver's Christ Church Cathedral to say their goodbyes. He was described as a gentle, loyal friend who never turned his back on his small-town Saskatchewan roots. At Jack's request, Dale Evans's "Happy Trails" was sung at the funeral. That was just like Jack, poking fun at the situation.

Jack was remembered fondly as "the father of the Games" by Premier Campbell. Friend and businessman Peter Brown high-lighted Jack's fun-loving and mischievous side. Everyone agreed Jack had a way of lifting one's burdens. I talked about how "he had taught us things not known to kings" and how Jack had convinced me to join him on this Olympic odyssey, saying that if I didn't do it he wouldn't either. "Like a three-year-old schoolboy I believed him," I told the congregation. "That was the first of a thousand times I was to be Jack Pooled."

WHEN JACK WAS a young man making his way in the business world, he would buy himself a new shirt whenever he had accomplished something worth celebrating. His first boss had failed to reward his performance, something that always bothered Jack. He figured if he didn't give himself a pat on the back once in a while, no one would.

Long after he had made millions and lost millions and made millions again in the development game, Jack would have one of the most breathtaking collections of fine shirts. After we started working together, Jack started to do the same thing with me—buy me a beautiful, expensive shirt after we accomplished something particularly noteworthy. He would call me on a good day and remark: "Almost a new shirt day, John."

A couple of months after he passed away, I was visiting Darlene at the couple's home in Vancouver. I wanted to see how she was doing. She left the room for a minute and returned with a box with a ribbon on it.

"Read the card first," Darlene said.

It was from Jack.

"Darlene," it read, "whatever happens, make sure you get John a new shirt for Christmas."

It was written just days before Jack passed away. I sat in my car on Point Grey Road after that visit and sobbed.

BUT THERE WASN'T much time to sit and ponder life without my good friend. Two days after Jack's funeral, I was back at the airport boarding that armed forces plane for the flight to Athens to bring the Olympic flame back to Canada. The sense of occasion was almost magnetic. However, what should have been a time of unmitigated joy and excitement felt a little less so. I wouldn't get over Jack's death easily.

The ceremony in Athens was held at the Panathenian Stadium, which was built in 1895 for the first Olympic Games of the modern era, held a year later. Its coliseum-like design would become the model for modern sports stadiums around the world. The ceremony involved more actresses playing the role of high priestesses, carrying out ancient traditions with utmost seriousness. Governor General Michaëlle Jean was there for the handover, as was Greek President Karolos Papoulias. The flame that had travelled from ancient Olympia was eventually used to light a torch held by Spyros Capralos, president of the Hellenic Olympic Committee, who then lit a torch I was holding. I was walking on a cloud, almost oblivious to all that was happening around me.

"Today we accept the Olympic flame with humility and respect," I told the thousands in the stands. It was a beautifully warm evening. Soon my torch was used to light a single miner's lantern. When that was lit I walked off the field with it, holding it high in the air to the delight of those watching. A picture of that moment became my personal favourite of the Games. And that lantern would become my number one memento of the Olympics.

Despite being completely exhausted, I didn't get much sleep on the 10-hour flight to Victoria. I don't think many of the others on the plane did either. Everyone was too excited to doze off, afraid they would miss something. It was all economy seating, save perhaps for the lantern and its siblings, flickering away in a row, strapped in seatbelts with RCMP officers on either side. I opened a few bottles of champagne so everyone could toast the fact that we were bringing the Olympic flame to Canada. At one point, we broke out in a chorus of "O Canada."

We were a little behind schedule because international aviation law said the pilots had to spend 18 hours resting in Greece before they could get behind the controls again. This was after we had developed a problem with the plane on the way over and had to make a pit stop in Prestwick, Scotland. The layover law also now meant a stopover in Iceland on the way back for a crew change.

We were about an hour late landing in Victoria, where Gregor Robertson walked off the plane carrying the flame shortly before 9 AM. The prime minister and premier were waiting on the tarmac to officially welcome the flame to Canadian soil. It was hard not to feel a sense of awe. We had a quick ceremony for the flame in an adjacent hangar, after which I drove into the city with the prime minister, who was just beginning to sense the scale of what we were doing. His presence added greatly to the occasion— validation that these were indeed Canada's Games. A moment in time for us all.

The flame, still in the miner's lantern, would make a grand entrance into Victoria's Inner Harbour about an hour later aboard a First Nations canoe. The First Nations members accompanying it were dressed in traditional costumes and sang and chanted as they paddled. The lantern was then carried to the steps of the legislature, where it was used to light a cauldron, which stubbornly refused to ignite for a couple of minutes that felt like an hour. I whispered to Darlene Poole that Jack was once again having fun at her expense as she tried to light the cauldron. But light it did, and it was quickly used to ignite a torch that was jointly held by Olympic gold medallists Simon Whitfield and Catriona Le May Doan. The pair carried the first torch together before handing it off to Olympic rower and bronze medallist Silken Laumann of Victoria and Quebec-born diver Alexandre Despatie, who won a silver medal in Athens. We were on the road to Vancouver—106 days to go.

Day one of the relay was everything I had imagined and more. The crowds were monstrous, everywhere. Victoria and outlying communities completely embraced the flame's arrival. The only blight on the day was a group of protesters who interrupted the relay's progress in the city the first night. We had to divert the route a little, and a couple of people lost their opportunity to run with the torch. (We would find spots for them a couple of days later.) But the public reaction to the protesters' antics was strongly negative and probably deterred other such groups across Canada from trying the same thing. Canadians were fine with protesters making a point, but they wouldn't tolerate ruining people's fun in the process.

My plan was to monitor the relay's progress and join up with it here and there over the next 105 days. I would often get updates from the road from Jim Richards, and I also got my relay fix by reading media reports from journalists on the road. CTV's Tom Walters did an amazing job, I thought, of capturing the joy and elation that the torch's journey inspired throughout the Far North, from Whitehorse to Iqaluit.

Most people seemed to be surprised at just how welcome these small, mostly Aboriginal communities made the torch relay team feel when it descended on their towns. Not me. I knew that spirit existed when I first visited them years earlier. Everywhere I went, Aboriginal leaders had asked if there was any chance the torch could come to their town, never in a million years imagining it would. A little Aboriginal community called Kugluktuk in Nunavut had even raised $60,000 to build an Inukshuk and move it to Whistler. They gave it to us as a gift and it now stands outside the Whistler information centre.

One of the wonderful by-products of the torch's journey throughout the north was the light it shone on the many problems that continue to exist there. I couldn't help but think how the travails of our Aboriginal friends in the High Arctic cause us southerners no pain, because we don't really know about them. So I thought one of the gifts we would eventually leave behind was the stories of these remote communities, the good and the bad. We also hoped to give the children something to dream about and aspire to.

Old Crow in Yukon may have been the ultimate achievement for the relay. On a per capita basis, I'm not sure any place in the country embraced the torch as strongly. It was incredible, from the moment the relay team's Air North 737 jet descended on the town's short runway. People stood on picnic tables and doghouses in their backyards, with cameras and cellphones to capture the historic moment. It was the first time a jet had ever landed in the town.

I remember reading an account of the day by Gary Mason in the *Globe and Mail.* In it he talked about a young man named Kyikavichik, who took to the stage to give an oral history of the Gwich'in people. Without referring to a single note, he talked about the hardship endured by his ancestors, and how food killed by one was food for everybody. He compared the obstacles and challenges of his forebears—and their sharing nature—with the torch relay, which too was founded on the notion of giving to many. "For that reason, I can't think of a better place for the torch to visit," the young man said.

There had been a strong expectation among some that Aboriginal Canada would reject the Games or use them as a platform to trumpet their causes—an expectation I never quite understood.

We decided early on to embed Aboriginal participation in the relay and treat their communities like any other.

One of my favourite moments happened in Quebec City, where the torch had arrived to a particularly hideous reception by Mother Nature. It was deadly cold and wet, yet thousands lined the route. Plans to carry the torch in a canoe had to be scotched because of the weather. Eventually, the torch ended up in Lévis, on the south shore of the St. Lawrence River opposite Quebec City. We took the 15-minute ferry ride to Lévis, which caused some mayhem as hundreds of passengers scurried to grab a photo of themselves holding the lantern. There was a celebration in Lévis, and everyone spoke French, which made my presence on the stage superfluous, so I wandered out into the crowd for a bit.

I eventually found myself standing beside a dignified-looking Aboriginal man, probably 75 or 80 years old. He was with his wife and several grandchildren and seemed to be mesmerized by what he was watching. Luckily for me he spoke three languages, including English. "What do you think?" I asked him. He told me how he had driven almost 100 kilometres in horrible weather to be there. And without taking his eyes off the cauldron burning onstage, he said, "I never thought I would live to be old enough to see our people involved in something like this."

What a moment that was.

But it wasn't always smooth sailing when it came to the torch's journey in Aboriginal communities. We were warned that our plan to bring the torch onto the Kahnawake reserve outside of Montreal was going to be met with resistance if we insisted on having our RCMP torch security detail there too. RCMP officers ran alongside the torch everywhere it went. The RCMP was our partner and did an outstanding job, but getting the torch onto the reserve was important to me. It was going to be run by Alwyn Morris, the Mohawk and Kahnawake resident who had won gold and bronze medals at the Los Angeles Olympics in 1984 in two-man canoeing.

The Mohawk leaders had told us we would have nothing to worry about if we left the RCMP behind for this part of the journey. They were just not welcome there. We had a dilemma: pass on Kahnawake or go in without the RCMP as the elders insisted. Adam Gray, a young VANOC executive from Australia with lots of Games savvy, was caught in the middle of all this. I said to him over the phone: "Adam, you have to understand one thing: the flame is bigger than everyone, so everyone has to get off their high horse so this can work. And everyone needs to look at this through the lens of the children living on the reserve." The word of the Mohawk leaders was good enough for me.

That's when all hell broke loose.

The RCMP didn't like this idea one bit. They thought any decision to leave them out of this portion of the relay diminished their authority and would damage team morale. Worse, it would be unsafe. Pretty soon a conference call was being arranged with Bud Mercer, head of security for the Olympics, RCMP deputy commissioner Gary Bass, Dave Cobb and a few others on my team. It was mentioned that if we went on the reserve without a police escort, the RCMP couldn't guarantee our safety. But the Natives have already guaranteed our safety, I said. "Guys, think about this. If we go in there and get into trouble and someone gets hurt and they put the flame out, what does that say about them? You don't think they care about the implications for their own reputation? They want this to work too. They have children and dreams and hopes like us."

I told them no one loved the RCMP more than me, but in this case I had to disagree with their opinion. We may not bring everybody on for this portion, but the flame is going on that reserve, I said. Anyone worried about their safety is free to stay back.

And the flame did go on the reserve, where it was a huge success. The Mohawk leaders did everything they said they would, and hundreds of kids got a chance to see the flame as it ran by in Alwyn's hands, a moment they would surely talk about for many years.

The run through Kahnawake was one of several days the relay spent in *la belle province*. Quebec was always a crucial player in our Olympic vision. Without French Canada, we wouldn't realize our dream of truly making these Canada's Games. It just wouldn't do to have everyone on board but not the second-largest province in the country. That is why I set about early to get Premier Jean Charest onside.

I told Charest in a meeting in 2005 that Quebec was the perfect partner for VANOC because of its culture of winter sports excellence. It had produced great Winter Olympic athletes, and it was likely that several Quebecers would win medals in Vancouver. I even suggested that we were exploring the idea of having the torch make an appearance in some of the legislatures in the country—and we thought Quebec's would be a natural. Although he liked the idea, Charest joked about bringing a torch into a place renowned for its passionate rancour. "Someone in here might try to use it to burn the place down," he joked.

There would be many more meetings over the next several months. But Jean, who was a former federal minister of sport, was ultimately an easy sell on the value of having an association with us. In October 2005, Quebec was the first province to sign a cooperative agreement with VANOC that pledged a partnership on everything, including sport, culture, economic development and volunteers. It was the first of similar deals we inked with the other nine provinces and three territories, which provided us with cash and other in-kind contributions. In exchange, they would have their own day at the Games during which the wonders and attributes of the respective province or territory would be promoted.

ON DECEMBER 10, 2009, we took the flame to Parliament Hill. I had been to the House of Commons many times during Question Period and was always struck by how mean-spirited it was. MPS yelled at each other all the time. If anything killed my appetite for a career in politics, that was it. But I thought the torch, if we could get it in there, might change all that, if only for a moment. If nothing else, we could get parliamentarians to stop, stand and let the flame do its thing. For a few seconds at least, the House would not be so divided, and the whole country would see images of what the flame could do in a place where tempers often flared.

Organizing the mission was not easy. One of our problems throughout had been reading Prime Minister Stephen Harper's enthusiasm for the Games. It was frustrating to try and figure him out. I was not sure his advisers had fully embraced the Olympics, and he seemed to be holding back a bit himself. And the opposition Liberals were immediately suspicious, thinking the government was behind the torch visit and that it was designed to make the Conservatives look good. I had to explain to Liberal House Leader Ralph Goodale that we weren't selling out to the Tories or anyone. This was about the country. Once we got House Speaker Peter Milliken to quarterback the torch's appearance on the Hill, suspicions seemed to ease and the stage was set.

Then the question became who would carry the torch. There was talk of asking the prime minister, but it would look too political and he might well have declined. So we chose Barbara Ann Scott, the figure skater from Ottawa who had won a gold medal at the 1948 Winter Games in St. Moritz. I tracked down the woman dubbed "Canada's Sweetheart" at her home in Florida and talked to her husband, ex-NBA player Tom King. When I got her on the phone initially she thought my call was some sort of hoax. Eventually she realized it wasn't and was honoured that we were asking her to do something so historic—it would be the first time an Olympic torch had been in the House of Commons.

That day Peter Milliken held a little reception in his office before the big moment. Soon we were standing outside the doors of the chamber itself. I held the lantern that we used to light Barbara Ann's torch, and the next thing we knew the doors to the House were being opened for her entrance. "This is going to be the most amazing thing you've ever done," I whispered to her before she walked in. "Enjoy it."

She was a bundle of nerves.

Her appearance was truly one of the highlights of the run-up to the Games. Members of both sides of the House were on their feet, clapping vigorously. Peter Milliken read into the record what had happened, one of the rare times that people other than elected politicians were allowed on the floor of the House. There were camera crews all over the place, recording the moment. I stood off in a corner, watching. The politicians broke into a chorus of "Go Canada Go! Go Canada Go!" After it was over, I ran into veteran political reporter Tom Clark from CTV, who told me it was one of the best moments he could remember in his long career covering the Hill.

Barbara Ann looked joyous, absolutely loving the spotlight. "Imagine an 81-year-old gal being asked to carry the torch into the Parliament Buildings," she would tell reporters. Imagine, indeed.

There were many more highlights as the torch made its way across the country. Toronto gave it a huge reception, as expected. Ditto Montreal and Winnipeg. I spent Christmas with the torch team and their families in London, Ontario. Instead of taking Christmas Day off, we decided to visit a children's hospital and bring the torch along. It made the kids' day and put smiles on the faces of everyone, including my teammates.

ONE OF THE MORE poignant stops along the way was in Mortlach, Saskatchewan, on January 10, 2010.

Mortlach was the small prairie town of a few hundred people in which Jack Poole was born and raised. Originally, Jack was supposed to run here, over his early objections to the idea. In producing our board chair, the town had made a major contribution to the Games and this would be a way to give something back. Jack eventually agreed and was starting to look forward to the idea when his cancer returned. After he died, I thought it would be great if Darlene could run in his honour. She agreed.

Mortlach looked very much like the town Jack had always described: a weather-beaten, Depression-era prairie town that didn't boast much in the way of modern amenities. Jack had had an enlarged black-and-white picture of the town's main drag on his office wall, showing a solid string of old clapboard houses. It reminded me of a village in Ireland we used to pass through called Inch. Blink and you would miss it. What it had in spades was heart, spirit and work ethic.

It was bitterly cold under a blue sky as Darlene ran the last lap of the relay up to the steps of the local school, where a special tribute was held and a cauldron lit. Darlene fought back tears as those in attendance gave her a long, heartfelt round of applause. Darlene spoke, telling the spectators, including some of Jack's friends who had flown out from Vancouver, that her husband had remained a prairie boy at heart, which is why it was important for her to bring the torch to Mortlach. She had taped a photo of Jack to her torch.

"He had to run with me," said Darlene. "This was his time. I couldn't run it alone so he helped."

Jack's oldest daughter, Gwen, was also there and said a few words. I told the crowd about how Jack often spoke about Mortlach in the many conversations we had had over the years. I knew how important the town was to him. Afterward we walked around the village. We saw inside the house where Jack grew up with no electricity and no running water. We all shook our heads and marvelled at how far Jack travelled from his humble beginnings.

Form Mortlach, the relay continued its journey westward. Calgary was another highlight, a homecoming of sorts. We arrived late in the day and were greeted by tens of thousands of people, many of whom who were wearing jackets and torch relay track suits from the '88 Games. My friend Frank King, the Calgary Games president who so generously had shared his thoughts and experience with me, was there cheering madly. It was great to see him.

On January 21, 2010, the relay left Banff for Golden. Crossing the B.C. border was a big deal for us. We could smell the magic of the Games now. Life was about to change. Former Alberta premier Peter Lougheed handed over the torch at the border to BC Lions football coach Wally Buono, who was excited about being involved in the relay. Premier Campbell was there to welcome the flame to British Columbia. The crowds were massive. It was bedlam everywhere the torch appeared, a reaction that exceeded many people's expectations but not mine. The Olympic spirit was quickly enveloping the province. Resistance was gone.

Less than a week later, the torch was going to be appearing in Prince George, my old stomping grounds. I had always planned to be there so I could celebrate its arrival with old friends and my son, Damien. Damien is as solid a citizen as you'll find and a major backer of the Games. I phoned him up the day the torch was arriving and said he needed to get to Exhibition Park with the family early because organizers were expecting big crowds. I could tell that Damien, who would be bringing my grandkids, Ethan, Max and Orla, thought that I was exaggerating just a bit about how enthused the community was going to be about the torch coming to town.

Sure enough, the place was jammed. Thousands showed up. It took Damien forever to find a parking spot. I brought Ethan up onstage with me. He was wide-eyed. I was asked to say a few words and talked about how great it was to be home in Prince George where my Canadian journey had started and how special it was to be celebrating the moment with my son and his family. The crowd gave me a loud, generous ovation. At this point, there were maybe 18,000 or 19,000 people jammed into the park.

Afterward, Ethan and I went looking for his father. Damien greeted his son with outstretched arms and me with a big smile. A quiet, introspective young man, my son seemed in awe. Later on, as we said our goodbyes, Damien looked at me proudly and said, "Jesus, Dad, from now on I'm going to be taking you a lot more seriously." We both laughed. It meant so much to me, and to Damien, to be able to share that moment together. It was a big day for him and Stacey, his expectant wife, and their children. I wished I could have done the same with all my kids.

The torch relay ended up being everything we ever hoped for, a unifying force like nothing we had ever experienced before as a country. It would lay the groundwork, I believe, for the passion that would spill over during the Games. If we hadn't touched so many people with the relay, the reaction in Vancouver and across the country may not have been so powerful. If we hadn't included our Aboriginal neighbours in the countrywide torch parade, who knows how their participation in the Games might have ultimately been remembered?

I only wished Jack could have been there. I knew he was watching, though. He was always watching.

8

Little **Big** Man

THE OPENING CEREMONIES are often viewed as the jewel of any Olympics. Anxiously awaited, they set the tone and mood for everything that follows. After the Games are long over, they are often remembered by a shining moment that occurred during opening ceremonies—Muhammad Ali lighting the cauldron in Atlanta, a ski jumper flying through the night sky in Lillehammer, the archer and flaming arrow in Barcelona, the fireworks spectacle in Beijing.

After the display that the Chinese put on in 2008, many in the media wondered how we would possibly match it on February 12, 2010. We weren't going to. Never planned to, never could. First, we didn't have that kind of money to play with. Second, and more importantly, that's not what our Games were about. We wanted our opening ceremonies to make Canadians proud, while at the same time tell the world our story. Our opening and closing ceremonies were always going to be about hearts and minds, about touching the soul of the country.

We needed to find someone special, someone who had the horsepower and creative ambition to stage a wondrous production that captured the deep essence of our country, striking a proud and emotional chord among those watching at home, while captivating those taking the ceremonies in live at BC Place Stadium.

Whoever we found would have to deal with the lingering albatross that was our bland contribution to the closing ceremonies in Turin in 2006. Fair or not, our production there had created doubt among some of our Olympic partners about our ability to pull off something as big, complex and important as the opening ceremonies.

After Turin, we formed a committee to find the right company to stage our ceremonies. We realized there were no more than three or four big players in the Canadian entertainment world who would be possible candidates. And then there were a number of international figures who had the depth of experience to handle something of this nature. We had Terry Wright put together detailed specs that set out the scope of the project and then we put out a call for tenders. We told prospective bidders to submit their credentials and tell us why they were especially qualified to do the job.

We realized that we were going to have to be somewhat kinder to any Canadian applicants. In an ideal world, the producer would be a homegrown talent. We got an excellent response and eventually put together a field of 16 contenders, including controversial impresario Garth Drabinsky. I met him a couple of times but discussions went nowhere. But we also got strong proposals from Scott Givens and Don Mischer, who produced the events in Salt Lake City; Andrew Walsh, an Australian who had a long list of high-profile events to his credit; and Blue Mountain Concerts, a B.C. firm.

Guiding our selection process was the notion that we wanted whoever got the job to weave together a uniquely Canadian story, using Canadian talent. We were looking for a giant in the industry and we found someone who was just over five feet tall: David Atkins.

We were not at all surprised when one of the most impressive submissions came from the creative and immensely likeable Australian. David had formidable credentials. His credits included the jaw-dropping fireworks show in Sydney Harbour that marked the close of the 2000 Summer Games. But he'd also put together the opening ceremonies for the 2006 Asian Games in Doha, which were considered among the best ever staged anywhere. The highlight occurred when Sheikh Mohammed Bin Hamad Al-Thani, riding a chestnut brown Arabian horse, mounted one hundred steps to light a giant cauldron in the form of an astrolabe. It was raining—the first time Doha had seen drops of water from the sky in 50 years, so I was told. Despite his horse slipping near the top, the sheikh pulled it off. It was brilliant and all on account of David's gutsy genius. That was difficult to ignore, as was his ability to inspire teamwork and confidence.

Even before the selection process began, many people, including me, assumed that we would end up choosing Cirque du Soleil, the Quebec-based entertainment company, admired and celebrated throughout the world. The Cirque has its own unique brand of show, a dazzling hybrid of street entertainment, space-age gymnastics and traditional circus fare (without the lions and tigers). One of the company's co-founders is Guy Laliberté, a former street entertainer who would later become known for paying to get on a flight into space. On one visit to Cirque's headquarters in Montreal, I discovered just why this company had such success: focus, creativity beyond description, state-of-the-art facilities and a cast of thousands, including hand-picked former Olympic stars. But the true secret of their success was practice, practice and more practice.

It was pretty clear to us that Cirque was of the view that it should be doing the opening *and* closing ceremonies, full stop, end of story. We knew that a lot of people, including some of our partners, would applaud a relationship with Cirque, given the company's reputation and expertise. A sure bet. Except we were looking for a collaborative relationship with whomever we chose.

As an organization we weren't willing to abandon our involvement in the process or set our vision aside. I know I had some pretty strong views about pieces that I wanted to see in both the opening and closing ceremonies if they were going to reach the soul of the country in the way we hoped. And I was not alone.

In our conversations with Guy Laliberté, he made it clear that he wanted the theme of the opening to be about water and, more specifically, about the fact that there was a water crisis in the world. I think he saw the ceremonies as a way to tell a story that he felt needed telling. No doubt it would have been beautiful, but it bothered me that Cirque never seemed to want to talk about or acknowledge the vision *we* had.

We got down to a small group of finalists and we had an open mind. Guy walked into the interview with his colleagues, and we could tell he just didn't want to be there. He was in a sullen mood and managed to annoy everybody. His whole attitude seemed to be "Look, give it to us, we will do a great job, this is what we do." To a person, the committee was flabbergasted. We were looking for a partner, not just a contractor. We weren't confident Cirque understood our goals. As a company, it had an independent streak that was personified by the genius Guy Laliberté himself.

Shortly after the final interviews, we got a call from his office informing us that Cirque was withdrawing from the process. The reason given was that the company didn't think it had the time to devote itself fully to this enterprise because of its other commitments around the world. True or not, the withdrawal was okay with us. It made our final decision that much easier.

In the end we picked David Atkins, largely because of his track record for greatness and the fact that he understood the complicated world of the IOC. There were expectations to be met, but David had the competitive instincts of a champion and knew how to handle adversity, which an opening and closing ceremonies producer always had to be prepared for. After all, you could count on one hand the list of global productions with this kind of complexity.

But what impressed so many of us was David's knowledge and love of Canada. He had schooled himself well on geography, history, Aboriginal Canada and weather and had honed a dazzling insight into our national culture. He seemed to know more about Canada than those interviewing him. And he had a real sense of what his challenge was going to be. He was an easy guy to embrace when he said his job was to extract a great story out of Canadians and tell it beautifully. He said the approach he wanted to take was to identify everyone in the country who might have a contribution to make to the planning and talk to them. Mine them for ideas of what the opening and closing ceremonies should include, who should sing and who shouldn't. He proposed staging a number of symposiums to give the cultural community a say in what might make it into the productions. He was going to hold them all over the country—and he did just that.

But David had another daunting responsibility as far as I was concerned.

"David," I told him one day, "one of the big jobs you are going to have to accept is you must be prepared to save us from ourselves. You need to stop us from making dumb decisions. You will need to have the courage to get in front of the bus and if necessary lie down on the road. Throw your body in front of it, if you have to, to prevent us from doing something that would make us look stupid or naïve."

We shook hands. He would remind me more than a few times along the way of our deal.

We announced David and his carefully selected team in September 2007. There were predictable grumbles from some quarters about our giving the job to a non-Canadian. So we had David agree to surround himself with some top-quality Canadians from the entertainment business, a group that included Vancouver-based music agents Sam Feldman and Bruce Allen; Nettwerk Records' Dan Fraser, and Jacques Lemay, co-founder of the Canadian College of Performing Arts, among others.

Shortly after, David made a great presentation to the board about his experiences elsewhere, specifically about how important it was to protect the integrity of the project by ensuring no details of the show ever got leaked. David came across as someone who was open-minded but would fiercely defend his show, who would demand a supreme effort and loyalty from everyone around him and inspire superb performances. No one was going to work harder than him, that's for sure.

(Years earlier, I had sought the broad, savvy advice of Salt Lake City Olympics CEO Mitt Romney, who would later go on to become a governor and candidate for the Republican presidential nomination. He had lots of good advice but most prominent was the wisdom he shared about the opening ceremonies. Stay no further than an inch away from them, he said. You will be judged harshly if they are a failure. I never forgot that, so my relationship with David was a priority and we became good friends.)

By 2009, the show was starting to take shape, and David and his team began framing it up. I was constantly in awe of what technology could do. David developed a computerized, 3-D version of the ceremonies, so as another piece of the story was crafted he could show us what it was going to look like. That gave us a pretty good idea of what kind of impact various elements of the show were likely to have. The first time I heard "O Canada" using David's system, my eyes welled up. Everyone in the room was blown away by the technology.

A huge variable from the beginning was the fact that we were staging the ceremonies indoors. The opening and closing ceremonies at all past Olympics, Summer or Winter, were held in outdoor stadiums, where the cauldron burned high and bright for all to see. Some thought having an indoor stadium gave us the advantage of having conditions we could rely on. Not entirely true. The roof, for instance, moves all the time because BC Place Stadium is pressurized. This was going to present issues if we tried to cast finite images on the roof. The light in the stadium was pretty bad as well. And let's face it, the building overall was a bit jaded and tired looking.

David felt valuable time had been wasted in the Beijing ceremonies with moving props and people on and off the performance area. He wanted the show to be a non-stop dazzler. To cut down on dead time in Vancouver, he conceived the idea of supporting the production from underneath the performance area. It would help make the stadium more intimate too. The crowd would be up close and personal with the performers. So that is how David came up with the idea of building a false floor, under which people and props would appear and later disappear. The new floor made the old stadium feel new again and gave us a far more efficient way to keep the production moving without long interruptions.

One of the most compelling aspects of the opening ceremonies should be the first few minutes. You want those early moments to be as powerful as possible, to have them make a heart-stopping impact, to create a "wow" moment upon which the entire production will build. As the show was developed, David started talking about this one-of-a-kind video idea with which he wanted to begin the show. It would be seen by those watching on television at home and on big screens inside the stadium.

David said the idea was to get a helicopter and shoot scenery of the host city and region and especially the pristine backcountry areas in the mountains. The video was going to be taken with cameras compatible with the latest high-definition technology, and it would feel to everyone watching as if they were in the helicopter, along for the ride. It would be that intimate, David said. And then the helicopter would hover over top of a mountain in Whistler and there, standing by himself, would be a lone snowboarder. The snowboarder would take off down the mountain with high-definition cameras in hot pursuit.

I remember thinking, "Boy, this is really out there." But David kept going. The snowboarder would blast through miles of flawless powder, performing a few daring stunts as he went along.

Images of the Maple Leaf would be emblazoned in the snow. He'd blast through an honour guard of people holding candles on the mountainside. The boarder would barrel along and then hit a breathtaking jump—right into the stadium, through a set of elevated Olympic rings, onto a ramp that takes him to the floor. And from there he would welcome the world to the Olympics in two different languages.

How about that for a show starter?

David proceeded to show us on his computer how it would all look. You could feel the confidence of people in the room surge. It was the first of many times I would murmur quietly to myself, "Looks incredible! My God, I hope he makes that jump inside the stadium." It was tricky and was going to take nerves of steel for the young boarder we finally selected for the assignment. If he wiped out, it would go viral within seconds. The trick could be a disaster, or it could be magnificent. It was a risk we were willing to take. I attended the practices and could see the risks and rewards. It was an awesome stunt.

Another idea David had was to fly Céline Dion in to sing the national anthem at the opening. He had David Pierce, the ceremonies' musical director, prepare a unique bilingual arrangement of "O Canada" specifically for Céline. He even somehow managed to put together a dead ringer of a soundtrack of what it would sound like—the best make-believe music I had ever heard. It was so breathtaking that everyone in the room demanded to hear it two or three times.

Unfortunately, Céline was trying to get pregnant around the time we needed her so she had to say no. That was a huge disappointment, as I think the public's expectations were pretty high that Céline would be involved in the opening ceremonies somehow. She was Canada's best-known international singing star—a face and name the world recognized. Thankfully her replacement and now rising global star Nikki Yanofsky performed beautifully on the night.

Céline wasn't the only star who couldn't make it. Comedian and actor Martin Short was supposed to be in the closing ceremonies, but had to back out at the last minute because his mother was ill. We tried to secure Leonard Cohen, Mike Myers and Jim Carrey, but again no luck.

Dealing with artists was a whole other experience. David would often fill me in on artists' demands and complications. The first question the stars or their agents invariably asked was, who else was going to be taking part? And what were those other artists being asked to do?

But David poured everything he had into this project. I had nothing but admiration for the effort he put into trying to understand who Canadians were, where we came from—the parts of our past that formed the vertebrae of this amazing country. As he learned we all learned.

For instance, as he put the broader story together, David wanted to include music associated with different parts of the country. In the process we found out from him how much fiddling is a part of Canadian culture—and not just Acadian culture. As it turned out, fiddling is an important part of Aboriginal culture as well. It's big in Newfoundland and Labrador, the Ottawa Valley, Cape Breton, the Prairies and even on the west coast. So it belonged in the show.

One difficult aspect of the show was the French element, and not for a lack of effort on our part. David's team had developed a spectacular segment around the well-known Quebec song "Mon Pays," a beautiful piece written and arranged in 1964 by well-known *chansonnier* Gilles Vigneault. David thought it would be perfect for the opening because it was such an iconic song in Quebec and it had a winter theme. The song's opening words are "Mon pays, ce n'est pas un pays, c'est l'hiver" (My country is not a country, it's winter). The lyrics talked about the winds, cold, snow, ice and solitude of wide-open spaces. I think David was also aware that the song had become a rallying anthem of sorts for Quebec nationalists. Gilles Vigneault was associated with the separatist movement, but we thought the song would send a strong message of how much we were embracing Quebec culture. After all, these were the Games for the many not the few. It was incredibly important to us that we had this song.

David had to clear every piece of music that was going to be in the show with the rights holder. In this case, that person was Gilles Vigneault. It didn't take him more than a second to inform us it was a no-go unless strict conditions were met. The first was that the song could not be performed anywhere where there was going to be a Maple Leaf displayed. And it could not be used in any kind of setting that effectively promoted Canada as a country that included Quebec. It was a devastating setback, as inflexible a position as I had ever encountered. Obviously, we were never going to give in to those outrageous demands.

I don't think David anticipated getting that kind of response. He had built an important section of the show around this song and poured his heart into it. It was going to be beautiful and emotional, sung by Quebec star Garou, and designed to make every Quebecer feel an enormous sense of pride and connection to the Games. And David had already spent a fair whack of our dough designing the opening ceremony with this song a key part of the portfolio of music that would be heard. Surely, something could be done to change this guy's mind, David said. He asked me to get involved.

I decided to start right at the top and try Jean Charest. I tracked him down in Russia, of all places. I asked if he could intervene and find someone with enough sway with Vigneault that he might acquiesce to our request. He tried but a few days later phoned me back to say he had had no luck. He felt terrible, as if he were letting us down. He had pulled out all the stops to get friends to put some subtle pressure on him, but none of it worked. The idea was now officially dead.

I was not happy. Here we were trying to do everything we could to design a powerful Quebec moment into the opening ceremonies, and we were being told we couldn't. I told the premier on the phone, and others later, that I was not going to allow my people to be criticized about the French content in the opening, given the fact we were trying to do everything we could and were getting rebuffed. In the end, we had to improvise and added a new song called "Un peu plus haut, un peu plus loin." We had Garou sing it just before the cauldron was lit, which was the climax of the show. Still, I think everyone on the inside was disappointed by the fact our original plans were scotched.

The other part of the show that prompted some debate inside the organization was the slam poet that David wanted to use in the show. To be honest, I had never heard of slam poetry before. A poetry slam is a competition at which poets read or recite original work and are judged by the audience. The work is often very political and a take on the hot social issues of the day. I wasn't sure how that fit into our program. But David thought it was important to have a mix of performers and include segments that had a little edge. He wanted Shane Koyczan to recite his poem "We Are More," which was about Canada.

While I saw David's logic, I was instinctively against it. I thought the poem might come across on television as Canadians talking to Canadians at the exclusion of the rest of the world that was watching. I didn't think it had the kind of humility we were looking for either. There was no French in it, which was also worrying me. I remember asking David at one point if there was any chance this guy, if he was included, could read some of his poem in French. David said no chance. This was art and you didn't mess with it. I could tell David was becoming increasingly annoyed with the French argument.

Anyway, as the lone holdout I got outvoted and, sure enough, we would be criticized later on for the fact that Shane's performance didn't include any French. Still, I must admit it was an incredibly popular part of the show, and Shane pulled it off brilliantly. The reviews around the world were uniformly glowing.

One of the biggest decisions we would have to make was the design of the cauldron, which was supposed to burn for the duration of the Games and be visible to members of the public at all times. Also, there were safety concerns associated with having a massive burning cauldron inside a closed stadium. The idea we had toyed with during the bid phase of having the rim of the stadium double as the cauldron—a veritable ring of fire that could be seen for miles—had been scrapped. For a thousand reasons it couldn't happen, not the least of which was the enormous cost. After the economy tanked in 2008, that discussion was moot.

David, as always, wanted something super-creative. He also wanted it to be a big surprise. In other words, he didn't want people to know until the last second what the cauldron looked like. He wanted something completely different—something that would produce an unforgettable memory. I thought he did an incredible job. He arrived at a design that included four silver, icicle-like arms that would be used earlier in the opening ceremonies production but disguised as Native totems, leaving people watching to wonder what on earth we planned to use for a cauldron. Secrecy was paramount, as the unveiling would be the show's most iconic moment.

It became evident that the structure of the cauldron and the associated hydraulic engineering needed to unveil it in the way we had planned, rising from the floor, was going to prevent us from wheeling it outside during the Games so people could see it. Nice idea but completely impractical. It was just not going to work. This meant that we were going to have to erect a second cauldron outside so we could abide by the IOC rules that stipulated it being on public view at all times while the Games were underway. Perhaps it could be a smaller version of the cauldron we envisioned for inside the stadium, some thought.

If we wanted to have an identical version of the cauldron outside, we were going to have to find a sponsor or donor who would pay for it. That is when David Podmore, the president of Concert Properties and a great friend of the Olympics, first suggested that Terasen

Gas might sponsor the second cauldron. David sat on Terasen's board and was also one of the champions for the inspired idea of naming the plaza located outside the new Convention Centre after Jack Poole. When it came time to thinking of possible locations to put a second cauldron, Jack Poole Plaza became a runaway favourite among all possible contenders.

The site had everything going for it: it was a wondrous spot with the North Shore Mountains and Burrard Inlet as a backdrop, and it was sure to get phenomenal media exposure. Finally, the location assured there would be plenty of foot traffic going by each day, which is just what we wanted. We never anticipated just how popular an attraction the cauldron would be. It was as if we had placed a grotto there.

One day in the late fall of 2009, I visited Terasen CEO Randy Jespersen to pitch the idea in person. He was immediately excited and could see the glow attached to the idea. For Terasen, the cauldron represented a perfect fit not just because it was a unique gas installation but also because it would be a long-lived legacy of the Games. As it turned out, Terasen would become our final Olympic sponsor—coming up with $3 million to have a replica second cauldron built and fed with gas for the duration of the Olympic and Paralympic Games. We had our solution at no extra cost.

It was a challenge having the cauldron built and installed without anyone knowing what was going on. We installed it behind a towering box so no one could see, but as the Games drew closer we would have to take a few risks and test it. We did so in the early hours of the morning, but the local CTV affiliate had somehow discovered what was inside the big wooden box. They rented a helicopter, got a shot of it while it was briefly exposed, and put it on the air. I was livid. I couldn't figure out why our Olympic partner would want to ruin this surprise for millions of Canadians.

In the months leading up to the opening, there was enormous speculation about who might light the cauldron—a guessing game that takes place before every Olympics. There are always lists drawn up by the media of the top contenders, lots of hearsay and debate.

Speculation seemed to centre around two possibilities: hockey superstar Wayne Gretzky and Betty Fox, mother of Marathon of Hope runner Terry Fox. I should say that wheelchair marathoner Rick Hansen was on many people's lists, as was Nancy Greene, the only Canadian woman to win a gold medal in Alpine skiing. But Gretzky and Betty Fox seemed to be the favourites with the public. An online petition to have Betty Fox light the cauldron received tens of thousands of signatures. Polls showed Gretzky was the choice of a majority of Canadians. There were people who felt we should have the oldest Canadian Olympian light it, or the youngest. There were people pulling for a First Nations chief. A cultural icon should do it, perhaps?

It would certainly have been simpler just to hand the job to the most popular choice. But then there would be no mystery, no excitement. And that's what we wanted. We didn't mind all the speculation, because it created a buzz around the process, but we were never going to be guided by what was being said in the media.

We talked to the Fox family and said we were still trying to figure out what role the family, and namely Betty, who was the public face of the Terry Fox Foundation, might play. We knew the family was probably wondering what was going on. At one point there were suggestions by media that we should have a hologram of Terry Fox light the cauldron. I met with Darrell Fox, Terry's younger brother who played a major role at the Terry Fox Foundation, and told him that we wanted to name an award after Terry. It would go to an athlete who best exemplified Terry's ferocious spirit and also his incredibly giving nature. (Circumstances during the Games caused us to reconsider and award it to two athletes.)

Eventually, given the cauldron's design, we were on our way to a completely different kind of surprise. We would need four people to light the four arms of the cauldron inside the stadium and a fifth to bring the torch in. This allowed us to deny almost every rumour outright, as it would be a team effort and not one person. And one of the four would also light the second cauldron down at the waterfront. For all intents and purposes, the second cauldron became the Olympic cauldron.

We talked long and hard about the type of people we needed lighting the cauldron inside the stadium, what their Olympic credentials needed to be. We strongly believed the four all had to be people of high character, who were virtually unassailable in the minds of the public. Canadian heroes. The type of name that triggered an "Of course, why didn't I think of that?" kind of response. We agreed each one had to be a former Olympian. We wanted that connection. The only people involved in this decision were David Atkins, Dave Cobb and I, and the pressure was intense. There were some people both in my executive and on the board who weren't happy about not being included in this exclusive little group. That was too bad. It was of the utmost importance that we maintain the integrity of the project above anything else. We couldn't afford this information leaking out. The fewer people who knew the better.

After a fair bit of back and forth, we decided on our four people: Wayne Gretzky, Catriona Le May Doan, Nancy Greene and Steve Nash. It was unanimous. All four met the criteria we had set out for the job: former Olympians of exemplary character. We were confident that most of the people watching the ceremonies at home, and outside of Canada, would know one if not all four. Three were gold medallists, and in Catriona's case she was the only Canadian to win gold in back-to-back Games in speed skating. Gretzky had won his gold as the general manager of the men's hockey team in Salt Lake City in 2002. Steve had only participated in one Olympics, in Sydney in 2000, but always gave his heart and soul during Olympic qualifying events. He was a British Columbian and an outstanding human being. He was a must. Nancy was a stellar person as well, and it would have been hard to overlook the woman named best Canadian female athlete of the twentieth century.

It then became my job to inform all four. I recall reaching Wayne while he was having lunch with his family. He excused himself from the table while I gave him the news and, as I did with the others, swore him to secrecy. We decided not to tell any of the four who their fellow lighters would be. We also told each of them that if word got out from them that they were taking part in the lighting, that would be it. They would be switched for someone else.

I caught Steve Nash while he was on a team bus heading to his hotel after a Phoenix Suns practice.

"You want me to do *what?*" he said, not quite believing his ears. "Tell you what, John," he said. "Call me back in 15 minutes and I'll be somewhere quiet."

I called him back when he was in his hotel room. I never heard someone sound so excited. It was like talking to a six-year-old on Christmas Day. The opening ceremonies were going to take place on the Friday of what was the NBA's all-star weekend, and Steve, fierce competitor that he is, said he fully intended to be playing in that game. I told him it wouldn't be a problem for him to make it there and if there were any issues we would work them out with the NBA. So he was onside. It was the same with Catriona and Nancy.

Nancy had wanted to participate in some way, so she was naturally very excited about the opportunity. We were a little concerned about her involvement getting out somehow. She was a Canadian senator now and lived in the leaky Ottawa fishbowl. I had to tell Nancy that if word got out that she was going to be a cauldron lighter we'd have to remove her from the role and put someone else in. "I'll deny we ever had this call," I told her.

She understood.

Now, I had this idea in my head that Rick Hansen should deliver the torch into the stadium, maybe breaking through a wall of dry ice. The place would go absolutely nuts when people recognized him. I believed that he would have a greater impact on the opening ceremonies playing this role than being one of the four cauldron lighters. His entry would be dramatic, and the focus would be on him and him alone. Also, he had a bit of experience in finishing tough journeys, and this was a big one at 45,000 kilometres.

David wasn't at all keen on the idea at first. Creatively, he didn't think it would produce the moment I was predicting. He thought Rick would have to wheel up this ramp onto the floor of the stadium and it would be slow and might put an awkward drag on things. David could become fairly fixed in his ideas, and I had the feeling he was going to be hard to persuade on this one.

"David," I said to him one morning, "I don't ask you for much and I'm really wanting you to consider this. I think it could be fantastic. I can hear the crowd. You have to know this guy is an icon in Canada. He deserves a very special moment in all this and he will not let you down—trust me."

David was mostly quiet. We didn't talk about it for a while after that.

Later on David came back to me. He said he had taken another look at the ramp, and there was no way that Rick would ever be able to get up it. He had even put himself in a wheelchair to prove the point, and fit as he was it was tough going for him. It was a performance ramp and not designed to be wheelchair-friendly.

"David," I said, "you do not know this guy. He will make it up that ramp, no problem."

"No, he won't," David insisted. "I tried. It's a brutal climb."

"Yes, he will," I barked back. "I guarantee you. You try telling him he can't make it up that ramp. I dare you. Let me tell you, David, I do not have the kind of courage a person needs to tell Rick Hansen he cannot do something. Get him over there. Let him try."

A few days later, David humoured me and got Rick to come over to the stadium to give it a whirl. Minutes later he called me at the office. "I thought I had seen everything," he said. "He went up the ramp on the first go. I can't believe it, and what a great sport he is. I think it's going to work."

Victory that time was mine.

The other big decision was who would carry in the Olympic flag, which was a highly prized, emotional moment. There would be eight people escorting the flag into the stadium on opening night, each holding a part of it. It was David who thought we should use the opportunity to showcase Canadian talent, specifically Canadians who the world might not know were Canadian. David, Dave Cobb and I put together a long list of possible candidates. The Canadian-born director James Cameron was on someone's list. Leonard Cohen on another. In the end we settled on actor Donald Sutherland, singer Anne Murray, astronaut Julie Payette, Betty Fox, hockey legend Bobby Orr, skating legend Barbara Ann Scott, Formula One racer Jacques Villeneuve and UN commander Roméo Dallaire. There was a view that a lot of people around the world probably thought that performers like Sutherland and Anne Murray were Americans, not Canadians. And they probably didn't know we had an astronaut program either. This assembly of fine Canadians would surprise some people.

It was a delight phoning them. I remember telling Bobby Orr that he would be in the last row holding a corner of the flag, because if he entered first the place would go nuts and we wouldn't be able to hear the announcer introducing the other flag-bearers. The Fox family was delighted with this role for Betty, who would walk in first, flanked by Donald Sutherland. So everyone seemed to be happy. I realized, as we informed the various individuals, why they were held in such high esteem by Canadians. Magnificent in their own right, sure, but each one was humble and patriotic. When asked, they all said, "Are you sure? There must be better choices."

When we finally decided on having the second cauldron, there wasn't much discussion about who would light it. We made the call that it should be Gretzky. I thought that because we were asking the networks to stay on the air for an extra five or 10 minutes to cover the lighting, the person we selected needed to be a compelling figure. Gretzky fit the mould perfectly. He was a known commodity. Pure star power. But how to get him from the stadium to the waterfront? There was some discussion about having him run with the torch to the second cauldron. But that was ruled out when we realized it would take too long. I thought, "Who cares if it gets on television?" There would be thousands of people lining the streets to watch it happen. An all-time Canadian hero waving to the crowd along the way. In my opinion, the route couldn't be long enough. But David said the police were concerned they couldn't properly protect the route so that idea was eliminated.

David decided to put Wayne in the back of a pickup truck. I didn't like the idea right from the start. It seemed odd and I couldn't picture it. Or I could and I didn't like what I was imagining. I thought it might make us look like hicks. I came up with another idea: Why don't we put Wayne in a specially designed basket that is carried by a helicopter and tracked by spotlights? Really, I thought it would have been fantastic. He would have been flying over the city, holding his torch, and then the helicopter would set him down at Jack Poole Plaza for the lighting. Are you kidding me? The networks would have been all over that. They wouldn't have dropped a second of coverage for the promise of that. It had all the drama they could have dreamed of. Again, David came up with a million reasons why it wouldn't work. In the end, I just gave up fighting. But I still think the helicopter idea was a winner that would have produced iconic images from our Games. Maybe someone else can steal the idea.

I thought the real gem of the opening ceremonies and where David showed his genius was with the athletes' walk-in. Over the years the walk-ins had become pretty perfunctory. They were always one of the highlights of the opening to be sure, and always produced camera-popping moments, but they had become a little bland and seemed to drag on. And they are predictable. David wanted to do something profound, make it something we would remember in Vancouver. Something uniquely Canadian. He thought we could use the moment to give the world a real insight into Canada's view of the Aboriginal community. David came up with the idea of having representatives from Canada's First Nations welcome the athletes of the world to their country. A brilliant but thoroughly complicated plan, and how to keep it secret?

The idea was to first identify top young people between the ages of 19 and 29 from all of Canada's several hundred Aboriginal communities. We would ask those communities to send us their best and brightest, their future leaders. Métis, Inuit, First Nations, they would all be represented. We would dress them in modernized versions of their tribal regalia to create the colour and pageantry for which we were striving. In practical terms, this was going to be hard to do. It would mean separate discussions or negotiations with someone from each of those native communities. And we had to get between 300 and 400 young people to Vancouver and keep them quiet about what they were here for once they arrived. We decided to invite them to Vancouver for a Native youth forum and added the confidential piece about the ceremonies when we had them locked in a hall in Squamish, a week or so before the Games.

David mapped the plan out and even mocked it up on his computer to show us. This piece was pivotal to the show's energy and authenticity. I was emotional just looking at the computer screen. But to make sure this was going to be okay, that Canada's Native organizations would be onside, we decided to seek the blessing of Phil Fontaine, who was then National Chief of the Assembly of First Nations. If there was a problem with what we were proposing, Phil would surely let us know. I knew Phil was a fan of the Games from an earlier meeting we'd had, but I also knew he would put his members above anything. So we brought him to David Atkins's office in downtown Vancouver to show him what we had in store. This was probably early in 2009.

"We are going to show you something that is completely confidential," I began. "And so everything that is said in this room today must stay here, regardless of what we end up agreeing or not agreeing on. It can't go out the door."

We started telling Phil what was going to take place. He sat with his glasses perched on his nose, his chin resting on his hands saying nothing. He wore no expression at all. He was impossible to read. So I took him through how the idea originated, how it centred around the notion of Canada's First Peoples welcoming the world, validating the Games and validating the opening ceremonies in the process.

"The chiefs of the four host nations would be like heads of state at the opening," I said. "And then the young native leaders would come in from east and west and north and south, and the whole country would be represented through them. And they would be on the floor singing and dancing with all their colour and charm forming the welcoming honour guard for the athletes of the world. It would be the duty of those young people to welcome the world to Canada."

Phil continued to regard me with a sober look. I had been talking for about 20 minutes by that point. I talked about the legacy that these young people would take from this, how they would go home enriched and pass on this experience to their kids, who would pass it on to their kids.

"Phil," I said, "that is what we'd like to do and what we need is your blessing. We may even need a bit of help because financially it's extremely difficult to do, but we want to do it. We think it could be an amazing moment, one that would make the entire country proud."

Phil continued to stare at me for a few more seconds before he slowly removed the glasses perched on the edge of his nose and placed them on the table. "John," he began, "if you do what you say you're going to do, exactly as you have laid it out, you will have done more to connect Aboriginal Canada with the rest of Canada than what we would have been able to achieve in a hundred years."

Sweet mother of mercy. It was music to my ears. Of all my Olympic memories this one is near the top. I quickly rolled up my papers and left to tell David Atkins we had liftoff.

PUTTING TOGETHER THE ceremonies is never without controversy, and we would have ours.

About a month before the event, Vancouver Symphony Orchestra conductor Bramwell Tovey told the media that he was refusing our invitation to pre-record the music for the opening ceremonies after being informed that he and the symphony would not all be performing in person at the ceremony and that their music would be mimed by other performers, which he called "fraudulent." We were all stunned to pick up the paper and see what Bramwell had said. We hadn't heard a word from him, or at least I hadn't. And I considered it poor sportsmanship to go to the media before coming to us and seeing if something could be worked out. Basically, he was taking exception to a process that was quite common for international live spectacles of the size and scope that we were putting on. It was standard practice to pre-record musical segments to ensure security of the broadcast transmission. The last thing a television network wanted was a bunch of dead air should something happen at the artist level. The pre-recorded music was all about achieving top quality results and certainty.

The story, however, seemed to have legs, because it just would not leave the front pages of the newspapers. I phoned Christopher Gaze, one of our Games ambassadors and a big player in the cultural community. It was his view that if we were going to get this story to go away I was going to have to phone Bramwell and explain our side of the story and hopefully talk him down from his position. Bramwell was having some personal air time at our expense, which I didn't think was very classy. I also thought he was saying things that weren't true and created the impression that the situation he was describing was akin to what happened in Beijing. An infuriating notion.

The Beijing organizing committee ran into trouble when it came out that they intended to have a young girl mouth the words to a song pre-recorded by someone else. The Chinese authorities thought the girl who would be mouthing the words would look better on television than the original singer. We weren't proposing anything of the sort.

I called Bramwell in Whistler and asked him about his position. He was still quite indignant. I told him we were not trying to offend him in any way. In the end, I had to fall on my sword. I apologized even though I didn't think he deserved an apology. I just wanted the story to go away and if that was what it took so be it. Bramwell made sure the media knew that I had called to apologize. I thought he ended up missing a great opportunity to be part of something that was remarkably special. Several, if not most, members of his orchestra ended up playing for us anyway. Proud, happy cast members in our country's most memorable artistic production.

There was lots of speculation in the final days before the cauldron was lit about how ready Vancouver was to host the event. There were even stories that suggested the city was pretty much indifferent and apathetic, that people didn't care. There were articles about people preparing to flee the city during the Games because of the chaos that the Olympics was going to create. Make-believe chaos.

I would talk to some of those people later. They were miserable that they had bought into all the spooky talk and missed an event that would be talked about for decades. Some complained they watched from Hawaii or Arizona feeling completely duped.

I wasn't picking up the lethargy toward the Games that others were talking about. I thought the opposite was true: that there was a very vocal 10 per cent who were major Games boosters and 10 per cent at the other end who didn't want anything to do with them.

In between there was an 80 per cent that was quietly looking forward to Vancouver becoming an Olympic city, with everything that entailed.

Comments that the citizens of Vancouver weren't ready to embrace the Games were an insult. If anything, I thought the city wasn't ready for how big this thing was going to be. I told Mayor Gregor Robertson that in person one day, just weeks before the opening ceremonies: "I honestly don't think you are prepared for what is coming. You need to get ready for a shocker. The celebration event being planned for David Lam Park the night the torch arrives in the city? I can tell you that site will not be nearly big enough to handle the crowds that are going to come out to see the magic of this thing."

The city was going to experience something it wouldn't experience again for generations. The fun was about to start.

9

Tragedy in Whistler

T HE WESTIN BAYSHORE was once the home to eccentric multimillionaire Howard Hughes. During the 2010 Winter Games, it became base camp for my executive team. We occupied makeshift offices in the hotel's northwest wing. The IOC was also headquartered in the hotel, making it easier to convene meetings of its coordination commission throughout the Games. The meetings were an opportunity for the IOC and VANOC to discuss any issues that might emerge during the Games. Given the hotel's occupants, the place was behind a security fence and on 24/7 lockdown, which meant no one entered the building without the highest level of security clearance.

On the morning of February 12, 2010, I arrived at the Bayshore early, feeling nervous but excited. My Canadian Armed Forces driver, a veteran of the war in Afghanistan, had arrived at my door at about 5 AM to transport me to the hotel, where I would stay for the duration of the Games. The big day had finally arrived. The spotlight was going to be fixed firmly on the Games now, our organization to be tested like never before. This was it. For 17 days we would be the world's biggest sports story.

I went to my office to prepare for the day. My office team was led by Monica Jako, or Mighty Mouse as she was affectionately known—tiny in stature but tough, relentless and completely loyal. Christine Chan, another tireless colleague, was already at her desk too, working on the French content in the speech I was to give that night at the opening ceremonies. Christine wore my mistakes as if they were hers. My whole team did, for that matter.

Dave Cobb and I met for breakfast at 6:30, as we would most days throughout the Games. We started to strategize over some of the items that would be on the agenda when Jacques Rogge convened the first meeting of the coordination commission early that morning. My team would be updating the IOC on everything from protests to the first official event that was scheduled to take place that day up in Whistler—ski jumping. We would be talking about transportation plans and laying out the general agenda for the day. After breakfast, we met up with Gilbert Felli, the IOC's director for the Games, to make sure everyone was on the same page and there were no unpleasant surprises when the coordination commission meeting began.

When it got underway seconds after 8 AM, spirits in the room were high. There was a lot of intelligence sharing. The IOC representatives and staff members in the room were complete pros, many of whom had worked at several Olympics. There was little they hadn't seen. Everyone was itching for the curtain to rise on this incredible show that had been over 10 years in the making. As we talked, the final day of the torch relay was underway, its long, 106-day journey about to wrap up. The energy on the streets had reached a fever pitch.

At Stanley Park, Sebastian Coe, the great British long-distance runner and Olympic gold medallist, was going to be accepting the torch from California Governor Arnold Schwarzenegger, who had flown up from Sacramento to take part. Sebastian was chair of the London 2012 organizing committee and had become a good friend of mine over the previous few years. He asked if I wouldn't mind coming down to Stanley Park, where he and the governor would undoubtedly be swarmed by a gang of reporters and camera operators. I could just imagine the atmosphere so I promised Seb I'd try my best.

After the meeting with the coordination commission, which went smoothly, I grabbed my Blue Jacket and asked my driver to head in the direction of Stanley Park, which wasn't that far away. We barely got around the corner from the hotel, however, when traffic came to a dead halt. It was people gridlock. It was as if everyone in Vancouver had decided they were not going to miss out. Thousands and thousands of people, young, old, some dressed in red and white, others in business suits and dresses. We moved maybe 100 metres in half an hour. There was no way we were getting anywhere near so we turned back for the hotel. I ended up watching the handoff on CTV.

It was some time after 10 in the morning when my BlackBerry rang. It was Dave Cobb. I could tell instantly it was a serious matter by the sober tone of his voice. He was shaking at the other end. There had been a catastrophic accident during a training run on the luge course, Dave said. The athlete involved was from Georgia, and the early word was he was not expected to survive. There were medical personnel on the scene almost instantly, and the athlete had been taken to hospital. I knew they would do everything humanly possible to save his life. Dave was understandably sombre and subdued, so different from his usual ebullient self. I told him to phone me back as soon as he heard anything definitive.

It was the beginning of a nightmare.

I sat in my office for a few minutes unable to move. All I could think about was this poor young man. Who was he? What was his Olympic story? What were his dreams? A young athlete with the world before him—likely gone. I could find no solace in the idea that if he died at least he died doing something he loved. He was 21 years old, and life was not supposed to end that young. After a couple of minutes I snapped to. I got up from my desk and closed the door.

Who to call? I thought about calling Jacques Rogge but realized he probably already knew. The IOC had dealt with matters this grave before. The Munich massacre came to mind. They would know what to do. But even as I went down a mental checklist of people I'd need to speak to, a part of me was grasping at the hope that the young man might somehow pull through. I wanted so badly to believe that was the next call I was going to receive: he's going to make it. Instead, the next call was from Dave. Nodar Kumaritashvili of Georgia had just been pronounced dead.

I felt as if I'd lost a son.

My face fell into my palms. I thought about my father and mother's deaths and my sister's untimely demise 10 years earlier from lupus. I had experienced the pain of great loss before. I felt empty. Lonely. Powerless.

I tried to come to grips with what this meant. I started to think about the boy's family in Georgia. Did his mother and father know they'd lost their son? Did the world know but not them? There was a minute or two where I wondered if this tragedy was beyond my capacity to manage. I'm typically pretty calm in crisis situations, but this had me rattled. I was also worried about my team—they would be devastated, I knew that. I needed to tap into a private well of strength I wasn't sure existed. I'd been to dozens of leadership and crisis seminars over the years, but none had prepared me for this. I'm not sure what could have. I was going to be relying on gut instinct to get me through the days to come.

I was concerned that members of my team were somehow going to feel responsible for what had happened, that they had contributed in some way. At times like this, one's mind is flooded with raging emotions and irrational thinking with almost no way of controlling them. But we were dealing with a matter that was going to be talked about around the world. It already was. It would pose an enormous communications challenge for the organization and drain its spirit, at least for a while.

When I finally emerged from my office, I could feel the penetrating eyes of the organization fall upon me. By that point the members of my team knew what had happened. It was all over the television. In the build-up to the Games we had developed protocols for just about every crisis scenario you could think of. We had confronted make-believe plane crashes, riots, major injuries, mustard gas—you name it and we had prepared for it. But never in our wildest dreams did we imagine the death of an athlete on opening day.

By now, we had learned more details about what happened. Nodar had lost control at the end of the course and was flipped over the side wall of the track into a pole. I saw the crash played on television once and would never watch it again, despite the networks showing it repeatedly for the next several days. Nodar was travelling at 143.3 kilometres an hour at the moment of impact. It was his final training run and his twenty-fifth time down the Whistler track.

A joint ad hoc meeting with the IOC was quickly convened. I had never felt a room so heavily burdened with sadness and grief. I looked at Jacques Rogge, who always seemed to be completely in control of his emotions. He seemed completely lost. He was not alone.

People were expressing views on what needed to be done, and for the first while everyone seemed to be talking at cross purposes. It was an uneasy environment. I remember looking over at Jacques sitting at the end of the table and listening to him say that our Games were now going to be remembered for this tragedy. No argument from me. I told him it was critical that we managed this moment with extraordinary dignity and compassion or the Canadian public would be deeply disappointed in us.

I told Jacques that it was imperative that we acknowledge without hesitation what had happened, be honest and forthright and not try and explain it as anything other than what it was. In other words, the worst thing we could do was to try and make excuses and sound defensive or rationalize the accident in any way. I felt we needed to lead first with our hearts.

This was a day to honour a young man who died pursuing his dream. We needed to express that in the most profoundly human way we could. His teammates would be devastated. Fellow lugers would be devastated. The people of Georgia would be grief-stricken—his family heartbroken beyond words. The athletes in Vancouver and especially in Whistler would be overcome with sadness. We also needed to start thinking about how we were going to address this loss in the opening ceremonies that night. On that point we all agreed.

Gilbert Felli was a commanding presence in the meeting. He did a good job of assuring people that, as dark as this moment was, we would get through it. We *had* to get through it. And we would respond with dignity and composure. I was willing to listen to any idea, provided it not diminish the empathy we both felt and needed to show.

Jacques and I would be attending a swiftly called news conference at the Main Press Centre later that morning to discuss the tragedy. Our communications staff tried to impress upon us the message we needed to impart to the media, but I wasn't interested in talking points. Not today. I didn't want to hear about what issues may or may not be in play. I had no intention of discussing the factors that may have contributed to the young man's death. I was simply going to be honest about how I was feeling: devastated, for the young man and his family. I wanted the public to know how wounded my team was by what happened. I was going to speak from the heart—that's all I knew how to do. There would be plenty of time in the days ahead to dissect exactly what had happened on the track.

In the meantime, there were practical matters to be dealt with such as an autopsy and returning Nodar's body to Georgia. What were our legal obligations? We discovered that Nodar's coach was his uncle and two of the athlete's teammates had been classmates.

Nodar's life was intertwined with the life of every villager where he lived in the mountains of Georgia. His uncle had the horrible task of phoning Nodar's family back home to give them the news. I ended up cancelling a number of events scheduled for that day, including one with the Governor General.

Jacques and I took separate cars to the Main Press Centre for the 11:30 AM news conference. We arrived early and sat in an ante room. Jacques was not someone who was comfortable expressing his emotions publicly. He was always so stoic, reserved, coming across as cold and detached at times. But for most of the morning he had looked on the verge of tears. I realized that I was going to need to help him get through this news conference and he was somehow going to need to help me. At one point while we waited we hugged one another. He told me that over his career as an orthopedic surgeon he had performed countless difficult surgeries, even lost some patients, but those experiences had not prepared him for this tragedy.

We were both barely able to hold back the tears we felt welling up. It was not the best shape to be in just before walking into a room to stare down the world's media, knowing they were going to have some tough questions about someone who had lost his life on our watch. If I had felt this lonely or vulnerable ever before, I could not remember.

I honestly don't recall much about the news conference. A lot of camera clicking and tape rolling. Every chair seemed to have someone in it. I remember Jacques having to stop and compose himself at one point. I patted his back to support him and help him along. I told reporters how heartbroken our organization was, how I felt I'd lost a son myself. Jacques said Nodar's death had cast a shadow over the Games.

There were questions about the speed of the track and whether it was too dangerous. I wasn't planning to spend much time answering hypothetical questions at this point. There were investigations underway and it wasn't a day to assign blame; it was a day to honour the life of an Olympic athlete who had died doing what he loved. A young man with the hopes of an entire country behind him. The media were quite decent and respectful during the press conference. Indeed, most there seemed to share the deep sense of grief that overwhelmed the day. I think the men and women in the room could tell our feelings were genuine, knew that we were in shock, that we were hurt, that we wanted to do the right thing for this young man's family. Not a good day to push anyone too hard.

Meanwhile the torch relay continued to the delight of tens of thousands of people jamming the streets, oblivious to what had happened. I was getting grateful e-mails every other minute from people telling me how this was the greatest thing that had ever happened to Vancouver. I wished I could have shared in that elation.

After the news conference, my attention turned to my staff working at the Whistler Sliding Centre, where the accident had occurred. I knew they would be on the verge of breaking down completely over the accident and I was especially worried about our top man there, Craig Lehto. This group was responsible for the operation of the track, so if anyone was going to feel responsible for Nodar's death it was these people. There were also big decisions to make. I called Craig later in the day to see how he was doing. A physically imposing but soft-spoken man, he was barely hanging on. I planned to see him the next day in person.

The track was immediately closed so police and others could do whatever forensic work was needed. There were even discussions about whether the luge events should be cancelled entirely.

In the meantime, we were learning more about Nodar and his family. We were informed that according to their customs, the body needed to be buried soon. Given the requirements of Canadian law and the autopsy and coroner's investigation that would need to be completed, it was unlikely we could repatriate his body back to Georgia before Thursday—a week away.

I also had to start thinking about the opening ceremonies and what we were going to do to acknowledge Nodar's death. The IOC had its ideas and I had mine. I would also have to change my opening night speech, as would Jacques. I phoned David Atkins and we talked about possible scenarios. David was the only person who would know exactly how we could achieve a level of balance between showing the appropriate respect and compassion for this young man while at the same time giving the world the opening ceremonies for which it had been waiting.

At first, the IOC wanted to open the ceremonies with a moment of silence. David was against that. He said that would start the ceremonies in the worst possible way. I felt for David at this moment and I trusted his judgment. Here he was preparing for an incredibly complex undertaking, getting the artists and the stadium ready and at the last minute we say to him: "Oh, by the way, David you need to incorporate a major change to your plans."

I repeated to him that if the event wasn't managed properly the public would be furious that we didn't demonstrate the proper respect while the world watched. We would never be forgiven for a bad blunder with something like this. The stakes were enormous. I told him that when the Georgia team walked into the stadium we could expect the loudest ovation of the night, next to that for the Canadians. But David knew all this intuitively anyway. The Nodar tragedy would remind me once again why our tiny friend from Australia was the perfect choice for the job. In my mind, he was a Canadian with an Aussie accent.

In the meantime, I was really worried about the capacity of the International Luge Federation (FIL) to handle this crisis. At the meeting with the IOC that morning, representatives from FIL seemed overwhelmed—shell-shocked and scared. They didn't have the communication skills and expertise to manage a problem of this enormity. They were going to be under relentless scrutiny and pressure from the media. Their organization was going to come under attack about the conditions of the track. There would be questions about what happened now. Would events go ahead? Would the track be changed? I remember telling Josef Fendt, the federation's president, that his organization needed to lean on us for help and support. I asked Renee Smith-Valade, our vice-president of communications, to assign someone to them right away. She was already on it. Managing this crisis was her biggest test too. It was important that we did everything possible to ensure that the athletes who would be competing had the best experience possible.

The day was evaporating on me. The relay was moving throughout the city to non-stop applause from the tens of thousands of people lining the route and would conclude sometime after noon. Given the events of the day, it was a bright spot and allowed me to feel a little joy amid the gloom. Even a protest flare-up on the east side of the city could not quell the spirit of the crowd.

In the afternoon, I went up to my hotel room to start getting ready for the opening ceremonies. I remember standing in front of the bathroom mirror putting on a black tie and thinking about how odd it all felt. I thought about my speech and was anxious that I strike the right chord when it came to acknowledging Nodar. I also wanted to ensure that people in the stadium still had a great experience. I practised my speech several times, still sweating over the few sentences in French. I had written the speech word for word myself, like every one I had ever given. Before the morning tragedy, I had been feeling good about the messages I was going to be communicating. Now I was distracted and my confidence was shaky.

At the stadium, I needed to visit with the folks at CTV, who had been there all day fine-tuning their evening coverage plans. I was going to be interviewed by Brian Williams, who was anchoring their coverage. I know Brian well and he's a terrific guy with loads of Olympic experience. But the interview felt awkward and uncomfortable almost from the start. The network was our Olympic partner, and yet at this moment I felt CTV standing back from us. It was almost as if Brian was trying to establish some professional distance. While I was talking to him, protests were going on outside. They made it difficult to concentrate, that's for sure. It was not my favourite interview.

The weather, meanwhile, was dreadful. A torrential downpour was creating havoc on the roads. Protesters were also helping to gum up traffic. Unfortunately, the protest got closer to BC Place Stadium than we anticipated. Originally, buses carrying media, IOC dignitaries and others were supposed to pull up outside the stadium seven and eight at a time, discharging people going to the show. But the protest not only slowed progress of the buses to the stadium, it also forced the police to restrict the number of buses stopping to one at a time. Those getting off the buses were being pelted with objects by the protesters. It was brutal.

Unfortunately, a few key people didn't get to the stadium on time to see the opening few minutes of the show. Some were clearly annoyed, including those IOC members who were late and not amused. The prime minister did make it on time but was not happy about the fact that some federal officials were late. Some PMO officials weren't too pleased either and vented hard. While they didn't come right out and suggest we had screwed up their transportation, that was the clear implication. But as I suspected at the time, and later confirmed, the late bus carrying federal officials and others was operated by Ottawa.

While the delay was just a few minutes, it seemed like a metaphor for the day. Everything was a little off.

The IOC members who were tardy had been a little too casual when it came time to leave their hotel for the stadium. I think they had assumed an effortless process. After that, we had to lay down the law with them and everyone else: the buses are going to leave at precisely the moment they are supposed to. You are either on that bus or not, but it's not waiting. It would end up being the last time we had problems getting IOC members or dignitaries on buses on time.

By the time I took my seat in the president's box at BC Place, an upscale section roped off for Jacques Rogge, the prime minister, the Governor General, the premier and others, the stadium was mostly packed. The late arrivals very quickly filled the place up. I was getting e-mails on my BlackBerry every five to 10 seconds at this point. There were notes of sympathy from friends who were wondering how I was holding up given the events of the day. But mostly there were e-mails from people telling me what a great day it had been in the city and how proud they were, Nodar's death notwithstanding. People around the world were sending messages of congratulations and wishing us well. It was nice to get the feedback because my brain was still too frozen and overflowing with painful thoughts about Nodar to focus on anything else. Darlene Poole was sitting beside me, lost in her own thoughts about her beloved Jack, how much he would have loved to have been there in the front row.

I remember being especially nervous about the opening scene of the ceremonies, which would end with snowboarder Johnny Lyall jumping through a set of Olympic rings in the stadium. I had witnessed him doing it successfully many times during practice. This was for real. There would be no second takes if it didn't work or he fell and crashed horribly. But Johnny nailed his part perfectly and from the floor welcomed the world in English and French. My heart immediately slowed by a few thousand beats. We were on.

As I sat watching the show, my mind wandered. The spectacle was wondrous. A great Canadian story was manifesting itself and the world was watching. But I couldn't stop worrying about my team. They had definitely been knocked off their game by Nodar's death. Dave Cobb, Terry Wright, Cathy Priestner Allinger and the rest of the executive had had a hellish day and were doing their own soul-searching. More than once that day, I recall thinking that we were going to find out pretty quickly how good an organization we really were. I'd be lying if I said I didn't worry about the situation deteriorating further. It's like the plane that starts falling out of the sky at 35,000 feet. If the pilot doesn't have control by 10,000 feet it's crashing. We were in that plane right now and it was my job to somehow bring us out of that free fall. If we didn't get the situation under control, all of the problems were going to be laid at my feet and everyone was going to say: "See, he was the wrong guy after all. He didn't have nearly the right experience. What were we thinking?"

Everywhere I looked inside the stadium people were smiling. Behind me sat the chiefs of the four First Nations whose traditional territories the Games were being held on. They represented the Squamish Nation, Musqueam Indian Band, Lil'wat First Nation and Tsleil-Waututh First Nation. They were being recognized as heads of state and sat behind the prime minister and Governor General. One of the most impressive and heartwarming parts of the evening was the welcome of the athletes by the Aboriginal peoples of Canada. This is where the hundreds of hand-picked young Native leaders, sent to us by their elders, came on to the floor to dance and sing and greet the athletes as they walked into the stadium. No other country could have presented this, not this way.

The show seemed to rivet the audience. I could sense the crowd was waiting for the team from Georgia to enter the stadium and when it did, with each of the athletes and coaches wearing a black armband in honour of Nodar, they received a prolonged, genuine Canadian standing ovation, just as I knew they would. It was both beautiful and a little heartbreaking to watch. My eyes were wet, but I was so proud of our country. We were reaching out the only way we knew—embracing our wounded visitors.

About halfway through the show, Jacques and I were beckoned to the green room in the bowels of the stadium to get ready for our appearance onstage. Makeup. Earphones. Sound checks. Pretty soon I was walking out with the IOC president and standing before the lectern, more nervous than I had ever been in my life. After Jacques delivered a joint statement of condolence, I was alone at the lectern, shaking and self-conscious.

"With Jack Poole and Nodar Kumaritashvili in our hearts," I began, "and standing on the shoulders of every Canadian, I commit that the men and women of Vancouver 2010 . . . are ready to deliver the performance of a lifetime."

I had hoped to reach out to the athletes, to let them all know how much we admired and respected what they did, on so many levels. I wanted to express that we had the utmost confidence and belief in them. But I also wanted to acknowledge the heavy hearts with which they would be competing. "At these Games you now have the added burden to shine and be united around your fallen comrade Nodar. May you carry his Olympic dream on your shoulders and compete with his spirit in your hearts."

I had given thousands of speeches in my life, but never with so many people watching, with so many people wanting to hear what I was going to say and how I was going to say it. Yet I had never felt more humbled in front of an audience.

I was also concerned about my French sentences. No matter how hard I tried, I was never going to sound like anything other than a person with little to no skills in Canada's other official language. Some friends liked to joke that I hadn't mastered English yet, let alone French. It was almost ridiculous how much I fretted about this, how much I obsessed on the amount of French content there was in the production. I knew we were going to be judged on how much French was spoken or sung: it couldn't just be subtitles on a screen; people needed to hear and feel the language. Still, I felt we had achieved a good balance, challenges notwithstanding.

I don't know what it is about me and French. When I read the pages of my speech that night, the French words seemed to be moving on the page. I wasn't helped by the fact that the lighting cast an awkward shadow so I couldn't see the page properly. I'm pretty sure I was awful. And if I had any doubt I certainly got enough e-mails reminding me. But I tried as hard as I could. Short of living in French for a year ahead of time, it was always going to be difficult for me.

"This journey has not been about the few but rather the many," I continued. "All Canadians—Aboriginal Canadians, new Canadians,

English- and French-speaking Canadians and the myriad of cultures, microcultures, languages and peoples that make Canada Canada.

"On this, the proudest night of my life, I thank my loyal, selfless teammates, our tireless Blue Jacket volunteers, our partners, our thoughtful leaders, the IOC and global Olympic family and our many friends and our families for their belief, their efforts, their sacrifice and their courage."

After Jacques and I finished, we walked back to our seats. I missed k.d. lang's haunting rendition of Leonard Cohen's "Hallelujah," a song that seemed more appropriate than ever. The audience radiated enthusiasm and didn't want the evening to end. My daughter Molly was waiting for me. She greeted me with her beautiful smile and a warm hug, which always has a way of making me feel good.

Then it was almost time for the Olympic flag to be brought into the stadium by Donald Sutherland, Betty Fox, Bobby Orr and the others. Betty looked radiant with her snow-white hair. After that, Hayley Wickenheiser took the oath on behalf of all of the athletes at the Games.

In minutes, Rick Hansen was going to push himself up that ramp that David Atkins feared he'd never be able to climb, and the cauldron lighting would begin. This part of the ceremony, the climax, the part everyone was waiting for, had been practised many times under strict scrutiny. Every time I attended a rehearsal, usually in the wee hours of the morning, all four arms of the cauldron rose up from the floor flawlessly. It was all so perfectly timed, like a well-crafted Swiss watch, and I couldn't wait to see the audience's reaction.

Rick powered his way onto the stadium floor through a thick veil of mist, as if he were crossing a snow-covered tundra. He immediately went to Catriona Le May Doan and used his torch to light hers. Catriona, in turn, ran to light Steve Nash's torch, who lit Nancy Greene's, who finally lit Wayne Gretzky's. David had organized this part perfectly. The identity of the four cauldron lighters was obscured until it was time for their individual torch to be lit, stringing out the surprise a little longer. Soon it was time for the lighting itself. I recognized within seconds that we had a problem on our hands. One of the arms of the cauldron was not coming up. The floor was frozen shut and the arm was locked down.

Oh my God, I thought. *Can this really be happening?*

The next 30 seconds felt like an hour. The four cauldron lighters, Canadian legends, stood at their positions waiting to get fresh instructions from David from his booth high up in the stadium. Each was wearing a hidden earpiece, which connected them to David precisely for a never-in-a-million-years moment like this. I could only imagine the private hell David was experiencing as we all looked down at the floor. Was someone down there trying to crank the cauldron up manually? I envisaged a chaotic scene underneath the stage floor, where many elements of the show were being organized.

The irony was that, unlike the television audience, most of the people watching in the stadium had no idea what was going on. Those watching at home were being told that an arm was malfunctioning, but the live audience just assumed that the cauldron had three arms. Steve, Nancy and Wayne lit the three arms of the cauldron that came up from the floor. Poor Catriona was the odd person out.

I was mortified. I remember joking to Darlene Poole that Jack was probably behind this screw-up. He would have enjoyed watching me squirm a little. I knew that had he been sitting beside me he would have had a crack or two that would have put a smile on my face. He would have tried anyway. It took a lot to faze that man and he would have known that a faulty cauldron wasn't life-and-death stuff. Without Jack there, however, the day was turning into the nightmare that just wouldn't end.

Nodar's death would frame everything that followed that first Friday. It would make the most mundane problem seem so many

times bigger. There are almost always niggly transportation problems on the opening day of the Olympics. At least there had been
at every one that I had attended, from Salt Lake City to Beijing. I
remember Gordon Campbell recalling how it took him four hours
to get back to his hotel after the opening ceremonies in Athens. It
takes a while to work the kinks out of the system. And what could
we do about the protests? That's democracy and this is Canada.

I thought the police handled the situation about as well as could
be expected. They approached that day with a good spirit. If anything, they went out of their way to avoid an ugly confrontation that
could lead to violence, triggering an event that might force them
to use tear gas or get into hand-to-hand combat. The last thing
we wanted or needed was bloody images on the television news
that would overshadow the opening ceremonies. But in showing
restraint, the police probably allowed the protesters to get a little
too close to the stadium, which had a negative impact on our transportation system. On top of all that we had the faulty cauldron.

By the next day, the word *glitch* had entered the commentary
surrounding the Games. It didn't seem particularly fair, but there
wasn't any point moaning or whining about it. Our job was to
plough ahead, to ensure doubt didn't start creeping into the minds
of those working at VANOC. I didn't want people feeling that perhaps we weren't ready for prime time.

I knew my immediate executive team and others working at
VANOC were looking to me for a signal that everything was going
to be okay. Wounded as I was on the inside, I tried to portray empathy and project a strong, calm demeanour. I wanted my team to
feel that they had support and could overcome adversity even if in
my heart I was far from being sure how. I instinctively decided to
assign key team members to key locations to shore up operations
and show we were facing our challenges head-on, which seemed to
help regenerate our focus. My staff had become complete disciples
of the project and committed believers in what we were trying to
accomplish. We were in a fast-paced environment with a million

moving parts. It was our aim to be in front of the parade, leading it. But we were mired in the middle of it at the moment.

I was particularly worried about my right-hand man, Dave Cobb. Dave had been such a warrior for us since the day he joined the team. He led the sponsorship drive that helped raise a record amount of money. He had a relentlessly positive attitude about everything. Underneath his gentle exterior beat the heart of a fearless competitor who wanted these Games to be the best in history. He took everything personally and his strength was important to us now.

But I could tell he was wounded by Nodar's death, deeply so. It was probably as tough a blow on him as anyone on the team. He was in charge of operations and felt a strong connection to what had happened in Whistler. Of course, Nodar's death was out of Dave's control, but the burden of it was his and he needed to be prepared to answer the tough questions, to take a lead role in making sure everything we did in connection with Nodar was handled with class and dignity and honour. And it was Dave who would have to watch over the restart of operations at the Sliding Centre. Every move he made now was so much weightier than before.

After the ceremony, I had to go to the Main Press Centre for a news conference involving David Atkins and some of the performers from the opening ceremonies. I sat beside David in the middle of an exhausted but very proud cast that included stars like Sarah McLachlan, k.d. lang, Nelly Furtado and others. I could tell instantly that David was torn up over what happened with the cauldron. I felt badly for him because I knew how much of himself he had poured into that ceremony, how badly he wanted it to all come off without a hitch. On top of the cauldron, he had been forced to redesign elements of the show at the last minute to incorporate various tributes to Nodar. In my book, David was a hero.

The problem with the cauldron notwithstanding, I thought the show was a masterpiece. And for him to have to sit there, after everything he had done, and be forced to answer question after question about the faulty cauldron seemed grossly unfair. But David did win rave reviews from Prime Minister Stephen Harper, who said it was the best show he'd seen in his life, and from Governor General Michaëlle Jean, who also praised the artistry.

But beyond those scarce kind words, however, I must say we didn't feel a lot of support from our 200 partners on that first day. It felt as if we were all alone, as if they didn't understand what was involved in getting the wheels of a machine this big rolling properly. Instead, we had to exchange stern words with officials in the PMO who were making unreasonable demands and unpleasant accusations and who should have been looking at themselves first before pointing fingers at others.

What bothered me was that in our darkest hour our friends seemed to be, if not abandoning us, suddenly indifferent toward us. I have never cherished fairweather friends who crave the front row when things are going great but don't want to be around you when times are tough. The one notable exception was Gordon Campbell, who stepped out of a meeting with some U.S. governors earlier in the day to phone and offer his support. "I just want you to know that I'm there for you. Whatever you need just ask," he said.

I appreciated the generosity of the gesture. The rest of our partners were in limbo. Oh, they would step forward and be happy to be seen with us eventually, once the stigma and pain of opening day had faded away and a few gold medals were won. Once it was clear that the Games were going to be among the greatest ever held, we had more friends than we could count. But the adage about hard times being when you learn who your true friends are certainly felt right.

I should acknowledge the support we received from senior staff at the IOC that first day. They were in this with us all the way, shoulder to shoulder. Our problems were their problems. At least that's the way they made it seem. There was no way the IOC was going to hang us out to dry. They realized how much we had put into preparing for these Games and that we had had some horrible luck on the opening day. Jacques Rogge helped me as much as I helped him. So did René Fasel and Gilbert Felli.

There wasn't a minute that I didn't miss my friend Jack Poole. I thought about him so much on that first day. "What would Jack have done?" I said to myself more than once. We would have talked a dozen times. We might have stayed up the entire night talking about what we did from here on. It would surely have been easier. I walked along the waterfront from the press centre after the news conference in the direction of my hotel. I passed the second cauldron sitting in the plaza named after Jack, and already crowds were surging around the fence to get a look, take pictures.

By the time my head hit the pillow that night I was mentally and physically knackered. The next day I was heading up to Whistler, where a downhill event was scheduled. There was a chance, we had been told, that the weather might prevent it from happening, which was not going to be the worst thing in the world from my perspective. It might give us a bit of a breather to deal with some of the issues that lingered in the wake of Nodar's death. I wanted to visit as many members of my team at the Whistler Sliding Centre as I could and spend time with the medical team members who had so valiantly tried to save Nodar's life. They would all need picking up. I would need to assure them all would be okay.

Little did I know there would be more tribulations to experience before the light would begin shining on us for good.

10

Cypress—Our **Special** Child

WHAT WOULD TODAY bring?

I rose from my bed around 4:30 the next morning after a fitful sleep. The mental gymnastics of the project had wreaked havoc on my sleep for years. A great night was four to five hours. It had been one of those nights.

I walked to the balcony of my room at the Bayshore to take a look at the second cauldron down at the waterfront. I wanted to make sure it was still burning. I was also optimistically on the lookout for any indication that the weather might give us a break. But all it did was rain.

My working day began with breakfast with Dave Cobb in the coffee shop at the Bayshore. We were typically the first to take a table. We talked about the events of the previous day and the fallout from Nodar's death that we were going to have to deal with over the next 24 to 48 hours. It was a pretty heavy discussion. I was heading up to Whistler later that morning to deal with the many Nodar-related issues that were now on our plate, among other things. After breakfast, Dave and I joined other members of the executive team in our private meeting room to talk about what each person would be doing and see if we needed to modify our plans.

Besides the heavy emotional toll that Nodar's death had had on our workers in Whistler, there was now a myriad of practical considerations. What was to happen to future luge events? Did we need to implement additional safety measures at the track to satisfy concerns being expressed in various quarters? When would the investigations into the accident place be completed? How was it all going to affect the timetable for other events that were supposed to be taking place at the Sliding Centre, such as skeleton and bobsleigh? And what about the athletes? What would their state of mind be, having to perform in the wake of a fellow competitor's death? Would they all be petrified? Who could have blamed them if they were?

This was no way to have to compete. The sliding sports are physically and mentally demanding. Competitors would need to be reassured that this track was safe, that it was no different from most around the world, that they could trust it if they trusted themselves.

There were mobs of media already in Whistler mid-Saturday and more were expected to descend on the town over the weekend to do follow-up stories on Nodar's death and to look into questions being raised about the track. A meeting with Felix Kumaritashvili, Nodar's uncle and the coach of the Georgian luge team, was hastily organized. Jacques Rogge was also going to be there, along with executives from the International Luge Federation.

Felix was wearing a Georgian team jacket. He was medium height, sturdy, with greying dark hair and a light stubble on his face. It was evident from the dark circles under his eyes that he'd spent the night tossing in his sleep. He looked like someone who had lived a hard life outdoors. One of Nodar's teammates, a fellow from the same small village, sat nearby with his back against the wall, motionless. There to support Felix, he never spoke.

I thought about the call he had had to make to his brother, David, the day before to tell him that his son was dead. I imagined the guilt Felix must have felt, that he was somehow partly responsible for the tragedy. That kind of self-inflicted psychological wound was only natural. Of course, none of it was his fault, but there was little I could say to relieve his anguish.

We spoke with Felix through an interpreter. It was a deeply humbling, emotional exchange with everyone searching for the right words of consolation. It was not a long conversation but it went on long enough for him to make clear that the family desperately wanted Nodar's body sent back home to Georgia as soon as possible. "Can you do anything, John?" Jacques asked me in front of Felix. "Leave this with me," I said. "These are statutory processes, but I will move heaven and earth to try and make this happen. I will do something, I promise."

After the meeting, I wandered about the Sliding Centre to see how our staff members and volunteers were coping and to chat quietly with officials from the luge federation. It didn't take long into my chat with FIL President Josef Fendt to determine that these guys were still lost, in an environment most of them had never ventured into before, surrounded by media trying to trip them up, to get them to say things that might be controversial, that would cast the Games or the sport in a negative light. Amid the avalanche of coverage surrounding Nodar's death were questions that flashed like a beacon: Was the track too dangerous? Did FIL officials, and by extension us at VANOC, have bloody hands in this affair?

That was certainly the subtext of many of the stories. Some of the papers in the U.K. were blaming the crash on Canada's Own the Podium program, suggesting we went so far as to speed up the track to give our team home-ice advantage, the logic being that because our athletes would be able to train on the track the most, they would be better able to handle its speed. It was a preposterous and repulsive suggestion unbecoming of any reporter. No one would ever put lives at risk to gain a competitive advantage. And we had given more practice time to visiting athletes than previous

Olympic host countries had. It was tough to read and listen to the coverage, but we had to deal with it.

By Saturday afternoon, there was a lot more information about what happened in the final seconds before the crash. I talked to the officer who had conducted the investigation into the accident for the RCMP. I had earlier wondered what expertise the RCMP could bring to bear on an accident that happened on a luge run. After all, what did the force's investigators know about the sport and this type of facility? But this guy was impressive and pretty much nailed what most authorities would conclude in due time.

Nodar was blazing down the course when he lost control of his sled in turn 15. His reaction was evident for all watching to see: he raised his left hand in the air and dropped his feet to the ice in an effort to slow himself down. By turn 16 he was high on the wall and completely out of control. In a split second, the gravitational forces at play acted to catapult Nodar out of his sled, over the wall and into a steel support pole. I was disappointed that broadcast outlets chose to show the tragedy over and over again. I failed to see the public service in this. I just couldn't imagine being the boy's parents and having to watch that.

By the afternoon, the investigations at the Sliding Centre were finished. It was decided to resume training runs in all of the sliding track sports, including luge. But the FIL made the arbitrary call that men competing in luge would now begin races from the women's start line, in an effort to reduce speeds and lower the psychological barrier now confronting their athletes. Also, walls at turn 16 were raised as a precautionary measure, and padding was put around support poles. Many luge competitors felt the decision ruined the event and said so. I could understand their feelings, but I also knew there were athletes competing in the sport who were nervous and may have welcomed the move. They just weren't going to say anything publicly for fear of incurring the wrath of their fellow competitors.

Over the next 10 days, there would be fewer accidents on the track than there were in Salt Lake City in 2002 and about the same as there were in Turin four years later, a reassurance that failed to make me feel any better.

My mind turned to helping Nodar's parents get their son's body back to Bakuriani, Georgia, as soon as possible. I phoned our chief medical officer for the Games, Dr. Jack Taunton, to see what the prospects were for getting this done at rocket speed. Jack explained the normal procedures and how much more complicated it was when the police and coroner were involved. But I still didn't see why, under the exceptional circumstances, we couldn't just speed the process up.

"Jack, this isn't good enough," I said. "We have to do better. You need to make these phone calls and explain our situation. And if you need to talk to the top officials in the country in charge of this, then it's time to talk to them now. You need to implore them to help us, to pull out all the stops, to go that extra distance to get Nodar on a plane back home in as short a time as humanly possible."

Jack, who possesses pit bull determination, said he would but he didn't seem very optimistic.

"Keep me in the loop," I told him. "I'm counting on you, Jack."

By the end of the day, Jack had worked some magic and managed to get the various authorities to speed things up, cutting three days off the length of time Nodar's body would remain in Canada. It was a small but important victory.

I wanted to spend as much time as I could over at the track, talking to our volunteers and full-time staff to make sure they were doing okay. I knew nerves would be frayed. I was worried about Craig Lehto, director of the Sliding Centre. Craig was one of the nicest people you'd ever meet, with a first-class knowledge of sliding centres. He had a huge heart and was loved by his team. We were lucky to have him.

When I saw him on Saturday, I told him that he was now in the midst of one of the most challenging moments in his career. In fact, there might never be one quite like it again. Over the next few days, he was going to need to show what kind of man he was and what kind of leader he was too. His team was going to draw off his body language, his mood and his strength. "This is not easy," I told Craig. "But people are going to be looking to you for signals, they are going to be looking to you for affirmation that everything is going to be okay and that some kind of order and calm is going to be restored. Mostly, Craig, they will be looking to you to show them, convince them, that you are all going to weather this storm. And whatever you need from me you will get—that I will promise."

I knew that, like many, he was unfairly wearing some of the responsibility for what had happened. I told him he needed to stop worrying about that now. He had to focus on running the project, to get the program he had developed over the last few years back on track. He couldn't let that slip away from him. There was too much riding on it. Craig would pass his test with flying colours.

Before heading back to Vancouver, I attended the lighting of the cauldron in Whistler, which was located in the town square. Thousands turned out, and yet the ceremony still felt quaint and warm and Canadian. I said a few words and probably didn't have the same upbeat lilt in my voice as I might have had under normal circumstances. But Whistler had responded brilliantly to its Olympic challenge, producing first-rate venues and an Athletes' Village that never got the recognition and kudos it deserved. From the stage, I could see the pride in the crowd over how the resort had come together. Its finest hour had arrived.

Because I needed to be in Whistler on Saturday, I was unable to take in Jenn Heil's performance at Cypress Mountain in women's moguls. Jenn is a five-foot-nothing dynamo from Spruce Grove, Alberta, with a smile that could light up a continent and a personality that could warm a small country. She represented our first legitimate chance of winning the first gold medal on Canadian soil. She had taken the gold in Turin. I knew Jenn wanted it badly and had trained her heart out to be the one here at home. When I got word that she had finished second, I felt a little sad for her because I knew that while a silver medal was nothing to sneeze at, gold was what she wanted. Gold was what we all wanted for her, and it certainly would have helped change the negative story lines that were being rolled out by the media.

I had been on the phone throughout the day Saturday, talking to various members of my team about new issues that were beginning to emerge. For one, we were receiving some early grief for what was perceived by a vocal few to be a lack of French content in the opening ceremonies. If there was one issue that could get my blood boiling throughout the Olympics, it was the tightrope we seemed to walk daily over the use of French.

As an organization, we had gone the extra mile and beyond to ensure the Games reflected Canada's linguistic duality. During the run-up phase, we had received heaps of praise from Canada's official languages commissioner, Graham Fraser, for ensuring that VANOC was fully bilingual. He applauded us for hiring bilingual staff in key positions. Almost a quarter of our staff spoke French. We were ensuring that all signage was in both languages. We had 4,500 volunteers who had driven or flown across the country, many from Quebec or other French-Canadian communities, to work on the Games. We had every document printed in both languages. We had signed memoranda of understanding with the Fédération des francophones de la Colombie-Britannique and the Fondation canadienne pour le dialogue des cultures to help us raise the profile of francophones living outside Quebec. Sure, Fraser had taken the odd shot at us, but by and large we had raised the bar on official languages.

And, of course, when it came to the opening ceremonies, few knew that we had tried to have the famous Quebec anthem "Mon Pays" in the lineup but were shot down by the song's author. Still, it wasn't enough to deflect criticism.

As fate would have it, one of my scheduled stops in Whistler was a reception hosted by the Organisation internationale de la

Francophonie, where I was to drop by and deliver a greeting on behalf of VANOC. The organization is made up of countries and states where French is the customary language. Given the events of the previous evening, and some of the reviews around French content that were in the morning newspapers, I wasn't sure what kind of greeting I would receive. As it turned out, although there were some private discussions among delegates at the function about the opening ceremonies, no one confronted me over it.

I did hear from some that they thought the show was spectacular, moving and emotional. Having said that, there was an elephant in the room—I could feel it. People were talking. The topic was doing the rounds. Still, I left mostly unscathed. It was funny because months later, in August 2010, I would get a letter of commendation from the president of the same organization in Switzerland praising our stellar efforts to recognize French at the Games. It said the organization also hoped Games organizers in London and Sochi were attempting to clear the high bar that we had set.

When it came to French content at the Olympics, Quebec premier Jean Charest said it best in one of the many conversations we had on the subject. "Whatever you do," said the premier, "it will never be enough for some. You will always have critics." And he was right. But the French debate, such as it was, was infused with politics. So when Heritage Minister James Moore, who represented a riding in suburban Vancouver and was also the minister responsible for official languages, came out and denounced the amount of French in the opening, I thought, Okay, this is clearly about votes in Quebec. But knowing that a big part of the conversation was political didn't help defuse my annoyance. I mean, as our head minister and partner, he had been intimately aware of our challenges as well as our plans. I had briefed him myself.

There we were, having spent years working to share these Games with the country, working to infuse the organization to the degree we could with the French spirit, and this was the respect we got? Not enough French in the opening? You had to be kidding.

I went back to Vancouver late Saturday night by car. All the way there I tried to answer some of the thousands of e-mails I had received in the previous 24 hours. Yes, there were a few denouncing my appalling French. But there were many more giving me marks for the courage of trying. There were lots urging me to keep my spirits up, giving me the same pep talk I was giving my team. It was gratifying that unknown Canadians cared enough to write me and tell me to hang in there. That the sun was going to shine . . . eventually.

We had experienced more transportation problems throughout the day. Who knew buses from California didn't like climbing hills? But beyond that, politicians and dignitaries were also creating problems. For instance, for buses going up to Cypress, there was a drop-off point halfway up the mountain, with security screening tents that spectators had to pass through as part of a strict protocol imposed by the IOC and the RCMP. But then a procession of black Escalades belonging to the security detail of U.S. Vice-President Joe Biden showed up and they weren't stopping at any checkpoint and having the president's number two man jump out to be searched and walk 800 metres. Not a chance.

If that wasn't enough, the vice-president's security detail also effectively stopped all traffic trying to get up the mountain. And it wasn't just Joe Biden. Arnold Schwarzenegger was another, and even the prime minister's entourage caused problems on the first day. At any given time we would have kings and queens and other royals visiting the Games, adding layers of protocol headaches behind the scenes.

Part of our challenge was getting these groups to understand that there was a way to access the venues smoothly and a way that would cause us enormous grief. I think there was a great deal of sympathy for us. The leaders knew we were managing a difficult situation, especially on Cypress, and after the first day we didn't have nearly as many problems with political processions.

I met with my staff first thing Sunday morning. We went over the list of issues that had emerged from the day before: the pesky transportation problems, more weather problems, the French fall-out from the opening, Nodar—the list went on and on. During my time in Whistler, it had become evident that confidence was fragile. Nodar's death had really caused people to spiral, but also the weather was getting everyone down (especially up at Cypress, where events were threatened with cancellation), and the international media were reacting negatively to some of the problems we were experiencing.

I felt it was important that we, as an executive, fan out and get to as many venues as possible, especially ones where there were problems—like the Sliding Centre in Whistler and in Cypress—and give the staff and volunteers on-site support and assurances that they were doing a great job and everything was going to be okay. We decided to double the executive presence at key soft spots, especially in the mountains.

For instance, I had Dan Doyle, our executive vice-president of venue construction, head up to Whistler and oversee things there for a bit. The idea wasn't to be looking over people's shoulders but rather just to have someone people could turn to if doubt started to creep into their decision making. More a guiding hand than anything and Dan was a pretty good shoulder to lean on. Donna Wilson, our vice-president of human resources, went to Cypress Mountain to boost morale of a Games team that was exhausted, wet and frustrated.

The warmest February in eternity was causing massive headaches at Cypress, and there was the rain to contend with. It was literally threatening to wash out events. This was leading to the second-guessing we'd anticipated about why we had planned so many events on Cypress instead of Whistler, where cold weather and snow were more of a sure thing. The short answer was that Cypress offered advantages that Whistler didn't. It was a lot closer to more people, for starters. That allowed us to get more Olympic tickets in the hands of more spectators. Not such a bad motivation. On a beautiful day, the view from Cypress over Vancouver was one of the most stunning in the world. And, frankly, we didn't anticipate we'd be dealing with weather that hadn't been seen in the area for more than a century. Whistler was already over capacity with five stadiums, an Athletes' Village, a Celebration Plaza and other facilities.

THE IOC HAD required us to stage test events in the period leading up to the Games. It was a chance for them to see us under the kind of pressure we would face at Games time. And for us it was an opportunity to face the stresses of competition, a chance to put ourselves through the wringer. Chances were that if there was a flaw or weakness it would reveal itself during these test events, and there would still be time to fix them.

We had scheduled 21 such events and boasted an impressive report card at the end. Almost straight A's. The program allowed our team to test transport, technology, security, accreditation, scoring systems and food and beverage. All the venues but one seemed a perfect fit: Cypress. The venue was tight, access tough, the owner not wildly enthusiastic that we were there, and there was always the worry that snow conditions might be problematic.

The test events at Cypress in 2009 were far from Olympic-calibre, with one postponement, so we had serious work to do. This fairly modest mountain was to face its stiffest test—ever. It had a year to become world-class. We worked hard to ready the hill, develop a spirit of teamwork on the site, recruit the best kinds of volunteers, install snow-making and lighting equipment and create an upbeat stadium atmosphere. By Games time, one of the most stylish grandstands ever built on a North American mountain was in place, a full 14 storeys top to bottom. Looking straight down on the finish corral for ski and snowboard cross (fairly recent Olympic disciplines) and other events, it looked like a giant Meccano model. Eventually the mountain, with its multiple venues, was transformed. We had turned water into wine. In its coverage, NBC favoured Cypress for its amazing vistas.

The organizing committee had taken painstaking measures to prepare for every kind of weather. Unique weather station technology had been installed in the mountains through a partnership with Environment Canada—the sole purpose to help us get in front of every imaginable winter challenge. Too much snow, too little snow, none at all, rain, sun, flying saucers—the system could tell. For years we watched, analyzed and tried to predict what was coming—usually with bang-on certainty. The data said don't worry. The data said we would manage. In Whistler, if the same weather technology said we'd have a clear window at 10 AM to start a downhill event, then *voilà* that's what we got. Pretty impressive stuff...until we needed it most.

In the months leading up to the Games, Cypress had looked good. But then conditions started to bounce around a bit. The mountain was acting strangely, just not co-operating. We thought that, based on previous years' data, it would right itself and the snow would come, and plenty of it. Just after Christmas the situation was beginning to look dire. No snow or so little it hardly mattered. The little snow that the mountain got was in the wrong places. On top of that, it wasn't cold enough to make any snow artificially.

Early work we had done on the mountain was destroyed by warm winds. January was the warmest in Vancouver since record-keeping began in 1937, with a mean temperature of 45 degrees Fahrenheit, or more than seven degrees higher than normal. It was El Niño Plus. At Capilano Golf and Country Club, a few kilometres from Cypress, men and women were playing golf in short sleeves. The fields of play on the mountain were breaking up. With the start of the Games closing in on us, the condition of Cypress had become the daily focus of our mountain operations team. New plans were drawn up. Still parts of the mountain were more brown than white, and pretty soon the media were going nuts with doom-and-gloom stories that went around the world. *Will they make it? Is there any hope?*

The pundits were having a field day predicting it was only going to get worse. The sport and venue teams collaborated endlessly, new money was found as contingencies for other things were reduced and major decisions were made to shore up our position. Creativity was the order of the day. We were now looking for bales of hay to protect and stabilize the runs, creating false but strong and effective bases to hold the snow. Meantime, we were hunting for other snow that was compatible with the snow on the mountain.

The crew was determined not to let the mountain defeat them. Every day was a new adventure with very little help from the sky. Every ounce of snow was taken from other sites on the mountain and stockpiled for emergencies above the runs. Erickson Air-Crane helicopters carrying the hay to key locations made for dramatic pictures, and when trucks started to haul snow from Manning Park it was clear to all it was game on—man versus mountain.

As the days ticked down, the mountain operations team, led by Paul Skelton, was exhausted after practically living on the mountain for weeks. I went up many times to see the work and cheer them on. Their Olympics had started and they were after a gold medal—nothing less. If something was humanly possible then they tried it. Dave Cobb, Terry Wright and Cathy Priestner Allinger worked day and night making key strategic decisions with the crew, and while there were many setbacks they chewed their way through each one. This was not going to be the site of the first-ever Olympic event outright cancellation.

To provide encouragement, I asked the premier to visit the workers. He had lunch with them and told them how proud he and the people of the province were of their heroic work. It meant the world to them.

A united House: The irresistible Barbara Ann Scott, figure skating gold medallist from 1948, carries the torch through the House of Commons for the first time in history.

ABOVE A proud Pittsburgh Penguins captain Sidney Crosby carries the torch through downtown Halifax.

TOP RIGHT Our First Peoples welcome the world at the opening ceremonies.

BOTTOM RIGHT The streets of Vancouver and Whistler teem with exuberant Canadians and their international visitors.

ABOVE Prime Minister Stephen Harper pauses for a moment at a memorial to pay his repects to Georgian luger Nodar Kumaritashvili.

TOP RIGHT 2010 saw the warmest January on record, and our Cypress Mountain operations team and volunteers worked in miserable conditions to ensure there was enough snow for the competitions.

BOTTOM RIGHT Alexandre the Great: Alexandre Bilodeau of Montreal won Canada's first gold medal on home soil in men's moguls.

TOP Snowboarders poised to conquer Cypress Mountain.

ABOVE Heroes in blue: 25,000 Blue Jacket volunteers were essential to pulling off a successful Olympic and Paralympic Winter Games.

TOP Joannie Rochette, Canada's girl, pours her heart into her performance despite her mother's death of heart failure days before.

ABOVE Captain Hayley Wickenheiser (#22) and her teammates celebrate winning a gold medal in women's hockey.

A joyous stadium awaits the athletes at the opening ceremonies of the Paralympics.

Other partners were rattled a bit and calling to hear me say how I thought it would all play out so they could reassure others who were calling them. I had faith in our team to pull it off. It's a wonderful thing to be surrounded by men and women who do not understand how to quit. One day in early February on Cypress, I mounted a snowcat to see the challenges up close. Paul Skelton, who was Australian and more commonly known as "Bones," said to me, "Worry about something else, boss. We won't let you down."

I knew they wouldn't.

Daily weather reports were painful to listen to and there was almost no point. One day we would get word snow was on the way—the next day it was forget it; now we're calling for rain and warm winds. Talk about breaking our hearts and kicking us when we were down. I sat in on some operations meetings and wanted to scream as Chris Doyle, VANOC's chief weather forecaster, outlined the what-if scenarios. I actually said to Chris at one meeting, "You can't talk anymore."

I couldn't handle it. He would say the weather was going to clear up in three days and it never would. I know Chris was as frustrated as I was. Like everyone else on the team he would have swum the length of the Fraser River if he thought it would give us snow. He wanted desperately to give us some good news. And any time he attempted to I'd spoil the moment: "Are you kidding me? Are you kidding me? Why should we believe you this time?" I eventually resigned myself to the fact I was only going to have faith in the weather when I woke up and saw a white mountain under a clear sky.

Mounting successful events on Cypress was clearly going to be all up to us. In the final days, as the athletes showed up and modified practices were scheduled, it was clear the entire country was cheering for the men and women toiling on Cypress. By Games time, the crew had endured unmerciful exhaustion but they had prevailed. The venue was ready.

SO THAT WAS the backstory to Cypress. It was an Olympian achievement that we were getting any events off on the mountain period, given what we were facing. But the first few days of the Games was more of the same, weatherwise. Heavy rain, warm temperatures. Cypress had become our "special child," in the immortal words of our hard-working and unflappable vice-president of communications, Renee Smith-Valade. We had growing concerns that some areas where spectators were supposed to stand could become unstable, which forced us to cancel 8,000 standing-room tickets the first weekend. It was a tough decision to take but we had no choice. The safety of our athletes and visitors was paramount.

The lack of snow wasn't the only problem on Cypress that first weekend. An electrical failure knocked out the concession stand. Lineups had been ridiculously long, especially for people wanting only a hot drink. Some buses were still struggling to get up the mountain. Some broke down in the process, leaving spectators in the pouring rain waiting for a bus to get them back downtown.

Within a couple of days, all those problems would be sorted out, except for the lack of snow. That would be an issue until the end. And while it would have been far preferable to have had an abundance of snow from the beginning, and perfect temperatures, the heroic work of our mountain team and the Blue Jackets that worked on Cypress in some of the worst conditions imaginable became a compelling story in itself. Their dedication and resilience were inspiring.

Despite the constant rain we were getting in Vancouver, crowds were already becoming a story. Tens of thousands poured into the downtown core the first weekend, with many hoping to catch a glimpse of the Olympic cauldron at Jack Poole Plaza. The cauldron was situated inside the security perimeter that we had set up. It had to be; the plaza in which it was located also contained the International Broadcast Centre and the Main Press Centre, which were only for journalists with proper credentials. What this meant was that the cauldron had to be behind the chain-link security fence we had set up around the area.

For security reasons, the fence was covered by blue tarps in different spots, which didn't exactly cater to those wanting a look. But these measures were mandated by the RCMP, and we took our obligations to protect Canadian and foreign journalists seriously. There were all sorts of people looking to draw attention to one cause or another.

Which is all to say that responding to early grumbling about the fence and its impact on cauldron viewing wasn't simple. But on the first Sunday I received a call from Mayor Gregor Robertson, who was adamant that we find some kind of solution because the complaints were getting louder by the hour. And the crowds bigger. Walking by one night, I heard a loud continuing chant from the crowd, I think partly in fun: "Mr. Furlong, take down that fence."

The truth is, no one anticipated that we'd get well past 30,000 people a day going down to the waterfront to see the cauldron. It became the biggest tourist attraction of the Games—by far. I phoned Terry Wright, our premier troubleshooter, and asked him what could be done. At first, Terry didn't think there was much we could do because of our security responsibilities.

But eventually, in discussions with the RCMP, we found a great solution, which involved moving the security fence closer to the cauldron and creating "windows" that allowed people to take unobstructed pictures. And we also managed to establish a roof-top viewing area west of the cauldron, which allowed people to get an eye-level view of the flame. The viewing area was a wing of the Convention Centre that was designed as a scenic outlook point and could accommodate about 150 people at any one time. From there, you could feel the flame's heat on your face. After it opened, the crowds seemed to grow even bigger.

While you could put the kerfuffle over the popular cauldron into the category of a nice problem to have, it became another thing that the media could lump into the problems we were experiencing and build into an early narrative that these were the "Glitch Games," and that we had got off to one of the worst starts in Olympic history.

By Sunday night, having heard a lot of the criticism, members of my executive team were bitter and very down at the complete lack of sympathy for our position. It's not like many of these problems were uncommon to the start-up of any Olympics, especially the transportation challenges. And I don't think we got enough credit for the stunning job our team on Cypress was doing just to have the venues competition-worthy. It was as if God himself was saying, "Anyone can stage this thing with snow. Let's see how good you are doing it without any."

On the afternoon of that first Sunday, I decided to head to the Richmond Oval, where a men's speed skating final was taking place. I was anxious to see the Oval in all its glory, packed with fans, many of them members of the famous Dutch orange army, all in awe of one of the most splendid Olympic settings seen in recent years. But I also wanted to shake hands and slap the backs of as many Blue Jacket volunteers as I could.

I hadn't been at the Oval long when I felt a tug on my arm. When I turned around it was one of our Blue Jackets.

"Mr. Furlong?" he said hesitantly.

"Yes."

"Jim Fowlie."

My eyes nearly popped out of my head.

"Jim Fowlie," I exclaimed. "What in the world are you doing here? I thought you were in Australia."

"I am," he said. "But there is no way on earth I was going to let this happen in my country and not be a part of it. So I volunteered and I'm your venue services manager here at the Oval."

"Wasn't anybody going to say anything to me?" I laughed.

I loved Jim Fowlie. I had known him from my earliest days in Canada, when I was athletic director at the high school in Prince

George. Unlike the other schools, which had dozens of swimmers, we had just five in the entire school when we entered the district swimming championships. Jim was an unbelievable swimmer, the best in the country in his age group. At the end of the competition there was only one event left: the 400-metre individual medley relay. Even with so few swimmers we had had lots of firsts and racked up the points, but to win it all we had to win the relay. But we didn't have a relay team. Heck, we barely even had a swim team.

So I went over to Dick Zarek, who was the head of the swim team at another school and our local swim czar. I said, "Dick, I'd like to give Jim Fowlie a chance to go in the relay as our team." Dick laughed at first. He thought I was joking.

"I'm serious," I said.

"Ridiculous," he countered. "You can't do that."

I asked why not and didn't he want to see just how good this kid was. So Dick went off to a corner to huddle with a few of the other coaches and organizers and came back a little later with a proposition: Jim could go in the relay as a one-man team but at the end of each length, he had to get out of the water, get up on the starter's block and jump back in.

"Okay," I said. "You've got a deal."

I found Jim and told him the terms of the pact. He had to swim 100 metres, get out of the pool and mount the block, dive back in and swim another 100 metres until he'd finished the 400 metres. To make a long story short, he won the race by a length—a length of the pool.

Jim ended up becoming world champion and record holder and eventually ended up in Australia working for the New South Wales Institute of Sport as a swim coach. It was great to see him again and even better seeing him in one of our Blue Jackets. What spirit! And all at his own cost.

As I wandered around the Oval, I didn't see any of the long and troubled faces among the volunteers and workers that I had witnessed up in Whistler the day before. Everyone was smiling, most of all those in the crowd, who were just loving the speed skating competition. I was routinely getting reports from my executive team telling me that competitions were going off flawlessly at other venues around Vancouver and up in Whistler. Even most of the bus problems had been fixed.

But those stories weren't making the news. By Sunday night the media, especially the foreign media, were obsessed with Nodar, the weather, French in the opening ceremonies, broken-down buses and the fencing around the waterfront cauldron.

I believe it was Sunday night when I heard the anchor on CTV say, "Look at what the world is saying about us." And it was a compendium of the worst headlines and stories from around the globe, but primarily from the British press. So our own Olympic coverage in our own city was centred on the views of others—hard to believe.

I got a nice respite from all the negativity on Sunday evening when I attended a U.S. Olympic committee reception staged partly in our honour. The committee members were over the moon with the Games to this point, particularly the hot start their athletes had got off to. There was a fantastic energy in the room. It made me feel better.

The big event that night for me was attending the first victory ceremony at BC Place Stadium. Jenn Heil would be getting her silver medal. Dave Cobb and I got over to the stadium a bit early. There was already a frisson of excitement in the building. Soon there would be 24,000 people filling the seats of the amphitheatre that we had designed for the celebration. The place looked spectacular.

But before Jenn had a chance to take to the stage, there was a commotion around one of the television sets in the area where we were standing. We went over to see what all the fuss was about. By now people were cheering and waving their hands in the air. Alexandre Bilodeau of Montreal had just won Canada's first gold medal on home soil. I wanted to drop to my knees in thankful prayer.

Alexandre had not been a medal favourite in men's moguls, but he turned in a performance of a lifetime on a miserable night on Cypress Mountain to give the country a wonderfully historic moment. What made it even more special was the warm human drama that was playing out around the victory. Waiting at the bottom of the hill on Alexandre's gold-medal run was his older brother, Frédéric, who suffers from cerebral palsy.

The image of a jubilant Frédéric cheering his brother's victory brought many Canadians to tears that night, including this Canadian. The story of the incredible bond the brothers enjoyed would be shared with the nation over the next several days as Alexandre, often with Frédéric in tow, went from one media interview to another. The Vancouver *Province* headline the next morning was perfect: "Alexandre the Great" it exclaimed. And he *was* great.

I was thrilled that such an incredible honour, the first gold in Canada, had been bestowed on such a worthy young man, someone who truly was a perfect role model for children around the country and who embodied everything that was good about sport. In fact, the victory and the tale around it represented the very best of what sport could be.

I was happy too for Quebec. It had developed so many great amateur athletes because it took amateur sports seriously and funded programs properly. Alexandre would be just the first of many French Canadians at the Games who would leave with a medal, including more gold. So I was happy that the people of Quebec, some of whom may have felt slighted by the opening ceremonies, would be dancing in the streets Sunday night and well into the following week. They had a new hero.

And selfishly, I was happy for the hard-working men and women at VANOC and the thousands and thousands of Blue Jackets. They all desperately needed some good news to help lift the gloom and this was it. If I could have somehow transported myself to Cypress Mountain at that moment, I would have sprinted over to Alexandre and given him the biggest hug he'd ever known. The entire nation wanted to hug the likeable 22-year-old.

After that, watching Jenn Heil get her silver medal was even more special. People in the stadium knew what had happened on Cypress by then, so the mood was buoyant. Everyone gave Jenn such a hearty, deserving ovation. The stadium rocked in her honour.

After it was over, Dave Cobb and I decided we'd walk back in the direction of the cauldron to see how things were looking there and on the streets. We hadn't yet fixed the viewing situation but would in a few days. By the time we got out of the stadium, the area around it was a mass of revellers. Even though it was raining the walk was fun. There were people everywhere, hooting and hollering. Young women on the shoulders of young men. The streets were rivers of red and white. I must have been stopped a hundred times for pictures. Dave became a go-to photographer, laughing away at the atmosphere building around us. Happiness was breaking out everywhere.

The news about Alexandre had evidently gone forth. Gold. Pure gold.

To say that this passion was nice to see was more than an understatement. I was praying that we were at the start of a turnaround. The day the story line began to change. But before I got too far in my thoughts I reminded myself that the next morning I would be brought back to earth—hard. I would be attending a memorial service for Nodar, as a pallbearer.

11

The Sun **Finally** Shines

WHEN I WALKED into the funeral home on Kingsway Street in Vancouver that Monday morning, I turned the corner into a modest, quiet chapel where a number of people had gathered. It's there that I saw the open casket with the still, athletic young body of Nodar Kumaritashvili lying inside, dressed in a dark suit he might have worn at his high school graduation.

A memorial service for Nodar had been put together over the weekend. It was a closed, intimate gathering of about 25 or so, including a few teammates and coaches from Georgia and some other athletes and Olympic officials. My old Irish friend Pat Hickey, now the head of the European Olympic Committees and a close friend of the Georgians, was there. While Pat had apparently offered to represent Jacques Rogge and the IOC, I thought the president might have been there himself.

The last time I had seen a body in an open casket was at my mother's funeral. I went up to Nodar's casket, touched his hand and quietly paid my respects. There was little evidence of the traumatic event that had cost him his life. It was difficult not to look at Nodar and think that just over 72 hours earlier he had been laughing and joking with his teammates, completely absorbing his experience in Whistler. He had undoubtedly been a little nervous and excited about the training run he had in front of him, a kid yet to enter the prime of his life. Now he was lying in this casket, far away from the excitement of the Games, surrounded by just a few. It was all too much to accept.

Nodar's uncle Felix was there, looking much like I had seen him on Saturday: broken, haunted, sad, lost. His difficult life had become that much more difficult. Private as the service was supposed to be, the funeral chapel started to fill up with Georgian Canadians who had come to support the young man. People came in and went up to the casket, some touching the body. There were quiet tears running down the faces of more than one person in the room; others sobbed uncontrollably. Some people dropped off flowers and left. Others knelt and prayed. Most wore black.

There was a short service. A minister offered a few informal words of comfort and prayers. When he was finished the coffin was sealed and I lined up to be one of the pallbearers who would wheel and then lift the hardwood coffin out to the waiting hearse. Pat Hickey was another one of the pallbearers. We were joined by some of Nodar's teammates, including the two who had grown up with the young luger and been in his class at school. I was struck by how heavy the casket was, even for the eight of us.

We walked outside into another grey morning. A light drizzle had earlier coated the streets with a fine sheen. But the rain had stopped during the service, so those who had been waiting outside to pay their respects were able to stay dry. Most were from the local Georgian community, but there were reporters there too and lots of cameras.

A squad of Vancouver police officers on motorcycles was lined up on the street about 30 metres to the west of the funeral home. They had come impromptu to escort the hearse from the service to the airport, where the body would be loaded onto a plane to be flown back to Georgia, escorted by the president of the Georgian National Olympic Committee. The officers were lined up perfectly in their bright yellow jackets and saluted the coffin as it came out, which I thought was incredibly moving and professional and spoke so well about our police forces in Canada. I crossed over to the officers to shake their hands. I just wanted to say thanks, on behalf of VANOC but really on behalf of all Canadians, for the remarkable service they were performing that morning. Such a spirit of giving.

As I shook their hands, I noticed the most remarkable thing: almost to a person the officers had tears in their eyes. It almost made me start crying. Here were these officers who put their lives on the line every day, some of the toughest individuals you'll find on the planet, and they were standing there in the rain shedding a tear for this kid from Georgia who had died in pursuit of a dream.

I was so proud of them that I wanted to embrace each one. Here we were in the middle of this nightmare, coming off this terrible weekend, and everyone outside the funeral home was feeling the same. These police officers wanted to do something, make a contribution in some way, and this is how they had decided to do it.

It was a profound moment. It said so much about our country and the people who make it what it is. Empathy is never in short supply in Canada. And we are a country that does not shirk its responsibilities. We help people. We show kindness. We do what's right. And that's what these officers were doing. Not because they were asked—they just felt it was right.

In the background that morning, I could hear a quiet rumble growing across the country, a low growl of encouragement. Canada was proud, I think, of the way we had responded to an extremely difficult situation. The Games would be dedicated to the spirit of Nodar and all the athletes like him. But Canadians wanted these Games to be great, they wanted us to shake off the criticism and courageously forge ahead. In some ways, we were like a hockey team that had fallen behind early in a game and now the crowd was encouraging us. It was a slow, silent cheer but it would be heard loud and clear later on.

When I hopped into the car after the service, I wanted everybody to be quiet. It was thinking time. The experience that morning would stay with me and ultimately inspire me to speak out on behalf of Canadians everywhere who were tiring of the attacks we were under, mostly from foreign media. But that chance wouldn't come immediately.

Soon enough, I was heading to the Main Press Centre, where I would meet the media for the first time since the news conference on that first Friday with Jacques.

As usual, I had Renee Smith-Valade beside me on the podium in the press room. Renee was the primary media spokesperson for VANOC and would be our representative at the daily news conference that was held throughout the Olympics. Some days she needed a Kevlar vest, the questioning was so tough. But she handled it like the complete pro that she was, in both official languages; her French flawless.

On this Monday morning, I was joined in the news conference by Quebec Premier Jean Charest. It was Quebec Day at the Games, something each province and territory was allocated as part of the partnership agreements we had signed with them earlier. He was still beaming from Alexandre Bilodeau's gold medal victory of the night before.

Inside the press conference room, a couple hundred journalists from Canada and around the world were waiting for us. It was an intimidating setting, no question. There was a bank of cameras stretched across the back of the room ready to catch every single breath we took. I had learned enough about the media that I knew everyone, especially in television, was looking for that one provocative statement, maybe a slip of the tongue, that reporters could hang their stories on. Body language was everything.

After congratulating Alexandre and the province of Quebec, I spoke for a few minutes about Nodar's memorial service. I noted how the body was on its way home. I talked a bit about our ongoing challenges up at Cypress. Jean talked for a few minutes about Quebec Day and also acknowledged Alexandre's historic win. Then it was time for questions.

The first one was for me. It was posed by a burly guy sitting right at the front. He had a shock of white hair and a white beard to match. It was Réjean Tremblay, a popular and influential columnist with *La Presse*. As I recall, he asked a question of me in French and asked that I answer it in French as well, a cheap shot intended to put me off balance.

So this is how it's going to be, I thought.

It was perhaps fitting that on Quebec Day the question of French content in the opening ceremonies would dominate the news conference. Not that anyone outside Quebec was much interested in the topic, but Réjean and another writer from Quebec did a pretty good job of monopolizing a good chunk of the time set aside for queries.

While I certainly had handled all types of questions in my time with the Olympics, I had rarely faced a journalist who was as hostile and surgical as Réjean was that morning. He wanted to know why there wasn't more French content in the opening and wasn't satisfied with any answer that I gave. So he continued to ask the same question several different ways, in an increasingly belligerent tone, until he elicited sighs from other journalists in the room who were as tired of the line of inquiry as I was.

Tempting as it was to take a run at the lack of cooperation we had received in Quebec trying to secure talent and music rights, I chose to take the high road instead.

It was a dead certainty that the pair were going to put Jean Charest on the spot and ask him what he thought of the opening. I knew what Jean was going to say. He loved the show but was disappointed and wished there had been more French throughout the production, though he was happy with VANOC's effort overall to promote and respect French Canada at the Olympics. If he hadn't said there should have been more French in the opening, he would have been fried by Réjean in his next widely read column, which would have led to some piling on by others in Quebec. That's how the media game often works. So I wasn't really upset that the premier said what he said. He had little choice. He was far from being an adversary.

But the French journalists wanted me to apologize for the opening and I refused. I said we had nothing to apologize for and that I was proud of the measures we had taken both during the opening and throughout the organizing of the Games to promote Canada's other language. I sure wasn't going to say sorry. "What we tried to do was include all the elements that we needed to do at various levels—words, music, artists," I said. "Let me be clear about what we are trying to do here—we are putting on the Olympic Games. It is a 17-day project and there are multiple, multiple layers." The show was unmistakably Canadian to any observer, I explained, and the global coverage was incredibly favourable and glowing with praise.

Eventually, we were able to move on to other topics, but the first 20 minutes or so of the press conference was no fun at all. It took every ounce of discipline in my body not to sound off and let the world know that this was trumped-up, pseudo-political opportunism intended to embarrass. But I remained composed, answered the questions the best I could and waited for the conversation to change.

Afterward, however, I was steaming at those who were attacking us about the French content for purely political reasons, a group that included federal Heritage Minister James Moore. Canada's Commissioner of Official Languages, Graham Fraser, also jumped on the bandwagon, announcing he would investigate the complaints that there wasn't enough French content in the show.

An investigation? This had to be some kind of joke.

The sum total of complaints Fraser had received, we were told, was about 30. Unlike his predecessor in the role, who had been a great collaborator and supporter of our efforts, Mr. Fraser pointed fingers from a distance but rarely pitched in with ideas or support. I told him more than once that his approach was not helpful and asked him to identify any project he had experience with that had outperformed us—he did not have one. Privately, he would tell me how impressed he was but in front of a parliamentary or senate committee he would bail on us. So proud was I of our efforts to deliver a bilingual Games, I invited Parliament and Senate committees for official languages to visit us and see what we were doing. We received no response.

Later that day, the Quebec government was hosting a reception at Quebec House, which was in a sparkling and innovative temporary building on the shores of False Creek, across from the Athletes' Village. Under the circumstances, it wasn't an event I was dying to attend. I knew it would be awkward from the moment I got there. But I'd be damned if I was going to be intimidated into not going. I wasn't going to run from anybody. Quebec had been our first provincial partner. Jean Charest had been there for us from the beginning, his mild but reasoned criticism of our opening aside.

When I arrived, the atmosphere inside was terrific. People were in a great mood, still high from Alexandre's gold medal run. Although no one was saying anything to me directly, I could feel the French controversy floating above the crowd. I wasn't there long before I saw James Moore heading toward me. James is a big guy you can see from anywhere. He has jet black hair combed straight back and always reminds me of someone from the cast of *Mad Men*. He was smiling. I doubt I was.

We shook hands.

"You're probably a little annoyed at me," James said, almost right off the bat.

"Well, I was certainly disappointed by your comments, no question," I said.

"Well, I hope you understand that I was just doing my job," James answered. "This isn't anything personal."

I told him I understood he was doing his job, but if he was going to criticize us I thought he at least needed to put the matter in context. When James was appointed Secretary of State for the 2010 Olympics, we gave him insider access to virtually all of our decisions. He was certainly aware of some of the challenges we had had trying to inject French content into the opening. And he knew about the myriad of other things we had done as an organization to reflect the French culture and influence in Canada, initiatives for which we had won wide praise. Instead, he just dumped on us for the lack of French in the opening, when we were still reeling from the death of Nodar. His timing was impeccable.

"You should know, James, that the number of people who are bilingual and working for VANOC is dramatically higher on a percentage basis than the number of bilingual people working for the federal government in Vancouver," I said, as I had many times before.

"I don't doubt it," he said.

The truth was the number of bilingual volunteers we had amassed to deliver the Games was equal in size to a mid-size Canadian town. By any measure, we had moved heaven and earth to live up to this obligation. And he knew it.

"James," I said, "I briefed you in person on this stuff and you had my direct line. All you had to do was pick up the phone and talk to me first and I might have helped give you a little background to everything that was going on to get French content into the opening. You are our partner and we deserved better. That's all I ask for. Just give us a chance to explain our side of the story before you go out there and attack us for not doing enough. I thought you were completely unfair. And frankly I didn't appreciate waking up Saturday morning and reading what you had to say in the paper."

By Monday there was mounting pressure from commentators like Réjean Tremblay and representatives from other cultural organizations to increase the amount of French content in the closing ceremonies to make up for the perceived lack in the opening.

Ironically, Réjean was in the crowd at the Quebec House reception too. We spoke and he told me he was just "doing his job" when he ripped into me at the press conference. And then he went on to say that, the ceremonies aside, he was having a perfectly bilingual experience and that these were the best Games he had ever experienced as a journalist. Too bad he hadn't put any of that in his column.

You can imagine how thrilled we were about demands for the closing ceremonies to incorporate more French. I phoned David Atkins to warn him about what was being said because it was going to reach him sooner or later. David was even more annoyed than I was. What did people honestly think? That we could be changing acts and inserting new production numbers at the last minute to suit the tastes of a few aggrieved people? I couldn't agree more with David. The show was long since ready to air.

It would be one of the biggest shows ever produced in Canada. It had been carefully put together over a couple of years. Rehearsals had been going on for months and would be ramped up throughout the course of the Games. The artists had already arrived and were rehearsing. All of the songs had already been recorded. Compact discs with all of the music would be coming out five minutes after the closing ceremony ended. Now people wanted us to just kick someone out of the lineup and insert someone who sang in French?

I knew already that there was more French in the closing than the opening. That was just how it was put together. But I couldn't be more specific without spoiling the surprise. Still, publicly I needed to be seen as listening to the complaints. I did not want to come across as rude or arrogant. But the matter was becoming a big problem because it was zapping energy out of our ceremonies team, who were already running on empty. And David Atkins was ready to blow a gasket at any moment.

I was hearing that we might soon be getting a call from the Prime Minister's Office about the matter. When I heard this I thought, "Okay, that's enough. I've got to put an end to this now." I managed to track down the number for the PMO through a friend. I told the woman who answered the phone that I needed to talk to the prime minister.

"Who is this?" she said.

"This is John Furlong," I replied. "I'm the chief executive officer of the Winter Games in Vancouver and this is a matter of considerable urgency."

The woman asked me what did urgent mean? Today? Tomorrow?

"No," I said. "Right now. I need to talk to the prime minister right now. This is a significant matter related to the delivery of the Games."

She said she would go and find out what his schedule was and get back to me. It couldn't have been more than a half-hour later when my cellphone rang. The voice on the other end said, "The prime minister would like to talk to you."

Deep breath.

I thanked Stephen Harper for calling me back and began outlining the predicament VANOC was facing generally but more so as it related to potentially making changes to the closing ceremonies to include more French content. I wanted him to know that we cared greatly about this issue and always had. I told him that there was going to be more French in the closing as it was and then explained what had happened with some of our attempts to beef up the French content in the opening. I also shared my thoughts with him about some of the personal criticism I was receiving for my efforts to speak French in my opening night address.

One blog I came across accidentally was merciless in its attack on me. "John Furlong's attempt at French was a disgraceful symbol of bilingualism," the person wrote. And for good measure he said my attempt at our second language was "atrocious" and "disgusting." Boy, that made me feel good.

I shared my frustration about this with the prime minister, whom I saw as an introverted and private man, just as I am. "This is not my language," I told him. "This is very, very difficult, sometimes terrifying for me."

The prime minister couldn't have been more thoughtful and sympathetic. "I've had the same challenge in my own career," he said. "I've had it my whole political life."

He told me that one of the ways he managed around it was to speak French early in his remarks. He found that francophones were more respectful when people made an attempt at French early on in such a situation. "This is the advice I would give you," he said. "Put the French up front and people will cheer you for it. Don't worry about the critics. The people in Quebec will be delighted that you made the effort. It's all about effort."

"But prime minister," I said. "You're a rock star at this compared to me. This is not comfortable for me. I look down at my notes and the words start moving on me."

He chuckled but was generous with his support and assurances.

We talked a bit about the demands for more French in the closing. I outlined the logistical realities of changing up the show at this late stage. He knew we weren't going to be making any big changes. "Do your best," he said to me. "Whenever there is an opportunity to include the spoken word in French put it in there. Just see what you can do. I know it will be wonderful and you guys will do a terrific job. The country is very proud of you. I'm really looking forward to it."

I explained that having our partners criticizing us over French content was making life very uncomfortable for a lot of people who were doing their damndest to make the country proud. Morale was suffering. I felt he heard what I was saying.

It was a great conversation, and the prime minister made me feel a whole lot better about the situation. To be honest, throughout the entire Games I thought Stephen Harper was a real leader and brought a great spirit to the Olympics. Just seeing him there cheering madly, living every moment as if he himself were playing, was reassuring. He certainly played his part with class and looked good in red. If he had been distant and unsure about the Games at one time he had morphed into a rabid supporter.

I wasn't quite finished with James Moore though. After the reception at Quebec House I would have a couple more conversations with him. And I was no less annoyed about the whole controversy.

"James," I said at one point, "we're partners, for God's sake. I mean, I'd never do this to you guys. I'd never get up publicly and say bad things about the federal government. I have never once criticized you guys for anything. I have always been thoughtful and respectful. And who, exactly, is benefiting from all this, James? People from all over the world are looking over our fence and we're fighting with each other. How does that look? We had the best opening ceremony imaginable and we're arguing about this and the world is watching."

And that was pretty much the last time we talked about it. I think the conversation with the prime minister had an effect because shortly thereafter the matter seemed to vaporize. When people approached James Moore looking for a quote he began telling reporters that there was nothing more to say and that the controversy was overblown.

(The only other time French was an issue was after the Games were over. We decided to send MPs, B.C. MLAs, senators and municipal council members from the host communities each a letter with a souvenir volunteer's Blue Jacket to thank them for their support over the years. I just wanted them to feel appreciated, and we had the inventory so the gesture wasn't coming at any extra cost. Universally the reaction was heart-felt, with one exception: the Bloc Québécois sent us a letter telling us that if we did not rewrite our letter to their members in French they would return all the jackets to us. The matter got resolved and they kept the jackets, but it was a final shot that didn't show a lot of class.)

THAT NIGHT, DAVE COBB and I went back to BC Place Stadium to watch Alexandre Bilodeau receive his gold medal. The morning papers had wall-to-wall coverage of his wonderful victory of the night before. The kid had taken a pretty significant monkey off the country's back and was getting the recognition he deserved for the honour. It seemed every time I looked at a television monitor, no matter where I was, they were replaying Alexandre's fabulous run that cinched first place. Displays of patriotism were breaking out all over the place. Delighted fans were soaking it up.

After it was over, Dave and I decided to take another walk outside and see what it was like on the streets. It was even wilder than it had been the night before. We made our way slowly along Robson Street, one of the streets that bisects the downtown core. A part of it had been closed to traffic and had subsequently become a non-stop party zone. Our own Red Square. Most days you could barely move on the street and on those around it. And it was no different on this Monday night. I was surprised by the number of people who seemed to know who I was. But people were coming up again and again and asking to get their pictures taken with me. Being treated like a celebrity in such a genuine way was touching, but I must admit it also felt awkward and embarrassing for someone as naturally shy and introverted as I am.

That said, to feel such positive energy from people was uplifting. Dave and I revelled in that walk, laughing and joking with perfect strangers. It was such a refreshing contrast to the negativity that I had been dealing with over the last few days. It was almost as if there were two worlds: the one inside the media bubble that was pretty grim, even hostile, and this other one, the one in the streets and at the venues that was completely different. People there were happy and having a great time, seemingly unaware of all the so-called controversies and brush fires that were flaring up all over the place.

Another fact that confirmed my two-worlds theory was the number of Canadians who had tuned in to watch Jenn Heil's medal ceremony the night before: about 8 million, give or take a few thousand. That was a stunning number, and the first time I remember thinking that the country was riveted by what was going on. They were tuning in the action and tuning out all the background noise about cauldrons and problems with buses, among other things.

I remember turning the corner to go down one street on that Monday night where the crowd was particularly dense and boisterous. A number of police officers were there. Dave and I stood back to see how the police were handling what was potentially a dicey situation. But they didn't have to worry. People were in such a great mood, and so were the officers. The fans were high-fiving the cops, shaking their hands, giving them hugs. People were getting their pictures taken with them. These were the same streets where in 1994 hundreds of people rioted after the Vancouver Canucks lost out in the Stanley Cup finals to the New York Rangers. The Olympic crowd couldn't have been more different. It was reaffirming to see. And no one seemed to mind that it was raining, though not nearly as hard as the night before.

If the streets of Vancouver and Whistler seemed like global gathering places full of delirious energy, the biggest Cultural Olympiad ever mounted deserved credit for fuelling much of the jubilation. The Cultural team led by Burke Taylor had magically woven together a pan-Canadian showcase of the best talent the country had to offer—on a shoestring budget. Over 2 million people attended events ranging from theatre and dance to music and film that highlighted the rich cultural diversity of Canada.

Performers also came from around the world, led by the Russians and the British, who arrived to give us a taste of what was to come at their Games. For Aboriginal Canada the Cultural Olympiad was a coming-out party. There was something for everyone and every facility that looked remotely like a staging area was used, and all were filled to bursting every night. Unique pavilions were erected to showcase Canada's many regions, and we cannot forget the 22,000 that crammed into the stadium every night to watch medals presentations and attend concerts.

BY TUESDAY OF that first week, the French controversy seemed to be behind us. But we had developed a problem with an Olympia ice-cleaning machine at the Richmond Oval and were having to truck a Zamboni—Olympia's rival—in from Calgary. We knew the media were going to have fun with that at our expense. We would also have to cancel more standing room tickets for Cypress—20,000 in fact. We hated to do it, of course, but the weather threatened to make the area where the spectators were to stand unstable. The last thing we needed was a serious injury. Combined with the 8,000 tickets previously cancelled a total of 28,000 tickets had to be refunded.

As I say, we felt horrible about it. But that is the nature of the Olympics, especially ones held in winter, when the weather can always wreak havoc. At the Calgary Games in 1988, 130,000 tickets had to be cancelled due to high winds. In Nagano 10 years later, 59,000 tickets had to be refunded because of rain and fog. One event had to take place with no spectators. So this sort of stuff was known to happen. It just seemed that given everything else that was going on, the ticket cancellations were being given bigger play than the story might have otherwise deserved.

Contrary to what the media were saying, I felt that we were quietly building some momentum. Many of the problems that had plagued us at the start were either solved or being addressed. Even though I refused to believe it, we were being told that good weather was on the way. What a break that would be. No place is as beautiful as Vancouver under sunny skies. And what wouldn't a little sunshine do to people's attitudes and dispositions? So, I definitely felt that by Tuesday we had turned a bit of a corner, even if the media, especially the British press, didn't want to. That was their problem.

I was stunned by the number of people who were e-mailing and texting me. Complete strangers. I had no idea how they even dug up my e-mail address, but somehow they did and they all seemed to want to tell me what a wonderful time they were having. They were people from all over the world. Some came from the United States. There were lots of Irish well-wishers, a few Aussies and even a bunch from England—decent folk angry as hell with their own press.

If I heard it once, I heard it a thousand times: thanks for making us feel so welcome and giving us such a truly wonderful experience, the e-mails said. But the majority of the notes came from Canadians who wanted to tell me that they had never felt more proud of their country. These were rank-and-file Canucks who badly wanted us to succeed, who were in their living rooms, or roaming the streets of Vancouver, who were cheering for us, in some cases loudly, in other cases quietly, but cheering us on and giving us their unqualified support.

Still, it was going to be important now to make sure we stayed on top of any potential issues and addressed them before they became something to write about. That was my message each day to my executive: Maintain a keen focus. Take nothing for granted. Let's look two and three days down the road and be dead certain we're not missing anything in terms of potential new land mines. If we felt there was going to be greater pressure on the transportation system on a certain day, we'd put more buses on the road. Cost aside, it would be far better to have too many of them than too few. It didn't matter how small an issue was, if it had the potential to bite us we had to deal with it. Service levels had to be maintained, so if we heard about some grumbling by volunteers about the lack of food at a particular venue we were all over it. The last thing we wanted was a bunch of Blue Jackets leaving us or losing their spirit.

For me, there were few things as important on my to-do list as getting out to as many venues as possible and thanking as many of our 25,000 volunteers as possible. You could have the best executive team in the world, the finest infrastructure, the most bulletproof plans, but if you didn't have a happy volunteer force you had problems.

I remember during the planning process having serious discussions about volunteers and exactly how many we were going to need. There were those who believed we were going to need far more than we ended up settling on because we had to factor in an attrition rate of 20 to 30 per cent. I found these predictions annoying. It was felt that a number of people would find the work too taxing, too unpleasant, especially if the weather was lousy, and they would pack it in after a while. After all, some of the jobs were menial and away from the limelight. Probably some would say, no thanks, I'm out of here. And many might not even give notice. They just wouldn't show up one day and you would be scrambling to find a replacement.

I refused to believe that we'd lose that many. I thought we'd have to be doing a pretty lousy job as an organizing committee to have that many people desert us. But a few of my colleagues insisted that it happened at every Games. It happened in Turin. It happened in Athens and Salt Lake. It happened at Games before those. I would say: we're not them. Canadians don't do that sort of thing. When they take on a job they stick with it until it's finished. It's not in our DNA to leave a task unfinished or to just walk out on somebody for no good reason. That is not the spirit on which this country was built, the spirit that allowed us to persevere and battle an often inhospitable climate. Canadians are better than that.

I was also of the view that to be Canadian was to give—I'd certainly seen enough evidence in my time in Canada to believe that was true. Once or twice in frustration I asked my colleagues how they would feel if we recruited substitutes in the event one of them didn't show up to work. They'd be insulted. A volunteer is as reliable as anyone else in my book.

I did think, however, that we were going to need to look at volunteers a little differently than others perhaps had in the past and take great care of them. I thought we needed to regard the volunteer who was working in a parkade somewhere as someone who was absolutely crucial to the success of the Games—and we needed to communicate that to him or her. We needed to communicate to them all just how important the work they were doing was. They needed to be treated like family. And we needed to constantly thank them for it and look after them and make sure they were being fed properly. That was our obligation to them.

I was going to try and do my part by hopping out of my car whenever I could to go up to any Blue Jacket I saw, to thank them for the wonderful sacrifice they were making in the name of their country. And it's with the greatest amount of humility that I say that all the volunteers I talked to seemed delighted when I approached them to say thanks and give them a hug or a pat on the back. They were happy to be so openly respected and appreciated. I remember going up to Cypress Mountain or out to the Callaghan Valley where the cross-country ski races and the ski jumping were taking place, and some days it was pretty darn cold with biting rain coming down, and there would be the Blue Jackets, braving it all, with smiles on their faces. If I have one regret it's that I missed some people during my rounds.

There was occasional grousing by the odd Blue Jacket about the lack or quality of food at some of the venues. When that happened, it was our problem and we fixed it. We did lose a few when all was said and done, but the numbers were minuscule. They were loyal to the Games and each other.

By late Tuesday, I had talked to enough volunteers to know that while they were doing their jobs and were mostly happy, there was a bit of resentment about the way the Games were being perceived by the international media in particular and about how even though so much was going right, the local media seemed preoccupied with what the foreign media, and especially the British press, was saying about us. I could tell this criticism was threatening to undermine morale.

Although I was not sure what exactly to do about it, I decided that night that I wasn't going to let it go on any longer without some sort of action. I needed to address what these reporters were saying, to take them on and challenge some of these British organizations to defend the stories they were publishing. I wanted people throughout our organization—all 50,000 of them—to see the optimism that I was feeling about the way the Games were going. They were waiting for us to fight back.

By this point, the *Guardian* had published a story suggesting our Games were a candidate to be "the worst ever held in Olympic history." Another British paper called them the "Calamity Games." The *Daily Mail* said we could now put our "Maple Leaf stamp on something more instantly tangible: the nondescript little box carrying the lifeless body of Nodar Kumaritashvili back to his home in Bakuriani, Georgia." People were writing this stuff, and other news organizations were printing it and validating it and shipping it all over the world, and the entire planet was talking about it.

It was suggested that some of these writers were taking vicarious shots at London 2012—a form of early target practice. The head of the London Olympic bid, Sebastian Coe, incensed at the British press, waded in more than once with rave reviews about the Vancouver experience, noting how London organizers would have their work cut out trying to match the celebratory atmosphere that had taken over the city. He said he was reading stories that bore no resemblance to what was actually happening. I obviously couldn't have agreed more.

The daily news conference was scheduled for 11:00 AM each morning in the imposing Gabriola conference room on the second floor of the Main Press Centre, a room decked out in the beautiful west coast look of the Games. I think that first Tuesday morning was the worst for Renee Smith-Valade, as reporters were still all over us for the cauldron-viewing situation, for which we were trying to secure a remedy. Unfortunately, Renee was not in a position at that point to announce the solution we were closing in on. So she had to sit there and absorb the punishment. I even had reporters who were there come up to me later and say they felt badly for her because of the abuse she took. It wasn't that reporters were being rude or personal. It was just that the questions were unrelenting, like being in a boxing ring and trying to bob and weave and duck the incoming blows knowing you were going to get tagged a few times.

So between the Tuesday news conference and the feeling I was picking up from my own executive team and the volunteers that somebody needed to stick up for the organization, I decided to make a surprise appearance at the regularly scheduled session on Wednesday morning.

Renee was aware that I was going to depart from our established protocol and was going to take the British media head-on. Normally, I was careful about what I said and what I didn't say. I hate the term "message box" but I was fairly good at staying within the parameters of whatever it was I was supposed to be talking about on any given day. I never took a reporter for granted and let my guard down much.

Renee knew she could count on me not to blurt out something that was going to create more problems for us. She also knew that I was going to speak the truth, or at least what I saw as the truth. If I didn't stand up for our organization who would? And I knew that there were members of the local media who also felt we weren't being treated fairly by the Brits. They shrugged it off as the way the British media worked: they yellowed things up, torqued up the most mundane events, to sell newspapers. It was a tried and true formula that British media had been using for years. Bottom-feeding, gutter talk, as my dad would say. Why would anyone expect them to make an exception with us?

I was aware that I had to be careful not to come across as arrogant or defensive. I wasn't going to try and absolve ourselves of blame in some of the problems that had occurred. There was criticism that was valid, the viewing area around the cauldron being one. We should have seen that coming. And then there was criticism that was not: the conditions on Cypress. Like we had any control over that. Okay, so only three legs of the cauldron came up during the opening ceremonies instead of four. This is a reason to smear a country internationally?

When we strode into the news conference room Wednesday morning, the media were surprised to see me. I think reporters were now anticipating some kind of announcement. I began by talking about how well I thought things were going. Yes, we had experienced some of the same teething problems that most Games endure at the beginning—transportation being one—but we had addressed them. What I wanted to impress upon the journalists in the room was the chasm that seemed to exist between some of the reporting and what was going on in the streets, at many of the pavilions that the provinces had set up and, most importantly, at the venues. I didn't make specific mention of the scathing reviews we were receiving from abroad. But to no one's surprise, I didn't have to wait long for a journalist to ask me about the British media's take on how the Games were going.

"I've read some things that I admit I didn't like reading and I don't believe are true or fair," I answered. "But having said that, when we make mistakes or when things don't go well, you have to fix them." I cited the cauldron as an example. But then I rhymed off a list of things that I thought were going well and perhaps were being overlooked by some of the media. The venues were sold out. The television audience numbers were astronomical. The athletes were raving about the experience. The downtown core was jammed. There had been none of the traffic chaos that had been predicted. In fact, the reverse was true. The city was operating beautifully.

"When I look at the first four or five days," I said, "I don't think there's anybody here and anyone in the city that would have been prepared to say 'I could have predicted this.' Today and yesterday were pretty darn good days and we're trying to build on that and show that we have the resilience and the thoughtfulness and the humility to manage the unexpected stuff that comes our way that is not welcome but that we have to deal with and will deal with. For me, one of the most pleasurable things that I've seen since we started is the quality of the sportsmanship in the crowd. People are embracing these young men and women who have come here from around the world." Canadian fans were rising to the occasion.

I said that I thought some of the criticism, especially from some of the British papers, had been manufactured nonsense that bore little resemblance to what was happening. Bad enough they were saying these things and that they were not true. Some of the writers were not even in the province but were blasting the way we were conducting business as if they were sitting in the bleachers. That was a bit much to stomach. As I talked, I could sense the mood shifting. Reporters wanted to cover my challenge of the British press. Even while I was talking, a request for an interview with me was coming in to Renee on her BlackBerry from the BBC.

I felt good about that news conference. I thought I had put the first four or five days in perspective. A month or so later, after the Games were long over, I received a lovely e-mail from a woman named Mary Conibear. Mary had a senior management role in the Main Operations Centre, which was based at VANOC headquarters on the east side of the city. It was our nerve centre, the place from which we kept an eye, literally, on everything going on at the Games. In her e-mail, Mary admitted to being quite down during the first four days of the Olympics. The criticism we faced was withering and morale destroying. Mary said that when she was at her lowest, I had come to a meeting at the MOC and told them that enough was enough, the media were ready to get on our side, we just needed them to report what was going on out there and show our stuff.

"That was the day you went to the press conference and in an unbelievably calm way straightened them out," Mary wrote. "We were literally cheering in the MOC like it was a sporting event. You'll never know how much that meant to me."

About 20 minutes after the Wednesday press conference I was sitting on a chair talking to James Pearce, a reporter with BBC Sport. We were on the northeast lower deck of the Broadcast Centre with the harbour and mountains in the background. He wanted me to reiterate some of the comments I had made at the news conference but also to use the opportunity to speak directly to our critics in the British papers. "We can't do this," Pearce told me before we began. "But we can give you a microphone so you can do it."

So I did. I told him that to read some of the comments that were being made about us in the *Guardian* and *Daily Mail*, among others, I had to wonder which Games these reporters were covering. James asked me a few more questions and then the camera was shut off. We chatted and he told me he understood my frustration. He marvelled at the atmosphere in the city. We shook hands and he promised to play my interview straight up and uncut. And he did.

I don't know if it was coincidence or what, but everything seemed to change that day. It was a turning point for us, no question. There would be little criticism after that morning. Instead, the focus would turn to how successful the Games were becoming. Reporters could feel the rumble of momentum building in the streets and in the living rooms of Canadians across the country.

And the sun came out. The glorious, glorious sun that we thought we might never see again. It made everyone feel better.

12

Owning the Podium

WITH MOST OF the early problems behind us—
although our fingers and toes would be always
crossed—the focus of Games coverage now
rightfully shifted to the athletes.

Alexandre Bilodeau had given the country the rarest of golden
moments for which it had long been waiting. And he'd conquered
Cypress Mountain to boot. In fact, in the first four days of competition, that mountain, our most vexing nemesis, had been exceedingly good to Canada's athletes. Besides Alexandre's gold, North
Vancouver's Maëlle Ricker also topped the podium in women's
snowboard cross, to the delight of a noisy cheering section of family and friends.

Cypress was also the scene of a couple of silver medal performances early in the Games, one being Jenn Heil's in moguls, the
other Mike Robertson's in men's snowboard cross. All four were
such stellar characters, such fine examples of athletes and young
citizens. There was so much to cheer for in all of their stories of
dedication and perseverance. The story behind Maëlle's gold medal

run was particularly meaningful to me as a Games organizer because of something not many people knew about at the time.

Maëlle had wonderfully supportive parents. Her mother, Nancy, was a retired biology professor. Her father, Karl, was a retired geologist. Karl had signed up to be a Blue Jacket during the Olympics and was assigned to Whistler to be part of the crew that got the mountain ready for competition each day. Karl became an invaluable member of his mountain-grooming crew. The day Maëlle was racing for gold, he was scheduled to be working on the mountain. His colleagues insisted that Karl take his shift off to go and see his daughter race. But Karl said that to do that would be letting his fellow volunteers down, so he decided to fulfill his obligations on the mountain. He missed Maëlle's wonderful run on Cypress but would hear all about it later. There was something in this story that embodied the spirit that existed among so many of our volunteers.

On Friday, the country had another gold and a truly iconic Canadian moment, thanks to one human fireball—Jon Montgomery. Jon was one of our top skeleton racers, yet not many were picking him to win at these Games. But underneath that mop of red hair and that unruly red beard beat the heart of a true champion. He had the run of his life and sure enough he ended up winning gold. It was on his way into the Whistler village afterward that he really cemented his place in the country's folklore.

Spectators and well-wishers had formed an honour guard that Jon walked through en route to the village square where he was scheduled to be interviewed by TSN. It was a beautiful clear night and everyone was screaming and yelling as Jon made his way through the crowd to TSN's outdoor stage. At one point, a woman with impeccable instincts handed Jon a pitcher of beer, and without missing a beat he began quaffing from the jug. After his first big swig, there was white foam all over his beard. The crowd ate it up. Heck, the country ate it up. Instant stardom: Canadians wouldn't be able to get enough of this charismatic prairie kid who wore a smile as wide as Saskatchewan throughout the Games. A day later, he would hop up on the podium at his victory celebration and endear himself to the country all over again with an off-key but full-throated rendition of "O Canada." What a character. A season earlier I had witnessed Jon at a media event in Whistler and noticed that look of steel in his eyes and thought there goes a real contender. And here he was now, the real McCoy, a new Canadian hero to whom we could all relate, with a gold medal hanging from his neck.

Saturday brought the first big hockey game of the Olympics for our men—Canada versus the United States. Many thought, and many prayed, that this was a prelude to the gold medal game. Certainly, NBC was hoping the two teams would compete. I had quietly hoped for Russia in the final, a clash of the traditional hockey superpowers—1972 all over again. While Canada was a clear gold medal candidate, along with the Russians, I thought the Americans would give us a good game. They have that "rise-to-the-occasion" mentality and never go away easily. The team's GM was Brian Burke, whose son Brendan had died tragically in a car accident shortly before the Games. He was bringing a broken heart to these Games. Brian was a tough, cagey guy and had spent much of the run-up to the Olympics playing down his team's chances of doing much, which should have been a signal to everyone that he thought the Americans had a great squad.

He was right.

I visited with Brian in a suite above the ice at Canada Hockey Place, where we grew to love him when he was GM of the Canucks. I wanted to welcome him home to Vancouver and express my regrets over his heartbreaking loss. As I opened the door I saw him sitting there studying his players, who were practising on the ice below. His face was red and puffy, evidence of some extremely hard nights in recent weeks. Here he was, I thought, a gladiator giving his team a lesson in life and showing the courage of 10 men.

We shared a few warm words of friendship and I wished him well. Walking down the hall, I thought that with Burkie in their corner the Americans were going to take everyone to the mat. And they did, starting with us.

With Martin Brodeur in net for Canada, the Americans played a great game, showing off their speed and exceptional goaltending. Ryan Miller was playing like the elite goaltender that he was. Canada ended up losing 5–3 and there were lots of sad, panicked faces in the arena and around the country after the game ended. I didn't share the pessimism. I thought the loss might have been just what we needed to shake off feelings of superiority or overconfidence our team might have had coming into the tournament.

Now the hockey tournament was starting to exhibit shades of Salt Lake in 2002, when the Canadian team that many thought was going to breeze through the preliminary round ran into trouble. But that adversity ended up being a good thing, something Wayne Gretzky would later credit for the team's gold medal. I thought the loss to the Americans represented the same opportunity for Canada. A chance to put things in perspective a bit and to demonstrate that nothing was going to be handed to this team. If it was going to win gold, it was going to have to earn every bit of it. The promise of real sporting drama was in the air and what could be the best Olympic hockey final ever was shaping up.

With that sobering loss to the U.S. and a few other hiccups, a definite nervousness, even anxiety, was beginning to surround the Canadian Olympic team as a whole. The Own the Podium program was coming under a new round of media scrutiny because a week into the Games our athletes weren't dominating the medal standings. Reporters began regurgitating quotes from the incoming Canadian Olympic Committee president, Marcel Aubut, who had said before the start of the Olympics that we would be good hosts but added, "These Games will be ours. We will own the podium." I loved the confidence he exuded but prayed the words wouldn't come back to bite Marcel, who would have pulled on a uniform himself to help the team win.

You could see and feel the pressure our athletes were under. It was evident in the voice of Mellisa Hollingsworth, who was seen as a medal cinch in women's skeleton. But when she failed to make the medal grade she crumbled emotionally, offering a tearful apology to the country for her performance. It was tough to watch. There were no apologies needed. She tried her heart out and on this particular day she just didn't have it—happens all the time in sport. I honestly thought it was a great sign because her tears were a manifestation of how badly our athletes wanted to win. They were in unison with Canadians everywhere who could see how hard the athletes were trying to give the country the success it was craving. This was the best of Canadian desire and humility all blended together.

By the end of the first week, Chris Rudge, the COC's outgoing chief executive officer, was telling reporters it was doubtful that we would finish in first place in the medal count, even though there was more than a week to go in the competition. The Americans, true to form, had jumped out to an impressive lead that Chris and others felt would be too hard to make up. I got wind of the fact that the COC was planning to hold a news conference to go public with its view that Canada was not going to "own the podium" as we had promised. When I heard this, I felt sick.

I thought holding a news conference would end up being a no-win race to the bottom and signal to our athletes that we were throwing in the towel on our ambitions to be number one. What kind of message did that send to the athletes who still had to compete? That we had no confidence in them? Besides, I didn't share the view that our team had performed that poorly, and when I looked at the schedule of events I saw a number of competitions left that we stood a great chance of medalling in. The people in the streets were positively euphoric about our successes so far, and to them a bugle-sounding retreat would seem ridiculous. Beyond that, however, I thought holding a news conference on the subject was completely unnecessary. Why prejudge what was going to happen? Why not just wait until the Games were over when we had something tangible to judge in the way of an overall performance?

I remember walking into the COC's offices at Canada Place around this time and I swear it was like walking into an Irish wake. Marcel was being the voice of optimism, whereas Chris Rudge and others seemed to be preparing for a gloomy proclamation of some sort. This was outside my mandate but I thought this news conference was a bad idea, and after biting hard on my lip for a while I decided to leave matters to them.

I thought that instead of casting the performance of our athletes in a negative light, we should be doing just the opposite, highlighting our biggest wins, especially on Cypress Mountain. We had won our first gold medal ever on Canadian soil—and they were going to hold a news conference that would generate stories about how poorly our athletes were doing. The last time an Olympics had been held in Canada we won five medals, total. Against that result we had crossed a great divide—big time.

As it turned out, the issue didn't explode into a huge story at the news conference, but a day later Chris was telling reporters we would likely fall short of our target. So in avoiding the first bullet we invited another. The Own the Podium program was about removing any obstacles standing between our athletes and their ability to perform at the top of their potential. To think every athlete we had was going to win was preposterous. On any given day in sports, anything can happen.

Kelly VanderBeek was one of our fiercest competitors in Alpine skiing and a real medal contender for Canada. She was a fearless human missile coming down that mountain. She had prepared exhaustively for these Games, and then the worst nightmare: she shattered her knee pouring herself into a race in Europe. Kelly would have climbed Everest on crutches to make the Olympic podium. But sports is full of this kind of misfortune. All she could do was watch and cheer and think about the next time.

Heartbreak is part of every athlete's story—and part of the story of every great competition like the Olympics.

THE IDEA OF the Own the Podium program had its genesis early in the Games' preparation. There was a view coming out of the Salt Lake City Olympics that the performance of the U.S. team there had helped the country embrace the Games in a way it might not have otherwise. At a time when Americans felt vulnerable because of 9/11, the performance of their athletes in Salt Lake gave them something to rally around. It was wonderful to see.

It was clear to us that no matter how we did as an organizing committee in Vancouver, to some degree our success would be determined by how our athletes performed. Even a flawless execution of the Games was not going to be enough to convince Canadians the whole exercise had been worth it. Canadians couldn't care less about how we got the buses to Whistler or if our technology was mind-blowing or if it was too cold in the media tent. To Canadians, the Olympics was about sports and athletes, full stop. In order to achieve our vision and have the country focus on the Games in the way we wanted, our Olympic team needed to be strong and confident. The strongest ever. Canadians needed to turn on their television sets and know the athletes' names as if they were family. They needed to hear "O Canada" played again and again and again. This was not something we had been able to achieve at past Olympic Winter Games.

It was after Salt Lake that I received a call from the COC's Chris Rudge asking me if we'd be interested in partnering with them in a study to look at what it would take for Canada to become the top-performing country at the 2010 Games as measured by the total number of medals. There had been discussions within the COC, largely led by the organization's wonderful director of sport, Mark Lowry, focusing on our performance in 2010. (Sadly, Mark passed away before he got to see the fruits of his genius.) Mark thought there was a way for us to achieve our greatest-ever success in Vancouver, even end up on top, if we applied ourselves fully. But it was going to take money and a plan and a realistic approach. A suggestion was made to have Cathy Priestner Allinger, a former Olympic medallist and seasoned, no-nonsense sport leader who had yet to join VANOC, put together a team and produce a report on what it would take to win the most medals at our Olympics.

The study was going to cost roughly $50,000. Chris Rudge phoned me to see if VANOC would pay half of the study's costs. He thought it would show good faith and demonstrate that VANOC and the COC were true partners. If we agreed on one thing it was that the athletes were the real key to the Games' success. My immediate thought was that although the cost was not huge, there was no way our board was going to approve the expenditure—at least not readily. But as I talked to Chris, I started to noodle the idea around a bit in my head. Given Canada's past performances at Winter Games, a knockout showing in Vancouver could be a game changer for the country. I also thought it was high time the athletes saw some real effort by the country's sport leaders to get them some winning tools. It was ridiculous to expect medals if we were trying to do it with Monopoly money and decade-old technology. Other winter sport nations like the United States, Germany and Norway had already turned winning into a science. To them, results mattered.

I told Chris I would take his proposal to the board, of which he was a member. There were six other COC members on it as well, and I knew I would have their support. The others I wasn't so sure about. Athlete support was usually left to the various national sport organizations, such as the COC. The organizing committees generally stayed out of this part of the Olympics. I felt we couldn't afford to.

When I made my pitch to the board, I tried to land the plane gently. I said that in my opinion the definition of success for us was going to be measured against three things: keeping our promises, delivering a great Games experience for athletes and spectators alike and performing well on the field of play. I believed that if our team didn't do well and haul home a lot of gold, Canadians were going to say, "Well, that was fun," but the experience and memory of the Games would evaporate in a nanosecond and the legacy potential would be lost. A generation of effort gone with little to show.

Despite my best sales pitch, a lot of board members were still not biting. They just didn't see supporting athletes as our job. A few thought I was out of line and felt we already had enough on our plate. They thought it was piling work on at a time when we barely had the capacity to handle what we had. They also wondered where it would go afterward. Would there be more costs? Ultimately, the board agreed to split the costs of the study. But that was as far as it was prepared to go—for now anyway.

Afterward, I said to Chris that the only way we were prepared to support the study was if the COC agreed that it would abide by whatever recommendations Cathy Priestner Allinger made. There would be no cherry-picking of ideas, no exceptions. It was all or nothing. We were going to go along with Cathy's proposals regardless of what they cost or we were out. Chris agreed.

Cathy assembled a small team to work on the project. A few months later she delivered her report, which analyzed every sport and how far we were away from gold, silver, bronze in each of them and what it was going to take to get onto the podium by 2010. Cathy costed out the equipment, coaching, travel, training and other things it would take to obtain our goal of being atop the podium. It wasn't going to be cheap: $110 million. For that sum we had a real shot, she said.

It was evident from the minute Cathy's report hit the table, and we digested the price tag associated with her recommendations, that there was no way the COC was going to be able to fund this venture by itself. I knew before anyone asked that VANOC was going to need to get involved to help bridge the funding gap. And once discussions began with the COC, it became clear we were going to have to find *all* of the money because it simply didn't have the funds to mount this kind of challenge. Even though the funding was going to be spread over five years, it was still a whopping $22 million a year. Where was it going to come from? I could barely get the VANOC board to agree to spend $25,000 on Cathy's study. How would we ever get it to support a decision to finance this endeavour?

It was going to take some creative thinking and a daring strategy, something out of an entirely new playbook. I believed the answer lay with our sponsors. Present the Games and the Olympic team to them as a package. Pitched properly, I thought they would all bite into the lure of helping create the greatest Canadian Olympic team ever. If it worked out the way Cathy Priestner Allinger envisioned, the sponsors that donated to Own the Podium would be able to declare victory alongside our athletes. Sure, this was not something that had been tried in the past, but I was discovering that sponsors liked the vision we were laying out and the performance of our team in Vancouver would be an important part of making sure that the big dream came true.

After the report came out and showed that winning was indeed possible, we had a fairly animated debate inside our own executive. Some sparks flew, to be sure. There was some nervousness about becoming a full-fledged partner in the plan. But vision ruled the day, and we went back to the board and told the directors that we simply had to find a way to make the findings in the report become a reality. If not us then who, I said to the board. Yes, even if it cost $110 million. So we pitched the idea of splitting the price tag with the federal government—without knowing, of course, if Ottawa would go along.

Beyond Jack and the seven COC directors, there was not what I would call resounding early support among the board. In fact, there was downright hostility from some. But I went back to my overarching theme: we had to make these Games more than just two weeks of sport. We had to make them about nation building and changing the country's view of itself. If our athletes failed, despite trying their best, it would make our mission almost impossible. Our dream would be lost. I really believed that. It was time to show some courage.

I also believed we could come up with the money because sponsors would want to have their name on the Own the Podium program. We debated the subject for a while longer before the majority of directors agreed to sign on with the plan, which, of course, was contingent on the feds going along with it. So that was one of our next hurdles—getting bureaucrats and ministers in Ottawa revved up about the idea. But there was one other potential stumbling block.

Anyone who had done a careful reading of Cathy's report would have noticed that it called for a big infusion of cash and effort in some sports and almost nothing for others. Cathy's feeling, after consulting with many experts, was you put your money squarely behind the sports you had the best chance of winning a medal in. This was a bit of a break from Canadian tradition, which often lacked that kind of cold, steely focus. For instance, she called for major bucks to be poured into our Alpine skiing program and next to nothing for ski jumping, a sport for which there was little culture in Canada. If we were going to be about winning in 2010, we had to give our best horses the best chance to win. No waste. Period.

This strategy was potentially going to complicate our conversation with the federal government. If we were going to convince Ottawa to fork over $55 million over five years, we had to go there united, that is, officials representing all the Winter sports federations had to be onside. If we had dissension, or if even one group claimed it was being discriminated against, the federal government would get nervous and shy away from the proposal. We arranged to have a meeting in Ottawa with Stephen Owen, the Liberal MP who was minister in charge of the Olympics at the time.

The day before the meeting, we got the group together for a strategy session in which I hammered home the unity message again. I said that in the past Ottawa had always been able to avoid these investments because we could never seem to show a united front. We were easy to dismiss. So everyone needed to understand that unless the group waved a green flag in the air signalling that the plan was a go, the government would sense there was a problem and back out. I guaranteed it, as did others.

I was also worried about what Sport Canada was going to say about the proposal. It had a huge influence over the outcome. Sport Canada was the federal department that advised the government on all matters related to amateur athletics. Ultimately, Stephen Owen would be getting a report from the federal agency on what to do about the funding request: grant or deny. At our strategy meeting that day was Tom Scrimger, director general of Sport Canada. It wasn't long into the discussion when I asked Tom what Sport Canada's vision was for the 2010 Games.

"Well," he said, "we don't have one."

"What do you mean, you don't have one?" I blurted. "You have to have one. I mean, surely you must be looking down the road at the Olympics and figuring out what Canada hopes to achieve."

I will never forget Tom's reply. "I don't have the luxury of being able to have a vision," he said. "That is for the minister, not me."

I nearly fell out of my chair.

"Tom," I continued, "you mean to tell me you don't have something, even something scribbled on a piece of paper somewhere and stuffed in a drawer, that says in a perfect world this is what we hope to achieve?" I could not believe he did not have his own bucket list of wishes to suggest to the minister.

Stephen Owen's political aide was in the room as well. He sat mostly expressionless. I was worried that we might be facing a situation in which Sport Canada really didn't believe in being part of the 2010 endeavour, which would mean a quick death for Own the Podium. I went back to my hotel room after the meeting and wasn't there long when the phone rang. It was Stephen Owen's assistant. He wanted to assure me that the minister had a vision for these Games and was a huge supporter. "I know what you heard today isn't what you wanted to hear," the young man said. "But don't be worried. The minister wants these Games to be a success. He has an open mind about the federal government's involvement and what form it might take, and if he believes in what you have to say he will fight for it."

I told him how relieved I was to hear that.

The next day, a group that included Cathy Priestner Allinger, Chris Rudge and representatives of all the sports sat down with Stephen Owen in a meeting room on Parliament Hill. I knew Stephen fairly well and considered him an ally of the Games. I thought that at the very least he would give us a fair hearing.

Cathy began by explaining the research behind her study and how she had reached the conclusions that she had. Hockey Canada's Wayne Russell spoke on behalf of the Winter sports federations, delivering the message of unity that was so important. And I finished by making the big pitch for the federal government's involvement, which outlined our overall vision and how Own the Podium meshed into it. You give us $55 million, I told the minister, and somehow we will come up with the rest. Fifty-fifty partners.

When Stephen took the floor, he began by telling us how impressed he'd been with Cathy's report. Good start. What he especially found intriguing about it was the possibility it held for being a test case of how to support high-level amateur sport in Canada. An important aspect of the plan was putting some sports on notice that they had to reach a certain threshold before they could expect big money for their athletes.

We were hoping Stephen would give us an answer within a few weeks because we needed to know where we stood with the program. He got back to us within days: yes, he said, we could count on Ottawa for the money. It was the fastest Ottawa turnaround I had ever heard of. What a huge victory for us—and one that may not have been given the prominence it deserved by the media. Without the federal government's support for this project, Lord knows where, or if, we could have mounted the program at all.

It was now going to be our very tall job to sell sponsors on the need for them to throw a little more cash in the kitty that could go toward Own the Podium and the national dream for our athletes that was embedded in our vision statement. I knew that if we could get a big opening sponsor donation toward OTP, the stage would be set for future ones. We needed a kingmaker. The $15 million that Bell Canada committed to its sponsor deal for OTP was just the tonic we were after. It sent the message that one very prominent and proud Canadian company was ready to stand up for the athletes. We had our champion. Every time a Canadian athlete mounted the podium Bell Canada could take a bow too.

As we moved along, I felt even more confident about what we were doing with OTP and our decision to get involved with funding the project, a place no organizing committee had so wholeheartedly gone before. I had to give Chris Rudge credit too, for kicking our door down. He knew the only chance of OTP coming to life was if we got involved. There was no way that the COC was going to raise $110,000, let alone $110 million. He realized that the spotlight was going to be on VANOC for the next five years, and we were the only ones who had the influence and leverage OTP needed. In the end, the federal government gave us some top-up money to help us meet the final target but it was mostly a 50–50 split.

With OTP we were going to try and ensure that for Vancouver things would be different, while recognizing that in an athletic competition anything can happen and there is no such thing as certainty. I think Chris Rudge might have said it best when he quoted that famous line of Victor Hugo's: "You can stop an advancing army but not an idea whose time has come." That's what Own the Podium was.

WHILE THE AMERICANS were having the Games of their lives in Vancouver, much to the relief of the NBC, whose Olympic coverage was enjoying a sky-high ratings bonanza, there was also something amazing going on in Canada. The country's focus on the Games was growing each day. It was topic number one at kitchen tables everywhere. It was certainly reflected in the stunning numbers that the CTV-led consortium was pulling in. But as the Olympics moved along, Canadians went from being casual watchers to full-time cheerleaders who were totally plugged in and experiencing every moment as if they too were on skates and skis. They got their pom-poms out and painted their faces, emptied their fridges and had the neighbours over to watch hockey, short-track speed skating, anything that included an Olympic athlete. This was an excitement you could feel from St. John's to Victoria.

Bars across the country were full at night with Canadians rooting for their athletes. There were impromptu Olympics parties being organized in thousands of living rooms across the nation. This phenomenon was becoming as big a story as the Games themselves, a national engagement the likes of which had only been witnessed a few times in the life of the nation.

Heading into the final week, I wanted us to be more vigilant about our preparation than ever. We could not afford to let our guard down. We needed to have a near-perfect run to the end. I wanted to make sure that our team didn't relax just because we seemed to be over the worst of the early hiccups and criticism, and because the tide of opinion was shifting in our favour.

I tried to get up to Whistler as often as I could. Every time I drove up there I marvelled at how beautiful and quick the drive was. Such stunning geography. Dick Ebersol of NBC Sports was right, I think, when he said that the only thing wrong with the road was that it wasn't long enough. I imagined what the athletes and visitors from around the world must have thought as they made their way past Howe Sound up into the mountains on a road vastly improved by the incredible work that had been done to make it wider and safer.

One of my favourite moments heading into the final week happened when I visited our medical clinic in Whistler. The death of Nodar was always in the air and was felt more profoundly by the people there than anywhere else in the Olympic environment, but when I saw them a week after the accident I sensed this horrible burden was lifting. They had fought so hard for him. These were amazing people, doctors, nurses, dentists, physiotherapists, who had taken time off from their jobs to volunteer to work at the clinic. And when I went up there to thank them, they seemed genuinely moved that I wanted to show respect for the contribution they were making on behalf of their country. To a person, they all said it was their privilege to be able to play a role in something that obviously meant so much to all Canadians.

Besides shaking the hands of as many Blue Jackets as I could, I also tried to take in some of the events in which we stood a solid chance of medalling. I was there when the Canadian women won another gold medal in hockey. What a juggernaut! Hayley Wickenheiser will surely go down as one of the greatest female athletes ever, a potential cauldron lighter the next time the Olympics return to Canada. I know there was a big deal made when the women returned to the ice after the gold medal game to drink a little champagne and light up a cigar or two. It never bothered me—just a media story more than anything, one that was horribly overblown. The girls were smart enough to offer a measured apology the next day to ensure the story died a quick death.

One of the most moving moments of the Games for me, and probably for Canadians across the country, was Joannie Rochette's skate in the long program in the women's figure skating final. Being an elite athlete is hard enough. The Olympics is a formidable, downright scary environment in which to compete. And figure skating, of all the Winter Olympic sports, has to be one of the most lonely, unforgiving, demanding and nerve-wracking. To skate with a clear mind in front of 15,000 people is hard enough. Having to do it with a broken heart is another thing entirely.

I don't think there was an athlete the nation cheered harder for than Joannie, after the country learned that her mother had died of heart failure shortly after arriving in Vancouver from Quebec to see her daughter compete. Many people thought it would all be too much for Joannie, that she'd never be able to pull off the incredibly difficult, complex jumps that are part of her routines. But Joannie gave one of the most amazing performances in Olympic history in the short program, which happened just days after her mother's death. And then for her to give another near flawless routine in the long program to win bronze was a stunning accomplishment. My five children were there that night. I watched them watch her. They were in awe, frozen with amazement. I thought that for years to come they would reflect on being present to see this real, raw human courage, the best example they would ever witness of how to face life's adversities head-on. Joannie Rochette is a rare kind of hero in my books, and to be there that night for her final skate was a transcendent experience.

It was clear as we headed into the home stretch that although we were not going to reach our goal of being atop the podium, our athletes were definitely starting to enjoy more success—everywhere. And so many great Canadian stories were being written in the process. Not many people were giving Jasey-Jay Anderson, a veteran of so many Olympics and Olympic disappointments, a chance in the men's parallel giant slalom. But with the support of a country at his back, he pulled off the unthinkable and won gold. We also won gold at the short track and our women took more gold in bobsleigh.

The country was captivated by the enthralling performance of Tessa Virtue and Scott Moir in the ice dance, another gold for Canada. The next morning they came to the Olympic cauldron for an interview with CTV, and I wandered over to share my happiness for them and tell them how proud we all were. Tessa, both classy and humble, held my hand warmly and told me she and Scott had sat in on an earlier presentation I had given where I had told the audience what the Games were going to do for our country. They both told me how I had inspired them to pour their hearts into these Olympics. That was a tall moment for me, with two beautiful Canadians who have inspired thousands of our youth to dream big.

And what more could be said about the amazing Clara Hughes, one of the finest Canadian Olympians ever, a woman whose first instinct is always to help others. What an inspiration! I can't wait to see what she does with the rest of her life—she has so much to offer. Her bronze in the ladies' 5000-metre speed skating event was such a wonderful capper to one of the truly great Olympic careers in our country's history.

I was in the crowd at Cypress when Ashleigh McIvor won gold in ski cross in front of a delirious crowd. A week earlier I had run into her and her boyfriend, teammate Chris Del Bosco, who was a medal hopeful in a men's event. They seemed so relaxed and happy. I stopped to see how they were doing and I could tell from Ashleigh's words, delivered in her modest way, that we were about to see something special from her. And we did. I think she visualized that golden moment a thousand times before it happened.

Despite the second-half surge by our athletes, there was still plenty of hand-wringing going on about the performance of the Canadian team. Forget first place, would we even finish in the top three, the media wondered. Chris Rudge seemed to be getting asked about Own the Podium just about every day. To me, it seemed bizarre that he was even having to defend it, but he was. By the end of the Games there weren't many who weren't giving OTP the credit for our best Olympics ever.

With just two days to go, it dawned on more than a few that a record medal haul was a possibility for Canada. All of a sudden history was there to be seized. We ended up winning 14 gold medals, the most ever by a host nation—and a total of 26 medals, also our best ever.

Outside of the field of play, the athletes were having the time of their lives. I made a point of visiting with them at the Athletes'

Villages in Whistler and Vancouver, and the competitors I talked to couldn't have been more complimentary about the experience they were having. The ones lucky enough to be staying in Vancouver were absolutely blown away by the accommodations, and why wouldn't they be? They were the most luxurious Olympic digs ever, with million-dollar views. No wonder so many athletes told me they didn't want to leave.

Both villages were in such contrast to the ones in Turin in 2006, where the rooms were drafty, there weren't enough blankets and the food was not good. We wanted to give the athletes the best experience. We wanted to make sure they were well protected while not suffocating them with our security arrangements. Time and again, the athletes would stop to be photographed with the police who embraced them so fully.

Everywhere I went now, whether it was to a competition, a medals ceremony, an event hosted by one of the provinces or a major sponsor, the feedback was the same: people were having the time of their lives. There wasn't a person who didn't seem happy, thrilled actually, that we had weathered the storms of the first few days and now had the wind at our backs. Even IOC members who had seemed to be hedging their bets in the early going, afraid to associate with an organizing committee that was having a few teething problems, couldn't say enough good things about us now. I could only smile and savour how hard my team had worked to pull it all together.

The downtown streets of Vancouver had become an Olympic lovefest, a huge organic party at which everyone was welcome. On the night our Canadian hockey women won their gold over their arch rival the U.S., I found myself standing on the second level of the International Broadcast Centre after doing an interview. I could hear the crowds outside singing "O Canada." Perfect strangers by the thousands, suddenly arm in arm, happy in the moment. Wild, happy patriotism was breaking out across the country. We were 34 million behaving as one.

During the closing days, every event seemed to top the one before it. Celebration Plaza in Whistler was electric every night as locals jammed every square metre of space. BC Place was at capacity every night as every athlete who arrived to collect his or her medal was treated as a hero. It didn't matter where they were from. Donald Sutherland, meanwhile, was like Waldo. He was everywhere. Wayne Gretzky too. Premier Campbell was running on empty cheering on the Olympic team from dawn to dark. Federal Sport Minister Gary Lunn was hoarse from screaming encouragements and the prime minister and Governor General were giving it all they had. It was as if the entire country was chasing something it wanted badly. The Games seemed to be touching everyone. Kings and queens, princes and princesses. Like a stone tossed into a pool of water, the Games were creating beautiful ripples.

The Games had become everything I had hoped for, if not more. The country had stopped what it was doing to put on its Team Canada jerseys and cheer. Every time I paused to think about the public's enthusiasm for even a second, I had to be careful.

It was easy to get overly emotional about what was taking place.

13

The **Closing** Curtain

A S LONG AND sometimes painful as the first few days felt, I was stunned at how quickly the Games were flying by. One day I was walking onstage to welcome the world to Vancouver and the next I was thinking about what I would say during the closing ceremonies.

I was physically and mentally exhausted by that point, but a full tank of adrenaline and nervous excitement were enough to keep me fuelled up. There was still a huge day to get through and a gold medal hockey game to watch. In other words, there was a lot still to happen on that closing Sunday, a lot that could still go terribly wrong and spoil the amazing atmosphere that had built up around the Games during the previous couple of weeks.

Dave Cobb and I met for breakfast at our usual time. All of a sudden, he was looking a little younger and less tense. We talked through preparations for the closing ceremonies, the potential for mayhem at the hockey final and the security and transportation arrangements that were going to be such a big part of the day's success. We also discussed the protest that was planned and the impact it might have on people's efforts to get to the ceremonies.

We did not want a repeat of what happened on opening day, when the best efforts of the police caused havoc to our transportation system. There were media obligations that I would need to take care of that morning, and there was an important 50-kilometre cross-country ski race in Whistler. A huge thing weighing on my mind was the speech I was going to have to give at the closing, particularly the French parts.

I planned to take the prime minister's advice and speak French as early in the speech as possible, but even his guidance and strategic suggestions weren't going to make it any easier. Some of the reviews from my effort during the opening were still blistering in my ears. I had received a little coaching over the previous couple of weeks on my pronunciation, but it was like trying to teach an English-speaking person Gaelic. I also didn't want to put words in the speech just because they might be easier to say. I wanted every word to have meaning, to count, to have earned its way into the speech. The more I thought about it all, the more stressed I got. Why hadn't I taken French more seriously in school?

But my primary mission in the speech was to thoughtfully convey, or at least attempt to convey, what had happened in the country over the previous 16 days. Yes, Canada had, at other times, celebrated loudly as a nation. But it said something about us, I think, that when you asked people about the last time they saw the country so elated, so proud, they often mentioned Canada's win over Russia in the 1972 hockey series. That was the last time we were so magically transfixed in every village, town and city at the same time over the same thing.

I don't think there's any question that the true personality of the country came out during the Games, and the entire world saw a side of us it didn't know was there. There were probably many who thought that we normally sober, self-effacing Canadians had received a personality transplant. However you describe the atmosphere, it was noticed and felt. Perhaps Jacques Rogge said it best when he said the IOC had never seen the Games embraced by its hosts on this scale before.

Never again were people going to say about Canadians that we were quiet, bashful, unpatriotic types. Never again were they going to say that we weren't flag wavers or that we weren't disposed to wearing our love of country on our sleeves. Time and again I heard the words "I have never been more proud to be Canadian." The Games showed we were more than happy to wear our patriotism on our sleeves, heads, chests, feet—and especially on our hands. Olympic Red Mittens had become the official hand-warmer of the country, and more than a few pair had made their way to the far corners of the globe. Everyone, it seemed, became Canadian for a fortnight and it felt great.

But the biggest indication of how smitten the country was with what was going on in Vancouver and Whistler was certainly in the television numbers, beginning with the opening ceremonies, when more than 13 million Canadians watched the entire three-and-a-half-hour production and 10 million more caught at least a part of it. These ratings made the ceremonies the most watched television event in Canadian history, marking an increase of more than 29 per cent over the previous benchmark of 10.3 million viewers for the gold medal hockey game at the 2002 Olympics in Salt Lake City. Another 3 million tuned into the opening using other platforms, including the Internet, radio and cellphones and other handheld devices.

The opening simply set the stage for what was about to come. Every other day, the CTV-led consortium seemed to be sending out a news release trumpeting staggering numbers for an Olympic final in which a Canadian stood a good chance of medalling. Millions were watching the medal ceremonies, for heaven's sake. Medal presentations were outscoring top NHL games by four and five times. And it maybe wasn't a great surprise when we later learned that 22 million Canadians had been glued to their sets for the gold medal men's hockey final. Makes you wonder who was running the country that day.

It was easy to look at what happened on the streets of Vancouver and in the living rooms of the nation during the Olympic fortnight and be surprised, shocked even, by what we were witnessing. A swagger we were not known for was now on full display. But honestly, for those who were paying attention it was obvious months earlier that something special was afoot. There were clear signals that the country was fully and completely engaged and ready to make the emotional investment in these Games that would later become so evident. Canadians seemed to take them over. Their fervent enthusiasm was there for all to see during the torch relay.

When we declared these to be Canada's Games, trying to make them relevant to all Canadians, no matter where they lived, there was a fair bit of eye-rolling. Many saw our plan as a vision too far. People said it would never happen. The country was too big. But it was during the relay, it turns out, that Canadians began to get inspired, and I mean all Canadians, of every colour and creed. That little flame seemed to touch everyone. That's when Canadians first swung open their doors and ventured outside to take a look, many wearing their red-and-white best.

While the performances of our athletes sent patriotism soaring through the roof, I doubt it would have happened, at least to the same degree, had the torch relay not touched down in every part of the country, allowing 90 per cent of Canadians to get up close and personal with the spirit of the Games. The relay is what ignited the fierce pride that would be on display during the Games. The relay gave us the momentum that would build throughout the 17 days of the Olympics.

These ideas had been swirling around in my head during my first run-throughs of my speech as I tried to find the words to express what Canadians might be feeling and expect on this day. I spent a good part of Sunday morning going over every word, tweaking parts here and there, practising my French aloud, cringing and sweating every time I did. But I was determined to be better. My mind was also full of emotions and imagery about the production itself and how the show was going to open. We had cooked up a bit of a surprise, to say the least.

It was about a week after the opening ceremonies, and that numbing poke in the eye we got when one of the arms of the cauldron embarrassingly failed to rise from the stadium floor, that David Atkins had beckoned me to his office for a closed-door chat. He wanted to talk about an idea he and a couple of others were kicking around for the closing ceremonies, which involved a significant departure from the original script: the crowd would take their seats and be greeted by an unlit cauldron still with only three arms, signs that it was indeed permanently disabled. The idea, David said, was to raise the fourth arm of the cauldron as part of the show and have it lit by Catriona Le May Doan, the torchbearer who had been left standing awkwardly in the cold when the arm she was to light stubbornly refused to operate on opening night. David envisaged a miming mechanic coming out of the floor and tugging on an imaginary rope to get the unseen cauldron arm into position. Then Catriona would appear to light the flame.

Forever the tease, David could see the smile building on my face as he outlined his plan. It was brilliant—on so many levels. First, it allowed us to poke a little fun at ourselves. Yes, the glitch on opening night had left a sour taste in some people's mouths. But now we were going to turn that lemon into lemonade. Canadians would be thrilled that Catriona, who had conducted herself with so much dignity and class on opening night, would get her moment in the spotlight as she deserved.

Second, our commitment to a bilingual Games wasn't just centred around how many French words were spoken but in how the duality of Canada was broadly reflected in everything we did. For the ceremonies, that could be achieved through the artists we chose, the dancers, music, imagery and the stories told, regardless of the language. By using a Montreal-based mime David was making a point: the mime was an artist who certainly reflected French culture but who also didn't speak a word.

I thought David had showed real ingenuity in the face of the pressure that we were getting from many fronts on the French issue, not to mention the sometimes unreasonable demands of the networks. On its part, NBC was not thrilled that we had ended the opening ceremonies with a song in French. For its mostly English-speaking American audience, the network would have preferred that we use a song that was more recognizable. Meanwhile, CTV was lobbying hard to have its Olympic theme song, "I Believe," inserted into the closing ceremonies. Not a chance, said David, and I wasn't going to argue with him. He was putting his foot down on all of the interference and lobbying that was coming from the bleachers, and who could blame him? I loved "I Believe" but was happy with the lineup of talent that David had already assembled. Besides, it wasn't our job to be a marketing company for CTV, great as their partnership with us was. Certainly, we weren't going to put their interests ahead of the greater good of the Games and David's well-crafted plan.

While part of me will forever crave the buzz and excitement of the Games, I will never miss the politicking and tug-of-war manoeuvring that went on behind the scenes, especially in regard to the opening and closing ceremonies.

BY LATE MORNING, I had made my way to Canada Hockey Place to take in the gold medal game. The building was a powder keg of excitement. Given the anxiety I was already feeling about the closing ceremonies, I probably could have done without the high drama that unfolded. But for the country, Sidney Crosby in over-time, wow, you couldn't have written it better if you were a Hollywood wordsmith. Our boy Sidney, our whole hockey team, gave Canada and the 2010 Olympics the defining moment that would be remembered and talked about for decades. It was the exclamation mark on a 17-day experience that brought Canadians together like never before.

It took a while to get from the rink to BC Place Stadium right next door after the game. I couldn't go two feet without someone approaching to talk about what had just happened in the rink and to congratulate VANOC on a superb job. The mood was ebullient. I eventually made it inside the stadium but I wasn't planning on making myself visible until right near the countdown to the start of the ceremonies, for a few reasons. First, I wanted to spend a little more time going over my speech and amending a part of it to incorporate the bit of hockey history that had just been made. We had managed quite an Olympic haul—14 gold medals, the most ever for a country at a Winter Games, host or not. What an achievement. What a validation of Own the Podium. That had to be recognized. I also wanted to go over my French parts just a bit more. Some last-minute cramming for the ultimate final.

I had earlier enlisted the assistance of Marcel Aubut, the president-elect of the Canadian Olympic Committee, the former owner of the Québec Nordiques and a legend in *la belle province*. I remember vividly when Marcel ran with the torch in Quebec. He had a huge following. I thought he could help me with some of my expressions, phrasing and elocution. Marcel immediately came up with several suggestions so that I might better express myself in French this time around. He even offered to help me in person, which is how we ended up together in the bowels of BC Place Stadium hours before the closing going over my French words. He made me repeat my phrases over and over and over again. He conducted his lessons with all the colour and flair of an animated choirmaster. "Not good enough," he'd bark. "Do it again." His hands were flying all over the place. His lips were moving a mile a minute. I would have burst out laughing if it hadn't all been so serious. He gave me a pretty thorough grinding, and when I was done I was beat. He helped me cross the line from complete hopelessness to 10 per cent Braveheart. I was ready to give it a shot.

The other reason I wanted to make myself scarce was because of what David had planned for Act One. Jacques Rogge and other members of the IOC were going to be staring down at an unlit cauldron, one that still had only three arms. But more significant was that it wasn't burning—a violation of Olympic protocol. Once you light the cauldron to begin the Olympics, it is supposed to remain lit until the Games are over and the world is beckoned to meet again in four years' time in the next host city. When people arrived for the closing, we should have had that cauldron burning, leaving everyone with the impression it had been glowing for 17 days.

Oops.

I could only imagine what everyone was thinking as they saw that poor, cold, unlit tripod, an arm still missing. For all they knew the embarrassment of opening night was about to be repeated.

I was also feeling a little anxious for my youngest daughter, Molly, who had grown from a small child into a beautiful young teenager during the life of this project. She was going to be dancing in the opening number, which was an ode to snowboarders. She had applied to be a dancer, auditioned quietly and been selected before I knew one word of her plan. All those years of dance classes had paid off. I was nervous and excited for her. I knew her stomach was probably a little queasy as well.

Eventually, it was time to find Darlene Poole, whom I was escorting to the president's box. When we got to our seats there was a frisson of expectancy in the air. Many people were looking at the cauldron and wondering what on earth gives. I leaned over to Darlene just before the voice of God came over the public address system to announce the show was starting momentarily. "Get ready for a doozy of a surprise," I whispered.

A few minutes later, with a burst of feathers, sparks and flames and the appearance of our mime dressed as a mechanic, the ceremonies began. It didn't take long for Catriona to make her dramatic appearance and for the crowd to realize what was taking place: a beautiful bit of self-deprecating humour to set the tone just right. The crowd went crazy, loving every bit of our self-inflicted comedy. Below me, Prince Willem-Alexander of the Netherlands looked over to Dave Cobb with a wide grin. "Genius," he said.

And it was. Pure David Atkins genius. He was worth every penny of his contract for that moment alone.

I didn't see Jacques Rogge's reaction to what had just happened on the stage floor but I'd like to think he was happy. Another inspired Olympic moment for him. I'm hoping he cracked a smile, regarded the moment for what it was and overlooked the breach in protocol. I didn't see it as a protocol gaffe so much as a protocol lift. People were going to be talking about this moment for a long time. It humanized us, not just the organizing committee but the country as a whole. I think it even helped make the IOC, an organization that guards its rules and traditions with the persistence and dedication of a Napoleonic army, seem less stodgy and hidebound. The moment seemed to mark the Games in a special way, showing Canadians for what they are: laid-back people who aren't afraid to poke a little fun at themselves, not slaves to tradition.

Our mime seemed to relax the whole stadium. Already in a great mood, the crowd was ready to have a good time now. Soon the floor was filled with hundreds of snowboard-carrying dancers dressed in white, swarming around the lit cauldron to the strains of a song called "Vancouver" led by the Winnipeg rock band Inward Eye. The dancers were mostly high school students, and out there among them was Molly, who had practised endlessly for her three minutes of fame. I strained to find her among the whirling-dervish frenzy taking place on the floor. No chance. It didn't stop me from being one proud father though.

The athlete parade, true to form, was a show of unity. No borders now as athletes abandoned tradition to link up with their global friends—black, white, brown, men, women, gay, straight. Uniforms and flags were traded around. It was as if the world was now just one country, a shining example of what could be. It was let-your-hair-down time, party time, as if the athletes were telling the rest of us that sport is truly life's greatest metaphor. I could only imagine the aspirations of children all over the earth whose Olympic dreams began right here.

I left my seat to make my way over to the stage, along with Jacques, to give my closing address. Although speeches from the CEO of the organizing committee are traditionally much shorter during the closing ceremonies than during the opening, I wanted mine to reflect the full story of what had happened in Vancouver and Whistler. It was not a time for useless words or trivia. I wanted Canadians to have someone enunciate for them what it was the country was feeling. So many profound things had happened over the course of the Games—so much and so many to acknowledge. A night to express genuine feelings and to be humble and gracious.

There is little question that this was the most anxious and tense that I have ever been before a speech—and it wasn't because billions would be watching. A blunder tonight would be with me my whole life. I was far less edgy before my speech at the opening, when the spotlight was even more intense. But I hadn't been so worried about my French in the opening. Now I was petrified.

As I stood backstage waiting to get signalled for my appearance, I could hear the delight of the crowd with everything that was taking place inside the stadium.

"You're on," someone said.

It's almost impossible to describe what it feels like to walk out onto the stage of a darkened arena knowing there are 60,000 sets of eyes trained on you. Excited and scared witless at the same time comes closest. Before I knew it, my trembling hands were putting my speech on the lectern in front of me. Jacques Rogge was just a few feet to my right waiting his turn. I had taken Prime Minister Harper's advice to heart: my opening acknowledgements to Dr. Rogge and members of the IOC, the prime minister, Governor General, provincial premiers, athletes, were all in French. I heard the PM's words in my head: "Speak French early and people will appreciate you for it, give you marks for trying."

I was off and running.

I talked about the remarkable demonstration of the power of sport that we had just finished witnessing, the force of which had the ability to unite, inspire and liberate us from feelings of hopelessness and despair. But now it was time to say goodbye and thank you. "And to perhaps compare for a moment the Canada that was with the Canada that now is," I said.

It was a line that I had settled on just a couple of days earlier, but one I thought was perhaps the most important of them all, one that acknowledged that something extraordinary had taken place, something profound, and that we were all a little taller than when we began. I was also suggesting to a watching world that it had come to know Canadians as we really are. And along the way a bunch of myths and preconceived notions had been tossed aside.

"That quiet, humble national pride we were sometimes reluctant to acknowledge seemed to take to the streets as the most beautiful kind of patriotism broke out all across the country... [Canadians] did not just cheer—rather you lived every glorious moment as if you yourselves were competing for gold."

Alexandre Bilodeau's first gold medal had given the country permission to feel and behave like champions. Our last gold medal in men's hockey would be remembered for generations.

I had to acknowledge the men and women without whose spirit and determination and hard work the Games could not have happened and certainly would not have been the success they were: the Blue Jackets, the undisputed heroes of the Olympics, some of whom had taken on a stubborn mountain and had defeated it. "May your contribution here be worn as a badge of honour for the rest of your lives," I said. "For you have, through your service, defined for all to see what it is to be a proud, generous Canadian."

I couldn't get through my final address without a reference to the tragedy that could easily have defined these Games but didn't.

"To the people of Georgia we are so sad and so sorry for your loss. Your unimaginable grief is shared by every Canadian and all those who have gathered here. May the legacy of your favourite son Nodar Kumaritashvili never be forgotten and serve to inspire youth everywhere to be champions in life."

The 2010 Winter Olympics would have many wonderful legacies, I said, yet I wished for just one: "That every Canadian child—be they from Chicoutimi, Moncton, Grande Prairie, Squamish or Niagara Falls—will have the chance to grow up to experience the pleasure of sport. No one left out. And that we of the global Olympic family will not rest until the right of every child to play across this planet is secured."

And with a "Vive le Canada" I was done.

As I walked from the stage, buoyed by a loud, warm ovation, I felt almost weightless. I could breathe again. The tension had melted from my body. I was happy to have survived. Before I even reached my seat my BlackBerry was buzzing. Two of the first messages I received were from James Moore, the federal culture minister I had battled with, and Marcel Aubut, both congratulating me on my French. I couldn't resist a smile. I knew, of course, it wasn't perfect, and probably offended the ears of the purists, but I had tried my best. Like the prime minister had told me, I was never going to please all the critics but I was going to get marks for having the courage to try hard.

To this day, I haven't been able to watch a video of my speeches, from either the opening or the closing. Maybe one day.

I was now going to be able to truly enjoy the rest of the show, which was designed as an outsized tribute to Canada, a spectacle that brought a smile to everyone's face, often at our own expense. We were going to play to some of the clichés rather than try to pretend they didn't exist or weren't partly based in fact. So when William Shatner came on and said, "I'm proud of the fact that we Canadians can have four beers and still pronounce the 'Strait of Juan de Fuca' without being censored," a knowing chuckle ripped right across the country. The highlight of the evening was Michael Bublé's rendition of "The Maple Leaf Forever."

The next day, I read a description of that segment that I thought nailed it perfectly. It was penned by Pete McMartin, of the *Vancouver Sun*, whose kind review was further noteworthy because the writer had been a critic of the Games from the start. "Bublé was perfect," Pete wrote, "and the Broadway production swirling around him was so wonderfully campy and so entertaining that I had the thought watching it that this was a new moment in Canada's image of itself. The squad of dancing Mounties, and then the giant wooden Mounties being wheeled out, and the dancing maple leaf babes, and the jigging coureurs de bois in their canoes, and the giant beavers and moose and best of all, the giant hockey table game, which was pure genius and a Canadian inside joke that caused a pang in the heart of every Canadian kid of a certain age (notice the gold medals on the hockey players?), it was brilliant, all of it. The joke on us, by us. All that was lacking was a giant pitcher of maple syrup to pour over everything."

A joke on us, by us. It was the perfect description. If there was any irony it was in how similar many parts of the production were to the one that was so severely criticized in Turin. It had been mocked for playing to every trite cliché there was about Canada. This one did the same, in many respects, and yet was hailed far and wide for being fun and entertaining and pitch perfect.

In the waning minutes, Canadian-born troubadour Neil Young brought the house down serenading the athletes with a rendition of his iconic hit "Long May You Run." It was a goodbye that seemed completely Canadian. The Games had served to remind the world of Canada's deep pool of homegrown but international talent.

As Neil took his leave, I could sense a strange feeling in the stadium. The flame now extinguished, people just did not want to let it go. I was delighted at the extent to which the crowd had embraced the entire production and thought they had played a starring role themselves. As I looked around, I was surprised by the number of people who continued to sit in their seats soaking up every last bit while others poured for the exits to continue the celebration. I turned to Darlene as we were heading out and told her that if Jack had been nearby, as I always felt he was, he would now know it was okay to slip away from us. His work was done. Somewhere out there he was smiling—this I know.

We set up for a press conference down at the Main Press Centre soon after the ceremonies were over and the mood heading into it couldn't have been more different from the one held after the opening ceremonies. I was so delighted for David, who was surely going to be hailed for the creative mastermind that he is. No questions about French or faulty cauldrons. Now he was going to be asked how he ever came up with the idea to begin the closing ceremonies in the brilliant way that he had. Some of the actors and singers were on the dais with David and me. I answered a few questions about how it felt to have the Olympics over. They aren't over, I answered, now we had to gear up for the Paralympics.

Overall, the news conference questions were kind and positive. The tone suggested that we had bounced back in a very Canadian way from some early setbacks and not only had won the big game but had set a whole new standard. Our successors would be measured differently now. I wasn't prepared to accept those kind of accolades that day and still don't. I was just happy that people weren't still saying the Games were the worst ever.

After the press conference, I wandered down to Jack Poole Plaza. Although the cauldron was extinguished, thousands of people were still milling around it. I stood there smiling, taking it all in, thrilled by the grand distinction that the cauldron had achieved. It had come to symbolize the heart of the Games. Tens of thousands had come to see it each day hoping to feel the warmth of its flame, to contemplate its storied history, the power of what it had come to symbolize over time. Mothers and fathers, children in hand, staring into the glow so full of wonder and hope. The Olympics have their flaws and have sometimes been dogged by scandal, this we know. But at the core is something good, with the potential to be life changing, earth changing, something with the power to unite a nation as it had ours. You can't say that about a lot of things today.

If the second cauldron had come to represent the soul and spirit of these Games, how appropriate, then, that it was situated in a plaza named after the person who I felt embodied the soul and spirit of these Olympics: Jack Poole. I sure missed my sage friend, perhaps never more so than on that final night when I most wanted to give him an embrace for everything he had done for me, everything he had come to mean to me. Ours was a relationship of a lifetime. Thirty-five years earlier I had lost my dad, John "Jack" Furlong, and now John "Jack" Poole was gone from me too. Both of them had made me feel I was worth their effort. I hope I was.

I eventually made my way back to the Bayshore, where the mood was relaxed and jubilant. Members of the IOC streamed up to me to tell me how proud my team should be with the way it had produced the best Games ever staged, the big guns from Sydney and Lillehammer among them. Quite the endorsement. While it all felt good, I was ready to crash and savour a few quiet hours in my room, call my kids and wind down a bit. There were parties everywhere and invitations to attend. I passed on them all. Besides, I had another early start the next morning and wanted to be out at the airport first thing to make sure everything went smoothly.

What was I thinking when my head hit the pillow that night? I've been asked that question a hundred times. What was I thinking? Relief, for sure. While my team wouldn't be able to fully exhale until the Paralympics were over, I knew that we had bounced back to achieve something special. Our goal was audacious, without question. We set out as dreamers hoping to be nation builders, to somehow do something great for our country, and when I lay down that night to think about whether we had achieved our goal I knew that pretty soon we would find out through the words and actions of others.

That night may have been one of the happiest, most serene experiences of my life. I was beginning to realize what we had accomplished; I could see it and feel it. And when you feel that good, it just fills you up. You think about things that make you happy, and so before I went to sleep that night I thought about my children and hoped that I had made them proud. I thought about how proud they all made me. I thought about my own family, particularly my mom and dad. What I would have given for them to be alive for this 17-day period in their son's life.

A part of me had always felt I had fallen a bit short with my father. To my dad, sport was an amateur endeavour. Sunday stuff. Not real work—not in Ireland in 1974 at least. When I told him I wanted to try to make a living through sport, he'd always shake his head and say he hoped I'd one day come to my senses. Dad would have been stunned had he been in the stadium that night.

My father was my hero and instilled in me all of the values that I liked to think I imbued in my organization. My mother taught me about honour and decency and doing the right thing and never disregarding the value of someone else's contribution. Those were also important tenets of my philosophy. So as I lay in bed that night, I thought of both of them and my sister, Rosemary, whom we lost during the bid period to lupus. She would have given anything to be here, to be with her brother.

I thought of all the children who would be waking up the next day, having dreamt all night of competing in an Olympics themselves one day, the next Sidney Crosby among them.

14

A Final **Farewell** to Nodar

T HE NEXT MORNING I was greeted with poetic headlines trumpeting the success of the Games. The positive reviews came from some of our harshest critics. "Londoners have a tough act to follow in 2012," declared London's *Daily Telegraph*, one of the British papers that had slammed us earlier. Its Fleet Street competitors expressed similar sentiments. David Atkins's master stroke in the closing ceremonies was universally applauded. Even the French content received positive reviews.

But March 1 meant it was time for tens of thousands of our visitors to begin heading home. The party was over, and now we faced a large army of very tired people descending on our airport. The experience that Olympic goers have at the airport can leave an indelible mark on their memories, which is why we always considered "Day 18" one of the most important on our Olympic calendar. The last thing we wanted was to have the special feelings that our visitors were leaving with sullied by their time getting checked in and passing through airport security.

As wonderful as the Games in Salt Lake had been, the lasting memory that many people had of those Olympics was the 10-hour lineups and utter chaos at the airport getting home. It was not a pretty sight, and frustrations boiled over on several occasions. We vowed not to let that happen here.

From the beginning, the Vancouver Airport Authority was a full partner in our Games. The airport was never going to be just a sterile place to land and leave from. We decided to make YVR a venue in itself, to give it a personality. So when people landed in Vancouver they knew instantly they were in an Olympic host city. Larry Berg, the CEO of the VAA, did a brilliant job along with members of our team in dressing the airport up in our Olympic colours and making arrivals feel as if they were being greeted by their own personal welcoming party.

After an early and happy breakfast at which my colleagues and I received the highly coveted Olympic Order from the IOC, I headed to the airport to see how things were going and to thank the Blue Jackets and airport volunteers who were there from early dawn making sure people's needs were met. By the time I arrived, the place was humming as exquisitely as the London Philharmonic. Thousands of passengers had already left. Security was a breeze and the planes were leaving on time.

In preparation, the airport had constructed what was tantamount to another terminal to handle the overflow customer traffic the Olympics created. Any time any of the lines got too long, people were directed to this temporary (now permanent) building, where they were processed almost immediately.

The IOC was especially impressed with how smoothly departure day was going, such a contrast to most Games. I think part of the problem was that other organizing committees had not seen the magic of having the airport as a full partner, one that was deemed to be crucial to the overall Games. It took effort to make sure that a partner that was only called upon to be at the top of its game for a brief period felt vital to the Games' success. All the training that Larry Berg had his staff take to be ready was paying off. There were Blue Jackets and airport volunteers everywhere, some handing out drinks and food. There was even music and other entertainment to keep those waiting in line amused.

Any exhaustion I felt was masked by the exhilaration I continued to experience. But the day was certainly bittersweet for me because it meant saying farewell to many special friends. There would be so many warm so-longs to people I hadn't known eight, nine years earlier. Now they were life-long friends, or so I liked to think. People like René Fasel, the president of the International Ice Hockey Federation, who had played such a critical role for us during the bid process. I was going to miss Gerhard Heiberg too. He was such a decent human being. I wondered when, if ever, I'd see him again.

"You did an unbelievable job, John," Gerhard told me as we said our goodbyes. Coming from Gerhard, this praise had special meaning. He had been CEO of the Winter Games that had established the highest standard for the event—Lillehammer 1994. If we were one day mentioned in the same company as those Games, that would be the highest compliment we could receive.

I would even miss Jacques Rogge, though we hadn't become especially close during my Olympic tenure. But Nodar's death did establish a bond between us that hadn't existed before, and when I shook Jacques's hand for the last time it felt different. He seemed more warm and human than the man I knew before the Games began. He's never going to be a bubbly, effervescent guy but I have enormous respect for Jacques, for his principles and his dedication to the Olympic cause. His is a tough job.

I spent a lot of my time at the airport talking to athletes from around the world. "The best Games ever" was a common expression used by many. It sure felt good. I met one guy who fell so in love with Vancouver he bought a condo in Coal Harbour, near where the second cauldron burned. "I couldn't help myself," he said.

AS THOUSANDS TOOK to the skies, a new entourage of excited visitors was landing and the customs hall was full again. The incoming hordes had been prepped for their visit by the massive global coverage of every second of the Olympics—now it was their turn to grab their credentials, board a Games vehicle and soak up the vibe.

The Paralympics would soon be upon us.

We were already in full transition mode. No time to rest or celebrate. My team was moving at rocket speed to take down the Olympic look and replace it with that of the Paralympics, a monster job of logistics. Venues were being prepared and modified for different uses. Some no longer in use were already being decommissioned. Volunteers who were getting ready for extended service, thousands of them, took off one badge and stuck on the "three agitos" Paralympic Games replacement—a cost-efficient measure we put in place as the money dried up. It worked beautifully.

I left the airport in the early afternoon satisfied we had played a near perfect game there. My teammates in the car were noticeably calmer and more at ease but still determined to pour on the effort. They had given blood for me, worried day and night about every detail, always ready to jump in to sort out even the tiniest complication. And they did not let me get away with anything. I was lucky to have them.

By day's end, I had heard from all my kids. They were high on pride and just too weary to contemplate normal life again. My son John Jr. called, dying to talk to me about his experience. "You know, Dad," he said, "I grew up knowing we lived next to a giant. They were bigger and stronger than us. They beat us at most things, they had all the money and the power and where they went we went. And it was okay to us that we lived in their shadow. The next generation will never know these feelings. Never again will we Canadians compete in sport or in anything and feel like we don't belong. From now on we will compete even up, feel like we can win and we will be confident we can achieve success in anything."

Wow, I thought, if that was the sole, lasting legacy from these Games, it would have all been worth it.

WHILE THERE WAS a tendency to want to savour and soak up the warm atmosphere, it was now time to tend fully to the three weeks still to come. We had but a few days to ready everything so the Paralympic athletes could settle in and acclimatize. By morning I would remind our executive that we must stay alert and not become complacent. On the streets the public was itching for Round Two. My colleagues assured me that all stations were manned and that we would be ready by mid-week. True to form we were.

The transition from Olympic to Paralympic was faultless to the point that we even had time on our hands. We had expected more challenges. By mid-week the athletes, coaches and officials were all on the ground, and the village atmosphere in both Whistler and Vancouver was comfortable. Technical experts and other event officials were busy putting final touches to everything and making sure the venues were at the required standard for competition.

One of the questions most often asked of me over the past 10 years is why are the Olympics and Paralympics not staged together? Surely there are efficiencies that could be realized by holding the two events at the same time? Surely it would be less costly? And wouldn't the Paralympians prefer to perform on the same grand stage as the other Olympians and not on one that comes with a little less glitz and glamour?

In the past, some Paralympic events have been showcased in the Olympics, but the fact is the IOC and IPC have no desire for an integrated event. Both want independence and a separate identity. Also, one is based in Switzerland and the other in Germany; integrating the two would add costs, not lessen them. Athletes' villages would have to be expanded to accommodate the extra competitors that would be on the ground at the same time. Food facilities would have to be bigger as well. The venues after the

Olympics are modified significantly for Paralympic use, so more venues would need to be built if events were to be staged simultaneously. And extra grandstands and a whole host of other support facilities would have to be built as well.

That said, it is difficult for an organizing committee like VANOC to start all over again after the Olympics have ended. The team is dead tired yet must immediately bounce back into action. We had seen this challenge coming and decided to organize the Games around a simple strategy—two Games inside a one-festival approach delivered by one team. In the past, the organization of the Paralympics has, at times, been contracted out to a separate agency (this is what they did in Turin, for example). But we felt that approach added unnecessary risk.

We knew that expectations would be high to deliver something special for the Paralympics and not treat them in any way as a second-tier event. So we committed ourselves to the same quality of delivery and transitioned very quickly.

It was time to turn my attention, at least in part, to the opening ceremonies. Patrick Roberge—the show's executive producer—and his team were already sweating in the stadium. Rehearsals had been a bit raw but were improving. Patrick had great confidence in the creative aspects of the show but had had no stadium time under his belt yet. If ever an executive producer faced serious adversity, it was Patrick. BC Place was the one venue where the transition had not been smooth. Patrick had the benefit of all the key Olympic staging and overlay materials but was frustrated about the general state he found the building in. It was like waking up the morning after a big party in your home and having to do all the clean-up, but with no part in making the mess. Patrick had expected an easier takeover.

His team tackled that building head-on, and by the weekend it too was sparkling and the cast was gelling. He needed every minute to practise and nail the surprise elements, and the artists were in overdrive getting the music and songs just right. The International Paralympic Committee (IPC) got an early look at some of the rehearsals and loved what was in store.

What was essentially a low-budget show was beginning to look exactly the opposite. Rumours circulated about broadcasting the opening ceremonies. One minute they were going to be live, then tape delay and then live again. The IPC was now freaking out. The public was watching closely and expected the Paralympics to be live too; in this country natural justice is expected. We had promised live and still hoped for it. CTV wasn't sure the show could hold a live audience for two hours.

By noon on March 2 we were on the road again, headed for Ottawa and the start of the Paralympic torch relay in the nation's capital. Jeff Mooney, one of our most dedicated, hard-working board members, could see how hard we were running and gave us, as he had before, complimentary use of his plane and pilot to get us safely to Ottawa and back. A lifesaver of a gesture. To us, Jeff was like the guy sitting on the bench always ready to leap over the boards and help out. The firepower and soul behind the A&W empire, he had contributed so much to VANOC, especially in the area of communications and marketing. On that day, Jeff was our favourite citizen.

Jim Richards, our torch relay director, and his advance team were already in Ottawa setting up the details for the traditional First Nations lighting event set to take place on Vancouver Island, before we took the flame to Parliament Hill in mid-morning. We were up at the crack of dawn. I must have done 10 interviews back to back before 8 AM. The country was still buzzing madly from the Olympics and did not want it to stop.

So we now had a new flame and were headed for Vancouver via some major centres. Before it was all over, throngs would run with the Paralympic torch or participate in some other way, including a 24-hour relay that was held in and around Vancouver. I knew for certain that Jim would execute the events flawlessly and make certain the flame's arrival at its final destination down to the second. Jim did not disappoint.

The executive team met at the Cannery Restaurant for a working lunch after the return from Ottawa. It had been a long time since we had had the luxury of a meal together. I couldn't help but notice the reduced stress on the faces of my teammates. They were younger looking, still united and happy with their work. They had been through a lot and I was deeply proud of each one of them. There were no big issues to report—the transition was buzzing along. The team was confident that all was locked down nicely and ready for the "Second Games." The restaurant staff fell over themselves to treat us well, and we each left with a gift—a thank you, they said, for what we "had done for our country."

Later that afternoon I stopped in to see Kyle Mitchell, who had recruited me and most of the executive team, and who was now giving us a hand to find new careers for our top people. He was determined to find them soft landings so they weren't worrying about being unemployed in a few short weeks, which would have distracted them from the task at hand. Kyle was a magician and would perform his magic yet again.

On March 5, Jeff Sherman, CEO of The Bay, ecstatic with the company's runaway Olympic success, hosted the executive for dinner and talked about the profound impact the Games was having on the iconic store. I thought back to that night, years before, backstage in Toronto with George Heller, the former CEO, and our handshake deal that was at the root of the years of effort and sweat that followed. Now here we were full circle—mission accomplished. The Bay was back. Jeff was gracious and thankful and gave each team member a patented Hudson's Bay striped blanket to celebrate and remember our partnership. When he said, midway through dinner, that "this was the first February in The Bay's history in which the company had made a profit," I felt more than a little bit good.

By Saturday, March 6, the torch had arrived in Victoria, and I and others were there to receive it. The premier was in fine form and Rick Hansen was too. After a stint as co-mayor of the Olympic Village in Vancouver—along with former Olympic rower Tricia Smith—Rick was on top of the world all over again. The incoming torch runners were beaming. A great community celebration followed. Media were out in full force, still juiced up and fighting their own exhaustion. Then to the Canadian Armed Forces base in Esquimalt for a visit and ceremony, and for me it was back on the float plane to Vancouver, where the work in my office was piling up and mail was coming in from all over. Letters from around the globe were pouring in from those who felt they had to say how appreciative they were. They came from Australia, Chile, the United States, Britain, France, Germany and, of course, from Canada. I felt how far we had come. How much we had already accomplished.

As the days passed and venues were declared ready, I was busy preparing to make my final progress report to the IPC, a considerably less daunting experience than facing the IOC. For the most part, things Paralympic fell under the leadership of the VANOC sport division. We had decided on a complete reversal of the Turin Games strategy, where on the surface the Paralympics looked as if they were organized by the Turin organizing committee but were in fact contracted out to a separate agency.

With only days to go now before the start of the Paralympics, ticket sales had taken off, the sledge hockey venue was almost sold out and curling was filling up. The opening ceremonies were within an inch of having the Sold Out sign placed on the door too.

Everything appeared right and ready, and the new look at the venues was impressive. Signs of the Olympics were now largely gone and replaced by a distinctive IPC appearance. While the athletes' villages were quieter, the new tenants from over 40 countries were buzzing with energy.

Later that week, with hundreds of practice runs complete and in the wake of a thousand small transition tasks, it was time to talk openly to the media about expectations. Sir Philip Craven, president of the IPC, was in his element, beaming with anticipation, and saying all the right things but also pushing buttons all over to keep the heat on the broadcasters to commit to live coverage. He was good at the pressure game, but he was also warm and thankful and noticeably eager to get on with it. I simply promised a continuation of the large crowds, Canadian medals and Blue Jacket heroics.

Originally, the plan was for the Paralympics to be entirely staged in Whistler. The IPC loved the intimacy of Whistler and felt the athlete experience would be enhanced if the Games were held in one place. And no doubt it would have been. But cost pressures forced us to take another look at this idea. Having some events in Vancouver, at venues that were ready, would save money. But we had made a promise to be in Whistler only. I felt we could go back on it only with the IPC's blessing, so I had flown to Manchester, England, for an audience with Sir Phil, a former wheelchair athlete himself and a standout on the basketball court. He had represented Great Britain at many Paralympics and other European championships.

I felt a little vulnerable sitting in his presence, in his home, where he would put me up for the night. It was not an easy conversation but I honestly believed the Paralympics would come out ahead if we held some of the big events in Vancouver, where they would get more exposure. I promised him that we would not back down from our commitment to make these Paralympics the best ever. While the request shook our relationship a bit, he thankfully let us off the hook.

As the athletes were bussed down from Whistler on March 12, the ceremonies team was removing any final blemishes from the stadium set-up. It was a beautiful and inviting atmosphere. We had a full house. The dress rehearsal the night before had gone well. The performers were giddy with excitement backstage—only Patrick Roberge was really biting his nails.

The night was free of the soul-searching tensions that were present exactly four weeks before. The high drama of the

Olympics was past now and the crowd was ready to let it all hang out one more time. Sold out it was. Spirits were high. The Governor General, prime minister, premier (decked out in red), local mayors and many others were all there as the countdown began. Performers gave it their all, sang their hearts out, and danced with joyous energy.

The athlete parade was beautiful, unprecedented for ambiance and oomph. It was emotional, energetic and every team was welcomed as if they were indeed the only one there, with the one possible exception—Canada. The arrival of Team Canada, including five-time gold medal winner-to-be Lauren Woolstencroft, seemed to electrify the crowd. The best kind of mayhem was happening.

The Governor General took the field early in the show, flanked by small children and beaming with pleasure, and the crowd responded warmly. We saw Rick Hansen and Betty and Rolly Fox, and were reminded time and again of the remarkable contribution people with disabilities have made to Canada and the world. The RCMP and Canadian Armed Forces were there in their finest protocol colours, delighted again to serve. It was a proud night for VANOC and a wonderful night for Canada.

In my speech I recognized the athletes whose lives were now interconnected forever because of these Games. I used the occasion to draw attention to the giving spirit of men and women of sport the world over: "Those who have made it their personal mission in life to use sport to build better lives, and inspire children... Sport is our common language and because so many in the world live in harm's way our message of peace through sport has never been more important."

It was a night to give thanks to so many. I concluded with a final wish for the athletes: "May this night be the beginning of the time of your life." And then I introduced Sir Phil, who was charming, strong and clear about the occasion this was. He spoke eloquently about values and gave thanks for the Paralympics' good fortune to be in Canada. If ever a man was in his element it was Sir Phil. If all he had done was sing the words of "Michael, Row Your Boat Ashore," the crowd of 60,000 would still have made him feel like Elvis. He was now every bit the great leader he had hoped to become when he took the reins at the IPC. He was strong, proud, vibrant, passionate, thoughtful and humorous. It was a night he would never forget. Paralympic Winter Sport was at centre stage and it was on live television. After having seen the rehearsals, the network did itself proud and put the ceremonies on for the entire country to enjoy in real time. We were the first Paralympic Winter Games organizing committee to broadcast the Games live. In the end, CTV delivered over 60 hours of coverage and millions watched—a runaway record. For the IPC, this was now the new standard. Sochi can expect to get pushed further in 2014. Sir Phil's relentless persuasion had paid off huge. He revelled in calling on Governor General Michaëlle Jean to declare the Games officially open.

The Paralympic flame arrived to great fanfare and was carried to centre field by Betty and Rolly Fox, as so many pondered the gift their heroic son had given to his country. The flame was passed around a ring of torchbearers and eventually handed to Zach Beaumont, a 15-year-old future Paralympic star who lit the cauldron as if life's greatest honour had been bestowed on him.

For me, the rest of the night was a blur, a media conference, a walk through the infectious atmosphere downtown before crashing into bed exhausted. Athletes were en route back to their villages, for one more sleep before game day, and all was set for competitions the next morning.

On Saturday, March 13, the athletes' wait was over. I woke up with a massive headache, seeing stars, and tried all kinds of medication just so I could manage. My migraines have become fewer in recent years but when they come they are brutal—like this one. Like a needle behind my eye. The day was at fever pitch by midmorning, so I needed to shake it off. The talk now was all about sledge hockey and whether the Canadian team had it in them to repeat their historic gold medal feat from Turin.

The team was now older, and though they were on the surface full of fire they had noticeably lost that edge. They gave it everything and made it to the semifinals, but there the dream ended. I had gotten to know these guys fairly well and marvelled at how they looked at life. These Games were everything to them and the prospect of repeating gold had been on their minds every minute since 2006. They had challenges to deal with that most of us cannot even contemplate, but they lived life fully and gave everything they had to the community.

On the ice, it was kamikaze-like action as our guys left not an ounce of effort unexpended. Missing that medal at home was devastating for them. Not getting even the bronze left them inconsolable. The U.S. managed to scramble a molecule of revenge for its gold medal loss to Canada in the men's hockey tournament at the Olympics by taking gold, stopping dead the three gold medals target Hockey Canada had set for itself. Putting a medal around the necks of the Americans and handing them flowers was a great privilege. They had the look of champions and sang their hearts out when their flag was raised. Not a single fan left the arena for the presentations, so their joy was fully shared and celebrated. Canadians stood and cheered—it looked good on us.

It's hard to imagine feeling excited watching wheelchair curling, which parallels a game of on-ice chess. But over at the Vancouver Paralympic Centre at Hillcrest Park the rules of decorum for curling were being tossed out. From the first rock at the Olympics to the last one at the Paralympics, fans took a vacation from all things normal, letting their instincts run amok. The curlers seemed buzzed at first but settled quickly into the craziness and antics of the crowd, which included the wave, numerous, spontaneous O Canadas, and thunderous ovations for even the most modest shot. This was twenty-first-century curling and it was great fun.

I dropped by the Athletes' Village in Vancouver mid-week and ran into Jim Armstrong, skip for Canada, once a world-class curler in his own right until his health forced him into a wheelchair. He admitted to being genuinely taken aback by the effervescent atmosphere, and to having underestimated the power of these Games. He was having the time of his life with his teammates and revelled sitting in the village cafeteria meeting the rest of the athletes, drenching himself in the excitement and colour of the Games.

It was dreams of gold for Jim, who had skipped his team to a world championship the year before, so we were all biting our nails as Korea chewed away at his big lead in the final game. But hang on he did to reprise the heroics of Turin. Watching him accept the gold medal was special, and many were in tears for what was to be our final gold of the Paralympics in Vancouver.

TWO GREAT CANADIAN stories unfolded in Whistler. Vancouverite Lauren Woolstencroft won five gold medals in Alpine skiing events, making her the darling of the Games. From the start gate to the finish line she was the favourite of the crowd. Blind cross-country skier Brian McKeever, who had made the Olympic team too but was not allowed to compete, gave the crowd at the Nordic Centre much to cheer about, winning three gold medals, which confirmed him as one of Canada's greatest Paralympians. The Canadian team had a great Paralympics, nailing their lofty Own the Podium third-place target.

Celebration Plaza in Whistler was full every night as medals were awarded and Canadians and visitors alike piled in to show their appreciation. The Paralympic athletes garnered a special kind of attention from everyone they met. The community showed extraordinary hospitality and had been determined to send everyone home with memories of a storybook place where the world came together. It was as if everyone had been given a key to the resort. Residents were well aware that the contributions they were making would pay a long-term dividend, as visitors would surely return for a repeat experience sometime down the road—that was how Whistler worked. Whistler had proven itself to be the little town that could and did. It had its own irresistible magic and knew it.

AS THE OLYMPICS were ending, I received an invitation from the parents of Nodar Kumaritashvili asking that I attend their son's funeral, due to take place, according to tradition, exactly 40 days after his death. Part of me thought it was a courtesy request and I wondered if indeed they really wanted me there. Their son had not been out of my thoughts since that tragic Friday. To visit his family would be healing for me as well. The problem was that getting to Georgia was near to impossible if I was to fulfill my duties at the Paralympic closing ceremonies in Whistler. So I had a dilemma and I was worried. My team went to work on logistics. Every kind of travel scenario was looked into.

If I took the last flight to London from Vancouver on Sunday night, I figured I could get to Tbilisi, Georgia's capital city, jump in a car and drive to the remote village of Bakuriani in time for the service. It would mean crossing the mountains on a slow, busy road, but I was prepared to do anything to get there. But everything would have to be on time for me to pull it off—and I would have to pass on the closing ceremonies, which would be a serious slight to the IPC.

I decided the ceremonies could be reworked and I could deliver my speech early if the IPC would agree to a protocol adjustment. But even then, there was the issue of getting to the airport in time to catch my flight. There was no commercial air or helicopter service available from Whistler. One thing at a time. First I pitched the change in the ceremonies program to Sir Phil. He agreed to go along and understood the significance of what I would be leaving for. I would now be on early in the lineup. My team got to work looking for a transport solution from Whistler, having secured a couple of seats on the last flight to London on Sunday night. Renee

Smith-Valade would be coming too, as we expected a media frenzy in Georgia.

At the eleventh hour, with no solution in sight, I went back to an old friend. I thought that if the Canadian Forces, which had thousands of personnel in the mountains, had choppers in the area they would surely be flying back and forth to Vancouver and might be able to help out. It was a Hail Mary option. Their helicopters were rough-and-ready machines designed for duty in war zones—not exactly passenger-friendly, but who cared? I would have been happy to stand in one. True to form, the army reworked its plans and scheduled a chopper flight to take off minutes after my speech. So failing a last-minute emergency at its end, we had an arrangement in place. It would be a basic flight in the dark that would get us to YVR on time for me to make my flight to London.

I liked my chances even if success meant flying for the better part of two days, stopping first in London, then Munich and then Tbilisi at 4 AM. It was one of those rare occasions when sleep seemed unimportant. I wanted us to be there and felt anything less would look bad on Canada and reflect badly on the Games. So I sent a note to Georgia that we were moving heaven and earth to get there. The IOC was sending Pat Hickey, the head of the European Olympic Committees, though I thought Jacques Rogge might travel too.

The last days of the Paralympics were pretty hectic. I went to every venue several times, shook as many hands as I could, hugged those Blue Jackets who were still going strong, attended many receptions and sponsor-hosted occasions and in the final hours attended the IPC closing reception, where the Paralympic Order was awarded to me and, posthumously, to Jack Poole. I practised my closing speech, making a final effort to get my French into better shape. I did some media interviews as well, where I revealed just how exhausted I was. But I also told reporters how much the Olympic experience had affected me. "I have an even greater appreciation today than I've ever had in my life about the power of a vision and about what happens when people pursue something with the kind of vigour you can," I said. "I think something pretty extraordinary has happened in the country and I am glad to have been a part of it."

And then I was off to the closing ceremonies.

At Whistler's Celebration Plaza, the rain had cleared. The athlete parade came down through the village, past rapturous crowds who were giving them a memorable send-off. The plaza was packed and Patrick Roberge and his backstage crew were ready to deliver a great show. Minutes into the ceremony, with the athletes all in place and after a beautiful rendition of "O Canada," I was at the podium in my Blue Jacket delivering my very last speech of the Games. "Tonight, together with our many partners, and in the name of all Canadians, we take our final steps across the finish line of Canada's Games," I said. "Our work is done. Our best has been given—our dear friend Jack Poole would be a very happy man tonight."

I thanked everyone who had made a contribution and especially paid tribute to the athletes, who had "dazzled us with your agility, your strength, your endurance and your sportsmanship. You reflect the best kind of character, integrity and focus and have shown that pain is no match for your courage."

Minutes later it was time to go.

"It is with humility and more than a little regret that we now say goodbye—it has been a true honour to serve. Thank you very much— Go Raibh Míle Maith Agaibh Go Léir. Slán Agus Beannacht." It was a traditional Gaelic farewell. My dad would have smiled.

The engine of the SUV was running outside, my bag loaded in the back. I walked off the stage and jumped in the back seat and we were off to the Heliport 15 minutes north of Whistler. It was a strange departure for sure. We met the two pilots and senior armed forces personnel on the tarmac, got our safety briefing, loaded ourselves in and were soon airborne. They were thrilled to help us out and treated this like any serious mission. Heading south, we passed the plaza as the ceremonies continued. There was a glow over the area. I was sad to miss the end and regretted not being there to hear what Sir Phil had to say.

Dave Cobb was ready to face the media and would take charge for the coming hours. We were in good, safe hands. The rest of the team would also be there. I was certain we would send our Paralympic friends home with the same efficiency and spirit we had for our Olympic guests.

This was one time I would have liked to wake up the next morning and read all about it. Sitting beside Admiral Pile, who was himself beaming with pride, I donned night goggles to see the amazing visuals below. As we headed toward Squamish I reflected in solitude on the men and women in uniform around me, and others like them who serve and protect us the world over. Courageous, loyal, proud and driven. My work was easy compared with theirs.

Forty-five minutes later we were all aboard for London. The trip was mostly a blur. After landing in London, we had to grab a connection to Munich. From Munich we flew to Tbilisi, a beautiful city that sits on the banks of the Mtkvari River. Not that there would be any time for sightseeing or exploring. Not long after landing we were being picked up by members of the Georgia National Olympic Committee and off in an entourage of Land Rovers for what we were expecting to be a three- to four-hour trek to Bakuriani, 160 kilometres to the west.

At least that is what the people with the Canadian consulate in Turkey had told us. Maybe with normal drivers behind the wheel but not the guys we had, professionals who took corners at great speeds. There were times where I was almost afraid to look at how fast we were going. When I did peek, the speedometer often said 170. More than once Renee and I exchanged glances, wondering if this was going to be our last ride together—our last ride, period.

But make it we did, arriving in the small town in the early afternoon. Bakuriani is situated on the northern slope of the Trialeti mountain range in the Borjomi Valley. It is covered by centuries-old fir and pine forests, and in Soviet times the area was considered an important ski centre. While it billed itself as a resort town, Bakuriani looked like a community that had seen more than its fair share of hard times. The homes were small. Many of the buildings were half-finished. When we pulled up to the home of Nodar's family there were dozens of people milling around. Everyone had been waiting for us. Nodar's home was a two-storey grey brick structure. A poster-sized picture of the fallen hero hung on the outside of the house, above the entranceway.

I was happy that my old friend Pat Hickey had joined us in Tbilisi. Pat was representing the European Athletic Association and I welcomed his moral support. He understood the importance of my presence. If I hadn't made every effort to get there it would have made everything I had said about Nodar's death seem like window dressing. But I was flat-out nervous and scared when we arrived. We were going into a community where everyone was clearly going to be devastated. Still, I thought, the people in Bakuriani, especially Nodar's parents, would have thought less of me if I hadn't shown up. They had invited me for a reason.

We walked inside their kitchen, which was crowded with family members. Nodar's mother, Dodo, was sitting on a couch dressed entirely in black. There was a table packed with food, a framed picture of Nodar sitting on it, his boyish face staring out at us. You could tell that someone had worked all day to make the place sparkling clean. There were also some reporters and TV cameras crowded into the room. Pretty soon people were giving speeches. I was asked to say a few words.

I hadn't been expecting it. So I just spoke from the heart, saying that I wished I had been visiting under different circumstances. I said I couldn't begin to comprehend the heartbreak of Nodar's parents, and that I thought it was important to be there in person to say how grief-stricken all Canadians felt. I didn't speak long, and when I finished the room went quiet for what seemed like minutes.

After the speeches, Renee and I were led behind the house to some makeshift stairs that took us up to a loft. It was Nodar's room. The bed was scattered with Olympic paraphernalia and other souvenirs from Canada. Above the bed hung a large picture of Nodar holding the Olympic torch, taken in Whistler. The humble surroundings made me realize just how much Nodar Kumaritashvili had had to overcome to get to the Olympics. It was clear he did not have the benefit of a well-to-do family with the kind of money and resources often necessary to support an Olympic dream. But I could also tell that he had the loving support of an entire town behind him.

Afterward, everyone drove to the church. We walked to Nodar's gravesite, which was still quite fresh. A robust, beautifully robed priest arrived, along with Nodar's father, David, and Dodo. There was a short service that was interrupted at one point when Dodo lay down on the grave and began sobbing uncontrollably. It was a profoundly emotional moment that would forever be seared into my memory.

After the service, everyone milled around for a little bit and then it was time to head to the community hall, where a feast had been planned. I needed to find a private moment to talk to Nodar's father. The family would be receiving the equivalent of CAN$150,000 insurance money as a result of Nodar's death. But who knew how long it was going to take for that to arrive? It was obvious the family could use money now. We had earlier decided to try and raise some cash the family could access while waiting for the insurance to arrive.

We had raised $25,000 by auctioning off one of the podiums that was used during the medals ceremonies at the Games. That money, which we converted to euros, was stuffed inside an envelope that was sitting in the breast pocket of my suit jacket. I had been trying to divine some sense of how this gesture would be greeted. I wanted to make sure the family would feel it was appropriate and not crass in any way. I knew Bakuriani had an all-cash culture, so writing a cheque, which we would normally have done, would have been problematic.

At the community hall, someone helped secure a room in which Renee and I joined David and his brother Felix, Nodar's Olympic coach. An interpreter was there as well. I explained that my executive team wanted to help the Kumaritashvili family until more money arrived. We figured David and his wife and daughter could use some support. I pulled out the envelope and handed it to him. I told him how much was in it.

His expression conveyed a multitude of emotions. He seemed slightly embarrassed but also relieved. I also saw the slightest hint of joy in that sad, burdened face. He'd have the pain of his loss for the rest of his life, but the money would help make that life easier. David came over and hugged me. I shook his hand, which was rough and strong, hardened by a lifetime outdoors. We walked into the hall where the feast was underway. It was a pretty sombre affair and reminded me of my grandfather's funeral. People were still in a state of shock and were doing what they could to comfort David and his wife. They too had also lost a son when Nodar died, that much was evident.

It was time to go. I said my goodbyes to Nodar's parents and Uncle Felix, and hopped into the back of the Land Rover idling outside. I was exhausted and dreading the marathon journey back to Canada. Evening was beginning to fall on the town as we pulled away. I looked back one last time to see the twinkling lights of Bakuriani fading in the cold night air. I lay my head against the window and closed my eyes.

I had done the best I could.

Epilogue

EVEN TODAY, THE commemorative DVD boxed set and other videos on the 2010 Winter Olympics sit on my living room coffee table unopened.

I'm not sure why I haven't been able to watch the beautifully packaged coverage of the Games, especially given that I missed so much while darting from event to event. Perhaps I don't want to listen to my nervous, self-conscious attempts at French in my opening and closing ceremonies speeches. More likely, however, it's because I'm not sure I can handle the tsunami of emotions that would roll to the surface at the first sight of the athletes, the Blue Jackets, the waterfront cauldron, the crowds, Nodar...

There will likely be a day when I'm ready to watch it, but not yet.

In the months since the Games ended I've run into thousands of people—on planes, restaurants, walking the streets—who have all insisted on telling me an Olympic story, their Olympic story, one that usually makes both of us smile. To say that listening to them makes me feel incredibly happy sounds trite, I know. But honestly, there is no other way to describe the warm feeling I get whenever

I talk to people who tell me how the Games touched their lives, made them feel prouder to be Canadian than at any other time.

One young Blue Jacket I met told me he had refused a $10,000 offer for his uniform—too proud to give it up, he said. Another who told me of her time volunteering at the Pacific Coliseum welled up with tears talking about it. There was the gentleman who slept in his car every night but never missed a shift in Whistler and the woman who came by bus all the way from Ontario to serve at the Games. These are the trophies I crave: stories of extraordinary Canadians who delivered profound heroics and considered themselves privileged to have volunteered.

I've had over 10,000 letters, cards, e-mails or calls from people around the world who felt the need to say thank you. They still trickle in and are all the proof I will ever need to know that the pebble of hope we tossed into a pond 14 years ago continues to ripple.

My team has long since been disbanded; happily, many of them are off to great new careers. I have taken scores of reference calls from employers looking to hire VANOC alumni. It's made me feel incredibly proud that their value is so high. Some of my colleagues did crash emotionally after the Olympics ended, at least for a while, as they tried to cope with no longer waking up to the high drama and excitement that had filled their lives for years. Some have been lured to London for the 2012 Games or Sochi in 2014 to do it all over again—they've become Olympic gypsies.

Hard as it was, the promises we made to balance the Games operations budget and build the venues have been kept. The venues were built for the $580-million budget we had and there will be no operating deficit. Our final report confirmed that about 90 per cent of the Games' operating budget revenue came from the private sector and from ticket buyers. Government invested in targeted areas like the torch relay and the opening and closing ceremonies.

As I write this, VANOC is a speck of its former size. From the 50,000 who came together in February 2010, only a few remain to pay the bills, clean up complex accounts, file reports and secure the archives for those who come to explore in the future. Our campus is now the new domain of the Vancouver Police Department. The sport venues were quickly decommissioned and are all functioning and serving their new legacy purpose. The next generation of athletes is already in training at some of them.

The Athletes' Village in Whistler has been converted to residential housing as planned and is a wonderful testament to the community's own sustainability vision. For Vancouver there is still work ahead to sell the remaining condominiums at Southeast False Creek, in what surely must be one of the most desirable housing developments on the continent. The Canada Line has hit its five-year passenger projections already, and the drive to Whistler is safer and faster. The Convention Centre in Vancouver is attracting global accolades and accelerated new business. In November, the prestigious FutureBrand global survey for the first time called Canada the world's top country brand, an honour attributed to the Olympics. The 2010 Games were also named the world's best-run event, beating out the FIFA World Cup, the Super Bowl, the World Series and the Tour de France.

I could go on.

Vancouver has a wider smile on its face now too—and is perhaps a little more extroverted and confident. The reluctance to believe and the angst that caused some to leave town before the Games hit have been replaced by deep pride and a "we can do anything" attitude.

I have travelled all over Canada, the U.S. and Europe over the past several months telling the story of the Games. To many, I think we were a puzzle. Even today, the most asked question is: How did you pull it off? Many want to know about what was happening behind the scenes—this book, I hope, tells that story.

I have heard scores of descriptions from people on the street— perfect strangers—who talk about their pride at being Canadian. A woman in Winnipeg well into her retirement years told me she had never watched sport in her life until the Vancouver Olympics. Her husband confirmed her transformation from holdout to superfan. I've heard of lawns decorated in Olympic colours and homemade Canadian flags, cauldrons and snowmen dressed as goaltenders. I've received poetry, art, music and lyrics from all over, and photographs of children exercising their Olympic imaginations in scores of different ways.

I admit to being filled with an undeniable bias about the power of international sport, so I may not be the best one to speak about the lasting legacy of Vancouver 2010. But I know that the example of Vancouver is something we must build on. We discovered so much about ourselves and so much happened here. We emerged a champion nation.

The Games lifted us up, filled us with confidence. George Cope, the CEO for Bell Canada, recalls being stuck in traffic, watching the women's hockey final with family members on his phone, realizing that he was gazing at the future. A few months later, George led the purchase of CTV and talked about that Olympic moment as being the inspiration for the gigantic move.

I have been through a deeply personal journey. I have seen so many places and met so many extraordinary people. Being CEO of the Vancouver Organizing Committee for the 2010 Olympic and Paralympic Winter Games was never a job; it was a cause. I believed in our mission from the moment I gazed at the heroics of Native American runner Billy Mills in Tokyo in 1964. I'm pretty sure that in many countries of the world, a man with a foreign accent like mine would not be given a chance to live such a dream. In Canada, no such barrier exists.

When I began my journey I had no grandchildren—I now have 11. My children Maria, John, Damien, Emma and Molly are closer to me than ever. The Games touched each of them in different ways, and they cheered for me every day and lived the difficult days too. I hope they will be filled with pride for all their days to come and pass it on to their own children and grandchildren.

Over the year since the Games ended I have received many honours. I won't lie, it is lovely to be recognized but the truth is mine was a shared adventure. The work was done by thousands. It's awkward to be singled out when in your heart you know that the credit belongs to so many. I wear my Officer of the Order of Canada and my Order of British Columbia pins with great pride and know I have them because my teammates did heroic things.

I now chair Own the Podium as a volunteer. My committee is dedicated and its members will be tireless advocates for giving our athletes the tools and support they need to succeed in London and Sochi. The Canadian Olympic team that came to Vancouver was living proof that we can compete with anyone and win.

Jack Poole was a man of his word. His handshake was more powerful than any contract. The last time we spoke, I promised him that no matter what happened we would keep our promises—all of them. I am most proud today that no one has suggested otherwise. Above all other things, this steadfastness would have mattered most to Jack. We can all learn from his example to exercise humility, trust more, give more, forgive the hurts we have endured and move on.

The death of Nodar Kumaritashvili will always fill a corner of my memory. A beautiful memorial is now in place at his burial site in Bakuriani. A new luge facility is being planned there in his honour. The chief coroner of British Columbia has handed down his report and found no blame, and we can only hope and pray that sport will never witness such a tragic accident again. The measures taken to make sport safer will never be foolproof, but they must be a continuing preoccupation for all of us.

This book was never a certainty. But as the games ended it seemed like a good way to move on. *Patriot Hearts* is intended to pay tribute to the remarkable heroics of so many—examples of Canadians' courage, conviction and remarkable teamwork. Vancouver 2010 was a celebration of the possible. The Games owe so much to

Canadians from a thousand communities who set everything aside to give their hearts unconditionally to this undertaking. No thanks will ever suffice. Their sole reward is in the knowledge and lasting pride of their accomplishments.

The stinging rebukes from the British media and others as the Games began were replaced by accolades and words of triumph as the flame was extinguished. The *Independent* signed off with, "And overall, for athletes, fans, the media, and the host nation especially, the Games were a triumph." The *Guardian*, merciless in its criticism at the beginning, concluded by saying, "Bottle that Vancouver enthusiasm and London 2012 will really hit the spot. The London Olympics can take their cue from Vancouver, its organizers and its volunteers."

The effect of the Games will take time to sink in. Prime Minister Harper has said, "Mark my words, some day historians will look back at Canada's growing strength in the twenty-first century and they will say that it all began here on the west coast, with the best Winter Olympic Games the world has ever seen." I believe he is right.

The Canada we all love was for a shining moment a place of genuine wonder, causing one U.S. reporter to poignantly ask "Why can't we be more like Canada?"

Now they know us, eh?

Acknowledgements

THE SUM OF all fears is forgetting to thank those whose heartfelt, generous contributions have touched your life and your work so completely. I hope I have not failed in this regard.

I had given up on the notion of writing about this story until Scott McIntyre showed up and put it to me that the Games had changed the country. A flattering notion, I have to admit, and he is a heck of a salesman.

If there was a book in me, I knew I would never extract it alone. It would still be locked away in my mind were it not for the magic touch of my good friend Gary Mason, who somehow managed to peel back my instinctive desire for privacy to find the words and the voice. Over these months, we have been friends and brothers and amid the thousands of e-mails and phone calls I have grown to appreciate Gary's intuitive mind and one-of-a-kind craftsmanship. To him, good enough was never going to be good enough. Thanks too to Marvin Storrow, our great friend who gave us the space to work and argue so we could bring this book to life.

To the entire team at Douglas and McIntyre, thank you for believing in this project and most especially to our gifted editor

Trena White for her patience and painstaking contribution to helping get the manuscript across the finish line. You are forgiven for any screaming you may have done in private.

The vision for Canada's Games would have evaporated into a slow, subtle retreat had some remarkable, pioneering presidents and CEOs not completely embraced our lofty mission of touching Canada's soul: George Cope of Bell Canada, Gord Nixon of RBC, Robert Dutton of Rona, Ron Brennerman of Petro-Canada, Arturo S. Elias of General Motors and Jeff Sherman of The Hudson's Bay Company. They and over 60 more CEOs of Canada's best companies and their employees and customers became champions and ambassadors in this mission of helping us make this about the many and not the few. They gave us our wings—far from traditional sponsors, they did much of the heavy lifting and became the very best kind of teammates.

I thank the thousands of men and women of VANOC, my dedicated executive team and those who toiled tirelessly outside my door trying to make me look and do good, and the heroes at every desk on every floor at headquarters, and of course those remarkable English- and French-speaking, blue-clad volunteers from all over for their selfless sacrifice. You gave and gave and gave again. This story is, in truth, your story. I will never forget you.

To Prime Minister Chrétien for a great start—and Prime Minister Harper for a great finish. To Premier Campbell, who always had our backs and your colleagues from every province and territory who joined you, thank you for believing in this one-of-a-kind adventure. To Olympic Ministers Owen, Emerson, Moore, Lunn, Hansen and McNeill, your support, your ideas, your courage and your friendship meant the world to us. To all those elected to high public office across the country—all sides and at all levels—thanks for caring and for never letting us down.

To the supportive board members of Vancouver 2010, past and present—great Canadians all of you—your service inspired us all.

To the RCMP, the courageous men and women in uniform, public servants, Games ambassadors and of course our remarkable athletes—your contributions were truly heroic. Warm appreciation to all at the IOC for helping us in the best and most difficult of times, and to Bob Storey, who taught me how the whole process works—a debt I will never be able to repay.

Ninety-nine per cent of Canadians watched the Games in person or on TV. You cheered, celebrated, wore red and lived every moment with us—you were the real difference makers. The title of this book, *Patriot Hearts*, was inspired by your embrace of these Games—thank you all.

I am blessed with wonderful friends—hundreds of them who cheered me on every day. To name them all would be impossible; they know who they are, but thanks to you I survived this and became a better human being.

To Jack and Darlene Poole, thank you for a remarkable journey, for never doubting me and for the deepest kind of unconditional friendship.

To my children, Maria, Johnnie, Damien, Emma and Molly and your children—your love, respect and support has meant the world to me. You paid a high price but never gave up on me when I was everywhere under heaven but at home. Because of you, I am the luckiest dad alive.

To Mom and Dad, wherever you are, I thank you for your sacrifices and your example and for teaching me about hard work, humility and how to live a better life. I promise I will never stop trying.

This book, just like the Games, was a walk on thin ice for me. A thousand times along the way I might have given up. I am grateful beyond words that I did not and am thankful for the support, encouragement, compassion, love, deep loyalty and inspiration of my dearest friend Catherine Bachand—demonstrated in a thousand ways. Hers is a patriot heart. Thank you so much!

Jack and John—the friendship of a lifetime.

Index

coordination commission
  meeting, 201
evaluation commission, 50–55
funding, 148
gifts, 57–58
letters, hand written, 61–62
member profiles, 39–40
Olympic Order, 301
Olympic Truce, 160–61
Paralympics, 304–5, 308
protests, 210
on sponsorships, 136
support for VANOC, 218–19, 282
transportation, 301
International Paralympic Committee
  (IPC), 304–5, 306, 308–9, 314
Inukshuk, 140, 167
Inward Eye, 292
IOC. *see* International Olympic
  Committee (IOC)
Irish Republican Army (IRA), 11
It's How You Play the Game (King), 151

Jack Poole Plaza, 188, 234, 297
Jackson, Roger, 51
Jacob, Gibby (Chief), 65, 71
Jako, Monica, 201
James, Carole, 114
Jarvis, Patrick, 88
Jean, Michaëlle, 164, 218, 310, 311
Jespersen, Randy, 188
journalists. *see* media
Jung, Chantal, 74

Kahnawake reserve, 168–70
Kim Un-Yong, 65
King, Frank, 83, 151, 173–74
King, Tom, 171
Kissinger, Henry, 73
Koyczan, Shane, 186
Kugluktuk, Nunavut, 167
Kulich, Marti, 63–64
Kumaritashvili, David, 221–22, 319
Kumaritashvili, Dodo, 318, 319

Kumaritashvili, Felix, 221–22,
  242–43, 320
Kumaritashvili, Nodar, 203–6, 217,
  220–24, 241–43, 279, 295, 314,
  318–20, 325
Kyikavichik, 167

Laliberté, Guy, 178–79
Lang, k.d., 214, 217
Laumann, Silken, 166
Lausuanne, Switzerland, 42–43
Lavigne, Avril, 133
Lay, Marion, 41
leadership workshops, 95
Lehman Brothers, 144
Lehto, Craig, 207, 224–25
Le May Doan, Catriona, 65, 72, 166,
  190–91, 214, 288
Lemay, Jacques, 180
letters to IOC, 61–62
Lévis, Quebec, 168
licensed products, 139–40, 147
Lillehammer Winter Olympic Games,
  1994, 51, 176, 302
Lil'wat First Nation, 212
logo design, 140–41
London, England, 139
London Summer Olympics,
  2012, 259
"Long May You Run" song, 296
Lougheed, Peter, 174
Lowry, Mark, 270–71
"lucky loonie," 70, 135
luge track, 207, 221, 222
Lunn, Gary, 157, 283
Luzhkov, Yuri, 46–47
Lyall, Johnny, 211

MacDiarmada, Padraig, 45
MacLachlan, Graham, 130
MacLachlan, Sarah, 217
MacMillan, Bruce, 30
Madrid, Spain, 56
Main Operations Centre, 262

Books of Merit

TRUE NORTH

TRUE
NORTH

Exploring the Great Canadian
Wilderness by Bush Plane

GEORGE ERICKSON

Thomas Allen Publishers
Toronto

Canadian Cataloguing in Publication Data

Erickson, George, 1932 –

True North: exploring the great Canadian wilderness by bush plane

Includes bibliographical references.

ISBN 0-919-28-38-1

1. Erickson, George, 1932 –   – Journeys – Canada, Northern.
2. Canada, Northern – Description and travel.
3. Air travel – Canada, Northern.   I. Title.

FC3956.E74 2000   917.1904'3   C00-931498-9

F1090.5.E74 2000

Design: Gordon Robertson
Editor: Alison Reid
Cover photographs: George Erickson
Author photograph: Sally Erickson

Published by Thomas Allen Publishers,
a division of Thomas Allen & Son Limited,
145 Front Street East, Suite 107,
Toronto, Ontario M5A 1E3 Canada

Printed and bound in Canada

This book is dedicated

To the Bernoullis, a family of seventeenth-century
scientists who fled to Switzerland to escape from persecution
by religious zealots. Daniel Bernoulli discovered the
principle that helps lift our wings to the sky.

To Nicolaus Copernicus, Galileo Galilei, Charles Darwin
and their many contemporaries who, often at great risk,
opened our eyes to grandeur and advanced the
sciences that provide our many comforts.

To Orville and Wilbur Wright, two independent thinkers
who, in 1903, achieved the world's first successful, powered,
piloted heavier-than-air flight. (The local paper didn't
consider the event worth reporting. The United States
Army later called the use of airplanes a "crazy" idea.)

To the bush pilots who bring supplies and
human contact to remote corners of the world,
and to all who seek new horizons.

Notes

This is a book of nonfiction. A few liberties were taken with the sequencing of events, but all of them actually happened.

The natives that we once called "Eskimos" prefer the word "Inuit," the Inuktitut word for "the people."

To convert Canadian costs to American, subtract approximately one-third.

In keeping with our antiquated U.S. system of weights and measures, temperatures are given in Fahrenheit, and volumes are listed in gallons.

Contents

Part Five

Part Six

TRUE NORTH

Preface

*T*HE ROOM where I write overlooks the tea-tinted waters of a northern Minnesota lake, a view that I share with a common loon. When I taxi my seaplane to and from our pier, the loon yodels a raucous theme while he performs his water-walking act. Convinced that he has once again decoyed my rumbling yellow bird away from his sanctuary, the loon settles low in the water, then gracefully slips beneath.

The loon and I share an interest in my Cub, but we do so from our own perspectives. Where the loon sees only an annoying interloper, I behold a magic carpet, the realization of a long-held dream. As a boy, I'd dash to the end of our log crib dock whenever I heard the stuttering start of a neighbor's seaplane. Enthralled by its reverberations and slow pirouettes while its engine warmed, I'd fidget in anticipation of power and spray. With one hand gripping our spruce-tree flagpole, I'd hang out over the water, my imagination riding co-pilot as the aircraft bounced from the waves and cleared the trees, then I'd return to reality as it faded from sight.

A lifetime later I write in a small, birch-bordered cabin overlooking the same log crib dock, thrice rebuilt. The wall to my right bears charts of Canada and Alaska, each map webbed with flights from my past, for the dreams that I dreamed at the end of the dock have changed from fiction to fact.

Rows of Kodachromes decorate the wall to my left: a crescent tundra beach where sandhill cranes cavort and cry, a herd of ten thousand caribou caught in midstep as they clatter past, and a Super Cub standing vertically on its prop and float tips at the edge of a northern lake.

The shelves above my desk hold stacks of books, clippings and travel notes. Some of the notes are neatly typed. Others, set down in a bobbing seaplane among the reeds of a mist-laden bay, are a barely legible scrawl. Still more settled into spiral notebooks beneath the canopy of a nylon tent or in the tar-paper austerity of an abandoned Arctic mission—its priest long missing, undoubtedly dead.

When I work with my notes, I often drift back to another time and place—to the turquoise waters of the Coppermine Gorge or to the banks of the Great Whale River, where arctic char played between my floats while I worked on a damaged engine.

My ninety horsepower Piper PA-11 is a transition model between the famous J-3 Cub and the beefier Super Cub, a descendant of the ornithopters envisioned by Leonardo da Vinci, the fifteenth-century scientist who saw birds not as fluff and feathers but as an "instrument working within mathematical law, which instrument it is within the capacity of man to reproduce with all its movements."

Equipped with long-range fuel tanks, the light and dependable Cub is ideal for lengthy tundra tours. On its cowling and on the vertical plates that cap the tips of the wings, its name is written in navy blue script: Tundra Cub.

The name is appropriate. The Cub has traversed the Yukon and measured the tides of Nome. Skimming the margins of Hudson Bay, it has dipped a wing to polar bears and delivered me to the banks of the Thelon River, where fifty yards into the bush I performed a nervous pirouette, surrounded by the shaggy descendants of worlds long past—musk oxen.

Now, with our long Minnesota winter just a memory, it's summer once again. The former Yugoslavia is still in fractured ferment. Inter-religious strife, overpopulation and hunger soil a globe beset with theologies of breed and the realities of greed.

Having written my legislators and paid up my dues, I will seek renewal in the sights and sounds and scents of the North, in its people, stories and myths. Flying a course determined by weather and whim, I'll return to the rotting cabin of three travelers who starved to death in the Thelon Sanctuary, and visit the Nahanni River's Headless Valley, where two brothers literally lost their heads in a fruitless search for gold.

Though I've no room to spare, I'll fly with Bernoulli, who supports my wings, and with centuries of his peers. In a fifty-year-old aircraft born of their contemplations, I'll renew my longstanding love affair with the North, escorted briefly by a common loon.

One

MINNESOTA TO
CHURCHILL,
MANITOBA

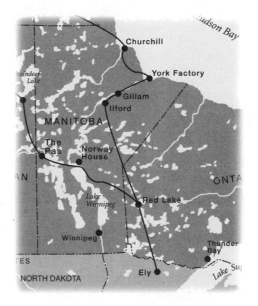

1

Minnesota to Ilford, Manitoba

*I am tormented with an
everlasting itch for things remote.*

— HERMAN MELVILLE

I T'S THE THIRD WEEK OF JULY. Soft summer winds have finally swept aside Lake Vermilion's amber pine-pollen veil. Rising from the depths, schools of whitefish lip watery ringlets where the last of the mayflies flutter down. As Sagittarius prowls the nighttime skies, fireflies twinkle in our evergreens, and it seems like Christmas once again.

Far to the north, the lakes of the Northwest Territories have finally shed their sheaths of ice. On Great Slave Lake, a diesel-driven barge is fighting a cold northeasterly wind as it struggles toward a tiny town called Snowdrift and an even more remote weather station named Reliance. Riding low, the barge is laden with machinery, building supplies, appliances, three-wheelers, groceries and a fifty-five-gallon barrel of aviation gas that bears my name.

In years past, I've been accompanied on my northern flights by a passenger, or occasionally by another aircraft, but this trip will be different, for the unforeseen has removed my companions, and I'm facing a solo flight.

A month ago I was one of four pilots eagerly reviewing maps and fueling sites, but appendicitis, loss of employment and a threatened divorce have sidelined the other three. Though I regret their difficulties and will miss their company, I'm buoyed by my freedom to choose destination and course without consultation, with only myself to please.

Flying alone doesn't worry me. I trust my equipment, my training and common sense. And though solo travel has its hazards, what good are our dreams if we lack the courage to follow?

Now, with its floats riding deep in the water, the Tundra Cub awaits. A mountain of gear has disappeared into its small baggage area, the back seat and compartmented floats. Beneath my seat, I've packed four books: Diane Ackerman's artful *Natural History of the Senses*, Carl Sagan's *Demon-Haunted World* and Barbara Walker's *Woman's Encyclopedia of Myths and Secrets*, which the London *Times* proclaimed the "best educational book of the year." The fourth is an old friend, Vilhjalmur Stefansson's *Friendly Arctic*, the intriguing book that first turned my thoughts to the North when a broken leg provided a brief vacation from high school.

A five-pound packet of sequenced maps lies atop the books. Removing the Winnipeg chart, I lay it over the cameras, bug dope notebooks and pens in the makeshift aluminum tray that hangs beneath the Cub's instrument panel.

Before leaving, I bend a two-foot length of clothes-hanger wire into a precise right angle and set it upright on the pier beneath the noonday sun, then point the horizontal arm directly north and file a nick in it to record the length of the shadow cast by the vertical arm. Packed away in one of the float compartments, my wire will emerge a few days later at the edge of an Arctic sea. There, with the two-thousand-year-old logic of Eratosthenes, I hope to measure the earth as he once did, with the shadow of the noonday sun.

Pushing away from the pier, I set the Cub's throttle to idle, flip the magnetos to Both, prime its engine with a few shots of fuel, step to the front of the float and give the prop a spin. The magnetos snap crisply. Another spin, another snap. "Now," I say to myself, for the Cub always fires on the third swing. Her engine snorts, then steadies to an even rumble.

As I settle into my seat, the Cub and I embrace. Webbed together with seat belt and shoulder harness, we become man/machine, making lazy circles as the engine warms.

My mind often shifts to the plural "we" whenever the Cub's in motion. Like a sailor romancing his ship, I call her Old Girl or Cubby. When her engine's ready, we pivot into a gentle southwesterly wind, building speed as I shove the throttle forward. She roars and shakes, first nose high like an accelerating motorboat, then level as she climbs onto the hydroplane-like step built into the bottoms of her floats, her knifelike keels slicing the water into sheets of spray.

We surge ahead, gaining speed as the chattering vibrations of our corrugated runway diminish, then cease. Transformed, the man/machine smiles and shivers, loving the vibrations that prickle our frames. Fusing thought with motion, we alter our wings with a touch of aileron, banking north toward a sparsely settled country that the Iroquois called Kanata.

The boreal forest below obscures the Canadian Shield, an ancient remnant of eroded mountains that spreads a granitic ellipse north from the Adirondacks and Lake Superior across two million square miles of Canada. Where the soil is sufficiently deep, tall stands of pine, birch and aspen masquerade as virgin forest, but they're really second growth. All of these hills were shorn like sheep just a hundred years ago.

After a short flight, the Tundra Cub passes the U.S. Customs facility at Crane Lake and descends toward a maple leaf flag on the shore of neighboring Sand Point Lake. There, a roadless Canadian Customs facility serves summertime boats and seaplanes. And although I'm "clean," I'm hoping that the agent won't ask me to unload my carefully packed gear. Fortunately, he remembers me from summers past and, clipboard in hand, sticks to the essentials.

"Where to this time?"

"Well, Churchill first. Then maybe the Arctic coast. If the weather cooperates, I'll head west to Alaska."

"How long will you be in Canada?"

"Two weeks for sure, no more than three."

"Are you carrying firearms?"

"I have a rifle. As you know, it's required that far north."

Nodding agreement, he signs my permit as a bulky de Havilland Beaver seaplane rumbles up to the pier, followed by an eighteen-foot fishing boat with three canoes in tow. The agent wishes me a good trip and turns to the Beaver, which is spilling tourists onto the pier.

As the Cub accelerates, her wings split the air into two layers. The lower layer flows straight back across the wings' flat undersides, while the upper layer, which must cross their longer, curved upper surfaces, becomes stretched like a rubber band. The space between the molecules in the upper layer increases, creating the area of low pressure that helps lift my wings and confirms the work of Daniel Bernoulli, who discovered that raising the speed of any fluid, including air, lowers its pressure.

Level again at a thousand feet, I head north across Rainy Lake, a lengthy portage-free section of the Voyageurs' Highway. For almost two centuries, thirty-foot birchbark canoes bearing up to three tons of supplies plied this watery thoroughfare that connected the Great Lakes to Winnipeg, Saskatoon and a tiny settlement called Edmonton until the canoes were displaced by rail near the time of our Civil War.

The Montreal-based North West Company, which dominated this "southern" fur-trade route, preferred short, stocky voyageurs—compact men who wouldn't usurp valuable cargo space but could still tote two ninety-pound "pieces" across the nine-mile Grand Portage from Lake Superior to the upper reaches of the Pigeon River. Urged on by a bonus, some carried three. Despite claims that it was easier to get into heaven than to portage the Grand, a few managed four. One voyageur, a hugely muscled black man named Pierre Bonga, is said to have portaged *five*—an amazing 450 pounds! And though they made their living on the water, most of the men couldn't swim, a shortcoming that the company actually preferred, believing that nonswimmers would take fewer risks with their valuable birchbark canoes.

Seine Bay appears, and with it a tugboat trailing a fat pendant of pine and aspen logs to International Falls and the mills of Boise Cascade. Over Redgut Bay, the Cub's shadow intercepts a linear, water-darkened log boom reminiscent of a Trident submarine that I once watched exit Pearl Harbor. As the cigar-shaped boom flattens the foam-flecked chop, I'm pleased that this slow-moving "vessel" will yield studs, rafters, plywood or paper, while the Trident held nothing but death.

Looking up, I scan the Rainy's westward flow in search of the Northwest Angle, the thirty-mile thumb that Minnesota pokes into Canada's belly to the west of Lake of the Woods, but it's lost in the afternoon haze. Believing (wrongly) that the Angle contained the source of the Mississippi River, the United States required the extension in the border-setting 1814 Treaty of Ghent.

When the Cub crosses the Trans-Canada Highway, I switch my radio to 121.5 megahertz, the emergency frequency that I usually monitor. Far above, a Boeing 767 strings a slender vapor trail toward Winnipeg. As the aircraft descends into warmer air, the frozen exhalations of its engines thin and disappear.

I wonder, could it be the same Boeing that I'd overheard one fine July evening in '83 as the Cub and I departed from Red Lake? While skipping through the frequencies to reach 121.5, I'd stumbled onto the transmissions of an Air Canada jet that had just lost power in both engines. Gripped by the gravity that tugs at every aircraft's wings, the huge jet had just begun a long, 140-mile glide toward Winnipeg from forty-one thousand feet.

When the captain realized that the 130-ton Boeing and its sixty-nine passengers would never reach Winnipeg, he turned toward a former World War II training base at Gimli, an Icelandic village on Lake Winnipeg's western shore. Lacking hydraulic pressure to lower the flaps or wheels, the crew cranked the gear down, but the nose wheel refused to lock into place.

The stricken 767 swept out of the sky toward the abandoned runway, then cleared the fence at 180 mph. Two of the main gear tires exploded; the front gear collapsed, igniting a fire as the Boeing skidded down the runway on its nose. But with no fuel to explode, what might have been a disaster turned into an outstanding success.

Now, as the Trans-Canada Highway falls behind, I envision the passengers and crew, first anxious, then frightened, then gloriously relieved, having found safety at that little town called Gimli, which in Icelandic means "Paradise."

When visions of Gimli's mouthwatering *ponnokokur* (crepes rolled in sugar) begin to prod my appetite, I remember stowing a sack of cherries behind my seat. Loosening my seat belt, I squirm around and grab the bag while the Cub flies itself. The deliciously sweet, succulent cherries tempt me to eat handfuls, but I'm restrained by vivid memories of the gluttony-induced diarrhea that I once suffered during the height of the plum and cherry season at Grand Junction, Colorado.

I'm the Johnny Cherrypit of Canada, spitting a pit out the open widow every ten seconds or so. Imagining that each will take root and survive, I envision perplexed canoeists in the midst of the Ontario wilderness gaping at ruby red cherry trees laden with luscious fruit.

An hour passes, then two. Boredom blows at me like a headwind. Kansans might be enthralled with the emerald forest below, but it's no different from northern Minnesota's, and I see that every day. Finally, when a dot on the horizon becomes the community of Red Lake, I lift the mike and transmit,

"Red Lake radio, this is Piper 4745 Mike."

"Piper Four five Mike, this is Red Lake."

"Red Lake radio, Four five Mike is fifteen south. Landing at Green's."

"Piper Four five Mike, altimeter is 30.02, wind is southwest at ten knots. Report on final."

At Green's seaplane base, the Tundra Cub wedges between a hulking radial-engined Norsemen and an equally impressive de Havilland Otter. In the sixties, I stood on this same wharf, chuckling at an ancient Fox Moth seaplane, a World War I–era biplane that housed three passengers directly behind the engine. The pilot sat above and *behind*, a reversal of the usual arrangement. Now, my 1947 Cub could also be called an antique.

As I secure the Cub, a woman arrives with a seagull cradled in her arms, its white breast stained with blood from a fishhook lodged in its mouth. Perhaps weakened or imbued with hidden wisdom, the gull waits calmly while I retrieve my tool kit, then remains surprisingly passive as I snip the hook and slide the shaft from its flesh. I return the gull to its feet, where it takes a few steps, then dashes my weakness theory by leaping into raucous, glaucous flight.

A huge part-Newfoundland dog ambles over. He leans against me, begging to be petted—and I discover that he's loaded with ticks. As I pluck them off, Large waits patiently, then rolls over for a more thorough job. Looking like six-legged burgundy grapes, the ticks make satisfying plops as I toss them into the lake, shattering flotillas of water beetles that are whirling away the day.

Fuel is expensive in Canada. Twenty-six U.S. gallons comes to $US90—more than twice what I'd pay at home. I offer my Master-Card to "Laura," Green's Airway's auburn-haired clerk, then phone the Department of Transport (DOT) to file a flight plan to Churchill. (In much of Canada, pilots are required to inform a responsible party of their route and destination.) As I turn to leave, "Laura" slips out from behind the counter and follows me through the door.

"I heard you file for Churchill," she says. "I've always wanted to go there. Not for long, though. It's too cold, you know."

"I don't blame you," I reply. "I've been there eight or nine times, and I haven't tired of it yet."

"It's the polar bears that intrigue me," she continues, "and the white whales, too. Everyone who stops here on their way south raves about them." Then, as I'm about to tell her about Churchill's abandoned forty-cannon fortress, she asks, "Are you just on a short holiday?"

"Two or three weeks. After Churchill I'm heading north to Baker Lake, then up to the Arctic coast. If the weather holds, I might end up in Alaska."

She stares at the plane, her eyes searching. "God," she sighs, looking directly at me, "I'd give *anything* to go along."

Surprised, I stammer, "Yeah, well . . ." then wave a hand at what she can plainly see—a passenger seat filled with gear. Besides, there's that thing called marriage, which my wedding ring proclaims.

As I taxi away from the pier amid a storm of fantasies, Large begins to howl. When I turn into the wind, "Laura" is stroking his huge head with one hand and waving with the other. I raise a hand to her, my fingers spread as if to grasp something, then lift the water rudder and pour on the gas.

The enlivened Cub snarls and rises shaking onto the step. Power flows through our frames as the hairs on the back of my neck begin to prickle in anticipation of flight. Temporarily freed from gravity, we climb toward a wider horizon and a broader, more unified view. When wings and rockets and things yet undreamed finally carry us to the edge of space, I wonder, will we ever grasp it all?

The land has changed. Back near the border, lighter greens of birch and aspen dapple dark forests of tall spruce and pine. But ahead, a mottled plain of shorter black spruce, jack pine and bog reaches for the horizon, encroaching on dwindling ghettos of aspen and birch that struggle in thinner soil and a cooler climate.

It's at least four hours to Ilford, so I climb to smooth air at eighty-five hundred feet as the afternoon sun highlights distant Lake Winnipeg, a two-hundred-mile-long remnant of Lake Agassiz, the immense flood that inundated northern Minnesota, much of North Dakota and most of Manitoba some ten thousand years ago. Fed by the waters of a dying ice age, Lake Agassiz honors Louis Agassiz, the brilliant young naturalist who, in the early 1800s, confronted the Swiss Society of Natural Sciences with two seemingly preposterous claims: that the deep Swiss valleys had once been filled by mile-thick mantles of ice, and that the great blocks of mountain granite that dotted the distant plains had been carried there by glaciers and not by Noah's flood. Instead, Agassiz proposed that "God's great plows," the glaciers, had slowly ground across Europe, overwhelming everything in their paths.

Because the Flood theory had provided a convenient compromise for geologists and theologians alike, Agassiz found only ridicule, and despite the evidence, the Genesis flood held sway. Nevertheless, after a long and often bitter campaign, Agassiz finally replaced the Flood with fact and won the posthumous honor of a glacial lake bearing his name.

Not long before he died, Agassiz wrote, "Every great scientific truth goes through three stages. First, people say it conflicts with the Bible. Next they say it has been discovered before. Lastly, they say they have always believed it."

His brilliance in one field, however, was no guarantee of wisdom in another. Applying some of the same arguments that had been used against him, Agassiz vehemently opposed the meticulous work of a methodical genius named Charles Darwin. Unfortunately, he died before learning that Darwin was right, and he had been wrong. In closing his mind to Darwin, Agassiz set a pattern for those who still promote schemes to have Genesis taught as science in the public schools today.

When Deer Lake draws near, I search for a small, amoeba-shaped lake with a granite-shouldered island that still bears grooves carved by Agassiz' rock-studded glaciers. On the island, a tiny cabin nestles in a balsam-rimmed cove, its red roof matted with russet pine needles and emerald green moss. The cabin, now empty, once belonged to a Deer Lake resident named Oscar Lindokken.

Oscar was pushing eighty when my younger son, Lars, and I taxied up to the Deer Lake seaplane base. Dressed in a red-plaid flannel shirt, jeans and rubber boots, lanky Oscar could have been the model for Jonathan Jo, the A. A. Milne character with "a mouth like an O and a wheelbarrow full of surprises."

Besides resembling Jonathan, Oscar turned out to be equally re-sourceful. Grabbing a wing as we taxied in, he helped secure the Cub, chatting all the while.

"Hi, I'm Oscar Lindokken. Nice Cub you've got there. A friend of mine had one just like it. Where you heading?"

"I'm not sure," I answered. "But we'd be happy with a decent place to camp and a few walleyes or trout."

"You can use my cabin," offered Oscar. "It's the only place on the lake. The keys are in the outhouse, and the boat and motor are ready to go. I haven't been there for a month—lots of fish along the north shore." As he marked the cabin on my map, he added, "And don't talk about payin' me. I'll be glad just to have the place looked at."

For two days Lars and I enjoyed Oscar's cabin, his secluded lake and its marvelous fishing, then left his outboard full of fuel and a big note saying thanks.

A year later, I returned to Deer Lake, only to learn that Oscar had died without seeing his island again. Now, as Oscar's sanctuary falls behind, I remember his generosity and how he typified the many Canadians I've met. Friendly, eager to be helpful and generous to a fault, Oscar truly embodied "the spirit of the North."

The southwesterly winds slowly switch to the north, bringing a solitary thunderstorm to block my path with gusts that bend the pines below as easily as prairie winds ripple fields of wheat. With a touch of rudder and aileron, I detour around the storm's western (and safest) flank while nature torches trees with shards of lightning, then douses them with torrents.

Hindered by the head wind, the Cub's wavering shadow slowly crosses concentric growths of jack pine, spruce and bog, then lazes across a fresh, forest fire burn softened by a haze of violet fireweed. An osprey with a fish in its talons descends to its nest. Moose tracks meander across the bottoms of shallow ponds, each one dotted with white sweet-scented water lilies, the North American version of the lotus that Buddhists revere, believing that if such a beauty can rise from the mud, there is hope for humans, too.

As the last rays of the setting sun gild the metal roof of the Hudson's Bay Company store, I measure the distance from Beaverhouse Lake to Ilford, my destination du jour. One hundred miles remain; the Cub cruises at ninety-two. Knowing that I'll need every bit of the long northern twilight for a landing well past sundown, I feed in full throttle, then crank in some nose-down trim to offset the climb that would otherwise follow. My airspeed rises to ninety-four.

Thirty miles pass. I add more nose-down trim to begin a long descent, and the downhill-running Cub hits one hundred, thirty mph *slower* than a Pete Sampras serve. By the time I level off above the trees, the western sky has dimmed from poppy red to rose, and we're back to ninety-four.

A string of bog-rimmed lakes parallels my course. As each lake passes and the sky slowly dims, I ask myself if there will be enough light to land on the *next* lake, and the answer is always yes. If in doubt, I'll land, for I'd rather spend a cramped night in the Cub than risk a landing on a surface that I can barely see. Finally, a pinprick of light appears on the horizon, and within minutes, the Cub crosses the nine-hundred-mile-long railroad that connects Winnipeg to Churchill, and Ilford flashes by.

Reducing power, I bank away from the purpling eastern sky, slowing the Cub as we clear the trees that encircle Moosenose Lake. The Cub responds to a gentle pull on the stick, raising her cowling toward the rosy afterglow of the Manitoba sky. She flares out over the water, her engine a quiet rumble, her slipstream receding to a gentle hiss. Hard-wired by hands, arms, body and brain, the Cub and I commune, sensing the subtleties of lift and drag that flow across our wings. Aided by peripheral vision, diminishing sound and softening control feedback, we descend like a bird, releasing speed as we plan the approaching stall. Three feet, two feet, then one. Raising the nose a trifle, we skim across Moosenose Lake, our floats slicing its serenity, then settling toward repose.

Ilford was once the hub of the North, home base to the cat-trains of the Sigfusson Line and Lindahl Transport. Fanning out over frozen bog and bay, the cat-trains hauled explosives to mines and supplies to Oxford House, God's Lake and a dozen or more remote outposts. But now, with the trains replaced by aircraft, and the dwindling town connected only by rail to the rest of the world, Ilford's population has shrunk dramatically. Only a few trappers and tourists remain, drawn by the "soft gold" of the North: fur and fish.

Ilford has three, maybe four, miles of road, all gravel, and since no one has noticed my arrival, I begin the trek to town, passing a sagging icehouse where crates of whitefish once chilled while awaiting transport south. On the opposite side of the road, tall columns of lavender fireweed camouflage ranks of rotting steel-shod sledges that once followed growling D-8 Cats. As if they were the dinosaurs of transport, their bones sag into the roadside heath.

Like a dog, I lift my head to inhale cool spruce-scented air still laced with summer's sweet perfumes—glad to be done with diesel exhaust and the clamor of sirens and horns.

In the sixties, pickups rattled down this road while I held my breath against their dust. At the Gold Trail Hotel, two trappers noisily vied for the floor—one eagerly guiding his audience through a visit to the girls at Split Lake, while the other told of the time that Sigfusson's "swing" dropped through the ice into sixty feet of water. This evening, however, barely an insect hums. In the distance, a dog barks; a three-wheeler whines.

Hoping to find my old acquaintances, Kip and Mickey Thompson, I knock on the door of the Gold Trail Hotel. Next to a sign reading "Licensed Beverage House" another complains "Closed Due to High Taxes." I wait, then knock again. No response. When I ask at a nearby house I'm told, "They're open—just pound harder." I again belabor the weathered door, finally bringing a light and a face to it.

Yes, they will rent me a room and rustle up some food, but the elder Thompsons are gone, replaced by their son, Kirk, as full-chested and straight-backed as his father. Later, when Mickey radios in from their Silsby Lake camp, we reminisce about bulldozing their Lake Waskiowaka airstrip out of the bush, and about the German shepherd pup they sold me many years ago.

The pup was supposed to have been a shepherd/Newfoundland cross, like her siblings that were born the year before. The mother was definitely a shepherd, but the Thompsons weren't so sure about Dad. After calling my wife, who said, "Well, OK—gee, maybe not ... I wonder if we should ..." I lured the pup out from beneath the hotel, where she'd been living on fish heads since her mother had been shot, looked her over, paid Kip $50, and carted her off to the plane.

One problem remained: what to tell the U.S. Customs agent. Because I didn't know the regulations for importing dogs and didn't want to detour to Kenora to get shots (and knew it would be stupid to try to hide her) I decided to let the inspector conclude that my new pup was *returning* to the U.S.

On arriving at Customs, I plunked her down in front of the inspector and began to secure the Cub. I answered the usual questions as he gave the Cub a cursory check and then turned to the dog. "What about the puppy?" he asked. "Got any papers?"

"No," I said, with a look of puzzlement, "I don't, but they didn't ask for any on the way out."

"Well," he said, "she looks OK, so you can go."

That night, I took Lady into the shower and removed what appeared to be eight pounds of dirt from a ten-pound dog.

The Thompsons' guess about her Dad turned out to be wrong, for Lady matured into a beautiful German shepherd, the guardian and friend of my wife and sons and my best buddy for eleven short years. When arthritis had almost totally immobilized her, I carried Lady to my veterinarian's office. There, as I cradled her in my arms, an injection stopped her heart.

During the long drive back to our country home, I fought the tears and the ache in my throat. Unable to continue, I pulled to the side of the road. Lowering our station wagon's tailgate, I buried my face in her still-warm fur, and my grief came pouring out.

The Gold Trail Hotel is showing its age: stair treads creak; floors sag and a few of the doors won't close. Thanks to the patchy permafrost below, the hotel tilts slightly toward the railroad tracks as if longing for the life and lights of Thompson, a nickel-mining town not far to the west.

During the night, I'm wakened by an unusual sound. At first I think I've startled myself with my own snoring, but there it is again. It's the call of the Muskeg Express, the train that I once rode to Churchill, ensconced in a sleeper that swayed to and fro while it "sped" along at thirty mph, its velocity restricted by a rail bed undermined by discontinuous permafrost.

I gawk from my second-floor window as the engine plows through daisy-strewn meadows and rafts of fog tinted pink by the predawn sky. Dogs howl; two elderly people get off, another on, delivered by a speeding three-wheeler just as the train departs.

Back in bed, I think again about the Muskeg Express—how my wife and I and four friends once took an airliner to Thompson, then boarded the train in midafternoon. Once we were under way, I sought out our neatly uniformed conductor and asked, "Any chance of riding with the engineer for a while?"

"I think so, sir," he replied. "When we stop at Wabowden, just climb out and walk to the front of the train. I'll tell the engineer that you're coming." Later, as I trudged toward the engine, I conjured up images of the engineer—probably a mature man, grayed at the temples like myself, a serious man with a uniform befitting someone who commands a few hundred tons of rolling freight and dozens of precious passengers.

Instead, I was greeted by a smiling, thirty-something engineer wearing a ripped oil-stained T-shirt, through which a portion of his ample belly protruded. However, as others have noted, clothes do not make the man, and our pleasant visit was surpassed only by the delicious breakfast we were served the following morning while the forest dwindled and miles of tripod telephone poles (the permafrost again) saluted our passage.

A shout from below says "Seven o'clock." By eight, I'm fed and back at Moosenose Lake, checking the oil and gas and pumping out the floats, which are divided into compartments to prevent a single leak from flooding the entire float. Fortunately, the Cub's floats are still quite tight, and I'm soon on my way to York Factory, a centuries-old fur-trading post on the eastern shore of an inland sea that's known as Hudson Bay.

2

Ilford to York Factory, Manitoba

What a pitiful business is the fur trade. . . .
Think how many mushquash and weasel skins the
Hudson's Bay Company piles up annually in their
warehouses leaving the bare, red carcasses on the
banks of the streams through all British America . . .
the place where Great Britain goes amousing.

– HENRY DAVID THOREAU

*A*HEAD LIES GILLAM, the final town on a dead-end road that may someday stop at Churchill. Wedged between the railroad and the Nelson River, Gillam was even smaller than Ilford until Manitoba Hydro dammed (many say "damned") the river and throttled the Nelson's flow.

Those who know bush pilot history might wonder if the town is named for Harold Gillam, the famous Alaskan pilot whose skill and luck earned him the title "Thrill 'em, chill 'em, never kill 'em Gillam," but it's not. Instead, the town takes its name from Zachariah Gillam, the master of the *Nonsuch*, the English ship that returned to England in 1668 with an eye-popping load of New World furs. Buoyed by Gillam's success, British investors quickly moved to form a company that would eventually rival the power of kings and become, for many, almost synonymous with Canada: the Hudson's Bay Company.

The river that flows beneath my wings, however, is nothing like the river that greeted Captain Gillam. Seven dams now hoard its flows, spinning out megawatts of electricity throughout the year to power-hungry homes and businesses along the U.S./Canadian border.

A few hundred miles upstream, water diverted into the Nelson from the Churchill River has eroded the shores of Southern Indian Lake. Manitoba Hydro claimed that the shorelines would stabilize within five years, but twenty years have passed and they still crumble. As the land has eroded, mercury once locked in permafrost and vegetation has found its way into fish, fowl and humans. The Southern Indian natives, with their resorts made worthless and their communities threatened, were forced to leave their homes and move even farther north. Large as it is, the Manitoba Project may eventually be dwarfed by projects on the eastern (Quebec) side of the bay, where an impoundment the size of France will inundate entire ecosystems and alter the weather as well.

The Cub's shadow leaps the Limestone dam as the river explodes from the penstocks into a wide, pasturelike valley. I descend to within fifty feet of the valley floor, weaving between ancient islands that have ridden springtime floods for thousands of years but now lie anchored in seas of grass.

The estuary broadens as it enters Hudson Bay, the inland sea named for Henry Hudson, an obscure British mariner who, after sailing the *Half Moon* up the Hudson River as far as present-day Albany, aimed his new ship, the *Discoverie*, farther north in 1610.

It was already fall by the time Hudson entered the bay. Gambling that the wide expanse of water would lead to the Pacific, he sailed on until it was too late to turn back. Hudson and his men barely survived a horrible winter, and when spring finally arrived, the crew mutinied, setting Hudson, his son and seven loyal sailors adrift in an open boat. The mutineers returned to England, where they somehow avoided death by hanging, but Hudson, his son and the seven sailors were never seen again.

Leaving the Nelson behind, I angle east across thirty miles of quagmire and bog toward the mouth of the nearby Hayes River and a historic post called York Factory, the center of the Hudson's Bay Company fur trade for almost two hundred years. The forest below seems solid and dry, but when I peer down through masses of alder and spruce, reflected sunlight continuously flashes upward from the water-filled sponge below. As a consequence, most of York Factory's few visitors arrive by canoe or by air. (Although the word "Factory" in Hudson's Bay Company place names seems to imply a product, it means that the head man, the factor, lived there.)

York Factory is looking up. Where I once tied to willows, compelled to regularly tend the Cub as the tides slipped up and down the Hayes, a floating dock offers safe mooring, and the airplane tends itself. Wooden stairs now climb the steep clay bank, and as I top the last step, I'm greeted by a slender Indian woman in a white sweatshirt bearing the image of a smiling polar bear beneath the word "Churchill." A baseball cap promoting Trapline guitars shades her dark brown eyes.

Offering her hand, she says, "Hi, I'm Betty Settee."

"Betty," I respond, "you haven't changed a bit since I stopped here maybe four or five years ago."

"Oh!" she exclaims, embarrassed at not having recognized me, "I thought you looked familiar. Are you back for another tour?"

"I sure am."

"OK," she replies, "but before we start, I just put the teapot on, so how about some tea and cakes?"

As I gingerly sip Betty's scalding tea, she reminds me that her husband, Jim, supervises the York Factory site, her job being to escort the occasional tourist when he's occupied.

"You know, Betty," I say, "when I first stopped here in '69, I slept in a little building with three archaeologists who were looking for fur-trade artifacts."

"That building," says Betty, "eventually became my living room."
Then, waving a hand at her new quarters, she adds, "but believe me,
I like *this* much better. It was finished in '94."

Relaxed and knowledgeable, Betty makes good company, and an
hour slips past while we exchange tales. She describes the thirty-to
forty-foot flat-bottomed York boats that replaced freighter canoes in
the early 1800s. Propelled by as many as eight oarsmen, each carried
up to four tons of goods and settlers upriver to Norway House and
Winnipeg, then up the Red River to homestead the northern plains.
The last boat, she says, was built in 1924.

I contribute that here, in 1930, two high school seniors named
Eric Sevareid and Walter Port ended an epic canoe trip that began
in Minneapolis—a trip that tested their endurance, their wits
and their friendship and provided Sevareid an entrée into journal-
ism by becoming the backbone of his first book, *Canoeing with
the Cree*.

As we stroll along the narrow boardwalk above a sprinkling of
red-lobed dewberries toward the Factory's stark-white three-story
centerpiece, I ask Betty, "Didn't the Hudson's Bay Company arrive
in the 1600s?"

"Yesssss," she says, drawing out her answer as she searches for
the date. "They built Fort York, as they called it then, in the 1680s.
But, you know, the Company, or the Bay, as we call it, actually
started out as the Governor and Company of Adventurers of
England Tradeing into Hudson's Bay, and it wasn't even a British
idea. It was proposed by two *French Canadians* named Radisson
and Groseilliers.

"Anyway, with the help of Prince Rupert, they got King Charles
II to give the company a monopoly on trade in Hudson Bay and its
entire drainage system in 1670. They called it Rupert's Land, and it
covered almost half of Canada plus parts of North Dakota and
Minnesota."

"Did you know," I ask, "that Radisson is French for 'radish' and
Groseilliers means 'gooseberries?' And didn't those two eventually
switch over to the French?"

"That's right," she replies. "They started a rival company called the Compagnie du Nord when the Bay wouldn't let them set up inland posts. Expecting to be welcomed, they took off for Quebec with two tons of English furs, but the New France officials seized their ships and fined them a fourth of their cargo for trading without a license. Groseilliers gave up and retired, but Radisson returned to the British, who'd finally realized the value of inland posts and welcomed his return.

"But the sad part is that Radisson, after years of service to the Company, returned to England broke. He begged the Company for work as warehouse keeper; they turned him down. He died at seventy-four and was buried in an unmarked grave."

"So, was it the railroad to Churchill that finally shut York Factory down?"

"I suppose so," she says, "but that was probably just the last straw. By the time the railroad reached Winnipeg in the mid-1800s, the post had already begun to decline. In 1870, the HBC—which some say means Here Before Christ—sold its land claims to Great Britain for $1.5 million. When World War II ended, they shut the Factory down and left it to rot. Now, the Bay is just another retailing chain.

"Most of my people moved inland to Shamattawa or God's Lake, or to the Split Lake reserve near Thompson. A few found work with the railroad or at the nickel mine. With a sweep of her hand, she adds, "Frankly, if it weren't for the government preservation work, all of this would be gone."

The depot—"the Big House"—is all that remains of York Factory's original fifty buildings, but it's still an impressive sight. Letitia Hargraves, the wife of one of the factors, was so impressed by the little community that she imported a Viennese piano and became the talk of the North. Her husband, however, took a more skeptical view, describing York Factory life as "nine months of winter varied by three of rain and mosquitoes."

Shaped like a square doughnut, the depot encloses an equally rectangular inner courtyard. One hundred twelve-pane windows look outward from its walls. On the side that faces the Hayes, a third floor supports a sentry's cupola.

Moving inside, we stroll across planks worn smooth by moccasins, mukluks and bales of fur. "Look up here," says Betty, pointing to a thick wooden wedge atop one of the many eight-by-eight posts that support the second floor. "Because the outer walls of the building rest on the ground, they rise and fall with the annual freezes and thaws more than these sheltered inner posts. To keep the floors level, they put wedges between the inner posts and the beams of the second floor. When the frost lifted the outer walls, they drove the wedges in, then hammered them back in the spring."

Spotting a pile of rusted ax blades, I ask Betty, "How old would these be?"

"A few are from the 1700s, but most are newer."

As I turn the battered blade in my hand, I begin to understand the success of the fur trade—why natives who had toiled with sharpened stones or a chunk of copper would covet a simple ax: a few strokes and a tree is felled—wood for a week in a day.

On the second floor, Betty stops beside a structure that runs ladderlike from floor to ceiling with but one four-by-eight "rung" set five feet above the floor. "This is all that's left of the fur presses," says Betty. The jack screw that the crosspiece held is gone, but carved across the frame of the press in boldface type is an aging record of its source: HARLAND, LONDON. Operated like an overgrown book press, the jack screw compressed ermine, mink, wolverine, fox and beaver pelts into bales for shipment to London, where, in the bustle of Garraway's Coffee House, a nearly spent candle urged bidders on; the last bid entered before the candle guttered out the winner. A variation involved a pin pressed into the side of the candle: the winner was the last to place a bid before the pin fell free.

For the most part, furs were eventually sewn into coats and robes. Beaver hats, however, were already de rigueur by the seventeenth century, thanks to a Charles I decree that proscribed materials other than beaver for the making of hats. (In 1661, the diarist Samuel Pepys recorded that he had he purchased a "bever [hat] which cost me 4 pounds, 5 shillings," a sum that exceeded the annual wages of many workers.) Besides being expensive, the hats caused a more insidious problem: the mercury used to manufacture the cheaper, look-alike rabbit-fur hats poisoned the workers, giving birth to the phrase "mad as a hatter."

"This," says Betty, as we leave the fur press behind, "is the stove room."

Thinking she said "throne room" I glance about, bewildered. Along the walls are the largest assortment of stoves I've ever seen. Rusted and bent, they stand at muster, ready to beat back the cold. Fronting their huge firebox of one of the stoves are doors wide enough to accept a two-foot log—sideways.

"These are Carron stoves, imported from England in sections and assembled on the spot," says Betty, moving between two of the largest and placing a hand on each—at shoulder height.

Beyond the stoves, an assortment of anchors, neatly coiled chains and an array of ship's hardware terminates in pyramids of two- to twenty-pound cannonballs. Most are unblemished, but a few have been plucked, scarred and spent of anger from the surrounding fields, their scent of powder gone.

Hefting one of the midsize balls, I say, "These would be great for lawn bowling."

"You're not the first to think of that," she replies. "After the Factory closed, vandals rolled those cannonballs down these halls into antique whiskey-bottle ten pins. They even tore siding from the building for fuel rather than cut brush."

Another stairway leads to the empty workmen's quarters of the third floor. Here, clay pipes once puffed and workers cheered when the first stoves arrived in 1841, bringing moderation to winters so severe that "the mercury in our thermometers froze so hard that it could be fired from a musket barrel without breaking." Despite the hardworking warehouse stoves, condensation on midwinter walls froze nightly into flowerlike blossoms.

Some sought relief from the relentless cold and isolation in liquor: during the week between Christmas and New Year's Day

1861, the average resident consumed two gallons. But liquor cuts two ways, and the fort's journals bear tales of suffering and suicide.

On the river side of the building, a ladder lifts us from the third floor into a confining cupola. Far below, near the banks of the Hayes, a sturdy foot-thick flagpole that was once a ship's mast lies in a carpet of grass. At its side, a cannon nestles in the heath. Gone without a trace is the hundred-yard-long six-foot-wide boardwalk that once connected the depot's front doors to the riverbank.

As my eyes scan the horizon, I imagine myself a sentry, shivering in the cold while far below the passing Swampy Cree sing to ward off the evil spirits that reside in the *Kihci-waskahikan*, "the Great House." My attention, however, is held not by the natives, but by a ship dropping anchor downstream at Five Fathom Hole. I strain to see her colors, wondering is she friend or foe? Does her hull hold rum, or ranks of soldiers intent on destroying the Fort and pirating the bales of "soft gold" that fill the floors below?

As we leave the building, Betty looks carefully in all directions, and I know the reason. Though we're only six hundred miles from Minnesota, we're surrounded by polar bears. In fact, Ontario's Polar Bear Provincial Park lies even farther *south*.

"Wapusk?" I ask, using the Swampy Cree word for "polar bear," and Betty nods her reply. "We had three yesterday. They're protected, you know. A shot will usually frighten them off, but if we have to, we're allowed to shoot to kill."

"Has that happened?"

"Not yet."

We leave the warehouse behind and stroll to the carriageless cannon. Squatting, I grasp its muzzle with both hands and make a ridiculous attempt to lift one end. As I withdraw my hand from its corroded bore, I remember two men named Thompson. The first was an American Loyalist named Benjamin Thompson (later Count Rumford) who returned to England in 1776, where he oversaw the manufacture of artillery pieces.

Struck by the extreme heat produced during the boring of cannon barrels, he immersed a section in water while it was being bored. The water eventually boiled. By careful weighing and measuring, Thompson disproved the idea that heat was a material substance, proved that heat was caused by motion, and the science of thermodynamics was born.

About the same time, an official of the Hudson's Bay Company sent a letter to London's Grey Coat School for orphaned boys, requesting "four boys trained in navigation." Only two were available. One, on learning his fate, ran away. The other was David Thompson, a charity student, age fourteen. Three months later, young Thompson landed at York Factory and began to survey the wilds to the west. (The town of Thompson bears his name.)

During his thirteen years of service, Thompson, like Radisson and Groseilliers, grew increasingly frustrated by HBC restrictions. Fed up, he quit the "mean and selfish" Bay in 1797 and joined its new and efficient rival, the Montreal-based North West Company.

When Thompson changed horses, no one was more pleased than an influential "North Wester" named Alexander Mackenzie, who was also destined to fame. With Mackenzie's support, Thompson surveyed some eighty thousand miles by canoe, foot and horseback, becoming the first to find a largely navigable route across Canada to the Washington coast. In so doing, Thompson won praise as "the greatest practical land geographer the world has ever produced."

By age forty-six, Thompson had aquired regular investments in the North West Company that allowed him to retire, but after moving his Métis (half native, half white) wife and his children east, he became restless and returned to work, surveying the new U.S./Canada border east from Minnesota's Lake of the Woods.

David Thompson tried to make the world a better place, but in the end, it proved his undoing. He loaned his congregation funds to build a church. They defaulted. He canceled their debt. He set his sons up in business. They failed. He paid their creditors.

Near the end of his life, having already pawned his treasured surveying instruments and his clothes, he had to borrow money for food from a friend. Like Radisson, he appealed for relief to the

Hudson's Bay Company, which had in the interim bought out the North West Company, but was rebuffed. Destitute, he was taken in by relatives in Longueuil, Quebec, where he combined his journals and memories into a manuscript called *Travels*. Lacking money to publish his memoirs, David Thompson died at eighty-five, ending a life of service, charity and honor.

Remembering that Betty hails from Churchill, I ask if she knew Gordon Paul, the Shell dealer who had befriended my father and I on our first trip to Churchill.

"He moved away," she says. "To Winnipeg, I think."

"Quite a man," I continue. "He offered my father and me free use of a fishing cabin that he'd purchased on South Knife Lake."

Her look softens.

"I grew up in that shack . . ." she says, her voice trailing off.

As I wipe my sweating forehead, Betty pauses beside a shaded thermometer. In one of the many ironies of the North, here in polar bear country where temperatures can fall to sixty below, it's ninety-three degrees.

When I fire up the Cub, it idles motionless beside the floating dock, its usual forward motion arrested by the current of the Hayes. With a wave to Betty, I add power. The Cub surges onto the step, accelerating as I lift the right wing to free one float from the river's drag. We spring into the air in a climbing turn, seeking the safety of altitude before we leave York Factory behind.

Far below, a small figure waves. At Betty's side stands her guardian against polar bears, her north country dog. A husky? A malamute? Perhaps a wolf/Alsatian cross? Of course not. Her protector is a feisty eight-pound Pomeranian!

3

York Factory to Churchill, Manitoba

*A lake is the landscape's most beautiful and expressive
feature. It is the earth's eye; looking into which the
beholder measures the depth of his own nature.*

— HENRY DAVID THOREAU

BENEATH A BLUE PORCELAIN SKY, the Tundra
Cub returns to the mouth of the Nelson River,
where hundreds of beluga whales rocket through
cool silty water in pursuit of herringlike fish called capelin.

Opening the Cub's windows to ease the full-bore heat of a mid-
July sun, I lean forward to expose my sweat-soaked back to the
swirling air. My sticky shirt dries, then peels away like shedding
skin. Fluttering, it sends cascades of goose bumps rippling across
my shoulders and down my arms.

In the distance, a rusting, two hundred-yard-long finger of steel
juts out from the Nelson's northern shore. The battered skeleton
of a dredge lies in ruin at one end of the pier, abandoned early in
the twentieth century when it failed to keep pace with the river's

silt-laden floods. At the other end, a handful of swaybacked, flattened buildings lie in ruins—the remains of Port Nelson.

Turning northeast, I descend to two hundred feet and begin to search the rock-studded flats and willow-fringed beaches for polar bears. As expected, the beach is loaded with bears, but whenever the Cub draws close, they mutate into bleached, hump-shouldered boulders. Then, directly ahead, one boulder moves, followed by two at its side—a mother bear and two cubs. The Cub flashes past as she pivots, confronting my big droning bird.

I've found polar bear heaven—single bears, bears in pairs and bears in groups up to five. Some lounge in azure sand-rimmed pools, while others loll on lush swamp grass. One bear, perhaps startled out of sleep by the Cub, jumps up and runs off with surprising speed, reminding me of the futility of trying to outrun a bear.

I suddenly develop a case of nerves. If my engine failed, I'd be forced to land in the shallows that David Thompson deplored two centuries ago: ". . . the sea, when the tide was in appeared deep; [but] by the Ebb retired to such a distance that the sea was not visible and showed an immense surface of Mud with immense boulders of rock from one to five to seven tons weight."

Once down, the Cub would be at risk from wind and wave beside a body of water that rivals the Mediterranean Sea. From its tiny antenna, my ELT (Emergency Location Transmitter) would be shouting to the satellites, "Here I am, here I am," while I counted rifle shells and tried to forget that a polar bear's strength and curiosity are exceeded only by its sense of smell.

I climb a thousand feet, then spot an eastbound freighter far out in the bay, its languid progress revealed by a feeble wake. If it holds course, in five hundred miles it will pass just south of the Belcher Islands. Farther on, it will steam into the bay's most striking feature: a semicircular, three-hundred-mile-wide bite taken out of its eastern shore.

Rugged and rocky, the eastern side of Hudson Bay is as vertical as the western side is flat—perhaps the result of a colossal meteorite strike far out in the bay. In fact, the arcs of the Belchers, the Nastapoka chain of islands and the land surrounding the bite, besides focusing on a common point, enclose an area laced with iron.

If the freighter continues, it will find shelter in the mouth of the Great Whale River, where years ago, I stood beside a different Cub with an engine cylinder in one hand and a connecting rod in the other.

I had flown across the top of Lake Superior to Ontario's Lake Nipigon, then followed the Missinaibi River north to food and fuel at Moosonee. Tired from the long flight, and not realizing that the James Bay tides reached upriver as far as Moosonee, I taxied through glass-smooth water toward the fuel dock and cut the engine, expecting to gently drift to a stop. But when the Cub continued to move briskly toward the pier, I realized that the deceptive, lakelike surface on which I'd landed was *tidal water* sliding rapidly back to James Bay. I was coasting downhill without brakes.

Fortunately, an alert dockhand flopped onto his stomach with arms outstretched to stop one float as I leaped to the front of the other, sat down and extended my legs. Thanks to his quick thinking and our human shock absorbers, the floats escaped damage and I learned yet another lesson about operating in unfamiliar surroundings.

When the fog cleared the following morning, I flew across the marshy terminus of James Bay, then north past the Rupert and La Grande Rivers, whose watersheds have been inundated by Hydro-Québec. Sixty miles south of Great Whale River, while cruising over rolling wooded terrain, I heard the sound of my engine begin to change. I removed my headset, only to have the noise vanish in the engine's roar. But with the headset back on, I could hear it again. Fortunately, I'd had enough hours behind the Continental engine to know its voice, and something was going wrong.

I tried the usual remedies: running on either of its two ignition systems instead of both. No change. Switched fuel tanks. No change. I pulled on the carburetor heat to melt any carburetor ice. No ice. (As an engine pulls air through its carburetor, the air pressure drops à la Bernoulli, accompanied by a drop in temperature. Add further cooling from vaporizing gasoline, and carburetor temperatures can run fifty degrees colder than the air they breathe, instantly freezing humidity to their walls. In times of high humidity, carburetors can slowly choke themselves with ice while inhaling seventy-degree air. Alert pilots notice the gradual drop in power and turn on "carb heat," which feeds the carburetor engine-warmed air from inside the cowling.) Out of ideas, I looked for a beach and landed.

By the time the Cub's floats nudged ashore, the clicking had become hammering. I opened the cowling but found only a trace of oil at the base of the left front cylinder. Suspecting a cracked cylinder, I disconnected its spark plug wires so that they couldn't fire (aircraft engines have *two* spark plugs for each cylinder) and started the engine. No buzzing and no hammering. Probably a cracked cylinder.

I decided that if the cylinder couldn't fire, it might hold together until I reached Great Whale River. If it blew, I'd shut the engine down and land on the nearest lake.

After tying the wires away from the plugs, I started the engine and took off on the remaining three cylinders. Down from its usual ninety horsepower to about sixty-five, the Cub struggled onto the step and began a lengthy takeoff run. I climbed until I had enough altitude to glide to the next lake, then turned north, flying with reduced throttle to ease the strain on the damaged engine.

When Great Whale River finally appeared on the horizon, I relaxed and, like a tourist, began to look around. Suddenly, between glances, half of the town disappeared behind a huge gray cloud, as if a tremendous explosion had blown it apart. Concern for my engine vanished with the town, then returned as the "smoke" dissipated and I spotted a Boeing 737 that had just landed on the village's gravel runway, its reversed jets whipping up an immense dust cloud that had hidden the tiny town.

Unbelievably, the first person I met as I hiked into town turned out to be a diesel mechanic who offered to lend me his tools.

Since aircraft engines, unlike car engines, have cylinders that can be individually replaced, I removed the suspect cylinder, ran a hand around its juglike interior and immediately found a crack extending almost all the way around. Had it completed its circuit, the cylinder head would have blasted through the Cub's cowling, an outstanding event that's guaranteed to attract even the most comatose pilot's attention.

Not knowing if any of the associated parts had been damaged, I ordered a complete assembly flown in from Timmins. Two days and a wad of money later, my "assembly" arrived *unassembled* amid another Boeing-generated explosion of dust. Fortunately, repairing the engine required only a careful reversal of the removal process, and in a few hours, with a smooth-running engine and a test flight completed, I headed north along the rugged Nastapokas toward distant Fort Chimo in search of the George River caribou herd and the tiger trout that prowl the rivers of northern Quebec.

As the freighter fades from sight, I turn inland toward the headwaters of the Owl River, one of the prime polar bear denning areas in all of the world. I'm flying along the tree line, a vague transition zone where forests dwindle and the tundra begins.

The tree line doesn't bisect Canada from west to east, as many assume. Instead, it follows the fifty-degree isotherm southeast from northern Alaska to Churchill, where it leaps Hudson Bay to wander through northern Quebec. Known as the "taiga," or the "Land of the Little Sticks," tree-line country varies from parklike beauty farther inland to the soggy mix of sparse forest, marsh, rock and bog that rims western Hudson Bay.

Because pregnant bears occasionally burrow into the fall tundra, then switch to snow dens as winter arrives, I descend when I reach the Owl, rolling the Cub from side to side as I slow-fly the winding river while searching for polar bear dens.

The Owl, like most rivers that flow through flat country, meanders across the land like ribboned Christmas candy. (The word "meander" derives from Turkey's convoluted Menderes River. The Greeks called it the Maiandras, the Romans the Maeander.) In time, erosion cuts through the narrow stem of land within the loop and builds a sandbar across the old channels to create an oxbow lake, its U shape a reminder of the loops that once confined the necks of laboring oxen.

As I roll out of a hard right turn, a yard-wide opening near the top of the bank catches my eye. I circle the area, searching for lingering bears, then line up with the river and ease back the throttle. As the Cub clears the tips of the stunted spruce, I push her nose down, drop the left wing and kick in right rudder, forward-slipping down between the river banks, then level out as the Cub's floats kiss the face of the Owl.

I secure the Cub to a boulder, slip the Marlin rifle from its case, lever a shell into the chamber, lower the hammer to Safety and climb the gravelly scree.

To avoid surprising any local residents—a badger, a wayward black bear, a skunk or a wandering polar bear—I shout "Hey!" as I climb. Twenty feet from the opening that I spotted, I stop and listen. Only blackbirds rasp a response.

I heave a stone into the den and wait. Climbing higher, I shine my flashlight inside. The shallow den extends inward only three to four feet. Claw marks score its walls. Lying scattered across the floor is an earthy mix of bone scraps, hair and musty leaves. Were the cave bigger, I'd be tempted to crawl inside despite its gamey odors, but with all of it visible, what's the point?

Leaving the den behind, I climb to the top of the bank. I hadn't noticed it from the air, but the grass is thoroughly flattened. Shallow holes dot its surface, as if fox or wolf cubs have been honing their digging skills. The lower branches of the trees have been chewed but not in the way that a deer, caribou or rabbit would strip away bark. Instead, the entire area looks like a wolf cubs' playground.

As I slide back down to the Cub, my stomach complains that Betty's tea and cakes don't make a proper lunch, so I dig out my thermos, the camp stove and a handful of fig bars, then retrieve a can of Dinty Moore beef stew from a float compartment. A few minutes later, the aromas of hot chocolate and beef stew rise above the playground.

The north is rife with insect horror stories, some accurate, some overblown and many of them preventable had their tellers chosen campsites away from running water to avoid blackflies, or in open windswept areas that keep mosquitoes at bay. But for some reason, on this windless day in prime mosquito country, there are very few insects. Those few, perhaps drawn to the heat and fragrance of the bubbling stew, dance in the vapors above the stove. As I watch, one of them plummets into the simmering gravy. Aha, I say to myself, a little extra protein.

With my hunger appeased, I crush the can under my heel and toss it into a bag for later disposal. I refuse to leave trash behind, and I won't travel with those who do. If we can carry full containers in, why shouldn't we haul the empties out?

Taxiing upstream to the end of the long curve on which I landed, I turn downriver and add full power. When the Cub climbs onto the step, I lift one wing to follow the river's arc. The Cub breaks free in seconds and leaves the Owl behind.

To my great surprise, the northwest horizon is hidden in fog. By the time I reach the north-running railroad, the billows have cut off Churchill, so I turn west toward Owl Lake in a race against the fog.

I cross a wide ribbon of sand. Stretching far to the north and south, this inland beach is another remnant of the ice age, a "raised" beach that once rimmed a larger Hudson Bay. While burdened by the mile-thick sheet of ice, the land slowly subsided, only to be flooded by the rising ocean as the ice age finally waned. Relieved of its immense load, the earth began a four-foot-a-century rebound. Now, the ancient beach lies seventy miles from and four hundred feet above Hudson Bay amid a sea of dwarf spruce and jack pine.

Fog is already spilling over the lake's western shore by the time I circle to check for shallows and snags. As I tail the Cub onto the beach, the mists slip in, visibility plummets to a hundred yards and the cool air suddenly quivers with the hum of a million mosquitoes. I retreat to the Cub. Why put up the tent in case the delay is brief?

The mosquitoes, however, have followed me in, and the Cub is filled with their whine. Retrieving a can of insecticide from the tray beneath the instrument panel, I give the cockpit a spray. The result is miraculous: mosquitoes go down like kamikazes, while the foot soldiers stagger and fall. With my life preserver for a headrest, I slump against the side of the cockpit and slide my hat over my eyes. A mist begins to fall as I slip into sleep, lulled by light rain hissing on the fabric of the Tundra Cub.

I awaken with a headful of hammers, then realize why the mosquitoes died so quickly—too much insecticide in such a small space. Squinting through my pain, I open a window to savor the air while hoping that the insects dancing in the shelter of the wing won't notice, but they do. How ironic. Here I am, finally surrounded by females who want me for my body—and they're mosquitoes.

Having driven myself from the plane, I've no choice but to pitch the tent. Fortunately, it's one of those pop-up jobs that's supposed to rise so quickly that one must stand back to avoid being injured. I hurriedly throw in my sleeping bag, rifle and camera, some M&Ms and my foam mattress. Then, after downing two aspirin for my aching head, I slaughter the mosquitoes that have followed me and seek relief in sleep.

It's still light when I awaken. Better yet, a thin glimmer of sunshine warms the western horizon. On my wrist, Mickey Mouse wears his perpetual smile, and proclaims it's 8:00 p.m. I'm famished. After retrieving my telescoping fishing rod from the Cub, I flick it out to full extension, attach a battle-scarred spoon and stroll along the beach, adding my footprints to an assortment of moose, heron and seagull tracks. At a likely-looking spot, I raise the rod, tip back my wrist and send the lure flying. As the red-and-white lure passes the midpoint of its arc, I suddenly realize that the mosquitoes are gone.

I have a theory, a mixture of observation and whimsy, about mosquitoes and other blood-sucking insects. Just as there are seasons for all things, there also seem to be schedules within the seasons. The chunky mosquitoes that clumsily drone about and painlessly probe my flesh appear at different times from the tiny whiners whose annoying sting always precedes an itching welt. To minimize competition, perhaps the ancient insects agreed to divide the territory and parse out the day.

The blackflies, weak fliers that mature in running water, saw the logic in staying near their place of their birth, so tend to plague those who frequent rivers and streams. The more agile mosquitoes, however, divided up the day: culex 1 patrols the dawn, culex 2 prowls at midday, with culex 3 assigned to dusk. Thus, some sort of insect is usually available across the liberally aquatic North. Nevertheless, at times they err, and, like gas stations, become either scarce or omnipresent.

The lure strikes the water. I begin a slow retrieve, then crank quickly for a few seconds. As the flickering spoon approaches, something strikes the lure. The line jerks, slicing a V through the water as I set the hook.

Holding the rod high, I let its arc absorb the frantic struggles from below the surface. With a sudden dash the fish overcomes the reel's clutch, stripping line from its spool. But a few minutes later, a three-pound northern pike lies exhausted on the beach, its gill-plates flaring—gasping for water and drowning in air. Though it has my sympathy, I will eat this fish for supper. And maybe breakfast, too.

I dispatch the pike with a blow to the head. Pressed into the sand, my paddle becomes a plank on which to fillet the pike. Knowing that northern pike, like their pickerel and muskellunge kin, have a *very* slippery coating, I get a good grip before I begin my first cut.

The flesh opens cold, firm and creamy white as my knife makes vertical slits behind the gill plates, then slices down its back from head to tail along each side of the spine. Guiding the blade downward along the outer curve of the ribs, I angle the blade inward toward the visceral cavity. A final slice down the belly separates the two fillets. I lay them skin-down on the paddle, then slide the blade between skin and flesh with a gentle sawing motion. Cleaned, buttered and floured, the fillets are soon sizzling in a battered frying pan atop my Coleman stove.

I once owned an ancient camp stove, a hand-me-down from my father-in-law. Like an antique blowtorch, it had a small reservoir beneath the fuel line that led to the burners. Releasing gas into the reservoir and igniting it vaporized the fuel in the line. For some reason, I always ended up with more gas than the tiny reservoir could hold, the overflow causing an eye-popping geyser of flame. As friends leaped back in alarm, I'd patiently wait for the blaze to subside, then explain that I'd attended the Incendiary School of Cooking with a major in Conflagration.

My new Coleman, however, needs no priming. Better yet, it burns any gasoline, so fueling is simple—just open a quick-drain on one of the Cub's wing tanks.

My menu will be pike fillets, cream of mushroom soup, a hard roll, raw carrots, coffee and a few Oreos. Unfortunately, I forgot the tartar sauce, but I'll take care of that in Churchill.

The northern, which my Canadian friends disdain, calling it a "jackfish," is delicious and could easily pass for a walleye. As I finish the last of my Oreos, I momentarily stop munching to appreciate the silence, then scrub my dishes and brighten my beach with a driftwood fire.

I've always liked the company of a fire, a small fire, an intimate, friendly fire that draws me close. Small fires are user-friendly, and better yet, they toss fewer sparks, a big plus near airplanes, forests and tents.

With the fire crackling and my clean-up done, I carry the northern's remains far down the beach and heave them into the lake. Since I'll be staying the night, I'd rather feed fish, turtles or herons than attract wolverines, skunks or bears.

The wide, almost level beach is rimmed with lichen and moss-encrusted dwarf jack pine, black spruce and birch. Except for the obstruction of an occasional pine that's grown beyond its grasp and toppled into the water, the beach could pass for a tilted sidewalk or a perfectly graded road. In the distance, a loon calls with a voice that's different from the call of my friend back home. It could be an arctic loon.

By the time I return to camp, a thin strip of sunset has transformed the jack pine horizon into the silhouetted teeth of a logger's two-man saw and the fire lies in embers. As I slide across the cool nylon exterior of my sleeping bag amid loon calls, forest fragrance and the fire's glow, I recall the opening sentence of Diane Ackerman's *Natural History of the Senses*: "How sense-luscious the world is." No one will ever say it better.

Morning brings the scent of sunlit tenting, the sight of clearing skies—and thoughts of a sweet roll rescued from the Gold Trail Hotel.

When the Cub rises from Owl Lake, the fog's still thick to the north, so I head west to the Little Churchill River. Thirty minutes later, I'm standing at the front of a float, flipping a jig ahead of the slowly drifting Cub. I let it settle for a second, then add a few twitches. Ziiinggg—it's time to start cranking.

It's a big walleye, quickly followed by several more, but I'd rather have a smaller fish, a two-pounder just for lunch. Finally, after releasing three of its large kin, I catch my next meal just as the current carries the Cub to a sunlit island with a sloping, granite shelf that will serve the Cub quite well.

I rope the Cub to a toppled pine, then return to my still-thrashing pike. As I drag him ashore, my eye catches a lens-shaped fragment of stone—a chip of my bedrock beach. I'm no expert on rocks, but I'm sure that my sharp-edged chip of the Canadian Shield is at least two billion years old. If so, it's just a youngster, for much of the Shield is older still. And as I finger my slender piece of our continent's backbone, which we now can date with ease, I remember that such precision wasn't always possible.

In the fourth century, St. Augustine, the venerated Church father who ordered non-Catholics to "convert or die," proclaimed creation to have occurred in 5500 B.C. Fourteen hundred years after Augustine, a seventeenth-century Irish bishop named James Ussher again took up the task. But with nothing more than the biblical "begats" to work with, the archbishop did even worse than Augustine, declaring with laughable precision that time began on "the beginning of the night that preceded the twenty-third day of October [my birthday, how nice!] in the year . . . 4004 B.C."

When humans were finally free to employ the tools of science without the hinderance of religious dogma, it soon became obvious that the earth was incredibly old. In pursuit of its age, some scientists estimated the time needed for erosion to bring the oceans to their then present salinity, while others worked with the probable cooling rate of an originally molten earth.

By the end of the nineteenth century, Lord Kelvin, who was the first to allow for the heat generated by gravitational contraction, had extended the age of the earth to fifty million years. Still, something was missing. That something turned up in the work of Antoine Henri Becquerel, who first described radioactivity in 1896, and in the laboratory of Marie Curie, who isolated radium a few years later, which, being 100,000 times more radioactive than uranium, eventually took her life. Her notebooks are still to "hot" to handle.

Upon learning that radium produced enough heat to melt an equivalent weight of ice every hour as it slowly "decayed" into lighter elements, scientists had to acknowledge that even Lord Kelvin's results had fallen far short of the mark. A few years later, when it was discovered that all of the unstable elements decay at predictable, uniform rates, scientists realized that the clock they'd sought had been hiding in the rocks themselves, and the door to the age of the earth sprang open.

Imagine, for the moment, that we have been given a pail filled with red marbles that we must count at noon every day. On the first day, all 512 marbles are red. The following noon, however, we're surprised to find that 256 (half) have turned blue, leaving 256 still red. On day three there are only 128 red marbles, the rest having turned blue. Day four yields 64 reds and day five only 32, as half of the remaining red marbles turn blue every day. Scientists, observing this transformation, would say that red marbles have a half-life of one day.

Now imagine that we've been given a pail with a *mixture* of red and blue marbles, then asked how long ago the pail was filled with red marbles. Knowing that the half-life of red marbles is one day, a quick count of each color would provide the answer. Half red—one day old; one-fourth red—two days old; an eighth red—three days old and so on. With such a clock, geologists have determined the age of the earth.

Geologists, however, work with elements that have immensely long half-lives. The half-life of carbon 14, for example, which all living matter contains, is 5,570 years. Near the far end of the scale is uranium 238, with a half-life of four billion years.

Equipped with half-life dating methods, scientists quickly verified what a few had long suspected, that the rocks of the Shield are among the oldest of all, ranging back some four billion years. In comparison, the half-billion-year-old rocks of the continental fringes are mere children. At the midatlantic ridge (or at any erupting volcano), new "land" is pouring forth.

I kill the walleye with a blow to the head, then decide to try my sharp-edged stone as a fish-cleaning knife—Modern Man Employs Stone Age Tool. Thirty seconds later, having gained new respect for my predecessors, I quit before I injure myself.

When the Cub heads north under clearing sunlit skies, I look down on the Little Churchill with fondness. It's a delightful river, a clear river, home to walleyes, grayling and char. Punctuated with mild rapids along its placid course, the Little Churchill is a recreational canoeist's dream. Its namesake, however, the emaciated Churchill River into which it flows, is a terrible disappointment. Rising far to the west in Saskatchewan, its voluminous flows once challenged voyageurs and canoeists with reaches of froth and foam. But now, with most its water diverted to the Nelson, the Churchill's withered remains expose a wide and rocky bed. Once a vigorous giant, the Churchill has become a feeble centenarian whose shriveled body no longer fits its bones.

Two

CHURCHILL TO BAKER LAKE, NUNAVUT

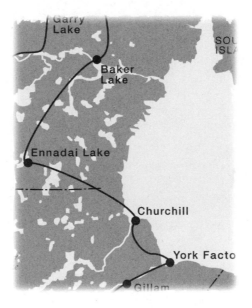

4

Churchill

Churchill brims with history—
most of it dismal.

[*S* CURVY CAUSED] "great pains in the loins, as if a thousand knives had been thrust there. . . . The body was discolored as when someone has a black eye, and all the limbs were powerless; all the teeth were loose, so that it was impossible to eat. . . . We seven miserable persons who were still lying there alive, looked mournfully at each other, hoping every day that the snow would thaw and the ice drift away," wrote Capt. Jens Munk.

The year was 1620. Three survived. Sixty-one died.

When Churchill's five-million-bushel grain elevator punctures the Cape Merry horizon, I select 122.2 mhz on my portable cigarette-carton-size transceiver, summon my most professional tone and casually announce, "Churchill radio, this is Piper 4745 Mike."

"Piper 4745, ahhh Mike, this is Churchill radio."

"Churchill radio, Four five Mike is twenty south, en route to the fort and the Ithaca. I'll need fuel at Landing Lake.

"Four five Mike, Altimeter is 29.86. Wind is south ten knots. Traffic is an inbound Convair twenty minutes north. Monitor this frequency and report on final."

To let the radio operator know that I've understood his transmission, I respond with "Four five Mike, Convair inbound, report final." Such brevity is only custom at remote fields like this, but at major airports that have a constant stream of transmissions, it's absolutely essential.

The Churchill River flares into western Hudson Bay as I swoop low to photograph a wharfside freighter, the first of some thirty ships that will call during a short July-to-November shipping season that's restricted by Hudson Strait ice. Riding low in the water, she's already burdened with prairie-province wheat.

Across the river, on the rock-strewn tundra of Eskimo Point, a centuries-old fiasco known as Fort Prince of Wales rises above the heath like a granitic flat-topped wart. After forty years a-building and eleven years of British use, the fort fell to the French, surrendered by a short-handed garrison in 1782.

As I cross the fortress, I lower a wing to scan the courtyard. Inside the battlements, tourists trailing a rifle-toting guide lift their heads to follow the Cub. Ghostlike, the Cub's shadow flits over the tundra, dances across the river's whitecaps and darts through the demarcation line between the beige silt-laden river and blue-watered Hudson Bay, where pods of torpedolike belugas roll among the swells.

Though we call them "whales," belugas are, in fact, large porpoises that run to sixteen feet and weigh about half a ton. The young wear suits of battleship gray; on maturing, they'll don the adults' white.

In 1961, the freighter *Ithaca* lost her steering and anchors in a colossal Hudson Bay storm. Driven aground a dozen miles from town, she squats among the boulders, dry-docked forever. There, despite her gale-canted funnel and a hull holed by cutting torches and wind-driven ice, her cranes still beg for a cargo as if she's ready to put out to sea.

As I orbit the ship, the afternoon sun cuts through the *Ithaca*'s wheelhouse, spreading golden light across a binnacle that's held its final course. I'm tempted to rent a car, bring a grappling hook and a rope ladder and climb aboard. I envision myself standing at the helm of the landlocked ship, grasping wheel handles worn smooth by a seaman's grip. If I lived here I'd have done it long ago, but I put it out of my mind. I haven't the time and it's too risky to try by myself.

The seaplane docks at Landing Lake are even shabbier than I'd remembered—a disintegrating assemblage of planks that threaten aircraft floats in any wind. The only decent dock is reserved for fueling, so I head that way, leaving tie-down decisions for later.

Someone calls when I remove my headset, and I swivel in search of the source. He calls again; I laugh at myself. It's an arctic loon.

Thirty minutes later, a Northwinds Shell truck rumbles into sight, backs up to the Cub, and out jumps Al. Thin as a strut and wearing a smile that begins at his ears, he yells, "Hi, there! Where'd you come from?"

"York Factory," I reply.

As I hoist the hose to the top of the wing, Al warns me, "Get a good grip on that hose. This pump is fast."

Although I take his warning seriously, the recoil almost rips the nozzle from my hands as the first of the Cub's two eighteen-gallon tanks fills in seconds, jetting a geyser of blue-tinted fuel into my face and eyes. I'm the victim of equipment designed for brutes with several hundred-gallon-tanks and sidewalk wings that you kneel on while the pump rams in the fuel. As I wipe hundred-octane gas from my burning eyes, Al apologizes, adding, "Hey, I'll take off a couple of gallons from the bill for spillage." At $3.84 a gallon, it's appreciated.

With the Cub secure, we jolt off toward town.

"You lived here long, Al?"

"Three years," he says, rolling his eyes. "Three lonnnnng years."

"So you're not planning to stay?

"No way," he replies. "My girlfriend's trying to find work for me in Winnipeg, but job or not, I'm leaving come winter." While Al laments his separation from his Winnipeg sweetie, I ponder a town of a thousand with an airport suited to a city a hundred times its size. Built and operated by the U.S. Air Force during World War II, the base reverted to Canada in 1945.

My driver is the antithesis of W. E. (Ernie) Senior, the enthusiastic publisher of *The Taiga Times*, Churchill's mimeographed "newspaper" during the sixties. Ernie, the quintessential booster, not only had great plans for Churchill, but he was also one of the few who cared about Churchill's minority ethnic groups, writing often on their behalf.

Ernie predicted (correctly) that tourism would someday provide a major boost to Churchill's economy, railed against Manitoba Hydro's diversion of the Churchill River and lobbied for an all-weather road from Churchill to Winnipeg. Forty years later, Ernie's road is still a dream.

As we follow the three-legged utility poles into town, I ask Al to take a turn past Churchill's unique Eskimo Museum, which has been curated since its 1941 inception by Brother John Volant, a walking encyclopedia of Inuit culture. There, I've spent hours under Brother John's wing while he patiently answered my questions in his breathy, cigar-scented, Brittany baritone. Captivated by his charm and the knowledge he'd accumulated during decades in the Arctic, my father and I once invited him to join us for supper. To our surprise he replied, "I'll have to ask the bishop for permission," and hurried off. That evening, we dined on T-bone steaks at the Hudson Hotel while Brother John served up tales of an Inuit culture that he knew as well as his own.

Perhaps only the natives stay in Churchill. When I ask if Brother Volant still runs the museum, I learn that he left for Winnipeg in 1991. Art Cripps, the dark-haired free spirit who shepherded tourists around town in the sixties is with Manitoba Hydro in Gillam. Gordon Paul, the friendly Shell dealer who purchased the shack in which Betty Settee was raised, has moved south to Winnipeg. The only Caucasian resident I've known who stayed to the end was Angus MacIver, the rawboned septuagenarian Scot who ferried tourists across to the fort in his freighter canoe and chronicled his adventurous life in a book titled *Churchill on Hudson Bay*.

Despite its frontierlike character, Churchill has gradually changed. In the seventies, the Hudson Hotel burned to the ground, leaving embers and rumors of arson. Later, the Churchill Hotel vanished in flames and similar speculation, leaving an opening for the Tundra Inn, the Arctic Inn and the Polar Hotel. But the most obvious improvement is a sprawling building called the Town Centre. Built in the seventies on the rock ridge that separates the town from Hudson Bay, the centre, with its wide expanses of glass overlooking the bay, is Churchill's administrative, recreational and health service hub. On its several floors, the centre houses a hospital, the school, a gymnasium, curling rink, bowling alley, movie theater, hockey arena, swimming pool and cafeteria.

The centre's halls abound with native images. Boldly colored, imaginative hangings of Inuit art line the corridor to the cafeteria, where an ingenious artist has sculpted a ten-foot tall polar bear statue/children's slide out of a huge block of spiked-together planks.

Architecturally, Churchill runs from Quonset hut to California modern, including an interesting tourist trap/trading post, an excellent restaurant, a supermarket/variety store, a bakery, a Parks Canada theater, a two-story wooden teepee and a co-op that sells Inuit carvings and native crafts—all of them dwarfed by the grain elevator that provides a big chunk of Churchill's seasonal economy.

Churchill's polyglot population of whites, Indians and Inuit rises each year with the mid-July to November tourist and shipping season. Then, when the summer sun has finally removed the ice (and prohibitive insurance rates) from the Hudson Strait, freighters steam into port, their crews adding bits of Polish, Danish or German to a Main Street accustomed to English, Inuktitut, Chipewyan and Cree.

Al drops me off at Steve Bosnjak's Churchill Motel. Steve, a hard-working Croatian immigrant and middle-aged bachelor, hires his tourist-season waitresses from southern Manitoba. He treats them well, calls them his daughters and they call him Dad.

The Muskeg Express has just pulled in, and Steve is too busy to talk, so I stow my gear and hike toward the river, eager to see how the Métis have fared. In the sixties, the Métis were still living in a grubby area beside the river called "the Flats." Unwanted by both natives and whites, and virtually ignored by the government, they survived in makeshift tarpaper hovels. There, they somehow managed a precarious hand-to-mouth existence in country that hosts five million mosquitoes to the acre and is known as the "home of the windchill."

As I walk, I'm surrounded by the sounds of industry: a tug working the harbor, trucks gearing down for the turn to the elevator, the idling diesel engine of the Muskeg Express. But in a single moment the din is displaced by the sensuous scent of the sea. Breathing deeply, I inhale not Ilford's delicate mix of wild rose and evergreen but the fecund tide of the estuary, rich with the fragrance of life.

A sun-warmed smile spreads across my face as I realize that the daisy-strewn fields that surround me were once the shantytown Flats. Aided by the support of an awakened government, the hovels of the Flats were finally razed and new housing provided. Today, rag-clothed Métis children no longer stand before their flimsy shacks to stare numbly into the cameras of well-dressed tourists from another world.

Churchill's social problems accumulated during decades of governmental mismanagement and indifference. Three hundred years ago, a fairly stable population of some ten thousand Chipewyans occupied the land to the west of Churchill. Then Europeans arrived, bringing alcohol, syphilis and smallpox. By the twentieth century, as few as a thousand remained. Of that thousand, about a third slowly gravitated to Hudson's Bay Company posts within a few days' paddle of Churchill.

When the railroad reached Churchill in 1929, the HBC moved their post one hundred miles northwest to Duck Lake to avoid competition from newly arrived free traders. According to *The Taiga Times*, "Except for the HBC manager, the servants and a few old men and women, no one lived at the Duck Lake Post for the entire year.

Trapping began in the fall and lasted until spring." Summer, with the band reunited, was more like a holiday. The event of the year, however, was Treaty Day, the natives' *ka-soniyaskak*, the "time of money," when the Indian agent arrived amid a great show of pomp, accompanied by a Mountie and sometimes a doctor and nurse. At the appropriate time the head of every family received his treaty money, after which he rushed to the Bay to buy whatever he could afford, except for alcohol, which was forbidden.

When the forties and fifties brought a slump in the market for long-haired fur, the Bay closed many of its inland posts, Duck Lake included. As *The Taiga Times* reported, "Faced with the Company's departure, the Indian Affairs branch decided to move the Chipewyan band to Churchill, where it would be closer to administration, schools and employment. A quick economic survey was conducted . . . concluding [some say falsely] that the Indians at Duck Lake are starving and Chipewyans are wantonly decimating the caribou herds."

In 1957, when the time came to move, the federal Indian Affairs department offered to transport the entire band by plane if they would abandon their dogs and sleds—their means of livelihood. The majority chose to move by aircraft, only to discover that space was extremely limited. As a result, many housekeeping goods, outboard motors and other essentials had to be left behind.

The Chipewyans were housed at a site called Camp 10, an area that one reporter charitably described as "extremely unattractive." Those who had driven their dog teams from Duck Lake camped across the Churchill River in small patches of brush while trying to eke out a living by fishing and trapping.

The Chipewyans quickly came to hate life at Churchill. Unable to speak English, and by nature shy and bush-like in attire and mannerism, they were ill equipped to compete for jobs and social status. Lacking education and organization, the Chipewyans bottomed out.

Years of unemployment and inactivity led to alcohol abuse. Unscrupulous whites profited by purchasing toboggans, traps and caribou meat from the Chipewyans for one-dollar bottles of wine. In

1960, when the sale of liquor to Indians became legal, the use of alcohol at Camp 10 soared: one Royal Canadian Mounted Policeman noted that 95 percent of work at Churchill involved Camp 10.

Time, intelligence and a change in governmental attitudes eventually brought improvements to the Chipewyans and to the Métis as well. The Camp 10 ghetto was abandoned in favor of a new settlement called Dene ("the people") village, and as the natives learned English, the job market slowly improved, and the process of integration began.

Like most frontier communities, Churchill had its share of entrepreneurs, but few have matched Johnny Bilenduke, the optimist who started a hog farm, feeding his hogs garbage from the air base. The polar bears, on discovering pork chop heaven, often had to be driven away six times a day. Finally, as Bilenduke lamented, "One day they learned how to climb my chain link fence, and that was the end of my hog farming days."

Canada is home to two-thirds of the world's twenty-five thousand polar bears, and Churchill rightly calls itself "the polar bear capital of the world." Visit Churchill in June, and most of the bears will still be out on the ice, hunting seals. But when the ice leaves the bay in July, the bears return to the coast to top off their season with jet black crow berries, blueberries and tidbits from the Churchill dump, where tourists photograph them from the safety of Tundra Buggies, a bit of four-wheel-drive entrepreneurism that has turned out very well.

In the late seventies, Len Smith decided to cash in on the tourist trade. Realizing that cabs and rental cars were unsuitable (a car window won't stop a determined bear) Len decided to build a safe off-road vehicle that could carry a couple of dozen passengers. Working from plans in his head and parts from a bucket loader and a few other vehicles, he topped his four-wheel-drive creation with a huge box, added floatation tires, put in a wood-burning stove and a bathroom and began carrying tourists. Today, up to thirty-six passengers can watch bears from a larger vehicle's open observation deck or from windows set well above their eight-foot reach. As his business grew, Tundra Buggy Tours added a fifty-foot bunkhouse-on-wheels that sleeps sixteen, plus a diner with a full kitchen and tables for twenty-eight.

Because polar bears tend to congregate in the Churchill area before freeze-up, they're plentiful from late August to November, but during the mild mid-July and August days that encourage trips across the river to the fort, a Tundra Buggy ride might yield only gulls, geese and ptarmigan—or, if you're lucky, a caribou or arctic fox. Then, pilots have the advantage, for the scattered bears are easily seen from the air.

Known to the Inuit as Tornarssuk, to the scientist as *Ursus maritimus*, and to much of the world as Nanook, the Ice Bears' circumpolar range makes them citizens of Canada, Greenland, Norway, Finland, Russia and the United States. Hunting the margins of the circumpolar pack, Nanook slides silently across the ice to stalk a sleeping seal, dives into the ocean for mussels and kelp and dines omnivorously through the summer on whatever the land provides. And although we call them "polar" bears, denning females have been found on James Bay, the southern tongue of Hudson Bay, just four hundred miles from Lake Superior. Pregnant bears remain ashore when the bay begins to freeze, digging into snowdrifts downwind from hummocks and ridges. Cubs, usually two, but occasionally one or three, are born in late December or early January. Weighing little more than a pound at birth, the cubs cannot hear for three weeks, and another week will pass before they can see. By the sixth, they're walking, and when mother breaks out of the den in late March or early April, the cubs are ready to roll.

Were it not for firearms, polar bears wouldn't need protection, as adult males can weigh 1,500 pounds, depending on the season and their success with the seals. (The largest polar bear on record weighed 2,210 pounds and stands in the Anchorage, Alaska, airport.) In 1956, the U.S.S.R. banned polar bear hunting, setting an example that eventually led to international limits on polar bear kills and to the creation of sanctuaries like Ontario's Polar Bear Provincial Park.

Unfortunately, Nanook's curiosity and fine sense of smell often lead to trouble with humans. Churchill-area cabin owners board up their shacks with plywood and lay spike-studded planks on their steps, but the bears routinely rip off the plywood and plunder the cabins. Even so, despite their power and occasional ferocity, Churchill area polar bears can be surprisingly amiable, sometimes even declining to dine on chained sled dogs in favor of playing with them, as evidenced by remarkable public television videos that have featured polar bears playfully wrestling, cavorting and hugging anxious-looking, chained sled dogs before flopping down beside them, exhausted from their play.

Still, the bears are not to be taken lightly. At Churchill, bears mauled people in '66 and '67, killed a child in '68, a man in '83 and a woman in '98. During the 1980s, an average of two bears a year were shot at Churchill alone.

On one occasion, a ground crewman guiding an airliner to a parking place became increasingly irritated when the pilot ignored his signals and kept flashing his taxi lights. Disgusted, the crewman turned to walk away and discovered a polar bear rearing up behind him. As the crewman ran to the plane, the pilot revved the engines and drove the bear away.

Most bear encounters result in retreats and, occasionally, a good laugh. When one bear ambled into the Legion Hall and headed straight for a group of dart throwers, the club steward, an old English army major, shouted, "You're not a member. Get out of here!" The bear left.

Perhaps because they're bear-free for much of the year, Churchill residents vigorously defend their bears. "Look at California," one resident said. "They once had 150,000 grizzlies. It's their state symbol. But they shot the last one in 1922."

After picking up a rental car from Polar U-Drive, I head toward the airport to search for *Miss Piggy*, a wrecked c-46 named for her once-rotund fuselage. After a few false starts down gravel roads that wander off to the Bay, I finally locate the wreck.

One account claims that the twin-engine transport lost an engine while far out over the bay. Heavily loaded, *Miss Piggy* slowly descended until it was within thirty feet of the rotting summertime ice. There, it flew in "ground effect," aided by a cushion of air trapped between the ice and the aircraft's wings. Barely flying, the C-46 labored on toward Churchill, but when it encountered the gentle mile-long uphill slope to the airport, *Miss Piggy* couldn't climb. Shearing off a scattering of black spruce, *Miss Piggy* smashed across truck-size boulders, her aluminum skin screeching as she slid to a stop. The crew survived because the pilot brought the aircraft in under control, saving lives with good airmanship and a sturdy hull.

Pushing the unlikely possibility of a bear encounter from my mind, I grab my camera and, leaving the car door open, climb from a boulder onto the port wing, then stride across the buckled aluminum sidewalk toward a fuselage bearing a red lightning stripe and the name LAMBAIR in bold black print.

I peer into the dimly lit, empty cargo compartment. Broken windows scatter slivers of light into the tunnel of the fuselage. Making my way forward, I discover that the instruments have been stripped from the panel, leaving behind an expanse of empty eye sockets from which wire nerves dangle. The windshield is shattered inward, broken not by the crash but by the rocks of vandals.

As I leave the fuselage, I stop for a moment beside a streamlined engine cowling faired into the top of the wing. At its front, a magnificent, eighteen-cylinder engine once poured out more than a thousand horsepower. But engines, like their builders, eventually tire and die, sometimes with little warning. The engine and its mate from the starboard wing have been removed, disassembled and inspected. Damaged parts became scrap. Still, I wouldn't be surprised if somewhere, a few of *Miss Piggy*'s cylinders have found new life on another crankcase and are still hauling freight and passengers for those who trust their aircraft and the engines that make them fly.

Spotting a dead six-foot-tall spruce near the end of the wing, I break it across my knee and smooth its stub with my pocket knife.

How many summers built this inch-thick trunk? I remove my glasses to combine my myopia with the magnifying power of my wide angle lens and begin counting. Three counts later, I know that my inch-thick spruce, if it died recently, took root during the term of President McKinley and struggled on for a hundred years.

The road to town passes little islands of stunted spruce trees wearing snow-blasted "bare midriffs" over drift-protected skirts of greenery. Above their barren waists, a few short branches struggle against the prevailing wind, while on their southeast sides, healthy branches stream away like windblown scarves. Like synchronized ballerinas frozen in midpirouette, their arms point away from the northwest wind.

As I motor past ponds littered with ducks, geese and shorebirds, I suddenly come upon two lounging roadside bears. I pull to a stop, and while they ignore me snap photos from fifteen feet. Perhaps they've heard about Ursus Alcatraz, the jail that provides an alternative to expensive helicopter rides out of town for trapped delinquent bears. But like its namesake in San Francisco Bay, this Alcatraz is also empty; no caged Nanooks pace to and fro while awaiting the reprieve of solid Hudson Bay ice.

The sun's still high, though it's 9:00 p.m.—definitely time for supper. At the Trader's Table, my placemat depicts two seated polar bears bending over steaming mugs of coffee while the amber glow of candlelight warms their pearlescent fur. By the time I've downed the last of my porterhouse steak, my evening plans are made: a bottle of Molson ale, a little television and a bed at the Churchill Motel. Life is hard on the northern frontier.

"Fred" tells me that he runs a river-taxi service "on the side," which means that he takes tourists across to the fort, but lacks a commercial license and insurance. But because Fred's attitude is "you're the boss," and he has a shotgun with firecracker shells to ward off inquisitive bears (and the price is right) I pass up Sea North's long and beamy, thirty-two passenger six-hundred-horsepower, aluminum launch and downsize to Fred's fourteen-foot Alumacraft and his twenty-horse Mercury. Besides, Sea North's vessel draws much more water than Fred's and must time its trips to the tides. Fred, however, can come and go at will, and he'll stop at Sloop's Cove, a concession that Sea North cannot make.

Fred's an old-timer, having lived at Churchill for thirty-six years. His short, bony, fiftyish frame shows surprising strength as he hoists the Merc onto the transom and, with one hand and a knee, shoves the Alumacraft into the river.

Fred turns upstream, and within a minute I spot jets of mist rising above the swells. "Belugas!" I shout, but Fred's already seen them. Seeing their exhalations is easy enough, but getting close quickly becomes a chore, for while we cruise back and forth on the surface, the whales make use of the depths.

When Fred cuts the motor as we enter Sloop's Cove, the brief silence is suddenly broken by a loud puuffffff directly behind us, and as we turn, another puuffffff. Four of the thousands of belugas that visit the Churchill River have followed us into the cove—three adults and one juvenile. Slipping through the water like alabaster columns, they pass within fifteen feet, their exhalations sounding like speech teachers demonstrating plosives to a diction class.

As we climb the weathered granite, Fred describes the beluga hunts that ended in '67: "Someone got the bright idea to can the blubber, sell the hides and market beluga meat for mink food. If I remember right, the going rate for a beluga was about $1.25 per foot. They'd motor up to the whales and shoot or spear them and tow them off to the plant. In case you're wondering, no one knows how many wounded belugas escaped, later to die in the bay.

"The factory was just a rough-board building on the edge of the tidal flats. They'd winch the whales into the plant and strip off the blubber. Outside, dozens of severed beluga heads were strewn about, each head oozing tiny streams of blood past green algae-coated boulders. The shallows had turned a faded pink.

"But the demand for muktuk never materialized, and the cannery failed. Later, the government found high levels of mercury in the meat."

Thirty yards from the shoreline, a deeply rusted mooring ring is pinned to the rock. Why so far from shore? Because post-ice-age rebound has raised the ring a good nine feet, adding yards of sloping shoreline during the 250 years since its anchoring-pin was driven home.

Fred slows when he reaches the top of the rise, taking care to avoid the inscriptions at his feet. Scattered across the light gray outcropping are more than a dozen names and dates, and one grim illustration.

One inscription, adorned at top and bottom with decorative scrolls, reads

Richard J Johnson

1773

A larger, more elaborate engraving remembers the last commander of Fort Prince of Wales:

S L Hearne

July ye 1 1767

The illustration, however, depicts a hanging. Chiseled into the stone by amateurish hands are the words "John Kelley—From the Isle of Wight" and "1765." According to Fred, Mr. Kelley stole a Christmas goose and in so doing cooked his own.

By the time we arrive at the fort, the rising tide has done us a great favor, inundating thirty yards of slippery algae-coated boulders. I persuade Fred to help me search for an Inuit grave that once lay close to the fort, but we come up empty-handed. Constrained by rock and permafrost, the Inuit simply covered their dead with stones, and though the mound was prominent thirty years ago, it's nowhere in sight today—perhaps carried off by the thoughtless who search for souvenirs.

The fortress squats under glowering stratus clouds like a dark Macbethan castle, its sixteen-foot-high limestone walls rising above the V-shaped stone ravelin that shielded its timber doors from frontal assault.

As we enter the fort, Flora Beardy, a stocky Parks Canada guide emerges with her flock of tourists. One vacationer keeps insisting that the lovely lavender fireweed surrounding the fort are lupines, while Flora, her moon face wreathed in smiles, tries to correct her. It's an uphill fight.

Fort Prince of Wales forms a square, a hundred yards on a side, with bastions like arrowheads protruding from each corner. The fort, which was begun in 1731, took forty years to complete. Built by the HBC to protect its fur trade, the fort with its forty cannons, still plays at guarding the only deep-water port on Hudson Bay. (Although the HBC claimed to oppose using liquor for pay, it awarded stonemason Thomas Smith an extra ten *gallons* of brandy a year for the risks he took while blasting out rock for the fortress's walls.)

When Samuel Hearne arrived in 1766, he found the fort commanded by an unscrupulous tyrant named Moses Norton, whom Hearne, a deist and an admirer of Voltaire, quickly grew to despise, describing Norton as "one of the most debauched wretches under the sun." (Norton, who was a notorious philanderer, and who had a handful of native "wives," two of whom he is said to have poisoned, required his men to listen to him preach about ethics and moral living.)

On hearing rumors of a river rich with copper far to the north and west, Norton sent Hearne to search it out but supplied him so poorly that the poor man almost starved. Worse yet, the guide Norton provided robbed and abandoned Hearne when they were hundreds of miles from the fort.

Hearne tried again the following year, again with bad "luck" when another of Norton's guides not only got lost but freely shared vital provisions with every native they met. Abandoned again, Hearne turned back, starving and alone. And then, in one of the great good luck stories of history, Hearne stumbled onto a Chipewyan chief named Matonabbee, who led him back to the fort.

Twelve days later, Hearne set out again, this time accompanied by Matonabbee and his eight wives, who, being traditional native women, did most of the work. Matonabbee proved far superior to Norton's guides, for he not only knew the terrain but he could also manage people. On his third attempt, Hearne finally reached the arctic coast near Coppermine. His journey, however, was marred by the massacre of an Inuit encampment that neither he nor Matonabbee could prevent at a place called Bloody Fall.

Nevertheless, Hearne's respect for Matonabbee held: "He had so much natural good sense and liberality of sentiment that he would not ridicule any particular sect on account of their religious opinion. He held them all in equal esteem, but was determined that as he came into this world, so would he go out of it—without professing any religion at all. Not withstanding, I have met few Christians who possess as many good qualities, or fewer bad ones." Hearne praised Matonabbee's "scrupulous adherence to truth . . . his benevolence and universal humanity to all . . . he was always the master of himself."

Toward the end of their return trek, they had nothing but tobacco and snow water. Hearne's toenails fell from his injured feet, leaving "the print of my feet in blood." No mine was discovered: only a few scraps of copper were found. But with his three attempts and five thousand miles of travel, Hearne finally proved that the long-sought inland waterway from Hudson Bay to the Orient simply didn't exist.

Shortly after his return, Norton ordered Hearne to establish an inland trading post far to the west on the Saskatchewan River. When Cumberland House was finally completed, a second stroke of luck fell to Samuel Hearne: Moses Norton died.

Promoted to commander, Hearne took charge of the fort and married one of Norton's Métis daughters, an attractive sixteen-year-old named Mary. Hearne, happily married and content to stay put, would later describe the following years as the best of his life. Unfortunately, they didn't last very long.

In 1782, the French privateer Comte Jean-François La Perouse, sailed up to the fort with three men-of-war at a very propitious time for the French. With only thirty-nine men in a fort that required at least three hundred to man its forty cannons, Hearne was compelled to surrender.

La Perouse torched the interior buildings and drove iron spikes into the cannon's ignition holes, transforming the great stone fort into a great stone folly. He then set off to attack York Factory. Hearne and his men were allowed to return to England, but the fort was never staffed again.

When Matonabbee learned that Hearne had become a prisoner of the French, he assumed that Hearne would be murdered. Believing also that the French would refuse to trade with him, he committed suicide. Without Matonabbee to assist them, his wives and children starved to death the following winter, along with Mary, Hearne's young wife. At about the same time, a smallpox epidemic swept up from the south, and half of the Chipewyan population perished.

The Hudson's Bay Company shipped Hearne back to Churchill in 1783 with orders to build a new post upriver from the damaged fort. Eager for a reunion with his wife and Matonabbee, Hearne arrived in midsummer, only to learn of their deaths. He resigned his command in 1787 and soon fell ill. He died at forty-seven. Chief Matonabbee, Hearne's friend and savior, is honored by a bronze plaque near the path that leads to the fort, but only the Sloop's Cove inscription keeps thoughts of Hearne alive.

Fred enters the fort and heads for a wooden ladder to climb to the top of the walls. By the time I mount the ladder, he's crossed to the windward side and is scanning Button Bay.

In the courtyard below, a few stone walls remain—remnants of buildings in which men shivered through seemingly endless winters, using heated cannonballs to warm frigid nights. Wine and beer, even when stored inside, froze solid. As a remedy, the men dug an eight-foot-deep pit and buried the spirits in horse manure. It worked.

I'm sighting along a cannon barrel toward Sea North's departing boat, when Fred softly calls my name. Pointing over the fortress wall, he silently mouths the word, "bear." I arrive just in time to see a polar bear disappear behind the six-foot-high V-shaped stone ravelin that protected the fortress's wooden doors from frontal assualt.

"Want to follow him?" asks Fred.

"OK," I answer, with a glance at his shotgun.

The bear is fifty yards away by the time we reach the ravelin, ambling toward the river at an angle that will take him through our scent. He stops, lifts his head and turns. Spotting us, he rises on his hind legs for a better look, then drops to all fours and casually strolls away. He might be annoyed, but he certainly isn't afraid.

The bear eases into the river and heads straight for Churchill.

"Jeez," says Fred, "we don't want him on Main Street, eh? Let's head him off with the boat."

By the time we idle alongside, he's a third of the way across, slipping through the water with easy grace, his pearly coat greened by algae growing within his hollow guard hairs. I marvel at his grace, how smoothly his big paddle-feet move him along, how *big* he is, though I guess his weight at no more than eight hundred pounds. Staying a few yards to one side, we slowly turn him back to the fort.

He suddenly dives, coursing through aquamarine water for twenty to thirty feet, then surfaces, as if expecting that we'd be gone. Having failed to elude us, he shakes his head in a halo of spray and heads back to Eskimo Point.

A shaft of sunlight enlivens the western sky as we drag Fred's boat ashore. Assuming that it's a harbinger of clearing skies, I ask Fred to wait outside the motel while I phone the airport. "Yes," they say, "the satellite shows that it's clearing from the west."

I file a flight note, grab my gear and ask Fred for a ride to the seaplane base, where I thank him for his help and pump a few pints of water from the floats. As I step from the end of the float to the slippery pier, my feet suddenly fly out from beneath me and I tumble into the lake. I prepare myself for a quick leap back to shore, but my feet find only soft, yielding muck. I climb out sputtering, remove my clothes and wring them out, then spot blood seeping from a scratch on my leg.

My clothes will dry in the heated Cub, so I struggle into them while smashing mosquitoes on my abundantly exposed skin. As I stow the rest of my gear, I notice the debris churned up by my plunge—great gobs of goose and loon excrement.

Tetanus! It's been *years* since my last tetanus shot, and I dare not leave without one. Fred, who has been smiling at my antics, agrees to run me back to the Town Centre, where a nurse provides my shot. When I offer to pay, I'm told to forget it. I'm a foreigner, and the paper work's too daunting.

The ever-obliging Steve Bosnjak lets me back into my room for a shower and a change of clothes, then drives me back to the Cub. Ninety minutes after my back flip, the Tundra Cub leaves Churchill's ramshackle docks behind. I contact Churchill Radio and report my next destination, Ennadai Lake.

The fort passes beneath my wings while I scan the tundra for Fred's polar bear, but it's nowhere in sight. In the transparent waters of Button Bay, hundreds of free-swimming belugas roll and dive. And as my camera preserves the moment, I regret that we capture these intelligent, social animals whose wanderings span hundreds of miles and imprison them in the bathtubs of our zoos.

"Churchill radio, Four five Mike is 20 miles northwest."

"Four five Mike, I have you leaving the zone at five five-[4:55]. Good day."

5

Churchill to Baker Lake, Nunavut

I am glad I shall never be young without wild country
to be young in. What avail are forty freedoms
without a blank spot on the map?

– ALDO LEOPOLD

*L*OOSENING MY SEAT BELT, I squirm around to retrieve a thermos of coffee from the back seat. It's already sugared and creamed, and it sets my mouth watering by the time I find its companion, a delicious Danish from the Churchill bakery. As I savor my in-flight meal, Caribou Lake slips beneath my wings, bringing memories of a trapper described in *Canada* (Life World Library).

"In the winter of 1947, a trapper named Shaback, lying in a makeshift shack . . . made this entry in his diary: '43rd day without food.' The previous September, finding little game and fearing starvation, he had begun to walk down the Caribou River toward civilization. Weakened by hunger, he had holed up in an empty shack. Awkwardly, Shaback carved three words on a piece of wood, went out into the thirty-degree-below-zero cold, nailed the piece of wood on the door of his shack and went inside again.

"Over a year later, a half-breed trapper found the shack and noticed the piece of wood nailed to the door. On it, Shaback had written: 'DEAD MAN HERE.'"

Shaback's story wouldn't have been unusual a century or two ago, but it happened in modern times. Because of Shaback and others like him, I carry extra food, fishing gear, a hatchet and rifle and of course my ELT. And because my dogleg route from Churchill to Baker Lake could easily empty my tanks, I'm carrying ten extra gallons of fuel in two collapsible jugs on the back seat, plus another five in the floats.

The Tundra Cub is a simple aircraft. Move the stick or push a rudder pedal and cables convey each input to ailerons, elevators and rudder. Designed to take off and land around forty mph, the Cub can almost promise that emergency landings will be injury free.

Like the Wright Flyer that skimmed the dunes of Kill Devil Hill, the Cub's fabric skin enfolds a framework of wood and steel. Given proper care, her dacron sheath will stay supple for more than thirty years.

The Cub's chrome-molybdenum tubing is a rust-resistant alloy of iron, the metal of meteorites, our only source of iron until we learned how to process ore. Her cowling, propeller and the spars of her wings are made of aluminum, a metal once so precious that the Washington monument originally wore an aluminum cap, and kings once preferred it to silverware. Her propeller, like that of the Flyer, is simplicity itself: two rotating airfoils with winglike cross sections that pull the Cub along. The Wrights' hand-carved prototype had a remarkable efficiency of 66 percent, but modern aluminum props like the Cub's have raised it to 88.

The Cub's spark plugs are fired by two magneto-driven ignition systems derived from the work of Michael Faraday, the English genius who discovered the relationship between electricity and magnetism in the early nineteenth century. Using his insights, the Cub's magnetos create pulses of electricity by whirling wires within a magnetic field. Were it not for people like Faraday, we'd still be riding horse-drawn buggies and dirty steam-driven trains; we'd be lighting coal oil lanterns and sweating through long summer nights.

With no hydraulics to leak, no starter, generator or battery to fail, the Cub's a Spartan but practical machine. Engine, propeller, airframe and a few instruments—that's all.

Because the Cub is thoroughly checked and relicensed every year, I don't worry about emergencies. Nevertheless, I always know which lake, river, meadow or bog (in that order) I can reach if my engine fails—a precaution that all instructors teach by suddenly closing the throttle and asking, "Where are you going to land?"

Alert students immediately slow to the speed at which the aircraft glides the farthest, then set up an approach to the area they've chosen. When the plane has descended to one or two hundred feet above the ground, the instructor restores power and comments on the student's choice and approach.

The sun returns, bathing the Cub in golden light as the tundra unrolls a carpet of ocher and green around lakes rimmed with orange lichens and butterscotch sand. Deepening, their waters shift from clear to aquamarine, and then to black as the Cub drones through indolent air above the deep, cold waters of Nueltin Lake that join Manitoba to Nunavut.

Well north of the tree line, Nueltin Lake was, for centuries, home to the band of inland Inuit that the Canadian writer Farley Mowat immortalized in *People of the Deer*. The "deer," of course, were caribou. Unlike their coastal counterparts, these Inuit had no ocean traditions, calling themselves the "People of the Willow Thicket." Compelled to move to Churchill in the fifties like the Chipewyans, they, too, found language barriers, intolerance, unemployment, segregated housing, liquor and, eventually, welfare checks.

The Cub angles into a land where winter lasts eight months and the main attractions are fish, game and minerals—and a paucity of people. In April 1999 the eastern half of the Northwest Territories

(20 percent of all Canada) became Nunavut, a new territory under aboriginal control, with a government like that of the Territories.

Looking into smoke-muted light that speaks of distant fires and splashes lakes and ponds with molten copper, I search the horizon for an antenna-studded island that housed the Ennadai Lake weather station, long since abandoned. The island is part of an esker, a long, wandering ridge of sand and gravel deposited by a glacial river. Trailing across the landscape for up to a hundred miles, eskers provide raised highways for migrating caribou and well-drained sites for denning badgers, foxes and wolves. Still, even when I'm sure that I have the island in sight, I can't see the antennas. Then, just as the Cub crosses the island's center, I spot buildings on its western shore, but the antennas are down, their twisted skeletons sprawled across the sandy hillocks like the vertebral columns of giant snakes.

I set up a long glide that will carry me to a landing near the station. To my surprise, two canoes loll at the edge of the beach, their sterns still awash, as if reluctant to leave the water. Far up the sandy slope, two tents flutter in the wind shadow of the bunkhouse. How nice, I think—a little company.

A tear in my chart precludes my reading the altitude of Ennadai Lake, so I arbitrarily set the Cub's altimeter to one thousand feet. Tomorrow morning, if the reading is significantly higher, I will know that a low pressure area is heading my way, and "lows" often bring dirty weather. If the altimeter reads much less than one thousand feet, a "high" is approaching and with it fair skies.

My altimeter is a gift from Evangelista Toricelli, Galileo's successor at the Florentine Academy, and from Blaise Pascal, his seventeenth-century contemporary—two scientists who concluded that we live at the bottom of an ocean of air (which is why it's so difficult to maintain a vacuum) and invented the barometer.

On observing that mercury always rose to the same height in different lengths of evacuated tubes that had their open, lower ends immersed in mercury, Toricelli reasoned that the weight of air could support only a limited column. The height of that column, the barometric pressure, is equivalent to the weight of the ocean of air over-head, an ocean that rises and falls like its watery counterpart, although not with such tidelike regularity.

Pascal, who had concluded that the weight of the air should change with altitude, took Toricelli's work one step further and devised a barometer that could measure mountains. My altimeter, which is a nothing more than a mechanical version of Pascal's baro-meter, converts air pressure into height above sea level. By setting it to the altitude on the chart (if it's recorded) or to an arbitrary alti-tude that I'll remember the next morning, I've a good idea what sort of weather's approaching, usually from the west.

Surprised that no one has arrived from the tents, I secure the Cub, then transfer the extra fuel to the wings and dig out the mak-ings of supper. Perhaps the paddlers are snoring in their sleeping bags, exhausted by their exertions. Perhaps they're semipurists, canoeists who fly to and from the barrens, but then claim that pass-ing aircraft sully their wilderness experience. As I haul my gear toward the tents, I consider a more likely possibility: they're proba-bly hiking the dunes where I wouldn't have seen them during my approach.

I pause a few yards from the tents, disgusted to see that every window in the nearby buildings has been shattered. Turning to the tents, I utter a quiet hello. No response. Another hello, a bit louder. Still no response.

Not wanting to waken them if they're sleeping, or to intrude if I'm being avoided, I trudge along one of the toppled antennas until I reach its concrete base, then face into a warm, humid breeze that keeps the mosquitoes at bay. I mustard my bread, add a few slices of ham, pour a cup of coffee and recall the very different Ennadai Lake that I found back in '68.

When my father and I taxied up to the pier, the crew streamed out of the buildings, helped secure the plane, rolled out a barrel of

Chuipka Airways fuel and worked the wobble pump to fill our tanks with gas.

They insisted we stay for coffee, which the cook transformed into a mouthwatering feast of fresh bread, sweet potatoes, a caribou roast and peach pie. Bribed with food by an isolated crew that was eager for company, we lingered in exchange for tales of Ennadai life: of feeding caribou by hand, of arctic foxes warming themselves against the chimney of the snow-covered cookhouse and of bulldozing a mile-long runway on eight-foot-thick ice for a Hercules transport with a fourteen-thousand-gallon fuel tank in its belly.

The following summer I stopped again at Ennadai Lake, where I found the same crew except for the cook, who, after so many years in the north, had succumbed to cabin fever. When his mood darkened during the short days of winter and he began to threaten violence, the government flew him out.

Two ravens begin to orbit my picnic site. Like their dapper cousins, the Canada jays, their intelligence and legendary sense of smell has won the respect of Indians and Inuit alike. Opening my pack, I remove two pieces of bread and toss them in different directions to ensure that my gift will be shared. When I'm a hundred feet away I stop and turn. The ravens are dining.

Back at the tents, I try another hello, but it, too, goes unanswered. They still can't be hiking, so I'm either being ignored or they're dead to the world and best left undisturbed.

Thinking that the vandalized cookhouse might provide an acceptable shelter, I step inside, but it's a shambles of glass, dirt and debris. Worse yet, it teems with mosquitoes. The shattered windows of the machine shop imply that it, too, will be useless, but I decide to look it over. Inside, shafts of light from the setting sun illuminate a scattering of empty barrels, a workbench and a few coils of wire. As I look about, I suddenly listen in disbelief—there are no mosquitoes. Despite its vacant windows and a wide-open door, not a single insect whines. I walk to the entrance, certain that they'll be drawn to me. A few venture in, but then turn back, repelled, perhaps, by the odor of diesel fuel rising from the oil-stained floor.

When I step outside to retrieve my gear, I'm captivated by an immense bronze sun angling toward the horizon in a scene that rivals the binary sunsets of Tatooine, Luke Skywalker's home. Though mosquitoes dance around me, I'm transfixed.

To the east, a gibbous moon slips yellow light through a toppled antenna. A minute later, its lower half turns toothy behind the meshwork of steel—a moon with orthodontics. And as the moon abandons its earthbound braces, I recall a tropical beach near Lighthouse Cay on the Barrier Reef of Belize.

Poo, our Mayan guide, had heard that my son, Chris, and I had planned to sleep outside. "Not sleep with moon on face," he warned us. When I asked him why, he replied, "Moon makes wrinkles." Poo may be right, but in the land of the Inuit, the moon brings a hunter luck and makes a woman fertile. And since I don't plan to hunt and I can't get pregnant, I'll sleep inside tonight.

I spread a sheet of plastic over the oil-stained concrete and stretch out on my sleeping bag. Eyes closed, I put everything from my mind while I absorb the sounds of evening. If I awaken to similar sounds, I'll quickly go back to sleep, but if I sense a change of wind or wave, I'll immediately check on the Cub. With the recording session over, I drift into the whispering reservoir of night while eau de diesel holds the skeeters at bay.

Just after three o'clock, the sound of a rising wind tugs me awake. When I reach the shore, the Cub is still secure, but the canoes are gone. I whirl in my tracks to confirm that the tents are still in place, then realize what has happened. The empty canoes, with their sterns awash, have been worked loose by waves slanting along the shore. Looking downwind, I spot one canoe bumping along the beach a hundred yards to the north. Beyond it, the predawn light reveals the second, rocking against a tiny spit of sand.

Ignoring the first canoe, I run for the second. If I can catch it, the first won't be a problem, but sprinting across the sloping sand is like running through a tilted bog—lots of effort but slow progress. I finally reach the distant canoe and grab its bow just as it's about to head off across forty miles of water. Panting, I anchor the canoe with my body while the wind cools me down. Then, with my breath regained, I tow it back to its companion and drag them both ashore.

Realizing that the wind will soon raise waves that could jeopardize a safe takeoff, I pack my gear and crank up the Cub. While the engine warms, I check the altimeter, which reads 1,180 feet. A "low" is definitely approaching. Since air flows counterclockwise around and into a low, my southerly winds indicate that the low must lie to the west. Tomorrow will probably bring the phantom canoeists clouds, drizzle and fog. But by then, I'll be far away, flying north out of Baker Lake.

The Tundra Cub breaks loose from the beach, her engine roaring, her wings lifting as she pivots into the wind. With the waves already spanning eight feet and the troughs deepening by the minute, I'm pushing the limits of safety.

Pulling back on the stick, I hold the Cub's nose higher than normal to avoid sucking spray into her carburetor. Even so, as we slam across the first two crests, she gasps on Ennadai spray. The third crest jolts her floats, sending her staggering into the air. The fourth is just a kiss—and we climb away. At two hundred feet I roll left, reverse course and streak past the station at 120 mph. While Ennadai brews a head of foam, the campers sleep on, their tent walls flapping in the wind.

The Cub hurries through the predawn light while I wonder what the campers will make of their wayward canoes. Will they decide that a midnight prankster prowls the shores of Ennadai Lake, or, if they heard the Cub, will they correctly reason that the pilot rescued their canoes? The longer I weigh the possibilities, the more irritated I become. Finally, convinced (unreasonably) that I was heard and ignored and that they will think that I deliberately messed with their canoes, I heave a sigh and push them from my mind.

The Cub's sole navigation instrument is a wet compass—"wet" meaning that its turbulence-induced oscillations are dampened by sealing it in high-grade kerosene. Like all compasses, my pole-seeking instrument is a descendant of the magnetite lodestones that were discovered near the town of Magnesia, Greece, around 550 B.C. Eventually, someone noticed that a needle rubbed against a lodestone would become "magnetized" and when floated, would align itself north and south.

First used by Europeans in the twelfth century, and common by the thirteenth, compasses escaped serious study until they attracted the attention of William Gilbert, the president of the London College of Surgeons, who realized that "the earth's globe is itself a great magnet," and published *De Magnete* in 1600. Gilbert, who denied the earth-centered astronomy of Luther, Calvin and the Vatican, was fortunate to live in a tolerant society—for its time. He was knighted and appointed the queen's physician, while across the Channel, the Inquisition was trying (and later executed) the philosopher and scientist Giordano Bruno for espousing similar views.

Staying low to watch for caribou, I toast the gentle warmth of the rising sun with a thermos of coffee and the last of my Danish rolls while steadying the stick with my knees. Where are the caribou, the wolves and the musk oxen? Have they returned to the hole in the earth from which Inuit legends says they came, pulled out bodily by the first woman?

Like vampires shrinking from the light of dawn, the horizons slowly recede. The sky brightens, and the monochrome tundra releases a mosaic of caramel, russet and green as the lakes slowly shift from gray to aquamarine. Then, faced with three hundred miles of glacier-scarred plain and with only my snoring engine for company, I begin to calculate how much air/fuel mixture the Cub's engine consumes each minute. After all, are the Cub and I not air breathers? Are we not internal-combustion heat-producing beings that fuel ourselves with hydrocarbons? Michael Faraday, the one whose work fires the Cub's spark plugs, would agree: "In every one of us there is a living process of combustion going on very similar to that of the candle...."

Since the Cub's two-hundred-cubic-inch engine "inhales" one hundred cubic inches of air a revolution (two of its four cylinders exhale as the other two inhale), it follows that at a cruise setting of 2300 rpm it consumes 230,000 cubic inches—about 130 cubic feet—a minute. That's seven refrigerators of air/fuel mix every minute, just to get the 20 percent that supports combustion. Today, we call that portion "oxygen," although Joseph Priestley, the Englishman who discovered it, called it "dephlogisticated air."

Priestley, a nonconformist if ever there was one, had the misfortune of being bright, contentious, personally unappealing and a Unitarian—believing in the unity of God instead of the Trinity—a very unpopular combination that inspired a religious mob to ransack his Birmingham, England, laboratory and set his home ablaze in 1791. Lucky Priestley! By escaping to America, where he renewed his acquaintance with Franklin and Jefferson, he fared better than Antoine Lavoisier, the French scientist and father of modern chemistry who gave us the word "oxygen." Charged with being sympathetic to the monarchy during the French Revolution, Lavoisier was brought before a Reign of Terror judge who is said to have sniffed, "The Republic has no need of scientists" and sent him to the guillotine.

My chart has abandoned English names in favor of native names like Angikuni, Tulemalu, Kaminuriak and Tebesjuak Lakes. But as the foam-streaked waters of Yathkyed Lake fall far behind, the Cub approaches Ferguson Lake, a small body of water that I landed upon long ago in order to stretch my legs.

As I secured the Cub, the drone of an outboard motor reached me, and a few minutes later, a boat carrying four men bumped ashore. When I expressed surprise at finding anyone, they countered, "We thought you were the charter pilot come to fly us out. He's two days overdue." All four were geologists, and all had foreign accents—not a Canadian in the lot. Hailing from Germany, Denmark, the Netherlands and India, they'd been employed by a French consortium to search for minerals of commercial value.

When an invitation to tea led to lunch, I updated them on the world they'd left behind. That done, we exchanged thoughts on everything from religion to politics. On the former, they professed indifference; on the latter, they politely advised the U.S. to "get out of Vietnam."

Hungry and ready for a stretch, I decide to land at Pitz Lake, a circular body of water with gently sloping shores that generate none of the turbulence that swirls downwind from steeper slopes. When the Cub's a foot above the whitecaps, I ease off the power, slide to a stop and carefully secure the Cub to a boulder, the only object to tie to on the treeless, barren shore. Should the Cub work loose, it's a twenty-mile hike to where she'd drift ashore.

I whip a Darcdevil far out over the lake, only to have my retrieve interrupted by a raucous cry, followed by a short duet. Dropping the rod, I peer over the gravelly ridge that separates beach from tundra. In the distance, two sandhill cranes cavort, perhaps performing a prenuptial dance or nesting display, despite it being late in July.

Creeping along the beach to within fifty yards of the gyrating cranes, I raise my head above the ridge. My hunger disappears, carried off by the dancing cranes on a stage of arctic cotton.

When I return to the Cub, it's six o'clock—breakfast time. But to my amazement, my casting draws a blank. I can't believe it. How can this be? Fishless for the first time in all of my travels, I fall back on my favorite quickie meal, a can of Dinty Moore stew before returning to the skies above the former Keewatin Territory. As large as Manitoba, the Keewatin, now part of Nunavut, has a population density of fewer than one person a square mile. Exclude the eleven hundred residents of Baker Lake, and the density drops to one for every *thousand* square miles.

Baker Lake still bears a few small rafts of ice, some of it delivered by the Thelon River, the main artery of the Thelon Wildlife Sanctuary. Rising far to south and west, the Thelon's tranquil flow offers hundreds of miles of safe river travel for canoeists who seek wild country and wild animals but not wild water. Like a sheltering oasis, the shallow Thelon valley hoards the warmth of the subarctic sun, encouraging growth within a long, fingerlike microclimate that probes a land of stone, brush, lichen and moss.

The Cub skips across the last hundred yards of Baker Lake, pushes through a jingle of candled ice and drifts to a stop at a unique beach where a seaplane that's displayed in the Smithsonian Air and Space Museum once eased ashore in 1931. Headed west to the Orient, the sleek six-hundred-horsepower Lockheed Sirius with a two thousand-mile range epitomized the technology that had developed during the twenty-eight years since the Wrights flew their Flyer to fame. The Sirius, however, was piloted by two who were well accustomed to acclaim: one was a shy Minnesotan named Charles. The other, his radio operator, journalist and wife, was Anne Morrow Lindbergh.

Three

BAKER LAKE TO GARRY LAKE, NUNAVUT

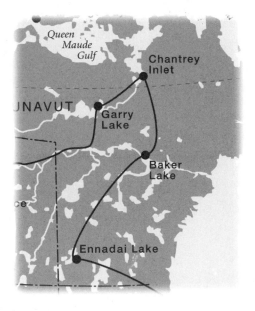

6

Baker Lake to Chantrey Inlet, Nunavut

Toward evening we came upon a grey, glassy lake, bounded by bleak shores a little higher than the marshes. On the shore, the only points of accent in the monotonous landscape, stood three or four white houses. This was Baker Lake.

— ANNE MORROW LINDBERGH,
North to the Orient, 1931

THE LINDBERGHS NEVER RETURNED to Baker Lake to see what a transformation a few decades would bring. No longer just "three or four white houses," Baker Lake boasts an airline, a rambling one-story hotel and restaurant, a craft store, a school, a government center and a herd of three-wheelers that never seem to stop. Newspapers arrive on scheduled flights instead of the yearly Churchill barge, and satellite communications have replaced the often unintelligible warblings of shortwave radio.

As I step ashore, two seaplanes bearing Minnesota registration stickers pull away from the beach. One has a canoe lashed to its floats, a practice that began with the Wrights, who strapped a canoe beneath their aircraft for a flight over New York harbor just in case their engine failed.

In the resoundingly busy Northern store I phone for a barrel of gas. I already know the drill: pay for all fifty-five gallons whether I can use them or not. A half hour later the truck arrives, drops off the barrel and adds $216 to my Visa account—about $US3 a gallon.

"Wow!" I exclaim as I sign the slip, "I used to think that your gas was expensive at $.95 a gallon, but look at it now."

"Yeah," he agrees. "It's plenty high. Just be glad you won't need it at Chantrey. It's even worse there—if you can get it."

Surrounded by a gaggle of bubbling children, I answer a stream of questions: "It's a Piper; it can fly six hundred miles on the wing tanks alone; I'm from Minnesota; I'm going to Chantrey Inlet and then Alaska; I was a dentist; yes, I'm traveling alone; I'm married, but my wife doesn't like flying; I have two sons; no, they don't fly either; it cruises at ninety mph; I carry a rifle, but only for an emergency."

A young entrepreneur stops to ask if I'll be needing all the gas. When I show him the vinyl bag in the floats, he wanders off. And as my hand pump slowly empties the barrel, I recall other years on this same beach, including a near disaster that happened in '81.

On arriving at Baker Lake in a rented Cessna 172 that required hundred-octane fuel, I called the gas truck, leaving a friend to fuel the plane while I headed to the Wildlife office to check on the caribou migration. By the time I returned, the fueling was done, and out of habit, I drained a bit from each wing tank to check for water. But instead of finding pale blue hundred-octane gas, the fuel I saw was clear, and the smell was definitely wrong.

Walking around to the far side of the barrel, I was stunned to read, "Jet-A," a kerosene fuel intended for jet engines. If I hadn't noticed the error, we'd have had just enough gasoline in the fuel lines to fly a mile or two. When the Jet-A reached the engine, we'd have been low over rocky terrain with a faltering engine or, more likely, a total failure.

After reassuring my non-pilot friend that the mistake was not his, I called the Shell office and told them to bring the fuel that I'd ordered. Ninety minutes later we had drained the tanks and fuel lines, flushed them twice, refueled with hundred-octane and were on our way after circling Baker Lake to be sure that the engine would perform as it should.

A few years later, when my longtime flying companion, Wesley Miller, and I arrived in identical Cubs, we were confronted by the pilot of a nearby Beaver who chewed us out for "running around up here in those little things."

"Just how long do you think you'd last in this water?" he grumbled, jabbing a finger at Baker Lake, which still held a few shards of ice. I was tempted to answer that Baker Lake in July was no worse than Minnesota in April, but I restrained myself. Later, we learned that our gruff adviser had wrecked his seaplane during an ill-advised takeoff in high waves. His training as a frogman saved his life, but his passengers drowned.

Returning from Chantrey Inlet another year, Wes and I hiked up to the Rainy Lake Airways camp for a hot meal, only to learn that "Pooch" Liesenfield, the company's senior pilot who had left Chantrey ahead of us, had yet to arrive.

Since the inlet's no more than two hours away, we were concerned, though not very seriously because the low ceilings that had posed no problem for our land-on-any-puddle Cubs could have forced a precautionary landing for Pooch's twin-engined Goose. Furthermore, the lack of radio contact meant nothing, for the Goose's line-of-sight signals would be blocked by the hills to the north and west of Baker Lake. The most reassuring factor, however, was that Pooch had been flying the bush since '36 and had yet to meet his match.

That evening, the Rainy Lake camp resembled a hospital waiting room. Deliberate small talk drifted back and forth above the steady hiss of gas lanterns, interrupted only by an occasional caller inquiring after the Goose. When daylight waned, we turned in, slept poorly and rose at five to pass another day of low ceilings, speculation and stilted conversation.

A second night came and went, bringing a wind shift and a slight increase in ceilings and visibility. By the time we'd finished breakfast, Wes and I had decided that the weather had improved enough to let us look for the Goose. Just as we were about to leave, the cook came running down, yelling that Pooch had radioed in. Even as he hollered, our ears picked up the distant, synchronous drone of the Goose's radial engines. Growing louder and louder, the sound grew to a skin-prickling roar as he buzzed the town and circled to land. Returning to camp, we found faces stretched with smiles of relief, and more than a few surreptitiously blinking back tears. As we had expected, low ceilings had prevented Pooch from using our direct route, and to stay within reach of the larger lakes, he'd veered to the west, where he landed to wait for the weather to change.

With fueling complete, I return to the store to ring up Father Joseph Choque, who exemplifies another major change—one of friendly co-existence between rival missionaries, and not just at Baker Lake, but in the arctic missionary field as a whole.

When I began reading about Alaska and the Canadian North, I was surprised at the frequent and often scathing criticism heaped upon northern missionaries. In *The Cruise of the Cachalot* (1899) First Mate Frank T. Bullen wrote, "No one who has travelled with his eyes open would assert that all missionaries are wise, prudent or even godly men; while . . . much is made of hardships, which in a large proportion of cases do not exist, the men who are supposed to be enduring them are immensely better off and more comfortable than they ever would have been at home."

Other authors observed that although whalers and trappers inadvertently destroyed the Inuit culture, those who arrived in the name of God had just that end in mind. Realizing that their success depended on their ability to eliminate the influence of Inuit medicine men, missionaries challenged shamans to prove their claims, a tactic that ignored the obvious: the challenging religion should provide similar proofs.

In the ensuing contest, missionaries used their ability to predict the annual return of the sun (which science, not religion, had provided) to embarrass shamans. Worse yet, according to missionary diaries, shamans who refused to convert were often severely beaten, receiving a promise of further abuse if they failed to yield to "reason."

James Houston, the Canadian artist, author and entrepreneur who lived with the Inuit from 1948 to 1962, wrote in *Confessions of an Igloo Dweller* that even in those days, missionaries still "demonstrated little kindness or charity toward each other . . ." Speaking of the native beliefs, Houston wrote, "Imagine a religion with no related priesthood, no written word, no head of church, no collection plates, no church! Shamanism can and does co-exist with Christianity in Inuit thinking. Why should it not? What kind of weak religion would shamanism be if after 16,000 years of its known existence it could be knocked down dead by a handful of new, squabbling missionaries who wandered in to the vastness of the arctic world less than a century ago."

In *An Arctic Man*, Ernie Lyall, HBC employee, entrepreneur, and founder of Spence Bay, told of Anglican/Catholic hatreds and the fruit they bore: "When I was in Pond Inlet, if there was one missionary visiting us and he'd see the other coming, he'd go out the back door before the other would come in the front door. Sometimes the people went haywire due to religion. . . . They'd get thinking about this [going to hell] so much they'd just get clear unbalanced. . . . Shamans and shamanism were looked down upon by the missionaries, both Protestant and Catholic, as a bad thing; but the way I look at it myself is that this was the Eskimos' religion then, and I think it should have been respected . . . Christianity was pushed too hard."

According to Lyall, the priest at Pond Inlet rang the church bell at six in the morning, at noon and again at six in the evening. The natives complained, saying, "There used to be seals in the morning out on the ice, and they liked to walk out to get them, but every time the seals heard these church bells they'd all go down their holes and disappear." Many missionaries even forbade Sunday hunting, a cruel and senseless prohibition, given the natives' survival needs.

Unfortunately, for every decent missionary, there were others who would, in the contest for souls, stoop to planting crosses on the graves of natives who'd refused to convert, then tell relatives that the deceased had experienced a last-minute conversion.

If Anglican churchmen reached a camp first, they'd baptize the "willing," and then warn them of evil men in black robes who dressed like women and would claim them for the devil. Catholic priests, in turn, worsened the natives' turmoil by threatening damnation upon those who refused to embrace the "one true faith."

Driven by contempt for native beliefs and their willingness to gain converts by unscrupulous methods, interfaith bickering between missionaries became so commonplace that during their brief stop at Baker Lake, even the Lindberghs noticed the friction, writing that the clergy were "not on speaking terms."

During this same period, Inuit children were suffering priestly abuse at church-run schools. Decades later, when lawsuits brought the offenses in nearby Chesterfield Inlet and other church-run schools to light, the Church that claims to be *the* source of ethics and morality hid behind the statute of limitations.

Unfortunately, the Chesterfield experience was not just an isolated incident in Catholic and Anglican schools. Most missionaries believed it was much more important for the Inuit to get into heaven than to be cured of tuberculosis or properly educated. As a result, by 1960, after half a century of mission-controlled government-supported "education," under 5 percent of Canadian Inuit could read, speak or write English. One in eight had a history of tuberculosis; infant mortality was one in five and Inuit life expectancy fell short of thirty years.

Unfortunately, Father Choque, whom I hope to thank for providing information about an abandoned mission at Garry Lake, is out of town, so I search out Henry Ford, a half-Inuit half-Caucasian entrepreneur who's lived in the Arctic for most of his life. Bright and remarkably agile for a man in his seventies, Henry is filling orders for native carvings at his store, Oopiktoyuk Arts, when I arrive.

When Henry mentions that he was about to check his nets, I offer to lend a hand. As we trudge back to the lake, a smiling Inuk makes a show of shielding his eyes. Henry and I glance at each other, then break into laughter. We're lighting up the cloud covered beach—Henry in his red-plaid hat and bright yellow slicker, and me in a gold Stearns windbreaker/inflatable life preserver and loud pink cap.

We climb into Henry's boat, paddle out to the near end of the net and begin untangling a mixed catch of yellow-flecked lake trout, red-spotted arctic char and silvery whitefish from its hundred-foot web. Most of the fish are stiff with rigor, but the recently ensnared thump noisily against the aluminum hull. Twenty minutes later, I photograph Henry beside eighty pounds of Baker Lake bounty, while imagining telling my friends of the time I pulled in twenty fish in just ten minutes. Faced with looks of disbelief, I'll add, "Of course, there was this net."

Over lunch at the Iglu hotel, I decide to hike past the Baker Lake cemetery to fish a small lake where one of my former passengers, Jim Kimball, an outdoor columnist for *The Minneapolis Star Tribune*, once fished for grayling. A half hour later, I puff to a stop amid a scattering of rock-covered graves and a mixture of wooden and iron rebar crosses. One rebar cross has fallen over, so I shove it into the ground, only to be stopped when the tip is six inches deep. I give it a twist and pull it out. The end bears a crystalline mix of earth and ice, a scraping from the great permafrost lens that spreads across the Arctic to a depth of four thousand feet.

One impressive marker rises above the tilting crosses—a memorial to Father Joseph Buliard, the priest who disappeared while serving at a primitive mission at distant Garry Lake. Chiseled into the granite headstone in English and Inuktituk are words of tribute to a man whom many considered a model of selflessness. But Buliard's remains lie elsewhere, for his body was never found. And as I stand before his memorial with my pants flapping in the wind, I wonder if I'll find a hint of his fate when I reach the Garry Lake mission, the last place to see him alive.

At Kimball's Lake I select one of my homemade lures, a removable flip top from an old pop can with a small treble hook attached to the tab, and clip the finger-ring end to my line. Within a few casts, I have a strike, then a solid take, and I soon slip my hand beneath the Arctic version of a sailfish, a fourteen-inch grayling. I lift it from the water, gently remove the hook and set the fish free. As the grayling's flaglike dorsal fin slips below the surface, I imagine it proclaiming that it had been hauled into another world by a gold-clad giant, from whom it escaped by playing dead.

I'd hoped to leave for Chantrey today, but by the time I return to town, it's late and I'm reluctant to battle a strong northwest wind that predicts a long, rough ride. Besides, the Iglu hotel has room to spare, so I grab my gear, check in and luxuriate in the shower's fluid warmth for several luscious minutes while ignoring my energy-sensitive conscience as it entreats, *That's enough*!

Steaming bowls of beef-and-broccoli stew are already circulating around the tables by the time I enter the dining room, and I'm well into my second helping when four Minnesotans walk in—the same four who had left when I arrived. Surprised to see them, I wave them to my table.

"Weather bad toward Churchill?" I ask as they sag into their chairs.

"You got it," the oldest replies, his voice a mixture of irritation and relief. "We hit some light rain, which wasn't too bad, but when we ran into patches of fog we decided to come back—and it's a good thing we turned around when we did. That cold front that came through after we left really slowed us down. Between the head wind and the drag of the canoe, I only had twenty minutes of fuel left when we landed."

They're tired and disgusted, but the stew and a few bottles of Labatt ale slowly work their charms, and we finish the evening over a cribbage board amid wild exaggerations and transparent lies—theirs, of course, not mine.

The youngest, a chunky black-haired lad claims to have caught such a huge trout that the photo weighed five pounds. Another reports a char so large that it took three huskies to bark at it, while a third swears that the local fuel truck driver radioed in to report that he'd finished fueling the Beaver that had just arrived. When the office replied, "What Beaver?" he discovered that he'd just pumped 120 gallons of avgas into one of Baker Lake's smaller mosquitoes.

Rainy Lake's Twin Beech shatters my sleep as it heads for Chantrey Inlet. It's 7:30 A.M. I toss down a breakfast of scrambled eggs, bacon and pancakes, then head for the DOT office, where I file a flight note and call my wife to ask how she's doing. I also check the weather, though it's just an empty gesture. I'll go anyway, ready to land if I must.

The Cessnas are already rumbling on the shoreline by the time I crank up the Cub. When they taxi out, I pull in about two hundred feet behind the last to leave the beach. With myself, my gear and thirty-six gallons of fuel in the wings plus thirty-five more in the cabin and floats, the Cub is heavy, the tails of her floats riding low in the water. Although I'm confident the Cub can climb onto the step quickly enough to avoid overheating her engine, I want that high-heat period to be as short as possible.

The lead Cessna adds power, its nose rising as it plows for fifty yards, then climbs up onto the step. The second follows suit, its 230-horsepower engine blasting a wind tunnel of air back at the Cub as I add full throttle. The Cub jumps onto the step as if helium filled, temporarily buoyed by the man-made blast that lifts her wings. Quivering in the Cessnas' prop wash, she races across their wakes, gaining speed as they pull ahead. As the Cessnas peel off toward Churchill, the Cub breaks free in a climbing turn to the north and levels off at one thousand feet.

Small flat-bottomed clouds like dollops of whipped cream enliven the morning sky. I alter my course to fly over one, then another. Leaping from billow to billow, the Cub's hurrying shadow is surrounded by a lovely rainbow—a colorful "glory" that encircles the Cub's fleeting image.

All sunlit aircraft bear hidden glories. Casting their delicate hues on ground and clouds alike, glories paint muted hoops of spectral light on the soft white flesh of clouds. And as my glory vaults from cloud to cloud, I find myself wishing that I could share the sight with an English genius who was born in 1642, the year that Galileo died.

As a young man, Isaac Newton alarmed the countryside with a candle-lit kite—a model 1660 UFO. Six years later, during the twelve-month period known in English history as the "annus mirabilis," the Year of Miracles, Newton worked out the laws of gravitation, invented calculus and the mirror telescope, formulated the Laws of Motion, wrote the Principia Mathematica and, while studying optics, employed prisms to investigate sunlight's rainbow spectrum of colors.

Enabled by Newton's work with prisms and light, later scientists developed spectroscopy, the unifying method of science that detects the distinctive fingerprints that elements emit when heated to incandescence. With the aid of spectroscopy, we've parsed the earth and probed the makeup of distant stars.

When the thickening clouds conspire to hide the earth, I descend toward the rolling rock-studded hills below. The overcast becomes solid; a mist begins to fall. By the time I'm down to four hundred feet, I spot the Twin Beech heeled up on the Back River's western shore—waiting out the weather. I begin a long glide that crosses the Arctic Circle, the southern limit of a land where the midsummer sun prefers not to set and, six months later, just as often fails to rise.

Though our senses would make us members of the Flat Earth Society, we know that the earth is round. Most of us also realize that the axis around which the earth revolves is tilted about twenty-three degrees from its orbital plane, which is why Northern Hemisphere days are longer when we tilt toward the sun and shorter when we tilt away.

Fortunately (for those in the Northern Hemisphere), the earth is a bit farther from the sun during the northern summer, which slightly reduces radiation to the already hot land masses "above" the equator. Six months later, we're a tad closer, which eases our northern winters.

Goose-down snow begins to fall as I tail the Cub ashore. Phalaropes twirl in the river-edge ponds as sandpipers tiptoe the beach, their heads bobbing as if to avoid the falling dime-size flakes.

Back inside the Cub, I reach for Barbara Walker's *Woman's Encyclopedia of Myths and Secrets*. An hour later, when I'm knee-deep in a bloody Crusade that murdered half of France for the crime of being judged insufficiently Catholic, I'm jolted alert by a pulsing roar as the Beech returns to the sky.

I taxi back to midstream while summoning Capt. George Back's 1835 description of Whirlpool Rapids, which I'm rapidly approaching: "The rapid looked as even and smooth as oil .... There was not, it is true, a single break in the smoothness of the surface, but with such wild swiftness were we borne along, that it required our extremest efforts, the very tug of life, to keep the boat clear of the gigantic waves below."

One hundred fifty years later, adventurer Robert Perkins, the author of *Into the Great Solitude*, paddled the Back during a low-water year and found the rapids tame. But this year the Back's running fast and high, promising a reprise of the rapids that impressed our Captain Back, the first to fully explore and chart the river.

Just for fun, I point the nose of the idling Cub downstream toward the approaching spray, letting the no-longer-subtle slope of the river draw the Cub toward the haystacks ahead. The river's hurrying surface bears not a ripple, its hidden speed revealed only when I glance toward shore. I wait. When my brain finally says, This is stupid, I feed the Cub's ninety horses well before I'd planned, rise from the oil-slick waters and leave Whirlpool Rapids behind.

Franklin Lake, the long expanse of dark, reef-studded water below, tapers off to the north and disappears into history. It's named for Sir John Franklin, the British captain whom the Canadian author Margaret Atwood had in mind when she wrote, "For Americans, of course, the name *Franklin* means Benjamin, or else a stove. But for Canadians it means a disaster."

The Franklin calamity began when Sir John, who had barely survived two earlier expeditions to the Arctic coast, loaded his presciently named ships, the *Erebus* (the dwelling place of the dead) and the *Terror*, with elegant silverware, stacks of *Punch* magazine, a mahogany desk and enough salt pork, beef, beer, potatoes and cabbage for a five-year voyage and set off to search for the Northwest Passage—the fabled water route to the Orient that explorers had been seeking for all of two hundred years.

On a spring morning in 1845, the Franklin expedition set off from the ominously named port of Gravesend and was never seen again. Following a century-and-a-half-long search that consumed five British ships and scores of lives, searchers finally located three graves far to the north of Franklin Lake, where they began to piece together the Franklin tragedy.

After his ships were entrapped by ice and wrecked during the first winter, Franklin and his crew of 128 men waited for rescue for two long years. When none came, they headed south in a desperate bid for safety before winter trapped them again. Abandoning once-precious items, they struggled on, burying their dead where they dropped, victims of famine, scurvy and probably lead poisoning—their canned goods had leaded seams. A few managed to reach Chantrey Inlet and the lake that bears Franklin's name. And then, for some strange reason, they turned back! Not a one survived.

My compass, waylaid by magnetic lines of force that have begun to dip downward, is becoming erratic. Seven hundred miles to the north, our footloose magnetic pole wanders about elliptically some fifty miles a day, perhaps in response to electrical currents generated by the earth's iron-rich core. Were the Cub to cross the magnetic pole and fly the additional eight hundred miles to the north geographic pole, its compass would become increasingly deceptive, wobbling about for a while before swearing we're heading south, though every minute would carry us farther north—toward the home of Santa Claus.

Halfway up Franklin Lake, a fifteen-foot-tall rooster tail high-lights the end of the Back River, the beginning of Chantrey Inlet and the site of the Rainy Lake camp. The Twin Beech is already unloading as I taxi through the whirlpools below the Back's final plunge, pulled first one way by the vortices, then another. When the largest spins me away from shore, I let the Cub complete its merry-go-round, then power out of its grip and idle ashore near the Rainy Lake camp.

As I retrieve a rope from a forward float compartment, I glance down through water like liquid glass. A ten-pound trout hovers beneath the float, idling in the current. Mesmerized by its powerful silhouette, I watch as it slowly swims away, only to be replaced by another, and another, and another.

7

Chantrey Inlet

Is it more beautiful than the country of the musk ox in the summer,
where sometimes the mist blows over the lakes, and sometimes
the water is blue and the loons cry very often?

– SALTATHA'S INQUIRY TO A MISSIONARY'S
PORTRAYAL OF HEAVEN

PERHAPS THE INUIT'S modest nature dissuaded them from naming places for people, as we so often do. Instead, they used descriptive words, naming the river that buoys my floats the Great Fish River. Here, the river validates its Inuit name. And as sleek-sided trout pass beneath my floats, I can hardly believe that on these same shores I once swore that I'd never return to Chantrey Inlet.

Three days of rain, snow showers and head winds had plagued me all the way from Churchill. I arrived so weary that even the Back's bountiful fishing couldn't overcome the finger-numbing cold of the Inlet's wind-driven sleet. That late-July night, as I lay wrapped in every scrap of clothing that I'd packed, I decided I'd had enough. When dawn arrived in a shroud of gray, I finally understood why explorers had called this country "the land God gave to Cain" and fled at the first opportunity.

By the following spring, my memories of discomfort had been replaced with visions of huge trout and an Inuit camp that I'd failed to visit. When July finally came, Wes and I headed north again, accompanied by weather that could well have been brewed on a different planet, arriving during a heat wave that peeled off our shirts and baked the shoreline from which we fished.

Slinging six-inch red-and-white spoons into the whirlpools, we hooked a trout or char on cast after cast. Most were much too large for a two-man meal, so we shuttled fish in and out of a rock-rimmed wier, replacing the largest with the smallest as we searched for our supper. Finally, too arm-weary to fish any longer, we settled for a five-pounder.

Across a hundred yards of thundering water, an Inuk stood, "trying his luck" with a spear. Luck, however, obviously played no role, for almost every thrust retrieved a struggling fish. We borrowed a boat from the Rainy Lake crew, then crossed to the Inuit camp, where a team of beautifully furred sled dogs howled us into camp.

A woman seated beside her canvas tent smiled and nodded permission when I held up my camera. She spoke no English, but her meaning was plain when she slipped her chubby child from beneath her parka and cradled him for a photograph.

When Wes pointed to a row of stone columns on a ridge beyond the tents, I remembered reading of Inuit constructions called "inukshuks" whose purpose varied by locale: an armless inukshuk was the counterpart of the lob-pine of the voyageurs—a beacon to head for—whereas an inukshuk with "arms" outstretched might indicate a valley or a body of water with outlets at either end.

This row, however, had served as a "drift-fence" to detour migrating caribou, whose notoriously poor vision apparently interpreted the posts as men or wolves. Pursued by women, the caribou would refuse to pass between the inukshuks, running parallel to them instead toward a place of ambush: a cliff or a body of water where they could be speared from kayaks. Now, although rifles have downgraded inukshuks from useful tools to relics, their crude silhouettes still speak of a time when everything, including life itself, depended on the hunt.

Turning to the clan's weathered patriarch, I pointed to the stone columns. "Inukshuk?" I asked. He beamed with surprise and nodded a reply as I hid my frustration at having only a few nouns in common. Unable to speak Inuktituk, I stood there mute while, with one callused hand, he gripped a four-pound chunk of green soapstone from which a seal was slowly emerging, liberated by the knife clutched in the three remaining fingers of his other hand.

How did this man lose the use of one opalescent, sightless eye? Were his missing fingers lost by accident or removed by the Arctic cold? What, I wondered, does a man who listens to the world on a transistor radio, but has lived the life of his seal-and-caribou-stalking ancestors, remember of that hazardous life?

Had he, like his father, ladled fresh water into the mouth of a dead seal to appease its spirit and slake the thirst it had acquired during a lifetime in saltwater? Did he believe that the seal would tell other seals that here was a considerate hunter—a man worth dying for? Or with his gift of fresh water, did he hope to escape the wrath of Sedna, the sea goddess who brings bad luck to those who treat animal spirits with contempt?

Had he stalked polar bears after silently apologizing to them, explaining his need to feed his family, and rewarded their spirits with a precious knife or an ulu—tools that bears must surely covet? Did he shelter their pelts and show them great respect for four days if a male's and five days if a female's? Following a season of poor hunting, did he change his name to escape the evil spirits that had plagued him?

Although most of the early missionaries and explorers called them "ignorant savages," the Chantrey Inuit somehow survived the ages without wood—not even driftwood—a truly remarkable feat. Here, wood is highly prized. As Gontran de Poncins wrote in the 1941 northern classic *Kabloona*, "The poverty of the natives . . . is so wretched that the least bit of string, the least stick of wood is a treasure in their existence." In a land that offered only hides and flesh, shrubs and stone, fish and bone, the Inuit somehow survived, while those who called them savages died until their successors adopted the Inuit way of life.

When attempts were made to explain World War I to the Inuit, the "savages" were aghast, saying that "white men ... were strangely unnatural and inhuman." Their language, which has dozens of words for the different types of snow, had none for war, which they decided to call "mass killings."

A gentle, modest people, the Inuit had no concept of illegitimacy and considered paternal lineage unimportant, as all children were related to the larger family. In a harsh land where life was truly treasured, they were tolerant parents who smiled at the misbehavior of children, replying to critics that it would be wrong to punish children who obviously "don't yet have all their brains."

If told that he was a good hunter, the traditional Inuk would claim that he had no skill, only luck. Likewise, a woman would deny being attractive and argue that X, or even Y, was much better-looking. Skill and innovation, however, not luck and modesty, ensured the survival of the Inuit: freezing animal hides onto precious sled runners to reduce wear and crafting seal-oil lamps from bone.

Unfortunately, one sensible Inuit practice brought them condemnation: their custom of wife sharing. Labeled sinful by all missionaries and some explorers, wife sharing was a logical response to the necessities of the harsh arctic environment. If a pregnant Inuk could not accompany her husband on a hunt, an agreeable woman exchanged duties with her, providing another set of eyes to search for game, another pair of hands to manage dogs and build a snow house and someone to cook and mend clothing. The mutual benefits of sexual variety were incidental to the exchange and only occasionally the primary reason.

Thus, it's not surprising that traditional Inuit had few of the sexual hang-ups that are found in "civilized" societies. Their practical approach to sex, their communal concept of a larger family and their willingness to share resources enhanced the odds of survival and produced less stressful lives.

Fifty yards from the patriarch, the young spearman stood beside a growing heap of arctic char and trout. One hand gripped a *kiki-vak*, a three-pronged, trident-like spear with a central shaft and two outer tines armed with inch-long barbs. Since two hands would be needed to spread the outer prongs, Wes asked the young Inuk how he removed the fish from the center tine. With a smile, he said, "Just watch."

Wading a yard into the river, he stood in the shallows, his spear raised as his eyes searched the sunlit ripples. Suddenly he made a quick thrust—and retrieved a struggling trout. Bending over, he spread the outer tines with his hands, bit the trout behind the head and pulled it free of the center shaft. He then thumbed an eye from its socket and popped it into his mouth. When he offered me its mate, I'm sorry to say I declined.

A small child ran down to the river, holding high over his head the primary symbol of change for the Arctic, if not the world—a bundle of twigs tied into the shape of an airplane. Though his grandmother might tell him that geese fly off to the Old Woman Who Never Dies every fall and return with the promise of spring, this child-of-the-airplane will also learn the facts of migrating birds. Airplane held aloft, he flopped onto a nearby caribou hide and flew his bundle high, his body cushioned in caribou hair, his mind far off in the sky.

Now, as I stare down into the cold waters of the Back, I miss my old friend, Wes, my traveling companion for many years, an easygoing, peace-loving *gentle*man who saddled himself with a shrew of a wife whom he steadfastly refused to divorce. Wes finally escaped into death many years ago, done in by twenty years of unrelenting bitchery and a kinder, briefer cancer.

Paul, one of the Rainy Lake guides, arrives and interrupts my thoughts. As we stroll to the camp through thousands of tiny flowers that are busily cramming a summer of life and reproduction into a few brief months, he holds up a hand and points toward a nearby boulder. I look carefully but see nothing. Looking again, I finally spot an immobile, beautifully camouflaged ptarmigan against a backdrop of dwarf willows.

"Want to hear Farley Mowat's ptarmigan poem?" I ask.

"Sure," he says.

"The ptarmigan—a kind of grouse
Lives in the Arctic with his spouse.
The ptarmigan is smart and perky,
And tastes much better than a pturkey."

Laughing, Paul asks if I've ever heard of an Alaskan town named Chicken. " 'Fraid not," I reply.

"Well, they really wanted to name it ptarmigan," he says, "but no one knew how to spell it, so they named it Chicken instead. It's between Dawson City and Tok."

Over lunch, Paul tells me that the campsite across the river hasn't been used for years. And the patriarch with the missing fingers and the opaque eye? Gone, like my old friend, Wes.

As I return to the Cub, I search the noon sky for a clearing trend, but the solid overcast makes it plain that I'll wait for another day. Grumbling, I put up my tent, a job that I'll dislike until someone invents a Viagra pill for tents—or one that springs to life at the touch of a remote. However, once my tent's up, I love its shelter and woodsy smells. With my foam pad, sleeping bag and pillow in place, I decide that a short rest will prepare me for an afternoon of tussling with trout, so I pull a stocking cap over my eyes and let the white sound of the Back's rooster tail sweep my cares away.

When I awaken, my watch reads 2:20—a little late, but not too bad. On looking again, I see that my bleary eyes have reversed Mickey's hands. It's 4:10! I've slept almost four hours! At supper, the cookhouse resounds with the chatter of tired fishermen. One fellow with a group of fishermen from Chicago ribs me, "You sure came a long way just to sleep."

"Yeah, well," I respond with a modest smile, "if I were going to be content with the minnows that I hear you guys have been catching, I wouldn't need much rest either. But I plan to do some big-time fishing this very evening. Matter of fact, here's the lure that I plan to use."

Lifting the lid of a battered cigar box, I hold up a stainless-steel teaspoon with a treble hook in its lip. Laughter erupts.

"Lemme see that thing," one burly fisherman says. As the spoon passes from hand to hand, one fisherman says that he'd love to set out spoons like that for uninvited company. Another rises to his feet, a Molson ale in one hand and the spoon held high in the other. "I christen thee the mother-in-law spoon," he announces while eyeing its gleaming barbs. "May she sup from you but once."

When I ask Paul about renting a boat for the evening, Phil, one of the Chicago fisherman invites me to join him, explaining that as the fifth in a party of five, he has room in his boat.

Later, as we motor into the Inlet, I realize that Phil, in addition to being a worrier, is way out of his element. Persuaded by his buddies to join them for what he thought would be an idyllic weekend in the woods, he almost turned back at Churchill and again at Baker Lake. Now he's just going through the motions, counting days until he can return to Chicago's Lake Shore Drive. Gripping the boat's gunwales whenever we cross a whirlpool, he's the picture of a man who'd prefer to get his wilderness experience by way of a good book and a comfortable recliner while a fire smiles from across the hearth.

Unfortunately, Phil's luck at fishing is as bad as his attitude. Thirty minutes pass, and he has caught one char to my four trout and two char. Having at first declined to try my productive "spoon," he finally relents when I offer it once again.

Phil casts beyond one of the whirlpools and begins a slow retrieve. Suddenly, he lets out a yell. Clutching his rod with both hands, he whips it into a U. "Phil," I say, as his line slices Chantrey foam, "you've got one helluva fish down there."

Five minutes pass, and we still haven't seen his fish. "It has to be a trout, a big trout," I tell Phil, keeping my voice low, then wondering why. More minutes pass. The nylon line that streamed from the reel after each retrieve now points straight down, quivering. "You've got him, Phil!" I exclaim. "He's worn out."

"What d'ya mean, *he's* worn out?" squeaks Phil, rolling his eyes as a grin spreads across his face. Phil cranks in twenty, then thirty feet of braided nylon. The fish takes off again, but his run is short. One more lunge and he's spent, lying alongside the boat. I slip a hand behind his gills and quickly heave him aboard. "Keeper?" I ask Phil.

"*Keeper?*" he says. "I'll say its a keeper! That trout's got a date with a taxidermist," Then, turning to the guide he asks, "Where's the scale?"

Phil's trout bottoms the scale at twenty-five pounds, its weight limited only by Phil's conscience and imagination. "What do you think?" he asks. "Thirty, maybe thirty-five pounds?"

"Probably," I reply, then add, with a wink to the guide, "that's the biggest trout I've ever seen."

After Phil returns my spoon with thanks commensurate to a loan of the Hope diamond, I return to battling trout. "This one," I boast to Phil, "is going to make yours look like an appetizer." Suddenly my line goes slack. When I reel it in, my spoon is gone. "Phil," I say, "You're a lucky man. That fish was so big we would have had to tow it back to camp. This way, you still have something to brag about."

As we troll through the Arctic twilight, I tell Phil that I'm hoping for sunshine tomorrow so I can repeat Eratosthenes' measurement of the earth. I start to explain, but we're interrupted so often by fish strikes that I give up. Finally satiated with fishing, I decide that this one's my last. I bring him to the side of the boat, my arms sore, my wrists shot. I'm worn out, but he's not. With a sudden swirl he slips the hook and disappears, leaving the rod drooping in my tired hands.

During the ride back to camp, Phil burbles, "Sure hope they have plenty of ice for the cooler? Do you have a photo of that spoon?" Then, looking over the side at his stringered trout, he exclaims, "My Gaaawwwd, that's a big fish!"

The guide and I haul the boat ashore as Phil races on ahead yelling, "Hey, hey, guys! Come and see what *I* caught!"

When a one o'clock nature call reveals a stunningly clear sky, my eyes seek Ursa Major, then leap to the polar star, which every mile of my northerly flight has lofted higher overhead. Although we Westerners call Ursa Major the Big Dipper, Homer saw the Bear That Never Bathes, passing on what every sailor knew: that in Mediterranean latitudes, the constellation never touched the sea. In France, our Big Dipper is called *le casserole*; in England, it's the plow; in China, the celestial bureaucrat.

Morning comes wreathed in fog. At breakfast, the cook tent resounds with conversation, much of it focused on talk of measuring the earth, which Phil has announced.

"How do you plan to do that?" asks one of Phil's friends.

"It's really just simple geometry," I reply, "which, by the way, means 'to measure the earth.' About two centuries B.C., a Greek named Eratosthenes became the first Westerner to calculate the size of the earth.

"His predecessor, Epicurus, had already theorized that matter consists of tiny, invisible particles like atoms. Besides rejecting gods as rulers of the world, he also proposed that many other worlds held life forms, all made from the same particles as ourselves. At about the same time, Aristarchus, who had proved that the sun was far larger than the earth, even proposed what we now know—that the smaller earth must orbit the larger sun."

Accompanied by the rattling of dishes as the tables are cleared, I continue. "Eratosthenes knew that on the longest day of the year the noontime sun shone directly down a deep well in the Egyptian city of Syene. Knowing also that the sun cast a shadow of approximately seven degrees at the same time in Alexandria, which lay some 500 miles to the north, he asked this question: If traveling 500 miles across a round earth produces a 7.5 degree change, how far would we travel with a change of 360 degrees? Since forty-eight 7.5 degree arcs equal 360 degrees, forty-eight 500-mile arcs yields a circumference of about 24,000 miles—a surprisingly accurate figure for its time."

When Phil asks, "Would ya run through that again?" I flip a dinner plate over onto the paper tablecloth and trace a circle—the earth. I follow with a straight line piercing the circle to terminate at its center—the beam of sunlight that shone down the well at Syene. Then I draw another radian from the circle's center outward, piercing it about an inch from Syene, and label the junction Alexandria.

"Think of this radian at Alexandria as another well and notice that the curve of the circle tilts it away from the radian at Syene, just as it would tilt a flagpole away from the sun, making it cast a shadow of about seven degrees. Because Eratosthenes had paid someone to pace off the distance between Syene and Alexandria, he knew that the 7.5 degree change represented 500 miles. If 7.5 degrees spans 500 miles, then 360 degrees must cover about 24,000 miles."

I pause, pleased to see nods of insight replacing furrowed brows.

"Before I left Minnesota, which is almost straight south of the inlet, I recorded the length of the shadow cast by the noonday sun on a right-angle wire. Even though I left home four days ago, and we're well north of the equator, the sun is high at this time of year, so Eratosthenes' method should work fairly well, especially since our known, 1,300-mile distance from where I started is probably more accurate than his paced-off span from Syene to Alexandria.

"So," I say, hoisting my mug of coffee, "here's to the science of the Greeks that almost died during the Dark Ages." Then, aware that I've been carrying on, I add, "End of speech."

To help pass the morning, I hike the poppy-strewn tundra with one of the Rainy Lake guides. Beneath our feet lies the same Canadian Shield that supports northern Minnesota, but the land here seems young and raw, and with good reason, for the ice age withdrew from the Arctic long after it left the States.

Rick, a student from the University of Toronto, has a double major in agriculture and astronomy—an odd mix that he obviously savors. Gathering up a bit of the thin, sandy soil, he lets it trickle from hand to hand. "Test this and you'll discover that it hosts only a thousandth as many bacteria as southern loams, which is one reason that plant productivity here is just a few percent of the yield you'd expect to find in the States.

He points to an orange two-inch lichen clinging to the south side of a granite slab. "You probably know that lichen are a blend of a fungus and an algae, but what most people don't realize is that they grow so slowly that photographs taken at fifty-year intervals reveal hardly any growth at all.

"Think of it," he says. "A lichen no wider than my hand might have begun life in the days of your friend Eratosthenes."

By the time we return to camp, the sun has begun to burn holes in the overcast. I retrieve my clothes-hanger wire, some duct tape and a file from the Cub, and get ready to measure the angle of the sun whenever it shows its face.

To my surprise, the experiment has gripped the camp. A dining room table has been carried outside, where it awaits adjustment with my pocket level and rock wedges. That done, I tape my L-shaped wire to its top with the horizontal arm pointing north and its vertical arm upright. There are cloud breaks everywhere, but none cross the camp. Finally, at twelve-fifteen, a huge opening admits a flood of sunlight, and I notch the wire at the end of the shadow cast by the vertical arm. Removing the tape, I lay the wire on a piece of paper, mark a dot at the tip of the wire, then a dot at the mark made in Minnesota and another at the new mark. With a folded paper for a straight edge, I connect the tip-of-the-wire dot with the Minnesota dot and also with the Chantrey dot to form an acute angle. As I take my protractor from my pocket, I'm struck by the silence of the men pressed against the table.

When I read off 18, maybe 19 degrees, Rick whips out his pocket calculator, then realizes he won't need it and talks his way through the math. "Let's see, 18 degrees goes into 360 degrees 20 times, and if a twentieth of the earth's circumference is 1,300 miles, then it's got to be 26,000 miles around. Nineteen degrees would make it about 5 percent less, say just under 25,000 miles—not bad, *not bad!*"

I suddenly realize that my aeronautical charts should verify the 18–19 degree difference. The camp turns out to be a shade north of

67 degrees, and my cabin just under 49, a difference of 19 degrees. Raising the chart, I announce that the precision of modern technology is hereby confirmed with a protractor, a level, a coat hanger and the common sense of Eratosthenes. Someone shouts, "I'll drink to that!" and we're off to the cookhouse for a pre-lunch beer.

As I dig into a heap of baked char, Phil pulls up a chair.

"Where did you get that earth-measuring idea?" he asks.

"Well," I say, "what got me going was an intriguing book and Public TV series called *The Ring of Truth* by Philip and Phylis Morrison. In a tribute to Eratosthenes, the Morrisons recorded the angular height of Arcturus on the side of a south-facing rental truck in northern Nebraska, then measured it again the next night when they were some 450 miles farther south. Using those figures, they calculated the earth's circumference at 26,500 miles. Knowing that I'd be traveling north for more than 1,000 miles, I thought I'd give it a try."

I settle up for my meals, find Rick and ask a favor. "If anyone comes looking for me, would you tell them that I left at noon today, and that I was heading up the Back to Garry Lake, then south to the Thelon River, then west to Reliance on Great Slave Lake, and then on to Yellowknife?" Before I can finish the sentence, Rick has his memo pad out and is taking notes.

A handshake and a wave later, the Cub again waltzes through Chantrey's whirlpools. It's the last of July, the month that the Inuit call Padlersersivik: "when there is no night." While the engine warms, I think back to my first departure from Chantrey Inlet—how I filled a float compartment with snow to cool two homeward-bound trout, then dribbled a few drops of oil onto the Cub's rudder and elevator hinges to prevent takeoff spray from locking them up in the subfreezing Chantrey air.

When the Cub's oil temperature gauge says go, I look around, knowing I'll never again see the inukshuks or hear thundering falls of the Great Fish River. But I'll remember the lure-thieving trout and the one-eyed frost-bitten elder—and a playful boy with a primitive plane on the shores of Chantrey Inlet.

8

Chantrey Inlet to Garry Lake, Nunavut

One midnight. In a time when most engines were round
and reciprocating. Four of them are hunched on
our wings, snoring through the night. I turn
to look over my shoulder at the navigator.
"Where are we?"
The navigator shrugs his shoulders.
"It beats me. So I suppose we're lost."
– ERNEST K. GANN, "Flying Circus"

WHEN PEOPLE ASK if I've ever been lost, I explain that with the extra fuel that I carry, the Cub can fly a thousand miles. "I can't get lost," I say, as I pull out my pocket map and drop a finger into the center of the Territories' "Zone of Inaccessibility."

"Head north and you run into the Arctic Ocean; fly east and there's Hudson Bay; to the west you'll hit the Slave or Mackenzie

River; head south and you'll find corn." Still, despite my bravado, the truth is that I've been briefly lost right here while accompanied by my friend Wesley Miller.

We were heading south from Chantrey Inlet in our Cubs, flying the same Back River that's slipping past below. Wes, in the lead plane, had cut overland to avoid following a westward bulge in the river. Forgetting that the Meadowbank River joined the Back in that area, Wes took the Meadowbank for the Back when it slowly came into view. Since I wasn't paying attention, I followed Wes along the slowly curving Meadowbank. Fifteen minutes later, out of habit, I checked my map.

"Wes," I radioed, "things don't look right."

After a long silence, Wes replied, "I guess not."

With our compasses unreliable and the sun obscured, we had lost two important tools. But then I remembered a dependable rule of thumb: if, over a short period, the weather hasn't changed, the wind probably hasn't either.

Since a northwest wind had been blowing when we left, and the weather hadn't changed, it should still have been northwest. Looking down at the wind-streaked lakes below, I could see that we were heading with the wind—forty-five degrees from the course we would have been flying if we were over the Back. Turning the map to line it up with the Meadowbank instead of the Back immediately snapped everything into place, and after we'd spent twenty minutes on a westerly course, the Back returned to view.

I scan the Cub's rudimentary but practical instrument panel. Housing nothing more than a tachometer, altimeter, airspeed indicator, oil pressure and temperature gauge, it is charitably described as a "basic" panel.

The Cub has no navigation radio, no Loran, no gyro horizon or gyro compass. I navigate by "pilotage," using a compass (when it works), common sense and a map, employing the same basic flight skills that led Lindbergh to Paris. Were I to plop one of my friends whose aircraft brim with electronic gadgets into my primitive Cub, he'd surely pop a stroke.

No fuel gauges disturb the panel's simplicity, their function being performed by two vertical glass tubes just above my head on each side of the cockpit. Connected to the wing tanks and set at the same level, the tubes house a small ball that floats at the same height as the fuel in the tanks. Although they're *almost* foolproof, the balls have been known to stick to the side of the tubes as the fuel is consumed, leading brain-dead pilots to fly on and on when a recalcitrant ball rides high. I like the Cub's austerity, but if I were to change one thing, I'd add a Global Positioning System, for even those who get lost in three-tree parks can cruise the globe with GPS. Just as sextants seek the light of stars, GPSs rely on satellite signals. Given a sextant and decent conditions, a trained navigator can locate his position within a mile or so, but a good GPS can fix my position with an accuracy of several yards.

Adding a touch of power, I follow the rising terrain while wishing that Wes, my caribou spotter, was here. Overdue for a new set of bifocals, Wes could barely read a map, but for spotting game he was superb. Where my eyes saw distant willow clumps, he discovered musk oxen; where I found nothing but a patch of brown vegetation or the shadow of a cloud, Wes would find a caribou herd. He was rarely wrong.

The Back suddenly changes character. Slick, fast and almost unbending near Franklin Lake, the inland Back rushes past granite lobes and ridges of glacial till, stringing turquoise ponds on a whitewater thread that descends from a pork-chop-shaped island at the far end of Garry Lake.

On the island's south-facing rib, a wide crescent-shaped beach gleams in the afternoon sun. Set deep in the Inuit's Nunassiaq ("beautiful land"), the island bears a tar-paper shack that years ago I wouldn't have noticed were it not for a tiny dot on my map and the word "mission."

Wes and I had been heading east from Coppermine on our way to Baker Lake. When I spotted the dot, I radioed Wes. "The map says there's a mission on an island ahead. It's close to our route and I'm getting hungry, so what say we stop for lunch?"

If either of us had expectations of finding a mission like those of the American southwest, they quickly disappeared. When I first spotted the tiny black shack, I took it for just another die-shaped glacial erratic, a remnant of the last ice age. This die, however, was precisely shaped and just a little too large.

As we taxied up to the island's Caribbean-like beach, the shack disappeared behind a ten-foot bluff. We set off toward the mission, only to be distracted by the chirp of a sik-sik, an arctic ground squirrel that is one of nature's few true hibernators. Like the dormouse (from the French *dormir*, meaning "to sleep") the sik-sik is poorly equipped to handle winter's extremes. So to conserve energy, sik-siks lower their body temperature below fifty degrees for months on end. Our chirping sik-sik, by slowing its metabolism, adds summers of life with long winter sleeps.

The twelve-by-fifteen-foot, tar-paper mission was equipped with a small entry and an attached storage space on its western side. Two small white crosses—painted sticks nailed together—decorated the roof. Like a black boulder carried to a barren island from the sheer walls of a distant fiord, the mission begged to be photographed under the deep blue Arctic sky.

We passed through the entry and peered inside. We hadn't expected comfort, but even so, we were surprised at the poverty that met our eyes. Against the east wall was a plywood bed. Above it, several shelves offered dozens of bottles, each containing a different remedy. All were labeled in French. As I tried to decipher their meaning, I remembered the tale of a sailor who had served aboard the *Passat*, a four-masted steel barque built in 1911. Because the owners of the *Passat* lacked funds for a doctor, they provided, instead, a small chest filled with bottled remedies numbered 1 through 7—number 1 for chills, 2 for fevers, 3 for ailments of the bowel, and so on. One day, finding the number 7 bottle empty, the first mate mixed a dose from numbers 3 and 4. The results were not reported.

On one windowsill, a red-and-gold icon of a saint glowed in sunlight softened by the dust-dimmed window, while across the barren room, the window's twin admitted muted shafts of light.

A small table stood beneath an open stovepipe through which decades of dust had descended, coating every surface a dull and even gray. On the table lay a scattering of French Bibles, English Bibles, religious comic books in English and Inuktitut and a few letters written in French.

Repelled by the dust and disorder, we took a few pictures and returned to the beach, accompanied by the chirp of the sik-sik, which we lured from its den with bread.

On arriving at Baker Lake, we learned that the mission had been hammered together in 1949. There (according to letters from Father Charles Choque of Baker Lake, Bishop John Robideaux of Churchill and reports in "Eskimo") Father Joseph Buliard, the man whose memorial dominates the Baker Lake cemetery, sought to convert the Inuit until he disappeared around Christmas 1956.

Joseph Paul Jean Marie Buliard began life in the little village of Le Barboux in southern France. In time, the boy with the large name grew into a small, big-eared, bespectacled man, a Mr. Peepers who might easily have been gobbled up by the world had he not turned to the Church. Following his indoctrination, Father Buliard became a congregant of the Oblates of Mary Immaculate (OMI), and in 1939 set sail from Le Havre, France, at the age of twenty-five. His destination: Churchill.

Churchill surprised him, being smaller and colder than he'd expected: "We are in the middle of summer and we have had . . . eight days below [freezing] . . ." That fall, Buliard and two other missionaries shipped out for an abandoned trading post at Repulse, a Hudson Bay inlet six hundred miles north of Churchill. There, they planned to proselytize whoever came their way.

Six weeks after freeze-up, Father Buliard fell through thin ice but managed to climb free and stagger back to the post. His arms and feet began to swell. When his companions thought they detected the scent of gangrene, they radioed for a rescue flight. Three weeks later, a single-engine Junker finally arrived to fly him out. Thus,

Buliard spent his first winter in the Churchill hospital, where, as his fingernails finally grew back, he became even more determined to return to the north.

FatherBuliard spent most of the next nine years in the rocky country to the north of Baker Lake. Often rejected, though occasionally accepted, he sought conversions during an era that saw some priests portraying their rivals as "wolves ravaging the one and only Fold of Christ."

His once-frozen hands proved a constant trial. Despite his best efforts, he often needed Inuit help because, unlike many missionaries, he shared the grim prospects of those he sought to convert while faulting himself for what he called his "meager success." Repeatedly reduced to ill health, Buliard would have to be ordered out for recuperation.

In August 1949, with Buliard restored and the materials on site at Garry Lake, the tar-paper Mission of Our Lady of the Rosary finally materialized on an island known to the Inuit as Siuradjuar—the big pile of sand. "From there, he attempted to convert the natives and reconvert Protestants in the area. Traveling alone or with an Inuit family for months at a time, he'd eventually return to his island, where in the winter "the walls became coated with frost, which it [the coal stove] could never entirely melt."

A strict observer of poverty, Buliard gave up his occasional treat of malted milk when he learned its Baker Lake price, saying that it was inappropriate for a minister to the poor to drink such an expensive beverage. He was offered a battery radio with which he could receive the Canadian Broadcasting Company that he missed so much, but he declined, unwilling to include a radio receiver on his list of needs. Unlike his superiors then and now, Buliard would have rejected a crystal palace or a grand cathedral. Neither would he have understood churches that shelter child-abusing clergy, or men like Swaggart, Bakker, Robertson and Falwell, or zealots like David Koresh.

Father Buliard often suffered from hunger, cold and exhaustion, but he rarely complained, the one exception involving the state of his hands, which ". . . make me powerless. I can't get them warm.

And at night, under the furs, when my circulation comes back, the pain and torment drive sleep away."

It comes as no surprise that his years in the Arctic almost certainly ended the way they began—with a plunge through the ice. He even predicted it: "Sooner or later, I'll finish by going through the ice, the rivers up here are so tricky in so many spots. . . ."

Some natives said that he went out in a storm to check his nets and never returned. Others said he drove his dogsled across thin ice that collapsed. Rumors circulated that he'd been murdered, a real possibility, given the Inuit's reluctance to reject their treasured beliefs and Buliard's insistence that they stop exchanging wives. The mission died with Father Buliard. A few months later, nineteen Garry Lake Inuit starved to death.

When I finally learned Buliard's story, I became determined to inspect the "big pile of sand" more closely. Decades had passed since his death, but I wanted to search for clues to his disappearance. From the distant clamor of city life, I yearned to sample the solitude that Buliard had accepted while he longed for the sight of a human face.

The island, like much of the Arctic, is a checkerboard of tundra polygons—hexagonlike "platters" of tundra just a few yards across. I secure the Cub to a half-buried gas barrel and begin to haul my gear to the mission.

A disheveled freighter canoe lies inverted near the entry, its canvas rotting, its stern hacked away for firewood. A wrecked snow-mobile sags nearby. The entry itself is much as Robert Perkins found it in 1987, containing "rubber gloves, used cans of motor oil, snowmobile parts, rusty traps, spools of nylon fishing line, nets." Inside, however, the contents are gone, perhaps carried off by souvenir hunters.

When I step outside, I discover an arctic hare just ten feet away from the steps. It stares at me as I stare back. I am not fox, or wolf, or snowy owl. As long as I stand still the hare remains motionless, the inbred reaction of animals that need to remain invisible in open country—don't move.

Remembering a *National Geographic* film of arctic hares bounding across the tundra on their hind legs, I let out a sudden yell. The startled hare leaps into flight. Sure enough, he's one of their finest. After a conventional bound, the hare rises to his hind legs and quickly disappears.

The cry of a gull tilts my head. Circling through the deep blue tundra sky, the ivory gull follows me as I begin my search. I inspect the western shoreline first but find only sand and solitude. Back at the mission, I mentally divide the surrounding tundra into ten-foot squares and begin to probe each square on my hands and knees. Halfway round the mission, I find several buttons beneath a clump of ground-hugging bearberry. Close by, I discover a packet of rusty needles and a few beads—the tip of a rosary protruding from years of windblown sand.

Near the north side of the building, my fingers find what the vegetation hides from sight—a sprinkling of leather tags about the size of 50-cent pieces. Unfortunately, the printing on all but one is unreadable.

In *An Arctic Man*, Ernie Lyall wrote that from 1941 to 1969, "Eskimos were given numbers because they generally had only one name and a lot of Eskimos had the same ones, and sometimes they even changed their name to something different. All this was very confusing. . . . So the government decided to give them numbers, which I think was a very good thing. Each settlement had its own number. . . . But later on, they started a program that they called 'Project Surname' and everybody was given a second name. . . . I guess whoever suggested getting rid of the numbers said why should Eskimos be known by numbers—it's only people in jails who have numbers."

I carry the disk to the sunlit side of the mission, where I see that one side carries a symbol of the crown rimmed by the words Eskimo Identification Canada. The other confirms Mr. Lyall, reading E.2-507 in its center. Along its lower rim is a handwritten name—Kowak-ferik—and the date 23-4-57.

Returning to the north side of the mission, I extend my sweep on hands and knees, carefully working my fingers through the ground cover like someone searching for a contact lens. An hour passes fruitlessly, then another with poor results. I'm laughing at myself, at my sore knees and tired back. If this were a job, I'd be demanding a rest period and better pay. Besides, the wind has begun to nibble, leaving goose bumps in its wake.

A sense of loneliness suddenly grips me, and as I return to the shelter of the mission, doubts about staying enter my mind. Cold and hungry, I toss a quarter pound of bacon on the Coleman, then stir in a can of Boston-baked beans as the bacon snaps and curls. Slathered on Baker Lake bread, my feast soon revives me, and I set off to explore the eastern half of the island.

When I reach the northern shore, I turn east along its rubble bank, the flesh of an esker laid bare by erosion. I consider looking for fossils, but on this pile that was scraped from the igneous Shield, it would be a waste of time. In the Arctic islands farther north, however, fossils are easily found. There, acres of petrified tropical forests prove that the earth is incredibly old, given the inconceivably slow drift of the continents.

A female caribou comes clopping round the point. The wind is wrong, so she cannot smell me, but at fifty feet she sees me well enough. I stand motionless, savoring her surprise while she swings her rudimentary antlers from side to side as she tries to catch my scent. With a sudden snort, she whirls about, trots into the lake and heads for the opposite shore.

A shiver spawned by the rising wind ripples across my back. A band of dark clouds is approaching, the harbinger of a rapidly advancing cold front. I quicken my pace, determined to reach the island's eastern end before I turn back. Just as I round the corner, it begins to pour. Parjanya, the one who brings monsoon rains to India, has gone a-traveling and soaks me in seconds.

As forty mile per hour gusts buffet me and the wind moans overhead, I break into a run. I'm tempted to head straight to the mission, but I race along the beach. I'm concerned for the Cub, and I'll certainly need dry clothes.

By the time I reach the Cub, it's thirty-six degrees. I'm soaked and shaking with cold—and plastered with wind-whipped sleet. As I near the mission, I'm seized by a shiver-driven urge to urinate. Hampered by trembling hands and bladder muscles that are losing their grip, I almost make a mess of it. Part of my brain whispers, Hypothermia, but the remainder says, Don't be silly—you can't get that cold in five minutes. But I am.

I fumble out of my wet clothes, grab a T-shirt, dry my sandpaper flesh and struggle into wool socks, a sweatshirt and pants. But when I jam myself into my sleeping bag, I can barely manage the zipper. I insanely contemplate retrieving a stocking cap from the Cub, but knowing that the bag's insulation will trap whatever heat I produce, I pull it over my head and begin doing sit-ups. Cold as I am, I laugh at myself as I flop around like a giant inchworm while trying to think warm thoughts.

As the heat of my efforts accumulates, I think of the time that I'd just turned twelve and was allowed to spend a midwinter night at our cabin while my parents went to town. Not realizing that our ancient wood burner leaked vast amounts of air, and reluctant to leave my bed to stoke the fire in the middle of a thirty-below night, I packed it full of wood, filling each crevice with ever smaller sticks. Then, as instructed, I filled the water pail with snow and set it on top of the stove.

Around two o'clock, I awoke, miserably hot and sweating. I rushed into the living room, where I found a red-hot wood burner, its ten-foot-long horizontal pipes aglow to within a yard of the wall as the last drops of water leaped and sizzled on the bottom of the pail.

I quickly propped open the cabin door. As steam billowed into the frigid night, I removed a burner lid and slowly dribbled water onto the inferno while taking care not to spill, which might crack the burner. Fifteen minutes later, the glowing stovepipes finally turned black, as did the stove, and I returned to bed, relieved that I hadn't burned down the cabin—and determined to keep my adventure to myself.

The following morning I noticed something I'd missed during my fright. Every one of our many candles had collapsed. Candles hung limply from wall sconces and lay flattened on windowsills. From the rim of our dining table centerpiece, more than a dozen fanned out like white daisy petals. Knowing that I couldn't explain away the flaccid candles, I confessed to my parents, who were understanding.

Years later, I came across a deformed candle that my mother had tucked away. I restored it to its holder, from which it flops across the windowsill like a dead snake. Visitors glance at it, wondering dare they ask? When they finally do, I smile and begin, "One winter evening, when I'd just turned twelve . . ."

The shaking finally slows, my fingers tingle and the shivering stops. Like the cold-blooded lizards that Australian aborigines believe brought life to earth, then lost their tails and stood erect as they warmed, I am once again a man.

Outside, the Arctic wind moans. Sleep descends amid visions of Buliard dropping through the ice, and of Laura from Red Lake, who had wanted to come along. I decide I will send her a card from Yellowknife saying, "You wouldn't like it."

Morning. Rested and rational again, I can't imagine sending such a message. Why should I prejudice her with a single unpleasant incident out of a hundred delightful events?

Over a makeshift breakfast of coffee, fig newtons and a handful of carrots, I'm embarrassed to admit that I've had enough of Siurad-juar's stark beauty, of the solitude that once seemed so attractive and of the mystery of a man who asked for so little and suffered so much.

In a way, it doesn't matter how Father Buliard died, for he held true to his beliefs and to those who shaped his mind. Nevertheless, with the exception of medical missionaries and those who provide a tangible benefit, I think that Robert Perkins had it right: "I've never been in favor of the missionary spirit. It is a bitter fruit that has destroyed many cultures."

Four

GARRY LAKE TO FORT ST. JOHN, BRITISH COLUMBIA

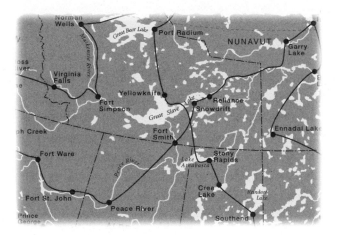

9

Garry Lake to Reliance, Northwest Territories

When men lack a sense of awe, there will be disaster.
– LAO-TZU

HE CUB'S PRIMITIVE HEATER roasts my feet but warms little else as it struggles against the cold, overcome by the cockpit's many air leaks that demand a turned-up collar, a pair of gloves and a stocking cap that's stretched over my headset. As Garry Lake fades from sight, the Tundra Cub slips across the northern boundary of the "Serengeti of the North," the Thelon Wildlife Sanctuary, which my chart delineates with a line of geese. And though every pond and river is V'ed with the wakes of molting geese, the twenty-one-thousand-square-mile sanctuary was set aside not just for waterfowl but for the protection of all wildlife within its borders. Now, while the sun warms my spirit, I scan the tundra for wildlife as the Cub hurries south toward one of North America's largest gatherings of caribou, the Beverly Lake herd.

The Beverly herd, like most of the other great herds, fell to a fourth of its former size during the twentieth century, reduced by mindless opportunists with repeating rifles and possibly by nuclear fallout absorbed by lichen that the caribou fed on. Fortunately, the North American herds are recovering, with recent estimates totalling a million animals.

Because we were loath to accept our responsibility for the caribou's decline, we sought a scapegoat—and found the wolf. Although we knew that wolves took few healthy caribou, we spread poison across the Territories and the provinces during the fifties, killing more than ten thousand wolves and countless other unfortunate animals lured by the scent of the bait. Even far-off Minnesota authorities became carried away, proposing to destroy two hundred wolves a year until the "wolf menace has been eliminated." Fortunately, when people like Farley Mowat, the author of *Never Cry Wolf*, rose to the wolves' defense, reason finally prevailed, and we "discovered" what the natives had always known: that wolves culled the weak, the ill and the injured.

In open country, large animals like musk oxen and caribou have nowhere to hide. Worse yet, the musk oxen's practice of encircling their young and threatening predators with their massive horns proved suicidal against trigger-happy hunters who often slaughtered with abandon. Alarmed at the obvious decline of the musk ox herds, John Hornby, a peripatetic ne'er-do-well who flitted across the Territories in the early 1900s, took it upon himself to become the chief promoter of the Thelon Wildlife Sanctuary and may well have saved the musk oxen from extinction. Had he been as concerned for his own welfare, he'd have lived to see the herds return, but his boundless enthusiasm disdained caution, and in 1927, the year that the sanctuary was created, he and two companions paid the ultimate price in the haven he'd sought to create.

As the Tundra Cub crests the Musk Ox Hills, I ease back the throttle to begin a long descent to the valley of the Thelon River.

Lakes, ponds, rivers and marsh fill every basin for as far as the eye can see—a seemingly incredible sight for an arid region that receives under ten inches of moisture a year.

I pick up the Thelon at Beverly Lake. Flowing east, the water will pass through Beverly, Aberdeen, Schultz and Baker Lakes before coursing the final two hundred miles to Hudson Bay. This year the lakes are ice-free, but in "bad" ice years large lakes like these can thaw very late, and occasionally not at all, creating a unpleasant surprise for canoeists who suddenly find their idyllic river voyage to Baker Lake suddenly slowed by a hundred miles of rotting lake ice.

Although it's early in the season, I'm hoping to come upon the fall caribou migration that so often follows the Thelon's shores— a migration like the one described by geologist and author J. W. Tyrrell in 1893: "Moving masses of caribou [covered] the valleys and hillsides for miles. . . . To estimate their numbers would be impossible. They could only be reckoned in acres or square miles."

Holding to a westerly course, I leave the rocky tundra behind as the Thelon meanders back and forth below. The scattering of trees slowly thickens as the Cub flies deeper into the evergreen oasis, soaring over spruce and willows that once again stand erect instead of hunching low to the ground.

Ursus Islands grow large through the Cub's invisibly spinning prop. Floating like green rafts on an azure river-sky melange, the islands are home to the Barren Ground grizzlies that have always evaded me, concealed by brush dense enough to hide a convention of bears. And though I search the dense alder canopy, the islands again fall behind once again without a single bear in sight.

No caribou, no bears and no musk oxen. If my luck doesn't change, I'll have to content myself with Musk Ox Hill, a sixty-foot-high blister that's rising on the horizon. Known to the Inuit as a *pingo*, meaning "conical hill," Musk Ox Hill is a cousin of the frost heaves that buckle our northern American roads. Pingos, like the sandy eskers deposited by glacial rivers and the gravelly moraines that trace a glacier's margins, are remnants of the Great Cold.

Exclusive to the Arctic, they form when runoff feeds a subsurface core of deep permafrost and freezes, expanding upward to burst through the overburden of silt and clay.

By the time the Tundra Cub passes the tiny cabin at Lookout Point I'm weary of searching for game, so I push the Cub's nose down until I'm twenty feet above the river, pour on the fuel and roll from side to side as I bank through the Thelon's turns. As the shoreline flashes past, waves of goose bumps wash up and down my spine. I am Walter Mitty, come to the rescue in my Spitfire, or perhaps in a Wart Hog—the ugly, low-level fighter bomber of the Gulf War. Darting up the Thelon at all of Mach .13, I hold my heading when the river turns, pull up abruptly to clear the trees, then shove the nose down again as the river rounds the bend.

With my ears monitoring the engine's roar, my eyes constantly measuring the height and distance of the oncoming trees and my muscles evaluating feedback from the Cub, I weave back and forth within the confines of the river's spruce-topped banks. I'm a surfer in the Banzai pipeline—the roaring surf my engine, the speeding surfboard my wings. Whipping up and down the breaker's face, I arc through three G turns, living on the edge while excusing myself with Robert Burns:

If there be life after death, he lies in bliss;
If not, he made the most of this.

Aiming again at a wall of trees, I pull up hard to leap another point of land. When I shove the nose down, I'm suddenly looking into an explosion of running musk oxen—huge mounds of fur startled into flight by the intruding Cub.

I pull back on the stick, bank left and gain two hundred feet. Scattered, but regrouping below, are more than twenty musk oxen bulls and cows and at least one calf. I throttle back to two thousand rpm, raise the window and circle for photos.

The musk oxen slowly drift back toward the point, pushing through shoulder-high brush as I slip the Cub to an unseen landing on the peninsula's opposite shore. I'm sure that I won't be able to get close to the herd, so I snap an 80–200 mm lens onto my camera, scramble up the riverbank and begin to push through the thickets.

Something to my left moves. I'm stunned to see a humped-shouldered, seven-hundred-pound bull musk ox staring at me. Less than thirty feet away and looking like an evolutionary throwback with an ominous brow and huge curved horns, he snorts and paws the ground. As his wooly-mammoth-like coat wavers in the wind, I center his bulk in the Nikon's viewfinder while reassuring myself of the musk ox's defensive nature and the claim that they rarely charge.

Musk oxen, like the Inuit, crossed the Bering land bridge from Asia thousands of years ago. But their name is misleading. Although the males emit a pungent, sweetish smell during the fall rut, they have no musk glands.

Known to the Inuit as Oomingmaq, meaning "the animal with skin like a beard," musk oxen are marvels of Arctic adaptation. Aided by short ears, stocky legs and an extremely efficient double coat of fur, the musk ox maintains a body temperature of 101 degrees in temperatures of 50 below and windchills that can exceed minus 90. A dense, wooly underfur called *qiviut* lies tucked within its two-foot-long guard hairs. As fine as vicuna or cashmere, qiviut is said to insulate eight times better than wool. Not surprisingly, qiviut products won't be found at the five and dime. Stocking caps start at $90, and scarves can top $200.

A twig snaps behind me. When I turn, I discover that I'm surrounded by musk oxen, having somehow walked into their midst in the head-high brush. Pivoting from side to side, I snap photos while trying to keep my cool. When I finally run out of film, I face an unexpected problem—how do I leave?

Fortunately, the musk oxen cooperate by drifting away—except for the big bull, who continues to stare at me with his dark brown eyes. As I slowly back away, I gather a handful of freshly shed qiviut from the brush, roll it into a ball and cup it in my hand. I'm astounded at how rapidly my palm overheats, as if I'd pulled on a fleece-lined mitten on a hot midsummer day.

Back at the Cub, I check the oil. She's used a quart since Baker Lake and about twenty-five gallons of fuel. Lifting the three five-gallon plastic bags of hundred-octane fuel from the back seat, I set them on the flat-topped floats, where they look like bulging bags of blueberry Kool Aid awaiting a Boy Scout picnic.

After rolling up my sleeves in anticipation of my usual spillage, I hoist the first bag overhead and pour the fuel into a filter-equipped funnel. In the midst of emptying the second container into the wing tank, a mosquito alights on my arm, followed by several of her friends who tank up while I steady the bag. For a moment I see them sympathetically—just fellow creatures trying to make ends meet. Oh sure, my inner voice interrupts, their ends—your meat. I sweep them into oblivion. When I reach for the last bag of fuel, I discover that it has slumped over the edge of the float and is slowly drifting downstream, which explains the quiet slurp that I heard and ignored while feeding mosquitoes. Not to worry. Gas is so much lighter than water that even steel drums full of fuel will float. Pulling off my boots, I wade into the river and retrieve the wayward bag.

I continue west when the river begins a long loop to the north. The odds of finding caribou will be better if I follow the river, but the overland route will save fuel, so I head for a ruined cabin and three small crosses at a place called Hornby Point.

The beach at Hornby Point runs from sand to platter-size stones. Shaped by exuberant springtime floods and polished by the abrasives of time, they've been sorted by the Thelon, leaving the fines near the waterline, the gravels higher and the boulders beyond it all, bulldozed high by rafts of ice.

Rocks roll beneath my feet as I climb toward a tiny opening at the edge of the trees—a clearing so small that even those who search for it often pass it by. In fact, as I step from the stones to the spruce-scented taiga, I begin to think that I've erred. No crosses greet me. Neither is there a hint of the cabin, which is not surprising, considering its ruinous state thirty years ago. But as I advance into the tiny clearing, I spot first one cross, then two more lying on a carpet of caribou moss, their flaking, dull white paint almost hidden by masses of russet needles and rotting leaves.

In 1968 the weathered crosses stood at odd angles near the entrance to a tiny shack. On a later visit, they wore a fresh coat of white—a tribute from passing canoeists who had come to explore Hornby's beloved sanctuary.

The cabin's roof had fallen in, lying broken within a small, knee-high rectangle of moss-covered logs that once were walls. As I stood beside the graves, the Hornby story came flooding back, filling me with sadness as I sensed the sorrow and quiet desperation that these walls had witnessed during a long, harsh winter that began in 1926.

In 1904, John Hornby, having failed his exams for the Diplomatic Corps, bade his parents goodbye and sailed from England at the age of twenty-three. Moving west from Montreal, he tried farming near Edmonton. When it held no appeal, he headed north, where he surveyed, prospected and hunted the barrens, becoming a resourceful, hardy individual who could persevere when old hands quit. As Hornby's trapper friend Jim Cooley put it, that fellow Hornby "could travel further on a diet of snow, air and scenery than a Lizzie [a model T Ford] can go on twenty gallons of gas."

At five foot four and a shade over a hundred pounds, Hornby was surprisingly fit. George Whalley, the author of *The Legend of John Hornby*, recalls that Hornby once "ran one hundred miles from Edmonton to Athabasca Landing in under twenty-four hours."

Hornby quickly learned the lessons of the bush, including how to tolerate starvation and began to prefer to live off the land like a native. As Whalley observed, "Hardship and starvation seemed to take on a positive value for him, as though they were the only substantial values left, as though an ascetic and masochistic spirit were driving him to some impossible consummation with the country he loved."

That consummation was predicted by his friend, D'Arcy Arden, who warned Hornby, "You go where there are no Indians, Jack, and you'll die. Every time you've starved, Jack, an Indian has come to your assistance. You get away from those Indians and you'll die like a rat." Hornby just smiled.

In the spring of 1926, having just returned from England with his cousin, a lad of seventeen named Edgar Christian, Hornby headed north from Edmonton with Edgar, accompanied by a twenty-seven-year-old Royal Air Force veteran named Harold Adlard. They arrived at the eastern end of Great Slave Lake during the long summer days of June.

With the arduous, three-and-a-half-mile, five-hundred-foot-high portage into Artillery Lake finally behind them, the trio began a leisurely trek across the barrens toward Hornby's beloved Thelon River, which they expected would carry them to the long chain of Beverly, Aberdeen and Schultz Lakes. After paddling the lakes, they'd ride the last miles of the Thelon to overwinter at Baker Lake.

Little is known of their journey across the barrens from the time they left Great Slave until October, and by then it was early winter. Lacking suitable clothing and knowing that the lakes leading to Baker Lake had already begun to freeze, Hornby decided that attempting to cross the remaining two hundred miles of open wind-swept tundra would be suicidal. Besides, he loved the Thelon valley. The river held fish, the forest provided shelter and he expected a surfeit of game.

By mid-October, the three adventurers had completed a one-room, dugout/log cabin in a spruce grove on the Thelon's northern shore, and young Edgar had begun to make regular entries in his neglected diary.

That fall, when the Hornby party failed to arrive at Baker Lake, few expressed concern, for Hornby's reputation as a skilled hunter, trapper and survivor led to the conclusion that the party had holed up on the Thelon and would arrive the following year.

Spring came, then summer. Weeks passed after the big lakes west of Baker had shed their sheaths of ice—time aplenty for the party to reach Baker Lake if they weren't disabled or dead. Searchers traveling as far west as Aberdeen Lake found no one, and a scarcity of aircraft and weeks of poor weather prevented a search farther west.

A midsummer party of canoeists following Hornby's route found a rock cairn near Deville Lake and in it a note from Hornby: "About August 5, 1926. Owing to bad weather and laziness, traveling slowly. One big migration of caribou passed. Expect to see you all soon. J. H."

Although travelers in the area had been urged to be on the look-out for the Hornby party, no one noticed the little cabin nestled in evergreens high on the Thelon's shore. Another year passed until, on July 21, 1928, four young canoeists finally spotted Hornby's shack.

Outside the cabin, the horrified men discovered two bodies wrapped in blankets. When their calls produced no response, they forced the door, which was secured from the inside, leading them to believe that another body lay within. There, illuminated by dim light that filtered through two tiny windows, lay a third blanket-covered body.

Kenneth Dewar, one of the canoeists, would later write in *The Beaver*, a Hudson's Bay Company publication, "The right hand bunk appeared to have something under the blanket, so I gave the blanket a slight pull. . . . With that little exercise, the bones of two feet fell off the foot of the bunk and the skull rolled off to the side." They belonged to Edgar Christian. Admitting later that a sort of panic propelled them, the men retreated to their canoes and began long days of furious paddling toward Baker Lake.

When RCMP made a more thorough search the following sum-mer, they discovered something that the distraught canoeists had missed: On the top of the sheet-metal stove lay a discolored note that read "WHOEVER . . . LOOK IN STOVE." There, they found a grim account of inch-by-inch starvation in the diary of Edgar Christian.

According to Edgar, by the time they had reached the sheltering spruce thickets of the Thelon valley, they were very late indeed. The plentiful caribou that they'd failed to hunt, thinking there would be hundreds more, had moved far off to the south. As the weeks stretched into months and the days grew short, Edgar Christian read and reread a loving and prophetic last letter from his father: "We think of you with hope & love & I know you look forward to success. But life is full of disappointments & disillusionments & things very seldom turn out as we hope."

As carefully rationed supplies slowly disappeared, their deprivation oscillated between serious and extreme. They managed to shoot or trap a few ptarmigan one week plus a fox or a wolverine in another, and by scavenging their dump for discarded caribou guts and fishheads, they persevered through the stingy light of winter in temperatures of fifty below. And though they took turns hunting, Hornby bore the brunt, repeatedly exhausting himself on ill-clad forays in the energy-sapping snow.

January came and slowly went. The warmest day was minus ten, the coldest, minus forty as Hornby further reduced his rations, having decided to sacrifice himself in the hope that the others might live.

February passed slowly, followed by the equinox with its increasing light and warmth. Edgar's diary: "Hope to god we get caribou soon as nothing seems to get in the traps . . . we are grovelling around for rotten fish."

On April 2, though too weak to hunt, Hornby took advantage of a spell of mild weather to struggle out to where Adlard had killed a small caribou and collected "a little blood which made an excellent snack."

Having arrived late in the fall, they had stored what little dry wood they could find. To conserve their supply, they tried green wood, which burned poorly and surrendered little heat. Finally, on April 6, when none had the strength to venture out, they burned their last scraps of dry wood. Four days later, Hornby wrote his will, bequeathing his all to Edgar Christian.

Edgar's diary: "16th April. Between us have prepared a meal of hide. . . . Jack still breathing but unconscious. . . . April 17. At 6:45 p.m. last evening poor Jack passed away . . . determined to pull through and go out to let the world know of the last days of the finest

The author's Tundra Cub, a 1947 Piper PA-11 Cub Special.

Erosion cuts through the stem of land, lays a sandbar across the channels,
and forms an oxbow lake near Manitoba's Owl River.

The freighter *Ithaca*, aground near Churchill, Manitoba.

Searching for hors d'oeuvres at the Churchill, Manitoba dump. PHOTO: DALE WALKER

A polar bear swims gracefully in Hudson Bay.

The author's innovative and productive lures.

One hand grips a *kikivak*, a three-pronged trident-like spear at Chantrey Inlet, Nunavut.

PHOTO: MATT OPAC

Fanning out across the Thelon River's broad beach, the caribou plunge into the current.

A lunch-size trout from Lockhart River, NWT.

Another pilot's unlucky landing on the shores of a remote lake in the NWT.

PHOTO: ELDON SORENSON

Crossing the Continental Divide, northwest of Fort Ware, B.C.

Soaring above snow-laden cirques and azure ponds in Northern B.C.

(left) Juneau's popular Mendenhall glacier towers above Mendenhall Lake, Alberta
(right) Glacier Lake leads the way to Mount Sir James MacBrien, NWT.

The Tundra Cub finds a novel hood ornament at Glacier Lake, NWT.

The Tundra Cub contemplates the Nahanni Range at Little Doctor Lake, NWT.

Communing with Unok beneath a black subarctic sky, Indin Lake, NWT.

man I have ever known and one who has made a foundation to build my life upon. Snowstorm all day. 20 degrees.

"May 4th. At 10:30 p.m. dear Harold passed away. . . . I cannot hunt, as walking around in soft snow is beyond my powers now, and the weather is bad."

Despite his weakness, Edgar somehow managed to wrap Adlard in a blanket and drag him outside. When Edgar crawled back into the silence of the spruce-log walls, Harold Adlard lay a few yards east of the cabin door beside the body of John Hornby.

"May 7th . . . as thin as a rake about my rump and my joints seem to jerk in and out of position instead of smoothly. This I believe to be exactly the same thing as happened to poor Jack and Harold. . . . May 17. If I cannot get grub tomorrow must make preparations. . . . Now June 1st. Yesterday I was out crawling . . . found fish guts. . . .

On June 2, as a bright spring sun flooded the tundra with warmth, blossoms and birds, Edgar wrote, "Weaker than ever . . . food on hand, but heart petering. Sunshine is bright . . . Make preparations now."

As Whalley later wrote, "Making preparations had been Hornby's term for doing the last things before death." In Edgar's case it meant writing separate letters to his mother and father in which he praised Hornby, writing, "Please don't Blame dear Jack."

Whalley continued, "When the fire had died out and he had decided that he would never light it again, Edgar Christian placed his two letters in the cool ashes of the stove, together with Hornby's will . . . and his diary. On the top of the stove he left his note.

"He was wearing a heavy gray sweater over a khaki shirt, gray flannel trousers held up by a silk handkerchief, a muffler around his neck, and winter moccasins with puttees. He turned in to his bunk and pulled two, red Hudson's Bay blankets over himself, covering his head." In the warmth of presolstice sunshine, Edgar Christian died in the solitude that Hornby had loved and that all three had come, too late, to respect.

Prior to setting out for the Thelon, Hornby had recommended in his Caribou Report that a sanctuary be created for musk oxen in the Thelon River District. In June 1927, shortly after Hornby died, but before his body had been discovered, the Thelon Wildlife Sanctuary was created to protect the remaining musk oxen and all other game as well.

Still thinking about the fallen crosses, I turn and head back to the Cub. Part of me says to leave them where they lie, while the other argues that the travelers deserve a marker. I stop briefly, undecided, then climb back to the clearing. Knowing that no matter what I do, nature will have its way, I brush away the debris and drive the crosses into the ground with a hefty river-worn stone.

When I untie the Cub, I spot a skipping stone beside the river's edge. Flat and well rounded, it fits perfectly within the arc of my thumb and fore-finger. As I send it bouncing across the Thelon, I think of Hornby, who hopped across the North like a stone skipping water, defying its pull for twenty-two years. After kissing the smooth-flowing river again and again, my stone encounters an unexpected ripple and, like John Hornby, Harold Adlard and Edgar Christian, quietly disappears into the depths of the Thelon Sanctuary.

The midafternoon sun pouring through the windshield demands a pair of sunglasses to mute the beautiful diamond-littered Thelon. Raising my camera to frame the river, I close one eye, rotate the polarizing filter—and everything goes black!

I sight through the camera again—still black. Turning the polarizer farther admits more light, but not enough. Has my camera failed—a near-disaster at this stage of the trip?

Removing my sunglasses, I carefully examine the Nikon while holding the stick with my knees. Nothing seems amiss, so I sight through the camera again. The lighting is now perfect, the windshield reflections gone as the Thelon gleams a sinuous, sequined blue. Puzzled, I stare at the camera as the Cub drones along, then notice my sunglasses lying in my lap and remember that they, too, are polarized. The answer's so obvious that I laugh out loud.

Polarized sunglasses reduce light in two ways: by their tint and because they are scored with tiny, invisible, parallel lines that admit light that "vibrates" in only one plane. When I first looked through the camera, the lines on the polarizing camera filter and the lines on my sunglasses happened to be aligned. Light that could pass through my glasses could also pass through the filter, just as a letter could pass through two closely aligned mailbox slots. But when I rotated the filter ninety degrees, the light it admitted arrived at right angles to the lines on my sunglasses, which wouldn't allow it to pass. In turning one of the mail slots, I'd stopped the sparkling panorama when it was halfway through.

Suddenly, a canoe flashes beneath my wing. Within it, two men frantically wave arms and paddles as if in distress while I circle to land.

As I drift up to their beached canoe, I examine the voyageurs. Scruffy beards proclaim two to three weeks in the bush. They're both in their fifties, and one of them sounds and looks exactly like Lee Marvin, the actor. Sunburned, sagging and semiclean, they introduce themselves while I try not to stare.

Their problem: the Thelon is too boring. Farther upstream they'd run a few challenging rapids, but for the last 150 miles, the river's millpondlike flow has been driving them mad. They'd originally planned to paddle up one of the Thelon's tributaries, then portage over to the Back River, but an early spring and a drier than normal summer has turned their tributary to a trickle, condemning them to the Thelon. Weary of its easy temperament, they ask me to arrange for a plane to fly them out when I reach Reliance.

"I could do that," I say, "but if I'm delayed or decide to follow a caribou herd I might not get to Reliance for three or four days. By then, you'd be halfway to Baker. Besides, no charter pilot is going to come looking for you on my say-so unless he's paid in advance." That stops them.

Actually, I have little sympathy for them. If they'd done some reading about this beautiful country, they'd have had other interests to follow when their much-anticipated contest with a lion became a stroll with a lamb.

As I push the Cub back into the current, I remember to ask if they've seen any game. "We sure did." One responds, "About fifteen musk oxen near Warden's Grove, and two days ago we ran across a God-awful herd of caribou."

The Cub's Continental barks to life as caribou fill my mind. Could the paddlers' herd have been the main migration? Two weeks from now, perhaps, but even that would be early. At any rate, finding that herd is unlikely, for two days of travel would have taken it well to the south of my route.

Grassy Island has always produced caribou, but this year's herd is disappointingly small—fewer than a hundred animals. Like leaves caught in a whirlpool, they circle in response to the orbiting Cub until I roll back on course to follow the millions of hoofprints that litter the Thelon's shores.

Far ahead, cloud shadows cast Rorschach patterns across sunlit sandbars. The shadows merge, becoming funnel shaped near the river. Wait a minute. Those aren't shadows—definitely not shadows. They're the lobes of an immense herd of caribou streaming down from the hills to the north. Fanning out over the Thelon's wide beach, the caribou plunge into the current, drifting sideways as they cross—like the Cub in a crosswind. On the opposite shore, they surge from the river, shaking rainbows of spray from their coats, then regroup into a wide column that extends as far as I can see. Like an immense swarm of procession caterpillars, the insects that travel head to tail in an endless game of follow the leader, the herd heads for the southern horizon. I stay with the herd for fifteen miles, and there's still no end in sight. As I roll into a 180, the herd plods on like a single-minded living carpet, drawn to the south by memories stored in their genes.

The Thelon falls behind as the Cub descends toward a Steel Lake island that will lower the odds of a midnight encounter with tundra grizzly bears.

Except for a tiny beach, the island's a confusion of frost-shattered rock. I secure the Cub to a stunted spruce and set off to search for a campsite. When I'm halfway to the top of the island, a fist-size chunk of rock nestled in a dark green bed of bearberry leaves catches my eye. On one glistening angular surface, a single inch-wide lichen lifts its face to the sun.

I hunch down on my knees and elbows like a Muslim at prayer to fill the Nikon's viewfinder with its yellow-on-maroon beauty mark of patient life. Delicate-looking but tough, these amazing life-forms endure summer's searing heat and the worst winter's cold to decorate the tundra with patches of mauve-gray and pink, with orange, red and black.

What a subarctic paradise! Blossoms speckle the tundra; fluffy, sheeplike cumulus clouds graze skies of royal blue; to the southwest, a straw-colored esker enlivens the horizon. Looking like the back of a giant lizard, the esker separates Steel Lake from Helen Falls and Dickson Canyon, two Hanbury River hazards that thin the ranks of migrating caribou.

Every spring, when the swift-running Hanbury bears rafts of ice, migrating caribou are swept downstream into a meat grinder of ice blocks and boulders called Dickson Canyon. Those that somehow survive the canyon plunge over Helen Falls to an almost certain death. In the placid water below the falls, however, caribou can cross with ease, swimming obliviously past the drifting bodies of their kin to graze away the short subarctic summer.

Drawn by the faint, characteristic clicking sound of caribou ankle bones, I turn to the northwest. The clicking fades, then returns more strongly, carried on the wind. A set of antlers rises over the crest of the island as a caribou bull grazes into sight. Approaching from upwind, he's unaware of me. I raise my camera to center him in the viewfinder—and discover a forest of antlers behind him.

When the bull is forty feet away, he spots me, snorts loudly and stops. Head tilted, he stares as he lifts his nose to the wind. He advances ten feet and stops again, legs spread in the characteristic alarm stance of caribou, then sidesteps around me, as others follow in a tympani of clicking and clacking hooves. They inspect me with their large round eyes, but not a one takes alarm when they pass downwind. Have I no meaning to them? Not being a grizzly, a wolf or a fox, am I, for all my human vanities, just an irrelevant collection of nonscents?

Brushing aside the insects that they've kicked out of the brush, I follow the herd until they slip into the lake and fan out behind the buck. They're soon halfway to the mainland, propelled by huge hooves and buoyed by coats of hollow hair and the summer's accumulation of fat. In their wake, a coating of caribou hair calms the wavelets of the Steel, bringing to mind a Hudson's Bay Company maxim: "If it doesn't have a caribou hair, it's not a proper cup of tea."

As I carry my tent to the island's only decent campsite, I'm suddenly strafed by a screeching bird. Whirling around to confront my assailant, I come face-to-face with an arctic tern that's beginning another pass.

When I scan the ground for the chicks that she must be protecting, I discover two fluffballs huddled beside a clump of arctic cotton just as their parent performs another wing-over and comes back like a dive bomber. I retreat to the Cub, clamp on a hat, retrieve my camera and catch the tern in midattack, its wings a blur of acceleration. Switching to telephoto, I lie down about twenty feet from the chicks for two quick photos.

Within a few weeks, these clumsy chicks will ride record-setting wings, for the arctic tern is the greatest traveler of all living things. Weighing just four ounces, these globetrotters "winter" in *southern* South America before returning to the Arctic for every northern spring.

Once supper is out of the way, I contemplate a quick bath. Unlike white-tail fawns, which are said to emit no predator-attracting scents, I'm awash in avgas, insect repellent, bacon grease, crushed insects and sweat. But my hands, still aching from washing dishes in the frigid water, protest that even ravenous grizzlies would be repelled by my malodorous melange. It's said that the wind goes to bed with the sun, and today is no exception. Within an hour, the breeze falls away, its sighs replaced by the annoying, high-pitched mating call of female mosquitoes as they summon mates with their vibrating wings. Seduced by the Joni-one-notes, the eager males take wing to find true love.

Mosquitoes, the Arctic's all-day suckers, pass through several stages before becoming adults: eggs yield larvae; larvae repeatedly shed their skins and become pupae; the pupae, bursting with energy, split down the back and out crawl miniature *aliens*. Chock-full of hormones, pheremones and eager to emit other moans, mosquitoes mate at the first opportunity. The females then search for blood, homing in on our warmth and our carbon dioxide-rich exhalations before laying eggs after every meal. Some species can survive mild freezing; a few can produce several generations on plant nectar alone, but all prefer blood, for its rich store of protein boosts egg production a hundredfold.

A mosquito alights on the back of my hand and becomes a tiny drilling rig, but luck is not with her. Finding a dry hole, she pulls the pipe, moves to one side and begins to drill at a slant like a wildcatter angling under his neighbor's property line. When her gusher comes in, she injects an anticoagulant, protein-laden saliva to prolong the flow. (It's the proteins that cause the itching and swelling.)

Back inside the tent, I try to focus on Diane Ackerman's *A Natural History of the Senses*, but I'm distracted by the horde of insects that are probing the netting in search of a meal. One queen-size mosquito repeatedly thrusts her "stinger" through the mesh, tempting me to grasp it between my fingernails, but, Gandhi-like, I decline. Another wobbles past. Overloaded with blood, she staggers through the air and lands on the *inside* of the netting, revealing that she too has supped—on me. Backlit by the lowering sun, she glows ruby red, a translucent, winged jewel.

I'm unwilling to have my blood fortify another horde, so I smear her vital cargo into a crimson B-positive streak. To my surprise, the blood fails to interest her relatives, who wander across the netting, oblivious to the treasure at their feet.

Returning to my reading, I begin the chapter on touch, with its captivating references to lovers and sexuality, only to be distracted by the sounds of snorting and snapping twigs. Through the tent's rear window, I spot several caribou heading for the river. The first pays the tent no mind, but the second stops, casting a maze of antler shadows across its yellow nylon walls. Turning its head, the caribou licks the tightly stretched fabric with its rasplike tongue. In the midst of its third lick, I curl a pointer finger into my thumb and give the tongue-depressed fabric a snap. The shadow leaps skyward and disappears in a clatter of hooves.

What a turnabout! A few hours ago, I had almost given up on caribou, and I'm again immersed in their flow. But now that the wind has dropped, this herd is beset with mosquitoes and flies. Tails flicking, their heads shaking and their backs shivering, they head for temporary relief in the lake.

Barren Ground Caribou are larger than Santa's Lapland-type reindeer, which dwarf the near-white, Peary's caribou of Canada's Arctic islands. These names, however, are white man's names. The Inuit, whose fortunes rose and fell with the herds, called their provider Tuktu—"the traveler." To them, Tuktu was a storehouse of vital food encased in an insulating hide that could shelter and warm their bodies and could be cut into useful ropey strips.

Tuktu is a marvel of evolution. Each spring, pregnant cows lead the trek north, arriving at the windswept barrens about a month ahead of the bulls. There they deliver calves that can stagger after their mothers within minutes of birth. A few days later, they'll out-run a human.

The fall retreat to the semishelter of the taiga is led by mature bulls carrying up to thirty pounds of back fat that serve as a reservoir of calories against the coming winter. For added protection, caribou muzzles are furred to reduce heat loss when they search for food beneath the snow.

As for the "caribou moss" that sustains Tuktu through the winter, it's not a moss; it's a lichen, and caribou are not the only ones who have prized this hardy plant-and-animal blend. Because lichen absorb and retain scents, tons of these symbiots were shipped to Europe during the eighteenth and nineteenth centuries, where, after being dried and packed in flowers, their finely ground remains brought enduring fragrance to sachets and powdered wigs.

With the exception of humans, caribou have only three enemies: grizzlies, wolves and insects, and because grizzlies and wolves feed primarily on the injured and aged, they're not a serious threat to the herd. And although it's hard to believe, even the millions of mosquitoes and blackflies are minor problems compared with the threat of two agile insects that can easily tolerate wind—and the caribou know it.

As a herd grazes lazily through a lush subarctic meadow, a caribou suddenly shakes its head violently and bolts, running wildly, as it flees from one of two villains, or possibly both: the warble fly and the nose bot fly.

Warble flies prefer thin, lightly furred skin on which to lay their eggs: the inner surface of a caribou leg or the soft hide of its belly. After hatching, the tiny saw-toothed larvae burrow into the animal's hide, then migrate through the flesh to the warmth of its well-furred back, where they overwinter in a fibrous sack. By spring each has become an aqueous grub about the size of a jelly bean. In June, two hundred or more grubs emerge through their often-infected breathing holes, which not only attract blowflies, but riddle the hide so badly as to render it worthless. Fortunately, the holes slowly close, making late-fall and winter hides useable.

Falling to the ground, the grubs pupate into warble flies, their life's ambition dictated by their genes: find a caribou leg or a belly and perpetuate your kind. Some of the grubs fall prey to birds, and, not surprisingly, to the Inuit, because, as survivors in a difficult climate, the Inuit developed eclectic tastes.

Gontran de Poncins in *Kabloona*, once shared these details about Inuit hors d'oeuvres: "They skinned the beast, and then one of them took the flesh in his fingers and pinched it sharply. Two enormous lice—worms, more truly—jumped out of the carcass . . . one after the other Kailek squeezed the worms out with his thumb and popped them into his mouth. I, who was determined to try anything once, took one up, shut my eyes, and put one in my mouth. It was sweetish inside its surprisingly fuzzy, raspberry-like skin, and I spat out the skin and had another, while Kailek sat with a heap of them before him on the snow."

While the warble fly attacks the caribou's legs and belly, the bee-like nose bot fly invades their nostrils, laying eggs that hatch into irritating larvae in the pharyngeal mucus of the animal. There, the wriggling mass restricts breathing, making the severely afflicted easy prey for wolves and bears. (In *People of the Deer*, Farley Mowat wrote of removing "one hundred and thirty of these giant maggots, each an inch long, from the throat and nostrils of a single doe.") Coughing and sneezing, caribou find relief only after the mature larvae return to the nostrils and fall to the ground, where they pupate into flies.

The last caribou departs, leaving only the hum of insects and the cry of a distant wolf. For a moment, I consider leaving the tent to howl a reply, but I'm dissuaded by the bugs. As the howling fades and the mosquitoes hum an endless reprise, I recall the thought-provoking words of Canadian biologist and author George Calef: "Like the caribou, the buffalo and the passenger pigeon were prodigious, gregarious species that made annual migrations. . . . Both are long gone, under the impact of fences and firearms, the ax and the plow."

As civilization moves ever northward, must the caribou herds go the way of the carrier pigeons and bison?

Leaving the Thelon Sanctuary behind, the Tundra Cub heads west across hundreds of miles of drumlin fields. Formed from glacial debris dropped behind resistant outcroppings of bedrock, the teardrop-shaped drumlins line up like compass needles, their tails revealing the direction of the last glacier's flow.

I've always had marvelous fishing where the Lockhart River tumbles into Artillery Lake, so I veer a bit to the north, and an hour later, the Cub bounces across the turbulent Lockhart and drifts to shore amid a swarm of blackflies. Here, where the river rushes down staircase rapids into a rippled backwater, blackfly larvae thrive.

Unlike mosquitoes, blackflies rip out a crater of flesh, then lap up the bloody flow. Mindful of their ferocity, I anoint my hands and wrists with repellent, tuck my pants into my socks and clamp on a hat and head net, taking care to cinch the net around my upraised collar. Only then do I open the door.

Beneath the floats and along the shoreline, every subsurface rock bears a mossy coating of blackfly larvae. At the water's edge, I cup my hands about my eyes and lower my face to the surface. In the seething nursery below, tiny, wormlike larvae cling to stones, straining nutrients from the passing water with iridescent, antennaelike filters mounted atop their heads.

Some have already encased their bodies in a tiny but growing bubble of air that will soon lift them free of the larval mass. As each bubble pops to the surface it ruptures, launching another hungry humpback into flight. But even as they mature, others are seeking them out, for trout and grayling fingerlings have a taste for blackfly larvae.

Clipping on a Daredevil, I send the red-and-white lure spinning out over the rapids, trapping the reel under my thumb as the lure strikes the water. The lure, restrained by twenty-pound line and pulled along by the Lockhart's flow, arcs shoreward as it's carried downstream, then enters a foam-laced eddy below several Volkswagen-size boulders.

I'm expecting a strike, but even so, a tremendous jerk almost rips the rod from my hands. This is *not* a grayling. It's a trout, and a big one that surprises me by heading upstream, leaving the calm water below the rapids to challenge my line in the river's fast-flowing core. As the trout drags me upstream, I slowly release line, afraid of losing him. When I'm down to a few yards on the reel, he pauses. I cannot move him, but neither can he move me. And then, when I'm almost convinced that my line is trapped beneath a boulder, the strain eases. Like a poker player who has seen one too many raises, he folds.

A minute later, a huge trout rests at my feet. I don't dare to lift him the way one might lift a smaller fish, so I drop to my hands and knees and scoop him into my arms. Staggering to my feet, I face my tripod-mounted camera and lift my head net to prove that this is me. Bad move.

Before I can lower the trout and replace the netting, the black-flies have found my face. I crush them against my skin, but a few escape the assault, leaving welts that will itch for days.

Working quickly, I measure the trout with my pocket tape. Thirty-two inches from his sour-faced jaw to the tip of his tail, he's thirty pounds for sure, maybe more. I slip him back into the river, then hold him upright while his wide mouth opens and closes, pumping oxygen-rich water past his gills. Sleek-finned and flecked with yellow, brown and gold, his streamlined body quickly broadens, then tapers to a lean and flexible tail that suddenly flicks—and he disappears.

Boosted by the fast-flowing river, the Cub leaps back into the air. Midway down Artillery Lake, a small resort sits astride the tree line. To the north lie the barrens, and a few miles to the south, the beginnings of the boreal forest. At the lake's southern end, where the Lockhart tumbles five hundred feet into Great Slave Lake near a settlement called Reliance, I begin to wonder if the barge has arrived with my fuel.

When I taxi in, I spot good news at the end of the pier—a fifty-five-gallon drum of avgas bearing an approximation of my name—"Erenson"—but what do I care? Were it labeled "Beelzebub," I'd claim it as my own.

As I roll the three-hundred-pound barrel to the Cub, a smiling man with a Kenny Rogers beard and a Willie Nelson body offers to lend a hand. On a shirt that's soon to see the rag bag, an embroidered pocket introduces me to Jake.

"So you're the one who ordered the fuel," says Jake. "Where're you heading?"

"West to Yellowknife," I reply.

"Uh-oh," says Jake. "I've got bad news for you. The weather that way is terrible. To the northwest, it's even worse."

"Well," I respond, "I suppose I'd better run up to the station anyway and talk to the weatherman."

"You already did," says Jake. "He's me!"

10

Reliance to Fort St. John, British Columbia

All men have stars, but they are not the same things for different people. For some, who are travelers, the stars are guides. For others, they are no more than lights in the sky.

– ANTOINE DE SAINT-EXUPÉRY,
The Little Prince

$\mathcal{I}$N THE EARLY 1900S, a Norwegian scientist named Vilhelm Bjerknes theorized that great domes and valleys of air circle the earth, changing the weather as they pass. Today, we call them "highs" and "lows." As new stations gradually filled in the gaps between distant reporting points, Bjerknes's son envisioned the cold and warm fronts that our weather maps now portray.

While weatherman Jake and I alternate on the wobble pump, whooshing a pint of avgas into the Cub with every stroke, Jake describes the classic low that's squatting over Yellowknife. On its western side, the counterclockwise winds that circle every low are driving dense arctic air southward, lofting thunderstorms along a four-hundred-mile cold front.

On its eastern side, between Reliance and Yellowknife, the same counterclockwise flow sweeps moisture-laden air up from the prairie provinces. Overrunning the milder northern air, the moist mass condenses, lowering ceilings and dropping visibility with rain, drizzle and fog. And though neither Jake nor I mention it, we both know that a forced landing in bad visibility opens the door to injury and death.

Accompanied by the distant throb of the weather station's diesel-driven generator, I tell Jake of a irrepressible friend who flew his Beechcraft Bonanza into the ground while searching for a Worthington, Minnesota, runway on a fog-shrouded summer night. The plane was found by a farmer when the fog lifted. His injured wife and two other passengers survived, but my friend was slumped cold and lifeless over the controls.

I've often wondered if his confidence began to erode as he orbited the airport, dropping lower with each revolution. Did his stomach churn, his guts turn greasy as his altimeter slowly unwound? Did his reason scream for a change of plans or did he descend serenely, only to have his optimism shattered by the blow that crushed his chest?

"Why don't you come up to the station for a cup of coffee while you decide about the weather?" suggests Jake.

As I finish my second cup, he asks, "Well, are you going to try for Yellowknife?

"Jake," I say, "I hate head winds, but waiting for Yellowknife's weather to change suits me even less, so I guess I'll angle south." Extending my hand, I add, "See you next year."

"Not here, you won't," he replies. "The station's closing. They'll probably have some sort of automatic reporting system, but there won't be any staff."

Nodding, I add, "And no free lunches, either."

Weighted down with sixty-five gallons of fuel, the Cub labors onto the step, hammers across a six-inch chop and rises from Great

Slave Lake. I circle to wave my thanks to Jake, who has promised to change the destination on my flight note to Fort Smith, which lies 240 miles to the southwest.

Except for the head wind, I'm pleased with the change of plans. Yellowknife can wait, and the detour might allow a stop at Snow-drift, Canada's most northerly Chipewyan settlement. Better yet, my course will follow Great Slave's spectacular East Arm, which is part of a 150-mile escarpment that's called the McDonald fault. Like the more famous San Andreas fault, the McDonald is visible proof that the earth's crust is webbed with globe-girdling cracks.

Between those cracks, and above the dense, semisolid mantle below, the lighter continental plates slowly perform a geological version of a bump and grind. Were they to be examined every million years or so, as with time-lapse photography, their sluggish wanderings would become the casual dance of the continents.

The plates are also fractured, one of the most obvious being the McDonald fault, where the Great Slave domain of the North American Plate grinds against the Churchill domain. In Christie and McLeod Bays, shorelines rise straight up for close to a thousand feet, creating vistas that moved George Back (of Back River fame) to write, "The scenery increased in grandeur and boldness; and never, either in Alp or Appenine, had I seen a picture of such rugged wildness."

Today, every well-educated person knows that the continents have been shuffling about for millions of years, but that now-well-proven theory received little but scorn when it was proposed by an early twentieth-century German astronomer-turned-meteorologist named Alfred Wegener, who became fascinated with geology while in Greenland. Wegener, in his 1915 book *The Origins of the Continents and Oceans*, proposed that the continents began as a single land mass that he called Pangaea, meaning "all land," which eventually split into several migrating plates, the continental plates that we speak of today. In so doing, Wegener challenged the science of the day, which claimed that continents and mountains arose from the wrinkling of a cooling, contracting earth. Poor Wegener—

he was derided as an outsider and told to stick to meteorology.

Perhaps Wegener had read that in the sixteenth century Sir Francis Bacon had noticed the fit of the Americas with the western coast of Africa, a fit that's even more precise when one uses the true borders of the continents, the margins of the continental shelves. Wegener's mass of evidence correlated the Cape Ranges of South Africa with comparable mountains that extend into Argentina, noted similar fossils on the opposing African and South American coasts, and included similarities in the Indian and southern oceans. He argued that the massive coal deposits in China and North America, which form from tropical forests, must have originated near the equator.

Finally, Wegener pointed to measurements suggesting that Greenland and Europe were slowly moving apart. Had he known of the fossilized forests in the Arctic islands, he'd have had further proof of our continents' wandering ways.

Though Wegener's *Origins* elicited little but yawns from his fellow Germans, it met a storm of criticism abroad. Harold Jeffreys, an eminent geophysicist, flatly stated that Wegener's proposals violated the laws of physics. "Continents," said Jeffreys, "cannot possibly plow through the earth's rocky mantle, which everyone knows is solid." Refusing to retreat, Wegener answered their objections in a second and third edition of *The Origins* and attended the 1928 American Association of Petroleum Geologists, where his work received a thorough pasting.

In 1930, Wegener returned to his beloved Greenland to study its glaciers. A few months later, after a successful 250-mile struggle in horrendous weather to bring supplies to two stranded members of his expedition, Wegener, on his fifieth birthday, set out with a companion to return to base. Neither was seen alive again, although Wegener's snow-covered body was eventually found.

Fortunately, science is a self-correcting discipline. By the fifties and sixties, most geologists favored Wegener, won over by the barrage of evidence from radiometric dating, from the discovery of the midocean ridges where upwelling magma drives the continents apart, and from the magnetic pole reversals recorded in the ridge-paralleling bands of hardened magma.

When lava is ejected onto the ocean floor it's much too hot to be magnetic, but as it cools, its iron particles align themselves with the earth's magnetic field. When radio-dating of rock became possible, surveys of the ocean floor revealed the chronology of the magnetic reversals. On each side of the midoceanic ridges, the history of the spreading ocean floor is revealed in bar code–like images of pole reversals trapped in the rocks—the code on one side of the ridge being a mirror image of the code on the other.

As Wegener had predicted, the oldest rocks lie far from the mid-ocean ridge. Like Agassiz, Wegener relied on the evidence, challenged the orthodox view and proved it wrong.

Chewing through the twenty mph head wind, the Tundra Cub finally reaches Snowdrift, but its piers are slick with spray. I'd like to stop, but since I've plenty of fuel, I decide not to risk the hazards of an unnecessary rough-water landing and an unprotected pier.

McDonald Lake crawls into sight. Dropping close to the foam to make my progress seem faster, I flit along the fault's ruler-straight escarpment within fifty feet of the soaring spruce that cling to McDonald's steeply rising shore.

I love the drama of vertical country. Its headlands, spires and chasms charm my flatlander eyes as I cruise past their battlements, ramps and towers, their massive shoulders of stone. Like a child fascinated by the glittering tinsel of a long-awaited Christmas, I'm dazzled by nature's ornaments. For thirty miles, I soar beside the fault, then turn south to head for Smith, and leave the fault behind.

The farther west I travel from Chantrey Inlet, Churchill or Minnesota, which lie south of *both* the geographic and magnetic poles, the larger my compass "error" becomes. Although compasses point to the more southerly *magnetic* pole, the *geographic* pole is the navigator's constant, and from my westerly perspective the two now lie

25 degrees apart. Consequently, to fly south, I need a compass heading of 155 degrees. Were I to fly a 180-degree heading, I'd miss Fort Smith by almost a hundred miles.

I'm weary and saddle sore. Except for fishing, fueling and eating, I've flown all day, and with Fort Smith still far away, I decide to camp. Besides, I'm surrounded with gorgeous campsites, while the country gets boggy near Smith. I scan my well-worn chart, searching for a pencilled *S* (for sand) alongside a T-shaped lake that I've visited once before.

I was also tired that day, when, after a long flight, I shook myself alert and lined up to land on T-bone lake. The lake, wide enough for two landings, was dead calm as I descended nose high with partial power, waiting for the floats to touch the invisible surface of T-bone's mirror-flat, invisible water. Like others before me, I was so confident that I could "put 'er where I want 'er" that I landed directly toward shore instead of parallel to it, which would have allowed an abundance of room.

Still airborne as the shoreline grew large in my windshield, I realized it was too late to add power and climb over the trees. The Cub touched down sixty yards from the beach, then skipped toward shore. I instantly shut down the engine, dropped the water rudder, shoved the stick left and the rudder right, doing everything I could think of to create drag. Planing into the shallows, the Cub slid to a stop with the tips of the floats overhanging the beach.

Were I inclined to deceive myself, I might call my landing a precision maneuver that few pilots could match. In fact, weariness had swayed my judgment, and I was lucky not to have damaged the Cub. Oddly enough, that same summer, another Minnesotan flying in the same area made the same mistake with more serious results.

Although they were flying similar aircraft, "Roger" had made fewer glassy-water landings than the pilot in the accompanying Cub. Moreover, their skills were not comparable. On seeing his partner make a successful landing directly toward the shore, Roger followed his example. Roger, however, carried a tad too much power, which extended his descent, and by the time his Cub touched down, he was rapidly closing on the shore.

Still planing along on the step, the Cub slid up the beach and jammed the tips of its floats into the ice-raised berm that rims so many northern shores. The aircraft's momentum lifted the tail skyward and stood the Cub on its nose as the prop bit into the brush. Fortunately, seaplane floats extend a foot or two beyond the prop, and the Cub came to a stop while pointing straight down—with the float tips resting on the beach and the prop on the berm—a perfect but unique three-point landing. Poised vertically, the Cub stood like a monument to all unlucky pilots—an obelisk with wings.

After Roger calmed down, the two pilots made a tripod from spruce trees, and with a rope sling, carefully lowered the tail. Fortunately, the Cub was undamaged except for the end of one propeller blade, which was slightly bent. But by roping a stout tree trunk to the blade and levering the tip forward, they soon had it tracking the same as the undamaged tip.

When the time came to fly his aircraft out, Roger lacked the nerve, for although the prop was fairly straight, it caused a disturbing vibration. The two pilots switched planes and flew to the next town, where they installed a new prop and continued on their way.

As I taxi toward my old campsite on the eastern shore, expecting nothing but sand and solitude, I spot a small shack set into the edge of the bush. A battered outboard protrudes from beneath an overturned boat. Behind the cabin, a moose hide is stretched on a black spruce frame.

After kicking aside a scattering of pinecones, I pitch my tent and rummage through my freeze-dried food for one of my favorites: beef stroganoff. I've finally learned to curb my impatience when cooking freeze-dried foods, so I force myself to stir the bubbling pot for the required time while savoring its scents and the sound of distant loons.

By the time I've scrubbed my dishes and pumped the fuel from floats to wing tanks, it's almost nine o'clock. I'm bone tired, but it's time for clean clothes and a bath. I strip, grab a bar of soap and run full speed into the dying whitecaps of T-bone Lake. The lake's not as cold as the Thelon, but it's frigid enough, and I emerge pink, goose-bumped—and quickly.

Later, dry and warmed by the southerly wind, I lean against a towering spruce as sparks from my campfire drift across the lake. Climbing like stars into the nighttime sky, they dance in the rising air, then flicker and die.

When the ancient Sumerians looked to the stars, they envisioned eternal lights that returned to the east by way of an underground river. Other cultures saw in the tiny lights the campfires of their ancestors. To Egyptians, the sun and stars rode courses not far above the canopies of their tents, and similar thinking led Chinese and Middle Eastern astronomers to scale stone towers to bring themselves closer to the heavens.

Anaxagoras, a fifth-century B.C. Greek philosopher, disagreed, lofting the sun to a height of some four thousand miles. A century later, Aristarchus, who had already proposed that the earth moves about the sun while spinning on its axis, reckoned the distance to the stars at approximately what we'd now call one light-year, an astoundingly perceptive conclusion in an era of astronomical ignorance.

Given such a promising start, one might expect that the science of the ancient Greeks would have flourished. It should have, and it could have, had it not been overcome by a new and powerful religion that, for centuries, opposed intellectual pursuits. Believing that the end was coming *soon*, early Christian leaders declared that it mattered not if the earth were round or flat, as it was already corrupt and doomed. As St. Ambrose put it, "To discuss the nature and position of the earth does not help us in our hope of the life to come."

Monks, acting on the orders of St. Cyril, stripped the living flesh from the woman geometer and librarian Hypatia with oyster shells and burned her corpse. Religious zealots plundered the famous half-million-volume library at Alexandria. When the Roman Emperor Justinian shut down Plato's Academy, scholars fled to the safety of a more tolerant Byzantium. Devoid of science and intellectual pursuits, Europe plunged into the Dark Ages, and the heavens, ruled once again by churchmen who saw the universe not as a stunning, lofty sphere, returned to the tent roofs of old, across which angels drove the stars.

A thousand years later, when men like Copernicus *again* proved that the earth orbited the sun, the Vatican's earth-centered theology began to crumble. And when observers noticed that the stars' brilliance remained unchanged despite our moving toward and away from them by the diameter of the earth's orbit (183 million miles) during our trip round the sun, the stellar lights returned to their rightful place. Today, no one believes that climbing a ziggurat will improve one's view of the stars.

In 1834, British astronomer Thomas Henderson used the diameter of the earth's orbit as a baseline to triangulate the distance to Alpha Centauri, which he thought was our nearest star. (Proxima Centauri is a tad closer.) His results, though half the true distance, lofted the stars even farther. Science, unfettered by dogma, was finally marching on.

Now, as soft winds whisper through the jack pines to fan the embers of my dying fire, I'm left to wonder which stars are titillating astronomers with evidence that they, too, have planets.

With so many to choose from, I turn to the child's game of "Star light, star bright, first star I see tonight." Which star should I wish upon, and for what should I wish? Certainly not a self-centered request like health or wealth. Perhaps world peace? An end to greed? A stable world population? Still not satisfied, I rummage through the alternatives and choose omniscience. Then, realizing that downloading omniscience might take a while, I lean back and let my imagination run while I wait. No longer superheated balls of gas, the stars become fireflies, sparks and Christmas lights, bits of radium glowing bright and astral clocks that light the night.

A southwesterly breeze confirms that yesterday's low still squats over Yellowknife. By 9:00 A.M., I've eaten and emptied the floats of the few cups of water that seep in every night. It's too long since I've thoroughly checked the Cub, so I examine it inch by inch, checking every cable and hinge. Opening the cowling, I examine the fuel lines and plug wires. As usual, a few of the cylinder head cover bolts are a quarter turn loose. I tighten them, then turn to the carburetor that hangs below the engine.

The Cub's carburetor is almost identical to the old Marvel-Schebler carburetor that once fed "Allis," my grandfather's tractor. Reliable and semi-efficient, my carburetor stems from an atomizer that caught the attention of a fledgling German automaker. After replacing the perfume with gasoline and making a few changes, he used this primitive carburetor to feed his first automobile, which he named for his daughter—Mercedes.

Satisfied that all is well, I fire up the Cub, and within the hour cross the Slave River near Fort Smith, just north of the Alberta border. Launch your boat here, in the heavily silted Slave, and thirteen hundred miles of deep-river water will carry you to the Arctic Ocean. Just upstream lie thirteen miles of rapids, followed by the equally navigable Slave, Athabasca and Peace Rivers.

As pelicans scoop whitefish from the rock-strewn eddies of the Slave, I think of a local guide who likes to tease his river-running guests. Before they enter the rolling foam, he relates how each set of rapids received its name. After explaining Mountain and Cassette Rapids, he says, "We call the third rapids Pelican, because it's the most northerly breeding ground for pelicans in North America. And then there's the Rapids of the Drowned." He waits.

When someone finally can't resist asking about *that* name, he replies, "Well, we call it that because every year some tourist dies while trying to run it, and no one's drowned in it this year—yet." He smiles for a moment, and then delivers the truth: the rapids found its name in 1786, when five canoeists perished after mistaking a hunter's volley for the OK signal of one of the party members who was scouting the river downstream.

Canada, like most countries, has many towns that are named for individuals: Fort Smith, Churchill, Gillam, Thompson, and so on. My favorite place-names, however, are those that spring from optimism. Some, like Fort Enterprise, Fort Reliance, Fort Confidence and Resolute ring of determination. When optimism waned, Fort Good Hope and the Bay of God's Mercy fell onto the map, while those beset with troubles left behind Dismal Lake, Repulse Bay and the Funeral Range.

As I taxi up to the pumps, a Beaver pulls away from Loon-Aire docks. I'm still long on fuel, but I need to add oil, and I want to call my wife. Having passed up the radio-telephone at Reliance in my rush to depart, I have not spoken to her since I called her from Baker Lake.

Peace River, my next stop, is only four hours away, so I empty the gas bags into the mains while Scott adds a liter of oil. Knowing that I'm an American because the Cub bears registration numbers (Canadian aircraft use letters) he asks where I've come from. When I explain he erupts: "My God, man, that's fantastic."

He slides a hand along the Cub's cowling. "I tell you," he says, "someday I'm going to buy one of these little beauties. I'll take off for two weeks straight—no, I'll take three—and see the country. God! I'd give anything to go along with you."

Laughing, I say, "I don't want to hurt your feelings, but a nice-looking gal back at Red Lake said those exact words, and I passed her up, so you know what the odds are for you."

As Scott fills out the charge slip, I ask if I can make a credit card call. "Sure," he replies. "Just go through that door and down the hall. The phone's in the first room on your left—under Georgia."

"Come again?"

"On your left under Georgia."

Figuring that they have a wall map of the United States with a pay phone over Florida, I head for the office, where I discover that Georgia is a gorgeous *Playboy* centerfold. "Wow!" I exclaim to the grinning clerk who's watching me, for I can't be the first to be stopped in his tracks by this eye-popping Georgia peach.

I stare at her. A bath towel V's suggestively upward from between two perfect legs to end conveniently an inch below her breasts. Her hazel-eyed gaze is direct and slightly inviting. She's stunning—a modern Rubens or Venus without the fat.

"Think you're man enough for her?" asks the grinning clerk as he eyes my graying hair.

"Sure am," I reply, and as my eyes sweep Georgia's curves, I tell him about the elderly gent whose friends expressed concern that bedding his bride of twenty-eight might become too much of a strain. "What the hell," he replied. "If she dies, she dies!"

While Georgia watches and the clerk listens, I try to call my wife. But the operator claims ignorance of my long distance phone company, and I'm forced to call collect.

"Hi, it's me," I say, forgetting that the operator has already told her. "I'm in Fort Smith."

"Where's that?"

"Northern Alberta," I respond, deliberately turning my back to Georgia, for I'm uncomfortable talking with my wife while my eyes cruise Georgia's curves.

"I thought you were going to Yellowknife," she says.

"Well, the weather forced a change of plans, so I'll probably stop there on the way back. I should reach Peace River today and Fort St. John—that's in British Columbia—tomorrow. You getting along OK?"

"Oh sure. You too?"

"I'm fine. Beautiful country north of here, you know."

"I suppose."

I pause, trying to think of something that might interest her, but she's heard it all before. Though our worlds intersect in many rewarding ways, flying isn't one of them, and as our conversation dwindles, I decide that the clerk and Georgia must think I'm terribly dull.

"Well, I'd better be going. I'll call from Fort St. John."

"OK. Take care. Good-bye."

"Miss you," I quickly add, telling myself that I *am* sincere and not just responding to Georgia's scenery. I wait for a response, but my wife is gone.

When I return to the Cub, a smiling Scott asks, "Did you find the phone?"

"Sure did," I reply. "I bet you have guys flying a hundred miles out of their way just to use that phone."

"Wouldn't be surprised," he says.

As I wipe a smudge from the Cub's yellow cowling, I think of Jim Kimball, my friend who fished for grayling in the fog at Baker Lake. After watching Wes and me fuss over our Pipers day after day, he claimed that pilots' wives would have a right to be jealous of the attention we heap on our planes.

"Think about it. You treat them like lovers, touching them, adjusting and loooooooobricating them," he said, drawing out the word with a leer. "You fuel them, polish them and fly off together, then do it again and again."

At the time I thought that Jim was either a little nuts or that he'd been away from home too long. But as I slide a hand along the Cub's rounded cowl and strap her idling, vibrating frame to my body, I wonder if maybe Jim wasn't right, and I'm the one who's been gone too long.

The Cub levels off over Wood Buffalo Park, Canada's largest national park, a wilderness puzzle of spruce islands, bogs and salt flats that straddles the Alberta/Northwest Territories border. In 1922, the Canadian government set aside 17,300 square miles for the protection of the last remaining herd of wood bison, then later imported some seven thousand plains bison with which the wood bison have interbred. Although the herd was reduced by an outbreak of anthrax a few decades later, it remains the largest concentration of bison in North America.

The overcast thins and disappears, revealing a veil of cirrus clouds. Far below, the fifty-mile-wide Peace River valley separates the domed plateau of the Birch Mountains from the slightly more prominent Caribous. To the east, Lake Athabasca, the sparkling tiara that joins northern Saskatchewan to Alberta, trails two hundred miles of glitter into the midday haze. To the south lie the Athabasca tar sands, which Alexander Mackenzie visited in 1789. Strip-mined like coal and then heated, the sands surrender thousands of barrels of petroleum products every day.

At age fifteen, Alexander Mackenzie began decades of service with the North West Company, the efficient rival of the stodgy Bay. Formed from independent French trappers when France lost Canada to the British, the North West Company quickly spread posts across southern and western Canada—posts that prospered under energetic, foresighted men like Mackenzie.

Mackenzie believed that the company's success depended on expansion and set off in 1789 to explore the Slave River, which flows north from Lake Athabasca. Misled by an optimistic map provided by his predecessor, a hot-tempered three-time murderer named Peter Pond, Mackenzie believed that the Pacific lay just two hundred miles west of Lake Athabasca and had good reason to hope that his voyage would reach those shores. He could hardly have been more wrong. As Mackenzie would eventually learn, the Pacific was seven hundred miles distant, with the Rockies in between.

Although Mackenzie's downstream two-thousand-mile "float" to the Arctic Ocean has been compared to Samuel Hearne's arduous journey from Churchill to Coppermine, Mackenzie's voyage was more like a cruise. Leaving his Lake Athabasca post (Fort Chipewyan), Mackenzie drifted down the Slave past today's Fort Smith to Great Slave Lake. Not knowing where the huge lake's outlet lay, he hired native "conductors" when he could and kidnapped them when he couldn't.

Mackenzie, depressed by the Slave's long northward run, took heart when the river ran west from Great Slave for all of three hundred miles. But then the natives' Deh Cho ("Great River") turned north, and as Mackenzie's hopes for a Pacific terminus began to fade, he named the watery highway the Disappointment River. In mid-July the river finally dissolved into the maze of channels, and the explorers camped on a low piece of land known as Whale Island. There, a rising midnight tide washed away any doubts that they'd reached the Arctic Ocean.

Undeterred by his failure to reach the Pacific Ocean via his Disappointment River, Alexander Mackenzie left Fort Chipewyan again in 1792, headed up the Peace, and overwintered near the site of Fort St. John. After an epic struggle, his party finally reached the Pacific in 1793, only to beat a quick retreat with hostile natives in pursuit. In so doing, Mackenzie crossed the North American continent twelve years before Lewis and Clark, who carried with them Mackenzie's account of his travels, *Voyages from Montreal*.

Unlike John Hornby, Mackenzie had no love for the North, saying, "I think it unpardonable in any man to remain in this country who can afford to leave it." He was knighted by King George III, purchased a substantial interest in the North West Company and retired early to Scotland. He died in 1820 at the age of fifty-six.

Because I've had nothing to eat but an OHenry and some fig bars since breakfast, four o'clock brings hunger pangs, but I'm too close to Peace River to stop. The Highway 2 bridge slips beneath as I radio the airport to have fuel delivered to Cardinal Lake. I'm sure I have enough gas for the 120-mile hop to Fort St. John, but I want to play it safe.

The fuel truck arrives, driven by Mack, a fellow pilot who brims with information—the best place to eat, where to stay and which pub has the best entertainment. As the tanks fill, Mack switches from his current events to history: "Bet you don't know how the Peace River got its name."

"I've no idea," I respond.

"Well," says Mack, "the natives around here had been at each other's throat for years. But the Bay needed trappers, not warriors, so they arranged a peace treaty not far from here. And that's why it's called Peace River."

Mack offers a ride to town, where, within minutes, I attack a chicken-fried steak. A cab ride later, the Cub and I head west in search of a small lake between Peace River and Fort St. John. On its western shore lies a tiny campsite that's highly recommended by a fuel-truck driver named Mack.

Skipping along the northern edge of farms lush with the radiant yellow beauty of canola (rapeseed) fields, I begin to daydream about author Richard Dawkins's "gently spinning, green and gold harvest festival of a planet"—and almost miss Mack's Shangri-la. At first glance the lake seems much too small, but flying its length at ninety mph takes eighteen seconds, so it's almost half a mile—plenty of room—especially since there are no obstructions at either end.

As the Cub drifts to a stop, I sense the campsite's charms. Unlike many farm country lakes that ground seaplanes in muck five yards from shore, Mack's small beach rises abruptly from the depths, marches inland fifty feet and disappears in a haze of willows and birch.

A solitary thunderstorm rumbles in from the west as I stow the last of my gear, bringing introductory mists, then droplets and a brief deluge, each phase backlit by the evening sun. The storm passes, trailing two rainbows, one nestled within the color-reversed arms of its contrarian mate while the soft light of evening sets buds and branches aglow.

The Cub's thermometer reads eighty-two degrees—just right for laundry and a swim, as I'm wearing my last clean clothes. Laden with an armful of sweaty garments and a bar of nonphosphate soap, I wade into Mack's lovely lake.

I sidestroke away from shore, savoring the lake's soothing, sensuous fluidity, blowing bubbles as cool currents caress my shoulders and thighs. Still too warm, I dive toward cooler bottom water, sending crayfish scuttling to safety. For twenty minutes I cavort like an otter, then turn to my laundry.

Later, dry and refreshed, I look around before turning in. To the west, Venus slowly descends toward distant Rocky Mountain peaks. I wonder if her nine-month orbit of the sun, a duration equal to that of a human pregnancy, is the reason that Venus is called the Goddess of Love?

Beyond the Cub, which is so festooned with drying laundry that it seems to be shedding its skin, a rising moon silhouettes a distant grove of tamaracks.

Edmond Rostand's nineteenth-century creation Cyrano de Bergerac suggested ascending to the moon by tying bottles of dew to the traveler, who'd be drawn aloft by the rising vapors. As an alternative, he considered tossing a magnet into the air from a light iron chariot, expecting the chariot to be pulled upward. The voyager would then catch the magnet and hurl it upward again, hauling himself to the moon by his gauss straps. (Even serious Isaac Newton might have smiled at that.)

Although my tent is shaded, it's still too hot for clothing and much too warm to even think of lying on my foam mattress or sleeping bag, so I shove it all aside, stretch out naked on the satiny tent floor, clasp my bands behind my head, close my eyes and turn my already moonstruck mind to a metaphorical tale from American author Diana Brueton's story collection *Many Moons*.

According to Brueton, certain aborigines believed that the moon was once an exceptionally fat man who truly loved women. Failing to attract any because of his size, he became very lonely. Night after night he'd sing to fair young girls and plead for a ride in their canoes.

Finally one pair relented. Swimming alongside, they towed the canoe to midstream, where they played for a while—and then upset it. The moon sank into the river, glowing faintly as he fell. Eventually, the moon climbed ashore and rose into the sky where, to this day, he beams down wistfully at the women of the world.

Five

FORT ST. JOHN TO FORT SIMPSON, NWT

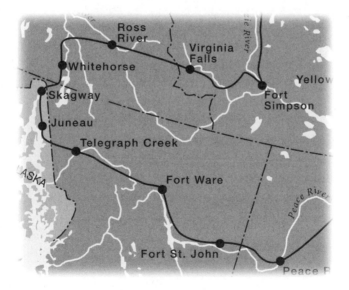

11

Fort St. John to Juneau, Alaska

The Tree which moves some to tears of joy is, in the Eyes
of others, only a Green thing that stands in the way.

– WILLIAM BLAKE

NINE O'CLOCK! I chastise myself for wasting a beautiful morning, then suddenly realize that I've found an excuse to delay breakfast: Fort St. John is just an hour away, so someone else can do the dishes. Still, even though I hop to it, it's almost ten by the time I taxi to the eastern end of the lake.

When the Cub pivots into the wind for takeoff, I'm surprised to discover a western horizon bulging with storm clouds. Figuring that I can reach the seaplane base before the deluge arrives, I pour on the gas, but twenty miles later, the Cub shudders into a wall of wind, and a semi heading to Fort St. John slowly leaves me behind. As lightning leaps from cloud to cloud, the British Columbia lion replaces Alberta, the lamb.

Determined not to return to Mack's lake, I red-line the Cub, then switch on my radio.

"Fort St. John, this is Piper 4745 Mike."

Silence.

"Fort St. John, this is Piper 4745 Mike."

More silence.

Realizing that my transmitter might be working, but not my receiver, I press the mike button and report: "Fort St. John, Piper 4745 Mike is a Piper PA-11, twenty east of Fort St. John for landing Charlie Lake."

Suddenly, I realize that I'm not getting any feedback in my headset. Either the entire radio is messed up or my batteries are dead. I try a few other frequencies without response. Probably batteries.

As the distant Rockies twist the wind into knots, the Cub, like a just-roped stallion, begins to leap and dive. I throttle back to reduce the stress on the Cub, then counter with stick and rudder as we struggle through turbulent air.

By the time Charlie Lake finally appears, the advancing squall line is already pummeling the far end of the lake. And as the Cub descends toward the whitecaps, I remember that eleven soldiers drowned just here while building the Alaska Highway in 1942–43.

I land close to the beach at the lake's southern end. If the breakers damage a float, or the wind and waves upset me, I'll be in shallow water, drifting toward the beach. But the same wind that churns the lake also cuts my landing speed, and after two jolts, I'm down and pitching on the waves. I momentarily consider drifting back to the beach, but without tie-downs the Cub would be at the mercy of the oncoming storm.

Pitching from crest to trough against the gusting wind, the rocking Cub makes little headway until I increase power. But the Cub's engine falters on the lake's spray, so I pull on carb heat, which directs cowling-protected spray-free air to the engine, and its gasps subside.

The tiny seaplane base isn't much more than a slot in the shoreline, but it looks like the Promised Land. After taxiing into its tree-rimmed shelter, I secure the Cub, then investigate a nearby house. When no one responds, I grab my bag and hit the road as rain drops like overripe grapes splatter down. A half minute later, a Chevy pickup stops and the passenger door opens. As I leap inside, the driver says, "Nice day, eh?

"From here, it's gorgeous," I reply, raising my voice above drumming on the roof, "but fifteen minutes ago it didn't look so good, and it's great to be on the ground."

"You need gas?" he asks.

"Just enough to top the tanks," I answer, "but I couldn't find anyone at the base."

"Rex is gone," he says. "I'm his neighbor, sorta. I saw you come in and figured you'd need a ride. I had to go to town anyway. If Rex isn't here when you come back, just gas up and leave a note with your name and address. The pump'll be on."

After turning down a cup of coffee, he drops me at the Coachman Inn, where I ask for a top-floor room so that nothing but rain can dance on my ceiling in the middle of the night.

A bed—a real bed. I stretch out on it, savoring its uniformity. No hidden pinecones here, no knuckled roots or unseen stones to jab my hips. And not just a bed, but television, a shower *and* a tub. Unable to resist it, I postpone eating, adjust the mirrored bathroom door so I can see the TV and slip into the steaming tub. To my great surprise, within a few minutes, the station turns to one of my heroes, a man whose work assisted Alexander Mackenzie: Galileo Galilei.

In 1609, when Galileo learned of the telescopes being demonstrated in Holland, he quickly grasped the principle and made not one but several telescopes. Although the ingenious, contentious and rather self-centered Galileo possessed an open mind, nothing could have prepared him for seeing mountains on the moon, a spotted sun or, perhaps most of all, for Jupiter's multiple moons.

The following year, Galileo published his observations in his book, *The Starry Messenger*, which created a sensation throughout Europe.

The Catholic Church, however, could no more abide spots that marred the perfection of the sun than they could accept Buddhism, Hinduism or Islam. Nevertheless, Galileo's sightings supported what Copernicus had feared to reveal: that the earth was *not* the center of the universe, an annoying fact that disproved the geocentric theology of the day, reaffirmed the sun-centered solar system of the pre-Christian Greeks and reduced our importance in the Grand Celestial Scheme. (Knowing that Cardinal Bellarmine had condoned, if not arranged, the murder of Giordano Bruno for defending the Copernican theory, Copernicus entrusted his *De Revolutionibus Orbium Coelestium* to Andreas Osiander, a Lutheran cleric, for publication after his death. *De Revolutionibus* was condemned by Rome, and by Calvin and Luther, who stated, as some fundamentalists still do, that "Joshua commanded the sun to stand still, and not the earth." The manuscript was placed on the Index of Prohibited books, a move that delayed its influence for more than a hundred years.)

Galileo, who was convinced that the evidence in his telescope outweighed biblical literalism and the speculations of theologians, soon ran afoul of the Church. When he was warned to stop teaching his "theories," he instead wrote a whimsical play in which the Church position was advanced by a rather dull character named Simplicius. In response, the pope ordered Galileo to appear before the Inquisition, where he was threatened with torture if he failed to recant.

Remembering the fate of Bruno, Galileo confessed to error. He was condemned to spend the rest of his life under house arrest, where he lost his eyesight from age and studying the sunspots that the Church said didn't exist.

Fort St. John, with a population of twelve thousand, is too large to inspect on foot, especially since the Coachman's on the fringe, so I strike up a conversation with Carla, a waitress who could easily work for the Chamber of Commerce.

"Well, first of all, we're the oldest settlement in B.C. If you want shopping, go to the Totem Mall. We've got a bunch of tour outfits that go to the mountains and Williston Lake, and if you like golf, there's the Country Club. Downtown we've got a new cultural center and the world's largest glass beehive."

"Really!" I exclaim, then dare to ask, "How do you know it's the largest?"

"I dunno," she replies with a toss of her head, "but it is."

She pauses, then adds, "Oh, yeah, there's a museum at the Bennett Dam with lots of fossils they dug up while making the dam and there's a mastodon trunk." Giggling at her mistake, she clasps a hand to her mouth and says, "I mean tusk."

One customer advises me not to miss the W.A.C. Bennett Dam, claiming that it backs up the world's largest reservoir, Williston Lake. Apparently a long-time resident, he ends many of his sentences with the stereotypical "eh?"

Resuming my role as visiting skeptic, I ask if he's certain that the reservoir is the world's largest, mentioning those created by the Hoover, Grand Coulee and Aswan Dams.

"Just a minute," he says, then yells to a uniformed woman seated at the far end of the counter. "Hey, Ruthie, isn't Williston the biggest reservoir in the world?"

"Yeah," says Ruthie.

As Carla hands me my bill, she says, "I just thought of something else. You might want to see the derrick."

While I wonder if the derrick is also the largest in the world, the cook shouts, "Carla!" and she dashes off.

Assuming that the derrick is an oil-drilling rig, I ask the cashier for directions. With a jerk of her thumb, she says, "Go that way a few blocks and you'll see it."

The derrick turns out to be a midsize drilling rig adjacent to the tourist bureau/museum/bookstore. The museum is small, but its collection of pioneer memorabilia and photographs of the construction of the Alaska Highway trap me for more than an hour. By restraining myself, I manage to leave the bookstore with just two volumes: Dick Turner's *Nahanni* and Shirlee Matheson's *Flying the Frontiers*.

I phone the weather bureau, which promises blue skies by morning, then call my wife to let her know I'll be in Juneau in a couple of days. "Miss you," I say, and this time she hears.

As the sky opens up and thunder booms, I flip on the television, belch a hint of Canadian bacon and open Ms. Ackerman's book to the chapter on *taste*.

It's clear. In the distance, mountain peaks rasp the base of a deep blue sky as I check the Cub, then top the tanks and leave Rex a note with my name, address and the amount of fuel I pumped.

Aided by cool, dense air that adds power and lift, the Cub leaps from Charlie Lake and climbs into a northwest breeze. What a difference! Yesterday, a sky wrenched with seizures. Today, a gently rolling swell. I love it, and the Cub loves it, too, for as I cross the Alaska Highway and head for Bennett Dam, the Continental has never sounded so smooth.

Scenic though it is, the Canyon of the Peace offers more than rugged peaks and wildlife. Beyond the dam, the Peace River coal block disappears beneath Williston Lake. Mined for more than a century, the coal now lies undisturbed, abandoned when immense reserves of cheap, clean-burning natural gas and oil were discovered near Fort St. John. Even so, energy still flows through Hudson Hope, generated by turbines in the concrete stopper that restrains Williston Lake, the largest reservoir in *British Columbia*.

When Williston Lake rose behind Bennett Dam, it inundated 640 square miles of farm and forest. Flooded-out homesteaders were relocated to areas of equal value. Whites whose traplines were submerged received consideration, and a method was even devised to provide substitute habitat for moose. But when it came to compensating the Sekani Indians who had hunted and fished the newly drowned valleys for centuries, nothing was done.

As the British anthropologist Hugh Brody wrote in *Maps and Dreams*, "Their reserves were destroyed; they were dispossessed of the entire area of their traditional homeland, expected to move along, make do, or somehow disappear."

Many of the Sekani moved up the Finlay River to a settlement called Fort Ware, the site of my next fuel stop and, according to folks at Fort St. John, the community with the highest murder rate in Canada. Bigotry and exaggeration, I tell myself. Prejudice of the worst sort. Still. . . .

Because Alexander Mackenzie knew that accurate maps were essential to the success of his employers, he carefully charted his travels by relying on star and sun sightings to determine his latitude (his north-south position). But when he needed to determine his longitude (his east-west position) Mackenzie was hampered by a less-than-reliable chronometer. In its place, he often substituted Galileo's infallible timepiece in the sky: the planet Jupiter and the clocklike regularity of its moons: "I had another observation of Jupiter and his satellites for the longitude . . ."

To understand why explorers had to know the time in order to determine their longitude, let's envision a popular fruit, an orange.

With your imagination, strip away the peel and cup it in your hand, stem end up. The stem end is the North Pole; the South Pole lies in the palm of your hand. Now draw a horizontal line around its belly—an equator. On the far side of your darkened room, a flashlight beams—the sun.

Your orange, for our convenience, has twenty-four wedges instead of the usual dozen or more. Lines drawn from pole to pole, like the lines between the wedges, are called meridians, or lines of longitude. Since the earth makes one revolution each day, it follows that the sun illuminates a new wedge every hour. Thus, each wedge equals a time zone of one hour, and because the earth is some twenty-four thousand miles in circumference, each of the earth's twenty-four wedges spans about a thousand miles *at the equator*.

If we could turn our orange as slowly as the earth revolves, we'd see that the time required for the flashlight beam to cross a single wedge/zone remains one hour *even to the north or south of the equator, where the wedges narrow on their way to the poles*. Although the wedges taper toward the poles, the number of degrees (fifteen) *in each zone and the time each zone represents remain the same*. Since the sun transits one wedge/zone every hour, and an hour equals fifteen degrees of longitude, time is related to distance. Consider now the fabled explorer Vasco da Swenson, two days out of Portugal in search of the legendary McDonald Islands and their Arches of Gold. If he sails north, the sun will move lower in the southern sky and the north star will rise higher; the farther he sails, the greater the change. Knowing the that earth is some twenty-four thousand miles around and by relying on sightings taken with an astrolabe, Vasco can pretty well fix his north/south location, his *latitude*. (Over the years, astrolabes shed superfluous parts, becoming quadrants, then sextants then octants, and now, thanks to GPS, obsoletants.)

But Vasco also needs to know his longitude—how far west he's travelled. And as Shakespeare so wisely observed, "Ay, there's the rub."

Out of sight of land, and with winds and currents of varying strength and direction, has poor Vasco averaged a hundred miles a day or two hundred? Depending on his fortunes with wind and wave, a week under sail could carry him a thousand miles from Lisbon's cantinas or as little as a few hundred. In which of those one-hour wedges is he located when the sun rides high at noon? Fortunately, there's a way out for Vasco, because even though he can't measure his east/west distance, we're going to let him measure its equivalent—time.

For a moment, let's present Vasco with a gift: a spring-driven chronometer from two hundred years in his future. So accurate is this timepiece that it varies less than a second per month. Unlike the inaccurate spring-driven clocks of Vasco's day or pendulum clocks that became useless when moved about, Vasco's chronometer is happy on pitching deck or jolting wagon. As the science writer Dava Sobel so vividly describes in her book *Longitude*, the chronometer was built over a period of forty years by John Harrison, clockmaker, in response to a British promise of a £20,000 reward. His eighteenth century timepiece could rival the best wind-up clock of today.

Because Vasco (the diligent) has taken care to keep his chronometer wound, it still tells Lisbon time. Three days out, under his first clear skies *with the sun directly overhead,* he checks his chronometer, which reads 12:20. Vasco, who is no dummy, quickly realizes that he is twenty minutes (five degrees) west of Lisbon.

Were Vasco on the equator, he'd have travelled 333 miles. However, since his westward course from Portugal crosses time zones that have narrowed to less than 1,000 miles, he first determines his latitude by observing the angle of the sun above the horizon. With his latitude known, his charts reveal that the zones at his latitude are only 780 miles across. Vasco therefore knows that he has sailed west for 260 miles.

With his old clock, which often varied by two minutes a day (most were much worse), he could be off by as much as a hundred miles—and in which direction, east or west? Having solved his problem, Vasco heaves a huge sigh of relief—and hides our miraculous clock.

Poor Vasco. That which we give, we can reclaim. However, to replace his treasured clock, which we cannot leave behind, we'll give him a celestial clock, the clock of Galileo's moons, the same moons relied on by Mackenzie in a world beyond Vasco's ken.

When Galileo trained his "optical tube" on Jupiter, he found four moons circling the planet with clock-like precision. Once their relative positions were carefully recorded, the "Galilean moons" became a universal clock that all could see at the same instant *regardless of their location*. Given a steady deck and a clear sky to grant good viewing, if Vasco's telescope shows the same arrangement of Jupiter's moons at 11:52 p.m. that the Lisbon tables show for midnight, he knows his old unreliable clock has lost eight minutes and must be reset. Periodically corrected by Galileo's moons, Vasco's clock can now be used to determine his longitude with greatly improved precision.

Within a decade of his death, Galileo's method for determining longitude had become widely accepted, especially on land, which always provided a stable platform. Thus equipped, geographers promptly set about resurveying the world—moving islands and shrinking nations. (Upon being presented with an updated map of his kingdom, King Louis XIV complained that he had lost more of France to the astronomers than to his enemies.)

Due in part to national pride, captains who sailed from London referred to London time, those from Venice to Venice time, and so forth. Fortunately, after a few centuries of printing different tables for every port, an international agreement finally named the meridian that runs through Greenwich, England, the Prime Meridian—zero degrees. Since then, all longitudes are measured from the "prime," as are times for navigation, which are given in Greenwich Mean Time, or GMT.

We now return to Vasco, who, with the aid of Galileo's celestial clock, finally reached the American coast, where he had a horrible nightmare in which huge garbage barges kept dumping their loads at sea. Disgusted with what the future might hold, Vasco turned south and came upon the Cayman Islands, where he established Los Bancos da Swenson to escape the taxes of his avaricious king.

Sprawling across the land like a recumbent T, Williston Lake begins at Bennett Dam. Seventy miles to the west, where the stem of the T joins the crossbar, I turn to the north, surrounded by malachite mountains that rise from Williston's chop. Far below, a tugboat strains against hundreds of chain-bound logs, heading south to Mackenzie's mills. A glance ahead reveals their source: entire mountains plucked bare.

Forests are renewable resources, but I fear the consequences of replanting them as single-species forests, which are more prone to disease and support a much smaller range of animal species than mixed forests. How sad it is that every day, almost everywhere, for our short-term convenience, we are shoving other species aside and driving them toward extinction.

Masquerading behind names that include the words "green," "environment," and "conservation," too many companies are following the lead of the Wise Use movement, a devious organization that talks "green" while opposing environmental concerns. In Alberta, where one pulp mill is expected to discharge twenty million gallons of questionable effluent into the Athabasca River every day, the provincial government has already leased a fourth of the province to clear-cutting pulp operations, most of them foreign owned.

Now, having denuded thousands of square miles of southern British Columbia timberland, industrial-strength clear-cutters have set their sights on the forests of the coastal range. According to a Canadian government report, at present cutting rates, all of the commercial old-growth forest will disappear in fewer than ten years. Meanwhile, the timber companies promise gifts and jobs, but common sense and experience tell us that the companies will leave when the trees are gone.

Yielding to summer's slow ascent, the higher peaks of Williston's northern arm bear shrinking robes of snow. Rivulets of meltwater pour from beneath their ermine mantles, joining to cascade down slopes laid bare. Clear streams that once watered verdant valleys dirty themselves with torn-up soil and stain the bays below. How much of this, I wonder, really stems from need? How much from waste?

Why should forests fall for junk mail? Why should trees be pulped for individuals, businesses and governments that refuse to use *both* sides of a sheet of paper? I envision Henry Thoreau and

Aldo Leopold grieving over prime forests and protesting the level-ing of the few old-growth stands that remain. I recall my grandfather describing the white pine forests of Michigan, Wisconsin and Min-nesota that were expected to last for centuries but disappeared in less than Lincoln's four score and ten.

Though I fly though grandeur, I hear chain saws and see the fal-ling forests of Malaysia and Brazil. I remember the words of Rena-tas, a Tanzanian park ranger quoted in William Calvin's *The River That Flows Uphill*: "After I be dead, others will follow. If people be killing killing, there will be no more buffalo, no rhino. If they be cut-ting cutting, there will be no more trees, no oxygen, no rain. Like a desert. What will my daughters think? They will come and there will be nothing. Our father was stupid, they will say."

Like Renatas, Thoreau railed against the abuse of nature: "most men . . . do not care for Nature and would sell their share in all her beauty. . . . It is for the reason that some do not care that we need to protect all from the vandalism of the few."

The Tundra Cub leaves Williston Lake behind and follows the Finlay River to a remote Sekani settlement set deep in the Wolverine Mountains. According to the *Water Aerodrome Supplement*, a publi-cation listing seaplane bases and the services they offer, Fort Ware's avgas is reserved for emergencies, but the Cub can burn car gas, so I'm really not concerned.

Although the *Supplement* advises landing upstream *into* the Finlay's twenty mph current, I line up with the current to reduce the sudden drag of touchdown, then drop between the towering ever-greens that line its serpentine banks. Engine muted, the Cub's noisy slipstream becomes a whisper. Swissssh. Piece of cake.

I turn upstream, then angle toward the shore, wincing as I slide a float firmly onto fist-size rocks. With the engine running to keep the Cub grounded, I climb onto the float, cut the ignition, then leap off and rope the Cub to a tree.

Just downstream, several natives are lounging near the center of a bridge that spans the Finlay. A dog romps at their feet. Suddenly, one of them scoops the animal up and tosses it over the side. As the dog falls, kicking, into the Finlay and struggles toward shore as the current sweeps it downstream, they laugh uproariously. I'm disgusted, but I'm also aware that this is a good place to mind my own business, so I lock the Cub and add another rope.

Thinking that a show of concern for the Cub might give them ideas, I avoid looking back as I jog toward the airport. When I find nothing that looks like a fueling site, I hail down a speeding three-wheeler.

"Who do I see for gas?"

"Over there," he says, pointing to a small building.

Inside, I discover what appears to be a store. The shelves along one wall are half-full, while those that line the rest are close to empty. In the center of the room, surrounded by benches strewn with books, clothing and personal gear, a white man sits, packing boxes. When he looks up, his face fills with surprise, then pleasure at seeing a stranger.

"Hi, there" I begin. "They say you're the man to see for gas."

"That's right," he replies.

"I've got a Cub on the river that could use about fourteen gallons. If you can't spare avgas, car gas will do."

"Sure, sure—I'm Andy," he says, extending a hand. Where'd you come from?"

"Fort St. John," I reply, "on my way to Juneau."

After looking around to make sure we don't have company, I tell Andy about the Indians who threw the dog in the river and ask if things are as bad as I've heard. With a voice tinged with anger, Andy begins.

"Well, I don't know what you've heard, but it's bad enough. The death rate for babies here is the highest in Canada. Accidents and violence among teens and adults are four times worse than elsewhere. As for tossing dogs in the river—that's called fun. He sighs, then adds, "In a month, I'm outta here. I thought this job would be a great getaway but it's been more like a sentence. "Look at me," he continues. "A month to go, and I'm already packing. Says it all, doesn't it?"

A woman passes by the open door. Andy waits a few seconds, then says, "That woman—that's Nettie—one of the Sekani elders. She's so disgusted with things in town that she's moving back into the bush."

When I pick up a can of corn, my eyebrows rise at its price. Andy notices my reaction. "Food costs here are the highest in British Columbia," he says. "And there isn't much money to begin with. The natives earn a little from trapping and fighting the odd fire, but a lot of it goes for booze."

As I fuel the Cub, I ask Andy what lies beyond the bridge, since I hadn't seen any roads on my way to Fort Ware.

"Oh, there's a road, all right," he answers. "But it's pretty well hidden. I've never been down it, but I hear it ends near Mackenzie at the south end of Williston Lake."

When the fueling is done, Andy holds my wing while I fire up the Cub. I yell, "Good luck!" then pour on the gas. The Cub fights the Finlay's current as it struggles onto the step. I glance to the side. We're already planing across the water, but the shoreline hardly moves. Nevertheless, as her ninety horses wind up and her wings begin to lift, the Cub slips back into the sky.

An hour later, the Tundra Cub crosses the Continental Divide and soars above the snow-filled cirques and aquamarine ponds on Mount Cushing's northern face. On either side, fluted pinnacles of stone rise like giant organ pipes, bringing to mind bits of Grieg's piano concerto, then *Finlandia* and the soaring centerpiece from Saint Saen's organ concerto.

Two hours out of Fort Ware, I measure the remaining distance to Juneau. It's almost three hundred miles. If all goes well, I could make it without a fuel stop, but if I run into head winds, or if coastal weather forces a return to Telegraph Creek, I'd be in trouble. Besides, the *Supplement* reports a "very strong current" in the Stikine River, which cools me on Telegraph Creek.

I head instead for Iskut, a tiny settlement on Highway 37 with a seaplane base just south of town. Nice long lake. Flat water. No current. And when I taxi in, no base. A passerby informs me that it's been moved south to the next lake. "Just fly along the shore," he says, then adds the inevitable "You can't miss it."

Ten minutes later the Cub noses onto a wooden ramp adjacent to the Stewart-Cassair Highway. I add a quart of oil, then fill the tanks while the base operator suggests a campsite on nearby Kakkidi Lake.

"It's a lovely spot," he says, "with a beautiful beach and maybe even some char."

I decide that Juneau can wait.

As the Cub rounds the steep flanks of Tuktsaada Mountain, I slip a wide-angle lens onto the Nikon, open the right window and maneuver close to the trees. Leaning out into the slipstream, I capture steeply wooded slopes that leap skyward from one wing and plunge away from the other, then throttle back, and the Cub soon coasts to a stop at a gently sloping beach rimmed with yellow fleabane. When I open the door, the wonderful silence seems magnified by the quiet tick, tick, tick of the Cub's cooling engine.

A nearby river as wide and smooth as a city street flows out from Kakkidi Lake. Clipping a Meps spinner onto my line, I follow a set of moose tracks to the river and, with a sweep of my arm, toss the spinner across the stream.

The water erupts in an explosion of spray, as a troutlike fish shakes its head, scattering sunlight from the whirling spinner, then dives and heads downstream. But it's a small fish, easily overcome, and I soon reel in a foot of red-speckled beauty—a Dolly Varden char. By the time the sun has slipped beyond the mountains, I'm sampling my first nonarctic char.

While searching for a pack of raisins, I come upon a pocket radio that I'd tossed in on a last-minute whim. Little bigger than a cigarette pack and cheaply made, it's probably useless here. Nevertheless, I thumb up the volume and begin to cruise the dial. Static mingles with beeps and yowls until, at 580 khz, the music of a bigoted but hugely talented German composer named Wagner rasps from the set. How can this be? With only one station, I'm favored with Wagner! Lying back, I walk my fingers back and forth to the march from *Tannhauser*.

Wagner finally fades away, and as the brightest stars begin to shine, I am reminded of Tycho Brahe, whose passion was astronomy.

Brahe, an excellent observer, began to doubt Ptolemy's earth-centered solar system (which we know had the support of the Church) when he discovered errors in his Ptolemy's work.

When Brahe's benefactor, Denmark's King Frederick II, drank himself to death, Brahe moved to Prague, where he hired a very unlikely assistant: Johannes Kepler, a neurotic, sickly, self-critical man. Kepler, however, had one saving grace: he was brilliant—so brilliant, in fact, that Immanuel Kant called him "the most acute thinker ever born."

The two despised each other, but Brahe needed Kepler's fine mind to unify his data into a comprehensive theory, while Kepler could do nothing without the precise observations that Brahe had so carefully amassed. In 1601, time, the salve that cures all ills, intervened when Tycho Brahe died. Suddenly granted unlimited access to the data that Brahe had been slowly sharing, Kepler set out to complete the task that Brahe, thinking it an impossible one, had assigned to him: determine the orbit of Mars.

For eight frustrating years, Kepler studied dozens of circular orbits, creating almost a thousand pages of calculations before he thought to try an ellipse, which worked beautifully, and not just for Mars but for all the planets as well. In vindicating Copernicus, the sickly, unappealing Kepler proved the Church and Ptolemy wrong and set the heavens right.

A few years later, in 1618, hatred between German Lutherans and German Catholics catapulted Europe into the bloody Thirty Years' War. Soldier-borne smallpox killed Kepler's son, Friedrich, age six. His wife, already stunned by the soldiers' atrocities, contracted typhus and died. His mother, accused of witchcraft, was narrowly acquitted, and then only through the intervention of the "imperial mathematician," her son. She died within six months.

To escape "the barbaric neighings" of religious intolerance, Kepler fled to the country, taking pains to avoid itinerant prophets who proclaimed the end of the world. Unable to collect money owed him or to find work to feed his children, he died at the age of forty-eight in the midst of the war he hated.

Although the Thirty Years' War put a premature end to Kepler's genius, a century later, another war, the Seven Years' War, persuaded a nineteen-year-old military-band oboist named William Herschel to turn from carnage to the cosmos and sail for England. There he set music aside and began to study the stars.

Within a decade, Herschel was producing Newtonian (mirror) telescopes without peer. He discovered Uranus, which doubled the diameter of the known solar system and garnered a grant from the king. With money in hand, Herschel sought a foundry to cast a thirty-six-inch mirror with three times the light-gathering ability of previous mirrors. When all refused, he decided to cast it himself.

After constructing a circular mold from densely packed horse manure in his basement, Herschel fired up his furnace and proceeded with the pour. The mold cracked. When he tried again, the furnace cracked, sending a fiery stream of molten metal flooding across the floor—and Herschel abandoned the casting business.

A few years later, the king's foundry finally provided a forty-eight-inch mirror for Herschel's new reflecting telescope. When the king invited the archbishop of Canterbury to the dedication, he reversed their usual roles, telling the archbishop, "Come, my Lord Bishop, I will show you the way to Heaven."

For breakfast, it's char for protein, pancakes sweetened with fresh blueberries for carbohydrates and vitamins and bacon for fat—a balanced meal, or close enough.

Under clear and windless skies, the Cub's unchanged altimeter proclaims a high-pressure dome that should take me to Juneau with ease. Before I depart, I spread out the Atlin chart and draw a course line from Kakkidi Lake to Telegraph Creek, then extend it west to Juneau's Tracy Arm. Thirty minutes should take me to Telegraph Creek, two more to Juneau.

While the Cub idles across the lake, I search my chart for the name of the mountain that towers above my camp: Edziza. Near its seven-thousand-foot level, I spot some eye-opening names: Williams Cone, Eve Cone and Cocoa Crater. I'm in Volcanoland!

Eager now, I feed in full throttle and climb toward Williams Cone. From a distance, both cones look like four-hundred-foot anthills—like the cinder cones of southern California. But up close, their thirteen-hundred-year-old mix of ocher, russet and black cinders speak of sulfur and iron compounds that escaped from deep in the earth.

It's Cocoa Crater, however, that really catches my eye, for Cocoa's more than a cinder cone, it's a crater where lava once leaped and splattered before hardening like wax in the crater's throat and on its flanks. As I circle Cocoa, sunlight dances across its glittering slopes.

My course briefly overlaps the valley of the Stikine River, the birthplace of the Raven, who in Tlingit lore is the creator of the world. I follow the rolling river downstream to the tiny town of Telegraph Creek. Built to serve a never-completed telegraph line between North America and Europe by way of the Bering Strait, the town clings to the steep north bank of the Stikine, lingering on, its future in communications severed by the transatlantic cable.

I flip my radio to 123.2 mhz, then lift the mike to ask Telegraph Creek to advise Juneau customs of my arrival time—a notification required, in part, by our endless war on drugs.

"Telegraph Creek, this is Piper 4745 Mike."

No response.

The feedback in my headset indicates that my new batteries are good, so I try 126.7, then 122.2.

Still no response.

Damn!

I'm unwilling to use the emergency frequency, because this is no emergency, but if the customs agent makes me empty the plane or dumps a fine on me, it will be. Switching back to 123.2, I keep calling as Telegraph Creek falls mutely behind.

At full throttle, the Cub climbs to eighty-five hundred feet, then levels off above a panorama of mountain peaks enrobed in snow—the white lava of the Alaskan Coastal Range. To my right, the Sawyer Glacier smothers whole mountains like a huge albino octopus, its gravel-striped tentacles slipping along rocky slopes to probe the valleys while I gawk at a thousand square miles of peaked meringue, or is it divinity, so pure and white?

The Continental abruptly loses two hundred rpm, then steadies. Probably carburetor ice. I pull on carb heat, flooding the carburetor with warm air from inside the cowling. Because warm air holds less oxygen than the same volume of cold air, the engine drops another hundred rpm. But, minutes later, the ice is gone and we're back to twenty-one hundred rpm. With the carb heat off, it rises to twenty-two.

I cruise across heaps and valleys of frozen cream while eyeing their graceful slopes. If I had to, I could land almost anywhere, as it's not that different from landing a seaplane on grass, which I've done many times. Once down, I'd flip on my Emergency Location Transmitter and wait for a chopper or ski plane to fly in a mechanic. For the takeoff, it's aim downhill, keep the nose up a tad and pour on the power.

The engine stumbles again, dropping to nineteen hundred rpm—not good, but enough to hold altitude if I raise the nose a bit. Carb heat on again—and I wait. With the peaks a thousand feet below, and the valleys even farther, there's plenty of time to melt the ice—and to cuss myself for not leaving the carb heat on until I'd flown into warmer air. I've left the dry inland air behind, and entered maritime air. Instead of being surprised, I should have expected ice.

The turquoise waters of Whiting Lake, British Columbia, lead to Alyeska, the "Great Land" that W. H. Seward, Lincoln's secretary of state, purchased from Russia for $7.2 million. In 1867, Seward's jeering critics promptly dubbed the purchase "Walrussia" and "Seward's Folly," and *The New York World* complained that "Russia has sold us a sucked orange." They couldn't have been more wrong, for Alaska's been more plum than orange. Twice as big as Texas, and with only 3 percent as many people, Alaska has barely been nibbled upon, let alone sucked dry.

Admiralty Island, a hundred-mile-long battleship of an island with mile-high peaks and a brown bear population of one per square mile, emerges from the Pacific haze as the Cub glides down the Sawyer's crevasses and soars over Tracy Arm, where, on truck-size slabs of swell-damping ice, harbor seals relax, safe from their chief predators—orcas, which we also call killer whales.

Surrounded by the waterfalls, I flit past a ship rimmed with waving sightseers, then turn up Stephen Passage. Suddenly, a dark form erupts from the ocean, focusing my panorama-scanning eyes on a single point as a breaching whale hangs briefly above the swells, then falls back in an explosion of spray. It's much too large for an orca, mostly likely a humpback whale that's returned from Hawaii to restore its forty-ton body in Alaska's krill and herring-rich waters.

Beyond the Cub's right wing, the advancing tongues of Taku, Norris and Wright Glaciers lick the waters of Taku Arm. The Taku glaciers, unlike most Alaskan glaciers, are considered "healthy," having advanced as much as eight miles since the turn of the century. Elsewhere, our warming climate has been more than a match for most of the world's glaciers, which are melting at a rate that exceeds their steady flow.

I send out a call to the Juneau tower.

"Juneau tower, this is Piper 4745 Mike."

No response.

I can hear the tower's more powerful transmitter directing other traffic, but they still can't hear me. Finally, as I pass Taku Harbor, Juneau responds, requests a call back on a one-mile final approach and confirms my request for customs.

Juneau clings to a narrow strip of land, hemmed in by Gastineau Channel cruise ships on one side and steep mountains on the other.

Descending, the Cub crosses the channel-spanning bridge that connects Juneau to West Juneau and the slopes of Douglas Island, then follows the channel north toward a long, two-hundred-foot-wide water-filled ditch—the seaplane waterway that parallels Juneau's main runway. A Boeing 727 descends from the opposite direction as if coming to meet me, its lowered gear reaching for the ground like the outstretched feet of a landing goose. When it touches down I pick up my mike.

"Juneau tower, Four five Mike is on one mile final."

"Four five Mike, cleared to land. Taxi to far end of the waterway. Mooring area will be on your left."

When I'm a half mile from the waterway, my peripheral vision picks up a huge blue-green wall—the terminus of the Mendenhall Glacier, one of the most visited glaciers in the world.

OK, I tell myself, let's not get distracted—gawking can get you killed. Carb heat already on. Fuel selector to fullest tank. Mixture already full rich. Power near idle. Trim the nose up until she slows to fifty-five, then fifty, then forty-five. With a prolonged hiss of keels kissing water, the Cub touches down and idles past a long row of colorful seaplanes, the taxis of the North.

Dropping the water rudder, I turn toward the mooring area while gawking at the glacier and ignoring the control tower now that I'm down. As I'm about to shut down the engine, I decide to taxi in a circle to photograph the glacier through the Cub's windshield.

"Four five Mike! You are crossing an active runway! Turn left immediately!"

Oops. Dumb move. (If I'd been paying attention, I'd have heard the tower clear another seaplane to land.)

Glancing to my right, I spot an Otter about to touch down. Fortunately, there's plenty of room, but my unauthorized 360 wasn't very bright—a legacy of operating from remote lakes and uncontrolled airports for far too long.

U.S. Customs officials require pilots to stay with their aircraft, but my bladder demands a quick trip to the bushes, where I meet an astonishing change. Ten feet from the asphalt ramp, I'm engulfed in evergreen-shaded, ankle-deep emerald green moss, the product of 130 inches of rainfall a year.

When the glowering customs officer finally arrives, clipboard in hand, he ignores me while he scans the Cub and writes down its registration number, then asks for my name, address and phone number.

"Why didn't you give us the *required* one-hour notice of arrival?" he asks.

"I tried to. But Telegraph Creek wouldn't respond to my request to relay the message. I tried all the frequencies except 121.5, but nothing worked. Then I couldn't raise Juneau until I was close because of the mountains."

He glares at me. I have broken a rule. He could fine me. He could make me unload every item from the plane and open every float compartment just to be difficult. He delays and ponders, playing me like a fish while I wonder if I will be released or tossed into the frying pan.

"Well," he finally grumbles, "You did *one* thing right. You had the tower call us before you landed."

Turning silent again, he collects the yearly $25 fee that private aircraft owners must pay for the privilege of returning to their own country and walks away. I'm free!

The Aero Service fuel truck brings a change of attitude: a friendly face, pleasant conversation and avgas at $2.54 a gallon—half the price at Fort Ware. Still, that's 60 cents more than I pay in the lower forty-eight.

I settle my bill while the driver calls Taku taxi, and within minutes a well-used Chevy arrives, driven by a loquacious retiree named Harry who's still got grip on the spirit of the North. It's a good eight miles to Juneau, but Harry, prompted by my many questions, makes like Hubert Humphrey all the way.

"It's gold that got Juneau going, you know," says Harry, whistling his *S*'s between a gap in his teeth. "The story is that a couple of prospectors named Joe Juneau and Harris found it back in 1880, [but the truth is that they were led to it by a Tlingit chief.] Why, just one of Juneau's mines has already coughed up ten times as much gold as the whole damn state cost! We're the capital, you know. Might've made sense when they did it, but it's a piss-poor idea now. They ought to move it north instead of dragging everybody down here. Prices are nuts, too. You'll see."

"I thought they decided to move the capital up near Anchorage. Whatever happened to that?" I ask.

"You're right," says Harry. "They voted to move the whole works back in the eighties. But when the time came to pay for the move, they wouldn't do it. How dumb can you get?

"Bald eagle perched on that crane," he remarks, jabbing a finger toward the channel. "They're here year-round, especially in the winter—after the salmon, you know. A bit north at Haines they have more eagles than people when winter sets in.

"There's the Gastineau fish hatchery," he adds. "Want to stop?"

I glance at the meter. I'd like to stop, but not with the meter running. Sensing my problem, Harry swings into the parking lot and shuts off the meter. "Tell you what," he says, "I'll take off a little time and show you through."

The Gastineau hatchery sits at the end of a stair-stepped fish ladder that switchbacks into the plant. A large window in the side of one of the ladders provides an underwater view of the salmon that are heading "upstream." Expecting to see just a few fish, I'm amazed to find dozens of huge chum and sockeye salmon lazing in swirls of dancing bubbles, while silver-sided cohos weave in and out of sight. Instead of spawning and subsequently dying, which is the fate of all Pacific salmon, the females will be stripped of up to ten thousand eggs, which are promptly fertilized with milt (sperm) squeezed from the males.

"What happens to the meat?" I ask.

"It's used for bait. Sometimes for dog or cat food or it's dumped into the channel.

"Why not for humans?"

"Well," says Harry, "you gotta remember that ready-to-spawn salmon stop feeding when they enter the rivers. The meat goes bad as they use up their bodies for energy."

"OK, but why not just let them spawn naturally? Why all this?" I ask, momentarily forgetting that my Minnesota Department of Natural Resources strips walleyes of eggs and sperm.

"Because the nursery gets a 90 percent hatch rate, but Ma Nature gets just 5!

"Wow."

Inside the hatchery, Harry pauses beside a cylindrical ceiling-high aquarium stocked with oceangoing fish. As the fish weave in and out of sight, he helps with their names.

"That's a sockeye," he says, pointing to five-pound red salmon. "When it comes to value, the sockeye's number one."

"And I suppose that's a silver," I add, as a chrome-plated salmon pauses, hanging eye-to-eye with me.

"That's right," says Harry, "but we call them cohos."

After pointing out the pink (humpbacked) salmon, Harry locates a dog salmon or chum, the least valuable of all.

"What about king salmon?" I ask.

Harold circles the aquarium. "Don't see any," he says. "The grown-ups'd be too big for this tank anyway. We call 'em Chinooks, you know. They run up to a hundred pounds."

A replica of a fish wheel draws me to a picture window overlooking the Gastineau Channel. Powered by river currents, fish wheels tirelessly scoop up migrating salmon and deliver them to adjacent holding pens via internal inclined ramps. As I examine the fish wheel, I'm reminded of another device that found use along this coast: a machine that was insensitively advertised as "The Iron Chink." Introduced in 1903, the revolving mechanism processed a salmon every second, replacing fifteen overworked and often underpaid Chinese.

As we return to the cab, I ask Harry to recommend a hotel, explaining that I'll take anything that offers beds without bugs. His first choice, the Prospector, has no vacancies. His second, the Alaskan, is also full, as is the Driftwood, but the Baranof will accept me for $132. Being tired and desperate, I settle up with Harry and sign in.

The Baranof takes its name from Alexander Baranof, the heavy-handed manager of the Russian American Company prior to 1817. Baranof, the "Lord of Alaska," drove his men to scour the coast for fur so thoroughly that by the end of his tenure, fur-bearing animals had almost become extinct. In his single-minded pursuit of furs, Baranof treated the Tlingits badly, practically enslaved the Aleuts and is said to have ordered a Russian shot for spreading rumors of gold.

In Juneau, price and quality don't always go hand in hand. The Baranof's main restaurant, the Gold Room, glows with a lushness appropriate to its pricey menu, but my $132 room is well-worn and only semiclean. Perhaps to compensate for its sixties furniture, its drab draperies and dated light fixtures, the bathroom bears a modern touch, the silly but obligatory strip of paper spanning the toilet seat "for your protection."

When the blast of a horn announces the arrival of another cruise ship, I raise my fourth floor window to watch it dock, only to be diverted by loud barking from across the street. Moments later, the door of the Taku Cab office opens and a malamute emerges. A hand slips his leash around the doorknob and disappears. Seconds later, the malamute lifts a leg to a nearby light post and emits a seemingly endless stream that flows down the sloping sidewalk, perversely avoiding the gutter as it trickles past four businesses before finally disappearing into a sidewalk crack. When I look up again, the ship has docked.

I consider a late lunch at the Red Dog Saloon but put it off in favor of checking out one of the cruise ships. I strike up a conversation with a couple heading toward the gangplank—just another happy camera-toting passenger heading home. Once inside, I realize that I forgot to read the ship's name. Oh well, if I'm questioned I'll just look blank and ask, "Isn't this the *New Amsterdam*?" the ship docked just ahead.

Without a floor plan, I don't know whether to head up, down, right or left. Up wins, as I want photos of Juneau's wharves from the upper decks. I wander through the immense ship from bow to stern and deck to deck until I come upon a huge, elegantly decorated dining room, the Coral Room, where I learn it's but one of three. I contemplate asking for a tour of the engine room but decide not to push my luck and head instead for the ramp.

The *New Amsterdam* lies beside the wharf like an enormous elongated beehive. On its Gastineau side, an endless procession of float-equipped Otters, Beavers and Cessnas buzz up to an opening in the hull near the waterline. Passengers leaving the aircraft gesticulate wildly, their words lost in the rumble of idling radial engines. Four, six and eight at a time, they're replaced by eager tourists ready to gawk at the sights of the Taku and Tracy Arm glaciers.

Having skipped lunch, I'm ready to treat myself to a seafood supper, no matter what the cost. The Fiddlehead, a highly regarded restaurant, has a prohibitively long waiting line, and another restaurant within walking distance won't open for an hour, so I return to Fisherman's Wharf, where I settle for a $16 seafood sampler, which arrives at my plastic table on a plastic plate, accompanied by plastic utensils. My scallops, fish, clam strips and potatoes arrive so overfried that they make the plate seem tempting, but I console myself with the knowledge that I won't have to worry about undercooked food.

While drizzle drips from the Wharf's shed roof into the channel, I grind away at the least brittle morsels while feeding a one-legged gull that begs from the railing beside my table.

"Here," I say. "You take it." He does.

When I return to the Eagan Street shops, the command "Repent" reaches my ears. A tall evangelist is holding forth beside a raised planting of petunias, nasturtiums and marigolds. As if numbed by his presentation, a city worker patiently waters the smiling pansies at his feet while it rains.

With boyish certainty, the young evangelist gushes gospel at indifferent passersby, rails against the "devil's doctrine—evolution" and urges all to "turn away from Hell and seek, instead, divinity." Smooth-faced, with his hair combed like Ralph Reid, he is Reid writ large as he fervently pitches a mixture of Jesus and Armageddon.

When he can't draw a crowd, I conclude that by ignoring him, passersby are obeying his admonition to reject the profane.

While the evangelist derides evolution, I think of Cornell University scientist Carl Sagan, who wrote in *The Demon-Haunted World* that much of the resistance to the fact of evolution "derives from our difficulty in imagining the passage of millennia, much less the aeons. What does seventy million years mean to beings who live only one millionth as long? We are like butterflies who flutter for a day and think it is forever."

The biologist William V. Mayer put it more bluntly: "Arrogance comes in a variety of forms. The arrogance of great wealth, the arrogance of great power, the arrogance of great beauty, and the arrogance of the great master are bearable because they rest on an acknowledged and measurable base. The arrogance of ignorance, however, is unbearable because it is rooted in the smug satisfaction of being isolated from the facts of the case. The anti-evolution plank in the platform of Christian Fundamentalism is a classic example of the arrogance of the know-nothings." Eager for a change of atmosphere, I spend a rewarding hour with the displays and photographs of the Alaska Museum, then head for its bookstore, where I promise myself that I won't buy more than one book, then begin to browse. Thirty minutes pass without notice, then forty-five. With four books in hand and the museum about to close, I force myself to choose just one—a lovely photo/essay book called *Searching Home: Pacific Salmon, Pacific People* by Natalie Fobes, Tom Jay and Brad Matsen.

In a nearby art store, I'm drawn to a bronze mottled-green statue of a standing polar bear that's a bit too large for the Cub. And at $4,400, it's also too big for my wallet. Still, I'm entranced by its graceful contours, its benign, inquisitive pose. Moving on, I buy cards and books for my wife, sons and grandchildren, then backtrack to the statue, not knowing that before leaving Juneau, I'll return again to stare.

It's already dusk by the time I get back to the Baranof. In the harbor below, the cruise ships have lit their rigging—a lovely sight marred only by the buildings that partially block my view. Thinking that I might get a better photo from the higher up, I head for the top floor and start knocking on doors.

The first, already vibrating before I knock, opens onto a raucous party.

"*May I take a picture from your window?*" I shout over the din.

"*Sure. Go right ahead,*" the host bellows back.

In less than a minute, I'm back in the hall. Half of me wishes they'd asked me to stay, but the half that hates chaos is relieved.

As I slip a new roll of Ektachrome into my camera, I remember passing a one-hour photo shop. They won't be able to process my slides, but they could develop the print film from my backup camera. Ninety minutes later, while the celebrants on the top floor keep their neighbors awake, I spread the photos across my bed, revisit my Steel Lake caribou and feast my eyes on the whipped-cream topping of the coastal range.

Following a delicious Baranof breakfast, I catch a Gray Line bus to the Mendenhall Glacier, only to be disappointed that the road ends a mile from the glacier's face. Fortunately, a paved walkway to Mendenhall Lake cuts the mile in half, and I'm soon gawking at the mountain of frozen Aqua Velva that rises from Mendenhall Lake. When someone mentions a trail leading to the glacier, I return to the starting point at the tourist center, locate the trail and head out.

According to the park map, I should be able to reach the glacier in about twenty-five minutes, snap a few pictures and be back in time for my bus. But what the map doesn't reveal is that the trail makes innumerable switchbacks, climbing some five hundred feet before descending to the glacier.

As I trudge upward through a soggy forest decked out in lichen and moss, my initially swift ascent slows. Forty minutes after leaving the tourist center, I puff to a stop at a river that cascades into Mendenhall Lake just as a returning group of hikers appears.

"How much farther to the glacier?" I ask, but receive only apologetic looks and a few words in German. Three hikers later I learn that the trail, which has been pretty good, gets worse. If I go on, I'll surely miss my bus. If I turn back now, I might catch it. I hesitate, then give up. I want to leave Juneau today, and if I'm late for the bus, that might become impossible.

Later, having missed the bus despite turning back, I stop for a final look at the glacier just as a pinnacle of ice crashes into the lake with the roar that the Tlingits call "white thunder."

With neither cabs nor buses in sight, I hike down the road, hoping that my cameras will help me look benign while my upraised thumb pleads, Brother, can you spare a ride? No one stops.

The road parallels a tributary of the Mendenhall, and when I stop to rest my legs, I'm surprised to find the stream swarming with jut-jawed salmon. Atlantic salmon can reproduce year after year, whereas spawning for Pacific salmon is a one time fling. In the river's gravelly bed, the fertilized eggs become "alevins," then "fry," ready to feast on nature's insect- and crustacean-rich cornucopia. Those who survive return in two to seven years, depending on their species. Guided by the chemistry of the stream in which they hatched, they journey upstream to spawn and die in the cradle where they were born.

As cars and tour buses hurry by a few feet from my back, hundreds of green-headed, russet-sided sockeyes weave back and forth in the final dance of their days while the tattered bodies of their spawned-out kin drift slowly back to the sea.

When a spawning female drives another salmon away from her "redd" (nest) of fertilized eggs, I suddenly find myself blinking back tears. What's going on here, I wonder. Why am I so moved? Do others feel this way?

Later, co-author Natalie Fobes's description of her first visit to a salmon run provides the answer: "A streak of crimson split the seams of the waterfall; I leaned forward to clear the fence from my sight. And then—a sockeye salmon floated in the air.

"Even today it is hard to describe the jumble of emotions I experienced during those moments.... I remember slowly turning to my father. His face had a look I had never seen, and before he turned away I saw his eyes were full of tears."

A car pulls over, its occupants curious to see what I'm photographing. As if fearful that talking would break some magic spell and they'd disappear, I silently point to the salmon. More cars stop—the beginning of a traffic jam. When I finally ride off with a couple from the *New Amsterdam*, I count myself lucky to have missed my bus and to have been denied a ride until I'd witnessed the spawning of the sockeye salmon.

12

Juneau to Whitehorse, Yukon Territory

Gold is a living god.
— PERCY BYSSHE SHELLEY

"Juneau Tower, Piper 4745 Mike is ready for takeoff.
Request north departure with a right turn.
Four five Mike cleared for north takeoff. Right turn approved.
Four five Mike cleared north with right turn."

ETTING the Cub's altimeter to ten feet, the elevation of the waterway, I advance the throttle. The Cub almost leaps into the sky, assisted by dense sea-level air.

A right turn quickly brings the Cub to the Mendenhall's gullied surface, where I hug the Nugget Mountains, leaving room for a quick turn if the glacier's slope begins to rise faster than the Cub can climb. Rolling from side to side, I photograph blue-green crevasses while wishing I'd done this yesterday, when the sun was still in bloom. When I've had my fill, I reverse course and glide toward the Lynn Canal, the ninety-mile-long fiord that leads to Haines and Skagway.

To my left, the navy blue waters of Icy Strait roll a gentle swell; on the right, Herbert Glacier pushes a frigid tongue toward a harbor brimming with gillnetters and seiners that can, at the height of the salmon run, net a fisherman $2,000 a day. In their midst I spot a few trawlers—boats that Harry despised: "Those goddamned bottom trawlers," he'd erupted when I asked about trawlers. "They crush and bury everything. What they don't catch they maim or kill. Compared to those damned trawlers, seiners are a just bunch of kids with dip nets."

A shaft of sunlight enlivens the pastel blues of Eagle Glacier as a column of rain descends on the Chilkoot Mountains. The closest drops will make their way to the Lynn Canal, but those that fall just a few miles inland will feed the Yukon River, with two thousand miles to travel to reach the Bering Sea. Dead ahead, an oncoming cruise ship tows a mile-long wake to Juneau.

A rapid hammering interrupts my reverie. The gauges read normal, but the hammering continues. Then my eye catches a blur at the front of the engine cowling where one end of the rub strip that fits between the cowling and the nose bowl is flailing against the cowl. It's not dangerous, but I'm not willing to let it go, so I land, locate a small roll of duct tape and begin to make repairs.

Just as I close the cowling, I'm interrupted by a loud whoosh, then several more. Spinning around, I'm surprised to see several four-foot-tall dorsal fins heading straight for the Cub. It's a pod of orcas.

I hurriedly retrieve my camera while my mind fills with stories of orcas upsetting rafts of ice to devour basking seals. I know that orcas are primarily salmon feeders and that kayakers routinely paddle among them, but even so, I chicken out and stay inside the Cub.

Feeling foolish for my retreat because if they wanted to they could easily sink the Cub, I raise the camera, then discover that I need to change the film.

The last orca in the pod lifts its head above the water and seems to examine the Cub. With eye patches of white, the black slick-skinned whale looks playful, the raccoon of the cetacean world. Close, yet worlds apart, we eye each other. I'm filled with wonder, but I'm also embarrassed to be part of the species that's imprisoned, maimed and murdered his kin. (At least a fourth of the orcas captured for aquariums during the sixties and seventies bore bullet wounds.) Does this orca know our past, I wonder. Would his thoughts make sense to me? Would mine to him?

Assisted by a strengthening tailwind, the Cub flits past one of the Alaska Marine Highway's many "blue canoes," the five-thousand-ton ferry *Matanuska*, which has just departed from Haines, her hull crammed with cars, buses, campers and semis, her railings lined with passengers bound for Juneau and Ketchikan.

By the time I reach Skagway (from a Tlingit word meaning "windy place"), the harbor is leaping with waves that are much too large for the Cub, so I fly on toward the ghost town of Dyea (pronounced Die-ee) where the wave-muting Taiya Inlet might permit a landing. If it does, I'll search out the Chilkoot Trail, the Gold Rush Highway to the Klondike.

Gold is a self-loving metal. Unlike gregarious carbon, which combines with other elements in half a million ways, gold consorts with just a few, and even then reluctantly. Conceited gold mimics Narcissus, the youth ensnared by his own reflection on the surface of a forest pool. But unlike the mythical waters that trapped Narcissus, water can set gold free.

In 1896, when a prospector named George Washington Carmack found flakes of placer gold near the Klondiuck River, a tributary of the Yukon, he set in motion a stampede that would enrich a few and impoverish many, build and destroy friendships and bring out the best in some and the worst in others.

Of the three main routes to the Klondike fields, the easiest was an all-water route through the Bering Sea to the tiny town of St. Michael. There, the stampeders boarded a sternwheeler and steamed up the Yukon to Dawson's fields of gold.

The remaining two routes involved a climb over one of two mountain passes—either Skagway's White Pass, which came to be known as Dead Horse Pass, or Dyea's Chilkoot Pass, which had a final ascent that was much too steep for horses. Although Chilkoot Pass stood six hundred feet higher than White Pass, prospectors had four good reasons to choose the Chilkoot: it was shorter by ten miles; it was open year-round; Dyea was safer than corrupt Skagway and, in the warm months, the Klondikers escaped the stench of the three thousand rotting horses that had died on the White Pass trail, "the pack animals' hell."

During the winter, packers struggled up fifteen hundred icy steps to the crest of the Chilkoot Pass, paying $1 a trip for their use. From dawn to dusk, a continuous line of gold seekers plodded carefully upward in the "Chilkoot Lock-Step." If an exhausted stampeder collapsed while climbing the "Golden Stairs," he could face an hour-long wait for a chance to get back in line. With the pass attained, some tobogganed back down on a shovel, but most rode the seat of their pants.

Faced with packing a ton of supplies over the pass (which the RCMP required to prevent starvation) prospectors had two choices: tote it themselves or hire natives who were quickly becoming rich. In addition, natives who had become Presbyterians refused to work on Sunday. Worse yet, halfway up the pass, some would set down their loads and "renegotiate" the rates.

When Skagway's George Bracket finally built a toll road twelve miles up White Pass, many were eager to use it, but no one was willing to pay, so he sold out a pair of railroad men named Thomas Tancred and "Big Mike" Heney, the latter having bragged, "Give me enough dynamite and snoose and I'll build a road to hell."

Two years and 450 tons of explosives later (and an unknown amount of snoose, or chewing tobacco), Heney made good his boast. But by then, the Rush was over. Nevertheless, the White Pass and Yukon railroad guaranteed that Skagway and the steamboats of the upper Yukon would make money for many years, while Dyea's days of glory would quickly fade.

During World War II, the WP&Y supplied most of the materials for the Alaska Highway. But when metal prices tumbled in the eighties, many Yukon mines shut down, taking the railroad with them. Today, the WP&Y is back in limited business, hauling loads of Skagway tourists to the summit of Dead Horse Pass.

I can't find Dyea. I'm beginning to think I've missed it, when I suddenly realize that the rubble passing below my wings is all of the town that remains.

To avoid taxiing into the last few spike-studded remnants of the mile-long wharf that had connected Dyea to saltwater, I land on the Taiya River, which is flush with salmon, the brown bears' food stamps, then set off across the tidal flats toward a wall-like stand of hemlock trees resplendent with bald eagles. Drawn by the spawning runs of chum, coho, sockeye and humpbacked salmon, the eagles' annual gathering of three thousand exceeds the population of Haines and Skagway combined.

As I stroll through Dyea's grassy remains, I can hardly believe that a town of five thousand once stood just here, with a main street two miles long. In the silence, I envision throngs of hopeful Klondikers hauling their gear past the clamor of Healy's Trading Post and crowded saloons until the bubble burst, replaced by the sighing wind and the cries of eagles and gulls. Now all ghost and no town, Dyea lies buried beneath fields of wavering goosegrass and lavender lupines.

Spotting a violet-rimmed mound of trash, I set my camera aside and, accompanied by the hum of bees, begin some prospecting of my own. Beneath scraps of deeply rusted iron, crumbling asphalt shingles and rotting wood lies a bed of broken glass, a handful of metallic slivers that once were nails and the disintegrating remains of corroded cans. As I carefully scrape aside each layer with an old strap hinge, my eyes search for the gleam of a long-lost $20 gold piece.

By the time I reach ground level, I'm down to the residue of a fire that must have died well before the shingles were dumped on top. Shaving off a quarter inch at a time, I sift through the ashes and toss them aside. Minutes later, something gleams—not gold, but silver. A key.

Its pitted nickel plated shaft bears a sculpted oval at one end and a small lock-engaging T at the other. Perhaps it's a skeleton key, the master key to old door locks. With no one to dispute me, I decide that it must be a skeleton key, having risen from Dyea's bones.

Pocketing the key, I head north through a scattering of blue-flag iris. The trail divides. One branch turns toward the western mountains, perhaps to join the Chilkat Trail, a little-used alternative to the Chilkoot. I explore it briefly, hoping to stumble onto an abandoned trapper's shack, but find only a lush patch of waist-high salmonberry bushes. Because grizzlies enjoy these large raspberry-like fruits too, I carefully scan the meadow for fifteen-hundred-pound mounds of fur, then pick a handful of the delicious-looking but disappointingly flavored berries.

A mosquito probes my wrist, reminding me of a Tlingit legend that tells of the sister of a chief, who, despite being told that she would never bear a child, soon became pregnant. The baby, born much too early, bore a heavy coat of hair and a mouthful of very sharp teeth. Growing rapidly, the child began to kill, for pleasure, every animal that crossed its path.

Because the child was related to the chief, no one dared to intervene. Finally, in desperation, the chief himself threw the incorrigible child into a roaring campfire. As the flames consumed the creature, a voice rose from within the flames, promising that it would drink human blood for a thousand years. The fire shot up, sending millions of ashes high into the sky, and each one became a mosquito.

Retracing my steps, I return to the gravel road that connects Skagway to Dyea, and follow it north toward the Chilkoot Trail until I come upon a sign that reads "Dyea Cemetery."

Although I prefer cremation, the soft, cool shade of the deeply wooded cemetery appeals to me. Sitka spruce and towering hemlocks spread layers of evergreen boughs over graves surrounded by nodding ferns, bunchberries and bell-blossomed pyrola. Their lofty branches whisper tales to the wind, but at ground level it's still and hushed.

Most of the wooden markers read "April 3, 1898"—Palm Sunday— the day that a Chilkoot Pass avalanche snuffed out sixty lives. On that day, a woman named Anne Maxon was struggling up the pass. Glancing up from beneath her load, she gasped as the onrushing avalanche swallowed the shouts and bodies of the fleeing stampeders above. Within seconds she, too, became trapped in the tumbling mass. Minutes passed as she grew cold. Her breathing became difficult; her cries for help weakened.

As she was about to lose consciousness, something poked her side, followed by shouts and frantic shoveling. Freed from her white coffin, she fled just as a second avalanche broke loose. The whirling mass roared downhill, caught the woman and again entombed her in a snowy shroud of white. Anne Maxon's good luck, however, was the equal of her bad. Once more she was discovered and quickly set free again.

Hailing from distant Maine, California, Minnesota and a host of other states and countries, the dead stampeders share their resting place with native graves surrounded by wooden fences. One granite headstone bears a finely detailed engraving of a beaver above a listing of those interred: Tagish Johns and his kin; Dyea Johns and his. At its base, ruby red strawberries mingle with the lacy ladderlike foliage of horsetails.

A glance at my watch persuades me to forgo the Chilkoot Trail. If I find it, I'll want to climb for at least an hour. Add the return trip and, if I still can't land at Skagway, I'd be late getting into White-horse. As I return to the road, I pause to pick a pyrola loaded with blossoms, then add a horsetail and slip the cluster into my shirt pocket—my Dyea boutonniere.

Horsetails, unlike much of the foliage that surrounds us, are truly ancient plants. Having found a niche that suited them well, they've changed very little from their fossilized ancestors, saying, in effect, "We're fine as we are."

Charles Darwin might have been surprised at such behavior, which seems to dispute evolution. Such arguments, however, miss the point, for evolution doesn't demand anything, including change. It's just what happens when nature comes upon a more efficient way.

When Darwin boarded the *Beagle* in 1831, he was a strict cre-ationist who reckoned the age of the earth at around ten thousand years. Imagine, then, his turmoil when he realized that millions of years must have been required to shrink volcanic islands to coral atolls and to write of the detailed fossil record that supported the suddenly obvious process of evolution.

As I retrace my steps down the rain-forest path, I imagine a wide-eyed Darwin clambering over Canada's richly fossilized Burgess Shales or ascending from the Grand Canyon's mile-deep floor. In its depths he'd find ancient rocks devoid of life. A third of the way up, near the four-hundred-million-year-old limestones, he'd marvel as fossils appeared—first shells and worms, all of them aquatic and primitive, without backbones, then, higher up, vertebrate creatures like armored fish. Climbing toward the younger two-hundred-mil-lion-year-old strata, he'd encounter the mineralized remains of rep-tiles and air-breathing fish, advanced forms of the aquatic life he'd seen below. With great luck, he might come upon the remains of a dinosaur. But he wouldn't find fossilized mammals.

Unfortunately, even the upper levels of the Grand Canyon are too old to record the onset of mammalian life. For that, he'd have to find younger sedimentary rocks that time hasn't worn away. Were he so fortunate, he'd notice that dinosaurs disappeared from the fossil record some sixty-five million years ago and that humanoids arrived just two or three million years in the past.

Darwin, who was an excellent observer, might also notice a thin, odd-looking layer of clay near the last dinosaur fossils. Below that layer, dinosaurs and a large variety of tiny creatures called foraminifera thrived, but above it, all evidence of the dinosaurs disappeared, and only a single species of foraminifera survived.

In 1978, a U.S. physicist named Luis Alvarez and his geologist son Walter decided to have the clay analyzed. To their great surprise, they learned that the layer was rich in iridium, an element that's rare on earth but common in meteorites. When subsequent studies revealed that the off-white stratum occurred worldwide, they proposed that the band was composed of dust from a huge meteorite strike that altered the earth's climate enough to end the reign of the dinosaurs.

Darwin's *The Origin of Species...*, like the man himself, was so well-organized and logical that his conclusions struck most readers as self-evident. In *The Origin ...*, Darwin demonstrated that reproduction, being imperfect, creates offspring with varying assets and liabilities. Those equipped with traits that prove advantageous to survival produce more offspring than those not so well equipped in a process he called "natural selection."

Fearing a storm of religious opposition, Darwin set his book aside for years, finally going public only when another scientist, Alfred Russell Wallace, contacted him with similar material that he planned to release. There, in 1859, the story should end, but it doesn't.

After sixteen years of ridicule and criticism from religious conservatives, Darwin answered back in a rather genial autobiography (to be published after his death) that included his personal beliefs. Speaking of his early years, Darwin confessed that "it never struck me how illogical it was to say that I believed in what I did not understand and what was in fact unintelligible," and concluded that "the Old Testament, from its manifestly false history of the world ... was no more to be trusted than the sacred books of the Hindoos, or the beliefs of any barbarian."

Unfortunately, Darwin's devout wife censored his autobiography, and the public remained ignorant of his thoughts until seventy years later, when his granddaughter discovered the original manuscript and ordered his words restored.

When I return to the Cub, I scrub my newly found key in sparkling river water. Then, struck by the contrast between its nickel plating and the emerald green algae-coated pebbles, I lay the key in the shallows and bring my camera close to capture another memory.

The sun, muted by a raft of cirrus clouds, becomes a pale yellow moon while I examine my key and search for the stories it holds. Did it open the door to Meyer's Saloon or secure John Healy's goods? Did the soft hand of a dance-hall girl enfold it as she locked a Palace Hotel door against yet another night? Did it rest in the cleavage of a prostitute? If so, had she come to her occupation by choice or was it a last resort? As I admire its still-gleaming patina and catenary curves, I wonder, was this nickel-plated keeper of secrets hanging on a nail when the fire came, or did it fall from burning clothing as its owner fled the flames?

The wind that sped me to Dyea becomes a head wind as the Cub struggles back to Skagway. It's not likely that the wind has shifted enough to let me land, but I press on anyway, for I'd really like to spend the night in Skagway.

On Skagway's infamous White Pass, the longer but lower of the two rival routes, the cost of getting a man's gear across the mountains often included the life of a horse. The adventurous author Jack London wrote, "Horses died like mosquitoes in a first frost. . . . From Skagway to Bennett, they rotted in heaps." Fortunately, the White Pass and Yukon railroad (and the dwindling gold rush) brought the carnage to an end.

At White Pass, as on the Chilkoot, the Mounties admitted only those with enough supplies to last a year. Without help, a man might need three months to haul such an outfit over the pass. Worse yet, every time he returned to Skagway, the Klondiker faced a different sort of hazard—a corrupt city run by a crafty con man named Soapy Smith.

Jefferson Randolph Smith picked up the nickname "Soapy" in the gold fields of Colorado, where he ran a bunco game using bars of soap with a $20 bill tucked under the wrapper. A few accomplices bought the marked bars, then flaunted their "good luck." Soapy, on hearing of the Klondike gold rush, promptly headed north, predicting that he would become Skagway's mayor. He also became its dictator.

Operating first out of Clancy's Saloon and later from Jeff's Place, Soapy and his congenial con men employed a multitude of schemes to separate the greenhorns from their money. Need to send a message home? Mr. Smith had a telegraph office. Never mind that it had no wires, no lines to anywhere. Just pay $5 and come back later for your reply, which (of course) always arrived collect. Freshly composed in the back room by Soapy's swindlers, the reply always included a desperate plea: wire money.

At Soapy's saloons, card sharks and watered whiskey whittled away a stampeder's reserves. If an alert gambler withdrew, a few drugged drinks or a mugging would follow.

On one occasion Soapy's "agents" solicited $35,000 (perhaps $200,000 in today's funds) in Skagway's bars, gambling halls and bawdyhouses to build the new pastor a church. Soapy, with great show, turned the money over to the preacher, then had him robbed while he slept.

Soapy, who had bought off the law, reigned supreme while Skagway paid the price. Warned that the town had become a stinkhole of crime, hundreds of stampeders bypassed Skagway's eighty saloons and sailed on to a quieter Dyea. Finally, when a group of vigilantes sprang to life, Soapy's days were numbered.

Emboldened by their swelling ranks and a common cause (the return of $2,600 in gold dust stolen from a prospector) they moved against Soapy, who packed two pistols and a rifle, and went to meet his fate. In the ensuing face-off, a vigilante named Frank Reid shot

Soapy, who died on the spot. Unfortunately, Reid also received a fatal wound, and twelve days later followed Soapy to the grave.

The wind at Skagway has indeed shifted—for the worse. Some other year I'll visit the Trail of '98 Museum that I can see so well below. Perhaps I'll lunch at Red Onion Saloon, its lusty past neutered by a large neon *Pizza* sign in its window. The women of the Red Onion, which was once a bordello, designated their availability by placing dolls bearing their names on a downstairs rack— upright for available and supine for engaged.

Lifting the Cub's nose with power, I head up the Skagway River as the WP&Y tourist train pulls out of town. With the highway on one side and the railroad looping to and fro on the other, finding the White Pass town of Fraser is simple, and after a quick stop at Canadian Customs, the Tundra Cub charges into the sky and heads for the first flat stretch of the prospectors' highway, the shining expanse of Bennett Lake.

In the spring of 1898, at the height of the Klondike Gold Rush, a sea of white canvas tents overspread the shores of Bennett and Lindemann Lakes. There, thirty-thousand gold seekers hammered and lashed together seven thousand rafts and boats, using green lumber whipsawn from trees on nearby mountain slopes. Each bore a number assigned by the Mounties, who kept a corresponding list of passengers.

One of those boats was captained by Lars Gunderson, the organizer of the sixteen-man Monitor Gold Mining and Trading Company. Mostly Norwegian Minnesotans, they arrived at Dyea from Minneapolis on the last day of January 1898.

The Monitors, as they called themselves, had expected to have the Chilkoot behind them within two weeks. But despite their diligent labors, three weeks of constant toil found them only halfway up, and three more weeks would pass before the last of their outfit topped the pass. Two weeks later, as they hauled the final load into their Bennett Lake camp and began to build their boats, they learned of the Chilkoot avalanches and the loss of sixty lives.

When 150 boats disintegrated in the Yukon's Miles Canyon, the Mounties began turning back unseaworthy and undermanned boats. Women and children were ordered to portage the Five-Mile Canyon and to leave the boats again at Squaw and Whitehorse Rapids.

At the tiller of one square-sailed skiff stood Jack London, who, after boasting that he could "outpack any Indian," had shouldered his gear over Chilkoot Pass without assistance. Moving downriver with spring toward a single, almost fatal, winter in the Yukon, he sampled the river's indifference and the dramas that lined its shores.

The following year London left the Yukon without a single regret, his pack loaded not with gold but with books by Darwin and Milton. Having learned firsthand the meaning of cold and scurvy, he left the Klondike gold behind and wrote his way to fame.

The Monitors, after surviving Miles Canyon and Whitehorse Rapids, floated on to Dawson, where they scraped their claims down to bedrock. When pay dirt failed to appear, they staked more, then survived by working for other miners. In August 1899, the Monitors disbanded. Most of them returned to Minnesota, but Lars Gunderson, the group's organizer, stayed on and became the U.S. commissioner and recorder for mining in the Seward Peninsula. The reward for their trials was paid not in wealth but in lifelong friendships. Like Jack London, they never found more than pocket-change gold.

The Cub slips through Bennett Valley on air like liquid glass. On either side, five-thousand-foot peaks hewn concave by glaciers reach up to touch the sky. At Carcross (caribou crossing), the sun returns to highlight the Caribou Hotel, the home of Polly, an alcoholic parrot that had been taught to sing "Onward Christian Soldiers" and to respond to queries of "Polly want a cracker?" with "Go to hell!" (Polly's death occasioned a special burial in the Carcross cemetery, a trainload of mourners from Whitehorse and a monumental wake at the Caribou Hotel.)

Turning north at the "smallest desert in the world," the Carcross desert, the Cub follows an emerald green string of marl-bottomed lakes north to the Alaska Highway and Whitehorse, the capital of the Yukon Territory—population sixteen thousand.

The reservoir formed by the Northern Power Commission dam swallowed the foaming horsetails and whitewater manes that inspired "Whitehorse Rapids," the source of the city's name. A fish ladder climbs the dam's eastern flank. Switching back and forth like a mountain highway, it shepherds salmon past the final obstacle on their two-thousand-mile odyssey from the Bering Sea to the streams of the Chilkoot Range.

Although evading nets and fish traps seems enough of a challenge, today's salmon face industrial pollution and spawning beds fouled by Yukon miners who are exempt from the Fisheries Protection Act. Not surprisingly, environmentalists and Canada's beleaguered salmon industry argue that the exemption has given the miners a license to pollute.

In response to shortsighted policies that depleted the stock of Newfoundland's Grand Banks and left fifty thousand Canadians jobless, and to claims that Alaskan fisheries are harvesting too many Canadian-spawned salmon, the Canadian government loaded its ambassador to the U.S., Raymond Chrétien, aboard a destroyer in 1995 and sent him off to discuss the salmon problem with Alaska's governor, Tony Knowles. Despite the military overtones, the meeting was cordial, but no one had expected a solution, and none was reached.

A year later, Canadian fishermen blockaded and egged the Alaskan ferry *Taku*, when it arrived at Prince Rupert, B.C. In 1997, an even larger group prevented the *Malaspina* from leaving port for several days.

Despite the decline in the Oregon, Washington and Canadian salmon harvest, which was caused by dams and the clear-cutting of forests, a burgeoning Alaskan "crop" in the early nineties sent prices tumbling. The temporary abundance, however, was due not to nature but to the success of the Gastineau-like hatcheries and to multinational salmon farms that feed so many fish in pens that half of the salmon consumed today are raised like chickens—in captivity. In Alaska, however, salmon farms have been banned since 1990, partly because the surrounding waters become polluted with high levels of excrement. Fish farms, though temporarily successful, fail to address the real problem: a warming biosphere and too many mouths. Unless we curb appetites that are taking giant tuna to the brink of extinction, the now-declining Alaskan harvest is doomed to share the fate of Newfoundland's once Grand Banks and California's near-barren fisheries near Monterey.

Whenever humans and nature have come into conflict, nature has usually lost. Will the salmon be an exception, or will we play yet another reprise of "screw the owls, the frogs and the wetlands" by refusing to limit our numbers?

The Tundra Cub taxis past stands of sweet-stemmed fireweed, the Yukon's official flower, and drifts to a stop at the pumps of Tagish Air. While the Cub accepts its precious load, I chat with Andy Jensen, a college student bound for Dawson.

Fortunately, my trip's gone better than Andy's. Since leaving Fort St. John, he's had two flats, an alternator fail and a rock crack the windshield of his battered '82 Ford.

"Any chance of a ride to town?" I ask.

"Sure thing," he replies, as he extracts a bald tire from the passenger seat and jams it into the back. "Hop in."

Andy drops me off at the *Klondike II*, a 170-foot duplicate of the original *Klondike* sternwheeler that ran aground in '36. The *Klondike II*, the last paddlewheel boat of the British Yukon Navigation

Company, is now a Parks Canada museum, and I'm just in time for the tour. Within minutes, Rod, our genial full-bearded guide, invites a woman tourist to ring the *Klondike*'s gleaming brass bell to begin our landlocked tour.

Inside, Rod pauses beside a huge firebox door. "You," he says, pointing to a paunchy middle-aged man, "will be the fireman. By the time we reach Dawson, you're going to be in fantastic shape, because you're going to feed this boiler fifty cords of wood. And that's just a warm-up, because when we return against the current, we'll use 140."

On the *Klondike*'s second deck, an encompassing array of sunlit windows warm the wicker chairs and sofas of an attractive passenger lounge. Moving on, we enter a surprisingly elegant dining room that served the first-class passengers, whose cabins take up the rest of the deck.

On the third deck (this thing is huge) we find the captain's cabin, which is topped by a semicircular wheelhouse. As Rod demonstrates the engine room controls, he continues his spiel: "More than two hundred of these riverboats plied the Yukon before World War II. Each carried up to two hundred tons of cargo. But one by one they disappeared. Some were scrapped; a few were wrecked; others were left to rot.

"When the all-weather road to Dawson was finished in 1955, it snuffed out the last of their fires. Two of them, the *Casca* and the *Whitehorse* were hauled onshore right here in Whitehorse, and they'd still be there if the mayor's son and a few of his friends hadn't had built a picnic fire on the *Casca*'s deck. When their fire got out of control, it took the *Whitehorse* with it."

The tour ends, and I head for the MacBride Museum, where, among exhibits of riverboat paraphernalia, I discover an old narrow-gauge locomotive that once chuffed up White Pass.

The Potbelly Restaurant (love that name) turns out to be deli-style, so I take my hunger to the hugely busy Talisman, where I wait twenty minutes for a table and another fifteen to order. The vegetable of the day is brussels sprouts—those yellow-green clumps of chlorophyll that should be fed only to convicted child molesters.

With my order finally accepted, I wait. Read paper. Ogle steaming platters of food destined for other diners. Reread menu. Speculate on the brown specks in the sugar dispenser. Level table with folded napkin. Food finally arrives. Damn fine sprouts. Hunger truly is the best sauce.

When a husky sixty-something man in an ill-fitting suit follows me to the register, I nod a greeting and ask, "You just passing through, like me, or do you live here?"

"I'm from Dawson," he replies, "but my son lives here. As soon as he's off work, we're hopping a plane to Las Vegas. Going to see the sights."

"I bet that'll set you back a couple of bucks!"

Smiling, he says, "Fortunately, money's not a problem. My wife and I had always planned to travel, but we never got around to it. A few years ago, she died, and now it's too late. Now, every day when I wake up, I wonder how I'm going to spend the money we saved. I don't want to make that mistake again, so now I take my kids."

Back at the seaplane base, a group of German tourists is having language problems with Bill, a local pilot who is trying to explain that he can't take them sight-seeing because he lacks a commercial license. Hampered by their limited English and his nonexistent German, Bill tries to explain that he'd like to but that by law he *can't*. With his point finally understood, the disappointed Germans head for their vans. As they depart, one of them mentions the Frantic Follies, a Gay Nineties stage show at the Westmark Hotel. I wonder what they'll make of *that*.

When I ask about a place to camp for the night, Bill purses his lips. "Well, lemme see," he says. "There's Fish Lake about twelve miles southwest. You'll find lots of grayling and a decent place to camp."

"That's great," I reply, "but I'm heading north, and I'd rather not backtrack."

"Gotcha," he says. "Thirty, thirty-five miles north of town there's a public campground on Fox Lake, just west of Lake Laberge—right next to the Dawson Highway. Just follow the Alaska to the Dawson Highway. When Laberge is on the right, Fox Lake'll be right on your nose."

As the Cub climbs away from Schwatka Lake, I scan the airport for the world's largest "windsock," a retired DC-3. Mounted on a huge pylon, the airliner still helps pilots make safe landings by pivoting into the wind, which, according to the forecast, is about to change. A deep low is moving in from the Gulf of Alaska. Fortunately, it's not due in Dawson for two more days, which is twice as long as I'll need.

A few miles north of Whitehorse, the Yukon River loops into Lake Laberge. There, when the cold breath of winter settles onto the lake's still water, ice forms more quickly than in the fast-flowing Yukon. And in the fall of 1900 the ice ensnared a steamer that was called the *Olive May*.

Hearing reports that the *Olive May* carried a miner dying from scurvy, a Dr. Sudgen hurried to the steamer but arrived a little too late. To dispose of the body, the resourceful Dr. Sudgen stoked up the *Olive May*'s firebox and used it as a crematorium. A few years later, a young Whitehorse bank clerk named Robert Service heard the story and promptly immortalized the steamer, the lake and the miner in "The Cremation of Sam McGee":

". . . The Northern Lights have seen queer sights,
But the queerest they ever did see,
Was the night on the marge of Lake Labarge,
I cremated Sam McGee . . .

In Service's poem, the *Olive May* became the *Alice May*, Laberge became Labarge, and the miner became a prospector bedeviled by the Yukon's cold. With the cremation supposedly finished, the miner's friends opened the firebox door. Inside sat a happy Sam, soaking up the heat. "Close the door," yelled Sam. "It's the first time I've been warm since leaving Tennessee."

As the Fox Lake sky turns crimson above the Miners' Range, I pour a steaming bowl of soup from my thermos, courtesy of the Talisman café. For dessert, it's fig bars and my last Mountain Dew. I should have bought more in Whitehorse. Oh well, I'll be in Dawson tomorrow.

13

Whitehorse to Fort Simpson, Northwest Territories

Three Laws of Thermodynamics:
You cannot win.
You cannot break even.
You must die to get out of the game.

— ANON

I T'S CLEAR TO THE SOUTH and east, but to the north, toward Dawson, rain clouds intrude. I reset the Cub's altimeter, which confirms the approaching low, then head for the derelict village of Lower Laberge, where the Cub rejoins the Yukon River.

When the Russians ascended the Yukon in the latter part of the seventeenth century, they used its Inuit name, the Kwikpak. But the Hudson's Bay Company, which arrived from the southeast, brought along its Athabascan name, the Youcon. The languages were different, but the meaning was the same—"big river."

From Laberge to Hootalingua, the Yukon twists through wind-polished canyons, hiding subsurface rocks that claimed twenty boats in a single day in the Rush of '98. In the notorious Thirty-Mile stretch, it loops so abruptly that sternwheelers winched their barges at an angle to the boat, then jackknifed their way through the turns. At Five Finger Rapids, Whitehorse-bound steamers had to winch themselves upstream with cables while their paddles churned the Yukon foam.

Split-up Island arrives. Legend says that here, incompatible Klondikers divided up their supplies and headed off on their own. One pair cut their boat in half, while another angry duo is reported to have sawed their only frying pan right down the middle.

The silt-laden Teslin River joins the Yukon near the abandoned RCMP post of Hootalingua, doubling its width. I'd planned to stop, but the decaying buildings persuade me to save the time for exploring a five-hundred-ton sternwheeler that's marooned downstream on Shipyard Island instead. Just when I begin to think I've missed it, I spot the sagging hulk atop an island not far from the western shore. She looks pretty good from bow to midships, but a giant has crushed her stern.

Skidding across gray-green Yukon water, the Tundra Cub noses into a dense stand of alders. The narrow trail that showed plainly from the air somehow eludes me, but after pushing through the alders, I'm soon standing beside the decaying sternwheeler that University of Wisconsin professor and author John Hildebrand described in *Reading the River*: "Its roof had slumped into the staterooms on the upper Texas deck and branches probed the pilot-house. The riverboat had been operated by two owners under different names, so *Norcom* had been painted above the water line on one side of the bow and *Evelyn* on the other—like a sailor with a tattoo for each romance."

Stepping carefully across her rotting deck, I explore the steamer's barren, half-lit interior. Strands of pale, sun-starved foliage struggle upward through breaks in her hull and quaking floor. Near midships, the scent of creosote spikes the humid air. Spotting an keyhole in an open door, I insert my Dyea key and give it a turn. The lock responds. How fitting—a skeleton key *should* work on a dead ship. Then, as I slowly enter the darkened, collapsing stern, the scent of a skunk turns me around.

Airborne again, I try to fly around the eastern edge of the advancing stratus. Ten miles pass, then twenty while the Cub cruises between peaks obscured by lowering clouds until I finally give up and turn east toward a brighter horizon and a town called Ross River. Dawson will have to wait.

At Ross River, the sun returns to highlight my skeleton key, which hangs, jittering, from the altimeter knob. Retrieving it, I turn it over in my hand. As the welcome sunlight slides along its shaft, I recall another sunny Ross River day that I'd just as soon have missed.

I'd been traveling with Stu Peel, one of the most gentlemanly traveling companions a man could want, and his son, Dan. Needing fuel, we decided to land on the river at the edge of the tiny town, where we'd fuel our Cubs with gas from a nearby station.

As Stu landed *downwind* and into the current of the swift flowing Pelly, I overflew the landing area, noting that the cables attached to the Canol Highway ferry ran straight up to pulleys near a suspended pipeline.

Seaplanes, with their long struts and tall floats, can nose over more easily than wheel aircraft during landing. Stu's Super Cub, with his 150-pound son on the rear seat and a pile of gear in the baggage, was considerably less prone to nosing over than my PA-11, which had little weight in the rear. Consequently, Stu had a good margin of safety when he landed *with* the wind and *into* the current to reach a sandy area just downstream from the ferry. After overflying the ferry to check the height of the cables again, I decided to fly upstream, turn around and land my Cub conventionally: into the wind and with the current. After landing, I'd just taxi under the pipeline to rejoin Stu and Dan.

Slowed by the head wind, the Tundra Cub settled gracefully onto the swift-flowing Pelly. Staying alert, I scanned the water for debris and obstructions while approaching the pipeline at fifteen mph, with about twelve mph provided by the Pelly's current and three by the Cub's idling engine.

I still don't know which I saw first—the thin, almost invisible second ferry cable hanging close to the water or Dan racing along the shore, frantically waving at me to turn around. As the rusty cable leaped into sight from its silty background, I stamped on the left rudder pedal and hit the throttle to hasten the turn.

As if trapped in a nightmare from which there was no escape, the Cub slowly began to turn in the suddenly molasseslike river, whose current, coupled with the Cub's beginning turn, hurried it toward the waiting cable. With the throttle and rudder pushed to the stops, I watched the woven steel approach. At fifty feet, the Cub, though turning, still drew closer to the snare. At thirty feet she finally began to point upstream. Two seconds from disaster, with her engine roaring and her propeller throwing spray across her shuddering tail, she finally held her own and snarled her way upstream.

Concentrating on staying in center stream, I pushed back images of my close call with disaster. Had I failed to see the cable or Dan's frantic signals, the river would have claimed the cable-ensnared Cub, riding up over her floats to pull her down. Had I been able to turn just ninety degrees before the cable rode up the sides of the float struts, she'd have gone under sideways. In either case, I'd have been scrambling out of the tumbling Cub and hoping to stay alive.

Minutes later, I soared above the pipeline, reversed course and followed Stu's example. For some reason, the seriousness of my close call hadn't sunk in by the time I nosed the Cub ashore. In fact, months passed before I really acknowledged how close I'd come to following the Cub through a slow and final roll beneath the river's swirls.

I dig out my Canada map and scan the country to the east. A few hundred miles away, on the Mackenzie River, I spot Fort Simpson. Now I'm more than pleased that I loaded extra fuel at Tagish Air. After crossing the Mackenzie Mountains, I'll intercept Canada's "Grand Canyon" of the South Nahanni River and land at Virginia Falls, a 315-foot-high spectacle that eclipses Niagara Falls. Perhaps I'll stop at Glacier Lake, a wilderness rival of Banff's Lake Louise, or, if the weather holds, camp beside a lovely beach at Little Doctor Lake.

The Cub climbs at full throttle toward the peaks of the Selwyn Range, where I cross the Continental Divide and return to the Northwest Territories. In dreamlike serenity, the Cub floats past 9,005-foot Mount Sir James MacBrien, soaring above sculpted snow fields as pristine as those of the Coastal Range until a glittering finger of water at Mount MacBrien's base finally slips into sight. I throttle back, letting the Cub slalom down to Glacier Lake, the crown jewel of the Ragged Range. S-turning through sweeping turns, the Cub and I descend through valley-cradled air.

As I coast to a stop beside a placid stream at the edge of a quiet beach, a stellar jay flits toward the mountain's vertical face. My eyes follow the jay, then climb six thousand feet of glistening rock to the pinnacles far above. At the foot of the mountain, a meadow bathes in sunlight, green and soft as a fantasy.

Spotting an odd-looking object protruding from the reeds, I remove my boots and socks, and wade through the frigid water toward what becomes a set of moose antlers. I'd love to take them home, but they'd never fit in the Cub, and they'd raise aerodynamic havoc if I strapped them to the floats. Still, I can't ignore such a find, so I haul the antlers to back to camp and hoist them onto the Cub for a unique photograph. Backed by MacBrien's towering columns, the yellow Cub gleams at the edge of a sparkling stream, sporting a dark brown moose-antler hood ornament.

Although it's early, I decide to stay the night, so I stow my gear, push off into the stream and drift into Glacier Lake. I clip my church-key lure to the end of my line and send it flying. Something immediately strikes the lure, then shakes loose. Casting again, I retrieve my supper, a three-pound trout.

Immersed in mountain silence, I stand at the end of the float, trout in hand as a majestic array of snow-capped peaks spreads mirror images across the lake's opalescent green. At the head of the lake, the highest peak in the Territories guards the Cirque of the Unclimbables, an amphitheater of vertical faces that are sought by skilled climbers from around the world. Surrounded by such Macchu Picchu–like beauty, I understand why so many native Americans honored the land and rejected the white man's heaven.

An appallingly thin lynx walks into camp in the midst of my supper. Long-legged, with big feet and pointed Spock-like ears, the lynx strolls calmly past, not far from my hissing stove. It must be aware of me, but the scruffy animal hardly gives me a glance. Perhaps it had just passed through the depths of the endless ten-year-long boom-and-bust cycle of hare and lynx populations, and it isn't about to let pointless distractions sap its strength.

As mountain shadows creep across the valley, I grab a handful of dried apricots and head for the tent. When I pull back the netting, I notice a spider shuttling back and forth between the tent and a wild rosebush. With its outlining triangle already in place, the tiny eight-legged wonder links the sides with bracing, radial threads, then weaves concentric orbs. Fifteen minutes pass before the spider retreats to the edge of her web. Like the Ross River cable that reached for me, her imperceptible strands lie in wait for the careless, the hurried or the just plain unlucky.

It's cold. Without looking out of the tent, I know that Dawson's weather has caught up with me overnight. Vibrantly green just yesterday, the mountain slopes beyond the lake have been powder-sugared with snow.

While the Cub's engine warms, I plan my escape. Fortunately, the clouds are high enough to let me slip into the valley of the Slavey Indians' Nahedah—the "powerful river"—a much more appropriate name than the one on my map: the South Nahanni.

Unlike the Tundra Cub, which joins the Nahanni in its tranquil middle third, canoeists usually reach the headwaters of the river by car. After a long portage from the road to the Moose Ponds, they race through the Rock Gardens, a wild section of the Nahanni that drops one thousand feet in forty-four miles, providing what many say is the finest whitewater canoeing in Canada. Leaving the gardens behind, the exhausted river then winds through a broad valley, its slow descent revealed in looping curves and intertwining channels, briefly becoming a braided river, silted beige.

When the river's attained, I dig out my Park Use Permit, which allows me to land "at Rabbit Kettle Lake and Virginia Falls" and requests that I minimize "low-level flight over the river corridor or park features." Except for a brief river-scraping flight that I plan for Virginia Falls, I'll be pleased to honor their request.

The Cub flies itself through the still morning air while I search for Rabbit Kettle Hot Springs. Like Yellowstone's Mammoth Hot Springs, Rabbit Kettle's mineral-rich water drips from one rimstone pool to the next, building terraced tufa domes that rise well above the surrounding trees. The domes, already ten thousand years old, rise a tenth of an inch a year. And as the Cub orbits the highest terraces, lenslike pools gaze upward from the centers of the domes, their azure pupils staring into my camera as I circle round and round.

Before leaving Glacier Lake, I attached my camcorder to the Cub's wing strut just beyond the propwash, then covered it with a small plastic bag. Now, as the Cub approaches the billowing spray from the cascades that lead to the falls, I slow to seventy mph, trim the nose up a tad, open the window and slowly lower the door. Removing my seat belt, I stow my glasses, lock a foot beneath the seat, grasp a brace with my left hand and slide to the right until I'm sitting on the edge of the door frame. Slowly forcing my hand, arm and shoulder, then head and chest into the slipstream, I remove the bag and switch on the camcorder. Back inside, I replace my seat belt and glasses, and descend to within a few feet of the Powerful River.

The South Nahanni, a. k. a. the River of Gold, has as its prize nugget a massive limestone spire bisecting Virginia Falls. Aiming just to the right of the tall flat-topped pyramid, I flit above the tumult as the river smashes through the Sluice Box to explode into mist against house-size slabs of stone. When the Nahanni's roar overcomes the Cub's noisy engine, I find myself glancing at the tachometer to confirm that the Continental is still running.

The Cub darts between layered walls of limestone and shale, bobbing in turbulent air while the river gnaws at its banks and plucks evergreens from its slopes. When the Cub soars over the falls, I briefly shove the nose down to capture the plunging water on tape, then add full throttle to climb out of the deep and twisting gorge. Reversing course, I fly upstream and land, then aim the camcorder backward for a rear-facing view of the falls. After editing, the tape will begin with spectacular cascades rearing against the Nahanni's midstream monolith, then end with acres of free-falling foam plunging over the falls.

When the filming's done, I land and secure the Cub to an improvement acquired by the Nahanni's status as a World Heritage Site—a pier just above the falls. Years ago, with neither beach nor pier available, I'd been forced to leap into the opaque river with a rope tied to the Cub in one hand while grabbing for a branch with the other. Although I'd hoped that the river would be shallow so close to shore, I wet my ankles all the way up to my armpits.

Now, in addition to the dock and a helicopter pad, campsites with fireplaces nestle in spruce and tamarack groves. Where I once staggered down a slippery trail to the bottom of the falls, a boardwalk undulates through blueberry bushes, leaving visitors free to savor the Nahanni's sights and scents and sounds.

A mist begins to fall. As Sunblood Mountain, the vanguard of the Sombre Range, probes the clouds across the river, I head downstream with my rifle in hand in case of Mr. Grizz, then stop at an enameled Park Service plaque set well back from the canyon's rim. At the top of the plaque, a canoe load of voyageurs paddle across a map of Canada. The plaque reads:

> The South Nahanni is one of the world's great wild rivers. Its visitors are treated to a unique blend of scenic grandeur, wilderness adventure and solitude. Tumultuous rapids and meandering calm water have cut deeply into the Mackenzie Mountains, creating three towering canyons and Virginia Falls, twice the height of Niagara. Deep caves puncture the walls of First Canyon. Rabbit Kettle Hotsprings have built the highest tufa mounds in Canada. In recognition of this unique heritage, the South Nahanni River has been proclaimed a Canadian Heritage River.

Minutes later, I'm standing at the brink, watching fifty-foot spruce go tumbling over the falls. Far below, tree trunks trapped in the deluge spin round and round, their bark sluiced away by the pummeling river, their amber skeletons pirouetting in swirls of foam. It occurs to me that I wouldn't mind dying in such a place, but then an absurdity strikes me—I'd soon tire of the noise. Give me Glacier Lake instead.

As the Cub climbs away from the river, I look down at the falls, remembering the cascade-generated rainbows of other years that so colorfully portrayed the Nahanni's Jekyll-like nature. But as the mist turns to rain, it's the valley's grim history that brings to mind Mr. Hyde.

Since the turn of the century, at least twenty men have died within the Nahanni's confining walls. Some drowned near Pulpit Rock, a huge spire that towers above the whirlpools below the falls. Others perished in the Rapids That Runs Both Ways, while a few froze nugget hard on their winter traplines.

The ill prepared or unlucky starved. Two burned to death in their cabins. Others vanished into the depths of the Funeral Range.

One winter, when five poorly supplied prospectors began to starve, one man tied a stick of dynamite to his chest and touched it off. Two of the survivors tried to hike out and disappeared, leaving two behind to tell their tale. And though Death Lake denotes a fatal seaplane crash, the most colorful of the maudlin tales occurred in Deadman's Valley, a. k. a. Headless Valley, which is named for two brothers who actually lost their heads in a fruitless search for gold.

Frank and Willie McCleod entered the Nahanni valley in 1904, accompanied by a fellow Scot. When they failed to return, a search party led by their brother, Charlie, stumbled onto their decapitated bodies. Some say that the McCleods had been tied to trees. Their companion was never found.

One Nahanni trader, on receiving a friend's jubilant message that he'd finally discovered gold, hurried off toward the prospector's claim, where instead of gold, he found a burned-out shack and another headless corpse.

In 1927, a Minnesotan-turned-Canadian named Albert Faille probed the Nahanni to its source, becoming, over the years, a legend of the North. As Albert aged, he was succeeded by Gus Kraus, a trapper and prospector who'd been roaming the Nahanni for close to fifty years, building cabins at Little Doctor Lake and at a twenty-acre hot-spring-fed oasis beside the Nahanni River called Kraus Hot Springs.

Despite being so far north, much of the Nahanni Valley managed to escape the last ice age; below Virginia Falls, the canyon has been ice-free for a quarter million years. As a result, the canyon has retained the nearly vertical walls carved by the river's tongue.

With wind, rain and sun constantly picking at the Nahanni's cliffs, I wonder if the sound of the passing Cub might loosen a chip from its limestone lip, descending not in miles per hour but in millions of years per layer as it falls to the river below. In its brief plunge, would it transit layers of geological time that span ten million years? Forty million? More?

The Cub soars through the depths of Third and Second Canyons, then descends farther below the rim as I search for openings in the ribboned dolomite of First Canyon, the most spectacular of all. Here, waterfalls spring like magic from thousand-foot cliffs, for this is karst country, a soluble land of underground rivers, limestone pinnacles, sinkholes and caves.

The karst caverns may be realms of wonder to geologists, but they're deadly traps for Dall sheep: more than a hundred Dall sheep skeletons lie in Valerie Caves alone. Closed not for safety but to protect the caves themselves, Ice Gallery and the opalescent formations of Igloo Cave have been declared off-limits to all but official visitors.

Near the end of First Canyon lies George's Riffle, the understatement of the park whose bucking-bronco waves and rollers as high as corn shocks point the way downstream toward the Liard River, brighter skies and flat, uninspiring terrain. I'm tempted to continue east to the safety of good weather and mundane surroundings, but instead I turn north toward a lovely but distant campsite that I've used many times before. Rimmed with blueberries and yellow potentilla, the beach tugs at me from beyond the mountain-enveloping clouds.

As I leave the Nahanni behind and head up Fishtrap Creek, I write the time, one-fifteen, on my map, then measure the distance to Little Doctor. It's fifty-seven miles. If the weather holds, I should be taxiing up to the beach in thirty-five minutes.

Fifteen minutes pass as the ceilings slowly descend. Visibility drops to five miles. Mud Lake, the halfway point to Little Doctor finally falls behind. The Cub crosses the height of land and enters the broad Tetcela River valley as I press on amid memories of a wrecked aircraft that I'd once spotted just ten miles off to the west. Upon reporting the wreck at Fort Simpson, I was told that it was an "old crash site—nothing to worry about."

One-forty brings a lowering five-hundred-foot ceiling. Forward visibility, which is always reduced by prop-shattered rain, has dropped to two miles. To either side, it's three or four. Hemmed in by clouds above, by the Franklin Mountains on the left and the Nahanni Range on the right, I fly on, ready return to Mud Lake if visibility drops to a mile.

I check my watch. Another minute gone and no lake in sight. Leaning forward in a mindless attempt to see better, I finger my skeleton key, then reach for the chart to compare its features to the convolutions of the Tetcela River. Surely two minutes have passed. I return to my watch. It's only forty seconds.

As the visibility drops, I think of Antoine de Saint-Exupéry. Lost at night over Egypt during an air race from Paris to Saigon, he descended through the darkness, searching for the lights of Cairo. Seeing nothing, he pressed his face against the window, tensely waiting for something, anything, to appear. "I was a man raking dead ashes, trying in vain to retrieve the flame of life in a hearth." He crashed—but survived.

Staying as high as possible, I scrape along the tattered underbelly of gray descending clouds. Another minute gone. Ceilings, 250 feet; visibility, two miles and shrinking. My hand complains, weary of crushing the stick in a snake-strangling grip. I change hands, then switch back, only to change again. Then, at one-forty-seven, thirty-two minutes after leaving the Nahanni, I see a light spot glowing through the mist. It's Little Doctor Lake.

Shaped like a round-nose arrowhead, the rain-stippled lake rams its tip through a three-thousand-foot cleft in the Nahanni Range toward a majestic beach. The Cub approaches tangent to the lake's curving lake shore, then slips between the treetops and taxis up to the beach.

Silence. Fresh from the tumult of Virginia Falls and the Cub's constant roar, I feel as if I've fallen into a feather bed. Under a nimbo-stratus blanket, the north country sleeps.

I hurriedly set up my tent, crushing spiderwebs bejeweled with mist. Later, with the flavor of vegetable beef soup still on my tongue and its heat comforting my body, I join the silence in sleep.

I awaken at six-thirty. It's still four hours until sunset, but the sky is almost dark. Only the steady hiss of rain assures me that the universe hasn't stopped. With my options reduced to reminiscing or reading, I turn again to Barbara Walker's revealing *Woman's Encyclopedia of Myths and Secrets*. An hour later, when the dwindling light censors my reading, it's still too early for sleep. Only memories remain.

When Wes Miller and I first arrived at Little Doctor, we had heard that Gus Kraus had built a tiny log cabin on the lake's western shore. However, since Gus spent most of his time in the Nahanni Valley, we were surprised to find not only Gus, but Mary, his Slavey Indian wife, and Mickey, their son. After introductions, I asked Gus how long he'd been roaming the Nahanni country.

"Maybe fifty years," he quietly replied as he hooked his thumbs in his broad suspenders, "except for a few months now and then in Fort Simpson."

Envisioning the long nights of the northern winters, I said, "I don't know if I'd be able handle a whole winter up here, but I might make it at those hot springs back in the canyon—if they're hot enough to make a difference."

"They are," replied Gus. "Even in January, the ground's warm enough to keep our cabin in the sixties. The snow across the river can be three feet deep, but we'll have bare ground outside. We only cut wood for cooking."

"How about gold?" I asked. "Did you ever find any gold?"

"No, I never did—but it's there. Someday they'll find it. Most likely a big outfit with a hired crew."

Then Wes said, "I've always wondered what it would be like to find gold. Not just a few flakes, you know, but some big chunks that would really add up."

"Me too," said Gus, as his weathered face stretched into a smile. "You want to know what I'd do if I stumbled onto a potful? Maybe get a new boat and motor." Then, with a sweep of his hand toward the Nahanni's peaks, he added, "But I'd never leave this."

That evening, as we watched the shadows creep up the sun-reddened Nahannis, Wes remembered Gus's suggestion that we use our binoculars to scan the range for sheep. Sitting on the beach, elbows on knees, he began the search. Within minutes, Wes said, "There they are."

Gus was right. Our ten-power binoculars easily transformed meaningless flecks into Dall sheep. And as the shadows climbed higher, we passed the binoculars back and forth, watching Dall sheep graze lofty meadows in the fading mountain light.

A few years after Wes died, the Tundra Cub again slid to a stop at the Little Doctor beach, this time accompanied by Ron Funk's Lake amphibian, a Piper Super Cruiser flown by Homer and Paul Bruggeman, and Stu Peel's Super Cub.

Earlier that day, as we crossed the rolling hills of Wood Buffalo Park, I'd radioed my companions, "Take a good look around, guys, and remember this when you're in the rest home!" Later, when someone complained that he was getting hungry, I urged him to fly another hundred miles, replying, "The weather's too good to quit. You can always eat, you know, but you can't fly in a rest home." Over the following hours, the rest-home line evolved into a standing joke as my companions listed additional delights we'd have to forgo when senility clipped our wings. That evening, we camped at Little Doctor Lake, ready to head for the mountains in the morning.

Daylight came. At five-thirty I looked out from my tent, saw no one and heard nothing but snores. Because we needed to get to Virginia Falls and back before the afternoon winds tied the mountain skies in knots, I noisily arose at six-thirty and began to prepare breakfast. When no one appeared, I yelled, "Come on, guys! You can sleep in the rest home!"

From inside one of the tents came the reply, "Not if you're around!"

Stu's packing philosophy and mine lie poles apart. Like John Hornby, I'm compulsive about traveling light. Do I really need this? Will A fit into B? As a result, I have less than Stu to carry, but I'm sometimes short on comfort.

Stu, on the other hand, packs all the refinements that I eschew. His cargo speaks of a wealthy trader, mine of an ascetic making do. Like Jonathon Jo's "wheelbarrow full of surprises," Stu's Super Cub seemed to me a cornucopia.

By the time we'd reached Little Doctor, I'd become accustomed to Stu's pulling his lawn chair up to his portable table beneath a sheltering tarp. Had he appeared in tails and addressed the evening's fillet with a glass of sauterne at his side, I wouldn't have been surprised. But that evening, Stu added yet another refinement, a tape player and a sampling of the classics. As a full moon climbed above the Nahanni Range, the soothing strains of Pachelbel's Canon in D rose above our campsite and wafted over the lake.

Thoughts of wine remind me of a treat in one of the floats—a twenty-five-ounce can of Foster's beer. With my Australian treasure in mind, I'd asked the Talisman's cook to hard-boil two eggs while I ate lunch. Then I sealed them in a plastic bag and stowed them away in a float compartment. Shaded by the wing and cooled by frigid lakes and rivers, my refrigerator-in-a-float works wonderfully well for up to several days.

I probe the darkness with my pocket flashlight. It's raining, but the drizzle doesn't dampen my passion for boiled eggs and beer, and after a quick dash to the shelter of the wing and back, I sit cross-legged, plate in lap, beneath a flashlight attached to the roof of the tent.

A tap or two on my knee and the eggs slip like wet ivory from within their shells. Before each bite, I touch them to a little mound of salt, though I know the extra salt will probably make my ears hiss, saying, I told you sssssso. One egg disappears, then the other, washed down with an abundance of beer. Twenty-five ounces, however, is more than I can manage, so I pour the excess out and enlarge the opening of the can with my pocket knife, knowing that during the night I'll need to return its contents. As barroom sages have observed from Nepal to Nairobi to Nome, "One doesn't purchase beer, one rents it."

Morning. Still raining. And *humid*. Visibility no more than a hundred feet. By ten o'clock, the fog has risen to fifty feet, but with the Cub's altimeter still unchanged, there'll be no flying today. Besides, I'd planned to stay for several days.

When the drizzle ends, I hike toward a stream that relieves Little Doctor Lake. I trudge along the beach, thinking about grayling until I come upon a string of bear tracks. Big as dinner plates, each print sports three-inch-long claws. Reversing course, I retrieve my Marlin rifle.

Before, I'd walked in silence. Now, I break into song, shattering the stillness with "Clementine," "The Beer Barrel Polka" and an occasional whistle. When I reach the river, I set the Marlin at the water's edge and toss my flip-top lure into its riffles.

The lure settles. I crank it in, then cast again and again. An hour later, I finally concede defeat and head back to camp, where I flip the lure fifty yards beyond the Cub's tail.

A fish shatters the surface with a twisting leap, stripping line from my reel as I walk along the beach to parallel its course. I'm sure it's a trout.

When the fish tires, I discover the largest grayling I've ever seen. Were it not for its sail-like russet-rimmed dorsal fin, its size alone might convince me that I'd found a new species. But it's definitely a grayling and, at over three pounds, a big one. Like all graylings, he wears the iridescent badge of his Arctic home, the aurora, but his colors seem to fade as I lift him from the lake. Were he smaller, he'd be my lunch. I let him go and opt for pancakes.

With coffee boiling and bacon sizzling on the stove, I dig out a container of mix, add water and a handful of blueberries, screw on the top and rhumba back and forth along the beach while shaking my batter like a James Bond martini. Fresh blueberry hot cakes, maple syrup, bacon and coffee. What a fantastic meal!

As I finish the dishes, a shower drives me back to my three-man tent, which really means two men if you plan to include any baggage. Rolling up my sleeping bag for a headrest, I finish Sagan's *Demon-Haunted World*.

Still raining. I sort through my gear while chuckling at myself for thinking that I, the proverbial rolling stone, could stay put for more than a day. I'm already becoming bored.

I lever the shells from the Marlin, insert a scrap of paper in the breech and sight through the barrel, pleased to see that the rifling's clean and sharp. Slipping my Bic pen into the Marlin's muzzle, I discover that Bic makes a .32 caliber pen, then drift into fantasy, envisioning a psycho writer using a pen-loaded pistol to dust off unfeeling reviewers who disdain his masterful works.

When the rain finally stops, I taxi to the base of the Nahanni Range. It's too wet for walking in the bush and, considering the bear tracks, maybe not too bright, but the lakeside edge of the rocky slope is almost brush-free.

Two weeks of flying have left me out of shape, so I take it easy. Even so, I soon puff to a stop. When I stretch out a hand to lean against a nearby pine, a blueberry squeezes from beneath its scaly bark. I check the other trees and find a scattering of berries. Something, perhaps a Canada or Stellar jay, has been stocking its winter larder.

Despite my complaining calves and quivering thighs, I delay resting until I reach the base of the clouds, which have risen some three hundred feet. Should I stop here, content to enjoy this gray yet marvelous view, or head farther up, perhaps high enough to break through the clouds into the pastures of the Dall sheep?

Since the Cub will be downhill and to the right when I return, I can't get lost, so I head into the clouds, taking care to angle away from the mountain's precipitous edge as I climb not so much into fog as into another world. As my vision is restricted, nearby evergreens leap into prominence. Every needle is sequined with dew. Spiderwebs sag, transformed by beads of moisture into strings of tiny seed pearls.

I climb for five minutes through the vaporous world, then stop to rest while my pulse pounds in my ears. How strange, I think, that the phenomenon that we call a "cloud" when we're outside of it, becomes "fog" when we're within. They're identical, of course, composed of billions of water droplets so fine that they float in billows. Then a new thought strikes me: Would radio-astronomy be the only possibility on a perpetually cloudy planet? What sort of eyes would evolve? How would we explain the seasons?

A flurry of sound upslope jerks me alert. Beginning as a rustle, it moves rapidly downhill, snapping twigs as it heads my way. Straining to see into the fog, I whirl around, thumb back the Marlin's hammer and point it toward the onrushing intruder. Crash! Thump! Splinter! Spotting motion in the mist, I raise my rifle as a boulder as big as a basketball comes barreling into view and bounces out of sight. I sigh with relief, then laugh out loud—I almost shot a rock.

The unseen rustling above continues, bringing visions of a busy wolverine or marmot. I consider climbing farther to see if I'm right, but I've had enough excitement. An hour later, in pouring rain, thunder rolls from peak to peak.

Toward evening, a lightening sky persuades me to build a fire. Since everything's soaked, I gather up a heap of wood, douse it with a cup or two of gasoline from the Cub, stand back and toss in a match. With an explosive *pow*!, the pile erupts into flame.

What a marvelous thing is fire. It lifts our sagging spirits, defeats the coldest morning and brightens flagstone skies. But the best fires are those that scent the air with the resinous vapors of pine, of tamarack or spruce. As if agreeing with me, my crackling blaze shoots off tiny rockets while it warms my face and paints shadows on the jackpine forest wall.

Too well rested to sleep and mesmerized by the dancing flames, I dredge up vivid camp stories of ravenous bears and narrow escapes, few of which probably happened.

My own encounters with bears include a hungry Yellowstone bear that climbed up onto my car, leaving a huge dent in the roof that I removed by lying on the back seat and pushing upward with my feet. Still, that's not the sort of bear that's on my mind. It's a young black bear that I shot a long, long time ago.

When I was sixteen, I bought a used 30-40 Krag, a relic of the Spanish-American War. That fall, when a bear came snooping around my parents' cabin, I ducked inside for the Krag. Then, after chambering a round with the rifle's unbelievably smooth, slick-sliding bolt, I slipped out the door.

The bear, some sixty yards distant and retreating, made the mistake of stopping when he heard the hinges squeal. Laying the sights on his chest, I touched the trigger. With a thunderous report, the rifle rammed my frame, digging its no-nonsense steel-plated stock into my bony shoulder.

The bullet caught the bear exactly where I'd aimed, throwing him, shrieking, ten feet into the brush. Still screaming like a human on a spit, he ran sixty feet and dropped. Rifle ready, I walked up to the gasping bear. Like Aldo Leopold, who, when young and "full of trigger itch," had watched the "fierce green fire" fade in a dying wolf's eyes, I was stunned. Accustomed to deer that obligingly fall without complaint, I'd expected a similar end. The bear's screams, however, stripped away my illusions and my isolation from the deed.

After peeling his hide from his suddenly gelatinous body, we sliced him into roasts and steaks. We ate the meat, but mine went down poorly. I sold the Krag. Tonight, sitting in my tent, as isolated as the last person on earth, I'm tempted to apologize like an Inuk, citing my need and respect. But, in truth, I was motivated only by "want" and, until the animal screamed had only felt indifference.

Fed up with bears, and prompted by a star glimmering through a tiny break in the overcast, I turn to a subject that surely must tantalize every lonely red-blooded male—Olbers' Paradox: If space is infinite and there are an infinite number of stars, as many propose, why is the night sky dark?

In 1823, Heinrich Olbers, a German physician and astronomer, reasoned that if space and the number of stars are infinite, the sky should blaze both day and night. However, as everyone knows, that simply isn't the case.

Scientists, philosophers and laymen offered solutions—most of them inferior to a theory that one gloomy American author proposed. In his *Eureka*, that writer suggested that the universe is still so young and the void so great that the light from the most distant stars has yet to reach us. Though we know him only as America's premier author of horror stories, Edgar Allan Poe's solution ranked with the best.

Later, others expanded on Poe, arguing that the unlimited but still empty universe surrounding the still-expanding star-filled universe within accounts for the paucity of starlight. Some postulated that in a fifteen billion-year-old-universe, many stars could have perished, leaving a void where once they gleamed.

What will happen, I ask myself, if a few billion years hence, our expanding universe slows to a halt, or, worse yet, begins to contract? As our skies brighten, what will we do with street lights, with headlights? What will become of the last drive-in movies? When the earth becomes a sauna, will our M&M's melt in our hands before they get to our mouths?

A shuffling sound wakens me—and it's definitely not a boulder. I quietly slip out of my sleeping bag, pull back the Marlin's hammer and point its barrel toward the approaching crackling. I expect the tent wall to bulge inward at any second, but the shuffling turns aside, then slowly moves away. I quietly slide to the front of the tent, ease it open and poke my head outside. Twenty feet away, a porcupine chews on a jack pine. I sag with relief.

"Hey, buddy!" I yell. "What are you doin', wakin' me up at this hour?" He examines me with his tiny black eyes.

Lowering the Marlin's hammer, I approach the porcupine and touch the rifle to his rear. Swat! His tail strikes out, scattering quills across the ground. I retrieve a few, then wrap them in duct tape—a gift for my grandchildren back home.

Preoccupied by the porcupine, I'm surprised to see clearing skies. Across the lake, the first sliver of a rising sun gilds the Nahanni Range as the last wisp of fog disappears and dew drips from the wings of the waiting Cub. Every bush is a liquid chandelier. Thousands of tiny spheres bejewel my tent. Unable to resist, I jar them into rivulets with a flick of my finger. Then, confronted with such a glorious day, I sail into a rendition of "Oh, What a Beautiful Morning..."

I glance at my watch. It's four o'clock! I could pack up and head for Simpson, but it's less than an hour away, and I'd end up sitting on the dock, waiting for the town to come to life. Besides, everything's wet.

Although I'm certain that my slumbers are done, I slip into my sleeping bag. As silhouetted beads of tent-wall dew coalesce before my eyes, I plunge back into sleep.

The Tundra Cub plows nose-high for a few seconds, then planes across the placid water of Little Doctor Lake. I lift one wing, letting the Cub skates along in a one-footed turn to follow the arc of the beach. The Cub breaks free, trailing tails of spray from floats and fuselage as it climbs into silken air.

Misty-eyed at leaving this Eden, I scan the lake, the forests and the surrounding peaks. Like a parting lover, I soak up every contour and curve and squeeze them into memory. Fifteen minutes later, the Nahanni Range lies miles behind, its bold peaks dwindling to dreams as they slowly disappear. After a third last look over my shoulder, I search the eastern horizon for a town by the name of Fort Simpson, just thirty minutes away.

Six

FORT SIMPSON
TO MINNESOTA

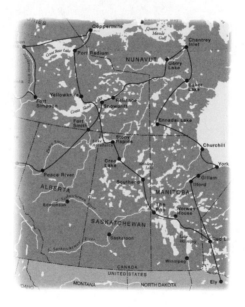

14

Fort Simpson to Coppermine, Nunavut

If a man would be alone, let him look at the stars.

— RALPH WALDO EMERSON

N 1804, THE HUDSON'S BAY COMPANY established the Fort of the Forks trading post on a long lens-shaped island near the junction of the Mackenzie and Liard Rivers. Renamed Fort Simpson in 1821, the town was until recently the end of the line for wheeled vehicles. But today, it's just a wayside stop, for the Mackenzie Road now follows the north-flowing river for another two hundred miles.

I tie up behind Simpson Air's multi-million-dollar twin turbo-prop Otter that's roped to the Mackenzie's riverside wharves. A flittering of dragonflies follows me to the top of the thirty-foot bank to search for a phone. Finding none, I return to the Cub and radio the airport, which relays my request for fuel. While I wait, the dragonflies patrol the riverbank, scooping mosquitoes out of the air as I contemplate the fates of two very different but related men who bore the name of Simpson. Both served the Hudson's Bay Company well, but one achieved wealth and acclaim, while the other died tragically, his character suspect.

As the winter of 1820 drew to a close, George Simpson, a polite, unprepossessing clerk at the Hudson's Bay Company post at Fort Chipewyan, could never have guessed that by year's end, thanks to his diligent work (and a lack of competition) he would have become Governor Simpson, the HBC's commander of all the North. Using tact, good sense and trust in his employees, the cherubic but demanding new governor promptly set out to ease old hatreds between the men of the just-wedded Hudson's Bay and North West Companies.

Simpson, by example and logic, persuaded former competitors who had even hunted each other to start anew. Aided by his excellent administrative skills and his open nature, Simpson would guide the Bay for close to forty years, a feat that earned him title of the Little Emperor, although never to his face. During Simpson's reign, and until the end of the nineteenth century, currency was virtually unknown in the North. Instead, the Bay used a barter system; one prime adult-size beaver pelt being the unit of trade—a practical solution that arose from the fact that in the beginning, the fur trade consisted almost exclusively of beaver pelts.

As other furs became popular, and a means of exchange based upon fractional values of a prime beaver pelt became necessary, the Company decided to "make a beaver" by establishing a smaller unit called a "Made Beaver" or MB. Near the close of the nineteenth century, one prime beaver pelt had a value of from ten to twelve MB. The standard in the lands farther north that lacked beavers was the pelt of a prime white fox.

After a trapper's pelts had been evaluated and their worth converted to an equivalent of Made Beaver, the trapper was paid with numbered disks made of ivory or shell or with quills (feathers or porcupine), depending on the post and availability. With these, he purchased whatever supplies he could afford, rarely leaving the post with any leftover MB, which, in most cases, could only be used at the issuing post. At various locations, "tokens" made of flat sticks, pieces of copper or lead embossed with the numeral 1 carried the value of one MB, but eventually, brass HBC tokens replaced them all.

Under this system, a large blanket might cost ten MB. Near the end of the nineteenth century, the same hatchet that Sears and Roebuck offered for 50 cents might cost one MB, and twelve could buy a rifle.

Guided by Simpson's frugal hand, Hudson's Bay stores remained cold long after stoves became available, for unheated stores saved money and were much less likely to burn. Furthermore, an unheated store not only discouraged loungers but also encouraged trapping. Damaged or worn-out boats were often burned to recover their nails, not so much as an economy measure but because nails were often in short supply.

Once relieved of the costs of competing with its old rival, the Bay quickly matured into an efficient, profitable company. During Simpson's time, dividends to shareholders always exceeded 10 percent, partly because the factors could charge whatever the traffic would bear, often exceeding the official Company rate of exchange by applying the "Factor's Standard." Simpson, who gradually turned the stodgy Bay into an upcoming giant, was knighted in 1841. He retired to a small town near Montreal, where he died in 1860.

Thomas Simpson, the governor's nephew, labored for the Company no less faithfully than his uncle, though often under miserable conditions. An excellent explorer and surveyor, Thomas canoed and backpacked the thousand difficult miles of Arctic coastline between Alaska's Point Barrow and Chantrey Inlet, twice enduring harrowing winters at a Great Bear Lake hovel called Fort Confidence. But instead of earning timely recognition that could have changed the course of his life, Thomas netted only a belated and useless reward.

After working faithfully for thirteen years, Simpson sought permission to explore the west coast of Baffin Island, a huge body of land lying well to the north of Quebec. The project carried his uncle's endorsement, but his repeated requests moved slowly through the London offices of the Bay.

Discouraged at the lack of response, Thomas in 1839 set out on a two-thousand-mile trek from the Arctic coast to Red River, a settlement near Winnipeg, Manitoba, where he hoped to receive a reply. Finding none, he snapped. With four companions, the embittered Simpson headed east for the nearest port. What happened next is still a source of debate. Within days, two of the five returned to Red River, where they claimed that Simpson had shot their two companions. The survivors fled, then retraced their steps after hearing another shot—and found Simpson dead.

If the survivors spoke the truth, Thomas Simpson died a murderer. If not, he was a tragic victim, murdered by those who returned to Red River, where, within days, a mail packet arrived. Within the packet, a letter addressed to Thomas Simpson approved his request and awarded him the Queen's Arctic medal with a life pension of £100 a year.

Coppermine, my next destination and the goal of Churchill's Samuel Hearne, lies five hundred miles to the north on an Arctic Ocean backwater called the Coronation Gulf. But today, I'll fly a dogleg course, first down the Mackenzie to Norman Wells, where I'll angle off to the northeast toward Coppermine.

When the Cub's finally fueled, I hike into town to Fat Daddy's Drive-In, where, undeterred, or perhaps spurred on by, the diner's name, I pack it in. Outside again, I ask a native lounging against the building for directions to the Dene monument, only to have him slump to the ground. I'm about to call for help when I'm assailed by the smell of booze. (Just as the people whom we once called Eskimos prefer the word Inuit, the aboriginal natives of the northern provinces and the Territories have chosen the word Dene, meaning "the people.")

Fortunately, I've a pretty good idea where the monument is, and I'm soon standing before a low, platformlike marker that commemorates the 1975 gathering of the Indian Brotherhood. Here, three hundred delegates met to adopt the Dene Declaration: a demand for self-determination, world recognition as a distinct people, recognition of the Dene Nation and independence within Canada.

As I contemplate their goals, I consider the problems: in the Territories (where liquor consumption is 50 percent higher than in the provinces), the suicide rate for Inuit and Dene youths between fifteen and twenty-five is six times the national average.

The Cub overtakes a Northern Transport barge. Its decks are jammed with pipe, vehicles, crated snowmobiles, building supplies, appliances and construction equipment from Hay River, the three-hundred-mile-distant rail terminus on Great Slave Lake's southwestern shore. By the time the barge reaches saltwater at Tuktoyuktuk, she'll have been ten days en route. Pressing on through the foulest weather with the aid of GPS, navigation buoys and shore-mounted reflectors, this diesel-powered barge and its crew of three or four is a far cry from old sternwheelers like the SS *Mackenzie*, whose sixteen stokers fed her firebox a cord of wood an hour.

A deckhand waves. As I rock the Cub in reply, I hope that Canadians have learned a lesson from our sewering of the Mississippi, which we now labor to restore. Thirty minutes later, the river becomes Mackenzie's Disappointment River when it turns north at Camsell Bend.

Bored with flying down the wide superhighway, I make a torpedo run at Berry Island, then set my sights on McGern. McGern Island, being much larger than Berry, is more stubborn, absorbing five of my mental torpedoes before it slips beneath the waves. Then, as Jones Landing falls behind, I lower the nose and hurtle down the Mackenzie a few feet above the waves, seeking the thrill of low-level seaplane flying that the English adventurer Sir Francis Chichester described in *Ride on the Wind*: "I was only a foot or two above the water ... The exhilaration of the flying stimulated and excited me til I felt half intoxicated with it. It was an almost incredible delight . . . and it left the once considered marvel of landplane flying as a dull old sow."

Cranking in a bit of nose-up trim as a safety measure, I counter the trim with a touch of forward pressure on the stick. (If I get distracted and release the stick, the nose-up trim will automatically cause the Cub to climb.) For twenty miles, the Cub roars along in ground effect just above the Mackenzie's face. Then, as the village of Wrigley appears on the horizon, my chart slips off my lap and disappears between the rudder pedals.

After climbing ten to fifteen feet, I duck my head beneath the panel and reach for the map, taking care not to push forward on the stick. It's quite a stretch, but within a few seconds my fingers close on the map. Just then, I spot a candy wrapper lying against the firewall and, in spite of warning myself to look around before I retrieve it, take a few extra seconds to get it within my grasp.

The Cub is a *light* airplane. Fully loaded, it weighs only thirteen hundred pounds. Shift just fifty pounds a few inches forward and her nose will begin to drop. And though I'm certain that I've cranked in enough trim to keep the nose up as I reach beneath the panel, I'm about to learn that I'm wrong.

As my head comes back above the panel and my hand returns to the stick, the Cub receives two almost simultaneous, staggering jolts as the keels of her floats slice into the Mackenzie at ninety miles per hour. Fortunately, I've just begun to pull back on the stick, and the Cub staggers skyward as I gasp in disbelief.

Fatalists might say that my time just wasn't up, but I credit the nose-up trim for flattening what could otherwise have been a fatal plunge. Without it, the Cub would have descended more steeply and flipped onto its back, like the Cessna of a Minnesota pilot who landed his seaplane with the nose too low. The aircraft flipped, ripping off the front four feet of both floats. The pilot died.

Although I'd known about that accident for many years, its lesson had never hit home. Now, as Wrigley slips past, I curse myself for a fool. Never again will I fly within fifty feet of *anything*, except when landing.

A few decades ago, events at Wrigley and several other northern villages prompted the bush pilot Mike Thomas to write scathingly about the government's entanglement with religion.

In an angry letter, Thomas told Yellowknife's *News of the North* how he'd been hired to fly children away from their homes to church-run schools in the Anglicans' *Norseman* while a friend, Buzz Gresl, flew for the Catholics.

"We'd fly into a settlement, park the plane, and when everybody came down to see the airplane, the Anglican hostel manager would start grabbing kids to take them off to school. Their parents didn't know what was going on.

"I'll never forget Fort Wrigley. . . . The priest and a nun were there grabbing kids and the Anglican guy was grabbing kids. . . . We flew back to Fort Simpson and we went back down the river again, grabbing kids. . . .

"I was back in Fort Wrigley at Christmas. I landed on the ice and this little lady came trudging down on snowshoes. She said 'Where did you take my kids?' She didn't know where her kids were from fall until Christmas. . . .

"Then I started having a better look at this. You see, the church-run schools were getting paid so much a head by the government for each kid they had in a hostel. It was a very competitive business."

Thomas's remarks brought an immediate response. "I got a visitor from Ottawa. He came right to Fort Simpson and he told me to mind my own business. I told him, 'Look, I'm not afraid of you. I don't work for the government. I'm not a Catholic, and I'm not an Anglican.'

"I never got another hour of flying from Northern Health; I never got another hour from Forestry. They completely grounded me. That was the way they worked in those days."

Before the Liard River was dammed, every flood carried a tangle of trees downstream to Fort Simpson, knitting branches and trunks into those contributed by the Nahanni. Reaching the Mackenzie, the aquatic "treeline" divided the big river into parallel halves for hundreds of miles—some say all the way to the ocean.

The first time I followed the waterborne ribbon of trees, a westerly wind had pushed it toward the river's eastern shore. But as Fort Norman approached, the linear snarl suddenly returned to center stream, moving *against* the wind. Puzzled at first, I soon spotted the driving force: the voluminous Great Bear River, the outflow of Great Bear Lake. When I finally left the Mackenzie at Norman Wells, I looked downriver, seeking the end of the backbone of trees. It wasn't in sight.

Expanding north along the Mackenzie River, the Hudson's Bay Company set up posts about every 150 miles, usually at the intersections of major waterways. At the junction of the Great Bear and Mackenzie Rivers, they established Fort Norman, a tiny community guarded by a hulking, spruce-topped headland. For a time, Fort Norman prospered, until the advent of barges and planes and the discovery of oil at Norman Wells, the next settlement downstream.

A few miles up the Great Bear River lies Fort Franklin, a tiny community named, for the same captain who eventually led his crews to their deaths near Chantrey Inlet. After barely surviving his first trek to the coast in 1821, Franklin again headed north from Fort Simpson in 1825. (Governor Simpson noted that Franklin was "incompetent" and "ill-prepared.")

Franklin even recorded native warnings in his journal, included the words of Akaitcho: "However, if . . . you are determined to go, some of my young men will join the party, because it shall not be said that we permitted you to die alone." Ignoring Akaitcho, Franklin set off for the Arctic Ocean—and survived only because of native charity. Undaunted, he returned to England, where he re-equipped with a store of delights for his table, then set off to search for the North West Passage and disappeared.

While I clean the flattened mosquitoes and blackflies from my windshield, Pete, the fuel truck driver tells me that he's lived at Norman Wells for close to forty years.

"So when did they find oil?" I ask.

"Just before World War I," he replies. "The Imperial Oil Company built a small refinery for local needs, but they didn't develop the field until the beginning of World War II. By the end of the war, we were pumping close to a million gallons a day through that little three-inch Canol pipeline to the refinery at Whitehorse. But when the war ended they cut production 85 percent and shut the pipeline down."

"Wow, that's a huge drop."

"Yeah," says Pete. "But the pipeline really never worked very well, and it was too expensive to maintain. In the sixties, when demand for fuel increased along the Mackenzie, Imperial added another refinery, and now we pump more oil than during the war. A lot of it heads south through a new pipeline, but nothing goes through the Canol."

An aircraft drones past, followed shortly by two more.

"Are you always this busy?" I ask.

"Most of the time," he says. "Between the airport and the seaplane base, we log about three thousand flights a year. It's the oil, eh? Not bad for a town of a few hundred."

Heavy with extra fuel, the Cub departs for Coppermine. I'll be able to fine-tune my course as soon as I spot massive Great Bear Lake, so I just settle for a northeast heading. But when the lake finally appears, it's directly in front of the cowling, though it should be off to the right.

On checking my chart, I discover that the compass deviation has risen to forty degrees, ten more than at Juneau. Were I to fly above or in the clouds with a ten degree error, I'd miss Coppermine by at least seventy miles.

The Cub angles across Great Bear's northern shore, then crosses the Arctic Circle near a scattering of gasoline drums. Empty fifty-five-gallon barrels, the "Alaskan State Flower," litter much of the North, their red, yellow, blue and white carcasses left to rust whenever the cost of removing them exceeds their value. Canadians call them "arctic poppies," another of our additions to the flora of the North.

Some of the barrels are put to use: docks float on them. They prop up buildings, store water and turn doors or planks into tables. Cut in half, they become basins, barbecues or bathtubs and, when sliced at an angle, the core of a makeshift wheelbarrow. With their ends removed, they find use as well-casings and culverts, and what traveler hasn't seen the empty drum's most frequent application: the barrel stove.

A massive wall of stone appears on the horizon. Rolling over hill and valley like the Great Wall of China, the "wall" is some forty feet across and sixty feet high. Geologists call these formations "dikes" when they're vertical, and "sills" when they're not. Both form when molten rock forces its way through a rift in the earth. As time erodes the softer surrounding rocks, the harder intrusion resists, and the once-buried wall slowly "rises" above the plain.

I decide to follow the wall to its northern end. Ten miles pass, then twenty, with still no end in sight, so I turn east toward a fifty-mile scimitar of water that's known as Dismal Lakes. Surrounded by thousand-foot sunlit hills, the maligned lakes look positively inviting, and I'm tempted to stop and camp despite their depressing name.

Vilhjalmur Stefansson, the Canadian-born American explorer who advanced Arctic exploration by adopting Inuit ways, explored this area in the early 1900s. After living comfortably along the Arctic coastline and on the pack ice for a total of nine years (getting to read his obituary twice) he wrote in *The Friendly Arctic* how Dismal Lakes was named.

> A young man by the name of Thomas Simpson had come direct from his home among the woods and hedges of England. . . . here for the first time in his life he was face to face with open country. He came to a lake about thirty miles long surrounded by hills of various form. There were trees at the east end, but he could only see them in the far distance. . . . He named it Dismal Lake. And in his book he goes nearly to the limits of the language in telling us how desolate and dreary, forlorn and forbidding, blasted and barren the country was.

Half a century later there grew up in England a man by the name of David Hanbury [the Hanbury River, with its caribou-devouring Dickson Canyon, bears his name]. . . . For one thing, he had purchased a ranch . . . in Wyoming. He was familiar with the prairie and even the uninhabited prairie. He had read Thomas Simpson's book and the adjectives had made enough impression on him so that when he approached he expected the place to live up to its name. . . . Perhaps partly as a reaction against Simpson, he goes to the other extreme and describes the lake as a wilderness paradise. I have lived a year in the vicinity of Dismal Lake and visited it both summer and winter, and I agree with Hanbury that a man who describes such a place as dismal, desolate and dreary is talking nothing of interest.

Though their beaches beckon, and their rapids promise grayling and char, I decide that Dismal Lakes are just too broad for my taste. I greatly prefer sheltered water, so I leave them behind and land on Elbow Lake, where I climb stiffly from the Cub and tail it onto the beach. Then, attracted by the sparkling ripples at my feet, I fill my hands with diamond-clear water and drink it down. Farther south, I wouldn't do this, but here there are no polluters, and certainly no beavers, which often dispense gut-wrenching giardia.

A sudden wail breaks the silence. Fifty yards away, a loon rides Elbow Lake. Drawing it close with my binoculars, I see it's an arctic loon. Neat and stately as his southern cousins, his body of gentleman's gray has vertical neck stripes of black and white, except for the front of his throat, which is spotlessly black. Unlike the common loon, which needs a long water run to become airborne, the arctic loon can lift off with a shorter, ducklike dash. His call, like his cousins', includes bursts of hysterical laughter and cries of deep despair.

When the ridge top behind my campsite beckons, I gather my binoculars, camera, rifle and a handful of Tootsie Rolls. The westerly breeze suggests I won't need a head net, but I take it anyway.

A narrow band of tussock grass separates the beach from my tent site, which is fleeced with arctic cotton. Spotting a cluster of yellow cinquefoil, I stoop to check their scent, only to find the knee-high brush teeming with wind-bound mosquitoes.

As I climb, my thoughts return to Stefansson, who walked these hills ninety years ago, having acquired an affinity for open country on the North Dakota plains and, as a friend noted, "an unabashed philosophy of eternal youth, complete with revolt and optimism." Combined with his logical mind, those characteristics almost guaranteed his success in the Arctic—a success that heightened his contempt for the British, whom Stefansson regarded as incompetent for having sacrificed so many lives while learning "next to nothing."

Stefansson reasoned that if the Inuit could survive for centuries with ingenuity and patience, those equipped with a rifle and the good sense to adopt their ways should fare at least as well. He also took a dim view of those who headed north in search of "adventure." Thus, when I think of my escapades, it's Stefansson who deflates me: "An adventure is a sign of incompetence."

Stefansson, despite being widely praised, refused to glorify his experiences, remarking that "everything you add to an explorer's heroism you have to subtract from his intelligence." Neither overly proud nor selfish, Stefansson took pains to share his moments of territorial discovery and promoted others' skills. Unlike Arctic explorers who shot their dogs to save weight and dog food on long trips, Stefansson loved his dogs. On the death of Lindy, his favorite, Stefansson wrote, "I lost my best friend in the world, whom I shall never forget."

Stefansson, always the optimist, saw great possibilities for the Canadian north. In 1922, recognizing the coming practicality of transpolar flights, he predicted, "It will be commonplace for Americans and Europeans to travel east by heading north. . . . We shall soon be booking passage from New York to Liverpool, or London to Tokyo . . . by plane in as matter-of-course a way as we now book passage by steamer."

Those who used the term "barren grounds" in Stefansson's presence seldom did so twice. In *The Friendly Arctic*, Stefansson wrote, "Barren Ground is a libelous name . . . better adapted to creating the impression that those who travel in the North are intrepid adventurers than it is for conveying to the reader a true picture of the country. If we want to be near the truth, we should rather follow Ernest Thompson Seton, who is so impressed with the grasslands of the North that he makes the expression, *The Arctic Prairies* the title of his book."

Stefansson scorned the way most hunters use binoculars: "The green man stands erect with his heels together, lifts the glasses jauntily to his eyes and spins slowly around on one heel. Then he announces that there is no game in sight.

"The experienced hunter . . . will lie down flat with his elbows on the ground. . . . There is never any pivoting or swinging motion as he brings the glasses to bear on successive fields of view. He examines one field thoroughly . . . then moves them so the second field overlaps the first. In calm weather . . . it takes about fifteen minutes for one good look around. . . . If, for instance, somewhere near the limit of the power of the glasses is seen a patch that may be a caribou, but which also may be a stone or wolf, it may take an hour of study to make sure."

Fortunately, the bald granite ridge holds no insects to harass me while I emulate Stefansson's methodical search for game. I lie down as instructed. Granite bites my elbows. Cushioning one with a handkerchief and the other with my head net, I stare for three minutes—motionless—then shift to the next field of view. Halfway through, my neck begins to hurt. I cheat by sitting with my elbows on my knees. A blurry butterfly flutters past, all of twenty feet away.

While searching the third field, my eyes begin to water. In the fourth, I find big game—a ground squirrel digging into a distant hillside. In the fifth, caribou antlers catch my eye, but on careful inspection become curved branches, dead and bleached. Discouraged and eye-weary, I rise and swivel like Stefansson's greenhorn and conclude there's "no game in sight."

On a whim, I raise the Marlin to my shoulder, aim at the center of Elbow Lake and squeeze the trigger. The rifle roars, rocketing a nearby well-camouflaged ptarmigan into flight. It's hard to say which of us is more surprised. I lever a new round into the chamber, lower the hammer and pick up the cartridge to savor the sharp but pleasant scent of spent powder. Bringing it to my lips, I blow across its rim, drawing forth a soft and sibilant *C*, then amble back to the Cub, picking poppies along the way.

Fed and soon to bed, I sit elbows on knees on the gently sloping beach with a fire at my side. Overhead, a blanket of cirrostratus clouds slips across the darkening sky to intercept the light of the thousands of stars that our unaided eyes can perceive. To circumvent my censored sight, I envision the Andromeda galaxy, which is said to be our twin, and I wonder whether on the beaches of distant worlds, are other life forms looking up and asking, "Is anybody out there?"

More than two thousand years ago, the Greek philosopher Metrodorus reasoned that "to consider the world the only populated world in infinite space is as absurd as to assert that in an entire field sown with millet, only one grain will grow." Epicurus agreed, as did Lucretius: "Nature is not unique to the visible world; we must have faith that in other regions of space there exist other earths inhabited by other people and animals."

Were Lucretius to return to us, he'd be pleased to find the scientific community firmly on his side, arguing that amino acids, the simple building blocks of life, are easily formed in the billions of galactic kitchens whose starry caldrons brim with primordial soups. In contrast, some fundamentalists embrace a doctrine of "just one earth, just for man." Really? And should pigeons believe that skyscrapers were assembled just for them?

Lucretius and I, being agreed that other life forms almost certainly exist, must respond to the question raised by the American nuclear physicist Enrico Fermi: "If there are others out there, then WHERE IS EVERYBODY?" I don't know, of course, and with Lucretius indisposed, I move on to a more easily answered question: Why don't we know?

In the first place, the distances between stars are so vast that even with fantastic speeds, the timetable for interstellar travel is reckoned in thousands of years.

Second, even if we try to communicate with other solar systems by radio, the time/distance problem is still enormous. Assume that the *nearest* star has planets. Assume that one of those planets shelters a technology equal to ours or better. Assume that their transceiver is aimed at our tiny portion of their sky and is scanning the frequencies we send their way. If *all* of this works, it would require at least ten years to send a message and receive a reply.

Warming to my subject, I conjure up Dr. Fermi and convince him that the odds of nearby celestial civilizations achieving technological parity at the same time as ours are not very good. Most other life-forms will either be primitive compared with our own or more advanced. The primitive society could not receive our signals, let alone reply.

As for the advanced civilization, Dr. Fermi suggests that we might have already been evaluated, using methods beyond our dreams. On observing that we still fight like children, they'd probably not return for several hundred years.

I offer a different approach: when we ask why others haven't contacted us, we assume that life on other worlds will evolve as it has on earth, producing beings with similar technologies. In so doing, we ignore the fact that with millions, perhaps billions of suitable planets to work with, the potential life-forms are limited only by time and the laws of physics. Perhaps there are *nonmaterialistic* intelligent beings out there that communicate among themselves, develop societies, loyalties and show compassion but lack technology.

Consider the whales and dolphins that we believe can communicate over great distances, or the societal patterns of the wolf pack and elephants that not only assist their injured but appear to grieve for their dead companions. Because communicating by radio with these creatures is not possible, does it mean they don't exist? Dr. Fermi, prompted by my mention of whales and elephants, might wryly add that if these great beasts can survive our brutality, they may yet evolve into creatures of brilliance and great sensitivity—and so may we.

Then, like Marley's Ghost of Christmas Past, another voice intrudes, and Lucretius appears. "There is yet another possibility," he says, "And a grim one it is."

"After a few million years of evolution, humans have developed technologies that can bring great comfort or destroy most of life on earth. Fail to use that energy wisely, and power-hungry primitives and fanatics who proclaim holy wars could snuff out our beacons of light when they've just begun to shine.

"Other worlds may well have evolved parallel technologies, broadcast for a few decades, then reaped the whirlwind and vanished into silence, only to begin again the long climb back from the stone age or beyond, if life survived at all."

Lucretius dims and vanishes. Fermi, too, is gone, leaving me to ponder what message I would send were I responsible for SETI, the Search for Extra-Terrestrial Intelligence. Relying on Lewis Thomas, American pediatrics professor and author of *Lives of a Cell*, I'd also use music: "perhaps the safest thing to do at the outset, if technology permits, is to send music." Though Thomas cast his vote for Bach, I'd send the soaring rhythms of Brahms's First Symphony or Tchaikovsky's disquieting "Pathétique" to probe the distant stars.

While tapping my breakfast toothbrush dry on a wing strut, I check the Cub's altimeter. My fair-weather high is moving on, but so will I. If it doesn't slip off too quickly, I just might remain within its embrace for several more sunlit days.

My chart says it's just fifty-six miles to Coppermine, but I call it seventy, for I plan to head east to the Coppermine River and then follow it north to the coast.

A sprinkling of lakes leads the Cub to an extension of the treeline that follows the Coppermine valley north from Great Bear Lake. As the valley steepens, the trees begin to lean tipsily downhill wherever the shallow tundra has slid across the underlying permafrost. Like signposts, they point the way to the Coppermine River, which I join at Sandstone Rapids, then follow its northward flow.

Near Escape Rapids, the river cuts through towering posts of black basalt; a hundred-foot waterfall plunges from the eastern rim, dissolving into mist; the trees disappear. And as the Coppermine expands into a four-mile-wide lake, I begin a long glide that will end at Bloody Fall.

By the time that Samuel Hearne, Matonabbee and his eight hard-working wives and packers finally reached the Coppermine River on their long trek from Churchill in 1771, they'd been joined by a party of Copper Indians. As the larger group passed Great Bear Lake and north along the Coppermine, Hearne began to suspect that the newcomers had come not to be helpful but to murder any Inuit they might encounter. Hearne took his concerns to Matonabbee, who convinced him that a protest or an attempt to leave the war party behind would mean their deaths. As each day carried them closer to the coast, Hearne, in rising turmoil, hoped that the river would end at a vacant beach, but that was not to be.

When they were just ten miles from the ocean, Copper scouts spotted five Inuit tents set beside some cascades. Near midnight, in the waning light of a long mid-July day, the Coppers attacked. Surprised and almost defenseless, the Inuit fought back as best they could.

A young woman ran to Hearne. "She fell down at my feet and twisted around my legs, so that it was with difficulty I could disengage myself from her dying gasps. Two Indian men were pursuing the unfortunate victim, and I solicited very hard for her life. The murderers . . . stuck both spears through her and transfixed her to the ground." More than twenty were slain that night, and the horror-struck Hearne named the site Bloody Fall.

The massacre over, the Indians destroyed the camp, feasted on arctic char and then joined Hearne to walk the last few miles to the ocean, where he claimed the coast for his employer, the Hudson's Bay Company. As for copper, only a single piece was discovered during their eleven-month trek back to Fort Prince of Wales.

I secure the Cub to the rocky shoreline just above the cascades. The air is thick with blackflies, so I slip on a head net, then grab my rod and head upstream over bedrock worn slippery smooth. On either side of the river, the tundra unrolls a blossom-flecked sea of green.

Because the arid Arctic receives about the same amount of precipitation each year as the Mojave Desert, tundra plants have evolved several moisture-conserving tricks. To compensate, saxifrages reduce transpiration with leathery leaves, while dwarf birch have developed evergreen leaves to save the energy required by a yearly renewal of growth.

Constrained by low temperatures and a short growing season, arctic plants fill every crevice that provides sufficient warmth, shelter and moisture. Poppies and Labrador tea increase their range by conserving heat and moisture with hairy stems. Others grow in tight, insulating clusters. Few bushes reach six feet, and then only in the shelter of a riverbank or some other feature that buries them in snow, where they escape winter's desiccating winds.

Animals have also evolved to cope with Arctic climes: the hollow hair of caribou and polar bears, superinsulating coats for musk oxen. Short legs and tiny ears help the arctic fox and musk oxen conserve heat, while willow ptarmigan have feathered their legs and feet to the very tips of their "toes."

A solitary sandpiper patrols the edge of a bay not far above the falls. Less than a hundred feet across, the bay's foam-streaked eddies are a perfect resting place for anadromous fish during their tiring upstream quest. I clip a red-and-white jig to my line, then toss the lure upstream while scanning the tundra for bears. At first, I crank rapidly to counter the river's flow, then slow when my lure meets the swirls.

Something hits the lure—a strike, or perhaps the jig bumping bottom. I cast again. This time, the jig is swallowed by Jaws himself. Line peels from my reel as I hustle along the shore, cranking in line during upstream runs and letting it run when he surges downstream. Suddenly, not twenty feet from shore, he leaps, tail wagging into the sky. It's an arctic char.

A few minutes later, eight pounds of orange-speckled crimson char lie exhausted at my feet. As the hook slides from its crescent jaw, his red belly prompts thoughts of the postmassacre feast held here at Bloody Fall, and I decide to set him free. I wade into the Coppermine and hold him upright until he leaves my supporting hand.

Keeping the windows open to blast away the blackflies, I take off for Coppermine. Within minutes, the rocky cliffs of the river's western shore dwindle, the eastern bank flattens into broad sandbars and the jadeite waters of the Coppermine River blend into the clear, salty water of the Coronation Gulf. A few miles seaward lie the Couper Islands and beyond them a continuous mass of ice.

Coppermine is playing ghost town. Although I look up one gravel street after another past rows of white, boxlike houses, there's not a soul in sight. No clothes flap on laundry lines; not a single four-wheeler whines. When I finally locate the store, it's closed, perhaps because it's lunchtime.

A forty-foot power-sailer has been hauled up onto the beach. Looking it over while I wait for Coppermine to come to life, I picture myself standing at the helm, dodging brash ice and bergy bits along the Arctic coast. As I'm about to wend my imaginary way into Cambridge Bay, someone says, "Hello."

Turning, I discover an Inuk woman with a child at her side. "Oh, hi," I answer. "I'd begun to wonder if the town was deserted. Where is everyone?"

"Oh, they're around," she says, with a casual wave that takes in land and sea.

"How about the store?" I ask.

"It's closed for the day," she replies. "But if you need gas, I can call the truck for you."

"Thanks, but I've plenty of fuel. However, I really should change the oil. If I leave a jug on the beach, will someone dispose of it?"

"Oh sure," she says. "The gas man pick it up."

As we stroll along the beach, I turn our conversation to her child. "And how old is this little guy?

"He's almost three."

"May I take his picture?"

When she answers, "That's OK," the child beams with delight. With the easy confidence of a professional model, he sets his baby bottle upright in the hub of a large bronze boat propeller lying on the beach, then pulls back his rabbit-fur hood and smiles a benevolent smile. Neither forward nor self-conscious, he stands at ease in rubber boots, plaid pants and a dark green parka. As the shutter captures his serene smile and Oriental ancestry, I think of the next Dali Llama—someone destined to fame.

Two husky pups crawl out from beneath a nearby overturned boat. Cuddly and roly-poly, they're dying for attention. One is pure white, the other a mixture of white, tan and gray. I squat down to rub their bellies and scratch their ears as they try to climb my legs. "My wife would love one of these," I say, then discover that the woman and child have moved on down the beach.

Back at the Cub, I slip a short length of hose onto the oil reservoir's quick drain and snap it open. Four quarts of hot black oil stream into a plastic milk jug that I've brought along for just this purpose. When it slows, I snap the drain shut, remove the hose and add four quarts of oil.

As the Cub climbs away from Coppermine's empty streets, an odd thought strikes me. I'm really not serious, but I can't help thinking that if my ancestors had been massacred so close to home, I might be reclusive, too.

15

Coppermine
to Yellowknife,
Northwest Territories

*Is civilization progress?. . . the final answer will be given
not by our amassment of knowledge, or by the discoveries
of our science, or by the speed of our aircraft, but by
the effect our civilized activities have as a whole
upon the quality of our planet's life—the life of
plants and animals as well as that of men.*

– CHARLES LINDBERGH

I**T'S BUMPY DOWN LOW**, so I climb to smooth air for the 150-mile flight to Port Radium. An hour later, as the Coppermine River skirts the September Mountains, the massive blue gemstone called Great Bear Lake peers over the horizon.

Great Bear is the world's seventh-largest lake, a ranking that includes the much larger Caspian Sea, which is really a lake, and the once-great Aral Sea, which, because of Russia's diversion of its headwaters for irrigation, is rapidly disappearing. Despite being larger than Lake Erie, Lake Ontario and eight of our fifty states, Great Bear and Great Slave Lakes are almost unknown within the United States.

Two hours out of Coppermine, the Cub crosses Great Bear's stony shoulders, lands on Echo Bay and drifts to a stop beside a rocky point that might well have written the end to World War II.

In 1900, two years before Marie Curie finally succeeded in extracting radium from pitchblende, MacKenzie Bell and Charles Campbell were cruising the Great Bear shores, taking samples of the region's copper and silver ores and of some odd-looking ocher deposits that they'd never seen before. Bell returned to Ottawa, where he reported the find to his government employers, and there the matter lay until a prospector named Gilbert Labine chanced upon Bell's report.

In 1930, Labine headed for Great Bear Lake, where he confirmed the presence of silver. But more important, Labine realized that the yellow ore was pitchblende, the source of two radioactive elements—uranium and its close relative radium—which, once refined, would bring a spectacular $400,000 an ounce. Ignoring the silver, Labine attacked the pitchblende, and Port Radium found its name. Although Labine didn't know it, he'd broken a monopoly, for until the Great Bear discovery, the Belgian Congo had been the world's only source of pitchblende.

Lacking a refinery, Labine had one built on Lake Ontario. For every *gram* of radium produced by the refinery, more than a thousand tons of pitchblende were removed from galleries reaching far beneath Great Bear Lake. And then came World War II.

The Canadian government took over the mines and began to ship refined uranium to the Manhattan Project, which produced the atomic bomb. Today, rumors persist that it was Great Bear Lake uranium that fueled Little Boy, the bomb that leveled Hiroshima and brought an end to World War II.

When the pitchblende ran out in 1960, the owners shut the Port Radium down, believing that the less valuable silver could not be profitably mined. They could hardly have been more wrong.

In 1962, Echo Bay Mines leased the property. Sinking shafts more than a thousand feet deep, they found ore that assayed a whopping 70 percent silver, and Echo Bay Mines quickly became the world's largest silver producer. (In many silver-bearing ores, the value lies in the copper and tin, and the silver is just a by-product.)

A decade later, when Wes asked mine manager John Zigarlich what the drums being rolled into a waiting Otter contained, Zigarlich casually replied, "Just silver."

"Ohhhh . . . and what about security?" asked Wes.

"First of all," said Zigarlich, "you might call us a company town, although, as you've noticed, there isn't any town. In addition, we're pretty isolated, so security isn't a big concern. Except for rare tourists like you, those barrels get no more attention than a stack of bricks in Edmonton."

"What about winter?" I asked. "What the heck do you do for entertainment?"

"Well," said John, "we play cards and billiards, and there's the radio." Then, pointing to Echo Bay, he added, "But when this turns to ice, we curl."

Not knowing if we understood what curling was, John played it safe. "It's like shuffleboard, only we slide forty-pound stones along the ice and sweep like mad in front of them with brooms to alter their speed and trajectory. Up here, curling's our winter sport. Given half a chance, we fly to Yellowknife whenever there's a bonspiel."

"A bonspiel?"

"That's right," he said, "a curling tournament."

As I transfer fuel from floats to wings, a raven flaps to a landing atop the fuselage, then hops toward me. Eye-to-eye, I talk to a bird that many natives revere.

"What a handsome fellow you are. Would you like some bread for that strong beak of yours?"

He nods, and I duck into the Cub to retrieve my food supply. Within minutes, the raven consumes a slice of bread, an Oreo and a chunk of cheese, the last lifted carefully from my fingers, then watches me, tilting his head from side to side as I resume transferring fuel from bags to wings.

A truck pulls up, "Quite a bird you have here," I say to the driver.

"Sure is," he answers, "and he's not the only one. Place is full of them, and they're first-rate panhandlers. But watch it if he takes a dump on your wing, eh. That stuff will bleach your paint, so be sure you rinse it off."

Eyeballing the raven, I say, "Watch it, buster." He behaves. As the Cub leaves Port Radium behind and races south across the open, parklike forest below, I imagine exploring the country by snowmobile. Weaving gracefully between the widely spaced jack pine and spruce, I'd hardly have to slow down.

Near Indin Lake, a grayling haven about halfway to Yellowknife, I descend to within a few hundred feet of the maze of rivers and lakes. Perched on a midstream boulder in the Snare River, a bald eagle tears at a fish in its talons—an innocuous, natural act. Yet years ago, when I read that Tibetan eagles were served human dead, their skulls smashed by priests to grant the eagles easy access, and that Indian Parsees similarly supplied corpses to the vultures of the Towers of Silence, I initially took offense. How could they do such a thing, I thought. I no longer share that bias.

Have we not, with great ceremony, fed bodies to the worms and delivered our dead to the creatures of the sea? In what way is confinement to casket and vault superior to dissolution by eagles, insects or fire?

The aviator-author Antoine de Saint-Exupéry accepted the rightness of a natural, unembellished death. Having sustained life-threatening injuries many times, once nearly drowning and, on another occasion, almost perishing from thirst, he made peace with death and gave up on conventional religion, which he saw as a construct built to ease human fears. "There is no more death when one meets it," wrote Saint-Exupéry. "When the body breaks apart, the essential is revealed. Man is only a knot of relationships."

The Snare River eventually leads to an Indin Lake esker that ends at a west-facing beach, then climbs from the depths on the opposite shore to continue its sinuous trek. My campsite will be a raised strip of level ground at the edge of the esker, where two hardy dandelions quiver in the breeze. Glowing brightly, they confirm my southward progress.

I'm eager to cast for grayling, but I force myself to clean and organize the Cub's interior, which has again degraded since leaving Little Doctor Lake. That done, I clip a silvery spoon to the end of my line and stroll down the beach while enjoying my favorite hyperbole—that *up here* you can hang a hook on a bowling ball and still catch plenty of fish.

As the lure arcs out over Indin Lake, I consider how spoiled I've become, accustomed to fishing that is often little more than cast, retrieve, remove fish; cast, retrieve, remove fish. Thus, I'm not surprised when my spoon is taken by a lunch-size grayling as I begin my first retrieve.

While the grayling simmers on the Coleman, I load two rumpled slices of Whitehorse bread with marmalade and decide how to end my day. Do dishes. Read. Build a fire. Take a hike. But with the dishes done, I'm too antsy to read, so I begin to assemble a fire.

Although making a fire should be one of our most satisfying acts, it's become unremarkable for most of us—like breathing. For me, fire building's a heart- and hand-warming art. Without fail, a budding fire's first wisps of nostril-biting smoke liberate visions of our prehistoric ancestors worshipfully urging flames from flint-struck sparks. In the first tiny flames, I see images from Jack London's masterful story "To Build a Fire," in which a freezing trapper struggles to fend off death.

After scraping aside the earth's mossy coverlet, I begin with a few candy wrappers and paper scraps, then add a mesh of tinder-dry twigs and move on to thicker branches before gently capping the assembly with bone white driftwood. Were I farther south, I'd begin with nature's pungent-burning, waterproof paper—birchbark.

In my pocket, I carry wax-coated wooden matches that can survive a dunking. Packed elsewhere are a flint, a propane cigarette lighter and a candle that can, with patience, ignite wet kindling. Triple O steel wool burns fast and hot. Given none of these, one might ignite gasoline with sparks struck from rocks or with almost any battery, its terminals bridged by a fine wire, which heats to incandescence, or with a camera lens to concentrate the heat of the sun.

I decide to try my widest diameter lens—a Tokina F2 80–200 mm telephoto. Opening it wide, I align the lens with the sun while adjusting its distance from a candy wrapper to concentrate the sunlight on a tiny, brilliant point.

A wisp of smoke appears, followed by a widening hole in the wrapper. Thin, glowing margins spread outward as the paper "burns," but not with an open flame. Laying a crumpled tissue on the smoldering wrapper, I gently blow across it. With a sudden puff, my fire bursts to life.

When the flames are well established, I wet the surrounding ground and stand a wide slab of rock at the fire's windward edge to foil the spark-carrying breeze. Then, with my camera and a little bug dope, I head for the crest of the esker that has formed my beautiful beach.

The esker's fifty-foot slopes are dappled with ground-hugging bearberry bushes and patches of caribou moss, but its well-worn crest has been denuded by thousands of migrating caribou. As I stroll above a sea of scattered treetops, a few blackflies dance in my wind shadow while the bug dope keeps them at bay.

How good it feels to be free from the confining Cub. I jog briefly, then settle into wide strides. Thirty minutes pass, and the esker finally ends as it began—at another beach, another lake.

Dropping onto the sun-warmed sand, I let my thoughts skip back through the years. I see an eight-year-old eagerly peddling sled-loads of homemade balsam Christmas wreaths. I recall a family friend who offered his mind-opening science fiction books to a bedridden fifteen-year-old to help him pass the time. I remember a college student who needed ten minutes to walk a single city block, impeded by a chronically collapsing lung that would require surgery just weeks before the blur of his final exams, his state and national board exams, his graduation, his wedding. I think of my wife and our marriage, once green, now mature. Finally, I remember my two sons, who mean so much to me, and things unsaid, undone. Suddenly lonely, I select a pristine stretch of sand and, with a slender wand of driftwood, inscribe my wife's name in sweeping script.

I stroll back to camp beneath a sky aglow with primrose light. Not far from the tent, I spot a skull-like dome protruding from the sandy soil. A touch confirms its bony nature, and a few finger scoops later, a human skull emerges. Probing further, I find no vertebrae, no ribs, no other bones.

If I'm to have company, my guest must have a name, and Yorick springs tritely to mind. Kneeling before the skull, I try to imagine its owner's past as Yorick evolves into Urok, then becomes Unok. A beretlike lichen decorates Unok's brow. Inches across, its maroon expanse testifies that Unok's skull has lain here for at least one hundred years.

"Unok," I softly inquire, "would you like to join me at one more campfire?" Hearing no response, I reverse our roles. Now Unok's the host and I'm the vacant skull. How would I respond to such an invitation? Yes, YES. Of course, YES!

With Unok's skull cradled in my hands, I return to the dwindling fire, add a few sticks of driftwood and blow its embers to life. Forcing a solid stick into the fireside tundra, I brace it with rock, then guide Unok's foramen magnum over the shaft so that his skull stands upright, supported on a spine of spruce. Beneath a purpling sky, Unok and I commune.

How many generations, how many millennia, have passed since our ancestral kinfolk shared a common fire, not knowing that some of their descendants would migrate north toward Scandinavia to become my ancestors, while others might eventually cross the Bering Strait to become native Americans, each to invent and refine stories of how the earth and the universe were born?

Some North American tribes tell of a muskrat that dove to the bottom of an eternal ocean and returned with a trace of mud; for others, a deep-diving loon retrieved the first lump of clay. Tahitians also created an aquatic myth, believing that their islands had been pulled from the ocean floor by gods. A hemisphere away, Sumerians claimed that the earth was formed from a clod of mud thrown by wrestling giants.

Letting my mind flow into the recesses of Unok's omniscient skull, I find an African tale to brighten the darkening sky: Bushmen tell of a lovely girl who dipped her hands into a fire and threw hot ashes into the sky to form the Milky Way. The sparks flew even farther, and now live on as stars.

As firelight flickers across Unok's brow and cheekbones, I have a brief qualm about moving his skull. As if in response, he fills my mind with a scene from ancient Egypt, where skeletons have been reverently seated beside feast tables as a reminder that the reward for life is death. "Live life while you can," whispers Unok. "Let judgment, not fear, be your guide."

With our fire reduced to embers, Unok and I search the darkening sky for a few of the thousands of meteors that plunge into our atmosphere every minute, escaping notice by day, and lighting tiny flares at night. As we watch, one spark after another streaks across the sky, adding tiny bits of mass to the earth in an accretion process that began billions of years ago.

When my neck cramps from looking upward, I lie back, cradle my head in my hands and smile. The northern sky has donned its luminous negligee of the night, the aurora borealis. Turning to Unok, I tilt him backward against a stabilizing mound of sand so he can enjoy the view.

Some of Unok's ancestors believed the aurora to be the spirits of dead elders playing with a walrus skull; others reversed the tale, allowing walrus spirits to toy with human heads. One Inuit group described an enormous wedding, with the guests arriving on glowing *komatiks* (sledges), and though some whistled to bring the aurora close, others whistled to hold it at bay. Point Barrow Inuit, believing that the numinous lights could attack with evil arms, kept their knives close at hand and threw dog excrement skyward to repel the ominous glow.

Finland's Sami warned their children that they'd be burned or turned to stone if they mocked the shifting lights, while in Norse mythology, the Vikings beheld a sky that mirrored Vulcan's forge. In their search for profits, Alaskan miners envisioned the glow of radium mines, while sixteenth-century explorers saw the reflections of polar ice.

In 1570, when an exceptional aurora illuminated central Europe, Bohemian scribes wrote that people were horrified: "No such gruesome spectacle had been seen or heard of within living memory." Fifteen hundred years earlier, when the lights lit Italian skies, the Roman senator Seneca reported that citizens rushed off to Ostia, expecting to find it in flames. (Seneca emphasized honor in ethics, science and philosophy, and rejected religion, saying, "Religion is regarded by the common people as true, by the wise as false and by the rulers as useful.")

Unok and I, however, see wavering curtains set aglow by the sun's charged-particle breath—the solar wind. Bestirred by the sun's exhalations, the earth's ionosphere blushes a palette-spanning array of nitrogen blues, hydrogen greens and oxygen yellows and reds. We also know that tonight's evanescent skies are only standard fare. Let the sun sneeze and its gusts can destroy communications, disrupt power transmission, induce electrical currents in the Alaskan pipeline, and, with ghostly humor, raise your garage's remote control door.

As the aurora flares above our evergreen-fringed amphitheater, I listen for the crackling sounds that so many claim to hear. But the skies have an antidote for eavesdroppers like me, and I soon succumb to sleep.

Later, awakened by the cooling night, I lift Unok from his wooden spine and, with the aid of my pocket flashlight, return him to his bed of flowers. When he's properly ensconced with his brow protruding from the sand and his lichen beret tilting jauntily to the south, I bid my friend good-night as the aurora borealis prances on through coal black skies.

Settling into my sleeping bag, I drift off to sleep. Far above, the aurora drapes the sky with curtains of shimmering light as the eyes of night follow skeins of migrating caribou, search the tundra for howling wolves and squint in puzzlement at a wilderness beach inscribed with the name Sally.

The western horizon bears popcorn clouds, but the sky overhead is clear. At my feet, scarlet-rimmed bearberry leaves proclaim that fall is on the way, and a glance at the Cub confirms what my hands already know: it's cold. The bushes sparkle with dew, but the Cub's easily cooled wings are white with dangerous frost. I'm unwilling to wait for the sun to melt it away, but I'm even more reluctant to take off with the innocent-looking frost, so I toss a few pails of Indin Lake onto the wings. Then, realizing that my wet hand might slip on the propeller, I dry my hands and the prop, for I don't want to repeat the mishap that crippled pilot J.

J. had run a bush operation for years, routinely hand-propping Cub-like planes to life and even larger aircraft whenever their batteries failed. After landing at a remote lake to cache a load of supplies, J. climbed into his Cessna and found his battery dead. Behind schedule and irritated at the delay, he scrambled onto the float and began to swing the prop.

My Cub, which produces 22.5 horsepower for each of its four cylinders, props fairly easily. But J.'s Cessna, which generates almost twice as much power per cylinder, required a muscular thrust. After propping the reluctant engine for a few minutes without success, J. began to tire. Frustrated, he gave the prop a mighty heave—and slipped—as the engine sprang to life.

The spinning prop severed his arm, sending blood spurting into the slipstream as he desperately clung to the plane. Climbing inside, he removed his belt and looped it around the bleeding stump, then pulled it tight with his teeth.

Knowing that he would die without help, J. poured on the power and flew back to his base, his teeth tugging on his life-saving belt while he fought the urge to faint. After making a passable landing, he ran the Cessna ashore, bringing help at a run. J. almost lost his life to impatience, but saved it with good sense and guts. And in so doing, he taught twitchy pilots like me a lesson: slow down.

Hindered by a southerly wind, the Cub drones toward a town that takes its name from the knives of the Copper Indians—Yellowknife. To the east of the capital of the Northwest Territories, lie millions of acres of tundra that are being "opened up" by prospectors seeking a new aurora: the reflections of garnets and diamonds, the mother lode of gems.

Unlike the prospectors of the Yellowknife Gold Rush of the thirties, today's geologists search not so much for gold as they do for kimberlite pipes—the remains of diamond-bearing volcanoes. Because kimberlite is softer than the surrounding rock, most of the surface ore has been scraped away by glaciers, leaving depressions that have turned into lakes. Thus, mining companies must either pump the lake dry when they find a pipe, a daunting project, or mine beneath them, which has hazards of its own.

After years of searching, a prospector named Charles Fipke realized that he'd have to head "upstream" toward the source of the glacial flows to find the origin of the diamond indicators that lay scattered across the Territories. Year by year, Fipke ranged farther east from the Mackenzie Mountains, discovering increasing numbers of "indicator stones" every few hundred miles.

By 1985, Fipke ran out of funds, and founded Dia-Met, selling stock for as little as 17 cents a share. That summer, while prospecting near Little Exeter Lake, Fipke took samples that fairly screamed of diamonds. Still, because he couldn't be sure of the pipe's location, he delayed staking (which would ensure a rush of competitors) until 1989, telling those who asked that he was searching for gold.

The following spring, Fipke hired a helicopter to speed up staking his claims. On the day that his money ran out, he landed beside a small oval lake. There, he found a tiny piece of chrome diopside, a kimberlitic mineral that usually disintegrates before it gets far from the pipe. Fipke promptly sold 51 percent of Dia-Met to Australia's Broken Hill Proprietary.

BHP began drilling immediately. One core yielded nearly a hundred small diamonds, many of gem quality, while later cores produced gems of even higher value. Within weeks, Fipke's find had attracted two hundred competitors, including De Beers Consolidated, which controls three-fourths of the world's diamonds.

Although the boom might be short-lived, its effects are bound to be huge. BHP alone proposes to spend $0.5 billion just to get into production. A single mineral analysis can cost $1,000, and the all-essential chopper goes for $700 an hour. In the long run, BHP expects to extract $25 billion of diamonds in twenty-five years while paying $2.5 billion in taxes. It's a gamble, too, for although kimberlite pipes exist in Africa, Australia and Siberia, until Fipke came along, not one major pipe had been found in North America.

Even so, Fipke's find is just one of a hundred pipes discovered to date. BHP owns twenty-five, including Misery, a misnamed pipe that's yielding a remarkable three carats a ton. As for Chuck Fipke, whose net worth has topped $400 million, he retained his well-worn pickup and shuns the trappings of wealth.

Development of the diamond fields is proceeding under tight scrutiny, as it should. In just one year, 8 percent of the area's grizzlies had already been shot by the expanding human population. As a result, many organizations, including the World Wildlife Fund, have asked the Canadian government to put BHP's permits on hold while the effects of development are evaluated. Once again, it's ecology versus economy. In the meantime, Yellowknife continues to live up to its Dogrib Indian name—"the money place."

Tuning my radio to 128.4 mhz, I listen to a recording of Yellowknife's landing conditions, then switch to the tower frequency. While I wait for a break in the pilot-tower transmissions, I offer thanks to Hertz and Marconi, two scientists whose work led to radio, television, cellphones and my small but potent transceiver. Because of them, our words can travel thousands of miles, and we're no longer limited to sending notes, waving flags, flashing lights and yelling into tubes.

After receiving clearance to land at Back Bay, I scan the land below for the hull of a DC-3 that undershot the airport in the forties, and crashed onto the first tee of Yellowknife's primitive golf course. Yellowknife golfers, being resourceful and disinclined to waste, promptly converted the twin-engined airliner into their first clubhouse.

At the Spur fueling dock, I find a locked office and a sign saying, "Back at 2:00." At 3:15 a pickup rattles up. The driver is all smiles and no apologies. I top off the Cub with thirty-one gallons of fuel.

By the time I eat lunch and hike to a two-story wooden box called the Igloo Hotel, then shower and wash a few clothes, it's almost three. Having agreed to pay $118.15 Canadian to stay in the Igloo's plywood cubicle splendor, I decide to economize by walking uptown. Besides, if the cabs follow the Igloo's example, they'll be called Comfort Econo-Cabs, run on square wheels and charge $40 a mile.

That said, it's easy to like Yellowknife, especially old Yellowknife, where a few Old Town shanties still bear tin cans nailed to their walls in which nasturtiums and marigolds bloom.

Spotting a granite dome topped by a stone obelisk, I briskly climb the stairs, then lean against the Bush Pilot's Memorial while drinking in the view. Here, from dawn to dusk, the skies reverberate the throaty roar of bush planes while the obelisk points a finger to the sky.

Located some six hundred miles north of Edmonton, Yellowknife sprang to life in 1933 when C. J. Baker and Herb Dixon discovered veins of gold-bearing quartz, the Slavey Indians' "rock fat."

Baker, using innovative spelling to capture Dixon's exclamation over their find, named the site Quyta Lake. Then another strike followed on Yellowknife Bay, and the rush was on, taking the price of a room at the Corona Hotel to all of $1 a night. By 1938, the year that Yellowknife poured her first gold bar, the town had fifty-two bootleggers and seven houses of prostitution. One saloon, the House of Horrors, found its name when a miner noticed the legs of a patron who'd drunk his last protruding from a water barrel beside the front door.

Like any frontier city, Yellowknife has had its heroes, and among them, a former Minnesotan named Vic Ingraham personified grit. It was late in October 1933 when Vic's tugboat caught fire while heading for Port Radium. Vic dove into the engine room to rescue two men. Driven back by burning gasoline that cost him his boots, his socks and his mittens, Vic and his companion, Stewart Curry, abandoned the flaming tug in a tiny life raft intended just for one. Adrift for hours in subfreezing temperatures on a lake that never warms above thirty-five degrees, Vic suffered severe frostbite on his hands and feet. For eighteen days, the pair awaited rescue on Great Bear's frigid shores. When rescue finally came, Vic was flown first to the Aklavik hospital at the mouth of the Mackenzie River, where the first of many operations began, and then to Minneapolis, where doctors finished the surgeries that left Vic with stubs for six of his fingers and no legs below the knees. His Yellowknife friends provided him with a new set of legs, and he headed north again, working as an agent for a barge operator on Great Slave Lake. When gold was discovered at Yellowknife, Vic turned his back on barging to build its first hotel. A larger replacement followed, and then a third, the Yellowknife Hotel, which he managed for the rest of his life. As word of Vic's ordeal and his resilience spread at the end of World War II, his story found print in *The Reader's Digest*, giving hope to the many disabled returning home from the war.

By the end of the war, Yellowknife had a few miles of road. Fifteen years later, the "highway" from the south finally reached town, thanks to a long Mackenzie River ferry ride that's still required today.

During the sixties, the smaller mines shut down, leaving only the Con (Consolidated Mining and Smelting) and the Giant. When labor troubles culminated in a fatal explosion at the Giant, the desk clerk advised against an evening on the town. Heading his advice, I confined myself to the Bush Pilot's Pub, where drinks are served on an aircraft-wing bar.

Designated the capital of the Northwest Territories in 1987, Yellowknife, then a town of only eight thousand, became the headquarters for a third of Canada. Now twice that population and growing, the capital boasts modern hotels, art galleries, fine restaurants, a Northern Heritage Centre to showcase the North's people, land and animals, and a $25 million legislature building with a round assembly chamber to inspire the consensus philosophy of government.

When I return to the Igloo Hotel, I tell the clerk that I'm surprised to see so few mosquitoes. "Is that normal?" I ask.

"Jeez, no," he replies. "It's been a dry year, eh? Most summers, it's almost as bad as camping in the bush."

"Oh . . . I thought you might have been spraying."

"Yeah, we tried that back in the eighties. The city funded a big drainage and pesticide program that was supposed to get rid of every mosquito within five miles of City Hall, but it flopped. When a wet summer came along, the bugs were as bad as ever."

He stops for a moment, smiling at a thought that he decides to share. "One old-timer who'd been living in a drafty log cabin even had to put up a tent in his living room so he could get some sleep. Then somebody introduced a referendum asking for more spraying. It won by a landslide, but the cost came close to a dollar a bug, so we gave it up. Better enjoy it, 'cause they'll be back next year."

Changing the subject, I ask a final question. "I understand why you have streets named for Hearne, Matonabbee and Franklin, but what about Bad Ass Road?"

With the look of someone compelled to answer an oft-asked question, he replies, "It's named for a mining consortium, but beyond that, your guess is as good as mine."

Back in my room, I scan *The Yellowknifer* and *News North* to take the community's pulse. Unfortunately, it's a slow news day, and Yellowknife's pulse, when I find it, is weak and thready. Even the letters section, always one of my favorites, is surprisingly mild, containing only a complaint about barking dogs and off-road vehicles, but there's nothing about national policy, as if such matters were a planet away.

In the classified ads, however, I strike it rich:

Dog team for sale—malamute/husky cross with harness. Healthy. Moving—best offer. (My wife loves dogs. Wouldn't she be surprised!)

Proven silver claim. Write Pete at xxxxxxx. Bargain for quick cash or might take partner.

Wrecked Cessna 185, 60 mile from YLKF. $9,000 as is, where is. Call room xxx at the hospital.

Hoping to catch the news, I turn on the television just in time to see a presentation about Canada's immigration policy, which has been revised to slow the country's growth on a planet that already houses some six billion people, the last billion having been added in just twelve years! Smiling now, I recall my irritation at once seeing a CBC television clip of then Prime Minister Brian Mulroney distributing awards to mothers of twelve or more children in his home province of Quebec. On returning home, I learned that our diocese had once again given its "Mother of the Year" award to one of its more prolific women.

Though I'm years removed from the events, I still fume. Why not give awards to rabbits, to hamsters or termites? Are they not infinitely more prolific? Grumbling, I wonder what our planet will be like by the time we begin to present awards to parents of one or two children. What might it be like if we'd heeded Thomas Malthus instead of plunging on, using unforeseen advances in agriculture to paint his predictions wrong?

Both Darwin and Wallace gave Malthus credit for the idea that led to their theories of natural selection. According to Darwin, "In October 1838 I happened to read for amusement, Malthus on population, and being well prepared to appreciate the struggle for existence which everywhere goes on . . . it at once struck me that under these circumstances, favorable variations would tend to be preserved and un-favorable ones destroyed. The result of this would be the formation of a new species. Here then I had a theory by which to work." Malthus, in turn, credited the philosopher/scientist/statesman Benjamin Franklin with remarks about population and the food supply that Malthus would later mature.

Turning to U.S. news, I see a commentator reporting that the Christian Coalition has mounted a new push for government funding of religious schools and has expanded its crusade against gays. Smoldering now, I wish I'd never turned the TV on.

Stephen Coonts, former Vietnam pilot, and author of *Flight of the Intruder*, summarized my opinion of these zealots in a comment in *Cannibal Queen*: "Little people in little rooms in little places purport to tell us the eternal truths. People who don't understand the most basic laws of physics tell us with straight faces that they have mastered the incomprehensible. How could they know?"

16

Yellowknife to Stony Rapids, Alberta

Wilderness is the one thing we can not build to order.
When our ciphers have choked out the last vestige of
the Unknown places, we cannot build new ones.

– ALDO LEOPOLD

I N THE LOG-WALLED Wildcat restaurant at the edge of the seaplane base, conversations focus on three related issues: forest fires, flying and the weather.

"Dry enough for you?"

"Hell, yes. Country hasn't been this thirsty since '88—or was it '89? Fires all over the place."

"Great year for business, eh?"

"You can say that again." (Charter operators do well during dry years by flying men and equipment to remote blazes.)

"Sid get back?"

"Yup—last night about ten. Says the Duncan Lake burn is still hot and there's a new one near Desperation Lake. Oh, yeah, there's a big one south of McDonald. He's flying two crews from Snowdrift to the McDonald burn today."

"That Sid—if we didn't have enough to keep us busy, he'd probably be tossing flares out the window right now." Laughter circles the table.

"Naw, Sid wouldn't do that," someone says, then adds, "not this year." More laughter.

Back Bay is mirror-perfect calm as the Cub rips across the smooth water and leaves its inverted image behind. I glance back over my shoulder at a taxiing Norseman, wishing now that I'd waited, for I love the throaty roar of radial engines. Unlike my diminutive Cub, the Norseman will shatter Back Bay's serenity, setting the pattern for yet another busy day.

Forty minutes pass. Far off to the north, a nuclear-bomb-like cloud billows up from the Duncan Lake burn, lifted high by an inferno hot enough to incinerate the tundra soil.

My destination is Utsingi Point, a long sliver of land at the tip of the Pethei Peninsula where I hope to find the stony remains of the organisms that brought to life all fish and fowl, all insects, reptiles and mammals. Called stromatolites, they're petrified colonies of blue-green algae, an early life-form that some two to three billion years ago began to produce oxygen in the shallows of our ancient seas.

An hour east of Yellowknife, I descend over Hearne Channel, turn north and follow Utsingi Point while searching its weathered limestone shore for stromatolite remains. Seeing nothing but elephant-skin-like rock, I descend even lower and skim the barren shore.

Finally, discouraged and unwilling to fly farther north, I land and taxi ashore. As I scan Utsingi's rippled surface for something to tie to, the scene suddenly snaps into focus. The entire shoreline is an exposed stromatolite reef! Expecting to see only isolated examples of the washtub-size colonies, I hadn't recognized the mottled mass of thousands as they passed beneath my wings. I'm surrounded by the petrified remains of the cells that breathed us into life, and filled with a sense of awe.

For aeons, the earth was a carbon-dioxide-rich oxygen-starved planet. But when early life-forms finally appeared, one of them, an algaelike organism called cyanobacteria, began to split water into hydrogen and oxygen by photosynthesis, then combined the hydrogen with carbon dioxide to make the forerunners of the carbohydrates that we enjoy today. In so doing, cyanobacteria changed the parameters of life on earth. Time passed, and as their numbers mushroomed, the cyanobacteria accumulated in colonial structures called stromatolites, which eventually formed the oceans' first biological reefs.

With an abundant supply of carbon dioxide and no competition, the thriving cyanobacteria soon became the ascendant lifeform. Oxygen, the algae's "waste product," accumulated for ages, fueling an explosive evolution of oxyphilic organisms while simultaneously protecting them from ultraviolet radiation with a byproduct called ozone, which we are now, to our peril, depleting.

Scientists now propose that many of the earth's iron deposits are the result of stromatolite activity: the cyanobacteria released oxygen into the ocean, which combined with dissolved iron, forming iron oxides that accumulated in the shallows. Thus, when prospectors discovered Minnesota's Mesabi Iron Range, they often found the ore beneath masses of unyielding, quartz-like rock, which they roundly cursed, unaware that it housed the remains of the algae that had laid down the ore that they prized. When the same Luis Alvarez who investigated the clay layer that marks the end of the dinosaur era thought to examine stromatolite sections with a microscope, we learned that these odd-looking rocks were formed from our humble precursors.

In the United States, fossilized reefs can be found on Lake Superior's northern shore, or in Wyoming's Medicine Bow Mountains. Fortunately, a few viable stromatolite colonies have survived. Some are actually thriving, the largest being located in Australia's Shark

Bay. Minnesota even hosts a few *living* colonies in the depths of its freshwater lakes, all of them spring fed, their locations kept secret to protect them from careless humans.

As I taxi away from Utsingi's rumpled shore, I recall reading that 99 percent of the earth's life-forms have already become extinct, and I'm immensely pleased that among the survivors are the simple algae colonies that brought us the breath of life.

Beneath an immaculate sky, the Tundra Cub slips past Redcliff Island's russet crags. And although the sky overhead is a great blue dome, far ahead, beyond the McDonald fault, the horizon is hidden in smoke.

Rutledge Lake looms through the smoky veil, but there are still no fires in sight. Rejuvenating myself with a candy bar, I push on as the visibility falls to eight miles, then six, then four while the smoke invades the cockpit. Though I'm miles from any fire, the scent bothers me, for no pilot relaxes when the cockpit smells of smoke.

I climb to four thousand feet, hoping to escape the acrid odor without losing sight of the earth, only to have it almost disappear behind a blanket of mahogany-tinted smoke. Dancing on the edge of instrument flight, which neither the Cub nor I are equipped to handle, I return to a thousand feet. With my nerves set a-jangle by the nostril-biting fumes, I cross the Talston River in two-mile visibility.

The earth's green face suddenly darkens. Burned just yesterday, or perhaps the day before, the forest lies in smoldering ashes. Blackened hills still flicker with orange fire where pitch-rich stumps burn on. Bouncing through a potholed sky, the Cub spans miles of blackened trees interspersed with water-lily-greened lakes. Like oases of color, they ride a pitch-black sea. Though they're widely scattered, clusters of still-verdant trees reveal a capricious fire that torched here, skipped there. I press on as, chart in my lap, I map a careful record of my progress. As I pencil in my track, sunlight gilds my skeleton key with brassy, smoke-obscured rays.

The Cub crosses a struggling, amoeba-shaped burn. Thwarted by nearby marshes, the fire has sent pseudopods flickering up the ridges in an attempt to pass them by. As the flames devour the wooded slopes, I see a cancer gnawing the forest's flesh—a very mis-leading vision, for when fire releases minerals from torched vegeta-tion, it renews a forest. Flooded with a sudden wealth of calcium, phosphorus and magnesium, seemingly lifeless burns soon erupt with shoots of fireweed, jack pine and aspen.

The air suddenly calms, as if I've flown into the eye of a hurri-cane, but within minutes I'm once again dancing in the hot breath of nearby smoke-hidden fires.

Visibility abruptly lifts to five miles. Dead ahead, a twenty-mile fire front dances in flames where a sinuous blaze is torching its way upwind. In the swirling air downwind from the ridges, flames rush upward, exploding evergreens in an incandescent storm. On the windward slope, the blaze gnaws its way downhill, opposed by both gradient and wind.

The Cub punches through bubbles of fire-heated air, leaves the flames behind and returns to a forest pockmarked with the scars of older burns. When a long, slender lake beckons, I angle into the wind, land and taxi toward acres of charcoal gray turf and ebony stumps that look like a black-and-white photo of a World War I battle zone.

This isn't a recent burn. On fresh burns, each step lifts clouds of ash. But here, though the acrid odor of charred wood still tweaks my nose, wind and rain have tidied up, and the ashes are all but gone.

At my feet, aspen shoots proclaim a burn that's a month or more old. I walk inland through a scattering of inch-high ferns. At the base of a charred pine ahead, I spot a cluster of emerald greenery. Moving closer, I discover a wild rose with a gloriously healthy blos-som that somehow escaped the flames and return to the Cub for my camera.

As the Nikon's shutter clicks, I'm struck by the absence of sound. No insect hums. No jays cry out, no ravens call. Here, with neither seeds nor berries, and very few insects, no bird will waste its time. In mid-August, a winterlike silence reigns. Still, like the ocean from which we arose, the lake remains a reservoir of life. Near its center, a common loon surfaces, fish in mouth, and with a toss of its head, gulps it down. Given time and moisture, the forest, too, will spring to life and rise like a phoenix from the ashes.

Heading south again, I follow the Tazin River toward a lake that bears the crème de la crème of northern campsites, which is a very high honor, given its many competitors. As the well-shaded moss-cushioned campsite passes below, I think of the first time that I saw this lovely spot.

The day was a hot one. By the time the Brugemmans' Super Cruiser and my Cub finally reached the Tazin River, I was flying with the windows open, with one arm resting on each sill like a kid in a narrow convertible. I'd been shedding my clothing for miles, carefully tucking each garment under my seat so they couldn't fly out a window. By the time we spotted the sandy point on the Tazin's eastern shore, I was down to nothing but shorts.

Baked by the full-bore incandescence of a midsummer sun that had lifted the temperature into the nineties, the Bruggemans soon followed my example as the three of us cast from the beach into deep Tazin water. Only northerns took our lures that day, and when I hooked forty-incher, Homer and I stopped for photographs while Paul stripped down for a swim. When Paul emerged from the Tazin, I yelled, "Hey, Paul, hold this pike in front of yourself and I'll take your picture!" A shutter click later, my camera captured a dripping naked Paul behind a discreetly positioned pike.

With Paul's permission, when I present programs about my travels, I include slides of our picturesque campsite. Next comes underwear-clad Homer, struggling to beach a thrashing pike, and laughter ripples through the crowd. When naked Paul appears, grinning above the fish, the audience roars.

I wait for the laughter to subside, then add, "According to my feeble and often inventive memory, I once asked Paul's wife what she thought of that photo. And though I'm no longer certain of her response, I like to think she replied, 'It's OK, but he could have used a smaller fish.'" And the audience roars again.

As the rolling Saskatchewan hills cup blue sapphire lakes in chaliced evergreen hands, the Cub nears Uranium City, a modern ghost town where, in the fifties, an entrepreneur named Gus Hawker greeted newcomers with cries of "stake your claim and make your fortune." Gus heeded his own advice, first becoming a store owner and then the president of his own mining company.

Uranium City boomed in response to the postwar demand for nuclear bombs and power plants, growing quickly into a town of ten thousand with a modern airport and first-class schools. But then priorities changed, and the mine shut down in '82. The town collapsed, leaving behind an empty city—no maple leaf flags, no laundry lines, no children, cars or dogs. Attracted to the barely used homes, entrepreneurs trucked a few to Lake Athabasca, then carted them over the frozen lake to begin life anew at Black Lake or Stony Rapids.

The Cub descends to a hundred feet and crosses Lake Athabasca. Along the lake's southern shore, submerged swirls of butterscotch sand break through the lake's frolicking surface, becoming sandbars fringed with foam. On the horizon, trees strangled by the Athabasca dunes reach for the sky like the masts of foundering ships.

A mile-wide lake at the edge of the dunes beckons, and I'm soon tying Cub to a bone white spruce that's protruding from lake's crater-like shoreline. But when I hoist a bag of fuel to the top of the wing and reach for the gas cap, it isn't there! I must have left it lying on top of the wing when I fueled in Yellowknife, an error I've made before. Fortunately, I used that tank first, so most of the fuel has been burned and not sucked overboard. Grumbling at my negligence, I empty the bag, dig out the duct tape and lay several overlapping strips across the opening, then poke a slit in the silvery patch with my pocket knife. (Fuel can't flow to the engine if air can't get into the tank.)

Although I leave the stove behind, getting my gear to the top of the shoreline dune takes three frustrating, back-sliding climbs. Then, with my camera and my ever-present compass clipped to my belt, I set out across the sand.

A hundred yards from camp, I stop to memorize the features surrounding my tent: the blank space with neither dunes nor trees that hints of the lake where the Cub awaits and a tall clump of spruce to the east. Another hundred yards later, I turn again. The tent has disappeared behind the dunes, but the landmarks remain.

The Athabasca dunes are interspersed with humps of low vegetation, little islands of struggling trees and patches of hard-packed clay. Around these islands weave ribbon-like dunes, breaking-wave dunes and dome-shaped dunes, not a one of them fifty feet high.

I've always liked sand dunes. Like ocean waves trapped in mid-curl, they wait for the wind to shift their shapes. Beguiled by their herringbone patterns and graceful contours, I've spent hours photographing their endless array of curvaceous crests under deep blue contrasting skies.

Because deserts are not necessarily deserted, I scan each slope and probe every island of struggling vegetation but find only insects, and even they are scarce. The plants, however, intrigue me. Stunted pine and birch rise from patches of yellow-green tansy and feathery sand heather. I've read that the Athabasca dunes contain fifty rare plants, plus ten that grow nowhere else, so I'm not surprised to come upon plants that I've never seen before. In part because of this rarity, the dunes became a Provincial Wilderness Park in 1993.

I climb to the top of the nearest dune and stretch out along its crest. As I bake in my sandy surroundings, I can easily believe that just 1 percent of the earth's water is fresh, with 2 percent locked up as ice and the remainder salted away in the seas. Like Coleridge's Ancient Mariner, who found "water, water everywhere, nor any drop to drink," I, too, ride an undrinkable sea, but here no wave breaks, no albatross hangs from my neck and no gulls or cormorants cry.

When the silence grows heavy, I begin to retrace my steps, then veer west to cover new terrain. I pause at a cluster of sand-blasted spruce, where I discover an empty bird nest. Poking around, I find a tiny anthill and, a few yards away, some small animal tracks heading north toward ninety miles of barren shoreline. They look like house-cat tracks, too small for a young fox or a bobcat. But a house cat? Here?

Because I've left the Coleman in the Cub, supper becomes an eclectic mix from package and can: a sardine sandwich, a handful of raw carrots, dried apricots, a half-dozen cookies and a can of soda. That done, I retrieve *A Natural History of the Senses*, and, as the sun descends, build a fire from the forest's bones. Maturing, it crackles, emitting explosions of sparks as if to confirm her opinion that "a campfire wouldn't be as exciting if it were silent."

I try to imagine a silent campfire. Seeking the real thing, I stuff my fingers in my ears. She's right, of course. Though the resinous scents, the radiant warmth and the leaping sparks remain, it really isn't the same.

As I set up the tent, a faint rumble turns my head to the west. An advancing line of thunderstorms is about to obscure the setting sun behind burgeoning castles of white. The storms probably won't be severe, but I quickly double the lines to the Cub and seal the gas-tank cap slit with another strip of tape. Thinking ahead, I slap a second piece onto the windshield as a reminder to unseal the tank tomorrow.

Back at the tent, I lay several logs across the tent stakes and heap sand against the lower six inches to keep the wind from getting underneath, then I lean against a jack pine and survey the approaching storm.

Advancing along a two-hundred-mile front, mature male cumulonimbus storms containing a half-million tons of water are muscling their way into the stratosphere, where the subarctic jet drags cirruslike streamers downwind. Because of their flat-topped profile, and perhaps in memory of Thor, we call these lofty tops "anvils." I imagine Thor hammering out a lightning overture while his hair streams off to the east as the sky darkens and drumrolls of thunder rumble over the dunes.

The female thunderheads, not quite tall enough to reach the jet stream, wear beautifully rounded but treacherous curves. Hidden within those soft whipped cream contours lie tumultuous cores of power that can rival nuclear bombs. Fly into one of these mobile explosions, and like a hungry spider, it can pluck your wings and eat you for lunch. As for her five-mile-high teenagers, they'd probably maul you and then let you pass. No sensible pilot will test them, for the cumulonimbus crowd is a violent, dangerous clan.

The thunderheads draw close, preceded by a low, ominous-looking roll cloud—the leading edge of a cold front, the tsunami of the sky. Wedging low, the roll cloud shovels lighter dune-warmed air into the growing storms. Rammed aloft on 150 mph updrafts, its moisture condenses, releasing heat, which further expands the air. The storms rocket higher as shards of lightning arc from cloud to cloud, and the families begin to commune.

As the sooty roll cloud advances, not a single raindrop falls, and the air is eerily calm. A mile to the west, stump-legged torrents of rain march forward. Black as basalt and as solid-looking as posts, they press on, their paths illuminated by pulses of lightning hotter than the surface of the sun. Like fleeing animals, dust devils waver ahead of the storm, racing a wall of wind.

Bracing myself against the quivering jack pine, I capture the storms' explosive drama with my wide-angle lens. Self-lit by their own internal strobes, the towering clouds glow white, gray, gold and purple while the wind pelts my face with sand. As the Nikon seizes the flashing scene, goose bumps flare across my flesh and fire up my brain. Blinded by lightning, deafened by thunder and peppered by wind-driven sand, I revel in Ms. Ackerman's "sense-luscious" world.

As huge drops of water begin to punch craters in the sand, a flurry of lightning reveals a sky streaked with green, and green means hail. Like a rabbit fleeing to safety, I scramble into my tent between great gobs of rain. Within minutes, the sky's green promise is fulfilled when hail the size of pearls begins to fall. Fortunately, my springy tent can tolerate marble-size hail, as can the drumlike skin of the Cub, but golf-ball-size hail or larger could reduce the tent and the Cub to rags, and larger hail can kill. Were the Cub to be trashed and I survive, having hidden beneath my foam mattress and sleeping bag, I'd be forced to wait for Search and Rescue planes to find me when I failed to reach Stony Rapids.

As hail, the farmers' "white plague," bruises parched spruce and birch, I sit in my shuddering tent. The pounding increases, leading me to the edge of worry, and then abruptly stops.

Outside, the crunch of inch-deep hail accentuates my steps. The deluge has bleached the yellow dunes, leaving snow-white drifts behind. Bedraggled foliage dangles from tree and shrub. But the stones are small; the tent is fine, and the Cub's unscathed.

I scan the storm's receding bulk. White-topped, with salmon pink backs rising from bulging purple bases, they rumble off to the east like a colorful crowd of Michelin men set aglow by the setting sun.

17

Stony Rapids to Minnesota

There's no place like home.
– FRANK BAUM, *The Wizard of Oz.*

THE CUB SLIPS ACROSS the freshly scrubbed forest in smoky orange light while I wonder if more fires await to the east, spawned by yesterday's storms. An hour later, with neither storms nor fires in sight, I arrive at Stony Rapids, where two Beavers are tied to a pier on the south side of the Fond du Lac River.

As I approach the only opening at the pier, a forty-foot space between the aircraft, I throttle back just enough to keep the Cub dead in the water, its forward speed canceled by the river's steady flow. With a touch of right rudder I angle the Cub toward the dock. When the side of the float bumps the pier, I kill the engine, leap out and secure the Cub.

An hour later, brimfull of Athabasca Airways fuel and stuffed with eggs and pancakes, the Cub and I leave Stony Rapids behind. On one wing, the Cub wears a rusty gas cap retrieved from a derelict truck, its $15 price the penalty for being careless in a sellers' market.

Turning south, I meet the northward flowing Cree where it winds through the Black Lake flats as if worn out from stringing sapphire ponds between rapids of pearly foam. An hour later, when Cree Lake finally becomes a slit on the horizon, I reach for my camera to capture its sunlit islands, its azure shallows and beaches of golden straw. Like a miniature Athabasca, Cree Lake's curvaceous shoals convert the lake's blue-green depths to a multi-hued topographical map.

Lazing along at seventy mph, I evaluate each beach: is the water too shallow, likely to leave a seaplane grounded ten feet from shore? Is it too exposed, or tucked into a sheltering bay? Are there open spaces beyond the sand on which to pitch a tent? Then, with my map bearing fourteen new *S*'s, I turn southeast toward an aptly named Reindeer Lake village called Southend.

From Cree Lake and Southend, a thriving forest rides a washboard of north/south ridges and valleys. Between the crests, linear lakes and streams flow through glacier-plowed troughs. One after another, the grayling-rich waters of the Wheeler, Geikie, Thompson, Wathaman, Foster and Pink Rivers pass below, their parallel flows herded northward by the lush corrugations of a deeply grooved earth.

When the Cub is refreshed with Southend fuel, I lay out a course to Fort Paskoyak, which everyone calls the Pas—pronounced "paw." Later, as Sandy Bay falls behind, I pass the time by recalling films with great flying scenes—films like *Mother Lode*, *Always* and *The Empire of the Sun*—then move on to my flying dreams.

For as long as I can remember, I've dreamed that I could fly. As a child, my dreams began with floating just above the ground with effortless block-long strides. While others plugged away, I'd float gracefully from step to step, immune to all but a tiny part of the earth's pervasive pull. Half realizing that I was dreaming as I glided from jeté to jeté, I'd tell myself, This is so easy; I *must* remember how to do this when I return to the light of day.

As the years progressed, I soared higher, flying prone like Superman while holding a small board in my hands, which I'd angle to direct my flight to lands that no others have seen. There was always a slight sense of danger, should I lose my grip on the board, but I soared through the nights for year after year and never fell out of the sky.

The nickel mines of Flin Flon lie far behind; to my right is Cumberland House, the Hudson's Bay Company post established by Samuel Hearne in 1774. Hearne knew that the Bay's competitors (whom they mockingly called "pedlars") had a post on the Saskatchewan River at the Pas, so he sited Cumberland House forty miles upstream to intercept the fur-laden eastbound trappers and promised his men a two-pound bonus for every trapper they induced to switch to the Bay. Recruiting a "pedlar" brought a munificent hundred-pound sterling reward.

When the Pas finally slips into sight, I open a window and thrash around in my seat. I'm stiff and weary from hours of sitting, so I grasp the overhead tubing and slide up and down to awaken my body and brain.

At Beaver Air Service, I ask Raymond, a Métis, for a ride into town, where I buy him lunch. Over burgers and chips, Raymond reports that the Pas is about half white and half Cree and Métis. Employment, according to Raymond, depends on the pulp mill and on the railroad (now owned by a U.S. firm) which divides at the Pas, sending one branch north to Lynn Lake and the other northeast to the nickel mines at Thompson and then on to Churchill.

As I down the last of my milkshake, I ask Raymond if he knew a local pilot whom I'd met in '92.

I'd just finished fueling the Cub when a dozer operator throttled down his Cat and walked over to ask where I'd been. Half expecting the usual display of envy, I said that I'd just arrived from Baker Lake by way of Reliance, Fort Smith and Lac La Ronge. That day, however, I was in for a surprise. In response, my questioner mentioned that he'd also made a rather nice trip—just that spring, in fact.

"Really," I said. "Where'd you go?"

"To the north pole."

In a classic role reversal, I became the slack-jawed amateur and he the veteran.

Knowing that flying to the north *magnetic* pole would not be a difficult task, I asked, "Do you mean the north magnetic pole?"

"No," he replied, "I mean the *geographic* pole. During the winter, I installed extra tanks in my Super Cub, put on a pair of wheel-skis so I could land on runways, ice or snow, and set off for the pole in April." Telling of places like Resolute, Eureka and Alert, he reduced my wanderings to minor suburban tours.

When I ask Raymond if he'd heard about the flight, he draws a blank.

"Surely it made the papers?"

When he replies, "Not that I know of—it's news to me," I begin to wonder if the cat driver was only pulling my leg.

The Tundra Cub rises from Grace Lake's weedy face and heads toward Norway House, a sprawling settlement of about three thousand at the north end of Lake Winnipeg. For close to two centuries, yearly brigades of voyageurs fanned out from Norway House, laden with goods for fur trade posts lying far to the north and west. The York boats carried homesteaders to farmlands along the Red River, while the big canoes headed west toward a tiny settlement called Edmonton, now reaching for 700,000.

Those who remained at Norway House planted potatoes and set nets for fish, twenty thousand being taken at Norway House alone in 1861. With the first crisp days of fall, the tide would turn, bringing a flood of fur from the north and west to Norway House, then down the Nelson and the Hayes to York Factory. But as roads and rail marched westward from the East Coast, the need for Norway House waned. By the twentieth century, it was just another HBC outpost, its administrative role having been usurped by Winnipeg.

But Norway House hangs on. Its schools, hospital and homes somehow survived a plague of forest fires that hopscotched through town in 1989. In that year alone, eleven hundred fires incinerated more than nineteen hundred square miles of forest, a comeuppance, perhaps, for years of extinguishing every little blaze, which stockpiled wood for '89, the year of the megaburn.

Descending to one hundred feet to follow Lake Winnipeg's scalloped shoreline, I pass one lovely crescent-shaped beach after another, their arcs separated by linear lichen-dappled outcroppings that rise like humpbacked whales from the lake's algae-laden depths. These long, fingerlike reefs reach far out into the shallow lake, making small boat travel treacherous when the wind comes up.

At Poplar River, I turn inland toward a hidden treasure at the east end of Black Birch Lake where, sheltered by aspen and birch-shaded slopes, I've often pitch my tent at the side of a reed-rimmed beach. An hour later, ripples chatter beneath my floats, the Cub slows and I toss a lure out the door.

Just as I enter the reeds, I feel a twitch, a tug and a flurry of jerks. I let the Cub ground itself while I crank in line. A few minutes later, I'm knee-deep in Black Birch Lake, filleting a gold-flecked walleyed pike on one of the Cub's flat-topped floats.

While I dine, my eyes wander past the Tundra Cub to the forest. Warm and inviting, every bush, needle, leaf and branch glows with the marmalade shades of evening.

A Canada jay floats down to a nearby branch, announcing its presence with a soft coo. When I toss a bit of bread across the fire, the jay cocks its head, then glides down to accept my gift. Playing its traditional role as a traveler's companion, my "Whiskey Jack" listens to whatever tales I offer while he eyes me from beyond the flames.

The more lyrical Cree called my guest wiska-zhon-shish, which is variously translated as "the little one that works at the fire" or "he who comes to the fire." Trappers dropped the ending "shish" to arrive at Whiskey John, then Whiskey Jack.

As dusk descends, I hike down the beach to stretch my legs. Shifting a few yards inland for my return, I discover a long-dead campfire. At its side, the fading light illuminates a small mound of metal. Moving closer, I discover a heap of rusting leghold traps and a crumbling snarl of snares. Someone, perhaps a native, once padded his income and warmed his body with these now-useless tools. The animals paid with their lives, of course, but their loss never stilled the trapper's lament: when prices are low, who gets skinned worse, the fox or the trapper?

When I was young and eager to own all the things that fur could buy, I sided with the trapper. Since then I've seen enough needless killing to make me change my mind: an otherwise principled friend who liked to shoot prairie dogs just for fun; a teenager threatened by cancer whose last wish is to kill a grizzly bear and films of whalers spearing mother whales while their calves continue to suckle.

As I draw my sleeping bag around my shoulders, my mind, still entangled with traps and snares, scrolls back through the decades to a forest scene and a boy just barely ten. It's the night of the winter solstice, a time of deep cold and long northern Minnesota nights. Under a black sky glittering with the sparks of distant stars, the border country sleeps.

Inside a small cabin, a pale hand slips from beneath a stack of gray woolen blankets, then moves from side to side to sense the cold. The hand gropes for a pair of wire-rimmed glasses and, having found them, disappears beneath the covers. A moment later, the hand returns to retrieve wool socks, long underwear, melton pants and a wool-flannel shirt. Beneath the blankets, the occupant curls himself around the clothing, preheating the layers that will have to keep him warm.

A clock strikes seven times. Poking his head from beneath the covers, the boy turns toward a window. Seven o'clock and still dark. He considers staying in bed a little longer. I'll wait for the sun, he thinks, but thoughts of his trapline widen his eyes.

He quickly pulls on his clothes, hurrying not so much because of the waiting riches, but to pile on the layers before they cool. As he turns to leave the room, he runs a finger down the frost-feathered window, carving a furrow a quarter-inch deep.

In the darkened living room, a wood burner smiles toothily through rectangular inlets beneath its cast-iron door. Feed me, it pleads. Quietly (his parents are still sleeping) he lays a few pieces of well split cedar on the coals, then blows across the radiant bed. The oily cedar bursts into flames. Birch follows, and the woodburner springs to life.

His boots, still warm from a night near the fire, exude the tarry aroma of Nor-V-gen boot grease. Bending over, the boy laces rawhide thongs through their tall ladders of hooks, then touches the pouch on the side of his boot to be sure that his pocket knife's there. He struggles into a jacket that was loose two years ago, fit last year but now grows tight. Pulling on a woolen cap, he lowers the earflaps, tugs a pair of leather choppers over wool mittens and quietly slips out the door.

Cold, dry air pinches his nostrils; the metal frames of his glasses bite into his nose and temples. Far out on the lake, a snow-muffled rumble ruptures the silence as the lake's lens of shore-fast ice contracts, shrinking from the cold until it cracks with the sound of distant thunder.

Guided by the feeble light of a dying aurora, the boy picks his way along a cement-hard trail. Squeaaach, squeaaach, squeaaach— his boots wrench protests from the bone-dry snow as he envisions the bicycle that a few more rabbits will buy—a red-and-white Schwinn with a battery-powered horn and headlight, two rearview mirrors and tasseled handle grips. The boy pauses beside a rock-hard brook to marvel at the change a few months can bring, then heads for a cluster of towering cedars that mark his first trap.

The leghold trap is empty. He carefully walks around it to admit the meager light of the purpling predawn sky. The trap is set correctly, but nothing has come this way.

The boy has but one leghold trap. All the rest are snares—supple braided-wire nooses that hang suspended just a few inches over the trail. A passing rabbit, accustomed to pushing its way through twigs and brush, feels nothing unusual until the noose draws tight around its neck. In the boy's mind, the rabbit dies quickly, aided by the numbing, merciful cold.

His first snare hangs as he'd set it—a perfect circle, a zero, a delicately frosted cipher hovering over the trail. Dropping to his knees to examine the pathway, he finds no tracks on its crystalline face.

The second sparkling loop reminds him of his mother's rhinestone choker. "Choker," he thinks, then retreats from the word with a twinge of regret.

When he finds his third snare empty, his dreams of a bicycle slowly begin to fade. He moves on, repeatedly wiping his dripping nose on the back of his choppers. Paralyzed by the subzero cold, the fine hairs that line his nostrils can no longer sweep back the flow, and the leather slowly hardens beneath a film of mucus ice.

The boy pushes his way through an alder thicket and carefully approaches his fourth snare. There, centered in the trail lies the largest rabbit he's ever seen, curled up as if sleeping—frozen solid. Slipping his knife from his boot, the boy slides the blade beneath the noose and pries it open. After ascertaining that the snare is still securely tied to it's heavy, club-like stick, he resets the snare, drops the rabbit into a burlap bag and heads for a pine-fringed bog. The sky, now indigo, dyes the snow the deepest blue.

As he nears the edge of the cranberry bog, something moves. He stops, motionless, scanning the trail. A rabbit materializes. Blue-white on blue-white, the rabbit is almost invisible in the slowly maturing light. The boy waits, hardly daring to breath, not knowing what to do. A minute passes. His unmoving feet protest the cold. Still he waits. A shiver runs down his body, and the rabbit races off down the trail—into a waiting snare.

Yanked off its feet, the rabbit tumbles, then dashes blindly back and forth, jerking against the drag as the noose tightens round its neck. The boy stands transfixed. It won't take long, he reassures himself as his eyes widen in disbelief at the animal's extraordinary gyrations.

The rabbit plunges on, thrashing violently through one long minute, then two, making frantic but futile attempts to escape. Anguished and hoping to put an end to its misery, the boy drops to his knees, reels in the convulsing animal and jerks the noose tight.

Caught in a ghastly scene of his own making, the horror-stricken boy pulls on the noose as tears yield to sobs of remorse. The rabbit, drawing on unimaginable reserves, twists and turns, striking out with its legs. Appalled at its frantic exertions, the boy whips off his mittens and tries to open the noose, but the wire, the strong, braided wire, has become so ensnarled in the animal's fur that release is impossible. Desperate to end the animal's pain and his horror, the boy pins the thrashing rabbit down with one hand and, with the other, raises high the club to which the snare is tied. Surely one blow will end its pain.

The first impact drives the rabbit's head into a cushioning pillow of snow. The second, though aimed through tear-flooded lenses, lands more solidly, squirting an eye from its socket in a gush of blood. Still the rabbit thrashes on, fighting for its life. The boy, totally undone and awash with pity, anguish, and a pain he's never known, strikes again and again. Frustrated by the pillowy snow and repelled by the crimson carnage, he pleads for an end to the horror, crying, "die, DIE, oh please, please Diiiieeee."

The rabbit finally quivers, then softens beneath his hand, taking with it his fantasy of quick and quiet, painless deaths. On his knees beside the limp body, the blood-spattered boy sobs while the silent forest watches. Far above, the first breath of dawn brushes crystals of frost from the towering Norway pines. Descending, they glitter the air.

With shaking hands steaming in melted snow, the sweating boy wipes his blood-smeared glasses while he tries to regain control. Opening his pocket knife, he saws away at the noose, then lays the limp body beside the trail. Still weeping, he carefully places the frozen rabbit alongside its companion and covers the bodies with snow.

The boy rises, shaking his lowered head, as he mourns an innocence lost. Racked with lingering sobs, he walks to the end of his trap line, pulling shut noose after noose after noose. He springs the leg-hold trap and leaves it behind to rust. As the boy trudges back to the cabin, his brow furrows at the thought of his mother, frightened by his empty-handed, blood-spattered return. When she asks, "Son! What happened? Are you alright?" What will I say? How will I hold back the tears?

I awaken at six o'clock. It's light enough to fly, but what's the rush. Scrunching down in my sleeping bag, I try to emulate the starlet who preferred to rise at the crack of noon, but hunger prods me awake.

When I taxi up to the Red Lake pier, there sits Large, his tail flopping from side to side. I slide a hand along his body, searching for ticks. But the season's waning, and his count is down to two. I pay my bill, then ask about Laura. "She's off today," they say.

At a nearby Waterfront restaurant, I hungrily toss down fried eggs, hash browns, bacon and cakes while two charter pilots try to one-up each other.

"Shit, Charlie," says one, "you've never seen such a head wind. It blew so hard that my shadow got left behind. Must have snuck in after dark though, 'cause it was right there in the morning."

Not to be outdone, Charlie begins a long-winded story about paddling his seaplane the length of Lake Winnipeg. I'd like to hear the ending, but I have to get back in the air.

Two hundred miles farther south, where Kanata ends and the Boundary Waters begin, I punch up 122.8 mhz on my radio and send out a call to Crane Lake.

"Crane Lake radio, this is Piper 4745 Mike, thirty minutes north for customs. Please confirm."

"Piper 4745 Mike. Crane Lake customs in thirty minutes."

The Cub descends through a gusting southwesterly wind, then taxis up to the pier. After greeting the sweating officer, I check the thermometer, which is pegged at ninety-four. Two minutes later, I'm free to go.

Just then, a slender, middle-aged man in an "I'd Rather Be Flying" T-shirt walks up.

"Excuse me," he begins, "aren't you the fellow who's done programs for the Seaplane Pilots Association?"

"I have," I respond.

"Oshkosh, too?"

"Yes."

"Loved 'em," he says, "Just loved 'em. You heading north?"

"I'm just getting back," I reply.

"Gosh," he says, "I'd love to take one of those trips, but I really don't think I should."

"Why is that?" I ask.

"Well, what if I got lost or something happened?"

"Look," I respond. "Would you fly from here to Red Lake?"

"Sure," he says.

"How about to Winnipeg?"

"I'd do that."

"Well, in the unlikely event of an engine failure, those heavily forested routes aren't as safe as flights in the open country farther north where a plane is easy to spot, and there are even more lakes to land on."

"Yeah, well," he says. "You're probably right. Still . . ."

As he searches for words, I consider telling him about Marion Hart, the grandmother who soloed a single-engine Beechcraft across the Atlantic Ocean at the age of seventy-four, but decide to let it go. Why should I pressure him or make him feel less a man?

When I taxi away, he stands on the pier, dreaming dreams that might never mature. He's owned a seaplane for fifteen years, but something's held him back. Do his maps bear the mythical beasts that rimmed the charts of old, or does he still hear the ancient cartographers' warning: beyond here lurk dragons!

Hot, gusting winds punish the Tundra Cub all the way to Lake Vermilion, where I fly the roughest approach of my life. When I'm four feet above the wind-whipped lake, the Cub enters rolling air, loses lift and slams into the water. Unbelievably, nothing breaks.

As the Tundra Cub drifts to a stop, a common loon trailed by two fluffy chicks cruises leisurely past my pier. I slump in my seat, glad to be home, then begin to unload the Cub. Before I call my wife, I drop into a chair and reach for the TV remote, only to discover that I've forgotten which of its faded buttons to press. Fortunately, it's news time. On the up side, the Israelis and Palestinians are still talking peace, and scientists have found even more fragments on earth that might have come from Mars, where a little robot called Sojourner once sampled the surface and sent home intriguing notes.

On the down side, graft and corruption are undermining Russia's struggling economy; inter-religious strife still troubles Ireland, the Middle East, India, Pakistan and the area that once was Yugoslavia while the wealthy still complain about taxes that force them to survive on a mere quarter million per year. Still, across much of the world, people are learning, caring and sharing, giving reason to hope that we'll someday outgrow our divisive superstitions, our greed and vicious squabbles and fall in love with life.

> Though our lives begin with a cry of surprise,
> and a question awaits at their close,
> in between lie days filled with wonder
> for all to slowly unfold.
>
> In forest and canyon cathedrals,
> in sacred libraries and halls,
> welcome them, open them, treasure them,
> for after the question, who *knows*?

A Brief Chronology of Powered Flight

1903   The Wright brothers make the first piloted, powered, heavier-than-air flight, flying 120 feet in twelve seconds.

1911   Glenn Curtiss flies the first seaplane.

1922   Jimmy Doolittle makes the first one-day flight across the United States.

1926   Robert Goddard demonstrates a liquid-powered rocket.

1927   Charles Lindbergh completes the first solo nonstop transatlantic flight.

1933   Wiley Post completes the first solo round-the-world flight.

1935   Howard Hughes sets a world speed record of 352 mph.

1942   The first commercial round-the-world flight is completed in a Pan American Pacific Clipper.

1947   Chuck Yaeger exceeds the speed of sound.

1954   The Boeing 707 becomes America's first jet transport.

1961   Yuri Gagarin orbits the earth.

1969   Apollo 11 astronauts Aldrin and Armstrong land on the moon.

1977   The Concorde completes the first commercial supersonic London to New York flight.

1977   The Gossamer Condor becomes the first human-powered heavier-than-air craft to sustain controllable flight.

1981   The first United States space shuttle is launched.

1986   Jeana Yeager and Dick Rutan complete the first nonstop round-the-world flight without refueling.

Bibliography

Ackerman, Diane. *A Natural History of the Senses*. New York: Random House, 1991.

Alexander, Bryan and Cherry. *The Eskimos*. New York: Crescent Books, 1988.

Anderson, Barry. *Lifeline to the Yukon*. Washington State: Superior Publishing, 1983.

Atwood, Margaret. *Strange Things: The Malevolent North in Canadian Literature*. New York: Oxford University Press, 1995.

Ballantyne, Robert. *Hudson's Bay*. New York: T. Nelson, 1848.

Bronowski, Jacob. *The Ascent of Man*. New York: Little, Brown & Company, 1973.

Bruemmer, Fred. *The Arctic*, New York: Quadrangle, 1974.

Bruemmer, Fred. *Encounters with Arctic Animals*. New York: American Heritage, 1972.

Brueton, Diana. *Many Moons*. New York: Prentice Hall, 1991.

Brody, Hugh. *Maps and Dreams*. New York: Pantheon, 1982.

Burke, James. *Connections*. Boston: Little, Brown & Company, 1978.

Berton, Pierre. *The Arctic Grail*. Toronto: McClelland & Stewart, 1988.

Berton, Pierre. *The Klondike Fever*. New York: Alfred A. Knopf, 1972.

Calef, George. *Caribou and the barren-lands*. Toronto: Firefly Books, 1995.

Coonts, Stephen. *The Cannibal Queen*. New York: Pocket Books, 1992.

Davis, Richard and Guravich, Dan. *Lords of the Arctic*. New York: Macmillan, 1982.

Dawkins, Richard. *The Blind Watchmaker*. New York: W.W. Norton, 1996.

De Poncins, Gontran. *Kabloona*. New York: Reynall and Hitchcock, 1941.

Dyson, John. *The Hot Arctic*. Boston: Little, Brown & Company, 1979.

Ferris, Timothy. *Coming of Age in the Milky Way*. New York: Morrow, 1988.

Freuchen, Peter. *Book of the Eskimos*. New York: World Publishing, 1961.

Frey, Jay. *How to Fly Floats*, Melville, New York: Edo Corporation, 1972.

Gingerich, Owen. *The Great Copernicus Chase*. Cambridge: Sky Publishing, 1992.

Hall, Sam. *The Fourth World*. New York: Random House, 1988.

Harrison, Edward. *Darkness at Night*. Cambridge: Harvard University Press, 1987.

Hearne, Samuel. *Journey From Prince of Wales Fort in Hudson's Bay to the Northern Ocean in the Years 1769-1772*. Philadelphia: Joseph and Jane Crukshank, 1802.

Helmericks, Harmon. *The Last of the Bush Pilots*. New York: Alfred A. Knopf, 1972.

Hildebrand, John. *Reading the River*. Boston: Houghton Mifflin, 1988.

Hing, Robert. *Tracking Mackenzie to the Sea*. Manassas: Anchor Watch Press, 1992.

Hummel, Monte. *Arctic Wildlife*. Toronto: Key Porter, 1984.

Innis, Harold. *The Fur Trade in Canada*. New Haven: Yale University Press, 1962.

Kurelek, William. *The Last of the Arctic*. Toronto: Pagurian Press, 1978.

Leopold, Aldo. *Sand Country Almanac*. New York: Random House, 1970.

Leslie, Edward. *Desperate Journeys, Desperate Shores*. Boston: Houghton Mifflin, 1988.

Lindbergh, Anne M. *North to the Orient*. New York: Harcourt Brace, 1963.

Lokke, Carl. *Klondike Saga*. Minneapolis: University of Minnesota Press, 1965.

Lopez, Barry. *Arctic Dreams*. New York: Bantam, 1987.

Lyall, Ernie. *An Arctic Man*. Edmonton: Hurtig Publishers, 1979.

MacDonald, Malcolm. *Down North*. New York: Oxford University Press, 1943.

Matheson, Shirlee Smith. *Flying the Frontiers*. Saskatoon: Fifth House Publishers, 1994.

McPhee, John. *Coming into the Country*. New York: Farrar, Straus & Giroux, 1976.

Mirsky, Jeannette. *To the North*. New York: Viking, 1934.

Morrison, Philip and Phylis. *The Ring of Truth*. New York: Random House, 1987.

Mowat, Farley. *Never Cry Wolf*. Boston: Little, Brown & Company: 1963.

Mowat, Farley. *Canada North*. Boston: Little, Brown & Company, 1962.

Mowat, Farley. *The Desperate People*. Boston: Little, Brown, 1959.

Mowat, Farley. *People of the Deer*. Boston: Little, Brown & Company, 1952.

Murie, Olaus. *Journeys to the Far North*. Palo Alto: America West Publishing Co., 1973.

Newman, Peter. *Company of Adventurers*. New York: Penguin, 1988.

Newman, Peter. *Empire of the Bay*. Toronto: Viking Canada, 1995.

Norment, Christopher. *In the North of Our Lives*. Camden: Down East Books, 1989.

Olesen, Dave. *North of Reliance*. Minocqua:NorthWord Press, 1994.

Patterson, R. M. *Dangerous River*. Toronto: Stoddart Publishing, 1989.

Perkins, Robert. *Into the Great Solitude*. New York: Bantam, 1991.

Place, Marian. *The Yukon*. New York: I. Washburn, 1967.

Raffan, James, ed. *Wild Waters*. Toronto: Key Porter Books, 1986.

Raymo, Chet. *The Crust of Our Earth*. New York: Prentice Hall, 1983.

Redfern, Ron. *The Making of a Continent*. New York: Random House, 1983.

Rytchetnik, Joe. *Alaska's Sky Follies*. Anchorage: Epicenter Press, 1995.

Sagan, Carl. *The Demon-Haunted World*. New York: Random House, 1995.

Seldes, George. *The Great Quotations*. Secaucus: Lyle Stuart Inc., 1960.

Shomon, Joseph. *Beyond the North Wind*. Cranbury: Barnes &Co, 1974.

Sobel, Dava. *Longitude*. New York: Penguin, 1996.

Stefansson, Vilhjalmur. *My Life with the Eskimo*. New York: Macmillan, 1922.

Stefansson, Vilhjalmur. *The Friendly Arctic*. New York: Macmillan, 1921.

Tryck, Keith. *Yukon Passage*. New York: Quadrangle, 1980.

Turner, Dick. *Wings of the North*. Surrey: Hancock House, 1980.

Turner, Dick. *Nahanni*. Surrey: Hancock House, 1975.

Weiner, Jonathan. *Planet Earth*. New York: Bantam, 1986.

White, Andrew. *A History of the Warfare of Science with Theology*. Gloucester: Peter Smith Publishers, 1896.

Walker, Barbara G. *The Woman's Encyclopedia of Myths and Secrets*. New York: Harper & Row, 1983.

Young, Steven. *To the Arctic*. New York: John Wiley & Sons, 1989.

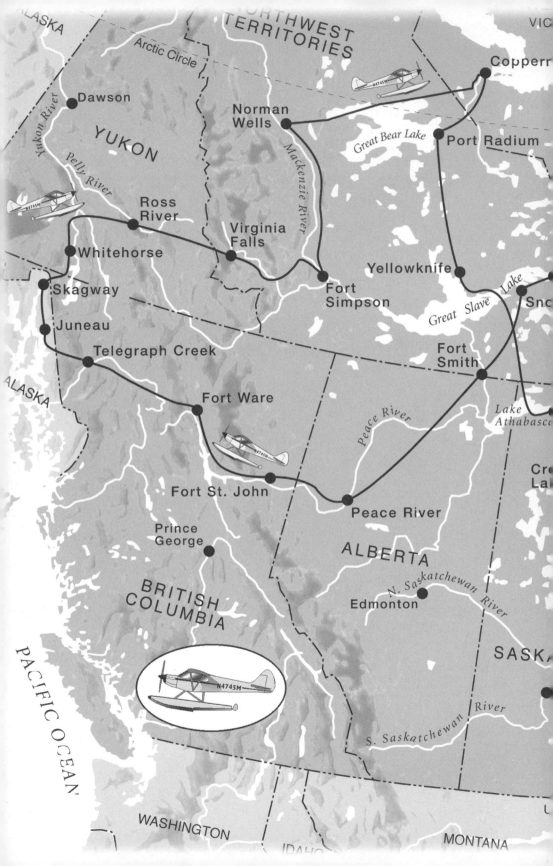